ENGLISH POEMS

THE UNIVERSITY OF CHICAGO PRESS
CHICAGO, ILLINOIS

Agents

THE BAKER & TAYLOR COMPANY
NEW YORK

———

THE CAMBRIDGE UNIVERSITY PRESS
LONDON AND EDINBURGH

ENGLISH POEMS

SELECTED AND EDITED, WITH ILLUSTRATIVE AND
EXPLANATORY NOTES AND BIBLIOGRAPHIES

BY

WALTER C. BRONSON, LITT. D.

Professor of English Literature, Brown University

THE NINETEENTH CENTURY

THE UNIVERSITY OF CHICAGO PRESS
CHICACO, ILLINOIS

Composed and Printed By
The University of Chicago Press
Chicago, Illinois, U.S.A.

PREFACE

This volume is the last in a projected series of four volumes of English poems, intended especially for use with college classes. The first volume will include Old English poems in translation, Middle English poems, a few specimens of the pre-Elizabethan drama, and old ballads. The second volume will cover the Elizabethan and Caroline periods. The third volume will cover the period of the Restoration and the eighteenth century. The present volume is devoted to poetry of the nineteenth century.

The series as a whole is designed for use in survey courses covering the entire field of English literature, and contains about all the poetry needed for reading in such courses. The separate volumes, except the first, will also, it is hoped, be found available for courses in single periods, as furnishing a sufficient basis for study in the classroom. The first volume, although elementary in nature, should increase considerably the value of the series for introductory courses; because, as every experienced teacher knows, the student gets far more well-defined and lasting impressions from actually reading the earlier portions of our literature, even superficially and in translation, than from merely studying a history of the literature or hearing lectures.

In the preparation of the present volume, authors and poems have been chosen both for their merit and for their significance in the history of English literature. The book is therefore not an anthology, or collection of the best poems. It is a collection of good poems that illustrate the different periods and phases of the work of individual poets, and the rise, growth, and decline of schools of poetry.

v

A judicious mean has been sought between the extremes of including too many minor authors and excluding them altogether. The first extreme would have robbed the greater poets of needed space, besides making the volume as a whole too scrappy. The other extreme would have seriously lessened the value of the book as the basis for a study of English poetry in the nineteenth century, since lesser writers often show the tendencies of an age quite as clearly as the greater writers, and in any case some knowledge of them is essential to the full understanding of a period.

Entire poems have been given whenever that was possible, and the bulk of the book is made up of them. But in order to represent some authors at all adequately it has been found necessary to admit a limited number of extracts. Most of these are complete and intelligible by themselves, and some of them come from poems which have no essential unity and therefore suffer little by dismemberment. A few rather fragmentary passages have been included, not for reading outside of the classroom, but to serve the teacher as illustrations of the thought, style, and verse of poems which could not be represented otherwise.

The latest text adopted by the author has been followed, without regard to the personal preferences of the editor. Spelling, capitalization, and punctuation have been modernized when it was necessary. But when the sense is doubtful, the original punctuation has been retained, or the changes made are recorded in the notes; and unusual spellings which were deliberately preferred by an author, such as "thro'" and "tho'" in Tennyson, have been allowed to stand.

The notes have been kept within moderate limits. Biographical sketches, and criticisms by the editor, have been excluded; for it is assumed that biography can be better supplied by a history of the literature, and criticism by the teacher. The notes include (1) the poet's theory of poetry and his philosophy of life when these can be given in his own words; (2) statements by the author or his friends which throw light on the meaning of a poem, or give circumstances connected with the composition of it, or illustrate the poet's method of work; (3) explanations of words, allusions, etc., which the average college student may find obscure; (4) variant readings of a few poems, such as "The Ancient Mariner" and "The Palace of Art," the reworking of which has special interest and significance; (5) quotations from sources and parallel passages, or references to them, to show the poet's literary relationships and his way of handling raw material; (6) specimens of contemporary criticisms on some of the leaders of new literary movements. A selected bibliography, adapted to the needs of undergraduates, follows the notes. It is believed that this material, some of which is not elsewhere easily accessible to college classes, will be welcomed by teachers as an aid in presenting to students the thought and art of the poets studied and the literary life of their times.

Essentially the same methods will be followed in the other volumes of the series.

I wish to express my thanks to Mr. T. J. Kiernan, of the Harvard College Library, for access to first editions and the Shelley manuscript; to my colleagues in the department of English, for various helpful suggestions; and to Professor F. G. Allinson, of Brown University, for aid on some points connected with Greek literature. The Macmillan Company have courteously allowed me to print several passages from the *Memoir* of Tennyson by his son; Ginn & Co., two notes from Professor Edward Dowden's edition of Wordsworth; and Professor V. P. Squires, a note from his edition of Tennyson's "In Memoriam." To my wife, who has aided me constantly by preparing the copy, collating texts, reading proof, making the indices, and writing notes (especially on matters relating to Greek life and literature), is largely due whatever accuracy the book may have.

W. C. B.

BROWN UNIVERSITY
July 17, 1907

CONTENTS

WILLIAM LISLE BOWLES

AT TYNEMOUTH PRIORY

As slow I climb the cliff's ascending side,
   Much musing on the track of terror past,
   When o'er the dark wave rode the howling blast,
Pleased I look back, and view the tranquil tide
That laves the pebbled shore: and now the beam   5
   Of evening smiles on the gray battlement,
   And yon forsaken tower that time has rent;
The lifted oar far off with transient gleam
Is touched, and hushed is all the billowy deep!
   Soothed by the scene, thus on tired Nature's breast   10
   A stillness slowly steals, and kindred rest,
While sea-sounds lull her, as she sinks to sleep,
Like melodies that mourn upon the lyre,
Waked by the breeze, and, as they mourn, expire!

1789.

THE BELLS, OSTEND

How sweet the tuneful bells' responsive peal!
   As when, at opening morn, the fragrant breeze
   Breathes on the trembling sense of pale disease,
So piercing to my heart their force I feel!
And hark! with lessening cadence now they fall!   5
   And now, along the white and level tide,
   They fling their melancholy music wide,
Bidding me many a tender thought recall
Of summer days, and those delightful years
   When from an ancient tower, in life's fair prime,   10
   The mournful magic of their mingling chime
First waked my wondering childhood into tears!
But seeming now, when all those days are o'er,
The sounds of joy once heard, and heard no more.

  1787.   1789.

SAMUEL ROGERS

FROM

THE PLEASURES OF MEMORY

Twilight's soft dews steal o'er the village green,
With magic tints to harmonize the scene.
Stilled, is the hum that through the hamlet broke,
When round the ruins of their ancient oak
The peasants flocked to hear the minstrel play,   5
And games and carols closed the busy day.
Her wheel at rest, the matron thrills no more
With treasured tales and legendary lore.
All, all are fled; nor mirth nor music flows
To chase the dreams of innocent repose.   10
All, all are fled; yet still I linger here!
What secret charms this silent spot endear?
    Mark yon old mansion frowning through the trees,
Whose hollow turret wooes the whistling breeze.
That casement, arched with ivy's brownest shade,   15
First to these eyes the light of heaven conveyed.
The mouldering gateway strews the grass-grown court,
Once the calm scene of many a simple sport,
When all things pleased, for life itself was new,
And the heart promised what the fancy drew.   20

. . . .

    As through the garden's desert paths I rove,
What fond illusions swarm in every grove!
How oft, when purple evening tinged the west,
We watched the emmet to her grainy nest;
Welcomed the wild bee home on weary wing,   25
Laden with sweets, the choicest of the spring!
How oft inscribed, with Friendship's votive rhyme,
The bark now silvered by the touch of Time;
Soared in the swing, half pleased and half afraid,
Through sister elms that waved their summer shade;   30
Or strewed with crumbs yon root-inwoven seat,
To lure the redbreast from his lone retreat!
    Childhood's loved group revisits every scene,
The tangled wood-walk and the tufted green;

Indulgent Memory wakes, and lo, they live!   35
Clothed with far softer hues than light can give.
Thou first, best friend that Heaven assigns below
To soothe and sweeten all the cares we know;
Whose glad suggestions still each vain alarm,
When nature fades and life forgets to charm;   40
Thee would the Muse invoke! to thee belong
The sage's precept and the poet's song.
What softened views thy magic glass reveals,
When o'er the landscape Time's meek twilight steals!
As when in ocean sinks the orb of day,   45
Long on the wave reflected lustres play,
Thy tempered gleams of happiness resigned
Glance on the darkened mirror of the mind.

1792.

WILLIAM WORDSWORTH

FROM

AN EVENING WALK

The bird, with fading light who ceased to thread
Silent the hedge or steaming rivulet's bed,
From his grey re-appearing tower shall soon
Salute with boding note the rising moon,
Frosting with hoary light the pearly ground,   5
And pouring deeper blue to æther's bound,
Rejoiced her solemn pomp of clouds to fold
In robes of azure, fleecy white, and gold,
While rose and poppy, as the glow-worm fades,
Checquer with paler red the thicket shades.   10
    Now o'er the eastern hill, where darkness broods
O'er all its vanished dells, and lawns, and woods.
Where but a mass of shade the sight can trace,
She lifts in silence up her lovely face;
Above the gloomy valley flings her light,   15
Far to the western slopes with hamlets white;
And gives, where woods the checquered upland strew,
To the green corn of summer autumn's hue.

Thus Hope, first pouring from her blessed horn
Her dawn, far lovelier than the moon's own morn;   20
Till higher mounted, strives in vain to cheer
The weary hills, impervious, b!ack'ning near;
Yet does she still, undaunted, throw the while
On darling spots remote her tempting smile.

. . . .

The song of mountain streams unheard by day,   25
Now hardly heard, beguiles my homeward way.
All air is, as the sleeping water, still,
List'ning th' aërial music of the hill,
Broke only by the slow clock tolling deep,
Or shout that wakes the ferry-man from sleep,   30
Soon followed by his hollow-parting oar,
And echoed hoof approaching the far shore;
Sound of closed gate, across the water borne,
Hurrying the feeding hare through rustling corn;
The tremulous sob of the complaining owl,   35
And at long intervals the mill-dog's howl;
The distant forge's swinging thump profound,
Or yell in the deep woods of lonely hound.

1787–89.   *1793.*

SIMON LEE

THE OLD HUNTSMAN

WITH AN INCIDENT IN WHICH HE WAS CONCERNED

In the sweet shire of Cardigan,
Not far from pleasant Ivor-Hall,
An old man dwells, a little man,—
'T is said he once was tall.
Full five-and-thirty years he lived   5
A running huntsman merry;
And still the centre of his cheek
Is red as a ripe cherry.

No man like him the horn could sound,
And hill and valley rang with glee   10
When echo bandied, round and round,
The halloo of Simon Lee.

In those proud days he little cared
For husbandry or tillage;
To blither tasks did Simon rouse   15
The sleepers of the village.

He all the country could outrun,
Could leave both man and horse behind;
And often, ere the chase was done,
He reeled and was stone-blind.   20
And still there's something in the world
At which his heart rejoices;
For when the chiming hounds are out,
He dearly loves their voices!

But oh the heavy change! bereft   25
Of health, strength, friends, and kindred, see!
Old Simon to the world is left
In liveried poverty.
His master's dead, and no one now
Dwells in the Hall of Ivor;   30
Men, dogs, and horses, all are dead;
He is the sole survivor.

And he is lean, and he is sick;
His body, dwindled and awry,
Rests upon ankles swoln and thick;   35
His legs are thin and dry.
One prop he has, and only one,—
His wife, an aged woman,
Lives with him, near the waterfall,
Upon the village common.   40

Beside their moss-grown hut of clay,
Not twenty paces from the door,
A scrap of land they have, but they .
Are poorest of the poor.
This scrap of land he from the heath   45
Enclosed when he was stronger;
But what to them avails the land
Which he can till no longer?

Oft, working by her husband's side,
Ruth does what Simon cannot do;   50

For she, with scanty cause for pride,
Is stouter of the two.
And though you with your utmost skill
From labour could not wean them,
'T is little, very little, all   55
That they can do between them.

Few months of life has he in store,
As he to you will tell;
For still, the more he works, the more
Do his weak ankles swell.   60
My gentle reader, I perceive
How patiently you 've waited,
And now I fear that you expect
Some tale will be related.

O reader! had you in your mind   65
Such stores as silent thought can bring,
O gentle reader! you would find
A tale in every thing.
What more I have to say is short,
And you must kindly take it;   70
It is no tale, but should you think,
Perhaps a tale you 'll make it.

One summer day I chanced to see
This old man doing all he could
To unearth the root of an old tree,   75
A stump of rotten wood.
The mattock tottered in his hand;
So vain was his endeavour
That at the root of the old tree
He might have worked for ever.   80

"You 're overtasked, good Simon Lee;
Give me your tool," to him I said;
And at the word right gladly he
Received my proffered aid.
I struck, and with a single blow   85
The tangled root I severed,
At which the poor old man so long
And vainly had endeavoured.

The tears into his eyes were brought,
And thanks and praises seemed to run   90
So fast out of his heart I thought
They never would have done.—
I 've heard of hearts unkind, kind deeds
With coldness still returning;
Alas! the gratitude of men   95
Hath oftener left me mourning.

1798.   1798.

LINES WRITTEN IN EARLY SPRING

I heard a thousand blended notes,
While in a grove I sate reclined,
In that sweet mood when pleasant thoughts
Bring sad thoughts to the mind.

To her fair works did Nature link   5
The human soul that through me ran;
And much it grieved my heart to think
What man has made of man.

Through primrose tufts, in that green bower,
The periwinkle trailed its wreaths;   10
And 't is my faith that every flower
Enjoys the air it breathes.

The birds around me hopped and played;
Their thoughts I cannot measure,
But the least motion which they made   15
It seemed a thrill of pleasure.

The budding twigs spread out their fan,
To catch the breezy air;
And I must think, do all I can,
That there was pleasure there.   20

If this belief from heaven be sent,
If such be Nature's holy plan,
Have I not reason to lament
What man has made of man?

1798.   1798.

EXPOSTULATION AND REPLY

"Why, William, on that old grey stone,
Thus for the length of half a day,
Why, William, sit you thus alone,
And dream your time away?

"Where are your books?—that light bequeathed   5
To beings else forlorn and blind!
Up! up! and drink the spirit breathed
From dead men to their kind.

"You look round on your Mother Earth,
As if she for no purpose bore you;   10
As if you were her first-born birth,
And none had lived before you!"

One morning thus, by Esthwaite lake,
When life was sweet, I knew not why,
To me my good friend Matthew spake,   15
And thus I made reply:—

"The eye, it cannot choose but see;
We cannot bid the ear be still;
Our bodies feel, where'er they be,
Against or with our will.   20

"Nor less I deem that there are Powers
Which of themselves our minds impress;
That we can feed this mind of ours
In a wise passiveness.

"Think you, 'mid all this mighty sum   25
Of things forever speaking,
That nothing of itself will come,
But we must still be seeking?

"Then ask not wherefore, here, alone,
Conversing as I may,   30
I sit upon this old grey stone,
And dream my time away."

1798.   1798.

THE TABLES TURNED

AN EVENING SCENE ON THE SAME SUBJECT

Up! up! my friend, and quit your books,
Or surely you'll grow double.
Up! up! my friend, and clear your looks;
Why all this toil and trouble?

The sun, above the mountain's head,   5
A freshening lustre mellow
Through all the long green fields has spread,
His first sweet evening yellow,

Books! 't is a dull and endless strife:
Come, hear the woodland linnet,   10
How sweet his music! on my life,
There's more of wisdom in it.

And hark! how blithe the throstle sings!
He, too, is no mean preacher.
Come forth into the light of things;   15
Let Nature be your teacher.

She has a world of ready wealth,
Our minds and hearts to bless—
Spontaneous wisdom breathed by health,
Truth breathed by cheerfulness.   20

One impulse from a vernal wood
May teach you more of man,
Of moral evil and of good,
Than all the sages can.

Sweet is the lore which Nature brings: 25
Our meddling intellect
Mis-shapes the beautious forms of things—
We murder to dissect.

Enough of Science and of Art;
Close up those barren leaves;   30
Come forth, and bring with you a heart
That watches and receives.

1798.   1798.

LINES

COMPOSED A FEW MILES ABOVE TINTERN ABBEY, ON REVISITING THE
BANKS OF THE WYE DURING A TOUR. JULY 13, 1798

Five years have past; five summers, with the length
Of five long winters! and again I hear
These waters, rolling from their mountain springs
With a soft inland murmur.   Once again
Do I behold these steep and lofty cliffs,   5
That on a wild secluded scene impress
Thoughts of more deep seclusion, and connect
The landscape with the quiet of the sky.
The day is come when I again repose
Here, under this dark sycamore, and view   10
These plots of cottage-ground, these orchard-tufts,
Which at this season, with their unripe fruits,
Are clad in one green hue, and lose themselves
'Mid groves and copses.   Once again I see
These hedge-rows—hardly hedge-rows, little lines   15
Of sportive wood run wild; these pastoral farms,
Green to the very door; and wreaths of smoke
Sent up, in silence, from among the trees,
With some uncertain notice, as might seem
Of vagrant dwellers in the houseless woods,   20
Or of some hermit's cave, where by his fire
The hermit sits alone.
                              These beauteous forms,
Through a long absence, have not been to me
As is a landscape to a blind man's eye;
But oft, in lonely rooms, and 'mid the din   25
Of towns and cities, I have owed to them,
In hours of weariness, sensations sweet,
Felt in the blood, and felt along the heart,
And passing even into my purer mind
With tranquil restoration; feelings too   30
Of unremembered pleasure, such, perhaps,
As have no slight or trivial influence
On that best portion of a good man's life,
His little, nameless, unremembered acts
Of kindness and of love.   Nor less, I trust,   35

To them I may have owed another gift,
Of aspect more sublime: that blessèd mood
In which the burthen of the mystery,
In which the heavy and the weary weight
Of all this unintelligible world,   40
Is lightened; that serene and blessed mood
In which the affections gently lead us on,
Until, the breath of this corporeal frame
And even the motion of our human blood
Almost suspended, we are laid asleep   45
In body, and become a living soul,
While, with an eye made quiet by the power
Of harmony and the deep power of joy,
We see into the life of things.
                        If this
Be but a vain belief, yet oh how oft—   50
In darkness and amid the many shapes
Of joyless daylight; when the fretful stir
Unprofitable, and the fever of the world,
Have hung upon the beatings of my heart—
How oft, in spirit, have I turned to thee,   55
O sylvan Wye! thou wanderer through the woods;
How often has my spirit turned to thee!
    And now, with gleams of half-extinguished thought,
With many recognitions dim and faint,
And somewhat of a sad perplexity,   60
The picture of the mind revives again;
While here I stand, not only with the sense
Of present pleasure, but with pleasing thoughts
That in this moment there is life and food
For future years. And so I dare to hope,   65
Though changed, no doubt, from what I was when first
I came among these hills; when like a roe
I bounded o'er the mountains, by the sides
Of the deep rivers and the lonely streams,
Wherever Nature led, more like a man   70
Flying from something that he dreads than one
Who sought the thing he loved. For Nature then
(The coarser pleasures of my boyish days,
And their glad animal movements, all gone by)

To me was all in all. I cannot paint   75
What then I was. The sounding cataract
Haunted me like a passion; the tall rock,
The mountain, and the deep and gloomy wood,
Their colours and their forms, were then to me
An appetite, a feeling and a love,   80
That had no need of a remoter charm,
Unborrowed from the eye. That time is past,
By thought supplied, nor any interest
And all its aching joys are now no more,
And all its dizzy raptures. Not for this   85
Faint I, nor mourn nor murmur; other gifts
Have followed, for such loss, I would believe,
Abundant recompense. For I have learned
To look on Nature, not as in the hour
Of thoughtless youth, but hearing oftentimes   90
The still, sad music of humanity,
Nor harsh nor grating, though of ample power
To chasten and subdue. And I have felt
A presence that disturbs me with the joy
Of elevated thoughts; a sense sublime   95
Of something far more deeply interfused,
Whose dwelling is the light of setting suns,
And the round ocean, and the living air,
And the blue sky, and in the mind of man;
A motion and a spirit, that impels   100
All thinking things, all objects of all thought,
And rolls through all things. Therefore am I still
A lover of the meadows and the woods
And mountains, and of all that we behold
From this green earth; of all the mighty world   105
Of eye and ear—both what they half create,
And what perceive; well pleased to recognise
In Nature, and the language of the sense,
The anchor of my purest thoughts, the nurse,
The guide, the guardian of my heart, and soul   110
Of all my moral being.
                              Nor perchance,
If I were not thus taught, should I the more
Suffer my genial spirits to decay:

For thou art with me here upon the banks
Of this fair river, thou my dearest friend,   115
My dear, dear friend; and in thy voice I catch
The language of my former heart, and read
My former pleasures in the shooting lights
Of thy wild eyes. Oh yet a little while
May I behold in thee what I was once,   120
My dear, dear sister; and this prayer I make,
Knowing that Nature never did betray
The heart that loved her: 't is her privilege,
Through all the years of this our life, to lead
From joy to joy; for she can so inform   125
The mind that is within us, so impress
With quietness and beauty, and so feed
With lofty thoughts, that neither evil tongues,
Rash judgments, nor the sneers of selfish men,
Nor greetings where no kindness is, nor all   130
The dreary intercourse of daily life,
Shall e'er prevail against us, or disturb
Our cheerful faith that all which we behold
Is full of blessings. Therefore let the moon
Shine on thee in thy solitary walk;   135
And let the misty mountain winds be free
To blow against thee; and in after years,
When these wild ecstasies shall be matured
Into a sober pleasure, when thy mind
Shall be a mansion for all lovely forms,   140
Thy memory be as a dwelling-place
For all sweet sounds and harmonies, oh then,
If solitude, or fear, or pain, or grief,
Should be thy portion, with what healing thoughts
Of tender joy wilt thou remember me,   145
And these my exhortations! Nor, perchance—
If I should be where I no more can hear
Thy voice, nor catch from thy wild eyes these gleams
Of past existence—wilt thou then forget
That on the banks of this delightful stream   150
We stood together; and that I, so long
A worshipper of Nature, hither came
Unwearied in that service—rather say,

With warmer love, oh with far deeper zeal
Of holier love! Nor wilt thou then forget   155
That after many wanderings, many years
Of absence, these steep woods and lofty cliffs,
And this green pastoral landscape, were to me
More dear, both for themselves and for thy sake.
1798.   1798.

ANIMAL TRANQUILLITY AND DECAY

  The little hedgerow birds,
That peck along the roads, regard him not.
He travels on, and in his face, his step,
His gait, is one expression: every limb,
His look and bending figure, all bespeak   5
A man who does not move with pain, but moves
With thought. He is insensibly subdued
To settled quiet; he is one by whom
All effort seems forgotten; one to whom
Long patience hath such mild composure given   10
That patience now doth seem a thing of which
He hath no need. He is by nature led
To peace so perfect that the young behold
With envy what the old man hardly feels.
1798.   1798.

THE SIMPLON PASS

  Brook and road
Were fellow-travellers in this gloomy pass,
And with them did we journey several hours
At a slow step. The immeasurable height
Of woods decaying, never to be decayed,   5
The stationary blasts of waterfalls,
And in the narrow rent, at every turn,
Winds thwarting winds bewildered and forlorn,
The torrents shooting from the clear blue sky,
The rocks that muttered close upon our ears,   10
Black drizzling crags that spake by the wayside
As if a voice were in them, the sick sight

And giddy prospect of the raving stream,
The unfettered clouds and region of the heavens,
Tumult and peace, the darkness and the light,   15
Were all like workings of one mind, the features
Of the same face, blossoms upon one tree,
Characters of the great Apocalypse,
The types and symbols of Eternity,
Of first, and last, and midst, and without end.   20

1799? or 1804.   1845.

INFLUENCE OF NATURAL OBJECTS

IN CALLING FORTH AND STRENGTHENING THE IMAGINATION IN BOY-HOOD AND EARLY YOUTH

Wisdom and Spirit of the universe!
Thou Soul, that are the Eternity of thought,
And giv'st to forms and images a breath
And everlasting motion! not in vain,
By day or star-light, thus from my first dawn   5
Of childhood didst thou intertwine for me
The passions that build up our human soul,
Not with the mean and vulgar works of man,
But with high objects, with enduring things,
With life and Nature, purifying thus   10
The elements of feeling and of thought,
And sanctifying by such discipline
Both pain and fear, until we recognise
A grandeur in the beatings of the heart.
    Nor was this fellowship vouchsafed to me   15
With stinted kindness. In November days,
When vapours rolling down the valleys made
A lonely scene more lonesome; among woods
At noon; and 'mid the calm of summer nights,
When, by the margin of the trembling lake,   20
Beneath the gloomy hills, homeward I went
In solitude; such intercourse was mine.
Mine was it in the fields both day and night,
And by the waters, all the summer long.
And in the frosty season, when the sun   25

Was set, and, visible for many a mile,
The cottage-windows through the twilight blazed,
I heeded not the summons: happy time
It was indeed for all of us; for me
It was a time of rapture! Clear and loud   30
The village-clock tolled six—I wheeled about,
Proud and exulting like an untired horse
That cares not for his home. All shod with steel
We hissed along the polished ice, in games
Confederate, imitative of the chase   35
And woodland pleasures—the resounding horn,
The pack loud-chiming and the hunted hare.
So through the darkness and the cold we flew,
And not a voice was idle: with the din
Smitten, the precipices rang aloud;   40
The leafless trees and every icy crag
Tinkled like iron; while far-distant hills
Into the tumult sent an alien sound
Of melancholy, not unnoticed, while the stars,
Eastward, were sparkling clear, and in the west   45
The orange sky of evening died away.
Not seldom from the uproar I retired
Into a silent bay, or sportively
Glanced sideway, leaving the tumultuous throng,
To cut across the reflex of a star,   50
Image that, flying still before me, gleamed
Upon the glassy plain. And oftentimes,
When we had given our bodies to the wind,
And all the shadowy banks on either side
Came sweeping through the darkness, spinning still 55
The rapid line of motion, then at once
Have I, reclining back upon my heels,
Stopped short; yet still the solitary cliffs
Wheeled by me—even as if the earth had rolled
With visible motion her diurnal round!   60
Behind me did they stretch in solemn train,
Feebler and feebler, and I stood and watched
Till all was tranquil as a summer sea.

1799.   1809.

SHE DWELT AMONG THE UNTRODDEN WAYS

She dwelt among the untrodden ways
   Beside the springs of Dove;
A maid whom there were none to praise,
   And very few to love:

A violet by a mossy stone   5
   Half hidden from the eye;
Fair as a star, when only one
   Is shining in the sky.

She lived unknown, and few could know
   When Lucy ceased to be;   10
But she is in her grave, and oh
   The difference to me!

1799.   1800.

LUCY GRAY

OR, SOLITUDE

Oft I had heard of Lucy Gray;
And when I crossed the wild,
I chanced to see at break of day
The solitary child.

No mate, no comrade Lucy knew;   5
She dwelt on a wide moor—
The sweetest thing that ever grew
Beside a human door!

You yet may spy the fawn at play,
The hare upon the green;   10
But the sweet face of Lucy Gray
Will never more be seen.

"To-night will be a stormy night—
You to the town must go;
And take a lantern, child, to light   15
Your mother through the snow."

"That, father, will I gladly do;
'T is scarcely afternoon—
The minster-clock has just struck two,
And yonder is the moon!"   20

At this the father raised his hook,
And snapped a faggot-band;
He plied his work; and Lucy took
The lantern in her hand.

Not blither is the mountain roe: 25
With many a wanton stroke
Her feet disperse the powdery snow,
That rises up like smoke.

The storm came on before its time:
She wandered up and down,   30
And many a hill did Lucy climb,
But never reached the town.

The wretched parents all that night
Went shouting far and wide;
But there was neither sound nor sight   35
To serve them for a guide.

At daybreak on a hill they stood
That overlooked the moor,
And thence they saw the bridge of wood,
A furlong from their door.   40

They wept, and, turning homeward, cried,
"In heaven we all shall meet!"
When in the snow the mother spied
The print of Lucy's feet.

Then downwards from the steep hill's edge   45
They tracked the footmarks small,
And through the broken hawthorn-hedge,
And by the long stone wall;

And then an open field they crossed;
The marks were still the same;   50
They tracked them on, nor ever lost,
And to the bridge they came.

They followed from the snowy bank
Those footmarks, one by one,
Into the middle of the plank;   55
And further there were none!

—Yet some maintain that to this day
She is a living child;
That you may see sweet Lucy Gray
Upon the lonesome wild: 60

O'er rough and smooth she trips along,
And never looks behind,
And sings a solitary song,
That whistles in the wind.

1799.   1800.

FROM
THE RECLUSE

On man, on Nature, and on human life
Musing in solitude, I oft perceive
Fair trains of imagery before me rise,
Accompanied by feelings of delight
Pure, or with no unpleasing sadness mixed;   5
And I am conscious of affecting thoughts
And dear remembrances, whose presence soothes
Or elevates the mind, intent to weigh
The good and evil of our mortal state.
To these emotions, whencesoe'er they come,   10
Whether from breath of outward circumstance,
Or from the soul—an impulse to herself,—
I would give utterance in numerous verse.
Of truth, of grandeur, beauty, love, and hope,
And melancholy fear subdued by faith;   15
Of blessed consolations in distress;
Of moral strength and intellectual power;
Of joy in widest commonalty spread;
Of the individual mind that keeps her own
Inviolate retirement, subject there   20
To conscience only, and the law supreme
Of that Intelligence which governs all—
I sing:—"fit audience let me find though few!"
So prayed, more gaining than he asked, the bard—
In holiest mood. Urania, I shall need   25
Thy guidance, or a greater muse, if such
Descend to earth or dwell in highest heaven!

For I must tread on shadowy ground, must sink
Deep, and, aloft ascending, breathe in worlds
To which the heaven of heavens is but a veil.   30
All strength, all terror, single or in bands,
That ever was put forth in personal form,
Jehovah with his thunder, and the choir
Of shouting angels, and the empyreal thrones,
I pass them unalarmed. Not Chaos, not   35
The darkest pit of lowest Erebus,
Nor aught of blinder vacancy, scooped out
By help of dreams, can breed such fear and awe
As fall upon us often when we look
Into our minds, into the mind of man,   40
My haunt, and the main region of my song.
Beauty—a living presence of the earth,
Surpassing the most fair ideal forms
Which craft of delicate spirits hath composed
From earth's materials—waits upon my steps,   45
Pitches her tents before me as I move,
An hourly neighbour. Paradise, and groves
Elysian, Fortunate Fields—like those of old
Sought in the Atlantic Main,—why should they be
A history only of departed things,   50
Or a mere fiction of what never was?
For the discerning intellect of man,
When wedded to this goodly universe
In love and holy passion, shall find these
A simple produce of the common day.   55
I, long before the blissful hour arrives,
Would chant, in lonely peace, the spousal verse
Of this great consummation: and, by words
Which speak of nothing more than what we are,
Would I arouse the sensual from their sleep   60
Of death, and win the vacant and the vain
To noble raptures; while my voice proclaims
How exquisitely the individual mind
(And the progressive powers perhaps no less
Of the whole species) to the external world   65
Is fitted; and how exquisitely, too—
Theme this but little heard of among men—
The external world is fitted to the mind;

And the creation (by no lower name
Can it be called) which they with blended might   70
Accomplish. This is our high argument,
—Such grateful haunts foregoing, if I oft
Must turn elsewhere—to travel near the tribes
And fellowships of men, and see ill sights
Of madding passions mutually inflamed;   75
Must hear humanity in fields and groves
Pipe solitary anguish; or must hang
Brooding above the fierce confederate storm
Of sorrow, barricadoed evermore
Within the walls of cities,—may these sounds   80
Have their authentic comment; that even these
Hearing, I be not downcast or forlorn!

1799?   1888.

MICHAEL

A PASTORAL POEM

If from the public way you turn your steps
Up the tumultuous brook of Green-head Ghyll,
You will suppose that with an upright path
Your feet must struggle, in such bold ascent
The pastoral mountains front you, face to face.   5
But courage! for around that boisterous brook
The mountains have all opened out themselves,
And made a hidden valley of their own.
No habitation can be seen; but they
Who journey thither find themselves alone   10
With a few sheep, with rocks and stones, and kites
That overhead are sailing in the sky.
It is in truth an utter solitude;
Nor should I have made mention of this dell
But for one object which you might pass by,   15
Might see and notice not. Beside the brook
Appears a straggling heap of unhewn stones;
And to that simple object appertains
A story, unenriched with strange events,
Yet not unfit, I deem, for the fireside,   20
Or for the summer shade. It was the first

Of those domestic tales that spake to me
Of shepherds, dwellers in the valleys, men
Whom I already loved—not verily
For their own sakes, but for the fields and hills　　25
Where was their occupation and abode.
And hence this tale, while I was yet a boy
Careless of books, yet having felt the power
Of Nature, by the gentle agency
Of natural objects led me on to feel　　30
For passions that were not my own, and think
(At random and imperfectly indeed)
On man, the heart of man, and human life.
Therefore, although it be a history
Homely and rude, I will relate the same　　35
For the delight of a few natural hearts,
And, with yet fonder feeling, for the sake
Of youthful poets, who among these hills
Will be my second self when I am gone.

Upon the forest-side in Grasmere Vale　　40
There dwelt a shepherd, Michael was his name;
An old man, stout of heart and strong of limb.
His bodily frame had been from youth to age
Of an unusual strength; his mind was keen,
Intense, and frugal, apt for all affairs,　　45
And in his shepherd's calling he was prompt
And watchful more than ordinary men.
Hence had he learned the meaning of all winds,
Of blasts of every tone; and oftentimes,
When others heeded not, he heard the south　　50
Make subterraneous music, like the noise
Of bagpipers on distant Highland hills.
The shepherd, at such warning, of his flock
Bethought him, and he to himself would say,
"The winds are now devising work for me!"　　55
And, truly, at all times, the storm, that drives
The traveller to a shelter, summoned him
Up to the mountains; he had been alone
Amid the heart of many thousand mists,
That came to him, and left him, on the heights,　　60
So lived he till his eightieth year was past.

And grossly that man errs who should suppose
That the green valleys and the streams and rocks
Were things indifferent to the shepherd's thoughts.
Fields, where with cheerful spirits he had breathed   65
The common air; hills, which with vigorous step
He had so often climbed, which had impressed
So many incidents upon his mind
Of hardship, skill or courage, joy or fear,
Which, like a book, preserved the memory   70
Of the dumb animals whom he had saved,
Had fed or sheltered, linking to such acts
The certainty of honourable gain;
Those fields, those hills—what could they less?—had laid
Strong hold on his affections, were to him   75
A pleasurable feeling of blind love,
The pleasure which there is in life itself.
      His days had not been passed in singleness.
His helpmate was a comely matron, old,
Though younger than himself full twenty years.   80
She was a woman of a stirring life,
Whose heart was in her house: two wheels she had
Of antique form; this large, for spinning wool;
That small, for flax; and if one wheel had rest,
It was because the other was at work.   85
The pair had but one inmate in their house,
An only child, who had been born to them
When Michael, telling o'er his years, began
To deem that he was old—in shepherd's phrase,
With one foot in the grave. This only son,   90
With two brave sheep-dogs tried in many a storm,
The one of an' inestimable worth,
Made all their household. I may truly say
That they were as a proverb in the vale
For endless industry. When day was gone,   95
And from their occupations out of doors
The son and father were come home, even then
Their labour did not cease, unless when all
Turned to the cleanly supper-board, and there,
Each with a mess of pottage and skimmed milk,   100
Sat round the basket piled with oaten cakes

And their plain home-made cheese. Yet when the meal
Was ended, Luke (for so the son was named)
And his old father both betook themselves
To such convenient work as might employ　　　　105
Their hands by the fireside; perhaps to card
Wool for the housewife's spindle, or repair
Some injury done to sickle, flail, or scythe,
Or other implement of house or field.

　　　Down from the ceiling, by the chimney's edge,　　　110
That in our ancient uncouth country style
With huge and black projection overbrowed
Large space beneath, as duly as the light
Of day grew dim the housewife hung a lamp;
An aged utensil, which had performed　　　　115
Service beyond all others of its kind.
Early at evening did it burn, and late,
Surviving comrade of uncounted hours,
Which, going by from year to year, had found
And left the couple neither gay perhaps　　　　120
Nor cheerful, yet with objects and with hopes,
Living a life of eager industry.
And now, when Luke had reached his eighteenth year,
There by the light of this old lamp they sate,
Father and son, while far into the night　　　　125
The housewife plied her own peculiar work,
Making the cottage through the silent hours
Murmur as with the sound of summer flies.
This light was famous in its neighbourhood,
And was a public symbol of the life　　　　130
That thrifty pair had lived. For, as it chanced,
Their cottage on a plot of rising ground
Stood single, with large prospect, north and south,
High into Easedale, up to Dunmail-Raise,
And westward to the village near the lake;　　　　135
And from this constant light, so regular
And so far seen, the house itself, by all
Who dwelt within the limits of the vale,
Both old and young, was named THE EVENING STAR.

　　　Thus living on through such a length of years,　　　140
The shepherd, if he loved himself, must needs

Have loved his helpmate; but to Michael's heart
This son of his old age was yet more dear—
Less from instinctive tenderness, the same
Fond spirit that blindly works in the blood of all,   145
Than that a child, more than all other gifts
That Earth can offer to declining man,
Brings hope with it, and forward-looking thoughts,
And stirrings of inquietude, when they
By tendency of nature needs must fail.   150
Exceeding was the love he bare to him,
His heart and his heart's joy! For oftentimes
Old Michael, while he was a babe in arms,
Had done him female service, not alone
For pastime and delight, as is the use   155
Of fathers, but with patient mind enforced
To acts of tenderness; and he had rocked
His cradle, as with a woman's gentle hand.
    And in a later time, ere yet the boy
Had put on boy's attire, did Michael love,   160
Albeit of a stern unbending mind,
To have the young one in his sight, when he
Wrought in the field, or on his shepherd's stool
Sate with a fettered sheep before him stretched
Under the large old oak, that near his door   165
Stood single, and, from matchless depth of shade,
Chosen for the shearer's covert from the sun,
Thence in our rustic dialect was called
THE CLIPPING-TREE, a name which yet it bears.
There, while they two were sitting in the shade,   170
With others round them, earnest all and blithe,
Would Michael exercise his heart with looks
Of fond correction and reproof bestowed
Upon the child, if he disturbed the sheep
By catching at their legs, or with his shouts   175
Scared them, while they lay still beneath the shears.
    And when by Heaven's good grace the boy grew up
A healthy lad, and carried in his cheek
Two steady roses that were five years old,
Then Michael from a winter coppice cut   180
With his own hand a sapling, which he hooped

With iron, making it throughout in all
Due requisites a perfect shepherd's staff,
And gave it to the boy; wherewith equipt
He as a watchman oftentimes was placed   185
At gate or gap, to stem or turn the flock;
And, to his office prematurely called,
There stood the urchin, as you will divine,
Something between a hindrance and a help,
And for this cause not always, I believe,   190
Receiving from his father hire of praise,
Though nought was left undone which staff, or voice,
Or looks, or threatening gestures could perform.

But soon as Luke, full ten years old, could stand
Against the mountain blasts, and to the heights, 195
Not fearing toil nor length of weary ways,
He with his father daily went, and they
Were as companions, why should I relate
That objects which the shepherd loved before
Were dearer now? that from the boy there came   200
Feelings and emanations—things which were
Light to the sun and music to the wind,—
And that the old man's heart seemed born again?

Thus in his father's sight the boy grew up;
And now, when he had reached his eighteenth year, 205
He was his comfort and his daily hope.

While in this sort the simple household lived
From day to day, to Michael's ear there came
Distressful tidings. Long before the time
Of which I speak, the shepherd had been bound   210
In surety for his brother's son, a man
Of an industrious life and ample means;
But unforeseen misfortunes suddenly
Had prest upon him; and old Michael now
Was summoned to discharge the forfeiture,   215
A grievous penalty, but little less
Than half his substance. This unlooked-for claim,
At the first hearing, for a moment took
More hope out of his life than he supposed
That any old man ever could have lost.   220
As soon as he had armed himself with strength

To look his trouble in the face, it seemed
The shepherd's sole resource to sell at once
A portion of his patrimonial fields.
Such was his first resolve; he thought again,   225
And his heart failed him. "Isabel," said he,
Two evenings after he heard the news,
"I have been toiling more than seventy years,
And in the open sunshine of God's love
Have we all lived; yet if these fields of ours   230
Should pass into a stranger's hand, I think
That I could not lie quiet in my grave.
Our lot is a hard lot: the sun himself
Has scarcely been more diligent than I;
And I have lived to be a fool at last   235
To my own family. An evil man
That was, and made an evil choice, if he
Were false to us; and if he were not false,
There are ten thousand to whom loss like this
Had been no sorrow. I forgive him;—but   240
'T were better to be dumb than to talk thus.
When I began, my purpose was to speak
Of remedies and of a cheerful hope.
Our Luke shall leave us, Isabel; the land
Shall not go from us, and it shall be free;   245
He shall possess it, free as is the wind
That passes over it. We have, thou know'st,
Another kinsman; he will be our friend
In this distress. He is a prosperous man,
Thriving in trade; and Luke to him shall go,   250
And with his kinsman's help and his own thrift
He quickly will repair this loss, and then
He may return to us. If here he stay,
What can be done? Where every one is poor,
What can be gained?"

                        At this the old man paused,   255
And Isabel sat silent, for her mind
Was busy, looking back into past times.
"There's Richard Bateman," thought she to herself,
"He was a parish-boy—at the church-door
They made a gathering for him, shillings, pence,   260

And halfpennies, wherewith the neighbours bought
A basket, which they filled with pedlar's wares;
And, with this basket on his arm, the lad
Went up to London, found a master there,
Who, out of many, chose the trusty boy   265
To go and overlook his merchandise
Beyond the seas; where he grew wondrous rich,
And left estates and monies to the poor,
And, at his birth-place, built a chapel floored
With marble, which he sent from foreign lands."   270
These thoughts, and many others of like sort,
Passed quickly through the mind of Isabel,
And her face brightened. The old man was glad,
And thus resumed: "Well, Isabel, this scheme,
These two days, has been meat and drink to me.   275
Far more than we have lost is left us yet.
We have enough—I wish indeed that I
Were younger;—but this hope is a good hope.
Make ready Luke's best garments, of the best
Buy for him more, and let us send him forth   280
To-morrow, or the next day, or to-night—
If he *could* go, the boy should go to-night."

    Here Michael ceased, and to the fields went forth
With a light heart. The housewife for five days
Was restless morn and night, and all day long   285
Wrought on with her best fingers to prepare
Things needful for the journey of her son.
But Isabel was glad when Sunday came
To stop her in her work; for when she lay
By Michael's side, she through the last two nights   290
Heard him, how he was troubled in his sleep,
And when they rose at morning she could see
That all his hopes were gone. That day at noon
She said to Luke, while they two by themselves
Were sitting at the door, "Thou must not go: 295
We have no other child but thee to lose,
None to remember—do not go away,
For if thou leave thy father he will die."
The youth made answer with a jocund voice;
And Isabel, when she had told her fears,   300

Recovered heart. That evening her best fare
Did she bring forth, and all together sat
Like happy people round a Christmas fire.

With daylight Isabel resumed her work; 305
And all the ensuing week the house appeared
As cheerful as a grove in spring. At length
The expected letter from their kinsman came,
With kind assurances that he would do
His utmost for the welfare of the boy;
To which requests were added that forthwith 310
He might be sent to him. Ten times or more
The letter was read over; Isabel
Went forth to show it to the neighbours round;
Nor was there at that time on English land
A prouder heart than Luke's. When Isabel 315
Had to her house returned, the old man said,
"He shall depart to-morrow." To this word
The housewife answered, talking much of things
Which, if at such short notice he should go,
Would surely be forgotten. But at length 320
She gave consent, and Michael was at ease.

Near the tumultuous brook of Green-head Ghyll,
In that deep valley, Michael had designed
To build a sheepfold; and before he heard
The tidings of his melancholy loss, 325
For this same purpose he had gathered up
A heap of stones, which by the streamlet's edge
Lay thrown together, ready for the work.
With Luke that evening thitherward he walked;
And soon as they had reached the place he stopped, 330
And thus the old man spake to him: "My son,
To-morrow thou wilt leave me; with full heart
I look upon thee, for thou art the same
That wert a promise to me ere thy birth,
And all thy life hast been my daily joy. 335
I will relate to thee some little part
Of our two histories; 't will do thee good
When thou art from me, even if I should touch
On things thou canst not know of.——After thou
First cam'st into the world—as oft befalls 340

To new-born infants—thou didst sleep away
Two days, and blessings from thy father's tongue
Then fell upon thee. Day by day passed on.
And still I loved thee with increasing love.
Never to living ear came sweeter sounds   345
Than when I heard thee by our own fireside
First uttering, without words, a natural tune,
While thou, a feeding babe, didst in thy joy
Sing at thy mother's breast. Month followed month,
And in the open fields my life was passed,   350
And on the mountains, else I think that thou
Hadst been brought up upon thy father's knees.
But we were playmates, Luke; among these hills,
As well thou knowest, in us the old and young
Have played together, nor with me didst thou   355
Lack any pleasure which a boy can know."
Luke had a manly heart, but at these words
He sobbed aloud. The old man grasped his hand,
And said, "Nay, do not take it so—I see
That these are things of which I need not speak.   360
Even to the utmost I have been to thee
A kind and a good father; and herein
I but repay a gift which I myself
Received at others' hands, for, though now old
Beyond the common life of man, I still   365
Remember them who loved me in my youth.
Both of them sleep together: here they lived,
As all their forefathers had done; and when
At length their time was come, they were not loth
To give their bodies to the family mould.   370
I wished that thou shouldst live the life they lived;
But 't is a long time to look back, my son,
And see so little gain from threescore years.
These fields were burthened when they came to me;
Till I was forty years of age, not more   375
Than half of my inheritance was mine.
I toiled and toiled; God blessed me in my work,
And till these three weeks past the land was free.
It looks as if it never could endure
Another master. Heaven forgive me, Luke,   380

If I judge ill for thee, but it seems good
That thou shouldst go."
                        At this the old man paused;
Then, pointing to the stones near which they stood,
Thus, after a short silence, he resumed:
"This was a work for us; and now, my son,   385
It is a work for me. But lay one stone—
Here, lay it for me, Luke, with thine own hands.
Nay, boy, be of good hope;—we both may live
To see a better day. At eighty-four
I still am strong and hale;—do thou thy part;   390
I will do mine.—I will begin again
With many tasks that were resigned to thee;
Up to the heights, and in among the storms,
Will I without thee go again, and do
All works which I was wont to do alone,   395
Before I knew thy face.—Heaven bless thee, boy!
Thy heart these two weeks has been beating fast
With many hopes; it should be so—yes—yes—
I knew that thou couldst never have a wish
To leave me, Luke; thou hast been bound to me   400
Only by links of love: when thou art gone,
What will be left to us?—But I forget
My purposes. Lay now the corner-stone,
As I requested; and hereafter, Luke,
When thou art gone away, should evil men   405
Be thy companions, think of me, my son,
And of this moment; hither turn thy thoughts,
And God will strengthen thee: amid all fear
And all temptation, Luke, I pray that thou
Mayst bear in mind the life thy fathers lived,   410
Who, being innocent, did for that cause
Bestir them in good deeds. Now, fare thee well—
When thou return'st, thou in this place wilt see
A work which is not here; a covenant
'T will be between us; but whatever fate   415
Befall thee, I shall love thee to the last,
And bear thy memory with me to the grave."
    The shepherd ended here; and Luke stooped down,
And, as his father had requested, laid

The first stone of the sheepfold. At the sight   420
The old man's grief broke from him: to his heart
He pressed his son, he kissèd him and wept;
And to the house together they returned.

Hushed was that house in peace, or seeming peace,
Ere the night fell. With morrow's dawn the boy   425
Began his journey, and when he had reached
The public way, he put on a bold face;
And all the neighbours, as he passed their doors,
Came forth with wishes and with farewell prayers,
That followed him till he was out of sight.   430

A good report did from their kinsman come,
Of Luke and his well-doing; and the boy
Wrote loving letters, full of wondrous news,
Which, as the housewife phrased it, were throughout
"The prettiest letters that were ever seen."   435
Both parents read them with rejoicing hearts.
So, many months passed on; and once again
The shepherd went about his daily work
With confident and cheerful thoughts; and now
Sometimes, when he could find a leisure hour,   440
He to that valley took his way, and there
Wrought at the sheepfold. Meantime Luke began
To slacken in his duty; and at length
He in the dissolute city gave himself
To evil courses; ignominy and shame   445
Fell on him, so that he was driven at last
To seek a hiding-place beyond the seas.

There is a comfort in the strength of love;
'T will make a thing endurable which else
Would overset the brain, or break the heart.   450
I have conversed with more than one who well
Remember the old man, and what he was
Years after he had heard this heavy news.
His bodily frame had been from youth to age
Of an unusual strength. Among the rocks   455
He went, and still looked up to sun and cloud,
And listened to the wind; and, as before,
Performed all kinds of labour for his sheep,
And for the land, his small inheritance.

And to that hollow dell from time to time 460
Did he repair, to build the fold of which
His flock had need. 'T is not forgotten yet
The pity which was then in every heart
For the old man—and 't is believed by all
That many and many a day he thither went 465
And never lifted up a single stone.
There, by the sheepfold, sometimes was he seen
Sitting alone, or with his faithful dog,
Then old, beside him, lying at his feet.
The length of full seven years, from time to time, 470
He at the building of this sheepfold wrought,
And left the work unfinished when he died.

   Three years, or little more, did Isabel
Survive her husband; at her death the estate
Was sold, and went into a stranger's hand. 475
The cottage which was named THE EVENING STAR
Is gone—the ploughshare has been through the ground
On which it stood; great changes have been wrought
In all the neighbourhood; yet the oak is left
That grew beside their door, and the remains 480
Of the unfinished sheepfold may be seen
Beside the boisterous brook of Green-head Ghyll.

  1800.   1800.

TO THE CUCKOO

   O blithe new-comer! I have heard,
   I hear thee, and rejoice.
   O cuckoo! shall I call thee bird,
   Or but a wandering voice?

   While I am lying on the grass 5
   Thy twofold shout I hear;
   From hill to hill it seems to pass,
   At once far off and near.

   Though babbling only to the vale,
   Of sunshine and of flowers, 10
   Thou bringest unto me a tale
   Of visionary hours.

Thrice welcome, darling of the spring!
Even yet thou art to me
No bird, but an invisible thing,   15
A voice, a mystery;

The same whom in my school-boy days
I listened to—that cry
Which made me look a thousand ways
In bush, and tree, and sky.   20

To seek thee did I often rove
Through woods and on the green;
And thou wert still a hope, a love—
Still longed for, never seen.

And I can listen to thee yet,   25
Can lie upon the plain
And listen, till I do beget
That golden time again.

O blessèd bird! the earth we pace
Again appears to be   30
An unsubstantial faëry place;
That is fit home for thee!

1802.   *1807.*

MY HEART LEAPS UP

My heart leaps up when I behold
    A rainbow in the sky:
So was it when my life began;
So is it now I am a man;
So be it when I shall grow old,   5
    Or let me die!
The child is father of the man;
And I could wish my days to be
Bound each to each by natural piety.

1802.   *1807.*

COMPOSED UPON WESTMINSTER BRIDGE, SEPTEMBER 3, 1802

Earth has not any thing to show more fair;
Dull would he be of soul who could pass by

A sight so touching in its majesty:
This city now doth, like a garment, wear
The beauty of the morning; silent, bare,   5
Ships, towers, domes, theatres, and temples lie
Open unto the fields and to the sky,
All bright and glittering in the smokeless air.
Never did sun more beautifully steep,
In his first splendour, valley, rock, or hill;   10
Ne'er saw I, never felt, a calm so deep!
The river glideth at his own sweet will;
Dear God! the very houses seem asleep;
And all that mighty heart is lying still!

1802.   1807.

IT IS A BEAUTEOUS EVENING, CALM AND FREE

It is a beauteous evening, calm and free;
The holy time is quiet as a nun
Breathless with adoration; the broad sun
Is sinking down in its tranquillity;
The gentleness of heaven broods o'er the sea: 5
Listen! the mighty Being is awake,
And doth with His eternal motion make
A sound like thunder—everlastingly.
Dear child! dear girl! that walkest with me here,
If thou appear untouched by solemn thought,   10
Thy nature is not therefore less divine:
Thou liest in Abraham's bosom all the year,
And worshipp'st at the Temple's inner shrine,
God being with thee when we know it not.

1802.   1807.

LONDON, 1802

Milton! thou shouldst be living at this hour;
England hath need of thee: she is a fen
Of stagnant waters; altar, sword, and pen,
Fireside, the heroic wealth of hall and bower,
Have forfeited their ancient English dower   5
Of inward happiness. We are selfish men:
Oh raise us up, return to us again;

And give us manners, virtue, freedom, power.
Thy soul was like a star, and dwelt apart;
Thou hadst a voice whose sound was like the sea;   10
Pure as the naked heavens, majestic, free,
So didst thou travel on life's common way,
In cheerful godliness, and yet thy heart
The lowliest duties on herself did lay.

1802.   *1807.*

THE GREEN LINNET

Beneath these fruit-tree boughs that shed
Their snow-white blossoms on my head,
With brightest sunshine round me spread
        Of spring's unclouded weather,
In this sequestered nook how sweet   5
To sit upon my orchard-seat,
And birds and flowers once more to greet,
        My last year's friends together!

One have I marked, the happiest guest
In all this covert of the blest: 10
Hail to thee, far above the rest
        In joy of voice and pinion!
Thou, linnet! in thy green array,
Presiding spirit here to-day,
Dost lead the revels of the May,   15
        And this is thy dominion.

While birds and butterflies and flowers
Make all one band of paramours,
Thou, ranging up and down the bowers,
        Art sole in thy employment;   20
A life, a presence like the air,
Scattering thy gladness without care,
Too blest with any one to pair,
        Thyself thy own enjoyment.

Amid yon tuft of hazel trees,   25
That twinkle to the gusty breeze,
Behold him perched in ecstasies,
        Yet seeming still to hover;

There! where the flutter of his wings
Upon his back and body flings   30
Shadows and sunny glimmerings,
    That cover him all over.

My dazzled sight he oft deceives,
A brother of the dancing leaves;
Then flits, and from the cottage eaves   35
    Pours forth his song in gushes,
As if by that exulting strain
He mocked and treated with disdain
The voiceless form he chose to feign,
    While fluttering in the bushes.   40

1803.   1807.

THE SOLITARY REAPER

Behold her, single in the field,
Yon solitary Highland lass!
Reaping and singing by herself;
Stop here, or gently pass!
Alone she cuts and binds the grain,   5
And sings a melancholy strain;
O listen! for the vale profound
Is overflowing with the sound.

No nightingale did ever chaunt
More welcome notes to weary bands   10
Of travellers in some shady haunt,
Among Arabian sands;
A voice so thrilling ne'er was heard
In spring-time from the cuckoo-bird,
Breaking the silence of the seas   15
Among the farthest Hebrides.

Will no one tell me what she sings?
Perhaps the plaintive numbers flow
For old, unhappy, far-off things,
And battles long ago;   20
Or is it some more humble lay,
Familiar matter of to-day?
Some natural sorrow, loss, or pain,
That has been, and may be again?

Whate'er the theme, the maiden sang 25
As if her song could have no ending;
I saw her singing at her work,
And o'er the sickle bending:
I listened, motionless and still;
And as I mounted up the hill, 30
The music in my heart I bore,
Long after it was heard no more.

Between 1803 and 1805. 1807.

TO THE MEN OF KENT

Vanguard of Liberty, ye men of Kent,
Ye children of a Soil that doth advance
Her haughty brow against the coast of France,
Now is the time to prove your hardiment!
To France be words of invitation sent! 5
They from their fields can see the countenance
Of your fierce war, may ken the glittering lance
And hear you shouting forth your brave intent.
Left single, in bold parley, ye of yore
Did from the Norman win a gallant wreath; 10
Confirmed the charters that were yours before:—
No parleying now! In Britain is one breath;
We all are with you now from shore to shore:
Ye men of Kent, 't is victory or death!

1803. 1807.

SHE WAS A PHANTOM OF DELIGHT

She was a phantom of delight
When first she gleamed upon my sight;
A lovely apparition, sent
To be a moment's ornament:
Her eyes as stars of twilight fair; 5
Like twilight's, too, her dusky hair;
But all things else about her drawn
From Maytime and the cheerful dawn;
A dancing shape, an image gay,
To haunt, to startle, and way-lay. 10

I saw her, upon nearer view,
A spirit, yet a woman too!
Her household motions light and free,
And steps of virgin liberty;
A countenance in which did meet   15
Sweet records, promises as sweet;
A creature not too bright or good
For human nature's daily food—
For transient sorrows, simple wiles,
Praise, blame, love, kisses, tears, and smiles.   20

And now I see with eye serene
The very pulse of the machine:
A being breathing thoughtful breath,
A traveller between life and death;
The reason firm, the temperate will,   25
Endurance, foresight, strength, and skill;
A perfect woman, nobly planned,
To warn, to comfort, and command;
And yet a spirit still, and bright
With something of angelic light.   30

1804.   *1807.*

I WANDERED LONELY AS A CLOUD

I wandered lonely as a cloud
That floats on high o'er vales and hills,
When all at once I saw a crowd,
A host, of golden daffodils,
Beside the lake, beneath the trees,   5
Fluttering and dancing in the breeze.

Continuous as the stars that shine
And twinkle on the Milky Way,
They stretched in never-ending line
Along the margin of a bay;   10
Ten thousand saw I at a glance,
Tossing their heads in sprightly dance.

The waves beside them danced, but they
Outdid the sparkling waves in glee:
A poet could not but be gay   15
In such a jocund company.

> I gazed—and gazed,—but little thought
> What wealth the show to me had brought:
>
> For oft, when on my couch I lie
> In vacant or in pensive mood,   20
> They flash upon that inward eye
> Which is the bliss of solitude;
> And then my heart with pleasure fills,
> And dances with the daffodils.

1804.   *1807.*

ODE TO DUTY

Stern Daughter of the Voice of God!
O Duty! if that name thou love
Who art a light to guide, a rod
To check the erring, and reprove;
Thou who art victory and law   5
When empty terrors overawe;
From vain temptations dost set free,
And calm'st the weary strife of frail humanity!

There are who ask not if thine eye
Be on them; who in love and truth,   10
Where no misgiving is, rely
Upon the genial sense of youth;
Glad hearts! without reproach or blot,
Who do thy work and know it not.
Oh, if through confidence misplaced   15
They fail, thy saving arms, dread Power, around them cast!

Serene will be our days and bright,
And happy will our nature be,
When love is an unerring light,
And joy its own security.   20
And they a blissful course may hold
Even now, who, not unwisely bold,
Live in the spirit of this creed,
Yet seek thy firm support according to their need.

I, loving freedom, and untried,   25
No sport of every random gust
Yet being to myself a guide,

Too blindly have reposed my trust;
And oft, when in my heart was heard
Thy timely mandate, I deferred   30
The task, in smoother walks to stray:
But thee I now would serve more strictly if I may.

Through no disturbance of my soul,
Or strong compunction in me wrought,
I supplicate for thy control,   35
But in the quietness of thought:
Me this unchartered freedom tires;
I feel the weight of chance-desires;
My hopes no more must change their name,
I long for a repose that ever is the same.   40

Stern Lawgiver! yet thou dost wear
The Godhead's most benignant grace;
Nor know we any thing so fair
As is the smile upon thy face:
Flowers laugh before thee on their beds,   45
And fragrance in thy footing treads;
Thou dost preserve the stars from wrong;
And the most ancient heavens through thee are fresh and strong.

To humbler functions, awful Power!
I call thee: I myself commend   50
Unto thy guidance from this hour;
Oh, let my weakness have an end!
Give unto me, made lowly wise,
The spirit of self-sacrifice;
The confidence of reason give;   55
And in the light of truth thy bondman let me live!
       1805.   1807.

ELEGIAC STANZAS

SUGGESTED BY A PICTURE OF PEELE CASTLE, IN A STORM, PAINTED BY
SIR GEORGE BEAUMONT

I was thy neighbour once, thou rugged pile!
Four summer weeks I dwelt in sight of thee;
I saw thee every day; and all the while
Thy form was sleeping on a glassy sea.

So pure the sky, so quiet was the air,　　　　　5
So like, so very like, was day to day,
Whene'er I looked, thy image still was there;
It trembled, but it never passed away.

How perfect was the calm! it seemed no sleep;
No mood, which season takes away or brings:　　10
I could have fancied that the mighty deep
Was even the gentlest of all gentle things.

Ah, then, if mine had been the painter's hand,
To express what then I saw, and add the gleam,
The light that never was, on sea or land,　　　15
The consecration, and the poet's dream,

I would have planted thee, thou hoary pile,
Amid a world how different from this!
Beside a sea that could not cease to smile,
On tranquil land, beneath a sky of bliss.　　　20

Thou shouldst have seemed a treasure-house divine
Of peaceful years, a chronicle of heaven;
Of all the sunbeams that did ever shine
The very sweetest had to thee been given.

A picture had it been of lasting ease,　　　　25
Elysian quiet, without toil or strife;
No motion but the moving tide, a breeze,
Or merely silent Nature's breathing life.

Such, in the fond illusion of my heart,
Such picture would I at that time have made,　　30
And seen the soul of truth in every part,
A steadfast peace that might not be betrayed.

So once it would have been,—'t is so no more;
I have submitted to a new control;
A power is gone, which nothing can restore;　　35
A deep distress hath humanised my soul.

Not for a moment could I now behold
A smiling sea, and be what I have been;
The feeling of my loss will ne'er be old:
This, which I know, I speak with mind serene.　　40

Then, Beaumont, friend! who would have been the friend
If he had lived, of him whom I deplore,
This work of thine I blame not, but commend;
This sea in anger, and that dismal shore.

O 't is a passionate work! yet wise and well,   45
Well chosen is the spirit that is here;
That hulk which labours in the deadly swell,
This rueful sky, this pageantry of fear!

And this huge castle, standing here sublime,
I love to see the look with which it braves,   50
Cased in the unfeeling armour of old time,
The lightning, the fierce wind, and trampling waves.

Farewell, farewell, the heart that lives alone,
Housed in a dream, at distance from the kind!
Such happiness, wherever it be known,   55
Is to be pitied, for 't is surely blind.

But welcome fortitude, and patient cheer,
And frequent sights of what is to be borne!
Such sights, or worse, as are before me here:
Not without hope we suffer and we mourn.   60

  1805.   1807.

NUNS FRET NOT AT THEIR CONVENT'S NARROW ROOM

Nuns fret not at their convent's narrow room;
And hermits are contented with their cells,
And students with their pensive citadels;
Maids at the wheel, the weaver at his loom,
Sit blithe and happy; bees that soar for bloom,   5
High as the highest peak of Furness-fells,
Will murmur by the hour in foxglove bells.
In truth, the prison unto which we doom
Ourselves no prison is; and hence for me,
In sundry moods, 't was pastime to be bound   10
Within the sonnet's scanty plot of ground,
Pleased if some souls (for such there needs must be),
Who have felt the weight of too much liberty,
Should find brief solace there, as I have found.

  1806?   1807.

THE WORLD IS TOO MUCH WITH US

The world is too much with us: late and soon,
Getting and spending, we lay waste our powers;
Little we see in Nature that is ours;
We have given our hearts away, a sordid boon!
This sea that bares her bosom to the moon;   5
The winds that will be howling at all hours,
And are up gathered now like sleeping flowers;
For this, for every thing, we are out of tune;
It moves us not.—Great God! I'd rather be
A pagan suckled in a creed outworn;   10
So might I, standing on this pleasant lea,
Have glimpses that would make me less forlorn—
Have sight of Proteus rising from the sea,
Or hear old Triton blow his wreathèd horn.

1806?   *1807.*

FROM

PERSONAL TALK

Wings have we, and as far as we can go
We may find pleasure: wilderness and wood,
Blank ocean and mere sky, support that mood
Which with the lofty sanctifies the low.
Dreams, books, are each a world; and books, we know,   5
Are a substantial world, both pure and good:
Round these, with tendrils strong as flesh and blood,
Our pastime and our happiness will grow.
There find I personal themes, a plenteous store,
Matter wherein right voluble I am,   10
To which I listen with a ready ear:
Two shall be named, pre-eminently dear—
The gentle lady married to the Moor,
And heavenly Una with her milk-white lamb.

Nor can I not believe but that hereby   15
Great gains are mine: for thus I live remote
From evil-speaking; rancour, never sought,
Comes to me not, malignant truth, or lie.
Hence have I genial seasons, hence have I
Smooth passions, smooth discourse, and joyous thought;   20
And thus from day to day my little boat

Rocks in its harbour, lodging peaceably.
Blessings be with them, and eternal praise,
Who gave us nobler loves and nobler cares—
The poets, who on earth have made us heirs 25
Of truth and pure delight by heavenly lays!
Oh might my name be numbered among theirs,
Then gladly would I end my mortal days.

1806.   1807.

ODE

INTIMATIONS OF IMMORTALITY FROM RECOLLECTIONS OF EARLY CHILDHOOD

I

There was a time when meadow, grove, and stream,
The earth, and every common sight,
            To me did seem
            Apparelled in celestial light,
The glory and the freshness of a dream. 5
It is not now as it hath been of yore;
            Turn wheresoe'er I may,
            By night or day,
The things which I have seen I now can see no more.

II

            The rainbow comes and goes, 10
            And lovely is the rose;
            The Moon doth with delight
Look round her when the heavens are bare;
            Waters on a starry night
            Are beautiful and fair; 15
    The sunshine is a glorious birth:
    But yet I know, where'er I go,
That there hath passed away a glory from the earth.

III

Now, while the birds thus sing a joyous song,
            And while the young lambs bound 20
            As to the tabor's sound,
To me alone there came a thought of grief;
A timely utterance gave that thought relief,
            And I again am strong:

The cataracts blow their trumpets from the steep;   25
No more shall grief of mine the season wrong;
I hear the echoes through the mountains throng,
The winds come to me from the fields of sleep,
   And all the earth is gay;
    Land and sea   30
   Give themselves up to jollity,
    And with the heart of May
   Doth every beast keep holiday;
    Thou child of joy,
Shout round me, let me hear thy shouts, thou happy
    shepherd-boy!   35

IV

Ye blessèd creatures, I have heard the call
  Ye to each other make; I see
The heavens laugh with you in your jubilee;
  My heart is at your festival,
   My head hath its coronal,   40
The fulness of your bliss, I feel, I feel it all.
   Oh evil day! if I were sullen
   While Earth herself is adorning,
    This sweet May morning,
   And the children are culling   45
    On every side,
   In a thousand valleys far and wide,
   Fresh flowers; while the sun shines warm,
And the babe leaps up on his mother's arm.
   I hear, I hear, with joy I hear!   50
   —But there's a tree, of many, one,
A single field which I have looked upon,
Both of them speak of something that is gone;
   The pansy at my feet
   Doth the same tale repeat: 55
Whither is fled the visionary gleam?
Where is it now, the glory and the dream?

V

Our birth is but a sleep and a forgetting;
The soul that rises with us, our life's star,
   Hath had elsewhere its setting,   60

And cometh from afar.
    Not in entire forgetfulness,
    And not in utter nakedness,
But trailing clouds of glory, do we come
    From God, Who is our home: 65
Heaven lies about us in our infancy!
Shades of the prison-house begin to close
    Upon the growing boy,
But he beholds the light, and whence it flows,
    He sees it in his joy!   70
The youth, who daily farther from the east
    Must travel, still is Nature's priest,
        And by the vision splendid
        Is on his way attended;
At length the man perceives it die away,   75
And fade into the light of common day.

VI

Earth fills her lap with pleasures of her own;
Yearnings she hath in her own natural kind,
And even with something of a mother's mind,
        And no unworthy aim,   80
        The homely nurse doth all she can
To make her foster-child, her inmate man,
        Forget the glories he hath known,
And that imperial palace whence he came.

VII

Behold the child among his new-born blisses,   85
A six years' darling of a pigmy size!
See where 'mid work of his own hand he lies,
Fretted by sallies of his mother's kisses,
With light upon him from his father's eyes!
See, at his feet, some little plan or chart,   90
Some fragment from his dream of human life,
Shaped by himself with newly-learned art:
    A wedding or a festival,
    A mourning or a funeral;
        And this hath now his heart,   95
        And unto this he frames his song;
        Then will he fit his tongue

To dialogues of business, love, or strife;
   But it will not be long
   Ere this be thrown aside,   100
   And with new joy and pride
The little actor cons another part,
Filling from time to time his "humorous stage"
With all the persons, down to palsied Age,
That Life brings with her in her equipage,   105
   As if his whole vocation
   Were endless imitation.

VIII

Thou whose exterior semblance doth belie
   Thy soul's immensity;
Thou best philosopher, who yet dost keep   110
Thy heritage, thou eye among the blind,
That, deaf and silent, read'st the Eternal Deep,
Haunted for ever by the Eternal Mind;
   Mighty prophet! seer blest!
   On whom those truths do rest   115
Which we are toiling all our lives to find,
In darkness lost, the darkness of the grave;
Thou over whom thy immortality
Broods like the day, a master o'er a slave,
A presence which is not to be put by;   120
Thou little child, yet glorious in the might
Of heaven-born freedom on thy being's height;
Why with such earnest pains dost thou provoke
The years to bring the inevitable yoke,
Thus blindly with thy blessedness at strife?   125
Full soon thy soul shall have her earthly freight,
And custom lie upon thee with a weight
Heavy as frost and deep almost as life!

IX

   O joy! that in our embers
   Is something that doth live;   130
   That nature yet remembers
   What was so fugitive!
The thought of our past years in me doth breed
Perpetual benediction—not indeed
For that which is most worthy to be blest,   135

Delight and liberty, the simple creed
Of childhood, whether busy or at rest,
With new-fledged hope still fluttering in his breast;—
  Not for these I raise
  The song of thanks and praise;   140
  But for those obstinate questionings
  Of sense and outward things;
  Fallings from us, vanishings;
  Blank misgivings of a creature
Moving about in worlds not realised;   145
High instincts before which our mortal nature
Did tremble like a guilty thing surprised;
  But for those first affections,
  Those shadowy recollections,
  Which, be they what they may,   150
Are yet the fountain-light of all our day,
Are yet a master-light of all our seeing,
  Uphold us, cherish, and have power to make
Our noisy years seem moments in the being
Of the Eternal Silence; truths that wake, 155
  To perish never,
Which neither listlessness, nor mad endeavour,
  Nor man nor boy,
Nor all that is at enmity with joy,
Can utterly abolish or destroy!   160
  Hence, in a season of calm weather,
  Though inland far we be,
Our souls have sight of that immortal sea
  Which brought us hither;
  Can in a moment travel thither,   165
And see the children sport upon the shore,
And hear the mighty waters rolling evermore.

x

Then sing, ye birds, sing, sing a joyous song!
  And let the young lambs bound
  As to the tabor's sound!   170
We in thought will join your throng,
  Ye that pipe and ye that play,
  Ye that through your hearts to-day
  Feel the gladness of the May!

What though the radiance which was once so bright   175
Be now forever taken from my sight,
    Though nothing can bring back the hour
Of splendour in the grass, of glory in the flower?
    We will grieve not, rather find
    Strength in what remains behind: 180
    In the primal sympathy
    Which, having been, must ever be;
    In the soothing thoughts that spring
    Out of human suffering;
    In the faith that looks through death;   185
In years that bring the philosophic mind.

XI

And O ye fountains, meadows, hills, and groves,
Forebode not any severing of our loves!
Yet in my heart of hearts I feel your might;
I only have relinquished one delight   190
To live beneath your more habitual sway.
I love the brooks which down their channels fret,
Even more than when I tripped lightly as they;
The innocent brightness of a new-born day
    Is lovely yet;   195
The clouds that gather round the setting sun
Do take a sober colouring from an eye
That hath kept watch o'er man's mortality—
Another race hath been, and other palms are won.
Thanks to the human heart by which we live,   200
Thanks to its tenderness, its joys, and fears,
To me the meanest flower that blows can give
Thoughts that do often lie too deep for tears.

1803–6.   *1807.*

INSIDE OF KING'S COLLEGE CHAPEL, CAMBRIDGE

Tax not the royal saint with vain expense,
With ill-matched aims the architect who planned—
Albeit labouring for a scanty band
Of white-robed scholars only—this immense
And glorious work of fine intelligence!   5
Give all thou canst; high Heaven rejects the lore

Of nicely calculated less or more:
So deemed the man who fashioned for the sense
These lofty pillars; spread that branching roof
Self-poised, and scooped into ten thousand cells, 10
Where light and shade repose, where music dwells
Lingering, and wandering on as loth to die;
Like thoughts whose very sweetness yieldeth proof
That they were born for immortality.
1820?   1822.

IF THOU INDEED DERIVE THY LIGHT FROM HEAVEN

If thou indeed derive thy light from heaven,
Then, to the measure of that heaven-born light,
Shine, poet, in thy place, and be content.
The stars pre-eminent in magnitude,
And they that from the zenith dart their beams 5
(Visible though they be to half the earth,
Though half a sphere be conscious of their brightness),
Are yet of no diviner origin,
No purer essence, than the one that burns,
Like an untended watch-fire, on the ridge 10
Of some dark mountain, or than those which seem
Humbly to hang, like twinkling winter lamps,
Among the branches of the leafless trees:
All are the undying offspring of one Sire.
Then, to the measure of the light vouchsafed, 15
Shine, poet, in thy place, and be content.
After 1813.   1827.

TO A SKYLARK

Ethereal minstrel! pilgrim of the sky!
Dost thou despise the earth where cares abound?
Or, while the wings aspire, are heart and eye
Both with thy nest upon the dewy ground?
Thy nest which thou canst drop into at will, 5
Those quivering wings composed, that music still!

Leave to the nightingale her shady wood;
A privacy of glorious light is thine,
Whence thou dost pour upon the world a flood

Of harmony, with instinct more divine: 10
Type of the wise, who soar but never roam,
True to the kindred points of heaven and home.

1825.   *1827.*

CALM IS THE FRAGRANT AIR

Calm is the fragrant air, and loth to lose
Day's grateful warmth, though moist with falling dews.
Look for the stars, you 'll say that there are none;
Look up a second time, and, one by one,
You mark them twinkling out with silvery light,   5
And wonder how they could elude the sight!
The birds, of late so noisy in their bowers,
Warbled a while with faint and fainter powers,
But now are silent as the dim-seen flowers.
Nor does the village church-clock's iron tone   10
The time's and season's influence disown;
Nine beats distinctly to each other bound
In drowsy sequence—how unlike the sound
That, in rough winter, oft inflicts a fear
On fireside listeners, doubting what they hear!   15
The shepherd, bent on rising with the sun,
Had closed his door before the day was done,
And now with thankful heart to bed doth creep,
And joins his little children in their sleep.
The bat, lured forth where trees the lane o'ershade,   20
Flits and reflits along the close arcade;
The busy dor-hawk chases the white moth
With burring note, which Industry and Sloth
Might both be pleased with, for it suits them both.
A stream is heard—I see it not, but know   25
By its soft music whence the waters flow;
Wheels and the tread of hoofs are heard no more;
One boat there was, but it will touch the shore
With the next dipping of its slackened oar—
Faint sound, that, for the gayest of the gay,   30
Might give to serious thought a moment's sway,
As a last token of man's toilsome day!

1832.   *1835.*

MOST SWEET IT IS WITH UNUPLIFTED EYES

Most sweet it is with unuplifted eyes
To pace the ground, if path be there or none,
While a fair region round the traveller lies
Which he forbears again to look upon;
Pleased rather with some soft ideal scene,   5
The work of fancy, or some happy tone
Of meditation, slipping in between
The beauty coming and the beauty gone.
If Thought and Love desert us, from that day
Let us break off all commerce with the Muse: 10
With Thought and Love companions of our way,
Whate'er the senses take or may refuse,
The mind's internal heaven shall shed her dews
Of inspiration on the humblest lay.

1833.   1835.

TO A CHILD

WRITTEN IN HER ALBUM

Small service is true service while it lasts;
Of humblest friends, bright creature! scorn not one:
The daisy, by the shadow that it casts,
Protects the lingering dew-drop from the sun.

1834.   1835.

SO FAIR, SO SWEET, WITHAL SO SENSITIVE

So fair, so sweet, withal so sensitive,
Would that the little flowers were born to live
Conscious of half the pleasure which they give!

That to this mountain-daisy's self were known
The beauty of its star-shaped shadow, thrown   5
On the smooth surface of this naked stone!

And what if hence a bold desire should mount
High as the Sun, that he could take account
Of all that issues from his glorious fount!

So might he ken how by his sovereign aid   10
These delicate companionships are made,
And how he rules the pomp of light and shade.

And were the sister-power that shines by night
So privileged, what a countenance of delight
Would through the clouds break forth on human sight ! 15

Fond fancies ! Wheresoe'er shall turn thine eye
On earth, air, ocean, or the starry sky,
Converse with Nature in pure sympathy :

All vain desires, all lawless wishes quelled,
Be thou to love and praise alike impelled,   20
Whatever boon is granted or withheld.
1844.   **1845.**

SAMUEL TAYLOR COLERIDGE

THE RIME OF THE ANCIENT MARINER

IN SEVEN PARTS

Argument

How a Ship, having passed the Line, was driven by storms to the
cold Country towards the South Pole; and how from thence she
made her course to the tropical Latitude of the Great Pacific Ocean;
and of the strange things that befell; and in what manner the
Ancyent Marinere came back to his own Country.

PART I

An ancient Ma-   It is an ancient Mariner,
riner meeteth
three gallants   And he stoppeth one of three.
bidden to a wed- "By thy long grey beard and glittering eye,
ding-feast, and
detaineth one.   Now wherefore stopp'st thou me?

The Bridegroom's doors are opened wide,   5
And I am next of kin;
The guests are met, the feast is set;
May'st hear the merry din."

He holds him with his skinny hand:
"There was a ship," quoth he.   10
"Hold off ! unhand me, grey-beard loon !"
Eftsoons his hand dropt he.

The Wedding-
Guest is spell-
bound by the
eye of the old
seafaring man,
and constrained
to hear his tale.
He holds him with his glittering eye—
The Wedding-Guest stood still,
And listens like a three years' child;　15
The Mariner hath his will.

The Wedding-Guest sat on a stone;
He cannot choose but hear;
And thus spake on that ancient man,
The bright-eyed Mariner.　20

"The ship was cheered, the harbour cleared,
Merrily did we drop
Below the kirk, below the hill,
Below the lighthouse top.

The Mariner
tells how the
ship sailed
southward with
a good wind and
fair weather, till
it reached the
line.
The sun came up upon the left,　25
Out of the sea came he;
And he shone bright, and on the right
Went down into the sea.

Higher and higher every day,
Till over the mast at noon"—　30
The Wedding-Guest here beat his breast,
For he heard the loud bassoon.

The Wedding-
Guest heareth
the bridal mu-
sic; but the
Mariner con-
tinueth his tale.
The bride hath paced into the hall,
Red as a rose is she;
Nodding their heads, before her goes　35
The merry minstrelsy.

The Wedding-Guest he beat his breast,
Yet he cannot choose but hear;
And thus spake on that ancient man,
The bright-eyed Mariner.　40

The ship driven
by a storm to-
ward the south
pole.
"And now the Storm-blast came, and he
Was tyrannous and strong;
He struck with his o'ertaking wings,
And chased us south along.

With sloping masts and dipping prow,　45
As who, pursued with yell and blow,
Still treads the shadow of his foe,

And forward bends his head,
The ship drove fast, loud roared the blast,
And southward aye we fled.   50

And now there came both mist and snow,
And it grew wondrous cold;
And ice, mast-high, came floating by,
As green as emerald.

The land of ice
and of fearful
sounds, where
no living thing
was to be seen.

And through the drifts the snowy clifts   55
Did send a dismal sheen;
Nor shapes of men nor beasts we ken—
The ice was all between.

The ice was here, the ice was there,
The ice was all around;   60
It cracked and growled, and roared and howled,
Like noises in a swound!

Till a great sea-
bird, called the
Albatross, came
through the
snow-fog, and
was received
with great joy
and hospitality.

At length did cross an Albatross,
Thorough the fog it came;
As if it had been a Christian soul,   65
We hailed it in God's name.

It ate the food it ne'er had eat,
And round and round it flew.
The ice did split with a thunder-fit;
The helmsman steered us through!   70

And lo! the Al-
batross proveth
a bird of good
omen, and fol-
loweth the ship
as it returned
northward
through fog and
floating ice.

And a good south wind sprung up behind;
The Albatross did follow,
And every day, for food or play,
Came to the mariners' hollo.

In mist or cloud, on mast or shroud,   75
It perched for vespers nine;
Whiles all the night, through fog-smoke white,
Glimmered the white moon-shine."

The ancient
Mariner inhos-
pitably killeth
the pious bird of
good omen.

"God save thee, ancient Mariner,
From the fiends that plague thee thus!   80
Why look'st thou so?"—"With my cross-bow
I shot the Albatross.

PART II

"The Sun now rose upon the right;
Out of the sea came he,
Still hid in mist, and on the left   85
Went down into the sea.

And the good south wind still blew behind,
But no sweet bird did follow,
Nor any day, for food or play,
Came to the mariners' hollo.   90

His shipmates
cry out against
the ancient Mar-
iner for killing
the bird of good
luck.

And I had done a hellish thing,
And it would work 'em woe;
For all averred I had killed the bird
That made the breeze to blow.
'Ah wretch!' said they, 'the bird to slay   95
That made the breeze to blow!'

But when the
fog cleared off,
they justify the
same, and thus
make them-
selves accom-
plices in the
crime.

Nor dim nor red, like God's own head,
The glorious Sun uprist;
Then all averred, I had killed the bird
That brought the fog and mist.   100
''T was right,' said they, 'such birds to slay,
That bring the fog and mist.'

The fair breeze
continues; the
ship enters the
Pacific Ocean
and sails north-
ward, even till it
reaches the line.

The fair breeze blew, the white foam flew,
The furrow followed free;
We were the first that ever burst   105
Into that silent sea.

The ship hath
been suddenly
becalmed.

Down dropt the breeze, the sails dropt down;
'T was sad as sad could be;
And we did speak only to break
The silence of the sea.   110

All in a hot and copper sky,
The bloody Sun, at noon,
Right up above the mast did stand,
No bigger than the Moon.

Day after day, day after day,   115
We stuck, nor breath nor motion;
As idle as a painted ship
Upon a painted ocean.

And the Alba-
tross begins to
be avenged.

Water, water, everywhere,
And all the boards did shrink;   120
Water, water, everywhere,
Nor any drop to drink.

The very deep did rot: O Christ!
That ever this should be!
Yea, slimy things did crawl with legs   125
Upon the slimy sea.

About, about, in reel and rout
The death-fires danced at night;
The water, like a witch's oils,
Burnt green, and blue, and white.   130

A spirit had fol-
lowed them;
one of the in-
visible inhabi-
tants of this
planet, neither
departed souls
nor angels; con-
cerning whom
the learned Jew,
Josephus, and
the Platonic
Constantino-
politan, Michael
Psellus, may be
consulted. They
are very numer-
ous, and there is
no climate or
element without
one or more.

And some in dreams assured were
Of the Spirit that plagued us so:
Nine fathom deep he had followed us
From the land of mist and snow.

And every tongue, through utter drought,   135
Was withered at the root;
We could not speak, no more than if
We had been choked with soot.

The shipmates,
in their sore dis-
tress, would fain
throw the whole
guilt on the an-
cient Mariner;
in sign whereof
they hang the
dead sea-bird
round his neck.

Ah! well-a-day! what evil looks
Had I from old and young!   140
Instead of the cross, the Albatross
About my neck was hung.

PART III

"There passed a weary time. Each throat
Was parched, and glazed each eye.
A weary time! a weary time!   145
How glazed each weary eye!
When, looking westward, I beheld
A something in the sky.

The ancient
Mariner be-
holdeth a sign
in the element
afar off.

At first it seemed a little speck,
And then it seemed a mist;   150
It moved and moved, and took at last
A certain shape, I wist.

A speck, a mist, a shape, I wist!
And still it neared and neared;
As if it dodged a water-sprite,   155
It plunged and tacked and veered.

At its nearer ap-
proach, it seem-
eth him to be a
ship; and at a
dear ransom he
freeth his
speech from the
bonds of thirst.

With throats unslaked, with black lips baked,
We could nor laugh nor wail;
Through utter drought all dumb we stood!
I bit my arm, I sucked the blood,   160
And cried, 'A sail! a sail!'

With throats unslaked, with black lips baked,
Agape they heard me call:

A flash of joy.

Gramercy! they for joy did grin,
And all at once their breath drew in,   165
As they were drinking all.

And horror fol-
lows; for can it
be a ship that
comes onward
without wind or
tide?

'See! see!' I cried, 'she tacks no more!
Hither to work us weal,
Without a breeze, without a tide,
She steadies with upright keel!'   170
The western wave was all a-flame.
The day was well-nigh done!

Almost upon the western wave
Rested the broad bright Sun;
When that strange shape drove suddenly   175
Betwixt us and the Sun.

It seemeth him
but the skele-
ton of a ship.

And straight the Sun was flecked with bars
(Heaven's Mother send us grace!),
As if through a dungeon-grate he peered
With broad and burning face.   180

'Alas!' thought I, and my heart beat loud,
'How fast she nears and nears!
Are those her sails that glance in the sun,
Like restless gossameres?

And its ribs are
seen as bars on
the face of the
setting Sun.
The Spectre-
Woman and her
death-mate, and
no other on

Are those her ribs through which the sun   185
Did peer, as through a grate?
And is that Woman all her crew?
Is that a Death? and are there two?
Is Death that woman's mate?'

board the skele-
ton ship. Like
vessel, like
crew!

Her lips were red, her looks were free,   190
Her locks were yellow as gold,
Her skin was as white as leprosy;
The Night-mare Life-in-Death was she,
Who thicks man's blood with cold.

Death and Life-
in-Death have
diced for the
ship's crew, and
she (the latter)
winneth the an-
cient Mariner.

The naked hulk alongside came,   195
And the twain were casting dice;
'The game is done! I've won! I've won!'
Quoth she, and whistles thrice.

No twilight
within the
courts of the
Sun.

The Sun's rim dips; the stars rush out;
At one stride comes the dark;   200
With far-heard whisper, o'er the sea,
Off shot the spectre-bark.

At the rising of
the Moon

We listened, and looked sideways up!
Fear at my heart, as at a cup,
My life-blood seemed to sip!   205
The stars were dim, and thick the night;
The steersman's face by his lamp gleamed white;
From the sails the dew did drip—
Till clomb above the eastern bar
The hornèd Moon, with one bright star   210
Within the nether tip.

one after an-
other,

One after one, by the star-dogged Moon,
Too quick for groan or sigh,
Each turned his face with a ghastly pang,
And cursed me with his eye.   215

his shipmates
drop down
dead.

Four times fifty living men
(And I heard nor sigh nor groan)
With heavy thump, a lifeless lump,
They dropped down one by one.

But Life-in
Death begins
her work on the
ancient Ma-
riner.

The souls did from their bodies fly,—   220
They fled to bliss or woe!
And every soul, it passed me by
Like the whizz of my cross-bow!"

PART IV

The Wedding-
Guest feareth
that a spirit is
talking to him;

"I fear thee, ancient Mariner!
I fear thy skinny hand!   225
And thou art long, and lank, and brown,
As is the ribbed sea-sand.

I fear thee and thy glittering eye,
And thy skinny hand, so brown."—

but the ancient
Mariner as-
sureth him of
his bodily life,
and proceedeth
to relate his
horrible pen-
ance.

"Fear not, fear not, thou Wedding-Guest!   230
This body dropt not down.

Alone, alone, all, all alone,
Alone on a wide, wide sea!
And never a saint took pity on
My soul in agony.   235

He despiseth
the creatures of
the calm.

The many men, so beautiful!
And they all dead did lie;
And a thousand, thousand slimy things
Lived on, and so did I.

And envieth
that they should
live, and so
many lie dead.

I looked upon the rotting sea,   240
And drew my eyes away;
I looked upon the rotting deck,
And there the dead men lay.

I looked to heaven, and tried to pray;
But or ever a prayer had gusht,   245
A wicked whisper came, and made
My heart as dry as dust.

I closed my lids, and kept them close,
And the balls like pulses beat;
For the sky and the sea, and the sea and the sky, 250
Lay like a load on my weary eye,
And the dead were at my feet.

But the curse
liveth for him
in the eye of the
dead men.

The cold sweat melted from their limbs,
Nor rot nor reek did they:
The look with which they looked on me   255
Had never passed away.

An orphan's curse would drag to hell
A spirit from on high;
But oh! more horrible than that
Is a curse in a dead man's eye!   260
Seven days, seven nights, I saw that curse,
And yet I could not die.

The moving Moon went up the sky,
And nowhere did abide;
Softly she was going up,   265
And a star or two beside.

Her beams bemocked the sultry main,
Like April hoar-frost spread;
But where the ship's huge shadow lay,
The charmèd water burnt alway   270
A still and awful red.

Beyond the shadow of the ship,
I watched the water-snakes:
They moved in tracks of shining white;
And when they reared, the elfish light   275
Fell off in hoary flakes.

Within the shadow of the ship
I watched their rich attire:
Blue, glossy green, and velvet black,
They coiled and swam; and every track   280
Was a flash of golden fire.

O happy living things! no tongue
Their beauty might declare:
A spring of love gushed from my heart,
And I blessed them unaware;   285
Sure my kind saint took pity on me,
And I blessed them unaware.

The selfsame moment I could pray;
And from my neck so free
The Albatross fell off, and sank   290
Like lead into the sea.

In his loneliness and fixedness he yearneth towards the journeying Moon, and the stars that still sojourn, yet still move onward; and everywhere the blue sky belongs to them, and is their appointed rest, and their native country and their own natural homes, which they enter unannounced, as lords that are certainly expected and yet there is a silent joy at their arrival.

By the light of the Moon he beholdeth God's creatures of the great calm.

Their beauty and their happiness.

He blesseth them in his heart.

The spell begins to break.

PART V

"Oh sleep! it is a gentle thing,
Beloved from pole to pole!
To Mary Queen the praise be given!
She sent the gentle sleep from heaven,   295
That slid into my soul.

By grace of the holy Mother, the ancient Mariner is refreshed with rain.

The silly buckets on the deck,
That had so long remained,
I dreamt that they were filled with dew;
And when I awoke, it rained.   300

My lips were wet, my throat was cold,
My garments all were dank;
Sure I had drunken in my dreams,
And still my body drank.

I moved, and could not feel my limbs;   305
I was so light, almost
I thought that I had died in sleep,
And was a blessed ghost.

He heareth sounds and seeth strange sights and commotions in the sky and the element.

And soon I heard a roaring wind;
It did not come anear,   310
But with its sound it shook the sails,
That were so thin and sere.

The upper air burst into life!
And a hundred fire-flags sheen,
To and fro they were hurried about!   315
And to and fro, and in and out,
The wan stars danced between.

And the coming wind did roar more loud,
And the sails did sigh like sedge;
And the rain poured down from one black cloud;   320
The Moon was at its edge.

The thick black cloud was cleft, and still
The Moon was at its side;
Like waters shot from some high crag,
The lightning fell with never a jag,   325
A river steep and wide.

The loud wind never reached the ship,
Yet now the ship moved on!
Beneath the lightning and the Moon
The dead men gave a groan.   330

They groaned, they stirred, they all uprose,
Nor spake, nor moved their eyes;
It had been strange, even in a dream,
To have seen those dead men rise.

The helmsman steered, the ship moved on;   335
Yet never a breeze up blew;
The mariners all 'gan work the ropes,
Where they were wont to do;
They raised their limbs like lifeless tools—
We were a ghastly crew.   340

The body of my brother's son
Stood by me, knee to knee;
The body and I pulled at one rope
But he said nought to me."

"I fear thee, ancient Mariner!"   345
"Be calm, thou Wedding-Guest!
'T was not those souls that fled in pain,
Which to their corses came again,
But a troop of spirits blest:

For when it dawned, they dropped their arms,   350
And clustered round the mast;
Sweet sounds rose slowly through their mouths,
And from their bodies passed.

Around, around, flew each sweet sound,
Then darted to the Sun;   355
Slowly the sounds came back again,
Now mixed, now one by one.

Sometimes, a-dropping from the sky,
I heard the sky-lark sing;
Sometimes all little birds that are,   360
How they seemed to fill the sea and air
With their sweet jargoning!

The bodies of
of ship's crew
are inspired,
and the ship
moves on;

but not by the
souls of the
men, nor by
dæmons of
earth or middle
air, but by a
blessed troop of
angelic spirits,
sent down by
the invocation
of the guardian
saint.

And now 't was like all instruments,
Now like a lonely flute;
And now it is an angel's song,   365
That makes the heavens be mute.

It ceased; yet still the sails made on
A pleasant noise till noon,
A noise like of a hidden brook
In the leafy month of June,   370
That to the sleeping woods all night
Singeth a quiet tune.

Till noon we quietly sailed on,
Yet never a breeze did breathe;
Slowly and smoothly went the ship,   375
Moved onward from beneath.

The lonesome Spirit from the south pole carries on the ship as far as the line, in obedience to the angelic troop, but still requireth vengeance

Under the keel nine fathom deep,
From the land of mist and snow,
The spirit slid; and it was he
That made the ship to go.   380
The sails at noon left off their tune,
And the ship stood still also.

The Sun, right up above the mast,
Had fixed her to the ocean;
But in a minute she 'gan stir,   385
With a short uneasy motion—
Backwards and forwards half her length,
With a short uneasy motion.

Then, like a pawing horse let go,
She made a sudden bound;   390
It flung the blood into my head,
And I fell down in a swound.

The Polar Spirit's fellow-dæmons, the invisible inhabitants of the element, take part in his wrong; and two of them

How long in that same fit I lay,
I have not to declare;
But ere my living life returned,   395
I heard, and in my soul discerned,
Two voices in the air.

relate one to the
other, that pen-
ance long and
heavy for the
ancient Mariner
hath been ac-
corded to the
Polar Spirit
who returneth
southward.
'Is it he?' quoth one; 'is this the man?
By Him Who died on cross,
With his cruel bow he laid full low   400
The harmless Albatross.

The spirit who bideth by himself
In the land of mist and snow,
He loved the bird that loved the man
Who shot him with his bow.'   405

The other was a softer voice,
As soft as honey-dew:
Quoth he, 'The man hath penance done,
And penance more will do.'

                    PART VI

                    FIRST VOICE

'But tell me, tell me! speak again,   410
Thy soft response renewing—
What makes that ship drive on so fast?
What is the ocean doing?'

                    SECOND VOICE

'Still as a slave before his lord,
The Ocean hath no blast;   415
His great bright eye most silently
Up to the Moon is cast—

If he may know which way to go;
For she guides him smooth or grim.
See, brother, see! how graciously   420
She looketh down on him.'

                    FIRST VOICE

The Mariner
hath been cast
into a trance;
for the angelic
power causeth
the vessel to
drive northward
faster than hu-
man life could
endure.
'But why drives on that ship so fast,
Without or wave or wind?'

                    SECOND VOICE

'The air is cut away before,
And closes from behind.   425

Fly, brother, fly! more high, more high!
Or we shall be belated;
For slow and slow that ship will go,
When the Mariner's trance is abated.'

The supernatu-
ral motion is re-
tarded; the Ma-
riner awakes,
and his penance
begins anew.

I woke, and we were sailing on   430
As in a gentle weather;
'T was night, calm night, the Moon was high,
The dead men stood together.

All stood together on the deck,
For a charnel-dungeon fitter;   435
All fixed on me their stony eyes,
That in the Moon did glitter.

The pang, the curse, with which they died,
Had never passed away;
I could not draw my eyes from theirs,   440
Nor turn them up to pray.

The curse is
finally expiated.

And now this spell was snapt; once more
I viewed the ocean green,
And looked far forth, yet little saw
Of what had else been seen—   445

Like one that on a lonesome road
Doth walk in fear and dread,
And having once turned round walks on,
And turns no more his head,
Because he knows a frightful fiend   450
Doth close behind him tread.

But soon there breathed a wind on me,
Nor sound nor motion made;
Its path was not upon the sea,
In ripple or in shade.   455

It raised my hair, it fanned my cheek
Like a meadow-gale of spring—
It mingled strangely with my fears,
Yet it felt like a welcoming.

Swiftly, swiftly flew the ship, 460
Yet she sailed softly too;
Sweetly, sweetly blew the breeze—
On me alone it blew.

And the ancient Mariner beholdeth his native country. Oh, dream of joy! is this indeed
The lighthouse top I see? 465
Is this the hill? is this the kirk?
Is this mine own countree?

We drifted o'er the harbour-bar,
And I with sobs did pray—
'O let me be awake, my God! 470
Or let me sleep alway!'

The harbour-bay was clear as glass,
So smoothly it was strewn!
And on the bay the moonlight lay,
And the shadow of the Moon. 475

The rock shone bright, the kirk no less,
That stands above the rock;
The moonlight steeped in silentness
The steady weathercock.

And the bay was white with silent light, 480
Till, rising from the same,
The angelic spirits leave the dead bodies, Full many shapes, that shadows were,
In crimson colours came.

and appear in their own forms of light. A little distance from the prow
Those crimson shadows were; 485
I turned my eyes upon the deck—
Oh Christ! what saw I there!

Each corse lay flat, lifeless and flat,
And, by the holy rood!
A man all light, a seraph-man, 490
On every corse there stood.

This seraph-band each waved his hand;
It was a heavenly sight!
They stood as signals to the land,
Each one a lovely light. 495

This seraph-band each waved his hand,
No voice did they impart—
No voice; but oh! the silence sank
Like music on my heart.

But soon I heard the dash of oars,   500
I heard the Pilot's cheer;
My head was turned perforce away,
And I saw a boat appear.

The Pilot and the Pilot's boy,
I heard them coming fast;   505
Dear Lord in Heaven! it was a joy
The dead men could not blast.

I saw a third—I heard his voice;
It is the Hermit good!
He singeth loud his godly hymns   510
That he makes in the wood.
He'll shrieve my soul, he'll wash away
The Albatross's blood.

PART VII

<table>
<tr><td>The Hermit of
the wood</td><td>"This Hermit good lives in that wood
Which slopes down to the sea.
How loudly his sweet voice he rears!
He loves to talk with marineres
That come from a far countree.</td><td>515</td></tr>
</table>

He kneels at morn, and noon, and eve—
He hath a cushion plump;   520
It is the moss that wholly hides
The rotted old oak-stump.

The skiff-boat neared; I heard them talk:
'Why, this is strange, I trow!
Where are those lights so many and fair,   525
That signal made but now?'

<table>
<tr><td>approacheth
the ship with
wonder.</td><td>'Strange, by my faith!' the Hermit said—
'And they answered not our cheer!
The planks look warped! and see those sails,</td></tr>
</table>

How thin they are and sere!   530
I never saw aught like to them,
Unless perchance it were

Brown skeletons of leaves that lag
My forest-brook along,
When the ivy-tod is heavy with snow,   535
And the owlet whoops to the wolf below,
That eats the she-wolf's young.'

'Dear Lord! it hath a fiendish look,'
The Pilot made reply;
'I am a-feared.'—'Push on, push on,'   540
Said the Hermit cheerily.

The boat came closer to the ship,
But I nor spake nor stirred;
The boat came close beneath the ship,
And straight a sound was heard.   545

The ship suddenly sinketh.

Under the water it rumbled on,
Still louder and more dread;
It reached the ship, it split the bay;
The ship went down like lead.

The ancient Mariner is saved in the Pilot's boat.

Stunned by that loud and dreadful sound,   550
Which sky and ocean smote,
Like one that hath been seven days drowned
My body lay afloat;
But swift as dreams myself I found
Within the Pilot's boat.   555

Upon the whirl, where sank the ship,
The boat spun round and round;
And all was still, save that the hill
Was telling of the sound.

I moved my lips—the Pilot shrieked,   560
And fell down in a fit;
The holy Hermit raised his eyes,
And prayed where he did sit.

I took the oars; the Pilot's boy,
Who now doth crazy go,   565
Laughed loud and long, and all the while
His eyes went to and fro.
'Ha! ha!' quoth he, 'full plain I see
The Devil knows how to row!'

And now, all in my own countree,   570
I stood on the firm land!
The Hermit stepped forth from the boat,
And scarcely he could stand.

The ancient
Mariner earn-
estly entreateth
the Hermit to
shrieve him;
and the penance
of life falls on
him.

'O shrieve me, shrieve me, holy man!'
The Hermit crossed his brow.   575
'Say quick,' quoth he, 'I bid thee say—
What manner of man art thou?'

Forthwith this frame of mine was wrenched
With a woful agony,
Which forced me to begin my tale;   580
And then it left me free.

And ever and
anon through-
out his future
life an agony
constraineth
him to travel
from land to
land,

Since then, at an uncertain hour,
That agony returns;
And till my ghastly tale is told,
This heart within me burns.   585

I pass, like night, from land to land;
I have strange power of speech;
That moment that his face I see,
I know the man that must hear me;
To him my tale I teach.   590

What loud uproar bursts from that door!
The wedding-guests are there;
But in the garden-bower the bride
And bride-maids singing are;
And hark the little vesper bell,   595
Which biddeth me to prayer!

O Wedding-Guest! this soul hath been
Alone on a wide, wide sea;
So lonely 't was that God himself
Scarce seemèd there to be.   600

O sweeter than the marriage-feast,
'T is sweeter far to me,
To walk together to the kirk
With a goodly company!

To walk together to the kirk,   605
And all together pray,
While each to his great Father bends,
Old men, and babes, and loving friends,
And youths and maidens gay!

and to teach by his own example, love and reverence to all things that God made and loveth.

Farewell, farewell! but this I tell   610
To thee, thou Wedding-Guest:
He prayeth well who loveth well
Both man and bird and beast.

He prayeth best who loveth best
All things both great and small;   615
For the dear God Who loveth us,
He made and loveth all."

The Mariner, whose eye is bright,
Whose beard with age is hoar,
Is gone; and now the Wedding-Guest   620
Turned from the bridegroom's door.

He went like one that hath been stunned,
And is of sense forlorn;
A sadder and a wiser man
He rose the morrow morn.   625

1797–98.   1798.

FRANCE: AN ODE

Ye clouds! that far above me float and pause,
   Whose pathless march no mortal may control!
  Ye ocean-waves! that, wheresoe'er ye roll,
Yield homage only to eternal laws!
Ye woods! that listen to the night-birds singing,   5
   Midway the smooth and perilous slope reclined,
Save when your own imperious branches, swinging,
   Have made a solemn music of the wind!
Where, like a man beloved of God,

Through glooms which never woodman trod,   10
    How oft, pursuing fancies holy,
My moonlight way o'er flowering weeds I wound,
    Inspired, beyond the guess of folly,
By each rude shape and wild unconquerable sound!
O ye loud waves! and O ye forests high!   15
    And O ye clouds that far above me soared!
Thou rising sun! thou blue rejoicing sky!
    Yea, every thing that is and will be free!
    Bear witness for me, wheresoe'er ye be,
With what deep worship I have still adored   20
    The spirit of divinest Liberty.

When France in wrath her giant limbs upreared,
    And, with that oath which smote air, earth, and sea,
    Stamped her strong foot, and said she would be free,
Bear witness for me, how I hoped and feared!   25
With what a joy my lofty gratulation
    Unawed I sang, amid a slavish band.
And when, to whelm the disenchanted nation,
    Like fiends embattled by a wizard's wand,
      The monarchs marched in evil day,   30
      And Britain joined the dire array;
    Though dear her shores and circling ocean,
Though many friendships, many youthful loves,
    Had swollen the patriot emotion,
And flung a magic light o'er all her hills and groves,   35
Yet still my voice, unaltered, sang defeat
    To all that braved the tyrant-quelling lance,
And shame too long delayed and vain retreat!
For ne'er, O Liberty, with partial aim
I dimmed thy light or damped thy holy flame;   40
    But blessed the pæans of delivered France,
And hung my head and wept at Britain's name.

"And what," I said, "though Blasphemy's loud scream
    With that sweet music of deliverance strove!
    Though all the fierce and drunken passions wove   45
A dance more wild than e'er was maniac's dream!
    Ye storms that round the dawning east assembled,
The Sun was rising, though ye hid his light!"
    And when, to soothe my soul, that hoped and trembled,

The dissonance ceased, and all seemed calm and bright;   50
   When France her front deep-scarred and gory
   Concealed with clustering wreaths of glory;
     When, insupportably advancing,
   Her arm made mockery of the warrior's ramp;
     While, timid looks of fury glancing,   55
   Domestic Treason, crushed beneath her fatal stamp,
Writhed like a wounded dragon in his gore;
   Then I reproached my fears that would not flee:
"And soon," I said, "shall Wisdom teach her lore
In the low huts of them that toil and groan;   60
And, conquering by her happiness alone,
   Shall France compel the nations to be free,
Till Love and Joy look round, and call the earth their own."

Forgive me, Freedom! O forgive those dreams!
   I hear thy voice, I hear thy loud lament,   65
   From bleak Helvetia's icy caverns sent;
I hear thy groans upon her blood-stained streams!
   Heroes that for your peaceful country perished,
And ye that, fleeing, spot your mountain-snows
   With bleeding wounds, forgive me that I cherished   70
One thought that ever blessed your cruel foes!
   To scatter rage and traitorous guilt
   Where Peace her jealous home had built;
     A patriot race to disinherit
Of all that made their stormy wilds so dear;   75
     And with inexpiable spirit
To taint the bloodless freedom of the mountaineer—
O France, that mockest Heaven, adulterous, blind,
   And patriot only in pernicious toils,
Are these thy boasts, champion of human kind?   80
   To mix with kings in the low lust of sway,
Yell in the hunt, and share the murderous prey;
To insult the shrine of Liberty with spoils
   From freemen torn; to tempt and to betray?

   The sensual and the dark rebel in vain,   85
   Slaves by their own compulsion! In mad game
They burst their manacles, and wear the name
   Of Freedom, graven on a heavier chain!
O Liberty! with profitless endeavour

Have I pursued thee, many a weary hour;　　　　　　90
　　But thou nor swell'st the victor's strain, nor ever
Didst breathe thy soul in forms of human power.
　　Alike from all, howe'er they praise thee
　　(Nor prayer nor boastful name delays thee),
　　Alike from Priestcraft's harpy minions,　　　95
　　And factious Blasphemy's obscener slaves,
　　　Thou speedest on thy subtle pinions,
The guide of homeless winds, and playmate of the waves!
And there I felt thee!—on that sea-cliff's verge,
　　Whose pines, scarce travelled by the breeze above,　　100
Had made one murmur with the distant surge!
Yes, while I stood and gazed, my temples bare,
And shot my being through earth, sea, and air,
　　Possessing all things with intensest love,
　　　O Liberty! my spirit felt thee there.　　　105

1798.　　　　　　　　　　　　　　　*1798.*

KUBLA KHAN

　　In Xanadu did Kubla Khan
　　A stately pleasure-dome decree,
　　Where Alph, the sacred river, ran
　　Through caverns measureless to man
　　　Down to a sunless sea.　　　　　5
So twice five miles of fertile ground
With walls and towers were girdled round;
And here were gardens bright with sinuous rills,
Where blossomed many an incense-bearing tree;
And here were forests ancient as the hills,　　　10
Enfolding sunny spots of greenery.

But O that deep romantic chasm which slanted
Down the green hill athwart a cedarn cover!
A savage place! as holy and enchanted
As e'er beneath a waning moon was haunted　　　15
By woman wailing for her demon-lover!
And from this chasm, with ceaseless turmoil seething,
As if this earth in fast thick pants were breathing,
A mighty fountain momently was forced;
Amid whose swift half-intermitted burst,　　　20
Huge fragments vaulted like rebounding hail,

Or chaffy grain beneath the thresher's flail;
And 'mid these dancing rocks at once and ever
It flung up momently the sacred river.
Five miles meandering with a mazy motion,   25
Through wood and dale the sacred river ran,
Then reached the caverns measureless to man,
And sank in tumult to a lifeless ocean;
And 'mid this tumult Kubla heard from far
Ancestral voices prophesying war!   30
    The shadow of the dome of pleasure
    Floated midway on the waves;
    Where was heard the mingled measure
    From the fountain and the caves.
It was a miracle of rare device,   35
A sunny pleasure-dome with caves of ice!

    A damsel with a dulcimer
    In a vision once I saw;
    It was an Abyssinian maid,
    And on her dulcimer she played,   40
    Singing of Mount Abora.
    Could I revive within me
    Her symphony and song,
    To such a deep delight 't would win me
That with music loud and long   45
I would build that dome in air,
That sunny dome! those caves of ice!
And all who heard should see them there,
And all should cry, "Beware! beware!
His flashing eyes, his floating hair!   50
    Weave a circle round him thrice,
    And close your eyes with holy dread,
    For he on honey-dew hath fed,
    And drunk the milk of Paradise."
1797 or 1798.   1816.

CHRISTABEL

PART THE FIRST

'T is the middle of night by the castle clock,
And the owls have awakened the crowing cock:

Tu—whit!——Tu—whoo!
And hark, again! the crowing cock,
How drowsily it crew.   5
    Sir Leoline, the baron rich,
Hath a toothless mastiff, which
From her kennel beneath the rock
Maketh answer to the clock,
Four for the quarters, and twelve for the hour;   10
Ever and aye, by shine and shower,
Sixteen short howls, not over loud:
Some say she sees my lady's shroud.
    Is the night chilly and dark?
The night is chilly, but not dark;   15
The thin gray cloud is spread on high,
It covers but not hides the sky;
The Moon is behind, and at the full,
And yet she looks both small and dull.
The night is chill, the cloud is gray;   20
'T is a month before the month of May,
And the spring comes slowly up this way.
    The lovely lady, Christabel,
Whom her father loves so well,
What makes her in the wood so late,   25
A furlong from the castle gate?
She had dreams all yesternight
Of her own betrothèd knight;
And she in the midnight wood will pray
For the weal of her lover that 's far away.   30
    She stole along, she nothing spoke,
The sighs she heaved were soft and low;
And naught was green upon the oak
But moss and rarest mistletoe.
She kneels beneath the huge oak tree   35
And in silence prayeth she.
    The lady sprang up suddenly,
The lovely lady, Christabel!
It moaned as near, as near can be,
But what it is she cannot tell.—   40
On the other side it seems to be,
Of the huge, broad-breasted, old oak tree.
    The night is chill; the forest bare;

Is it the wind that moaneth bleak?
There is not wind enough in the air   45
To move away the ringlet curl
From the lovely lady's cheek;
There is not wind enough to twirl
The one red leaf, the last of its clan,
That dances as often as dance it can,   50
Hanging so light, and hanging so high,
On the topmost twig that looks up at the sky.
    Hush, beating heart of Christabel!
Jesu, Maria, shield her well!
She folded her arms beneath her cloak,   55
And stole to the other side of the oak.
    What sees she there?
    There she sees a damsel bright,
Drest in a silken robe of white,
That shadowy in the moonlight shone;   60
The neck that made that white robe wan,
Her stately neck and arms were bare;
Her blue-veined feet unsandalled were,
And wildly glittered here and there
The gems entangled in her hair.   65
I guess 't was frightful there to see
A lady so richly clad as she—
Beautiful exceedingly!
"Mary Mother, save me now!"
Said Christabel; "and who art thou?"   70
    The lady strange made answer meet,
And her voice was faint and sweet:
"Have pity on my sore distress,
I scarce can speak for weariness:
Stretch forth thy hand, and have no fear!"   75
Said Christabel, "How camest thou here?"
And the lady, whose voice was faint and sweet,
Did thus pursue her answer meet:—
    "My sire is of a noble line,
And my name is Geraldine.   80
Five warriors seized me yestermorn,
Me, even me, a maid forlorn;
They choked my cries with force and fright,
And tied me on a palfrey white.

The palfrey was as fleet as wind, 85
And they rode furiously behind.
They spurred amain, their steeds were white;
And once we crossed the shade of night.
As sure as Heaven shall rescue me,
I have no thought what men they be; 90
Nor do I know how long it is
(For I have lain entranced, I wis)
Since one, the tallest of the five,
Took me from the palfrey's back,
A weary woman, scarce alive. 95
Some muttered words his comrades spoke:
He placed me underneath this oak;
He swore they would return with haste;
Whither they went I cannot tell—
I thought I heard, some minutes past, 100
Sounds as of a castle bell.
Stretch forth thy hand,"—thus ended she—
"And help a wretched maid to flee."
    Then Christabel stretched forth her hand,
And comforted fair Geraldine: 105
"Oh well, bright dame, may you command
The service of Sir Leoline;
And gladly our stout chivalry
Will he send forth, and friends withal,
To guide and guard you safe and free 110
Home to your noble father's hall."
    She rose; and forth with steps they passed
That strove to be, and were not, fast.
Her gracious stars the lady blest,
And thus spake on sweet Christabel: 115
"All our household are at rest,
The hall as silent as the cell;
Sir Leoline is weak in health,
And may not well awakened be;
But we will move as if in stealth, 120
And I beseech your courtesy,
This night, to share your couch with me."
    They crossed the moat, and Christabel
Took the key that fitted well;
A little door she opened straight, 125

All in the middle of the gate,
The gate that was ironed within and without,
Where an army in battle array had marched out.
The lady sank, belike through pain,
And Christabel with might and main   130
Lifted her up, a weary weight,
Over the threshold of the gate;
Then the lady rose again,
And moved, as she were not in pain.

    So free from danger, free from fear,   135
They crossed the court; right glad they were.
And Christabel devoutly cried
To the lady by her side,
"Praise we the Virgin all divine,
Who hath rescued thee from thy distress!"   140
"Alas, alas!" said Geraldine,
"I cannot speak for weariness."
So, free from danger, free from fear,
They crossed the court; right glad they were.

    Outside her kennel, the mastiff old   145
Lay fast asleep, in moonshine cold.
The mastiff old did not awake,
Yet she an angry moan did make!
And what can ail the mastiff bitch?
Never till now she uttered yell   150
Beneath the eye of Christabel.
Perhaps it is the owlet's scritch;
For what can ail the mastiff bitch?

    They passed the hall, that echoes still,
Pass as lightly as you will!   155
The brands were flat, the brands were dying,
Amid their own white ashes lying;
But when the lady passed, there came
A tongue of light, a fit of flame;
And Christabel saw the lady's eye,   160
And nothing else saw she thereby,
Save the boss of the shield of Sir Leoline tall,
Which hung in a murky old niche in the wall.
"O, softly tread," said Christabel,
"My father seldom sleepeth well."   165
    Sweet Christabel her feet doth bare;

And, jealous of the listening air,
They steal their way from stair to stair,
Now in glimmer, and now in gloom,
And now they pass the Baron's room,   170
As still as death, with stifled breath!
And now have reached her chamber door;
And now doth Geraldine press down
The rushes of the chamber floor.

   The moon shines dim in the open air,   175
And not a moonbeam enters here.
But they without its light can see
The chamber carved so curiously,
Carved with figures strange and sweet,
All made out of the carver's brain,   180
For a lady's chamber meet:
The lamp with twofold silver chain
Is fastened to an angel's feet.

   The silver lamp burns dead and dim;
But Christabel the lamp will trim.   185
She trimmed the lamp, and made it bright,
And left it swinging to and fro,
While Geraldine, in wretched plight,
Sank down upon the floor below.

   "O weary lady, Geraldine,   190
I pray you, drink this cordial wine!
It is a wine of virtuous powers;
My mother made it of wild flowers."

   "And will your mother pity me,
Who am a maiden most forlorn?"   195
Christabel answered: "Woe is me!
She died the hour that I was born.
I have heard the gray-haired friar tell
How on her death-bed she did say
That she should hear the castle bell   200
Strike twelve upon my wedding day.
O mother dear, that thou wert here!"
"I would," said Geraldine, "she were!"

   But soon, with altered voice, said she,
"Off, wandering mother! Peak and pine!   205
I have power to bid thee flee."
Alas! what ails poor Geraldine?

Why stares she with unsettled eye?
Can she the bodiless dead espy?
And why with hollow voice cries she,   210
"Off, woman, off! this hour is mine—
Though thou her guardian spirit be,
Off, woman, off! 't is given to me."

    Then Christabel knelt by the lady's side,
And raised to heaven her eyes so blue.   215
"Alas!" said she, "this ghastly ride—
Dear lady! it hath wildered you!"
The lady wiped her moist cold brow,
And faintly said, "'T is over now!"

    Again the wild-flower wine she drank: 220
Her fair large eyes 'gan glitter bright,
And from the floor whereon she sank,
The lofty lady stood upright;
She was most beautiful to see,
Like a lady of a far countrée.   225

    And thus the lofty lady spake:
"All they who live in the upper sky
Do love you, holy Christabel!
And you love them, and for their sake
And for the good which me befell,   230
Even I in my degree will try,
Fair maiden, to requite you well.
But now unrobe yourself; for I
Must pray, ere yet in bed I lie."

    Quoth Christabel, "So let it be!"   235
And as the lady bade, did she.
Her gentle limbs did she undress,
And lay down in her loveliness.

    But through her brain of weal and woe
So many thoughts moved to and fro   240
That vain it were her lids to close;
So half-way from the bed she rose,
And on her elbow did recline
To look at the lady Geraldine.

    Beneath the lamp the lady bowed,   245
And slowly rolled her eyes around;
Then, drawing in her breath aloud,
Like one that shuddered, she unbound

The cincture from beneath her breast:
Her silken robe and inner vest   250
Dropt to her feet, and, full in view,
Behold! her bosom and half her side—
A sight to dream of, not to tell!
Oh shield her! shield sweet Christabel!

    Yet Geraldine nor speaks nor stirs;   255
Ah, what a stricken look was hers!
Deep from within she seems half-way
To lift some weight with sick assay,
And eyes the maid and seeks delay;
Then suddenly, as one defied,   260
Collects herself in scorn and pride,
And lay down by the maiden's side!
And in her arms the maid she took,
      Ah well-a-day!
And with low voice and doleful look   265
    These words did say:
"In the touch of this bosom there worketh a spell,
Which is lord of thy utterance, Christabel!
Thou knowest to-night, and wilt know to-morrow,
This mark of my shame, this seal of my sorrow;   270
    But vainly thou warrest,
      For this is alone in
    Thy power to declare,
      That in the dim forest
    Thou heard'st a low moaning,   275
And found'st a bright lady, surpassingly fair,
And didst bring her home with thee in love and in charity,
To shield her and shelter her from the damp air."

THE CONCLUSION TO PART THE FIRST

It was a lovely sight to see
The lady Christabel, when she   280
Was praying at the old oak tree.
    Amid the jagged shadows
    Of mossy leafless boughs,
    Kneeling in the moonlight,
    To make her gentle vows;   285
Her slender palms together prest,
Heaving sometimes on her breast;

Her face resigned to bliss or bale—
Her face, O call it fair, not pale!
And both blue eyes more bright than clear,   290
Each about to have a tear.
　　With open eyes (ah, woe is me!)
Asleep, and dreaming fearfully,
Fearfully dreaming, yet, I wis,
Dreaming that alone which is—   295
O sorrow and shame! Can this be she,
The lady, who knelt at the old oak tree?
And lo! the worker of these harms,
That holds the maiden in her arms,
Seems to slumber still and mild,   300
As a mother with her child.
　　A star hath set, a star hath risen,
O Geraldine, since arms of thine
Have been the lovely lady's prison.
O Geraldine, one hour was thine—   305
Thou 'st had thy will! By tairn and rill,
The night-birds all that hour were still.
But now they are jubilant anew,
From cliff and tower: tu—whoo! tu—whoo!
Tu—whoo! tu—whoo! from wood and fell!   310
　　And see! the lady Christabel
Gathers herself from out her trance;
Her limbs relax, her countenance
Grows sad and soft; the smooth thin lids
Close o'er her eyes; and tears she sheds—   315
Large tears that leave the lashes bright!
And oft the while she seems to smile
As infants at a sudden light.
　　Yea, she doth smile, and she doth weep,
Like a youthful hermitess,   320
Beauteous in a wilderness,
Who, praying always, prays in sleep.
And if she move unquietly,
Perchance 't is but the blood so free,
Comes back and tingles in her feet.   325
No doubt she hath a vision sweet.
What if her guardian spirit 't were?
What if she knew her mother near?

But this she knows, in joys and woes,
That saints will aid if men will call;   330
For the blue sky bends over all!
1797.

PART THE SECOND

"Each matin bell," the Baron saith,
"Knells us back to a world of death."
These words Sir Leoline first said,
When he rose and found his lady dead;   335
These words Sir Leoline will say,
Many a morn to his dying day!
    And hence the custom and law began,
That still at dawn the sacristan,
Who duly pulls the heavy bell,   340
Five-and-forty beads must tell
Between each stroke—a warning knell,
Which not a soul can choose but hear
From Bratha-Head to Windermere.
    Saith Bracy the bard, "So let it knell!   345
And let the drowsy sacristan
Still count as slowly as he can!
There is no lack of such, I ween,
As well fill up the space between.
In Langdale Pike and Witch's Lair,   350
And Dungeon-ghyll so foully rent,
With ropes of rock and bells of air
Three sinful sextons' ghosts are pent,
Who all give back, one after t' other,
The death-note to their living brother;   355
And oft too, by the knell offended,
Just as their one, two, three, is ended,
The Devil mocks the doleful tale
With a merry peal from Borrowdale."
    The air is still! through mist and cloud   360
That merry peal comes ringing loud;
And Geraldine shakes off her dread,
And rises lightly from the bed,
Puts on her silken vestments white,
And tricks her hair in lovely plight,   365
And, nothing doubting of her spell,

Awakens the lady Christabel:
"Sleep you, sweet lady Christabel?
I trust that you have rested well."
   And Christabel awoke and spied   370
The same who lay down by her side—
O rather say, the same whom she
Raised up beneath the old oak tree!
Nay, fairer yet, and yet more fair!
For she belike hath drunken deep   375
Of all the blessedness of sleep.
And while she spake, her looks, her air,
Such gentle thankfulness declare,
That (so it seemed) her girded vests
Grew tight beneath her heaving breasts.   380
"Sure I have sinned!" said Christabel;
"Now Heaven be praised if all be well!"
And in low faltering tones, yet sweet,
Did she the lofty lady greet
With such perplexity of mind   385
As dreams too lively leave behind.
   So quickly she rose, and quickly arrayed
Her maiden limbs, and, having prayed
That He Who on the cross did groan
Might wash away her sins unknown,   390
She forthwith led fair Geraldine
To meet her sire, Sir Leoline.
   The lovely maid and the lady tall
Are pacing both into the hall,
And, pacing on through page and groom,   395
Enter the Baron's presence-room.
   The Baron rose, and while he prest
His gentle daughter to his breast,
With cheerful wonder in his eyes
The lady Geraldine espies,   400
And gave such welcome to the same
As might beseem so bright a dame.
   But when he heard the lady's tale,
And when she told her father's name,
Why waxed Sir Leoline so pale,   405
Murmuring o'er the name again,
Lord Roland de Vaux of Tryermaine?

Alas! they had been friends in youth;
But whispering tongues can poison truth,
And constancy lives in realms above,   410
And life is thorny, and youth is vain,
And to be wroth with one we love
Doth work like madness in the brain.
And thus it chanced, as I divine,
With Roland and Sir Leoline.   415
Each spake words of high disdain
And insult to his heart's best brother:
They parted—ne'er to meet again!
But never either found another
To free the hollow heart from paining.   420
They stood aloof, the scars remaining,
Like cliffs which had been rent asunder;
A dreary sea now flows between:
But neither heat, nor frost, nor thunder,
Shall wholly do away, I ween,   425
The marks of that which once hath been.

Sir Leoline, a moment's space,
Stood gazing on the damsel's face;
And the youthful Lord of Tryermaine
Came back upon his heart again.   430

Oh then the Baron forgot his age;
His noble heart swelled high with rage;
He swore by the wounds in Jesu's side
He would proclaim it far and wide,
With trump and solemn heraldry,   435
That they who thus had wronged the dame
Were base as spotted infamy!
"And if they dare deny the same,
My herald shall appoint a week,
And let the recreant traitors seek   440
My tourney court—that there and then
I may dislodge their reptile souls
From the bodies and forms of men!"
He spake; his eye in lightning rolls,
For the lady was ruthlessly seized, and he kenned   445
In the beautiful lady the child of his friend.

And now the tears were on his face,
And fondly in his arms he took

Fair Geraldine, who met the embrace,
Prolonging it with joyous look.   450
Which when she viewed, a vision fell
Upon the soul of Christabel,
The vision of fear, the touch and pain!
She shrunk and shuddered, and saw again
(Ah, woe is me! was it for thee,   455
Thou gentle maid, such sights to see?),
Again she saw that bosom old,
Again she felt that bosom cold,
And drew in her breath with a hissing sound;
Whereat the Knight turned wildly round,   460
And nothing saw but his own sweet maid
With eyes upraised, as one that prayed.

    The touch, the sight, had passed away;
And in its stead that vision blest
Which comforted her after-rest,   465
While in the lady's arms she lay,
Had put a rapture in her breast,
And on her lips and o'er her eyes
Spread smiles like light!
            With new surprise,
"What ails then my belovèd child?"   470
The Baron said. His daughter mild
Made answer, "All will yet be well!"
I ween she had no power to tell
Aught else, so mighty was the spell.

    Yet he who saw this Geraldine   475
Had deemed her sure a thing divine,
Such sorrow with such grace she blended,
As if she feared she had offended
Sweet Christabel, that gentle maid!
And with such lowly tones she prayed   480
She might be sent without delay
Home to her father's mansion.
                "Nay!
Nay, by my soul!" said Leoline.
"Ho! Bracy, the bard, the charge be thine!
Go thou, with music sweet and loud,   485
And take two steeds with trappings proud,
And take the youth whom thou lov'st best,

To bear thy harp and learn thy song,
And clothe you both in solemn vest,
And over the mountains haste along,   490
Lest wandering folk that are abroad
Detain you on the valley road.

   "And when he has crossed the Irthing flood,
My merry bard! he hastes, he hastes
Up Knorren Moor, through Halegarth Wood,   495
And reaches soon that castle good
Which stands and threatens Scotland's wastes.
Bard Bracy! bard Bracy! your horses are fleet,
Ye must ride up the hall, your music so sweet
More loud than your horses' echoing feet!   500
And loud and loud to Lord Roland call,
'Thy daughter is safe in Langdale hall!
Thy beautiful daughter is safe and free—
Sir Leoline greets thee thus through me.
He bids thee come without delay   505
With all thy numerous array,
And take thy lovely daughter home;
And he will meet thee on the way
With all his numerous array
White with their panting palfreys' foam!'   510
And by mine honor! I will say
That I repent me of the day
When I spake words of fierce disdain
To Roland de Vaux of Tryermaine!
For since that evil hour hath flown,   515
Many a summer's sun hath shone;
Yet ne'er found I a friend again
Like Roland de Vaux of Tryermaine."

   The lady fell, and clasped his knees,
Her face upraised, her eyes o'erflowing;   520
And Bracy replied, with faltering voice,
His gracious hail on all bestowing:
"Thy words, thou sire of Christabel,
Are sweeter than my harp can tell.
Yet might I gain a boon of thee,   525
This day my journey should not be;
So strange a dream hath come to me
That I had vowed with music loud

To clear yon wood from thing unblest,
Warned by a vision in my rest.   530
For in my sleep I saw that dove,
That gentle bird whom thou dost love,
And call'st by thy own daughter's name,
Sir Leoline! I saw the same,
Fluttering, and uttering fearful moan,   535
Among the green herbs in the forest alone.
Which when I saw and when I heard,
I wondered what might ail the bird;
For nothing near it could I see,
Save the grass and green herbs underneath the
          old tree.   540
     "And in my dream methought I went
To search out what might there be found,
And what the sweet bird's trouble meant,
That thus lay fluttering on the ground.
I went and peered, and could descry   545
No cause for her distressful cry;
But yet for her dear lady's sake
I stooped, methought, the dove to take,
When lo! I saw a bright green snake
Coiled round its wings and neck!   550
Green as the herbs on which it couched,
Close by the dove's its head it crouched;
And with the dove it heaves and stirs,
Swelling its neck as she swelled hers!
I woke; it was the midnight hour,   555
The clock was echoing in the tower;
But though my slumber was gone by,
This dream it would not pass away—
It seems to live upon my eye!
And thence I vowed this self-same day   560
With music strong and saintly song
To wander through the forest bare,
Lest aught unholy loiter there."

     Thus Bracy said: the Baron, the while,
Half-listening heard him with a smile;   565
Then turned to Lady Geraldine,
His eyes made up of wonder and love,
And said in courtly accents fine,

"Sweet maid, Lord Roland's beauteous dove,
With arms more strong than harp or song,   570
Thy sire and I will crush the snake!"
He kissed her forehead as he spake,
And Geraldine in maiden wise
Casting down her large bright eyes,
With blushing cheek and courtesy fine,   575
She turned her from Sir Leoline,
Softly gathering up her train,
That o'er her right arm fell again;
And folded her arms across her chest,
And couched her head upon her breast,   •   580
And looked askance at Christabel—
Jesu, Maria, shield her well!
    A snake's small eye blinks dull and shy:
And the lady's eyes they shrunk in her head,
Each shrunk up to a serpent's eye;   585
And with somewhat of malice, and more of dread,
At Christabel she looked askance!—
One moment—and the sight was fled!
But Christabel, in dizzy trance
Stumbling on the unsteady ground,   590
Shuddered aloud, with a hissing sound;
And Geraldine again turned round,
And like a thing that sought relief,
Full of wonder and full of grief,
She rolled her large bright eyes divine   595
Wildly on Sir Leoline.
    The maid, alas! her thoughts are gone;
She nothing sees—no sight but one!
The maid, devoid of guile and sin,
I know not how, in fearful wise   600
So deeply had she drunken in
That look, those shrunken serpent eyes,
That all her features were resigned
To this sole image in her mind,
And passively did imitate   605
That look of dull and teacherous hate!
And thus she stood in dizzy trance,
Still picturing that look askance
With forced unconscious sympathy,

Full before her father's view—   610
As far as such a look could be
In eyes so innocent and blue.
  And when the trance was o'er, the maid
Paused awhile, and inly prayed;
Then, falling at the Baron's feet,   615
"By my mother's soul do I entreat
That thou this woman send away!"
She said; and more she could not say,
For what she knew she could not tell,
O'ermastered by the mighty spell.   620
  Why is thy cheek so wan and wild,
Sir Leoline? Thy only child
Lies at thy feet, thy joy, thy pride,
So fair, so innocent, so mild;
The same for whom thy lady died!   625
O, by the pangs of her dear mother
Think thou no evil of thy child!
For her, and thee, and for no other,
She prayed the moment ere she died;
Prayed that the babe for whom she died   630
Might prove her dear lord's joy and pride.
That prayer her deadly pangs beguiled,
  Sir Leoline!
And wouldst thou wrong thy only child,
  Her child and thine?   635
  Within the Baron's heart and brain
If thoughts like these had any share,
They only swelled his rage and pain,
And did but work confusion there.
His heart was cleft with pain and rage,   640
His cheeks they quivered, his eyes were wild,
Dishonoured thus in his old age,
Dishonoured by his only child,
And all his hospitality
To the insulted daughter of his friend   645
By more than woman's jealousy
Brought thus to a disgraceful end,
He rolled his eye with stern regard
Upon the gentle minstrel bard,
And said in tones abrupt, austere,   650

"Why, Bracy! dost thou loiter here?
I bade thee hence!" The bard obeyed,
And, turning from his own sweet maid,
The aged knight, Sir Leoline,
Led forth the lady Geraldine!   655

1800.

THE CONCLUSION TO PART THE SECOND

A little child, a limber elf,
Singing, dancing to itself,
A fairy thing with red round cheeks,
That always finds, and never seeks,
Makes such a vision to the sight   660
As fills a father's eyes with light;
And pleasures flow in so thick and fast
Upon his heart, that he at last
Must needs express his love's excess
With words of unmeant bitterness.   665
Perhaps 't is pretty to force together,
Thoughts so all unlike each other,
To mutter and mock a broken charm,
To dally with wrong that does no harm.
Perhaps 't is tender too and pretty   670
At each wild word to feel within
A sweet recoil of love and pity.
And what if in a world of sin
(O sorrow and shame should this be true!)
Such giddiness of heart and brain   675
Comes seldom save from rage and pain,
So talks as it's most used to do.

1801?   1816.

INSCRIPTION FOR A FOUNTAIN ON A HEATH

This sycamore, oft musical with bees,
Such tents the patriarchs loved. O long unharmed
May all its agèd boughs o'er-canopy
The small round basin, which this jutting stone
Keeps pure from falling leaves. Long may the spring,   5
Quietly as a sleeping infant's breath,
Send up cold waters to the traveller

With soft and even pulse; nor ever cease
Yon tiny cone of sand its soundless dance,
Which at the bottom, like a fairy's page,   10
As merry and no taller, dances still,
Nor wrinkles the smooth surface of the fount.
Here twilight is, and coolness; here is moss,
A soft seat, and a deep and ample shade.
Thou may'st toil far and find no second tree.   15
Drink, pilgrim, here! Here rest! And if thy heart
Be innocent, here too shalt thou refresh
Thy spirit, listening to some gentle sound,
Or passing gale or hum of murmuring bees.

                                        1802.

WORK WITHOUT HOPE

All Nature seems at work. Slugs leave their lair—
The bees are stirring—birds are on the wing—
And Winter, slumbering in the open air,
Wears on his smiling face a dream of Spring!
And I the while, the sole unbusy thing,   5
Nor honey make, nor pair, nor build, nor sing.

    Yet well I ken the banks where amaranths blow,
Have traced the fount whence streams of nectar flow.
Bloom, O ye amaranths! bloom for whom ye may;
For me ye bloom not! Glide, rich streams, away!   10
With lips unbrightened, wreathless brow, I stroll.
And would you learn the spells that drowse my soul?
Work without Hope draws nectar in a sieve,
And Hope without an object cannot live.
1827.   1827.

ROBERT SOUTHEY

THE HOLLY TREE

O reader, hast thou ever stood to see
        The holly tree?
The eye that contemplates it well perceives
        Its glossy leaves
Ordered by an intelligence so wise   5
As might confound the atheist's sophistries.

Below, a circling fence, its leaves are seen
    Wrinkled and keen;
No grazing cattle through their prickly round
    Can reach to wound;   10
But as they grow where nothing is to fear,
Smooth and unarmed the pointless leaves appear.

I love to view these things with curious eyes,
    And moralize;
And in this wisdom of the holly tree   15
    Can emblems see
Wherewith perchance to make a pleasant rhyme,
One which may profit in the after time.

Thus, though abroad perchance I might appear
    Harsh and austere,   20
To those who on my leisure would intrude
    Reserved and rude,
Gentle at home amid my friends I'd be,
Like the high leaves upon the holly tree.

And should my youth, as youth is apt, I know,   25
    Some harshness show,
All vain asperities I day by day
    Would wear away,
Till the smooth temper of my age should be
Like the high leaves upon the holly tree.   30

And as when all the summer trees are seen
    So bright and green,
The holly leaves a sober hue display
    Less bright than they;
But when the bare and wintry woods we see,   35
What then so cheerful as the holly tree?

So serious should my youth appear among
    The thoughtless throng;
So would I seem amid the young and gay
    More grave than they;   40
That in my age as cheerful I might be
As the green winter of the holly tree.

1798.   1799.

BISHOP BRUNO

Bishop Bruno awoke in the dead midnight,
And he heard his heart beat loud with affright;
He dreamt he had rung the palace bell,
And the sound it gave was his passing knell.

Bishop Bruno smiled at his fears so vain,   5
He turned to sleep and he dreamt again:—
He rang at the palace gate once more,
And Death was the porter that opened the door.

He started up at the fearful dream,
And he heard at his window the screech-owl scream; 10
Bishop Bruno slept no more that night,—
Oh, glad was he when he saw the day-light!

Now he goes forth in proud array,
For he with the Emperor dines to-day;
There was not a baron in Germany   15
That went with a nobler train than he.

Before and behind his soldiers ride,
The people thronged to see their pride;
They bowed the head, and the knee they bent,
But nobody blest him as he went.   20

So he went on stately and proud,
When he heard a voice that cried aloud,
"Ho! ho! Bishop Bruno! you travel with glee;
But I would have you know, you travel to me!"

Behind and before and on either side,   25
He looked, but nobody he espied;
And the Bishop at that grew cold with fear,
For he heard the words distinct and clear.

And when he rang at the palace bell,
He almost expected to hear his knell;   30
And when the porter turned the key,
He almost expected Death to see.

But soon the Bishop recovered his glee,
For the Emperor welcomed him royally;
And now the tables were spread, and there   35
Were choicest wines and dainty fare.

And now the Bishop had blest the meat,
When a voice was heard as he sat in his seat:
"With the Emperor now you are dining with glee;
But know, Bishop Bruno! you sup with me!" 40

The Bishop then grew pale with affright,
And suddenly lost his appetite;
All the wine and dainty cheer
Could not comfort his heart that was sick with fear.

But by little and little recovered he, 45
For the wine went flowing merrily,
Till at length he forgot his former dread,
And his cheeks again grew rosy red.

When he sat down to the royal fare,
Bishop Bruno was the saddest man there; 50
But when the masquers entered the hall,
He was the merriest man of all.

Then from amid the masquers' crowd
There went a voice hollow and loud:
"You have passed the day, Bishop Bruno, in glee; 55
But you must pass the night with me!"

His cheek grows pale, and his eye-balls glare,
And stiff round his tonsure bristled his hair;
With that there came one from the masquers' band,
And took the Bishop by the hand. 60

The bony hand suspended his breath,
His marrow grew cold at the touch of Death;
On saints in vain he attempted to call—
Bishop Bruno fell dead in the palace hall.

1798.   1799.

FROM

THALABA THE DESTROYER

So on a violet bank
The Arabian maid laid down,
Her soft cheek pillowed upon moss and flowers.
She lay in silent prayer,

Till prayer had tranquillized her fears, 　　　　5
And sleep fell on her. By her side
　　　Silent sate Thalaba,
　　　And gazed upon the maid,
　　　And, as he gazed, drew in
　　　New courage and intenser faith, 　　　10
And waited calmly for the eventful day.

Loud sung the lark; the awakened maid
Beheld him twinkling in the morning light,
And wished for wings and liberty like his.
　　　The flush of fear inflamed her cheek, 　　15
　　　But Thalaba was calm of soul,
　　　　　Collected for the work.
　　　　He pondered in his mind
　　　　How from Lobaba's breast
　　　　His blunted arrow fell. 　　　　20
　　　　Aloadin too might wear
　　　Spell perchance of equal power
　　　To blunt the weapon's edge.

　　　　Beside the river-brink
Grew a young poplar, whose unsteady leaves 　　25
　　　Varying their verdure to the gale,
　　　　With silver glitter caught
　　　　　His meditating eye.
　　　Then to Oneiza turned the youth,
　　　　And gave his father's bow, 　　　30
　　　And o'er her shoulders slung
　　　　The quiver arrow-stored.
　　"Me other weapon suits," said he;
　　"Bear thou the bow: dear maid,
The days return upon me, when these shafts, 　　35
True to thy guidance, from the lofty palm
Brought down its cluster, and thy gladdened eye,
Exulting, turned to seek the voice of praise.
　　O, yet again, Oneiza, we shall share
　　Our desert-joys!" So saying, to the bank 　　40
　　　He moved, and stooping low,
With double grasp, hand below hand, he clenched,
　　　And from its watery soil
　　　Uptore the poplar trunk.

Then off he shook the clotted earth, 45
    And broke away the head
    And boughs and lesser roots;
    And, lifting it aloft,
Wielded with able sway the massy club.
"Now for this child of hell!" quoth Thalaba; 50
    "Belike he shall exchange today
    His dainty Paradise
For other dwelling, and its cups of joy
    For the unallayable bitterness
    Of Zaccoum's fruit accursed." 55

With that the Arabian youth and maid
Toward the centre of the garden went.
It chanced that Aloadin had convoked
    The garden-habitants,
    And with the assembled throng 60
Oneiza mingled, and the Appointed Youth.
    Unmarked they mingled; or if one
With busier finger to his neighbour notes
    The quivered maid, "Haply," he says,
    "Some daughter of the Homerites, 65
Or one who yet remembers with delight
Her native tents of Himiar." "Nay!" rejoins
His comrade, "a love-pageant! for the man
Mimics with that fierce eye and knotty club
    Some savage lion-tamer; she forsooth 70
Must play the heroine of the years of old!"

Radiant with gems upon his throne of gold
    Sate Aloadin; o'er the Sorcerer's head
Hovered a bird, and in the fragrant air
    Waved his wide winnowing wings, 75
    A living canopy.
    Large as the hairy cassowar
    Was that o'ershadowing bird;
    So huge his talons, in their grasp
The eagle would have hung a helpless prey. 80
    His beak was iron, and his plumes
    Glittered like burnished gold,
And his eyes glowed as though an inward fire
    Shone through a diamond orb.

The blinded multitude   85
Adored the Sorcerer,
And bent the knee before him,
And shouted forth his praise:
"Mighty art thou, the bestower of joy,
The Lord of Paradise!"   90
Then Aloadin rose and waved his hand,
And they stood mute and moveless
In idolizing awe.

"Children of Earth," he said,
"Whom I have guided here   95
By easier passage than the gate of Death,
The infidel Sultan, to whose lands
My mountains stretch their roots,
Blasphemes and threatens me.
Strong are his armies, many are his guards,   .100
Yet may a dagger find him.
Children of Earth, I tempt ye not
With the vain promise of a bliss unseen
With tales of a hereafter heaven,
Whence never traveller hath returned!   105

Have ye not tasted of the cup of joy
That in these groves of happiness
Forever over-mantling tempts
The ever-thirsty lip?
Who is there here that by a deed   110
Of danger will deserve
The eternal joys of actual Paradise?"

"I!" Thalaba exclaimed;
And, springing forward, on the Sorcerer's head
He dashed his knotty club.   115

Aloadin fell not, though his skull
Was shattered by the blow,
For by some talisman
His miserable life imprisoned still
Dwelt in the body. The astonished crowd   120
Stand motionless with fear,
Expecting to behold

Immediate vengeance from the wrath of Heaven.
  And lo! the bird—the monster bird—
    Soars up—then pounces down   125
      To seize on Thalaba!
     Now, Oneiza, bend the bow,
    Now draw the arrow home!—
True fled the arrow from Oneiza's hand;
   It pierced the monster bird,   130
    It broke the talisman;—
  Then darkness covered all;—
Earth shook, heaven thundered, and amid the yells
    Of evil spirits perished
     The Paradise of Sin.   135

   At last the earth was still;
  The yelling of the demons ceased;
Opening the wreck and ruin to their sight,
The darkness rolled away. Alone in life,
  Amid the desolation and the dead,   140
Stood the Destroyer and the Arabian maid.
They looked around: the rocks were rent,
  The path was open, late by magic closed.
Awe-struck and silent down the stony glen
  They wound their thoughtful way.   145

1800.   *1801.*

MY DAYS AMONG THE DEAD ARE PAST

My days among the dead are past:
  Around me I behold,
Where'er these casual eyes are cast,
  The mighty minds of old;
My never-failing friends are they,   5
With whom I converse day by day.

With them I take delight in weal,
  And seek relief in woe;
And while I understand and feel
  How much to them I owe,   10
My cheeks have often been bedewed
With tears of thoughtful gratitude.

My thoughts are with the dead: with them
    I live in long-past years;
Their virtues love, their faults condemn,   15
    Partake their hopes and fears,
And from their lessons seek and find
Instruction with an humble mind.

My hopes are with the dead; anon
    My place with them will be,   20
And I with them shall travel on
    Through all Futurity,
Yet leaving here a name, I trust,
That will not perish in the dust.

1818.   *1823.*

THOMAS CAMPBELL

FROM

THE PLEASURES OF HOPE

At summer eve, when heaven's ethereal bow
Spans with bright arch the glittering hills below,
Why to yon mountain turns the musing eye,
Whose sunbright summit mingles with the sky?
Why do those cliffs of shadowy tint appear   5
More sweet than all the landscape smiling near?
'T is distance lends enchantment to the view,
And robes the mountain in its azure hue.
Thus, with delight, we linger to survey
The promised joys of life's unmeasured way;   10
Thus, from afar, each dim-discovered scene
More pleasing seems than all the past hath been,
And every form, that Fancy can repair
From dark oblivion, glows divinely there.
    What potent spirit guides the raptured eye   15
To pierce the shades of dim futurity?
Can Wisdom lend, with all her heavenly power,
The pledge of Joy's anticipated hour?
Ah, no! she darkly sees the fate of man—
Her dim horizon bounded to a span;   20

Or, if she hold an image to the view,
'T is Nature pictured too severely true.
With thee, sweet Hope! resides the heavenly light
That pours remotest rapture on the sight;
Thine is the charm of life's bewildered way,   25
That calls each slumbering passion into play.
Waked by thy touch, I see the sister-band,
On tiptoe watching, start at thy command,
And fly where'er thy mandate bids them steer,
To Pleasure's path, or Glory's bright career.   30
    Primeval Hope, the Aönian Muses say,
When Man and Nature mourned their first decay;
When every form of death and every woe
Shot from malignant stars to earth below;
When Murder bared her arm, and rampant War   35
Yoked the red dragons of her iron car;
When Peace and Mercy, banished from the plain,
Sprung on the viewless winds to Heaven again;
All, all forsook the friendless, guilty mind,
But Hope, the charmer, lingered still behind.   40

1796?–99.   *1799.*

YE MARINERS OF ENGLAND

Ye mariners of England,
That guard our native seas;
Whose flag has braved, a thousand years,
The battle and the breeze!
Your glorious standard launch again   5
To match another foe,
And sweep through the deep,
While the stormy winds do blow;
While the battle rages loud and long,
And the stormy winds do blow.   10

The spirits of your fathers
Shall start from every wave!
For the deck it was their field of fame,
And Ocean was their grave.
Where Blake and mighty Nelson fell   15
Your manly hearts shall glow,

As ye sweep through the deep,
While the stormy winds do blow;
While the battle rages loud and long,
And the stormy winds do blow.   20

Britannia needs no bulwarks,
No towers along the steep;
Her march is o'er the mountain waves,
Her home is on the deep.
With thunders from her native oak   25
She quells the floods below,
As they roar on the shore,
When the stormy winds do blow;
When the battle rages loud and long,
And the stormy winds do blow.   30

The meteor flag of England
Shall yet terrific burn,
Till danger's troubled night depart,
And the star of peace return.
Then, then, ye ocean warriors!   35
Our song and feast shall flow
To the fame of your name,
When the storm has ceased to blow;
When the fiery fight is heard no more,
And the storm has ceased to blow.   40

1799–1800.   1801.

HOHENLINDEN

On Linden, when the sun was low,
All bloodless lay th' untrodden snow,
And dark as winter was the flow
Of Iser, rolling rapidly.

But Linden saw another sight,   5
When the drum beat at dead of night,
Commanding fires of death to light
The darkness of her scenery.

By torch and trumpet fast arrayed,
Each horseman drew his battle-blade,   10
And furious every charger neighed,
To join the dreadful revelry.

Then shook the hills with thunder riven,
Then rushed the steed to battle driven,
And louder than the bolts of heaven   15
Far flashed the red artillery.

But redder yet that light shall glow
On Linden's hills of stainèd snow,
And bloodier yet the torrent flow
Of Iser, rolling rapidly.   20

'T is morn; but scarce yon level sun
Can pierce the war-clouds, rolling dun,
Where furious Frank and fiery Hun
Shout in their sulphurous canopy.

The combat deepens. On, ye brave,   25
Who rush to glory, or the grave!
Wave, Munich, all thy banners wave,
And charge with all thy chivalry!

Few, few shall part where many meet!
The snow shall be their winding-sheet,   30
And every turf beneath their feet
Shall be a soldier's sepulchre.

1802.   1802.

BATTLE OF THE BALTIC

Of Nelson and the North
Sing the glorious day's renown,
When to battle fierce came forth
All the might of Denmark's crown,
And her arms along the deep proudly shone;   5
By each gun the lighted brand,
In a bold determined hand,
And the Prince of all the land
Led them on.

Like leviathans afloat,   10
Lay their bulwarks on the brine,
While the sign of battle flew
On the lofty British line;
It was ten of April morn by the chime.

As they drifted on their path,   15
There was silence deep as death;
And the boldest held his breath,
For a time.

But the might of England flushed
To anticipate the scene;   20
And her van the fleeter rushed
O'er the deadly space between.
"Hearts of oak!" our captains cried, when each
    gun
From its adamantine lips
Spread a death-shade around the ships,   25
Like the hurricane eclipse
Of the sun.

Again! again! again!
And the havoc did not slack,
Till a feeble cheer the Dane
To our cheering sent us back;   30
Their shots along the deep slowly boom—
Then ceased—and all is wail,
As they strike the shattered sail,
Or in conflagration pale
Light the gloom.   35

Out spoke the victor then,
As he hailed them o'er the wave:
"Ye are brothers! ye are men!
And we conquer but to save;   40
    So peace instead of death let us bring.
But yield, proud foe, thy fleet,
With the crews, at England's feet,
And make submission meet
To our King."   .45

Then Denmark blessed our chief,
That he gave her wounds repose;
And the sounds of joy and grief
From her people wildly rose,
As Death withdrew his shades from the day;   50
While the sun looked smiling bright

O'er a wide and woeful sight,
Where the fires of funeral light
Died away.

Now joy, old England, raise   55
For the tidings of thy might,
By the festal cities' blaze,
Whilst the wine cup shines in light!
And yet, amidst that joy and uproar,
Let us think of them that sleep,   60
Full many a fathom deep,
By thy wild and stormy steep,
Elsinore!

Brave hearts! to Britain's pride
Once so faithful and so true,   65
On the deck of fame that died,
With the gallant good Riou;
Soft sigh the winds of heaven o'er their grave!
While the billow mournful rolls,
And the mermaid's song condoles,   ·   70
Singing glory to the souls
Of the brave!

1804–05.   *1809.*

LORD ULLIN'S DAUGHTER

A chieftain, to the Highlands bound,
    Cries, "Boatman, do not tarry!
And I 'll give thee a silver pound
    To row us o'er the ferry."

"Now who be ye, would cross Lochgyle,   5
    This dark and stormy water?"
"O, I 'm the chief of Ulva's Isle,
    And this, Lord Ullin's daughter.

"And fast before her father's men
    Three days we 've fled together,   10
For should he find us in the glen,
    My blood would stain the heather.

"His horsemen hard behind us ride;
  Should they our steps discover,
Then who will cheer my bonny bride   15
  When they have slain her lover?"

Outspoke the hardy Highland wight:
  "I'll go, my chief—I'm ready;
It is not for your silver bright,
  But for your winsome lady.   20

"And by my word! the bonny bird
  In danger shall not tarry;
So though the waves are raging white,
  I'll row you o'er the ferry."

By this the storm grew loud apace,   25
  The water-wraith was shrieking;
And in the scowl of heaven each face
  Grew dark as they were speaking.

But still as wilder blew the wind,
  And as the night grew drearer,   30
Adown the glen rode armed men—
  Their trampling sounded nearer.

"O haste thee, haste!" the lady cries,
  "Though tempests round us gather;
I'll meet the raging of the skies,   35
  But not an angry father."

The boat has left a stormy land,
  A stormy sea before her,—
When, oh! too strong for human hand,
  The tempest gathered o'er her.   40

And still they rowed amidst the roar
  Of waters fast prevailing:
Lord Ullin reached that fatal shore—
  His wrath was changed to wailing.

For sore dismayed, through storm and shade,   45
  His child he did discover:
One lovely hand she stretched for aid,
  And one was round her lover.

"Come back! come back!" he cried in grief,
   "Across this stormy water; 50
And I'll forgive your Highland chief,
   My daughter!—oh, my daughter!"

'T was vain:—the loud waves lashed the shore,
   Return or aid preventing;—
The waters wild went o'er his child, 55
   And he was left lamenting.

1795–1805.   *1809.*

WALTER SCOTT

FROM

THE LAY OF THE LAST MINSTREL

The feast was over in Branksome tower,
And the Ladye had gone to her secret bower,
Her bower that was guarded by word and by spell,
Deadly to hear, and deadly to tell—
Jesu Maria, shield us well! 5
No living wight, save the Ladye alone,
Had dared to cross the threshold stone.

The tables were drawn, it was idlesse all;
   Knight and page and household squire
Loitered through the lofty hall, 10
   Or crowded round the ample fire;
The stag-hounds, weary with the chase,
   Lay stretched upon the rushy floor,
And urged, in dreams, the forest-race
   From Teviot-stone to Eskdale-moor. 15

Nine-and-twenty knights of fame
   Hung their shields in Branksome Hall;
Nine-and-twenty squires of name
   Brought them their steeds to bower from stall;
      Nine-and-twenty yeomen tall 20
      Waited, duteous, on them all:
      They were all knights of metal true,
      Kinsmen to the bold Buccleuch.

Ten of them were sheathed in steel,
With belted sword, and spur on heel;   25
They quitted not their harness bright,
Neither by day nor yet by night;
  They lay down to rest
  With corslet laced,
Pillowed on buckler cold and hard;   30
  They carved at the meal
  With gloves of steel,
And they drank the red wine through the helmet
  barred.

Ten squires, ten yeomen, mail-clad men,
Waited the beck of the warders ten;   35
Thirty steeds, both fleet and wight,
Stood saddled in stable day and night,
Barbed with frontlet of steel, I trow,
And with Jedwood-axe at saddle-bow;
A hundred more fed free in stall: 40
Such was the custom of Branksome Hall.

Why do these steeds stand ready dight?
Why watch these warriors, armed, by night?
They watch to hear the blood-hound baying;
They watch to hear the war-horn braying,   45
To see St. George's red cross streaming,
To see the midnight beacon gleaming;
They watch against Southern force and guile,
  Lest Scroop or Howard or Percy's powers
  Threaten Branksome's lordly towers,   50
From Warkworth or Naworth or merry Carlisle.

Such is the custom of Branksome Hall.
  Many a valiant knight is here;
But he, the chieftain of them all,
His sword hangs rusting on the wall,   55
  Beside his broken spear.
  Bards long shall tell
  How Lord Walter fell:
When startled burghers fled, afar,
The furies of the Border war;   60
When the streets of high Dunedin

Saw lances gleam, and falchions redden,
And heard the slogan's deadly yell;
Then the Chief of Branksome fell.

Can piety the discord heal,   65
    Or stanch the death-feud's enmity?
Can Christian lore, can patriot zeal,
    Can love of blessed charity?
No! vainly to each holy shrine,
    In mutual pilgrimage, they drew;   70
Implored, in vain, the grace divine
    For chiefs their own red falchions slew.
While Cessford owns the rule of Carr,
    While Ettrick boasts the line of Scott,
The slaughtered chiefs, the mortal jar,   75
The havoc of the feudal war,
    Shall never, never be forgot!

In sorrow o'er Lord Walter's bier
    The warlike foresters had bent,
And many a flower and many a tear   80
    Old Teviot's maids and matrons lent;
But o'er her warrior's bloody bier
The Ladye dropped nor flower nor tear!
Vengeance, deep-brooding o'er the slain,
    Had locked the source of softer woe;   85
And burning pride and high disdain
    Forbade the rising tear to flow;
Until, amid his sorrowing clan,
    Her son lisped from the nurse's knee,
"And if I live to be a man,   90
    My father's death revenged shall be!"
Then fast the mother's tears did seek
To dew the infant's kindling cheek.

All loose her negligent attire,
    All loose her golden hair,   95
Hung Margaret o'er her slaughtered sire,
    And wept in wild despair;
But not alone the bitter tear
    Had filial grief supplied,
For hopeless love and anxious fear   100

Had lent their mingled tide,
Nor in her mother's altered eye
Dared she to look for sympathy.
Her lover 'gainst her father's clan,
　　With Carr in arms had stood,   105
When Mathouse-burn to Melrose ran
　　All purple with their blood;
And well she knew her mother dread,
Before Lord Cranstoun she should wed,
Would see her on her dying bed.   110

Of noble race the Ladye came;
Her father was a clerk of fame,
　　Of Bethune's line of Picardie.
He learned the art that none may name,
　　In Padua, far beyond the sea: 115
Men said he changed his mortal frame
　　By feat of magic mystery;
For when in studious mood he paced
　　St. Andrew's cloistered hall,
His form no darkening shadow traced   120
　　Upon the sunny wall!

And of his skill, as bards avow,
　　He taught that Ladye fair,
Till to her bidding she could bow
　　The viewless forms of air.   125
And now she sits in secret bower,
In old Lord David's western tower,
And listens to a heavy sound
That moans the mossy turrets round.
Is it the roar of Teviot's tide,   130
That chafes against the scaur's red side?
Is it the wind that swings the oaks?
Is it the echo from the rocks?
What may it be, the heavy sound,
That moans old Branksome's turrets round?   135

At the sullen, moaning sound,
　　The ban-dogs bay and howl;
And, from the turrets round,
　　Loud whoops the startled owl.

In the hall, both squire and knight 140
   Swore that a storm was near,
And looked forth to view the night;
   But the night was still and clear!

From the sound of Teviot's tide,
Chafing with the mountain's side, 145
From the groan of the wind-swung oak,
From the sullen echo of the rock,
From the voice of the coming storm,
   The Ladye knew it well!
It was the Spirit of the Flood that spoke, 150
   And he called on the Spirit of the Fell.

RIVER SPIRIT

"Sleep'st thou, brother?"

MOUNTAIN SPIRIT

     "Brother, nay—
On my hills the moonbeams play.
From Craik-cross to Skelfhill-pen,
By every rill, in every glen, 155
   Merry elves their morris pacing,
     To aërial minstrelsy,
   Emerald rings on brown heath tracing,
     Trip it deft and merrily.
Up, and mark their nimble feet! 160
Up, and list their music sweet!"

RIVER SPIRIT

"Tears of an imprisoned maiden
   Mix with my polluted stream;
Margaret of Branksome, sorrow-laden,
   Mourns beneath the moon's pale beam. 165
Tell me, thou, who view'st the stars,
When shall cease these feudal jars?
What shall be the maiden's fate?
Who shall be the maiden's mate?"

MOUNTAIN SPIRIT

"Arthur's slow wain his course doth roll, 170
In utter darkness, round the pole;
The Northern Bear lowers black and grim;
Orion's studded belt is dim;

Twinkling faint and distant far,
Shimmers through mist each planet star;   175
  Ill may I read their high decree!
But no kind influence deign they shower
On Teviot's tide and Branksome's tower,
  Till pride be quelled and love be free."

The unearthly voices ceast,   180
  And the heavy sound was still;
It died on the river's breast,
  It died on the side of the hill.
But round Lord David's tower
  The sound still floated near;   185
For it rung in the Ladye's bower,
  And it rung in the Ladye's ear.
She raised her stately head,
  And her heart throbbed high with pride:
"Your mountains shall bend,   190
  And your streams ascend,
    Ere Margaret be our foeman's bride!"
  1802-04.   *1805.*

LOCHINVAR

O, young Lochinvar is come out of the west!
Through all the wide Border his steed was the best;
And save his good broadsword he weapons had none;
He rode all unarmed, and he rode all alone.
So faithful in love, and so dauntless in war,   5
There never was knight like the young Lochinvar.

He stayed not for brake, and he stopped not for stone;
He swam the Eske river where ford there was none;
But ere he alighted at Netherby gate,
The bride had consented, the gallant came late: 10
For a laggard in love, and a dastard in war,
Was to wed the fair Ellen of brave Lochinvar.

So boldly he entered the Netherby Hall,
Among bride's-men, and kinsmen, and brothers, and all.
Then spoke the bride's father, his hand on his sword, 15
(For the poor craven bridegroom said never a word):
"O come ye in peace here, or come ye in war,
  Or to dance at our bridal, young Lord Lochinvar?"

"I long wooed your daughter; my suit you denied;
Love swells like the Solway, but ebbs like its tide;   20
And now am I come, with this lost love of mine
To lead but one measure, drink one cup of wine.
There are maidens in Scotland more lovely by far,
That would gladly be bride to the young Lochinvar."

The bride kissed the goblet; the knight took it up,   25
He quaffed off the wine, and he threw down the cup.
She looked down to blush, and she looked up to sigh,
With a smile on her lips, and a tear in her eye.
He took her soft hand, ere her mother could bar—
"Now tread we a measure!" said young Lochinvar.   30

So stately his form, and so lovely her face,
That never a hall such a galliard did grace;
While her mother did fret, and her father did fume,
And the bridegroom stood dangling his bonnet and plume;
And the bride-maidens whispered, "'T were better by far 35
To have matched our fair cousin with young Lochinvar."

One touch to her hand, and one word in her ear,
When they reached the hall-door, and the charger stood near;
So light to the croupe the fair lady he swung,
So light to the saddle before her he sprung!   40
"She is won! we are gone, over bank, bush, and scaur!
They 'll have fleet steeds that follow!" quoth young Lochinvar.

There was mounting 'mong Graemes of the Netherby clan;
Forsters, Fenwicks, and Musgraves, they rode and they ran;
There was racing and chasing, on Cannobie Lee,   45
But the lost bride of Netherby ne'er did they see.
So daring in love and so dauntless in war,
Have ye e'er heard of gallant like young Lochinvar?

1806–08.   1808.

CORONACH

He is gone on the mountain,
  He is lost to the forest,
Like a summer-dried fountain,
  When our need was the sorest.

The font, reappearing,   5
    From the rain-drops shall borrow,
But to us comes no cheering,
    To Duncan no morrow!

The hand of the reaper
    Takes the ears that are hoary,   10
But the voice of the weeper
    Wails manhood in glory.
The autumn winds rushing
    Waft the leaves that are searest,
But our flower was in flushing   15
    When blighting was nearest.

Fleet foot on the correi,
    Sage counsel in cumber,
Red hand in the foray,
    How sound is thy slumber!   20
Like the dew on the mountain,
    Like the foam on the river,
Like the bubble on the fountain,
    Thou art gone, and forever!

1809–10.   1810.

FROM

THE LADY OF THE LAKE

BATTLE OF BEAL' AN DUINE

The minstrel came once more to view
The eastern ridge of Benvenue,
For, ere he parted, he would say
Farewell to lovely Loch Achray—
Where shall he find, in foreign land,   5
So lone a lake, so sweet a strand!—
    There is no breeze upon the fern,
        No ripple on the lake;
    Upon her eyrie nods the erne,
        The deer has sought the brake;   10
    The small birds will not sing aloud,
        The springing trout lies still,
    So darkly glooms yon thunder-cloud,

That swathes, as with a purple shroud,
  Benledi's distant hill.   15
Is it the thunder's solemn sound
    That mutters deep and dread,
Or echoes from the groaning ground
    The warrior's measured tread?
Is it the lightning's quivering glance   20
    That on the thicket streams,
Or do they flash on spear and lance,
    The sun's retiring beams?—
I see the dagger-crest of Mar,
I see the Moray's silver star,   25
Wave o'er the cloud of Saxon war,
That up the lake comes winding far!
  To hero bound for battle-strife,
    Or bard of martial lay,
  'T were worth ten years of peaceful life,   30
    One glance at their array!

Their light-armed archers far and near
    Surveyed the tangled ground;
Their centre ranks, with pike and spear,
    A twilight forest frowned;   35
Their barbèd horsemen, in the rear,
    The stern battalia crowned.
No cymbal clashed, no clarion rang,
    Still were the pipe and drum;
Save heavy tread, and armour's clang,   40
    The sullen march was dumb.
There breathed no wind their crests to shake,
    Or wave their flags abroad;
Scarce the frail aspen seemed to quáke,
    That shadowed o'er their road;   45
Their vaward scouts no tidings bring,
    Can rouse no lurking foe,
Nor spy a trace of living thing
    Save when they stirred the roe.
The host moves like a deep sea-wave   50
Where rise no rocks its pride to brave,
    High-swelling, dark, and slow.
The lake is passed, and now they gain

A narrow and a broken plain,
Before the Trosach's rugged jaws;   55
And here the horse and spearmen pause,
While, to explore the dangerous glen,
Dive through the pass the archer-men.

At once there rose so wild a yell
Within that dark and narrow dell   60
As all the fiends from heaven that fell
Had pealed the banner-cry of hell!
 Forth from the pass in tumult driven,
 Like chaff before the wind of heaven,
  The archery appear: 65
 For life! for life! their flight they ply—
 And shriek, and shout, and battle-cry,
 And plaids and bonnets waving high,
 And broadswords flashing to the sky,
  Are maddening in the rear.   70
 Onward they drive in dreadful race,
  Pursuers and pursued;
 Before that tide of flight and chase,
 How shall it keep its rooted place,
 The spearmen's twilight wood?   75
"Down! down!" cried Mar, "your lances down!
 Bear back both friend and foe!"
 Like reeds before the tempest's frown,
 That serried grove of lances brown
  At once lay levelled low;   80
 And, closely shouldering side by side,
 The bristling ranks the onset bide.
 "We'll quell the savage mountaineer,
  As their Tinchel cows the game!
 They come as fleet as forest deer,   85
  We'll drive them back as tame!"
Bearing before them, in their course,
The relics of the the archer force,
Like wave with crest of sparkling foam,
Right onward did Clan-Alpine come.   90
 Above the tide, each broadsword bright
 Was brandishing like beam of light,
  Each targe was dark below;

And with the ocean's mighty swing,
When heaving to the tempest's wing,⠀⠀⠀⠀95
They hurled them on the foe.
I heard the lance's shivering crash,
As when the whirlwind rends the ash;
I heard the broadsword's deadly clang,
As if an hundred anvils rang!⠀⠀⠀⠀100
But Moray wheeled his rearward rank
Of horsemen on Clan-Alpine's flank—
⠀⠀"My banner-man, advance!
I see," he cried, "their column shake.
Now, gallants! for your ladies' sake,⠀⠀⠀⠀105
⠀⠀Upon them with the lance!"
The horsemen dashed among the rout,
⠀⠀As deer break through the broom;
Their steeds are stout, their swords are out,
⠀⠀They soon make lightsome room.⠀⠀⠀⠀110
Clan-Alpine's best are backward borne—
⠀⠀Where, where was Roderick then!
One blast upon his bugle-horn
⠀⠀Were worth a thousand men.
And refluent through the pass of fear⠀⠀⠀⠀115
⠀⠀The battle's tide was poured;
Vanished the Saxon's struggling spear,
⠀⠀Vanished the mountain-sword.
As Bracklinn's chasm, so black and steep,
⠀⠀Receives her roaring linn,⠀⠀⠀⠀120
As the dark caverns of the deep
⠀⠀Suck the wild whirlpool in,
So did the deep and darksome pass
Devour the battle's mingled mass;
None linger now upon the plain,⠀⠀⠀⠀125
Save those who ne'er shall fight again.

Now westward rolls the battle's din,
That deep and doubling pass within.
Minstrel, away! the work of fate
Is bearing on; its issue wait⠀⠀⠀⠀130
Where the rude Trosachs' dread defile
Opens on Katrine's lake and isle.—
Gray Benvenue I soon repassed;

Loch Katrine lay beneath me cast.
  The sun is set; the clouds are met;   135
    The lowering scowl of heaven
  An inky hue of livid blue
    To the deep lake has given;
Strange gusts of wind from mountain glen
Swept o'er the lake, then sunk again.   140
I heeded not the eddying surge;
Mine eye but saw the Trosachs' gorge,
Mine ear but heard the sullen sound
Which like an earthquake shook the ground,
And spoke the stern and desperate strife   145
That parts not but with parting life,
Seeming, to minstrel ear, to toll
The dirge of many a passing soul.
Nearer it comes—the dim-wood glen
The martial flood disgorged again,   150
  But not in mingled tide:
The plaided warriors of the North
High on the mountain thunder forth,
  And overhang its side;
While by the lake below appears   155
The dark'ning cloud of Saxon spears.
At weary bay each shattered band,
Eyeing their foemen, sternly stand;
Their banners stream like tattered sail
That flings its fragments to the gale,   160
And broken arms and disarray
Marked the fell havoc of the day.

Viewing the mountain's ridge askance,
The Saxon stood in sullen trance,
Till Moray pointed with his lance,   165
  And cried, "Behold yon isle!
See! none are left to guard its strand
But women weak, that wring the hand.
'T is there of yore the robber band
  Their booty wont to pile.   170
My purse, with bonnet-pieces store,
To him will swim a bow-shot o'er,
And loose a shallop from the shore.

Lightly we'll tame the war-wolf then,
Lords of his mate and brood and den."   175
Forth from the ranks a spearman sprung,
On earth his casque and corslet rung,
   He plunged him in the wave.
All saw the deed—the purpose knew;
And to their clamours Benvenue   180
   A mingled echo gave:
The Saxons shout, their mate to cheer,
The helpless females screamed for fear,
And yells for rage the mountaineer.
'T was then, as by the outcry riven,   185
Poured down at once the lowering heaven;
A whirlwind swept Loch Katrine's breast,
Her billows reared their snowy crest.
Well for the swimmer swelled they high,
To mar the Highland marksman's eye;   190
For round him showered, 'mid rain and hail,
The vengeful arrows of the Gael.
In vain; he nears the isle, and lo!
His hand is on a shallop's bow.
—Just then a flash of lightning came;   195
It tinged the waves and strand with flame:
I marked Duncraggan's widowed dame,
Behind an oak I saw her stand,
A naked dirk gleamed in her hand;—
It darkened—but amid the moan   200
Of waves, I heard a dying groan;—
Another flash!—the spearman floats
A weltering corse beside the boats,
And the stern matron o'er him stood,
Her hand and dagger streaming blood.   205

"Revenge! revenge!" the Saxons cried;
The Gaels' exulting shout replied.
Despite the elemental rage,
Again they hurried to engage;
But ere they closed in desperate fight,   210
Bloody with spurring came a knight,
Sprung from his horse, and, from a crag,
Waved 'twixt the hosts a milk-white flag.

Clarion and trumpet by his side
Rung forth a truce-note high and wide,   215
While, in the Monarch's name, afar
An herald's voice forbade the war,
For Bothwell's lord, and Roderick bold,
Were both, he said, in captive hold.

1809–10.   1810.

PROUD MAISIE

Proud Maisie is in the wood,
    Walking so early;
Sweet Robin sits on the bush,
    Singing so rarely.

"Tell me, thou bonny bird,   5
    When shall I marry me?"
"When six braw gentlemen
    Kirkward shall carry ye."

"Who makes the bridal bed,
    Birdie, say truly?"   10
"The grey-headed sexton,
    That delves the grave duly.

"The glow-worm o'er grave and stone
    Shall light thee steady;
The owl from the steeple sing,   15
    'Welcome, proud lady.'"

1818.   1818.

COUNTY GUY

Ah, County Guy, the hour is nigh,
    The sun has left the lea,
The orange-flower perfumes the bower,
    The breeze is on the sea.
The lark, his lay who thrilled all day,   5
    Sits hushed his partner nigh;
Breeze, bird, and flower confess the hour—
    But where is County Guy?

The village maid steals through the shade,
    Her shepherd's suit to hear;   10

To beauty shy, by lattice high,
    Sings high-born Cavalier.
The star of Love, all stars above,
    Now reigns o'er earth and sky;
And high and low the influence know—   15
    But where is County Guy?

1823.   1823.

BONNY DUNDEE

To the Lords of Convention 't was Claver'se who spoke:
"Ere the King's crown shall fall there are crowns to be broke;
So let each Cavalier who loves honour and me
Come follow the bonnet of Bonny Dundee.

    Come fill up my cup, come fill up my can,   5
    Come saddle your horses and call up your men,
    Come open the West Port and let me gang free,
    And it 's room for the bonnets of Bonny Dundee!"

Dundee he is mounted, he rides up the street;
The bells are rung backward, the drums they are beat; 10
But the Provost, douce man, said, "Just e'en let him be;
The Gude Town is weel quit of that Deil of Dundee."
    Come fill up my cup, etc.

As he rode down the sanctified bends of the Bow,
Ilk carline was flyting and shaking her pow;   15
But the young plants of grace they looked couthie and slee,
Thinking, "Luck to thy bonnet, thou Bonny Dundee!"
    Come fill up my cup, etc.

With sour-featured Whigs the Grassmarket was crammed,
As if half the West had set tryst to be hanged!   20
There was spite in each look, there was fear in each e'e,
As they watched for the bonnets of Bonny Dundee.
    Come fill up my cup, etc.

These cowls of Kilmarnock had spits and had spears,
And lang-hafted gullies to kill Cavaliers;   25
But they shrunk to close-heads, and the causeway was free,
At the toss of the bonnet of Bonny Dundee.
    Come fill up my cup, etc.

He spurred to the foot of the proud Castle rock,
And with the gay Gordon he gallantly spoke: 30
"Let Mons Meg and her marrows speak twa words or three,
For the love of the bonnet of Bonny Dundee."
    Come fill up my cup, etc.

The Gordon demands of him which way he goes—
"Where'er shall direct me the shade of Montrose!   35
Your Grace in short space shall hear tidings of me,
Or that low lies the bonnet of Bonny Dundee.
    Come fill up my cup, etc.

"There are hills beyond Pentland and lands beyond Forth;
If there's lords in the Lowlands, there's chiefs in the North; 40
There are wild Duniewassals three thousand times three,
Will cry *hoigh!* for the bonnet of Bonny Dundee.
    Come fill up my cup, etc.

"There's brass on the target of barkened bull-hide;
There's steel in the scabbard that dangles beside;   45
The brass shall be burnished, the steel shall flash free,
At a toss of the bonnet of Bonny Dundee.
    Come fill up my cup, etc.

"Away to the hills, to the caves, to the rocks—
Ere I own an usurper, I'll couch with the fox!   50
And tremble, false Whigs, in the midst of your glee;
You have not seen the last of my bonnet and me!"
    Come fill up my cup, etc.

He waved his proud hand, and the trumpets were blown;
The kettle-drums clashed, and the horsemen rode on,   55
Till on Ravelston's cliffs and on Clermiston's lee
Died away the wild war-notes of Bonny Dundee.

    Come fill up my cup, come fill up my can,
    Come saddle the horses and call up the men,
    Come open your gates and let me gae free,   60
    For it's up with the bonnets of Bonny Dundee!

        1825.   1830.

GEORGE GORDON BYRON

LACHIN Y GAIR

Away, ye gay landscapes, ye gardens of roses!
 In you let the minions of luxury rove;
Restore me the rocks where the snow-flake reposes,
 Though still they are sacred to freedom and love.
Yet, Caledonia, beloved are thy mountains,   5
 Round their white summits though elements war;
Though cataracts foam 'stead of smooth-flowing fountains,
 I sigh for the valley of dark Loch na Garr.

Ah, there my young footsteps in infancy wandered;
 My cap was the bonnet, my cloak was the plaid;   10
On chieftains long perished my memory pondered,
 As daily I strode through the pine-covered glade.
I sought not my home till the day's dying glory
 Gave place to the rays of the bright polar star;
For fancy was cheered by traditional story,   15
 Disclosed by the natives of dark Loch na Garr.

"Shades of the dead! have I not heard your voices
 Rise on the night-rolling breath of the gale?"
Surely the soul of the hero rejoices,
 And rides on the wind o'er his own Highland vale.   20
Round Loch na Garr while the stormy mist gathers,
 Winter presides in his cold icy car:
Clouds there encircle the forms of my fathers;
 They dwell in the tempests of dark Loch na Garr.

"Ill-starred, though brave, did no visions foreboding   25
 Tell you that fate had forsaken your cause?"
Ah, were you destined to die at Culloden,
 Victory crowned not your fall with applause:
Still were you happy in death's earthy slumber,
 You rest with your clan in the caves of Braemar;   30
The pibroch resounds, to the piper's loud number,
 Your deeds on the echoes of dark Loch na Garr.

Years have rolled on, Loch na Garr, since I left you,
 Years must elapse ere I tread you again;

Nature of verdure and flowers has bereft you,   35
   Yet still are you dearer than Albion's plain.
England, thy beauties are tame and domestic
   To one who has roved on the mountains afar;
Oh, for the crags that are wild and majestic,
   The steep, frowning glories of dark Loch na Garr!   40

                 1807.

FROM

ENGLISH BARDS AND SCOTCH REVIEWERS

Behold! in various throngs the scribbling crew,
For notice eager, pass in long review:
Each spurs his jaded Pegasus apace,
And rhyme and blank maintain an equal race;
Sonnets on sonnets crowd, and ode on ode;   5
And tales of terror jostle on the road;
Immeasurable measures move along,
For simpering Folly loves a varied song,
To strange mysterious Dulness still the friend,
Admires the strain she cannot comprehend.   10
Thus Lays of Minstrels—may they be the last!—
On half-strung harps whine mournful to the blast;
While mountain spirits prate to river sprites,
That dames may listen to the sound at nights;
And goblin brats, of Gilpin Horner's brood,   15
Decoy young Border nobles through the wood,
And skip at every step, Lord knows how high,
And frighten foolish babes, the Lord knows why;
While high-born ladies in their magic cell,
Forbidding knights to read who cannot spell,   20
Despatch a courier to a wizard's grave,
And fight with honest men to shield a knave.

. . . .

   Oh, Southey! Southey! cease thy varied song!
A bard may chant too often and too long.
As thou art strong in verse, in mercy spare!   25
A fourth, alas, were more than we could bear.
But if, in spite of all the world can say,
Thou still wilt verseward plod thy weary way,
If still in Berkeley ballads most uncivil

Thou wilt devote old women to the Devil,   30
The babe unborn thy dread intent may rue:
"God help thee," Southey, and thy readers too.
    Next comes the dull disciple of thy school,
That mild apostate from poetic rule,
The simple Wordsworth, framer of a lay   35
As soft as evening in his favourite May;
Who warns his friend "to shake off toil and trouble,
And quit his books, for fear of growing double";
Who, both by precept and example, shows
That prose is verse, and verse is merely prose,   40
Convincing all, by demonstration plain,
Poetic souls delight in prose insane,
And Christmas stories tortured into rhyme
Contain the essence of the true sublime.
Thus, when he tells the tale of Betty Foy,   45
The idiot mother of "an idiot boy,"
A moon-struck, silly lad, who lost his way,
And, like his bard, confounded night with day,
So close on each pathetic part he dwells,
And each adventure so sublimely tells,   50
That all who view the "idiot in his glory"
Conceive the bard the hero of the story.

. . . .

    Health to immortal Jeffrey! once, in name,
England could boast a judge almost the same;
In soul so like, so merciful, yet just,   55
Some think that Satan has resigned his trust,
And given the spirit to the world again,
To sentence letters, as he sentenced men.
With hand less mighty, but with heart as black,
With voice as willing to decree the rack;   60
Bred in the courts betimes, though all that law
As yet hath taught him is to find a flaw;
Since well instructed in the patriot school
To rail at party, though a party tool,
Who knows, if chance his patrons should restore   65
Back to the sway they forfeited before,
His scribbling toils some recompense may meet,
And raise this Daniel to the judgment-seat?
Let Jeffreys' shade indulge the pious hope,

And, greeting thus, present him with a rope:　　　　70
"Heir to my virtues! man of equal mind!
Skilled to condemn as to traduce mankind,
This cord receive, for thee reserved with care,
To wield in judgment, and at length to wear."
. . . .

　　Thus far I've held my undisturbed career　　　75
Prepared for rancor, steeled 'gainst selfish fear.
This thing of rhyme I ne'er disdained to own—
Though not obtrusive, yet not quite unknown;
My voice was heard again, though not so loud,
My page, though nameless never disavowed;　　　80
And now at once I tear the veil away:—
Cheer on the pack! the quarry stands at bay,
Unscared by all the din of Melbourne house,
By Lambe's resentment, or by Holland's spouse,
By Jeffrey's harmless pistol, Hallam's rage,　　　85
Edina's brawny sons and brimstone page.
Our men in buckram shall have blows enough,
And feel they too are "penetrable stuff";
And though I hope not hence unscathed to go,
Who conquers me shall find a stubborn foe.　　·　90
The time hath been when no harsh sound would fall
From lips that now may seem imbued with gall;
Nor fools nor follies tempt me to despise
The meanest thing that crawled beneath my eyes.
But now, so callous grown, so changed since youth,　95
I've learned to think, and sternly speak the truth;
Learned to deride the critic's starch decree,
And break him on the wheel he meant for me;
To spurn the rod a scribbler bids me kiss,
Nor care if courts and crowds applaud or hiss.　　100
Nay more, though all my rival rhymesters frown,
I too can hunt a poetaster down;
And, armed in proof, the gauntlet cast at once
To Scotch marauder and to Southern dunce.
Thus much I've dared; if my incondite lay　　　105
Hath wronged these righteous times, let others say.
This, let the world, which knows not how to spare,
Yet rarely blames unjustly, now declare.

　　1807–09.　　　　　　　　　　　　1809.

SHE WALKS IN BEAUTY

She walks in beauty, like the night
   Of cloudless climes and starry skies
And all that's best of dark and bright
   Meet in her aspect and her eyes,
Thus mellowed to that tender light   5
   Which heaven to gaudy day denies.

One shade the more, one ray the less,
   Had half impaired the nameless grace
Which waves in every raven tress,
   Or softly lightens o'er her face,   10
Where thoughts serenely sweet express
   How pure, how dear, their dwelling-place.

And on that cheek, and o'er that brow,
   So soft, so calm, yet eloquent,
The smiles that win, the tints that glow,   15
   But tell of days in goodness spent,
A mind at peace with all below,
   A heart whose love is innocent!

1814?   *1815.*

WHEN WE TWO PARTED

When we two parted
   In silence and tears,
Half broken-hearted
   To sever for years,
Pale grew thy cheek and cold,   5
   Colder thy kiss;
Truly that hour foretold
   Sorrow to this.

The dew of the morning
   Sunk chill on my brow—   10
It felt like the warning
   Of what I feel now.
Thy vows are all broken,
   And light is thy fame;
I hear thy name spoken,   15
   And share in its shame,

They name thee before me,
    A knell to mine ear;
A shudder comes o'er me—
    Why wert thou so dear?   20
They know not I knew thee,
    Who knew thee too well;
Long, long shall I rue thee,
    Too deeply to tell.

In secret we met—   25
    In silence I grieve
That thy heart could forget,
    Thy spirit deceive.
If I should meet thee
    After long years,   30
How should I greet thee?
    With silence and tears.

1815?   1816.

THE PRISONER OF CHILLON

My hair is grey, but not with years,
    Nor grew it white
    In a single night,
As men's have grown from sudden fears.
My limbs are bowed, though not with toil,   5
    But rusted with a vile repose,
For they have been a dungeon's spoil,
    And mine has been the fate of those
To whom the goodly earth and air
Are banned and barred—forbidden fare.   10
But this was for my father's faith
I suffered chains and courted death:
That father perished at the stake
For tenets he would not forsake;
And for the same his lineal race   15
In darkness found a dwelling-place.
We were seven—who now are one;
    Six in youth and one in age
Finished as they had begun,
    Proud of Persecution's rage: 20

One in fire and two in field,
Their belief with blood have sealed,
Dying as their father died,
For the God their foes denied;
Three were in a dungeon cast,   25
Of whom this wreck is left the last.

There are seven pillars of Gothic mould
In Chillon's dungeons deep and old;
There are seven columns massy and grey,
Dim with a dull imprisoned ray,   30
A sunbeam which hath lost its way,
And through the crevice and the cleft
Of the thick wall is fallen and left,
Creeping o'er the floor so damp,
Like a marsh's meteor lamp: 35
And in each pillar there is a ring,
    And in each ring there is a chain;
That iron is a cankering thing,
    For in these limbs its teeth remain,
With marks that will not wear away   40
Till I have done with this new day,
Which now is painful to these eyes,
Which have not seen the sun so rise
For years—I cannot count them o'er,
I lost their long and heavy score   45
When my last brother drooped and died,
And I lay living by his side.

They chained us each to a column stone,
And we were three—yet each alone;
We could not move a single pace,   50
We could not see each other's face
But with that pale and livid light
That made us strangers in our sight.
And thus together, yet apart,
Fettered in hand but joined in heart,   55
'T was still some solace, in the dearth
Of the pure elements of earth,
To hearken to each other's speech,
And each turn comforter to each
With some new hope, or legend old,   60

Or song heroically bold:
But even these at length grew cold;
Our voices took a dreary tone,
An echo of the dungeon stone,
 A grating sound—not full and free   65
 As they of yore were wont to be;
 It might be fancy, but to me
They never sounded like our own.

I was the eldest of the three,
 And to uphold and cheer the rest   70
 I ought to do—and did—my best;
And each did well in his degree.
 The youngest, whom my father loved
Because our mother's brow was given
To him, with eyes as blue as heaven,   75
 For him my soul was sorely moved:
And truly might it be distressed
To see such bird in such a nest;
For he was beautiful as day—
 (When day was beautiful to me   80
 As to young eagles, being free)—
 A polar day, which will not see
A sunset till its summer's gone,
 Its sleepless summer of long light,
The snow-clad offspring of the sun;   85
 And thus he was as pure and bright,
And in his natural spirit gay,
With tears for naught but others' ills,
And then they flowed like mountain rills,
Unless he could assuage the woe   90
Which he abhorred to view below.

The other was as pure of mind,
But formed to combat with his kind;
Strong in his frame, and of a mood
Which 'gainst the world in war had stood,   95
And perished in the foremost rank
 With joy—but not in chains to pine:
His spirit withered with their clank;
 I saw it silently decline—
 And so perchance in sooth did mine;   100

But yet I forced it on to cheer
Those relics of a home so dear.
He was a hunter of the hills,
    Had followed there the deer and wolf;
    To him this dungeon was a gulf,   105
And fettered feet the worst of ills.

    Lake Leman lies by Chillon's walls:
A thousand feet in depth below
Its massy waters meet and flow;
Thus much the fathom-line was sent   110
From Chillon's snow-white battlement,
    Which round about the wave inthrals;
A double dungeon wall and wave
Have made—and like a living grave.
Below the surface of the lake   115
The dark vault lies wherein we lay:
We heard it ripple night and day;
    Sounding o'er our heads it knocked;
And I have felt the winter's spray
Wash through the bars, when winds were high   120
And wanton in the happy sky;
    And then the very rock hath rocked,
    And I have felt it shake, unshocked,
Because I could have smiled to see
The death that would have set me free.   125
I said my nearer brother pined,
I said his mighty heart declined;
He loathed and put away his food:
It was not that 't was coarse and rude,
For we were used to hunter's fare,   130
And for the like had little care.
The milk drawn from the mountain goat
Was changed for water from the moat;
Our bread was such as captive's tears
Have moistened many a thousand years,   135
Since man first pent his fellow men
Like brutes within an iron den.
But what were these to us or him?
These wasted not his heart or limb:
My brother's soul was of that mould   140

Which in a palace had grown cold
Had his free breathing been denied
The range of the steep mountain's side.
But why delay the truth?—he died.
I saw, and could not hold his head,   145
Nor reach his dying hand—nor dead,—
Though hard I strove, but strove in vain,
To rend and gnash my bonds in twain.
He died—and they unlocked his chain,
And scooped for him a shallow grave   150
Even from the cold earth of our cave.
I begged them, as a boon, to lay
His corse in dust whereon the day
Might shine—it was a foolish thought,
But then within my brain it wrought,   155
That even in death his freeborn breast
In such a dungeon could not rest.
I might have spared my idle prayer—
They coldly laughed, and laid him there:
The flat and turfless earth above   160
The being we so much did love;
His empty chain above it leant,
Such murder's fitting monument!

But he, the favourite and the flower,
Most cherished since his natal hour,   165
His mother's image in fair face,
The infant love of all his race,
His martyred father's dearest thought,
My latest care, for whom I sought
To hoard my life, that his might be   170
Less wretched now, and one day free;
He, too, who yet had held untired
A spirit natural or inspired,
He, too, was struck, and day by day
Was withered on the stalk away.   175
Oh, God! it is a fearful thing
To see the human soul take wing
In any shape, in any mood:
I've seen it rushing forth in blood,
I've seen it on the breaking ocean   180

Strive with a swoln convulsive motion,
I 've seen the sick and ghastly bed
Of Sin delirious with its dread;
But these were horrors—this was woe
Unmixed with such—but sure and slow.   185
He faded, and so calm and meek,
So softly worn, so sweetly weak,
So tearless, yet so tender—kind,
And grieved for those he left behind;
With all the while a cheek whose bloom   190
Was as a mockery of the tomb,
Whose tints as gently sunk away
As a departing rainbow's ray;
An eye of most transparent light
That almost made the dungeon bright;   195
And not a word of murmur—not
A groan o'er his untimely lot;
A little talk of better days,
A little hope my own to raise,
For I was sunk in silence—lost   200
In this last loss, of all the most;
And then the sighs he would suppress
Of fainting nature's feebleness,
More slowly drawn, grew less and less:
I listened, but I could not hear—   205
I called, for I was wild with fear;
I knew 't was hopeless, but my dread
Would not be thus admonishèd;
I called, and thought I heard a sound—
I burst my chain with one strong bound,   210
And rushed to him:—I found him not;
I only stirred in this black spot,
I only lived—*I* only drew
The accursed breath of dungeon-dew;
The last—the sole—the dearest link   215
Between me and the eternal brink,
Which bound me to my failing race,
Was broken in this fatal place.
One on the earth, and one beneath—
My brothers—both had ceased to breathe: 220
I took that hand which lay so still,

Alas! my own was full as chill;
I had not strength to stir or strive,
But felt that I was still alive—
A frantic feeling, when we know　　　　　225
That what we love shall ne'er be so.
　　　I know not why
　　　I could not die;
I had no earthly hope—but faith,
And that forbade a selfish death.　　　　　230

What next befell me then and there
　　I know not well—I never knew.
First came the loss of light and air,
　　And then of darkness too:
I had no thought, no feeling—none;　　　　235
Among the stones I stood a stone,
And was, scarce conscious what I wist,
As shrubless crags within the mist;
For all was blank, and bleak, and grey;
It was not night—it was not day;　　　　　240
It was not even the dungeon-light,
So hateful to my heavy sight,
But vacancy absorbing space,
And fixedness—without a place;
There were no stars—no earth—no time—　　245
No check—no change—no good—no crime—
But silence, and a stirless breath
Which neither was of life nor death;
A sea of stagnant idleness,
Blind, boundless, mute, and motionless!　　250

A light broke in upon my brain—
　　It was the carol of a bird;
It ceased, and then it came again,
　　The sweetest song ear ever heard;
And mine was thankful till my eyes　　　　255
Ran over with the glad surprise,
And they that moment could not see
I was the mate of misery.
But then by dull degrees came back
My senses to their wonted track:　　　　　260
I saw the dungeon walls and floor

Close slowly round me as before;
I saw the glimmer of the sun
Creeping as it before had done,
But through the crevice where it came   265
That bird was perched, as fond and tame,
   And tamer than upon the tree;
A lovely bird, with azure wings,
And song that said a thousand things,
   And seemed to say them all for me!   270
I never saw its like before,
I ne'er shall see its likeness more:
It seemed like me to want a mate,
But was not half so desolate;
And it was come to love me when   275
None lived to love me so again,
And, cheering from my dungeon's brink,
Had brought me back to feel and think.
I know not if it late were free,
   Or broke its cage to perch on mine;   280
But knowing well captivity,
   Sweet bird, I could not wish for thine!
Or if it were, in wingèd guise,
A visitant from Paradise;
For—Heaven forgive that thought, the while   285
Which made me both to weep and smile—
I sometimes deemed that it might be
My brother's soul come down to me;
But then at last away it flew,
And then 't was mortal, well I knew,   290
For he would never thus have flown,
And left me twice so doubly lone,—
Lone—as the corse within its shroud,
Lone—as a solitary cloud,
   A single cloud on a sunny day   295
While all the rest of heaven is clear,
A frown upon the atmosphere,
That hath no business to appear
   When skies are blue and earth is gay.

A kind of change came in my fate.   300
My keepers grew compassionate;

I know not what had made them so,
They were inured to sights of woe,
But so it was:—my broken chain
With links unfastened did remain,   305
And it was liberty to stride
Along my cell from side to side,
And up and down, and then athwart,
And tread it over every part,
And round the pillars one by one,   310
Returning where my walk begun,
Avoiding only, as I trod,
My brothers' graves without a sod;
For if I thought with heedless tread
My step profaned their lowly bed,   315
My breath came gaspingly and thick,
And my crushed heart fell blind and sick.

I made a footing in the wall:
  It was not therefrom to escape,
For I had buried one and all   320
  Who loved me in a human shape,
And the whole earth would henceforth be
A wider prison unto me;
No child—no sire—no kin had I,
No partner in my misery;   325
I thought of this, and I was glad,
For thought of them had made me mad;—
But I was curious to ascend
To my barred windows, and to bend
Once more, upon the mountains high,   330
The quiet of a loving eye.

I saw them—and they were the same,
They were not changed like me in frame;
I saw their thousand years of snow
On high—their wide long lake below,   335
And the blue Rhone in fullest flow;
I heard the torrents leap and gush
O'er channelled rock and broken bush;
I saw the white-walled distant town,
And whiter sails go skimming down: 340
And then there was a little isle,

Which in my very face did smile,
    The only one in view;
A small green isle, it seemed no more,
Scarce broader than my dungeon floor,   345
But in it there were three tall trees,
And o'er it blew the mountain breeze,
And by it there were waters flowing,
And on it there were young flowers growing,
    Of gentle breath and hue.   350
The fish swam by the castle wall,
And they seemed joyous each and all;
The eagle rode the rising blast,
Methought he never flew so fast
As then to me he seemed to fly;   355
And then new tears came in my eye,
And I felt troubled—and would fain
I had not left my recent chain;
And when I did descend again,
The darkness of my dim abode   360
Fell on me as a heavy load;
It was as is a new-dug grave,
Closing o'er one we sought to save,—
And yet my glance, too much oppressed,
Had almost need of such a rest.   365

It might be months, or years, or days—
    I kept no count, I took no note;
I had no hope my eyes to raise,
    And clear them of their dreary mote:
At last men came to set me free;   370
    I asked not why, and recked not where;
It was at length the same to me,
Fettered or fetterless to be;
    I learned to love despair.
And thus when they appeared at last,   375
And all my bonds aside were cast,
These heavy walls to me had grown
A hermitage—and all my own!
And half I felt as they were come
To tear me from a second home: 380
With spiders I had friendship made,

And watched them in their sullen trade;
Had seen the mice by moonlight play,
And why should I feel less than they?
We were all inmates of one place,   385
And I, the monarch of each race,
Had power to kill—yet, strange to tell!
In quiet we had learned to dwell;
My very chains and I grew friends,
So much a long communion tends   390
To make us what we are:—even I
Regained my freedom with a sigh.

1816.   1816.

TO THOMAS MOORE

My boat is on the shore,
    And my bark is on the sea;
But before I go, Tom Moore,
    Here's a double health to thee!

Here's a sigh to those who love me,   5
    And a smile to those who hate;
And whatever sky's above me,
    Here's a heart for every fate.

Though the ocean roar around me,
    Yet it still shall bear me on;   10
Though a desert should surround me,
    It hath springs that may be won.

Were't the last drop in the well,
    As I gasped upon the brink,
Ere my fainting spirit fell,   15
    'T is to thee that I would drink.

With that water, as this wine,
    The libation I would pour
Should be—Peace with thine and mine,
    And a health to thee, Tom Moore!   20

1816–17.   1821.

CHILDE HAROLD'S PILGRIMAGE

(From Canto I)

SPAIN

Oh, lovely Spain! renowned, romantic land!
Where is that standard which Pelagio bore,
When Cava's traitor-sire first called the band
That dyed thy mountain streams with Gothic gore?
Where are those bloody banners which of yore   5
Waved o'er thy sons, victorious to the gale,
And drove at last the spoilers to their shore?
Red gleamed the cross, and waned the crescent pale,
While Afric's echoes thrilled with Moorish matrons' wail.

Teems not each ditty with the glorious tale?   10
Ah such, alas, the hero's amplest fate!
When granite moulders and when records fail,
A peasant's plaint prolongs his dubious date.
Pride! bend thine eye from heaven to thine estate,
See how the mighty shrink into a song!   15
Can volume, pillar, pile, preserve thee great?
Or must thou trust Tradition's simple tongue,
When Flattery sleeps with thee, and History does thee
      wrong?

Awake, ye sons of Spain! awake! advance!
Lo, Chivalry, your ancient goddess, cries;   20
But wields not, as of old, her thirsty lance,
Nor shakes her crimson plumage in the skies:
Now on the smoke of blazing bolts she flies,
And speaks in thunder through yon engine's roar;
In every peal she calls—"Awake! arise!"   25
Say, is her voice more feeble than of yore,
When her war-song was heard on Andalusia's shore?

Hark! heard you not those hoofs of dreadful note?
Sounds not the clang of conflict on the heath?
Saw ye not whom the reeking sabre smote,   30
Nor saved your brethren ere they sank beneath
Tyrants and tyrants' slaves?—the fires of death,
The bale-fires, flash on high;—from rock to rock
Each volley tells that thousands cease to breathe;

Death rides upon the sulphury Siroc,   35
Red Battle stamps his foot, and nations feel the shock.

Lo, where the Giant on the mountain stands,
His blood-red tresses deepening in the sun,
With death-shot glowing in his fiery hands,
And eye that scorcheth all it glares upon;   40
Restless it rolls, now fixed, and now anon
Flashing afar,—and at his iron feet
Destruction cowers, to mark what deeds are done;
For on this morn three potent nations meet,
To shed before his shrine the blood he deems most sweet.   45

By Heaven! it is a splendid sight to see
(For one who hath no friend, no brother, there)
Their rival scarfs of mixed embroidery,
Their various arms that glitter in the air!
What gallant war-hounds rouse them from their lair,   50
And gnash their fangs, loud yelling for the prey!
All join the chase, but few the triumph share;
The Grave shall bear the chiefest prize away,
And Havoc scarce for joy can number their array.

Three hosts combine to offer sacrifice;   55
Three tongues prefer strange orisons on high;
Three gaudy standards flout the pale blue skies;
The shouts are France, Spain, Albion, Victory!
The foe, the victim, and the fond ally
That fights for all, but ever fights in vain,   60
Are met—as if at home they could not die—
To feed the crow on Talavera's plain,
And fertilize the field that each pretends to gain.

There shall they rot—Ambition's honoured fools!
Yes, Honour decks the turf that wraps their clay!   65
Vain sophistry! in these behold the tools,
The broken tools, that tyrants cast away
By myriads, when they dare to pave their way
With human hearts—to what? a dream alone.
Can despots compass aught that hails their sway?   70
Or call with truth one span of earth their own,
Save that wherein at last they crumble bone by bone?

1809.   1812.

(From Canto II)

GREECE

Fair Greece! sad relic of departed worth!
Immortal, though no more; though fallen, great!
Who now shall lead thy scattered children forth,
And long accustomed bondage uncreate?
Not such thy sons who whilome did await,   5
The hopeless warriors of a willing doom,
In bleak Thermopylæ's sepulchral strait—
Oh, who that gallant spirit shall resume,
Leap from Eurotas' banks, and call thee from the tomb?
. . . .

When riseth Lacedemon's hardihood,   10
When Thebes Epaminondas rears again,
When Athens' children are with hearts endued,
When Grecian mothers shall give birth to men,
Then may'st thou be restored; but not till then.
A thousand years scarce serve to form a state;   15
An hour may lay it in the dust; and when
Can man its shattered splendour renovate,
Recall its virtues back, and vanquish Time and Fate!

And yet how lovely in thine age of woe,
Land of lost gods and godlike men, art thou!   20
Thy vales of evergreen, thy hills of snow,
Proclaim thee Nature's varied favourite now.
Thy fanes, thy temples, to thy surface bow,
Commingling slowly with heroic earth,
Broke by the share of every rustic plough: 25
So perish monuments of mortal birth,
So perish all in turn, save well-recorded worth;

Save where some solitary column mourns
Above its prostrate brethren of the cave;
Save where Tritonia's airy shrine adorns   30
Colonna's cliff, and gleams along the wave;
Save o'er some warrior's half-forgotten grave,
Where the grey stones and unmolested grass
Ages, but not oblivion, feebly brave,
While strangers only not regardless pass,   35
Lingering like me, perchance, to gaze, and sigh "Alas!"

Yet are thy skies as blue, thy crags as wild,
Sweet are thy groves, and verdant are thy fields,
Thine olive ripe, as when Minerva smiled,
And still his honied wealth Hymettus yields;　　40
There the blithe bee his fragrant fortress builds,
The freeborn wanderer of thy mountain-air;
Apollo still thy long, long summer gilds,
Still in his beam Mendeli's marbles glare;
Art, Glory, Freedom, fail, but Nature still is fair.　　45

Where'er we tread 't is haunted, holy ground;
No earth of thine is lost in vulgar mould,
But one vast realm of wonder spreads around,
And all the Muse's tales seem truly told,
Till the sense aches with gazing to behold　　50
The scenes our earliest dreams have dwelt upon.
Each hill and dale, each deepening glen and wold,
Defies the power which crushed thy temples gone;
Age shakes Athena's tower, but spares grey Marathon.

The sun, the soil, but not the slave, the same:　　55
Unchanged in all except its foreign lord,
Preserves alike its bounds and boundless fame
The battle-field where Persia's victim horde
First bowed beneath the brunt of Hellas' sword,
As on the morn to distant Glory dear,　　60
When Marathon became a magic word;
Which uttered, to the hearer's eye appear
The camp, the host, the fight, the conqueror's career;

The flying Mede, his shaftless broken bow;
The fiery Greek, his red pursuing spear;　　65
Mountains above, Earth's, Ocean's, plain below;
Death in the front, Destruction in the rear:
Such was the scene—what now remaineth here?
What sacred trophy marks the hallowed ground,
Recording Freedom's smile and Asia's tear?　　70
The rifled urn, the violated mound,
The dust thy courser's hoof, rude stranger, spurns around.

Yet to the remnants of thy splendour past
Shall pilgrims, pensive but unwearied, throng;

Long shall the voyager, with th' Ionian blast, 75
Hail the bright clime of battle and of song;
Long shall thine annals and immortal tongue
Fill with thy fame the youth of many a shore;
Boast of the agèd! lesson of the young!
Which sages venerate and bards adore, 80
As Pallas and the Muse unveil their awful lore.

1810–1814. 1812, 1814.

(From Canto III)

BYRON AND CHILDE HAROLD

Is thy face like thy mother's, my fair child!
Ada! sole daughter of my house and heart?
When last I saw thy young blue eyes they smiled,
And then we parted,—not as now we part,
But with a hope.—

 Awaking with a start, 5
The waters heave around me; and on high
The winds lift up their voices: I depart,
Whither I know not; but the hour's gone by,
When Albion's lessening shores could grieve or glad mine
 eye.

Once more upon the waters! yet once more! 10
And the waves bound beneath me as a steed
That knows his rider. Welcome to their roar!
Swift be their guidance, wheresoe'er it lead!
Though the strained mast should quiver as a reed,
And the rent canvas, fluttering, strew the gale, 15
Still must I on, for I am as a weed,
Flung from the rock, on Ocean's foam, to sail
Where'er the surge may sweep, the tempest's breath prevail.

In my youth's summer I did sing of one,
The wandering outlaw of his own dark mind; 20
Again I seize the theme, then but begun,
And bear it with me, as the rushing wind
Bears the cloud onwards. In that tale I find
The furrows of long thought, and dried-up tears,
Which, ebbing, leave a sterile track behind, 25
O'er which all heavily the journeying years
Plod the last sands of life, where not a flower appears.

Since my young days of passion—joy or pain—
Perchance my heart and harp have lost a string,
And both may jar; it may be that in vain   30
I would essay as I have sung to sing.
Yet, though a dreary strain, to this I cling:
So that it wean me from the weary dream
Of selfish grief or gladness, so it fling
Forgetfulness around me, it shall seem   35
To me, though to none else, a not ungrateful theme.

He who, grown agèd in this world of woe,
In deeds, not years, piercing the depths of life,
So that no wonder waits him; nor below
Can love, or sorrow, fame, ambition, strife,   40
Cut to his heart again with the keen knife
Of silent, sharp endurance,—he can tell
Why thought seeks refuge in lone caves, yet rife
With airy images, and shapes which dwell
Still unimpaired, though old, in the soul's haunted cell. 45

'T is to create, and in creating live
A being more intense, that we endow
With form our fancy, gaining as we give
The life we image, even as I do now.
What am I? Nothing: but not so art thou,   50
Soul of my thought! with whom I traverse earth,
Invisible but gazing, as I glow
Mixed with thy spirit, blended with thy birth,
And feeling still with thee in my crushed feelings' dearth.

Yet must I think less wildly:—I *have* thought   55
Too long and darkly, till my brain became,
In its own eddy boiling and o'erwrought,
A whirling gulf of phantasy and flame;
And thus, untaught in youth my heart to tame,
My springs of life were poisoned. 'T is too late!   60
Yet am I changed; though still enough the same
In strength to bear what time can not abate,
And feed on bitter fruits without accusing Fate.

Something too much of this:—but now 't is past,
And the spell closes with its silent seal.   65
Long absent Harold reappears at last,

He of the breast which fain no more would feel,
  Wrung with the wounds which kill not, but ne'er heal;
  Yet Time, who changes all, had altered him
  In soul and aspect as in age: years steal   70
  Fire from the mind as vigour from the limb;
And life's enchanted cup but sparkles near the brim.

His had been quaffed too quickly, and he found
  The dregs were wormwood; but he filled again,
  And from a purer fount, on holier ground,   75
  And deemed its spring perpetual—but in vain!
  Still round him clung invisibly a chain
  Which galled forever, fettering though unseen,
  And heavy though it clanked not; worn with pain,
  Which pined although it spoke not, and grew keen,   80
Entering with every step he took through many a scene.

Secure in guarded coldness, he had mixed
  Again in fancied safety with his kind,
  And deemed his spirit now so firmly fixed
  And sheathed with an invulnerable mind,   85
  That, if no joy, no sorrow lurked behind;
  And he, as one, might 'midst the many stand
  Unheeded, searching through the crowd to find
  Fit speculation, such as in strange land
He found in wonder-works of God and Nature's hand.   90

But who can view the ripened rose, nor seek
  To wear it? Who can curiously behold
  The smoothness and the sheen of beauty's cheek,
  Nor feel the heart can never all grow old?
  Who can contemplate Fame through clouds unfold   95
  The star which rises o'er her steep, nor climb?
  Harold, once more within the vortex, rolled
  On with the giddy circle, chasing Time,
Yet with a nobler aim than in his youth's fond prime.

But soon he knew himself the most unfit   100
  Of men to herd with man, with whom he held
  Little in common; untaught to submit
  His thoughts to others, though his soul was quelled
  In youth by his own thoughts; still uncompelled,
  He would not yield dominion of his mind   105

To spirits against whom his own rebelled,
Proud though in desolation, which could find
A life within itself, to breathe without mankind.

Where rose the mountains, there to him were friends;
Where rolled the ocean, thereon was his home;   110
Where a blue sky and glowing clime extends,
He had the passion and the power to roam.
The desert, forest, cavern, breaker's foam,
Were unto him companionship; they spake
A mutual language, clearer than the tome   115
Of his land's tongue, which he would oft forsake
For Nature's pages glassed by sunbeams on the lake.

Like the Chaldean, he could watch the stars,
Till he had peopled them with beings bright
As their own beams; and earth, and earth-born jars,   120
And human frailties, were forgotten quite.
Could he have kept his spirit to that flight,
He had been happy; but this clay will sink
Its spark immortal, envying it the light
To which it mounts as if to break the link   125
That keeps us from yon heaven which wooes us to its brink.

But in man's dwellings he became a thing
Restless and worn, and stern and wearisome,
Drooped as a wild-born falcon with clipt wing,
To whom the boundless air alone were home.   130
Then came his fit again, which to o'ercome,
As eagerly the barred-up bird will beat
His breast and beak against his wiry dome
Till the blood tinge his plumage, so the heat
Of his impeded soul would through his bosom eat.   135

Self-exiled Harold wanders forth again,
With naught of hope left, but with less of gloom;
The very knowledge that he lived in vain,
That all was over on this side the tomb,
Had made Despair a smilingness assume,   140
Which, though 't were wild—as on the plundered wreck
When mariners would madly meet their doom
With draughts intemperate on the sinking deck,—
Did yet inspire a cheer, which he forbore to check.

1816.   *1816.*

WATERLOO

Stop! for thy tread is on an Empire's dust!
An Earthquake's spoil is sepulchred below!
Is the spot marked with no colossal bust,
No column trophied for triumphal show?
None; but the moral's truth tells simpler so: 5
As the ground was before, thus let it be;—
How that red rain hath made the harvest grow!
And is this all the world has gained by thee,
Thou first and last of fields, king-making victory?

And Harold stands upon this place of skulls,   10
The grave of France, the deadly Waterloo.
How in an hour the Power which gave annuls
Its gifts, transferring fame as fleeting too!
In "pride of place" here last the Eagle flew,
Then tore with bloody talon the rent plain,   15
Pierced by the shaft of banded nations through;
Ambition's life and labours all were vain—
He wears the shattered links of the world's broken chain.

Fit retribution! Gaul may champ the bit
And foam in fetters;—but is Earth more free? 20
Did nations combat to make *one* submit,
Or league to teach all kings true sovereignty?
What! shall reviving Thraldom again be
The patched-up idol of enlightened days?
Shall we, who struck the Lion down, shall we 25
Pay the Wolf homage, proffering lowly gaze
And servile knees to thrones? No! *prove* before ye praise!

If not, o'er one fallen despot boast no more!
In vain fair cheeks were furrowed with hot tears
For Europe's flowers long rooted up before   30
The trampler of her vineyards; in vain years
Of death, depopulation, bondage, fears,
Have all been borne, and broken by the accord
Of roused-up millions: all that most endears
Glory, is when the myrtle wreathes a sword 35
Such as Harmodius drew on Athens' tyrant lord.

There was a sound of revelry by night,
And Belgium's capital had gathered then
Her Beauty and her Chivalry, and bright

The lamps shone o'er fair women and brave men;   40
A thousand hearts beat happily; and when
Music arose with its voluptuous swell,
Soft eyes looked love to eyes which spake again,
And all went merry as a marriage-bell—
But hush! hark! a deep sound strikes like a rising knell!   45

Did ye not hear it? No; 't was but the wind,
Or the car rattling o'er the stony street.
On with the dance! let joy be unconfined;
No sleep till morn, when Youth and Pleasure meet
To chase the glowing Hours with flying feet—   50
But hark! that heavy sound breaks in once more,
As if the clouds its echo would repeat;
And nearer, clearer, deadlier, than before!
Arm! arm! it is—it is—the cannon's opening roar!

Within a windowed niche of that high hall   55
Sate Brunswick's fated chieftain; he did hear
That sound the first amidst the festival,
And caught its tone with Death's prophetic ear;
And when they smiled because he deemed it near,
His heart more truly knew that peal too well   60
Which stretched his father on a bloody bier,
And roused the vengeance blood alone could quell:
He rushed into the field, and, foremost fighting, fell.

Ah, then and there was hurrying to and fro,
And gathering tears, and tremblings of distress,   65
And cheeks all pale, which but an hour ago
Blushed at the praise of their own loveliness;
And there were sudden partings, such as press
The life from out young hearts, and choking sighs
Which ne'er might be repeated; who could guess   70
If ever more should meet those mutual eyes,
Since upon night so sweet such awful morn could rise?

And there was mounting in hot haste: the steed,
The mustering squadron, and the clattering car
Went pouring forward with impetuous speed,   75
And swiftly forming in the ranks of war;
And the deep thunder, peal on peal afar,

And, near, the beat of the alarming drum,
Roused up the soldier ere the morning star;
While thronged the citizens with terror dumb,　　80
Or whispering, with white lips—"The foe! they come!
　　they come!"

And wild and high the "Cameron's Gathering" rose!
The war-note of Lochiel, which Albyn's hills
Have heard, and heard, too, have her Saxon foes.
How in the noon of night that pibroch thrills,　　85
Savage and shrill! But with the breath which fills
Their mountain-pipe, so fill the mountaineers
With the fierce native daring which instils
The stirring memory of a thousand years,
And Evan's, Donald's, fame rings in each clansman's ears!　90

And Ardennes waves above them her green leaves,
Dewy with nature's tear-drops, as they pass,
Grieving, if aught inanimate e'er grieves,
Over the unreturning brave,—alas,
Ere evening to be trodden like the grass　　95
Which now beneath them, but above shall grow
In its next verdure, when this fiery mass
Of living valour, rolling on the foe
And burning with high hope, shall moulder cold and low.

Last noon beheld them full of lusty life,　　100
Last eve in Beauty's circle proudly gay;
The midnight brought the signal-sound of strife,
The morn the marshalling in arms, the day
Battle's magnificently stern array!
The thunder-clouds close o'er it, which when rent,　　105
The earth is covered thick with other clay,
Which her own clay shall cover, heaped and pent,
Rider and horse—friend, foe—in one red burial blent!
1816.　　　　　　　　　　　　　　1816.

LAKE LEMAN IN CALM AND STORM

Clear, placid Leman! thy contrasted lake,
With the wild world I dwelt in, is a thing
Which warns me, with its stillness, to forsake

Earth's troubled waters for a purer spring.
This quiet sail is as a noiseless wing　　　　　　5
To waft me from distraction : once I loved
Torn Ocean's roar, but thy soft murmuring
Sounds sweet as if a sister's voice reproved
That I with stern delights should e'er have been so moved.

It is the hush of night, and all between　　　　　10
Thy margin and the mountains, dusk, yet clear,
Mellowed and mingling, yet distinctly seen,
Save darkened Jura, whose capt heights appear
Precipitously steep; and drawing near,
There breathes a living fragrance from the shore,　　15
Of flowers yet fresh with childhood; on the ear
Drops the light drip of the suspended oar,
Or chirps the grasshopper one good-night carol more.

He is an evening reveller, who makes
His life an infancy, and sings his fill;　　　　　20
At intervals, some bird from out the brakes
Starts into voice a moment, then is still.
There seems a floating whisper on the hill;
But that is fancy, for the starlight dews
All silently their tears of love instil,　　　　　25
Weeping themselves away, till they infuse
Deep into Nature's breast the spirit of her hues.

Ye stars! which are the poetry of heaven!
If in your bright leaves we would read the fate
Of men and empires, 't is to be forgiven　　　　30
That in our aspirations to be great
Our destinies o'erleap their mortal state,
And claim a kindred with you; for ye are
A beauty and a mystery, and create
In us such love and reverence from afar　　　　35
That fortune, fame, power, life, have named themselves a
　　　star.

All heaven and earth are still—though not in sleep,
But breathless as we grow when feeling most,
And silent as we stand in thoughts too deep.
All heaven and earth are still: from the high host　　40

Of stars, to the lulled lake and mountain-coast,
All is concentered in a life intense,
Where not a beam, nor air, nor leaf is lost,
But hath a part of Being, and a sense
Of that which is of all Creator and Defence. 45

Then stirs the feeling infinite, so felt
In solitude, where we are *least* alone;
A truth, which through our being then doth melt
And purifies from self: it is a tone,
The soul and source of music, which makes known 50
Eternal harmony, and sheds a charm
Like to the fabled Cytherea's zone,
Binding all things with beauty;—'t would disarm
The spectre Death, had he substantial power to harm.

Not vainly did the early Persian make 55
His altar the high places and the peak
Of earth-o'ergazing mountains, and thus take
A fit and unwalled temple, there to seek
The Spirit in Whose honour shrines are weak,
Upreared of human hands. Come, and compare 60
Columns and idol-dwellings, Goth or Greek,
With Nature's realms of worship, earth and air,
Nor fix on fond abodes to circumscribe thy prayer!

The sky is changed!—and such a change! Oh night,
And storm, and darkness, ye are wondrous strong, 65
Yet lovely in your strength, as is the light
Of a dark eye in woman! Far along,
From peak to peak, the rattling crags among,
Leaps the live thunder! Not from one lone cloud,
But every mountain now hath found a tongue; 70
And Jura answers, through her misty shroud,
Back to the joyous Alps, who call to her aloud!

And this is in the night:—most glorious night!
Thou wert not sent for slumber! let me be
A sharer in thy fierce and far delight— 75
A portion of the tempest and of thee!
How the lit lake shines, a phosphoric sea,
And the big rain comes dancing to the earth!
And now again 't is black,—and now the glee

Of the loud hills shakes with its mountain-mirth,   80
As if they did rejoice o'er a young earthquake's birth.

Now, where the swift Rhone cleaves his way between
Heights which appear as lovers who have parted
In hate, whose mining depths so intervene
That they can meet no more, though broken-hearted;   85
Though in their souls, which thus each other thwarted,
Love was the very root of the fond rage
Which blighted their life's bloom, and then departed;
Itself expired, but leaving them an age
Of years all winters, war within themselves to wage;—   90

Now, where the quick Rhone thus hath cleft his way,
The mightiest of the storms hath ta'en his stand—
For here, not one, but many, make their play,
And fling their thunderbolts from hand to hand,
Flashing and cast around;—of all the band,   95
The brightest through these parted hills hath forked
His lightnings,—as if he did understand
That in such gaps as desolation worked
There the hot shaft should blast whatever therein lurked.

Sky, mountains, rivers, winds, lake, lightnings! ye   100
With night, and clouds, and thunder, and a soul
To make these felt and feeling, well may be
Things that have made me watchful: the far roll
Of your departing voices is the knoll
Of what in me is sleepless—if I rest.   105
But where of ye, oh tempests! is the goal?
Are ye like those within the human breast?
Or do ye find, at length, like eagles, some high nest?

Could I embody and unbosom now
That which is most within me,—could I wreak   110
My thoughts upon expression, and thus throw
Soul, heart, mind, passions, feelings, strong or weak,
All that I would have sought, and all I seek,
Bear, know, feel, and yet breathe, into *one* word,
And that one word were Lightning, I would speak;   115
But as it is, I live and die unheard,
With a most voiceless thought, sheathing it as a sword.

1816.   1816.

(From Canto IV)

VENICE

I stood in Venice, on the Bridge of Sighs,
A palace and a prison on each hand;
I saw from out the wave her structures rise
As from the stroke of the enchanter's wand;
A thousand years their cloudy wings expand   5
Around me, and a dying glory smiles
O'er the far times when many a subject land
Looked to the wingèd Lion's marble piles,
Where Venice sate in state, throned on her hundred isles.

She looks a sea Cybele, fresh from ocean,   10
Rising with her tiara of proud towers
At airy distance, with majestic motion,
A ruler of the waters and their powers:
And such she was; her daughters had their dowers
From spoils of nations, and the exhaustless East   15
Poured in her lap all gems in sparkling showers;
In purple was she robed, and of her feast
Monarchs partook, and deemed their dignity increased.

In Venice Tasso's echoes are no more,
And silent rows the songless gondolier;   20
Her palaces are crumbling to the shore,
And music meets not always now the ear.
Those days are gone—but Beauty still is here:
States fall, arts fade,—but Nature doth not die,
Nor yet forget how Venice once was dear,   25
The pleasant place of all festivity,
The revel of the earth, the masque of Italy!

1817.   1818.

ROME AND FREEDOM

Oh Rome! my country! city of the soul!
The orphans of the heart must turn to thee,
Lone mother of dead empires! and control
In their shut breasts their petty misery.
What are our woes and sufferance? Come and see   5.
The cypress, hear the owl, and plod your way
O'er steps of broken thrones and temples, ye

Whose agonies are evils of a day—
A world is at our feet as fragile as our clay.

The Niobe of nations! there she stands,   10
Childless and crownless, in her voiceless woe,
An empty urn within her withered hands,
Whose holy dust was scattered long ago:
The Scipio's tomb contains no ashes now;
The very sepulchres lie tenantless   15
Of their heroic dwellers. Dost thou flow,
Old Tiber! through a marble wilderness?
Rise, with thy yellow waves, and mantle her distress.

The Goth, the Christian, Time, War, Flood, and Fire
Have dealt upon the seven-hilled city's pride;   20
She saw her glories star by star expire,
And up the steep barbarian monarchs ride,
Where the car climbed the Capitol; far and wide
Temple and tower went down, nor left a site:—
Chaos of ruins! who shall trace the void,   25
O'er the dim fragments cast a lunar light,
And say here was, or is, where all is doubly night?

. . . .

And thou, the thunder-stricken nurse of Rome,
She-wolf! whose brazen-imaged dugs impart
The milk of conquest yet within the dome   30
Where, as a monument of antique art,
Thou standest; mother of the mighty heart,
Which the great founder sucked from thy wild teat,
Scorched by the Roman Jove's ethereal dart,
And thy limbs black with lightning,—dost thou yet   35
Guard thine immortal cubs, nor thy fond charge forget?

Thou dost; but all thy foster-babes are dead—
The men of iron; and the world hath reared
Cities from out their sepulchres; men bled
In imitation of the things they feared,   40
And fought and conquered, and the same course steered,
At apish distance; but as yet none have
Nor could the same supremacy have neared,
Save one vain man, who is not in the grave,
But, vanquished by himself, to his own slaves a slave—   45

The fool of false dominion, and a kind
Of bastard Cæsar, following him of old
With steps unequal; for the Roman's mind
Was modelled in a less terrestrial mould,
With passions fiercer, yet a judgment cold,   50
And an immortal instinct which redeemed
The frailties of a heart so soft, yet bold,
Alcides with the distaff now he seemed
At Cleopatra's feet,—and now himself he beamed,

And came—and saw—and conquered! But the man   55
Who would have tamed his eagles down to flee,
Like a trained falcon, in the Gallic van,
Which he, in sooth, long led to victory,
With a deaf heart which never seemed to be
A listener to itself, was strangely framed: 60
With but one weakest weakness—vanity,—
Coquettish in ambition, still he aimed—
At what? can he avouch, or answer what he claimed?—

And would be all or nothing, nor could wait
For the sure grave to level him; few years   65
Had fixed him with the Cæsars in his fate,
On whom we tread:—for *this* the conqueror rears
The arch of triumph! and for this the tears
And blood of earth flow on as they have flowed,
An universal deluge, which appears   70
Without an ark for wretched man's abode,
And ebbs but to reflow!—Renew thy rainbow, God!

What from this barren being do we reap?
Our senses narrow, and our reason frail,
Life short, and truth a gem which loves the deep,   75
And all things weighed in custom's falsest scale;
Opinion an omnipotence,—whose veil
Mantles the earth with darkness, until right
And wrong are accidents, and men grow pale
Lest their own judgments should become too bright,   80
And their free thoughts be crimes, and earth have too
        much light.

And thus they plod in sluggish misery,
Rotting from sire to son, and age to age,

Proud of their trampled nature, and so die,
Bequeathing their hereditary rage   85
To the new race of inborn slaves, who wage
War for their chains, and, rather than be free,
Bleed gladiator-like, and still engage
Within the same arena where they see
Their fellows fall before, like leaves of the same tree.   90

I speak not of men's creeds—they rest between
Man and his Maker—but of things allowed,
Averred, and known, and daily, hourly seen:—
The yoke that is upon us doubly bowed,
And the intent of tyranny avowed,   95
The edict of Earth's rulers, who are grown
The apes of him who humbled once the proud,
And shook them from their slumbers on the throne—
Too glorious, were this all his mighty arm had done.

Can tyrants but by tyrants conquered be,   100
And Freedom find no champion and no child
Such as Columbia saw arise when she
Sprung forth a Pallas, armed and undefiled?
Or must such minds be nourished in the wild,
Deep in the unpruned forest, 'midst the roar   105
Of cataracts, where nursing Nature smiled
On infant Washington? Has Earth no more
Such seeds within her breast, or Europe no such shore?

But France got drunk with blood to vomit crime,
And fatal have her Saturnalia been   110
To Freedom's cause, in every age and clime;
Because the deadly days which we have seen,
And vile Ambition, that built up between
Man and his hopes an adamantine wall,
And the base pageant last upon the scene,   115
Are grown the pretext for the eternal thrall
Which nips life's tree, and dooms man's worst, his second,
       fall.

Yet, Freedom! yet thy banner, torn but flying,
Streams like the thunder-storm *against* the wind;
Thy trumpet voice, though broken now and dying,   120
The loudest still the tempest leaves behind;

Thy tree hath lost its blossoms, and the rind,
Chopped by the axe, looks rough and little worth,
But the sap lasts, and still the seed we find
Sown deep, even in the bosom of the North: 125
So shall a better Spring less bitter fruit bring forth.
1817.   1818.

THE OCEAN

There is a pleasure in the pathless woods,
There is a rapture on the lonely shore,
There is society, where none intrudes,
By the deep sea, and music in its roar:
I love not man the less, but Nature more,   5
From these our interviews, in which I steal
From all I may be, or have been before,
To mingle with the Universe and feel
What I can ne'er express, yet cannot all conceal.

Roll on, thou deep and dark blue Ocean—roll!   10
Ten thousand fleets sweep over thee in vain;
Man marks the earth with ruin—his control
Stops with the shore; upon the watery plain
The wrecks are all thy deed, nor doth remain
A shadow of man's ravage, save his own,   15
When, for a moment, like a drop of rain,
He sinks into thy depths with bubbling groan,
Without a grave, unknelled, uncoffined, and unknown.

His steps are not upon thy paths, thy fields
Are not a spoil for him,—thou dost arise   20
And shake him from thee; the vile strength he wields
For earth's destruction thou dost all despise,
Spurning him from thy bosom to the skies,
And send'st him, shivering in thy playful spray
And howling, to his gods, where haply lies   25
His petty hope in some near port or bay,
And dashest him again to earth:—there let him lay.

The armaments which thunderstrike the walls
Of rock-built cities, bidding nations quake,
And monarchs tremble in their capitals;   30
The oak leviathans, whose huge ribs make
Their clay creator the vain title take

Of lord of thee, and arbiter of war,—
These are thy toys, and as the snowy flake
They melt into thy yeast of waves, which mar   35
Alike the Armada's pride, or spoils of Trafalgar.

Thy shores are empires changed in all save thee—
Assyria, Greece, Rome, Carthage, what are they?
Thy waters washed them power while they were free,
And many a tyrant since; their shores obey   40
The stranger, slave, or savage; their decay
Has dried up realms to deserts:—not so thou,
Unchangeable save to thy wild waves' play;
Time writes no wrinkle on thine azure brow—
Such as creation's dawn beheld, thou rollest now.   45

Thou glorious mirror, where the Almighty's form
Glasses itself in tempests; in all time,
Calm or convulsed—in breeze, or gale, or storm,—
Icing the pole, or in the torrid clime
Dark-heaving,—boundless, endless, and sublime—   50
The image of Eternity—the throne
Of the Invisible; even from out thy slime
The monsters of the deep are made; each zone
Obeys thee; thou goest forth, dread, fathomless, alone.

And I have loved thee, Ocean! and my joy   55
Of youthful sports was on thy breast to be
Borne, like thy bubbles, onward: from a boy
I wantoned with thy breakers—they to me
Were a delight; and if the freshening sea
Made them a terror, 't was a pleasing fear,   60
For I was, as it were, a child of thee,
And trusted to thy billows far and near,
And laid my hand upon thy mane—as I do here.
1817–18.   1818.

DON JUAN

(From Canto II)

THE SHIPWRECK

The ship was evidently settling now
    Fast by the head; and, all distinction gone,

Some went to prayers again, and made a vow
   Of candles to their saints—but there were none
To pay them with; and some looked o'er the bow,   5
   Some hoisted out the boats; and there was one
That begged Pedrillo for an absolution,
Who told him to be damned—in his confusion.

Some lashed them in their hammocks; some put on
   Their best clothes, as if going to a fair;   10
Some cursed the day on which they saw the sun,
   And gnashed their teeth, and, howling, tore their hair;
And others went on as they had begun,
   Getting the boats out, being well aware
That a tight boat will live in a rough sea,   15
Unless with breakers close beneath her lee.

The worst of all was that in their condition,
   Having been several days in great distress,
'Twas difficult to get out such provision
   As now might render their long suffering less—   20
Men, even when dying, dislike inanition;
   Their stock was damaged by the weather's stress:
Two casks of biscuit, and a keg of butter,
Were all that could be thrown into the cutter.

But in the long-boat they contrived to stow   25
   Some pounds of bread, though injured by the wet;
Water, a twenty-gallon cask or so;
   Six flasks of wine: and they contrived to get
A portion of their beef up from below,
   And with a piece of pork, moreover, met,   30
But scarce enough to serve them for a luncheon—
Then there was rum, eight gallons in a puncheon.

The other boats, the yawl and pinnace, had
   Been stove in the beginning of the gale;
And the long-boat's condition was but bad,   35
   As there were but two blankets for a sail,
And one oar for a mast, which a young lad
   Threw in by good luck over the ship's rail;
And two boats could not hold, far less be stored,
To save one half the people then on board.   40

'T was twilight, and the sunless day went down
  Over the waste of waters; like a veil,
Which if withdrawn would but disclose the frown
  Of one whose hate is masked but to assail.
Thus to their hopeless eyes the night was shown,   45
  And grimly darkled o'er the faces pale,
And the dim desolate deep: twelve days had Fear
Been their familiar, and now Death was here.

Some trial had been making at a raft,
  With little hope in such a rolling sea,   50
A sort of thing at which one would have laughed,
  If any laughter at such times could be,
Unless with people who too much have quaffed,
  And have a kind of wild and horrid glee,
Half epileptical and half hysterical:—   55
Their preservation would have been a miracle.

At half-past eight o'clock, booms, hencoops, spars,
  And all things for a chance, had been cast loose,
That still could keep afloat the struggling tars,
  For yet they strove, although of no great use.   60
There was no light in heaven but a few stars;
  The boats put off o'ercrowded with their crews;
She gave a heel, and then a lurch to port,
And, going down head foremost—sunk, in short.

Then rose from sea to sky the wild farewell—   65
  Then shrieked the timid, and stood still the brave—
Then some leaped overboard with dreadful yell,
  As eager to anticipate their grave.
And the sea yawned around her like a hell,
  And down she sucked with her the whirling wave,   70
Like one who grapples with his enemy,
And strives to strangle him before he die.

And first one universal shriek there rushed,
  Louder than the loud ocean, like a crash
Of echoing thunder; and then all was hushed,   75
  Save the wild wind and the remorseless dash
Of billows; but at intervals there gushed,
  Accompanied with a convulsive splash,

A solitary shriek, the bubbling cry
Of some strong swimmer in his agony. 80

The boats, as stated, had got off before,
    And in them crowded several of the crew;
And yet their present hope was hardly more
    Than what it had been, for so strong it blew
There was slight chance of reaching any shore; 85
    And then they were too many, though so few—
Nine in the cutter, thirty in the boat,
Were counted in them when they got afloat.

. . . .

As they drew nigh the land, which now was seen
    Unequal in its aspect here and there, 90
They felt the freshness of its growing green,
    That waved in forest-tops, and smoothed the air,
And fell upon their glazed eyes like a screen
    From glistening waves and skies so hot and bare—
Lovely seemed any object that should sweep 95
Away the vast, salt, dread, eternal deep.

The shore looked wild, without a trace of man,
    And girt by formidable waves; but they
Were mad for land, and thus their course they ran,
    Though right ahead the roaring breakers lay: 100
A reef between them also now began
    To show its boiling surf and bounding spray;
But finding no place for their landing better,
They ran the boat for shore—and overset her.

But in his native stream, the Guadalquivir, 105
    Juan to lave his youthful limbs was wont;
And having learnt to swim in that sweet river,
    Had often turned the art to some account:
A better swimmer you could scarce see ever;
    He could, perhaps, have passed the Hellespont, 110
As once (a feat on which ourselves we prided)
Leander, Mr. Ekenhead, and I did.

So here, though faint, emaciated, and stark,
    He buoyed his boyish limbs, and strove to ply

With the quick wave, and gain, ere it was dark,   115
   The beach which lay before him, high and dry.
The greatest danger here was from a shark,
   That carried off his neighbour by the thigh;
As for the other two they could not swim,
So nobody arrived on shore but him.   120

Nor yet had he arrived but for the oar,
   Which, providentially for him, was washed
Just as his feeble arms could strike no more,
   And the hard wave o'erwhelmed him as 't was dashed
Within his grasp; he clung to it, and sore   125
   The waters beat while he thereto was lashed.
At last, with swimming, wading, scrambling, he
Rolled on the beach, half senseless from the sea.

There, breathless, with his digging nails he clung
   Fast to the sand, lest the returning wave,   130
From whose reluctant roar his life he wrung,
   Should suck him back to her insatiate grave.
And there he lay, full length, where he was flung,
   Before the entrance of a cliff-worn cave,
With just enough of life to feel its pain,   135
And deem that it was saved, perhaps, in vain.

With slow and staggering effort he arose,
   But sunk again upon his bleeding knee
And quivering hand; and then he looked for those
   Who long had been his mates upon the sea;   140
But none of them appeared to share his woes,
   Save one, a corpse from out the famished three,
Who died two days before, and now had found
An unknown barren beach for burial ground.

And as he gazed, his dizzy brain spun fast,   145
   And down he sunk; and as he sunk, the sand
Swam round and round, and all his senses passed;
   He fell upon his side, and his stretched hand
Drooped dripping on the oar (their jury-mast),
   And, like a withered lily, on the land   150
His slender frame and pallid aspect lay,
As fair a thing as e'er was formed of clay.

1819.   1819.

JUAN AND HAIDÉE

And thus a moon rolled on, and fair Haidée
    Paid daily visits to her boy, and took
Such plentiful precautions that still he
    Remained unknown within his craggy nook.
At last her father's prows put out to sea,   5
    For certain merchantmen upon the look,
Not as of yore to carry off an Io,
But three Ragusan vessels, bound for Scio.

Then came her freedom, for she had no mother,
    So that, her father being at sea, she was   10
Free as a married woman, or such other
    Female as where she likes may freely pass,
Without even the incumbrance of a brother,
    The freest she that ever gazed on glass:—
I speak of Christian lands in this comparison,   15
Where wives, at least, are seldom kept in garrison.

Now she prolonged her visits and her talk
    (For they must talk), and he had learnt to say
So much as to propose to take a walk;
    For little had he wandered since the day   20
On which, like a young flower snapped from the stalk,
    Drooping and dewy on the beach he lay.
And thus they walked out in the afternoon,
And saw the sun set opposite the moon.

It was a wild and breaker-beaten coast,   25
    With cliffs above, and a broad sandy shore,
Guarded by shoals and rocks as by an host,
    With here and there a creek, whose aspect wore
A better welcome to the tempest-tost;
    And rarely ceased the haughty billow's roar,   30
Save on the dead long summer days, which make
The outstretched ocean glitter like a lake.

And the small ripple spilt upon the beach
    Scarcely o'erpassed the cream of your champagne,
When o'er the brim the sparkling bumpers reach,   35
    That spring-dew of the spirit! the heart's rain!

Few things surpass old wine; and they may preach
    Who please—the more because they preach in vain;—
Let us have wine and woman, mirth and laughter,
Sermons and soda-water the day after.   40

Man, being reasonable, must get drunk;
    The best of life is but intoxication:
Glory, the grape, love, gold, in these are sunk
    The hopes of all men, and of every nation;
Without their sap, how branchless were the trunk   45
    Of life's strange tree, so fruitful on occasion!
But to return—get very drunk; and when
You wake with headache, you shall see what then.

Ring for your valet—bid him quickly bring
    Some hock and soda-water, then you 'll know   50
A pleasure worthy Xerxes, the great king;
    For not the blest sherbet, sublimed with snow,
Nor the first sparkle of the desert-spring,
    Nor Burgundy in all its sunset glow,
After long travel, ennui, love, or slaughter,   55
Vie with that draught of hock and soda-water.

The coast—I think it was the coast that I
    Was just describing—yes, it *was* the coast—
Lay at this period quiet as the sky,
    The sands untumbled, the blue waves untost;   60
And all was stillness, save the sea-bird's cry,
    And dolphin's leap, and little billow crost
By some low rock or shelve, that made it fret
Against the boundary it scarcely wet.

And forth they wandered, her sire being gone,   65
    As I have said, upon an expedition;
And mother, brother, guardian, she had none,
    Save Zoe, who, although with due precision
She waited on her lady with the sun,
    Thought daily service was her only mission,   70
Bringing warm water, wreathing her long tresses,
And asking now and then for cast-off dresses.

It was the cooling hour, just when the rounded
    Red sun sinks down behind the azure hill,

Which then seems as if the whole earth it bounded,   75
  Circling all Nature, hushed, and dim, and still,
With the far mountain-crescent half surrounded
  On one side, and the deep sea calm and chill
Upon the other, and the rosy sky,
With one star sparkling through it like an eye.   80

And thus they wandered forth, and hand in hand,
  Over the shining pebbles and the shells,
Glided along the smooth and hardened sand,
  And in the worn and wild receptacles
Worked by the storms, yet worked as it were planned,   85
  In hollow halls, with sparry roofs and cells,
They turned to rest; and, each clasped by an arm,
Yielded to the deep twilight's purple charm.

They looked up to the sky, whose floating glow
  Spread like a rosy ocean, vast and bright;   90
They gazed upon the glittering sea below,
  Whence the broad moon rose circling into sight;
They heard the waves' splash, and the wind so low,
  And saw each other's dark eyes darting light
Into each other—and beholding this,   95
Their lips drew near and clung into a kiss.

. . . .

Alas, the love of women! it is known
  To be a lovely and a fearful thing;
For all of theirs upon that die is thrown,
  And if 't is lost, life hath no more to bring   100
To them but mockeries of the past alone,
  And their revenge is as the tiger's spring,
Deadly and quick and crushing; yet, as real
Torture is theirs, what they inflict they feel.

They are right; for man, to man so oft unjust,   105
  Is always so to women; one sole bond
Awaits them, treachery is all their trust;
  Taught to conceal, their bursting hearts despond
Over their idol, till some wealthier lust
  Buys them in marriage—and what rests beyond?   110
A thankless husband, next a faithless lover,
Then dressing, nursing, praying, and all 's over.

Some take a lover, some take drams or prayers;
   Some mind their household, others dissipation;
Some run away, and but exchange their cares,   115
   Losing the advantage of a virtuous station;
Few changes e'er can better their affairs,
   Theirs being an unnatural situation,
From the dull palace to the dirty hovel;
Some play the devil, and then write a novel.   120

Haidée was Nature's bride, and knew not this;
   Haidée was Passion's child, born where the sun
Showers triple light, and scorches even the kiss
   Of his gazelle-eyed daughters; she was one
Made but to love, to feel that she was his   125
   Who was her chosen—what was said or done
Elsewhere was nothing; she had naught to fear,
Hope, care, nor love, beyond,—her heart beat *here*.
   1819.   1819.

(From Canto XIV)

THE SCEPTIC AND HIS POEM

If from great Nature's or our own abyss
   Of thought we could but snatch a certainty,
Perhaps mankind might find the path they miss—
   But then 't would spoil much good philosophy:
One system eats another up, and this   5
   Much as old Saturn ate his progeny;
For when his pious consort gave him stones
In lieu of sons, of these he made no bones.

But System doth reverse the Titan's breakfast,
   And eats her parents, albeit the digestion   10
Is difficult. Pray tell me, can you make fast,
   After due search, your faith to any question?
Look back o'er ages, ere unto the stake fast
   You bind yourself and call some mode the best one.
Nothing more true than *not* to trust your senses;   15
And yet what are your other evidences?

For me, I know naught; nothing I deny—
   Admit—reject—contemn: and what know *you*,

Except perhaps that you were born to die?
   And both may after all turn out untrue;   20
An age may come, Font of Eternity,
   When nothing shall be either old or new.
Death, so called, is a thing which makes men weep,
And yet a third of life is passed in sleep.

A sleep without dreams, after a rough day   25
   Of toil, is what we covet most; and yet
How clay shrinks back from more quiescent clay!
   The very suicide that pays his debt
At once without instalments (an old way
   Of paying debts, which creditors regret)   30
Lets out impatiently his rushing breath,
Less from disgust of life than dread of death.

'T is round him, near him, here, there, everywhere;
   And there's a courage which grows out of fear,
Perhaps of all most desperate, which will dare   35
   The worst to *know* it:—when the mountains rear
Their peaks beneath your human foot, and there
   You look down o'er the precipice, and drear
The gulf of rock yawns, you can't gaze a minute
Without an awful wish to plunge within it.   40

'T is true, you don't—but, pale and struck with terror,
   Retire: but look into your past impression!
And you will find, though shuddering at the mirror
   Of your own thoughts, in all their self-confession,
The lurking bias, be it truth or error,   45
   To the *unknown;* a secret prepossession,
To plunge with all your fears—but where? You know not,
And that's the reason why you do—or do not.

But what's this to the purpose? you will say.
   Gent. reader, nothing; a mere speculation,   50
For which my sole excuse is—'t is my way.
   Sometimes with and sometimes without occasion
I write what's uppermost, without delay;
   This narrative is not meant for narration,
But a mere airy and fantastic basis,   55
To build up common things with commonplaces.

You know, or don't know, that great Bacon saith,
  "Fling up a straw, 't will show the way the wind blows":
And such a straw, borne on by human breath,
  Is poesy, according as the mind glows;   60
A paper kite which flies 'twixt life and death,
  A shadow which the onward soul behind throws;
And mine's a bubble, not blown up for praise,
But just to play with, as an infant plays.

The world is all before me—or behind: 65
  For I have seen a portion of that same,
And quite enough for me to keep in mind;
  Of passions, too, I have proved enough to blame,
To the great pleasure of our friends, mankind,
  Who like to mix some slight alloy with fame—   70
For I was rather famous in my time,
Until I fairly knocked it up with rhyme.

I have brought this world about my ears, and eke
  The other; that's to say, the clergy, who
Upon my head have bid their thunders break   75
  In pious libels by no means a few.
And yet I can't help scribbling once a week,
  Tiring old readers, nor discovering new.
In youth I wrote because my mind was full,
And now because I feel it growing dull.   80

    1823.   *1823.*

FROM

THE VISION OF JUDGMENT

The varlet was not an ill-favoured knave;
  A good deal like a vulture in the face,
With a hook nose and a hawk's eye, which gave
  A smart and sharper-looking sort of grace
To his whole aspect, which, though rather grave,   5
  Was by no means so ugly as his case;
But that indeed was hopeless as can be,
Quite a poetic felony *"de se."*

Then Michael blew his trump, and stilled the noise
  With one still greater, as is yet the mode   10

On earth besides; except some grumbling voice,
　　Which now and then will make a slight inroad
Upon decorous silence, few will twice
　　Lift up their lungs when fairly overcrowed;
And now the bard could plead his own bad cause,　　15
With all the attitudes of self-applause.

He said—I only give the heads—he said
　　He meant no harm in scribbling; 't was his way
Upon all topics; 't was, besides, his bread,
　　Of which he buttered both sides; 't would delay　　20
Too long the assembly (he was pleased to dread),
　　And take up rather more time than a day,
To name his works—he would but cite a few—
"Wat Tyler"—"Rhymes on Blenheim"—"Waterloo."

He had written praises of a regicide;　　25
　　He had written praises of all kings whatever;
He had written for republics far and wide,
　　And then against them bitterer than ever;
For pantisocracy he once had cried
　　Aloud, a scheme less moral than 't was clever;　　30
Then grew a hearty anti-jacobin—
Had turned his coat—and would have turned his skin.

He had sung against all battles, and again
　　In their high praise and glory; he had called
Reviewing "the ungentle craft," and then　　35
　　Become as base a critic as e'er crawled—
Fed, paid, and pampered by the very men
　　By whom his muse and morals had been mauled;
He had written much blank verse, and blanker prose,
And more of both than anybody knows.　　40

He had written Wesley's life:—here turning round
　　To Satan, "Sir, I'm ready to write yours,
In two octavo volumes, nicely bound,
　　With notes and preface, all that most allures
The pious purchaser; and there's no ground　　45
　　For fear, for I can choose my own reviewers;
So let me have the proper documents,
That I may add you to my other saints."

Satan bowed, and was silent. "Well, if you,
    With amiable modesty, decline   50
My offer, what says Michael? There are few
    Whose memoirs could be rendered more divine.
Mine is a pen of all work; not so new
    As it was once, but I would make you shine
Like your own trumpet. By the way, my own   55
Has more of brass in it, and is as well blown.

"But talking about trumpets, here's my 'Vision'!
    Now you shall judge, all people; yes, you shall
Judge with my judgment, and by my decision
    Be guided who shall enter heaven or fall.   60
I settle all these things by intuition,
    Times present, past, to come, heaven, hell, and all,
Like King Alfonso. When I thus see double,
I save the Deity some worlds of trouble."

He ceased, and drew forth an MS.; and no   65
    Persuasion on the part of devils, saints,
Or angels, now could stop the torrent; so
    He read the first three lines of the contents;
But at the fourth the whole spiritual show
    Had vanished, with variety of scents,   70
Ambrosial and sulphureous, as they sprang,
Like lightning, off from his "melodious twang."

Those grand heroics acted as a spell;
    The angels stopped their ears and plied their pinions;
The devils ran howling, deafened, down to hell;   75
    The ghosts fled, gibbering, for their own dominions
(For 't is not yet decided where they dwell,
    And I leave every man to his opinions);
Michael took refuge in his trump—but, lo!
His teeth were set on edge, he could not blow!   80

Saint Peter, who has hitherto been known
    For an impetuous saint, upraised his keys,
And at the fifth line knocked the poet down;
    Who fell like Phaeton, but more at ease,
Into his lake, for there he did not drown;   85
    A different web being by the Destinies

Woven for the Laureate's final wreath, whene'er
Reform shall happen either here or there.

He first sank to the bottom—like his works;
　　But soon rose to the surface—like himself,　　90
For all corrupted things are buoyed like corks,
　　By their own rottenness, light as an elf,
Or wisp that flits o'er a morass: he lurks,
　　It may be, still, like dull books on a shelf,
In his own den, to scrawl some "Life" or "Vision,"—　95
As Welborn says, "'the Devil turned precisian."

As for the rest, to come to the conclusion
　　Of this true dream, the telescope is gone
Which kept my optics free from all delusion,
　　And showed me what I in my turn have shown.　100
All I saw farther, in the last confusion,
　　Was that King George slipped into heaven for one;
And when the tumult dwindled to a calm,
I left him practising the hundredth psalm.

1821–22.　　　　　　　　　　　　　　*1822.*

ON THIS DAY I COMPLETE MY THIRTY-SIXTH YEAR

'T is time this heart should be unmoved,
　　Since others it hath ceased to move:
Yet, though I cannot be beloved,
　　　　Still let me love!

My days are in the yellow leaf;　　　　　　5
　　The flowers and fruits of love are gone;
The worm, the canker, and the grief
　　　　Are mine alone!

The fire that on my bosom preys
　　Is lone as some volcanic isle;　　　　　　10
No torch is kindled at its blaze—
　　　　A funeral pile!

The hope, the fear, the jealous care,
　　The exalted portion of the pain
And power of love, I cannot share;　　　　　15
　　　　But wear the chain.

But 't is not *thus*—and 't is not *here*—
   Such thoughts should shake my soul, nor *now*,
Where Glory decks the hero's bier,
     Or binds his brow.   20

The sword, the banner, and the field,
   Glory and Greece, around me see!
The Spartan, borne upon his shield,
     Was not more free.

Awake! (not Greece—she *is* awake!)   25
   Awake, my spirit! Think through *whom*
Thy life-blood tracks its parent lake,
     And then strike home!

Tread those reviving passions down,
   Unworthy manhood!—unto thee   30
Indifferent should the smile or frown
     Of Beauty be.

If thou regret'st thy youth, *why live?*
   The land of honourable death
Is here:—up to the field, and give   35
     Away thy breath!

Seek out—less often sought than found—
   A soldier's grave, for thee the best;
Then look around, and choose thy ground,
     And take thy rest.   40

1824.   1824.

THOMAS MOORE

THE HARP THAT ONCE THROUGH TARA'S HALLS

The harp that once through Tara's halls
   The soul of music shed,
Now hangs as mute on Tara's walls
   As if that soul were fled.
So sleeps the pride of former days,   5
   So glory's thrill is o'er;
And hearts that once beat high for praise
   Now feel that pulse no more!

No more to chiefs and ladies bright
 The harp of Tara swells;   10
The chord, alone, that breaks at night,
 Its tale of ruin tells.
Thus Freedom now so seldom wakes,
 The only throb she gives
Is when some heart indignant breaks, 15
 To show that still she lives!

LESBIA HATH A BEAMING EYE

Lesbia hath a beaming eye,
 But no one knows for whom it beameth;
Right and left its arrows fly,
 But what they aim at no one dreameth.
Sweeter 't is to gaze upon   5
 My Nora's lid that seldom rises;
Few its looks, but every one,
 Like unexpected light, surprises!
  Oh, my Nora Creina, dear,
 My gentle, bashful Nora Creina, 10
   Beauty lies
   In many eyes,
 But Love in yours, my Nora Creina.

Lesbia wears a robe of gold;
 But all so close the nymph hath laced it, 15
Not a charm of beauty's mould
 Presumes to stay where nature placed it.
Oh, my Nora's gown for me,
 That floats as wild as mountain breezes,
Leaving every beauty free   20
 To sink or swell as Heaven pleases.
  Yes, my Nora Creina, dear,
 My simple, graceful Nora Creina,
   Nature's dress
   Is loveliness—   25
 The dress *you* wear my Nora Creina.

Lesbia hath a wit refined;
 But when its points are gleaming round us,

Who can tell if they're designed
   To dazzle merely, or to wound us?   30
Pillowed on my Nora's heart,
   In safer slumber Love reposes—
Bed of peace! whose roughest part
   Is but the crumpling of the roses.
     Oh, my Nora Creina, dear,   35
My mild, my artless Nora Creina!
      Wit, though bright,
      Hath no such light
As warms your eyes, my Nora Creina.

OH, COME TO ME WHEN DAYLIGHT SETS

Oh, come to me when daylight sets;
   Sweet! then come to me,
When smoothly go our gondolets
   O'er the moonlight sea;
When Mirth's awake, and Love begins,   5
   Beneath that glancing ray,
With sound of lutes and mandolins,
   To steal young hearts away.
Then, come to me when daylight sets;
   Sweet! then come to me,   10
When smoothly go our gondolets
   O'er the moonlight sea.

Oh, then's the hour for those who love,
   Sweet! like thee and me;
When all's so calm below, above,   15
   In heaven and o'er the sea;
When maidens sing sweet barcarolles,
   And Echo sings again
So sweet that all with ears and souls
   Should love and listen then.   20
So, come to me when daylight sets;
   Sweet! then come to me,
When smoothly go our gondolets
   O'er the moonlight sea.

OFT, IN THE STILLY NIGHT

Oft, in the stilly night,
    Ere Slumber's chain has bound me,
Fond Memory brings the light
    Of other days around me:
        The smiles, the tears,   5
        Of boyhood's years,
    The words of love then spoken;
        The eyes that shone,
        Now dimmed and gone,
    The cheerful hearts now broken!   10
Thus in the stilly night,
    Ere Slumber's chain has bound me,
Sad Memory brings the light
    Of other days around me.

When I remember all   15
    The friends, so linked together,
I've seen around me fall,
    Like leaves in wintry weather,
        I feel like one
        Who treads alone   20
    Some banquet-hall deserted,
        Whose lights are fled,
        Whose garlands dead,
    And all but he departed.
Thus in the stilly night,   25
    Ere Slumber's chain has bound me,
Sad Memory brings the light
    Of other days around me.

TWOPENNY POST-BAG

LETTER V

From the Countess Dowager of C——rk to Lady ————.

My dear Lady ————! I've been just sending out
About five hundred cards for a snug little rout—
(By the bye, you've seen Rokeby?—this moment got mine—
The Mail-Coach Edition—prodigiously fine!)
But I can't conceive how, in this very cold weather,   5

I'm ever to bring my five hundred together;
As, unless the thermometer's near boiling heat,
One can never get half of one's hundreds to meet.
(Apropos—you'd have laughed to see Townsend, last night,
Escort to their chairs, with his staff, so polite,   10
The "three maiden Miseries," all in a fright;
Poor Townsend, like Mercury, filling two posts,
Supervisor of *thieves,* and chief-usher of *ghosts!*)

But, my dear Lady ———, can't you hit on some notion,
At least for one night to set London in motion?—   15
As to having the R–g–nt, *that* show is gone by—
Besides, I've remarked that (between you and I)
The Marchesa and he, inconvenient in more ways,
Have taken much lately to whispering in doorways;
Which—considering, you know, dear, the *size* of the two—   20
Makes a block that one's company *cannot* get through;
And a house such as mine is, with doorways so small,
Has no room for such cumbersome love-work at all.—
(Apropos, though, of love-work—you've heard it, I hope,
That Napoleon's old mother's to marry the Pope,—   25
What a comical pair!)—but, to stick to my rout,
'T will be hard if some novelty can't be struck out.
Is there no Algerine, no Kamchatkan, arrived?
No Plenipo Pacha, three-tailed and ten-wived?
No Russian, whose dissonant consonant name   30
Almost rattles to fragments the trumpet of fame?

I remember the time, three or four winters back,
When—provided their wigs were but decently black—
A few Patriot monsters, from Spain, were a sight
That would people one's house for one, night after night.   35
But—whether the Ministers *pawed* them too much—
(And you know how they spoil whatsoever they touch)
Or, whether Lord G—rge (the young man about town)
Has, by dint of bad poetry, written them down,
One has certainly lost one's *Peninsular* rage;   40
And the only stray Patriot seen for an age
Has been at such places (think how the fit cools!)
As old Mrs. V–gh–n's or Lord L–v–rp—l's.

But, in short, my dear, names like Wintztschitstopschinzoudhoff
Are the only things now make an evening go smooth off;   45
So, get me a Russian—till death I'm your debtor—

If he brings the whole Alphabet, so much the better.
And—Lord! if he would but, *in character,* sup
Off his fish-oil and candles, he'd quite set me up!
   Au revoir, my sweet girl—I must leave you in haste— 50
Little Gunter has brought me the liqueurs to taste.
Postscript
By the bye, have you found any friend that can construe
That Latin account, t'other day, of a Monster?
If we can't get a Russian, and *that thing* in Latin
Be not *too* improper, I think I'll bring that in. 55
  1813.
                                      1813.

FROM

LALLA ROOKH

Who has not heard of the Vale of Cashmere,
  With its roses the brightest that earth ever gave,
Its temples, and grottoes, and fountains as clear
  As the love-lighted eyes that hang over their wave?
Oh, to see it at sunset, when warm o'er the lake 5
  Its splendour at parting a summer eve throws,
Like a bride, full of blushes, when ling'ring to take
  A last look of her mirror at night ere she goes!
When the shrines through the foliage are gleaming half shown,
And each hallows the hour by some rites of its own. 10
Here the music of prayer from a minaret swells,
  Here the Magian his urn, full of perfume, is swinging,
And here, at the altar, a zone of sweet bells
  Round the waist of some fair Indian dancer is ringing.
Or to see it by moonlight, when mellowly shines 15
The light o'er its palaces, gardens, and shrines,
When the water-falls gleam, like a quick fall of stars,
And the nightingale's hymn from the Isle of Chenars
Is broken by laughs and light echoes of feet
From the cool, shining walks where the young people meet: 20
Or at morn, when the magic of daylight awakes
A new wonder each minute, as slowly it breaks,—
Hills, cupolas, fountains, called forth every one
Out of darkness, as if but just born of the Sun;
When the spirit of fragrance is up with the day, 25
From his haram of night-flowers stealing away,

And the wind, full of wantonness, wooes like a lover
The young aspen-trees, till they tremble all over;
When the East is as warm as the light of first hopes,
 And Day, with his banner of radiance unfurled,   30
Shines in through the mountainous portal that opes,
 Sublime, from that valley of bliss to the world!
   But never yet, by night or day,
   In dew of spring or summer's ray,
   Did the sweet valley shine so gay   35
   As now it shines—all love and light,
   Visions by day and feasts by night!
   A happier smile illumes each brow,
    With quicker spread each heart uncloses,
   And all is ecstasy, for now   40
    The valley holds its Feast of Roses;
   The joyous time, when pleasures pour
   Profusely round, and, in their shower,
   Hearts open, like the season's rose,—
    The flow'ret of a hundred leaves   45
   Expanding while the dew-fall flows,
    And every leaf its balm receives.
   'T was when the hour of evening came
    Upon the lake serene and cool,
   When Day had hid his sultry flame   50
    Behind the palms of Baramoule,
   When maids began to lift their heads,
   Refreshed from their embroidered beds,
   Where they had slept the sun away,
   And waked to moonlight and to play.   55
   All were abroad—the busiest hive
   On Bela's hills is less alive,
   When saffron-beds are full in flower,
   Than looked the valley in that hour.
   A thousand restless torches played   60
   Through every grove and island shade;
   A thousand sparkling lamps were set
   On every dome and minaret;
   And fields and pathways, far and near,
   Were lighted by a blaze so clear   65
   That you could see, in wandering round,
   The smallest rose-leaf on the ground.

Yet did the maids and matrons leave
Their veils at home, that brilliant eve;
And there were glancing eyes about,   70
And cheeks that would not dare shine out
In open day, but thought they might
Look lovely then because 't was night.
And all were free and wandering,
  And all exclaimed to all they met   75
That never did the summer bring
  So gay a Feast of Roses yet;
The moon had never shed a light
  So clear as that which blessed them there;
The roses ne'er shone half so bright,   80
  Nor they themselves looked half so fair.
And what a wilderness of flowers!
It seemed as though from all the bowers
And fairest fields of all the year
The mingled spoil were scattered here.   85
The lake, too, like a garden breathes
  With the rich buds that o'er it lie,—
As if a shower of fairy wreaths
Had fallen upon it from the sky!
And then the sounds of joy:—the beat   90
Of tabours and of dancing feet;
The minaret-crier's chaunt of glee
Sung from his lighted gallery,
And answered by a ziraleet
From neighbouring haram wild and sweet;   95
The merry laughter, echoing
From gardens where the silken swing
Wafts some delighted girl above
The top leaves of the orange-grove,
Or from those infant groups at play   100
Among the tents that line the way,
Flinging, unawed by slave or mother,
Handfuls of roses at each other.
Then the sounds from the lake:—the low whispering in boats,
 As they shoot through the moonlight; the dipping of oars; 105
And the wild, airy warbling that everywhere floats,
 Through the groves, round the islands, as if all the shores,
Like those of Kathay, uttered music, and gave

An answer in song to the kiss of each wave.
But the gentlest of all are those sounds full of feeling,   110
That soft from the lute of some lover are stealing,
Some lover who knows all the heart-touching power
Of a lute and a sigh in this magical hour.
Oh, best of delights as it everywhere is
To be near the loved *one*,—what a rapture is his   115
Who in moonlight and music thus sweetly may glide
O'er the Lake of Cashmere, with that *one* by his side!
If woman can make the worst wilderness dear,
Think, think what a heaven she must make of Cashmere!

    1811–16.   1817.

PERCY BYSSHE SHELLEY

FROM
QUEEN MAB

   Spirit. I was an infant when my mother went
To see an atheist burned. She took me there.
The dark-robed priests were met around the pile;
The multitude was gazing silently;
And as the culprit passed with dauntless mien,   5
Tempered disdain in his unaltering eye,
Mixed with a quiet smile, shone calmly forth.
The thirsty fire crept round his manly limbs;
His resolute eyes were scorched to blindness soon;
His death-pang rent my heart! The insensate mob   10
Uttered a cry of triumph, and I wept.
"Weep not, child!" cried my mother, "for that man
Has said, 'There is no God.'"
    Fairy.   There is no God!
Nature confirms the faith his death-groan sealed.
Let heaven and earth, let man's revolving race,   15
His ceaseless generations, tell their tale;
Let every part depending on the chain
That links it to the whole, point to the hand
That grasps its term! Let every seed that falls
In silent eloquence unfold its store   20
Of argument. Infinity within,

Infinity without, belie creation;
The exterminable spirit it contains
Is Nature's only God; but human pride
Is skilful to invent most serious names   25
To hide its ignorance.
    The name of God
Has fenced about all crime with holiness,
Himself the creature of his worshippers,
Whose names and attributes and passions change—
Seeva, Buddh, Foh, Jehovah, God, or Lord—   30
Even with the human dupes who build his shrines,
Still serving o'er the war-polluted world
For desolation's watchword; whether hosts
Stain his death-blushing chariot-wheels, as on
Triumphantly they roll whilst Brahmins raise   35
A sacred hymn to mingle with the groans;
Or countless partners of his power divide
His tyranny to weakness; or the smoke
Of burning towns, the cries of female helplessness,
Unarmed old age, and youth, and infancy,   40
Horribly massacred, ascend to heaven
In honour of his name; or, last and worst,
Earth groans beneath religion's iron age,
And priests dare babble of a God of peace
Even whilst their hands are red with guiltless blood,   45
Murdering the while, uprooting every germ
Of truth, exterminating, spoiling all,
Making the earth a slaughter-house!

1812–13.   1813.

FROM

ALASTOR

Earth, Ocean, Air, belovèd brotherhood!
If our great Mother has imbued my soul
With aught of natural piety to feel
Your love, and recompense the boon with mine;
If dewy morn, and odorous noon, and even,   5
With sunset and its gorgeous ministers,
And solemn midnight's tingling silentness,
If Autumn's hollow sighs in the sere wood,
And Winter robing with pure snow and crowns

Of starry ice the grey grass and bare boughs,   10
If Spring's voluptuous pantings when she breathes
Her first sweet kisses, have been dear to me;
If no bright bird, insect, or gentle beast
I consciously have injured, but still loved
And cherished these my kindred; then forgive   15
This boast, belovèd brethren, and withdraw
No portion of your wonted favour now!
    Mother of this unfathomable world,
Favour my solemn song! for I have loved
Thee ever, and thee only! I have watched   20
Thy shadow, and the darkness of thy steps,
And my heart ever gazes on the depth
Of thy deep mysteries. I have made my bed
In charnels and on coffins, where black Death
Keeps record of the trophies won from thee;   25
Hoping to still these obstinate questionings
Of thee and thine by forcing some lone ghost,
Thy messenger, to render up the tale
Of what we are. In lone and silent hours,
When night makes a weird sound of its own stillness,   30
Like an inspired and desperate alchemist
Staking his very life on some dark hope,
Have I mixed awful talk and asking looks
With my most innocent love, until strange tears,
Uniting with those breathless kisses, made   35
Such magic as compels the charmèd night
To render up thy charge. And though ne'er yet
Thou hast unveiled thy inmost sanctuary,
Enough from incommunicable dream,
And twilight phantasms, and deep noonday thought,   40
Has shone within me, that serenely now
And moveless, as a long-forgotten lyre
Suspended in the solitary dome
Of some mysterious and deserted fane,
I wait thy breath, Great Parent, that my strain   45
May modulate with murmurs of the air,
And motions of the forests and the sea,
And voice of living beings, and woven hymns
Of night and day, and the deep heart of man.

1815.   1816.

HYMN TO INTELLECTUAL BEAUTY

The awful shadow of some unseen Power
    Floats though unseen among us, visiting
    This various world with as inconstant wing
As summer winds that creep from flower to flower:
Like moonbeams that behind some piny mountain shower,   5
    It visits with inconstant glance
    Each human heart and countenance;
  Like hues and harmonies of evening,
    Like clouds in starlight widely spread,
    Like memory of music fled,   10
    Like aught that for its grace may be
Dear, and yet dearer for its mystery.

Spirit of Beauty, that dost consecrate
    With thine own hues all thou dost shine upon
    Of human thought or form, where art thou gone?   15
Why dost thou pass away, and leave our state,
This dim vast vale of tears, vacant and desolate?
    Ask why the sunlight not forever
    Weaves rainbows o'er yon mountain river;
Why aught should fail and fade that once is shown;   20
    Why fear and dream and death and birth
    Cast on the daylight of this earth
    Such gloom; why man has such a scope
For love and hate, despondency and hope.

No voice from some sublimer world hath ever   25
    To sage or poet these responses given;
    Therefore the names of demon, ghost, and Heaven
Remain the records of their vain endeavour,—
Frail spells, whose uttered charm might not avail to sever,
    From all we hear and all we see,   30
    Doubt, chance, and mutability.
  Thy light alone, like mist o'er mountains driven,
    Or music by the night wind sent
    Through strings of some still instrument,
    Or moonlight on a midnight stream,   35
Gives grace and truth to life's unquiet dream.

Love, hope, and self-esteem, like clouds, depart
    And come, for some uncertain moments lent.
    Man were immortal and omnipotent,
Didst thou, unknown and awful as thou art,   40
Keep with thy glorious train firm state within his heart.
    Thou messenger of sympathies
    That wax and wane in lovers' eyes,
Thou that to human thought art nourishment,
    Like darkness to a dying flame,   45
    Depart not as thy shadow came!
    Depart not, lest the grave should be,
    Like life and fear, a dark reality!

While yet a boy I sought for ghosts, and sped
    Through many a listening chamber, cave, and ruin, 50
    And starlight wood, with fearful steps pursuing
Hopes of high talk with the departed dead.
I called on poisonous names with which our youth is fed:
    I was not heard, I saw them not;
    When, musing deeply on the lot   55
Of life, at that sweet time when winds are wooing
    All vital things that wake to bring
    News of birds and blossoming,—
    Sudden thy shadow fell on me;
I shrieked, and clasped my hands in ecstasy!   60

I vowed that I would dedicate my powers
    To thee and thine—have I not kept the vow?
    With beating heart and streaming eyes, even now
I call the phantoms of a thousand hours
Each from his voiceless grave: they have in visioned bowers 65
    Of studious zeal or love's delight
    Outwatched with me the envious night;
They know that never joy illumed my brow
    Unlinked with hope that thou wouldst free
    This world from its dark slavery,   70
    That thou, O awful Loveliness,
Wouldst give whate'er these words cannot express.

The day becomes more solemn and serene
    When noon is past; there is a harmony
    In autumn, and a lustre in its sky,   75

Which through the summer is not heard or seen,
As if it could not be, as if it had not been!
    Thus let thy power, which like the truth
    Of nature on my passive youth
Descended, to my onward life supply   80
    Its calm,—to one who worships thee,
    And every form containing thee;
    Whom, Spirit fair, thy spells did bind
To fear himself, and love all human kind.

1816.   **1817.**

ODE TO THE WEST WIND

I

O wild West Wind, thou breath of Autumn's being,
Thou from whose unseen presence the leaves dead
Are driven, like ghosts from an enchanter fleeing,

Yellow, and black, and pale, and hectic red,
Pestilence-stricken multitudes; O thou   **5**
Who chariotest to their dark wintry bed

The wingèd seeds, where they lie cold and low,
Each like a corpse within its grave, until
Thine azure sister of the Spring shall blow

Her clarion o'er the dreaming earth, and fill   **10**
(Driving sweet buds like flocks to feed in air)
With living hues and odours plain and hill;

Wild Spirit, which art moving everywhere;
Destroyer and preserver; hear, O hear!

II

Thou on whose stream, 'mid the steep sky's commotion,   **15**
Loose clouds like earth's decaying leaves are shed,
Shook from the tangled boughs of heaven and ocean,

Angels of rain and lightning; there are spread
On the blue surface of thine airy surge,
Like the bright hair uplifted from the head   **20**

Of some fierce mænad, even from the dim verge
Of the horizon to the zenith's height,
The locks of the approaching storm. Thou dirge

Of the dying year, to which this closing night
Will be the dome of a vast sepulchre,   25
Vaulted with all thy congregated might

Of vapours, from whose solid atmosphere
Black rain, and fire, and hail will burst; O hear!

III

Thou who didst waken from his summer dreams
The blue Mediterranean, where he lay,   30
Lulled by the coil of his crystalline streams,

Beside a pumice isle in Baiae's bay,
And saw in sleep old palaces and towers
Quivering within the wave's intenser day,

All overgrown with azure moss and flowers   35
So sweet the sense faints picturing them! Thou
For whose path the Atlantic's level powers

Cleave themselves into chasms, while, far below,
The sea-blooms, and the oozy woods which wear
The sapless foliage of the ocean, know   40

Thy voice, and suddenly grow grey with fear,
And tremble and despoil themselves; O hear!

IV

If I were a dead leaf thou mightest bear;
If I were a swift cloud to fly with thee;
A wave to pant beneath thy power, and share   45

The impulse of thy strength, only less free
Than thou, O uncontrollable! if even
I were as in my boyhood, and could be

The comrade of thy wanderings over heaven,
As then, when to outstrip thy skyey speed   50
Scarce seemed a vision; I would ne'er have striven

As thus with thee in prayer in my sore need.
Oh, lift me as a wave, a leaf, a cloud!
I fall upon the thorns of life! I bleed!

A heavy weight of hours has chained and bowed   55
One too like thee—tameless, and swift, and proud.

v

Make me thy lyre, even as the forest is;
What if my leaves are falling like its own!
The tumult of thy mighty harmonies

Will take from both a deep, autumnal tone,   60
Sweet though in sadness. Be thou, Spirit fierce,
My spirit! Be thou me, impetuous one!

Drive my dead thoughts over the universe,
Like withered leaves, to quicken a new birth!
And, by the incantation of this verse,   65

Scatter, as from an unextinguished hearth
Ashes and sparks, my words among mankind!
Be through my lips to unawakened earth

The trumpet of a prophecy! O Wind,
If Winter comes, can Spring be far behind?   70
1819.   *1820.*

THE INDIAN SERENADE

I arise from dreams of thee
In the first sweet sleep of night,
When the winds are breathing low,
And the stars are shining bright:
I arise from dreams of thee,   5
And a spirit in my feet
Hath led me—who knows how?—
To thy chamber window, sweet!

The wandering airs, they faint
On the dark, the silent stream;   10
And the champak's odours fail
Like sweet thoughts in a dream;

The nightingale's complaint,
It dies upon her heart,
As I must on thine, 15
Oh, belovèd as thou art!

Oh, lift me from the grass!
I die! I faint! I fail!
Let thy love in kisses rain
On my lips and eyelids pale. 20
My cheek is cold and white, alas!
My heart beats loud and fast:
Oh, press it to thine own again,
Where it will break at last.

1819. *1822.*

THE MASK OF ANARCHY

As I lay asleep in Italy,
There came a voice from over the sea,
And with great power it forth led me
To walk in the visions of Poesy.

I met Murder on the way— 5
He had a mask like Castlereagh;
Very smooth he looked, yet grim;
Seven bloodhounds followed him.

All were fat; and well they might
Be in admirable plight,
For one by one, and two by two, 10
He tossed them human hearts to chew,
Which from his wide cloak he drew.

Next came Fraud, and he had on,
Like Lord Eldon, an ermined gown; 15
His big tears, for he wept well,
Turned to mill-stones as they fell;

And the little children, who
Round his feet played to and fro,
Thinking every tear a gem, 20
Had their brains knocked out by them.

Clothed with the Bible as with light,
And the shadows of the night,
Like Sidmouth, next Hypocrisy
On a crocodile rode by.   25

And many more Destructions played
In this ghastly masquerade,
All disguised, even to the eyes,
Like bishops, lawyers, peers, and spies.

Last came Anarchy; he rode   30
On a white horse splashed with blood;
He was pale even to the lips,
Like Death in the Apocalpyse.

And he wore a kingly crown;
In his hand a sceptre shone;   35
On his brow this mark I saw—
"I am God, and King, and Law!"

With a pace stately and fast,
Over English land he passed,
Trampling to a mire of blood   40
The adoring multitude.

And a mighty troop around
With their trampling shook the ground,
Waving each a bloody sword
For the service of their Lord.   45

And with glorious triumph they
Rode through England, proud and gay,
Drunk as with intoxication
Of the wine of desolation.

O'er fields and towns, from sea to sea,   50
Passed that pageant swift and free,
Tearing up, and trampling down,
Till they came to London town.

And each dweller, panic-stricken,
Felt his heart with terror sicken,   55
Hearing the tempestuous cry
Of the triumph of Anarchy.

For with pomp to meet him came,
Clothed in arms like blood and flame,
The hired murderers who did sing,   60
"Thou art God, and Law, and King.

"We have waited, weak and lone,
For thy coming, Mighty One!
Our purses are empty, our swords are cold:
Give us glory, and blood, and gold."   65

Lawyers and priests, a motley crowd,
To the earth their pale brows bowed;
Like a bad prayer not over-loud,
Whispering, "Thou art Law and God!"

Then all cried with one accord,   70
"Thou art King, and God, and Lord!
Anarchy, to thee we bow;
Be thy name made holy now!"

And Anarchy, the Skeleton,
Bowed and grinned to every one,   75
As well as if his education
Had cost ten millions to the nation.

For he knew the palaces
Of our kings were rightly his;
His the sceptre, crown, and globe,   80
And the gold-inwoven robe.

So he sent his slaves before
To seize upon the Bank and Tower,
And was proceeding with intent
To meet his pensioned Parliament,   85

When one fled past, a maniac maid,
And her name was Hope, she said;
But she looked more like Despair,
And she cried out in the air:

"My father Time is weak and grey   90
With waiting for a better day;
See how idiot-like he stands,
Fumbling with his palsied hands!

"He has had child after child,
And the dust of death is piled
Over every one but me—
Misery! oh, misery!"

95

Then she lay down in the street
Right before the horses' feet,
Expecting with a patient eye
Murder, Fraud, and Anarchy:—

100

When between her and her foes
A mist, a light, an image rose,
Small at first, and weak and frail,
Like the vapour of a vale;

105

Till, as clouds grow on the blast,
Like tower-crowned giants striding fast,
And glare with lightnings as they fly,
And speak in thunder to the sky,

It grew—a shape arrayed in mail
Brighter than the viper's scale,
And upborne on wings whose grain
Was as the light of sunny rain.

110

On its helm, seen far away,
A planet like the morning's lay;
And those plumes its light rained through,
Like a shower of crimson dew.

115

With step as soft as wind it passed
O'er the heads of men—so fast
That they knew the presence there,
And looked—but all was empty air.

120

As flowers beneath May's footstep waken,
As stars from Night's loose hair are shaken,
As waves arise when loud winds call,
Thoughts sprung where'er that step did fall.

125

And the prostrate multitude
Looked—and, ankle-deep in blood,
Hope, that maiden most serene,
Was walking with a quiet mien;

And Anarchy, the ghastly birth,   130
Lay dead earth upon the earth;
The Horse of Death, tameless as wind,
Fled, and with his hoofs did grind
To dust the murderers thronged behind.

A rushing light of clouds and splendour,   135
A sense awakening and yet tender,
Was heard and felt; and at its close
These words of joy and fear arose,

As if their own indignant Earth,
Which gave the sons of England birth,   140
Had felt their blood upon her brow,
And, shuddering with a mother's throe,

Had turnèd every drop of blood
By which her face had been bedewed
To an accent unwithstood,   145
As if her heart had cried aloud:

"Men of England, heirs of glory,
Heroes of unwritten story,
Nurslings of one mighty Mother,
Hopes of her and one another;   150

"Rise like lions after slumber,
In unvanquishable number!
Shake your chains to earth like dew
Which in sleep had fallen on you!
Ye are many, they are few.   155

"What is Freedom?—Ye can tell
That which Slavery is too well,
For its very name has grown
To an echo of your own.

"'T is to work and have such pay   160
As just keeps life from day to day
In your limbs, as in a cell
For the tyrants' use to dwell;

"So that ye for them are made
Loom, and plough, and sword, and spade;   165

With or without your own will, bent
To their defence and nourishment.

"'T is to see your children weak
With their mothers pine and peak,
When the winter winds are bleak—   170
They are dying whilst I speak.

"'T is to hunger for such diet
As the rich man in his riot
Casts to the fat dogs that lie
Surfeiting beneath his eye.   175

"'T is to let the ghost of gold
Take from toil a thousandfold
More than e'er its substance could
In the tyrannies of old;

"Paper coin—that forgery   180
Of the title-deeds which ye
Hold to something from the worth
Of the inheritance of Earth.

"'T is to be a slave in soul,
And to hold no strong control   185
Over your own wills, but be
All that others make of ye.

"And at length when ye complain
With a murmur weak and vain,
'T is to see the tyrant's crew   190
Ride over your wives and you—
Blood is on the grass like dew!

"Then it is to feel revenge,
Fiercely thirsting to exchange
Blood for blood, and wrong for wrong: 195
Do not thus when ye are strong!

"Birds find rest in narrow nest,
When weary of their wingèd quest;
Beasts find fare in woody lair,
When storm and snow are in the air.   200

"Horses, oxen, have a home
When from daily toil they come;
Household dogs, when the wind roars,
Find a home within warm doors.

"Asses, swine, have litter spread,   205
And with fitting food are fed;
All things have a home but one—
Thou, O Englishman, hast none!

"This is Slavery: savage men,
Or wild beasts within a den,   210
Would endure not as ye do—
But such ills they never knew.

"What art thou, Freedom? Oh, could slaves
Answer from their living graves
This demand, tyrants would flee   215
Like a dream's dim imagery.

"Thou art not, as impostors say,
A shadow soon to pass away,
A superstition, and a name
Echoing from the cave of Fame.   220

"For the labourer thou art bread,
And a comely table spread,
From his daily labour come,
In a neat and happy home.

"Thou art clothes, and fire, and food,   225
For the trampled multitude—
No, in countries that are free
Such starvation cannot be
As in England now we see.

"To the rich thou art a check;   230
When his foot is on the neck
Of his victim, thou dost make
That he treads upon a snake.

"Thou art Justice—ne'er for gold
May thy righteous laws be sold,   235
As laws are in England; thou
Shield'st alike both high and low,

"Thou art Wisdom—freemen never
Dream that God will damn forever
All who think those things untrue   240
Of which priests make such ado.

"Thou art Peace—never by thee
Would blood and treasure wasted be,
As tyrants wasted them when all
Leagued to quench thy flame in Gaul.   245

"What if English toil and blood
Was poured forth, even as a flood?
It availed, O Liberty!
To dim but not extinguish thee.

"Thou art Love—the rich have kissed   250
Thy feet, and, like him following Christ,
Give their substance to the free
And through the rough world follow thee;

"Or turn their wealth to arms, and make
War for thy belovèd sake   255
On wealth and war and fraud, whence they
Drew the power which is their prey.

"Science, Poetry, and Thought
Are thy lamps; they make the lot
Of the dwellers in a cot   260
Such they curse their Maker not.

"Spirit, Patience, Gentleness,
All that can adorn and bless,
Art thou—let deeds, not words, express
Thine exceeding loveliness.   265

"Let a great Assembly be
Of the fearless and the free,
On some spot of English ground
Where the plains stretch wide around.

"Let the blue sky overhead,   270
The green earth on which ye tread,
All that must eternal be,
Witness the solemnity.

"From the corners uttermost
Of the bounds of English coast;   275
From every hut, village, and town,
Where those, who live and suffer, moan
For others' misery or their own;

"From the workhouse and the prison,
Where, pale as corpses newly risen,   280
Women, children, young and old,
Groan for pain, and weep for cold;

"From the haunts of daily life,
Where is waged the daily strife
With common wants and common cares,   285
Which sows the human heart with tares;

"Lastly, from the palaces,
Where the murmur of distress
Echoes, like the distant sound
Of a wind alive, around   290

"Those prison-halls of wealth and fashion,
Where some few feel such compassion
For those who groan, and toil, and wail,
As must make their brethren pale;—

"Ye who suffer woes untold,   295
Or to feel or to behold
Your lost country bought and sold
With a price of blood and gold;

"Let a vast Assembly be,
And with great solemnity   300
Declare with measured words that ye
Are, as God has made ye, free!

"Be your strong and simple words
Keen to wound as sharpened swords;
And wide as targes let them be,   305
With their shade to cover ye.

"Let the tyrants pour around
With a quick and startling sound,
Like the loosening of a sea,
Troops of armed emblazonry.   .   310

"Let the charged artillery drive,
Till the dead air seems alive
With the clash of clanging wheels
And the tramp of horses' heels.

"Let the fixèd bayonet   315
Gleam with sharp desire to wet
Its bright point in English blood,
Looking keen as one for food.

"Let the horsemen's scimitars
Wheel and flash, like sphereless stars   320
Thirsting to eclipse their burning
In a sea of death and mourning.

"Stand ye calm and resolute,
Like a forest close and mute,
With folded arms, and looks which are   325
Weapons of unvanquished war.

"And let Panic, who outspeeds
The career of armèd steeds,
Pass, a disregarded shade,
Through your phalanx undismayed.   330

"Let the laws of your own land,
Good or ill, between ye stand,
Hand to hand, and foot to foot,
Arbiters of the dispute;

"The old laws of England, they   335
Whose reverend heads with age are grey,
Children of a wiser day,
And whose solemn voice must be
Thine own echo, Liberty!

"On those who first should violate   340
Such sacred heralds in their state,
Rest the blood that must ensue;
And it will not rest on you.

"And if then the tyrants dare,
Let them ride among you there,   345
Slash, and stab, and maim, and hew:
What they like, that let them do.

"With folded arms and steady eyes,
And little fear and less surprise,
Look upon them as they slay,　　　　　　350
Till their rage has died away.

"Then they will return with shame
To the place from which they came,
And the blood thus shed will speak
In hot blushes on their cheek.　　　　　　355

"Every woman in the land
Will point at them as they stand;
They will hardly dare to greet
Their acquaintance in the street.

"And the bold true warriors,　　　　　　360
Who have hugged Danger in wars,
Will turn to those who would be free,
Ashamed of such base company.

"And that slaughter to the nation
Shall steam up like inspiration,　　　　　365
Eloquent, oracular;
A volcano heard afar.

"And these words shall then become
Like Oppression's thundered doom,
Ringing through each heart and brain,　　　370
Heard again—again—again!

"Rise like lions after slumber
In unvanquishable number!
Shake your chains to earth, like dew
Which in sleep had fallen on you—　　　　375
Ye are many, they are few!"

1819.　　　　　　　　　　　　　　1832.

THE CLOUD

I bring fresh showers for the thirsting flowers,
　　From the seas and the streams.
I bear light shade for the leaves when laid
　　In their noonday dreams.

From my wings are shaken the dews that waken   5
 The sweet buds every one,
When rocked to rest on their mother's breast,
 As she dances about the sun.
I wield the flail of the lashing hail,
 And whiten the green plains under,   10
And then again I dissolve it in rain,
 And laugh as I pass in thunder.

I sift the snow on the mountains below,
 And their great pines groan aghast;
And all the night 't is my pillow white,   15
 While I sleep in the arms of the blast.
Sublime on the towers of my skyey bowers,
 Lightning my pilot sits;
In a cavern under is fettered the thunder,
 It struggles and howls at fits: 20
Over earth and ocean, with gentle motion,
 This pilot is guiding me,
Lured by the love of the genii that move
 In the depths of the purple sea;
Over the rills and the crags and the hills,   25
 Over the lakes and the plains,
Wherever he dream, under mountain or stream,
 The spirit he loves remains;
And I all the while bask in heaven's blue smile,
 Whilst he is dissolving in rains.   30

The sanguine sunrise, with his meteor eyes,
 And his burning plumes outspread,
Leaps on the back of my sailing rack,
 When the morning star shines dead;
As on the jag of a mountain crag,   35
 Which an earthquake rocks and swings,
An eagle alit one moment may sit
 In the light of its golden wings.
And when sunset may breathe, from the lit sea beneath,
 Its ardours of rest and of love,   40
And the crimson pall of eve may fall
 From the depth of heaven above,
With wings folded I rest, on mine airy nest,
 As still as a brooding dove.

That orbèd maiden, with white fire laden,   45
   Whom mortals call the moon,
Glides glimmering o'er my fleece-like floor,
   By the midnight breezes strewn;
And wherever the beat of her unseen feet,
   Which only the angels hear,   50
May have broken the woof of my tent's thin roof,
   The stars peep behind her and peer;
And I laugh to see them whirl and flee,
   Like a swarm of golden bees,
When I widen the rent in my wind-built tent,   55
   Till the calm rivers, lakes, and seas,
Like strips of the sky fallen through me on high,
   Are each paved with the moon and these.

I bind the sun's throne with a burning zone,
   And the moon's with a girdle of pearl;   60
The volcanoes are dim, and the stars reel and swim,
   When the whirlwinds my banner unfurl.
From cape to cape, with a bridge-like shape,
   Over a torrent sea,
Sunbeam-proof, I hang like a roof;   65
   The mountains its columns be.
The triumphal arch, through which I march,
   With hurricane, fire, and snow,
When the powers of the air are chained to my chair,
   Is the million-colored bow;   70
The sphere-fire above its soft colors wove,
   While the moist earth was laughing below.

I am the daughter of earth and water,
   And the nursling of the sky;
I pass through the pores of the ocean and shores;   75
   I change, but I cannot die:
For after the rain, when with never a stain
   The pavilion of heaven is bare,
And the winds and sunbeams with their convex gleams
   Build up the blue dome of air,   80
I silently laugh at my own cenotaph,
   And out of the caverns of rain,
Like a child from the womb, like a ghost from the tomb,
   I arise and unbuild it again.

1820.   1820.

TO A SKYLARK

Hail to thee, blithe spirit!
   Bird thou never wert,
That from heaven, or near it,
   Pourest thy full heart
In profuse strains of unpremeditated art.   5

Higher still and higher
   From the earth thou springest
Like a cloud of fire;
   The blue deep thou wingest,
And singing still dost soar, and soaring ever sing-
      est.   10

In the golden lightning
   Of the sunken sun,
O'er which clouds are bright'ning,
   Thou dost float and run;
Like an unbodied joy whose race is just begun.   15

The pale purple even
   Melts around thy flight;
Like a star of heaven,
   In the broad daylight
Thou art unseen, but yet I hear thy shrill delight,   20

Keen as are the arrows
   Of that silver sphere,
Whose intense lamp narrows
   In the white dawn clear,
Until we hardly see—we feel that it is there.   25

All the earth and air
   With thy voice is loud,
As, when night is bare,
   From one lonely cloud
The moon rains out her beams, and heaven is over-
      flowed.   30

What thou art we know not;
   What is most like thee?
From rainbow clouds there flow not
   Drops so bright to see
As from thy presence showers a rain of melody.   35

Like a poet hidden
In the light of thought,
Singing hymns unbidden,
Till the world is wrought
To sympathy with hopes and fears it heeded not; 40

Like a high-born maiden
In a palace tower,
Soothing her love-laden
Soul in secret hour
With music sweet as love, which overflows her
bower; 45

Like a glow-worm golden
In a dell of dew,
Scattering unbeholden
Its aërial hue
Among the flowers and grass, which screen it from
the view; 50

Like a rose embowered
In its own green leaves,
By warm winds deflowered,
Till the scent it gives
Makes faint with too much sweet these heavy-
wingèd thieves; 55

Sound of vernal showers
On the twinkling grass,
Rain-awakened flowers,
All that ever was
Joyous and clear and fresh, thy music doth surpass. 60

Teach us, sprite or bird,
What sweet thoughts are thine;
I have never heard
Praise of love or wine
That panted forth a flood of rapture so divine. 65

Chorus hymenæal,
Or triumphal chaunt,
Matched with thine, would be all
But an empty vaunt,
A thing wherein we feel there is some hidden want. 70

What objects are the fountains
    Of thy happy strain?
What fields or waves or mountains?
    What shapes of sky or plain?
What love of thine own kind? what ignorance of
        pain?   75

With thy clear keen joyance
    Languor cannot be;
Shadow of annoyance
    Never came near thee;
Thou lovest, but ne'er knew love's sad satiety.   80

Waking or asleep
    Thou of death must deem
Things more true and deep
    Than we mortals dream,
Or how could thy notes flow in such a crystal
        stream?   85

We look before and after,
    And pine for what is not;
Our sincerest laughter
    With some pain is fraught;
Our sweetest songs are those that tell of saddest
        thought.   90

Yet if we could scorn
    Hate and pride and fear,
If we were things born
    Not to shed a tear,
I know not how thy joy we ever should come
        near.   95

Better than all measures
    Of delightful sound,
Better than all treasures
    That in books are found,
Thy skill to poet were, thou scorner of the
        ground!   100

Teach me half the gladness
  That thy brain must know,
Such harmonious madness
  From my lips would flow,
The world should listen then, as I am listening
      now.   105

    1820.   *1820.*

FROM

EPIPSYCHIDION

The day is come, and thou wilt fly with me!
To whatsoe'er of dull mortality
Is mine remain a vestal sister still;
To the intense, the deep, the imperishable—
Not mine but me—henceforth be thou united,   5
Even as a bride, delighting and delighted.
The hour is come:—the destined star has risen
Which shall descend upon a vacant prison.
The walls are high, the gates are strong, thick set
The sentinels—but true love never yet   10
Was thus constrained; it overleaps all fence:
Like lightning with invisible violence
Piercing its continents; like heaven's free breath,
Which he who grasps can hold not; liker Death,
Who rides upon a thought, and makes his way   15
Through temple, tower, and palace, and the array
Of arms: more strength has love than he or they;
For it can burst his charnel, and make free
The limbs in chains, the heart in agony,
The soul in dust and chaos.
                              Emily,   20
A ship is floating in the harbour now;
A wind is hovering o'er the mountain's brow;
There is a path on the sea's azure floor,—
No keel has ever ploughed that path before;
The halcyons brood around the foamless isles;   25
The treacherous ocean has forsworn its wiles;
The merry mariners are bold and free:
Say, my heart's sister, wilt thou sail with me?
Our bark is as an albatross, whose nest

Is a far Eden of the purple East; 30
And we between her wings will sit, while Night
And Day and Storm and Calm pursue their flight,
Our ministers, along the boundless sea,
Treading each other's heels, unheededly.
It is an isle under Ionian skies, 35
Beautiful as a wreck of Paradise;
And, for the harbours are not safe and good,
This land would have remained a solitude
But for some pastoral people native there,
Who from the Elysian, clear, and golden air 40
Draw the last spirit of the age of gold,—
Simple and spirited, innocent and bold.
The blue Ægean girds this chosen home,
With ever-changing sound and light and foam,
Kissing the sifted sands and caverns hoar; 45
And all the winds wandering along the shore
Undulate with the undulating tide:
There are thick woods where sylvan forms abide,
And many a fountain, rivulet, and pond,
As clear as elemental diamond, 50
Or serene morning air; and, far beyond,
The mossy tracks made by the goats and deer
(Which the rough shepherd treads but once a year)
Pierce into glades, caverns, and bowers, and halls
Built round with ivy, which the waterfalls 55
Illumining, with sound that never fails
Accompany the noonday nightingales:
And all the place is peopled with sweet airs;
The light clear element which the isle wears
Is heavy with the scent of lemon-flowers, 60
Which floats like mist laden with unseen showers,
And falls upon the eyelids like faint sleep;
And from the moss violets and jonquils peep,
And dart their arrowy odour through the brain,
Till you might faint with that delicious pain: 65
And every motion, odour, beam, and tone
With that deep music is in unison,
Which is a soul within the soul; they seem
Like echoes of an antenatal dream.
It is an isle 'twixt heaven, air, earth, and sea, 70

Cradled and hung in clear tranquillity;
Bright as that wandering Eden, Lucifer,
Washed by the soft blue oceans of young air.
It is a favoured place. Famine or blight,
Pestilence, war, and earthquake, never light   75
Upon its mountain-peaks; blind vultures, they
Sail onward far upon their fatal way.
The wingèd storms, chaunting their thunder-psalm
To other lands, leave azure chasms of calm
Over this isle, or weep themselves in dew,   80
From which its fields and woods ever renew
Their green and golden immortality.
And from the sea there rise, and from the sky
There fall, clear exhalations, soft and bright,
Veil after veil, each hiding some delight;   85
Which sun or moon or zephyr draws aside,
Till the isle's beauty, like a naked bride
Glowing at once with love and loveliness,
Blushes and trembles at its own excess.
Yet, like a buried lamp, a soul no less   90
Burns in the heart of this delicious isle,
An atom of the Eternal, whose own smile
Unfolds itself, and may be felt, not seen,
O'er the grey rocks, blue waves, and forests green,
Filling their bare and void interstices.   95
But the chief marvel of the wilderness
Is a lone dwelling, built by whom or how
None of the rustic island-people know:
'T is not a tower of strength, though with its height
It overtops the woods; but for delight   100
Some wise and tender ocean-king, ere crime
Had been invented, in the world's young prime,
Reared it, a wonder of that simple time,
An envy of the isles, a pleasure-house
Made sacred to his sister and his spouse.   105
It scarce seems now a wreck of human art,
But, as it were, Titanic; in the heart
Of Earth having assumed its form, then grown
Out of the mountains, from the living stone,
Lifting itself in caverns light and high: 110
For all the antique and learnèd imagery

Has been erased, and in the place of it
The ivy and the wild vine interknit
The volumes of their many-twining stems;
Parasite flowers illume with dewy gems   115
The lampless halls, and, when they fade, the sky
Peeps through their winter-woof of tracery
With moonlight patches, or star-atoms keen,
Or fragments of the day's intense serene,—
Working mosaic on their Parian floors.   120
And, day and night, aloof, from the high towers
And terraces, the Earth and Ocean seem
To sleep in one another's arms, and dream
Of waves, flowers, clouds, woods, rocks, and all that we
Read in their smiles, and call reality.   125
     This isle and house are mine, and I have vowed
Thee to be lady of the solitude.
And I have fitted up some chambers there
Looking towards the golden Eastern air,
And level with the living winds which flow   130
Like waves above the living waves below.
I have sent books and music there, and all
Those instruments with which high spirits call
The future from its cradle, and the past
Out of its grave, and make the present last   135
In thoughts and joys which sleep, but cannot die,
Folded within their own eternity.
Our simple life wants little, and true taste
Hires not the pale drudge Luxury to waste
The scene it would adorn; and therefore still   140
Nature with all her children haunts the hill.
The ring-dove, in the embowering ivy, yet
Keeps up her love-lament, and the owls flit
Round the evening tower, and the young stars glance
Between the quick bats in their twilight dance;   145
The spotted deer bask in the fresh moonlight
Before our gate, and the slow silent night
Is measured by the pants of their calm sleep.
Be this our home in life; and when years heap
Their withered hours, like leaves, on our decay,   150
Let us become the overhanging day,
The living soul of this Elysian isle,

Conscious, inseparable, one. Meanwhile
We two will rise, and sit, and walk together,
Under the roof of blue Ionian weather,   155
And wander in the meadows, or ascend
The mossy mountains, where the blue heavens bend
With lightest winds, to touch their paramour;
Or linger where the pebble-paven shore,
Under the quick, faint kisses of the sea,   160
Trembles and sparkles as with ecstasy,—
Possessing and possessed by all that is
Within that calm circumference of bliss,
And by each other, till to love and live
Be one: or, at the noontide hour, arrive   165
Where some old cavern hoar seems yet to keep
The moonlight of the expired night asleep,
Through which the awakened day can never peep;
A veil for our seclusion, close as night's,
Where secure sleep may kill thine innocent lights;   170
Sleep, the fresh dew of languid love, the rain
Whose drops quench kisses till they burn again.
And we will talk, until thought's melody
Become too sweet for utterance, and it die
In words, to live again in looks, which dart   175
With thrilling tone into the voiceless heart,
Harmonizing silence without a sound:
Our breath shall intermix, our bosoms bound,
And our veins beat together; and our lips,
With other eloquence than words, eclipse   180
The soul that burns between them; and the wells
Which boil under our being's inmost cells,
The fountains of our deepest life, shall be
Confused in passion's golden purity,
As mountain-springs under the morning sun.   185
We shall become the same, we shall be one
Spirit within two frames—oh, wherefore two?
One passion in twin-hearts, which grows and grew,
Till, like two meteors of expanding flame,
Those spheres instinct with it become the same,   190
Touch, mingle, are transfigured; ever still
Burning, yet ever inconsumable;
In one another's substance finding food,

Like flames too pure and light and unimbued
  To nourish their bright lives with baser prey,   195
  Which point to heaven and cannot pass away:
One hope within two wills, one will beneath
Two overshadowing minds, one life, one death.
One heaven, one hell, one immortality,
  And one annihiliation!

                  Woe is me!   200
The wingèd words on which my soul would pierce
Into the height of love's rare universe
Are chains of lead around its flight of fire.
I pant, I sink, I tremble, I expire!

1821.   *1821.*

ADONAIS

I weep for Adonais—he is dead!
O, weep for Adonais! though our tears
Thaw not the frost which binds so dear a head!
And thou, sad Hour, selected from all years
To mourn our loss, rouse thy obscure compeers,   5
And teach them thine own sorrow: say, "With me
Died Adonais; till the Future dares
Forget the Past, his fate and fame shall be
An echo and a light unto eternity!"

Where wert thou, mighty Mother, when he lay,   10
When thy son lay, pierced by the shaft which flies
In darkness? where was lorn Urania
When Adonais died? With veilèd eyes,
'Mid listening Echoes, in her paradise
She sate, while one, with soft enamoured breath,   15
Rekindled all the fading melodies,
With which, like flowers that mock the corse beneath,
He had adorned and hid the coming bulk of death.

O, weep for Adonais—he is dead!
Wake, melancholy Mother, wake and weep!—   20
Yet wherefore? Quench within their burning bed
Thy fiery tears, and let thy loud heart keep,
Like his, a mute and uncomplaining sleep;
For he is gone where all things wise and fair

Descend: oh, dream not that the amorous Deep　　25
Will yet restore him to the vital air;
Death feeds on his mute voice, and laughs at our despair.

Most musical of mourners, weep again!
Lament anew, Urania!—He died,
Who was the sire of an immortal strain,　　　　30
Blind, old, and lonely, when his country's pride
The priest, the slave, and the liberticide
Trampled and mocked with many a loathèd rite
Of lust and blood; he went, unterrified,
Into the gulf of death; but his clear sprite　　35
Yet reigns o'er earth, the third among the sons of light.

Most musical of mourners, weep anew!
Not all to that bright station dared to climb;
And happier they their happiness who knew,
Whose tapers yet burn through that night of time　40
In which suns perished; others more sublime,
Struck by the envious wrath of man or God,
Have sunk, extinct in their refulgent prime;
And some yet live, treading the thorny road
Which leads, through toil and hate, to Fame's serene abode. 45

But now thy youngest, dearest one has perished,
The nursling of thy widowhood, who grew
Like a pale flower by some sad maiden cherished
And fed with true-love tears instead of dew;
Most musical of mourners, weep anew!　　　　50
Thy extreme hope, the loveliest and the last,
The bloom whose petals, nipt before they blew,
Died on the promise of the fruit, is waste;
The broken lily lies—the storm is overpast.

To that high capital where kingly Death　　　55
Keeps his pale court in beauty and decay,
He came; and bought, with price of purest breath,
A grave among the eternal.—Come away!
Haste, while the vault of blue Italian day
Is yet his fitting charnel-roof! while still　　60
He lies as if in dewy sleep he lay!
Awake him not! surely he takes his fill
Of deep and liquid rest, forgetful of all ill.

He will awake no more, oh, never more!
Within the twilight chamber spreads apace   65
The shadow of white Death, and at the door
Invisible Corruption waits to trace
His extreme way to her dim dwelling-place;
The eternal Hunger sits, but pity and awe
Soothe her pale rage, nor dares she to deface   70
So fair a prey, till darkness and the law
Of change shall o'er his sleep the mortal curtain draw.

O, weep for Adonais!—The quick Dreams,
The passion-wingèd ministers of thought,
Who were his flocks, whom near the living streams   75
Of his young spirit he fed, and whom he taught
The love which was its music, wander not,
Wander no more, from kindling brain to brain,
But droop there, whence they sprung; and mourn their
    lot
Round the cold heart, where, after their sweet pain,   80
They ne'er will gather strength, or find a home again.

And one with trembling hands clasps his cold head,
And fans him with her moonlight wings, and cries,
"Our love, our hope, our sorrow, is not dead!
See, on the silken fringe of his faint eyes,   85
Like dew upon a sleeping flower, there lies
A tear some Dream has loosened from his brain."
Lost angel of a ruined paradise!
She knew not 't was her own, as with no stain
She faded, like a cloud which had outwept its rain.   90

One from a lucid urn of starry dew
Washed his light limbs as if embalming them;
Another clipt her profuse locks, and threw
The wreath upon him, like an anadem,
Which frozen tears instead of pearls begem;   95
Another in her wilful grief would break
Her bow and wingèd reeds, as if to stem
A greater loss with one which was more weak,
And dull the barbèd fire against his frozen cheek.

Another Splendour on his mouth alit,   100
That mouth whence it was wont to draw the breath

Which gave it strength to pierce the guarded wit,
And pass into the panting heart beneath
With lightning and with music: the damp death
Quenched its caress upon his icy lips;   105
And, as a dying meteor stains a wreath
Of moonlight vapour, which the cold night clips,
It flushed through his pale limbs, and passed to its eclipse.

And others came—Desires and Adorations,
Wingèd Persuasions and veiled Destinies,   110
Splendours, and Glooms, and glimmering Incarnations
Of hopes and fears, and twilight Fantasies;
And Sorrow, with her family of Sighs,
And Pleasure, blind with tears, led by the gleam
Of her own dying smile instead of eyes,   115
Came in slow pomp;—the moving pomp might seem
Like pageantry of mist on an autumnal stream.

All he had loved, and moulded into thought,
From shape, and hue, and odour, and sweet sound,
Lamented Adonais. Morning sought   120
Her eastern watch-tower, and her hair, unbound,
Wet with the tears which should adorn the ground,
Dimmed the aërial eyes that kindle day;
Afar the melancholy thunder moaned;
Pale Ocean in unquiet slumber lay,   125
And the wild winds flew round, sobbing in their dismay.

Lost Echo sits amid the voiceless mountains,
And feeds her grief with his remembered lay,
And will no more reply to winds or fountains,
Or amorous birds perched on the young green spray,   130
Or herdsman's horn, or bell at closing day,
Since she can mimic not his lips, more dear
Than those for whose disdain she pined away
Into a shadow of all sounds:—a drear
Murmur, between their songs, is all the woodmen hear. 135

Grief made the young Spring wild, and she threw down
Her kindling buds, as if she Autumn were,
Or they dead leaves; since her delight is flown,
For whom should she have waked the sullen year?

To Phœbus was not Hyacinth so dear,   140
Nor to himself Narcissus, as to both
Thou, Adonais: wan they stand and sere
Amid the faint companions of their youth,
With dew all turned to tears, odour to sighing ruth.

Thy spirit's sister, the lorn nightingale,   145
Mourns not her mate with such melodious pain;
Not so the eagle, who like thee could scale
Heaven, and could nourish in the sun's domain
Her mighty youth with morning, doth complain,
Soaring and screaming round her empty nest,   150
As Albion wails for thee: the curse of Cain
Light on his head who pierced thy innocent breast,
And scared the angel soul that was its earthly guest!

Ah, woe is me! Winter is come and gone,
But grief returns with the revolving year;   155
The airs and streams renew their joyous tone;
The ants, the bees, the swallows, reappear;
Fresh leaves and flowers deck the dead Seasons' bier;
The amorous birds now pair in every brake,
And build their mossy homes in field and brere;   160
And the green lizard and the golden snake,
Like unimprisoned flames, out of their trance awake.

Through wood and stream and field and hill and ocean,
A quickening life from the Earth's heart has burst,
As it has ever done, with change and motion,   165
From the great morning of the world when first
God dawned on Chaos; in its stream immersed,
The lamps of heaven flash with a softer light;
All baser things pant with life's sacred thirst,
Diffuse themselves, and spend in love's delight   170
The beauty and the joy of their renewèd might.

The leprous corpse, touched by this spirit tender,
Exhales itself in flowers of gentle breath;
Like incarnations of the stars, when splendour
Is changed to fragrance, they illumine death,   175
And mock the merry worm that wakes beneath.
Naught we know dies. Shall that alone which knows

Be as a sword consumed before the sheath
By sightless lightning?—th' intense atom glows
A moment, then is quenched in a most cold repose.　　180

Alas! that all we loved of him should be,
But for our grief, as if it had not been,
And grief itself be mortal! Woe is me!
Whence are we, and why are we? of what scene
The actors or spectators? Great and mean　　185
Meet massed in death, who lends what life must borrow.
As long as skies are blue, and fields are green,
Evening must usher night, night urge the morrow,
Month follow month with woe, and year wake year to sorrow.

He will awake no more, oh never more!　　190
"Wake thou," cried Misery, "childless Mother, rise
Out of thy sleep, and slake, in thy heart's core,
A wound more fierce than his with tears and sighs!"
And all the Dreams that watched Urania's eyes,
And all the Echoes whom their sister's song　　195
Had held in holy silence, cried, "Arise!"
Swift as a Thought by the snake Memory stung,
From her ambrosial rest the fading Splendour sprung.

She rose like an autumnal Night, that springs
Out of the East, and follows wild and drear　　200
The golden Day, which, on eternal wings,
Even as a ghost abandoning a bier,
Had left the Earth a corpse. Sorrow and fear
So struck, so roused, so rapt Urania;
So saddened round her like an atmosphere　　205
Of stormy mist; so swept her on her way
Even to the mournful place where Adonais lay.

Out of her secret paradise she sped,
Through camps and cities rough with stone, and steel,
And human hearts, which, to her airy tread　　210
Yielding not, wounded the invisible
Palms of her tender feet where'er they fell;
And barbèd tongues, and thoughts more sharp than they,
Rent the soft form they never could repel,
Whose sacred blood, like the young tears of May,　　215
Paved with eternal flowers that undeserving way.

In the death-chamber for a moment Death,
Shamed by the presence of that living Might,
Blushed to annihilation, and the breath
Revisited those lips, and life's pale light   220
Flashed through those limbs, so late her dear delight.
"Leave me not wild and drear and comfortless,
As silent lightning leaves the starless night!
Leave me not!" cried Urania: her distress
Roused Death; Death rose and smiled, and met her vain
      caress.   225

"Stay yet awhile! speak to me once again;
Kiss me, so long but as a kiss may live;
And in my heartless breast and burning brain
That word, that kiss, shall all thoughts else survive,
With food of saddest memory kept alive,   230
Now thou art dead, as if it were a part
Of thee, my Adonais! I would give
All that I am to be as thou now art!
But I am chained to Time, and cannot thence depart!

"O gentle child, beautiful as thou wert,   235
Why didst thou leave the trodden paths of men
Too soon, and with weak hands though mighty heart
Dare the unpastured dragon in his den?
Defenceless as thou wert, oh where was then
Wisdom the mirrored shield, or scorn the spear?   240
Or hadst thou waited the full cycle, when
Thy spirit should have filled its crescent sphere,
The monsters of life's waste had fled from thee like deer.

"The herded wolves, bold only to pursue;
The obscene ravens clamorous o'er the dead;   245
The vultures, to the conqueror's banner true,
Who feed where Desolation first has fed,
And whose wings rain contagion,—how they fled,
When, like Apollo, from his golden bow
The Pythian of the age one arrow sped,   250
And smiled!—The spoilers tempt no second blow;
They fawn on the proud feet that spurn them lying low.

"The sun comes forth, and many reptiles spawn;
He sets, and each ephemeral insect then
Is gathered into death without a dawn,   255
And the immortal stars awake again.
So is it in the world of living men:
A godlike mind soars forth, in its delight
Making earth bare and veiling heaven; and when
It sinks, the swarms that dimmed or shared its light   260
Leave to its kindred lamps the spirit's awful night."

Thus ceased she. And the mountain shepherds came,
Their garlands sere, their magic mantles rent:
The Pilgrim of Eternity, whose fame
Over his living head like heaven is bent,   265
An early but enduring monument,
Came, veiling all the lightnings of his song
In sorrow; from her wilds Ierne sent
The sweetest lyrist of her saddest wrong,
And love taught grief to fall like music from his tongue.   270

Midst others of less note, came one frail form,
A phantom among men; companionless
As the last cloud of an expiring storm,
Whose thunder is its knell: he, as I guess,
Had gazed on Nature's naked loveliness,   275
Actæon-like, and now he fled astray
With feeble steps o'er the world's wilderness,
And his own thoughts, along that rugged way,
Pursued, like raging hounds, their father and their prey.

A pardlike spirit beautiful and swift;   280
A love in desolation masked; a power
Girt round with weakness—it can scarce uplift
The weight of the superincumbent hour;
It is a dying lamp, a falling shower,
A breaking billow—even whilst we speak,   285
Is it not broken? On the withering flower
The killing sun smiles brightly; on a cheek
The life can burn in blood, even while the heart may break.

His head was bound with pansies overblown,
And faded violets, white and pied and blue;   290

And a light spear topped with a cypress cone,
Round whose rude shaft dark ivy-tresses grew,
Yet dripping with the forest's noonday dew,
Vibrated, as the ever-beating heart
Shook the weak hand that grasped it: of that crew   295
He came the last, neglected and apart;
A herd-abandoned deer struck by the hunter's dart.

All stood aloof, and at his partial moan
Smiled through their tears; well knew that gentle band
Who in another's fate now wept his own,   300
As in the accents of an unknown land
He sung new sorrow. Sad Urania scanned
The stranger's mien, and murmured, "Who art thou?"
He answered not, but with a sudden hand
Made bare his branded and ensanguined brow,   305
Which was like Cain's or Christ's—oh, that it should be so!

What softer voice is hushed over the dead?
Athwart what brow is that dark mantle thrown?
What form leans sadly o'er the white death-bed,
In mockery of monumental stone,   310
The heavy heart heaving without a moan?
If it be he who, gentlest of the wise,
Taught, soothed, loved, honoured the departed one,
Let me not vex with inharmonious sighs
The silence of that heart's accepted sacrifice.   315

Our Adonais has drunk poison—oh,
What deaf and viperous murderer could crown
Life's early cup with such a draught of woe?
The nameless worm would now itself disown:
It felt, yet could escape, the magic tone   320
Whose prelude held all envy, hate, and wrong,
But what was howling in one breast alone,
Silent with expectation of the song
Whose master's hand is cold, whose silver lyre unstrung.

Live thou, whose infamy is not thy fame!   325
Live! fear no heavier chastisement from me,
Thou noteless blot on a remembered name!
But be thyself, and know thyself to be!

And ever at thy season be thou free
To spill the venom when thy fangs o'erflow. 330
Remorse and self-contempt shall cling to thee;
Hot shame shall burn upon thy secret brow,
And like a beaten hound tremble thou shalt—as now.

Nor let us weep that our delight is fled
Far from these carrion kites that scream below; 335
He wakes or sleeps with the enduring dead;
Thou canst not soar where he is sitting now.
Dust to the dust! but the pure spirit shall flow
Back to the burning fountain whence it came,
A portion of the Eternal, which must glow 340
Through time and change, unquenchably the same,
Whilst thy cold embers choke the sordid hearth of shame.

Peace, peace! he is not dead, he doth not sleep—
He hath awakened from the dream of life.
'T is we who, lost in stormy visions, keep 345
With phantoms an unprofitable strife,
And in mad trance strike with our spirit's knife
Invulnerable nothings. *We* decay
Like corpses in a charnel; fear and grief
Convulse us and consume us day by day, 350
And cold hopes swarm like worms within our living clay.

He has outsoared the shadow of our night;
Envy and calumny and hate and pain,
And that unrest which men miscall delight,
Can touch him not and torture not again; 355
From the contagion of the world's slow stain
He is secure, and now can never mourn
A heart grown cold, a head grown grey in vain;
Nor, when the spirit's self has ceased to burn,
With sparkless ashes load an unlamented urn. 360

He lives, he wakes—'t is Death is dead, not he;
Mourn not for Adonais. Thou young dawn,
Turn all thy dew to splendour, for from thee
The spirit thou lamentest is not gone!
Ye caverns and ye forests, cease to moan! 365
Cease, ye faint flowers and fountains; and thou air,
Which like a mourning veil thy scarf hadst thrown

O'er the abandoned earth, now leave it bare
Even to the joyous stars which smile on its despair!

He is made one with Nature: there is heard   370
His voice in all her music, from the moan
Of thunder, to the song of night's sweet bird;
He is a presence to be felt and known
In darkness and in light, from herb and stone,
Spreading itself where'er that Power may move   375
Which has withdrawn his being to its own,
Which wields the world with never wearied love,
Sustains it from beneath, and kindles it above.

He is a portion of the loveliness
Which once he made more lovely; he doth bear   380
His part, while the one Spirit's plastic stress
Sweeps through the dull dense world, compelling there
All new successions to the forms they wear,
Torturing th' unwilling dross that checks its flight
To its own likeness, as each mass may bear,   385
And bursting in its beauty and its might
From trees and beasts and men into the heaven's light.

The splendours of the firmament of time
May be eclipsed, but are extinguished not;
Like stars to their appointed height they climb,   390
And death is a low mist which cannot blot
The brightness it may veil. When lofty thought
Lifts a young heart above its mortal lair,
And love and life contend in it for what
Shall be its earthly doom, the dead live there,   395
And move like winds of light on dark and stormy air.

The inheritors of unfulfilled renown
Rose from their thrones, built beyond mortal thought,
Far in the Unapparent. Chatterton
Rose pale,—his solemn agony had not   400
Yet faded from him; Sidney, as he fought
And as he fell, and as he lived and loved,
Sublimely mild, a spirit without spot,
Arose; and Lucan, by his death approved:
Oblivion as they rose shrank like a thing reproved. 405

And many more, whose names on earth are dark,
But whose transmitted effluence cannot die
So long as fire outlives the parent spark,
Rose, robed in dazzling immortality.
"Thou art become as one of us," they cry;   410
"It was for thee yon kingless sphere has long
Swung blind in unascended majesty,
Silent alone amid an heaven of song.
Assume thy wingèd throne, thou Vesper of our throng!"

Who mourns for Adonais? oh, come forth,   415
Fond wretch! and know thyself and him aright.
Clasp with thy panting soul the pendulous earth;
As from a centre, dart thy spirit's light
Beyond all worlds, until its spacious might
Satiate the void circumference; then shrink   420
Even to a point within our day and night;
And keep thy heart light lest it make thee sink,
When hope has kindled hope, and lured thee to the brink.

Or go to Rome, which is the sepulchre—
Oh, not of him, but of our joy: 't is naught   425
That ages, empires, and religions there
Lie buried in the ravage they have wrought;
For such as he can lend, they borrow not,
Glory from those who made the world their prey;
And he is gathered to the kings of thought   430
Who waged contention with their time's decay,
And of the past are all that cannot pass away.

Go thou to Rome,—at once the paradise,
The grave, the city, and the wilderness;
And where its wrecks like shattered mountains rise,   435
And flowering weeds and fragrant copses dress
The bones of Desolation's nakedness,
Pass, till the spirit of the spot shall lead
Thy footsteps to a slope of green access,
Where, like an infant's smile, over the dead   440
A light of laughing flowers along the grass is spread.

And grey walls moulder round, on which dull Time
Feeds, like slow fire upon a hoary brand;

And one keen pyramid with wedge sublime,
Pavilioning the dust of him who planned   445
This refuge for his memory, doth stand
Like flame transformed to marble; and beneath
A field is spread, on which a newer band
Have pitched in heaven's smile their camp of death,
Welcoming him we lose with scarce extinguished breath. 450

Here pause: these graves are all too young as yet
To have outgrown the sorrow which consigned
Its charge to each; and if the seal is set,
Here, on one fountain of a mourning mind,
Break it not thou! too surely shalt thou find   455
Thine own well full, if thou returnest home,
Of tears and gall. From the world's bitter wind
Seek shelter in the shadow of the tomb.
What Adonais is, why fear we to become?

The One remains, the many change and pass;   460
Heaven's light forever shines, Earth's shadows fly;
Life, like a dome of many-coloured glass,
Stains the white radiance of Eternity,
Until Death tramples it to fragments.—Die,
If thou wouldst be with that which thou dost seek!   465
Follow where all is fled!—Rome's azure sky,
Flowers, ruins, statues, music, words, are weak
The glory they transfuse with fitting truth to speak.

Why linger, why turn back, why shrink, my heart?
Thy hopes are gone before; from all things here   470
They have departed: thou shouldst now depart!
A light is past from the revolving year,
And man, and woman; and what still is dear
Attracts to crush, repels to make thee wither.
The soft sky smiles, the low wind whispers near;   475
'T is Adonais calls! oh, hasten thither!
No more let Life divide what Death can join together.

That Light whose smile kindles the Universe,
That Beauty in which all things work and move,
That Benediction which the eclipsing curse   480
Of birth can quench not, that sustaining Love

Which, through the web of being blindly wove
By man and beast and earth and air and sea,
Burns bright or dim, as each are mirrors of
The fire for which all thirst, now beams on me,　　485
Consuming the last clouds of cold mortality.

The breath whose might I have invoked in song
Descends on me; my spirit's bark is driven
Far from the shore, far from the trembling throng
Whose sails were never to the tempest given;　　490
The massy earth and sphèrèd skies are riven!
I am borne darkly, fearfully, afar;
Whilst, burning through the inmost veil of heaven,
The soul of Adonais, like a star,
Beacons from the abode where the Eternal are.　　495

　　1821.　　　　　　　　　　　　1821.

THE WORLD'S GREAT AGE BEGINS ANEW

The world's great age begins anew,
　　The golden years return,
The earth doth like a snake renew
　　Her winter weeds outworn;
Heaven smiles, and faiths and empires gleam　　5
Like wrecks of a dissolving dream.

A brighter Hellas rears its mountains
　　From waves serener far;
A new Peneus rolls his fountains
　　Against the morning star;　　10
Where fairer Tempes bloom, there sleep
Young Cyclads on a sunnier deep.

A loftier Argo cleaves the main,
　　Fraught with a later prize;
Another Orpheus sings again,　　15
　　And loves, and weeps, and dies;
A new Ulysses leaves once more
Calypso for his native shore.

Oh, write no more the tale of Troy,
　　If earth Death's scroll must be!　　20

Nor mix with Laian rage the joy
  Which dawns upon the free,
Although a subtler Sphinx renew
Riddles of death Thebes never knew.

Another Athens shall arise,   25
  And to remoter time
Bequeath, like sunset to the skies,
  The splendour of its prime;
And leave, if nought so bright may live,
All earth can take or heaven can give.   30

Saturn and Love their long repose
  Shall burst, more bright and good
Than all who fell, than one who rose,
  Than many unsubdued;
Not gold, not blood, their altar dowers,   35
But votive tears and symbol flowers.

Oh cease! must hate and death return?
  Cease! must men kill and die?
Cease! drain not to its dregs the urn
  Of bitter prophecy!   40
The world is weary of the past,—
Oh might it die or rest at last!

1821.   *1822.*

TO ——

One word is too often profaned
  For me to profane it,
One feeling too falsely disdained
  For thee to disdain it;
One hope is too like despair   5
  For prudence to smother,
And pity from thee more dear
  Than that from another.

I can give not what men call love,
  But wilt thou accept not   10
The worship the heart lifts above
  And the heavens reject not—

The desire of the moth for the star,
  Of the night for the morrow,
The devotion to something afar   15
  From the sphere of our sorrow?

1821.   1824.

TO NIGHT

Swiftly walk over the western wave,
    Spirit of Night!
Out of the misty eastern cave,
Where all the long and lone daylight
Thou wovest dreams of joy and fear,   5
Which make thee terrible and dear,—
    Swift be thy flight!

Wrap thy form in a mantle grey,
    Star-inwrought!
Blind with thine hair the eyes of Day;   10
Kiss her until she be wearied out;
Then wander o'er city, and sea, and land,
Touching all with thine opiate wand—
    Come, long-sought!

When I arose and saw the dawn,   15
    I sighed for thee;
When light rode high, and the dew was gone,
And noon lay heavy on flower and tree,
And the weary Day turned to his rest,
Lingering like an unloved guest,   20
    I sighed for thee.

Thy brother Death came, and cried,
    "Wouldst thou me?"
Thy sweet child Sleep, the filmy-eyed,
Murmured like a noontide bee,   25
"Shall I nestle near thy side?
Wouldst thou me?" And I replied,
    "No, not thee!"

Death will come when thou art dead,
    Soon, too soon;   30

Sleep will come when thou art fled;
Of neither would I ask the boon
I ask of thee, belovèd Night—
Swift be thine approaching flight,
    Come soon, soon! 35

1821. 1824.

LEIGH HUNT

FROM

THE STORY OF RIMINI

A noble range it was, of many a rood,
Walled round with trees, and ending in a wood;
Indeed the whole was leafy, and it had
A winding stream about it, clear and glad,
That danced from shade to shade, and on its way 5
Seemed smiling with delight to feel the day.
There was the pouting rose, both red and white,
The flamy heart's-ease, flushed with purple light,
Blush-hiding strawberry, sunny-coloured box,
Hyacinth, handsome with his clustering locks, 10
The lady lily, looking gently down,
Pure lavender, to lay in bridal gown,
The daisy, lovely on both sides,—in short,
All the sweet cups to which the bees resort,
With plots of grass, and perfumed walks between 15
Of citron, honeysuckle, and jessamine,
With orange, whose warm leaves so finely suit,
And look as if they shade a golden fruit.
And midst the flowers, turfed round beneath a shade
Of circling pines, a babbling fountain played; 20
And 'twixt their shafts you saw the water bright,
Which through the darksome tops glimmered with shower-
    ing light.
So now you walked beside an odorous bed
Of gorgeous hues, white, azure, golden, red;
And now turned off into a leafy walk, 25
Close and continuous, fit for lovers' talk;
And now pursued the stream, and, as you trod

Onward and onward o'er the velvet sod,
Felt on your face an air, watery and sweet,
And a new sense in your soft-lighting feet;   30
And then perhaps you entered upon shades,
Pillowed with dells and uplands 'twixt the glades,
Through which the distant palace, now and then,
Looked lordly forth with many-windowed ken.
A land of trees, which, reaching round about,   35
In shady blessing stretched their old arms out,
With spots of sunny opening, and with nooks
To lie and read in, sloping into brooks,
Where at her drink you started the slim deer,
Retreating lightly with a lovely fear.   40
And all about, the birds kept leafy house,
And sung and sparkled in and out the boughs;
And all about, a lovely sky of blue
Clearly was felt, or down the leaves laughed through;
And here and there, in every part, were seats,   45
Some in the open walks, some in retreats,
With bowering leaves o'erhead, to which the eye
Looked up half sweetly and half awfully,—
Places of nestling green, for poets made,
Where, when the sunshine struck a yellow shade,   50
The rugged trunks, to inward peeping sight,
Thronged in dark pillars up the gold green light.

　　But 'twixt the wood and flowery walks, halfway,
And formed of both, the loveliest portion lay,
A spot that struck you like enchanted ground.   55
It was a shallow dell, set in a mound
Of sloping shrubs, that mounted by degrees,
The birch and poplar mixed with heavier trees;
From under which, sent through a marble spout,
Betwixt the dark wet green, a rill gushed out,   60
Whose low sweet talking seemed as if it said
Something eternal to that happy shade.
The ground within was lawn, with plots of flowers
Heaped towards the centre and with citron bowers;
And in the midst of all, clustered with bay   65
And myrtle, and just gleaming to the day,

Lurked a pavilion—a delicious sight,—
Small, marble, well-proportioned, mellowy white,
With yellow vine-leaves sprinkled—but no more,—
And a young orange either side the door.   70
The door was to the wood, forward and square;
The rest was domed at top, and circular;
And through the dome the only light came in,
Tinged, as it entered, with the vine-leaves thin.
    It was a beauteous piece of ancient skill,   75
Spared from the rage of war, and perfect still;
By some supposed the work of fairy hands,
Famed for luxurious taste and choice of lands,—
Alcina or Morgana, who from fights
And errant fame inveigled amorous knights,   80
And lived with them in a long round of blisses—
Feasts, concerts, baths, and bower-enshaded kisses.
But 't was a temple, as its sculpture told,
Built to the nymphs that haunted there of old;
For o'er the door was carved a sacrifice,   85
By girls and shepherds brought, with reverend eyes,
Of sylvan drinks and foods, simple and sweet,
And goats with struggling horns and planted feet;
And round about, ran on a line with this,
In like relief, a world of pagan bliss,   90
That showed, in various scenes, the nymphs themselves—
Some by the water-side, on bowery shelves
Leaning at will; some in the water sporting,
With sides half swelling forth, and looks of courting;
Some in a flowery dell, hearing a swain   95
Play on his pipe till the hills ring again;
Some tying up their long moist hair; some sleeping
Under the trees, with fauns and satyrs peeping,
Or, sidelong-eyed, pretending not to see
The latter in the brakes come creepingly,   100
While from their careless urns, lying aside
In the long grass, the straggling waters slide.
Never, be sure, before or since was seen
A summer-house so fine in such a nest of green.

1812–16.   1816.

JOHN KEATS

ON FIRST LOOKING INTO CHAPMAN'S HOMER

Much have I travelled in the realms of gold,
   And many goodly states and kingdoms seen;
    Round many western islands have I been
Which bards in fealty to Apollo hold.
Oft of one wide expanse had I been told   5
   That deep-browed Homer ruled as his demesne;
    Yet did I never breathe its pure serene
Till I heard Chapman speak out loud and bold:
Then felt I like some watcher of the skies
   When a new planet swims into his ken;   10
Or like stout Cortez when with eagle eyes
   He stared at the Pacific—and all his men
Looked at each other with a wild surmise—
   Silent, upon a peak in Darien.

1816.   1816

FROM

I STOOD TIPTOE UPON A LITTLE HILL

I stood tiptoe upon a little hill.
The air was cooling, and so very still
That the sweet buds which with a modest pride
Pull droopingly, in slanting curve aside,
Their scantly-leaved and finely tapering stems,   5
Had not yet lost those starry diadems
Caught from the early sobbing of the morn.
The clouds were pure and white as flocks new shorn,
And fresh from the clear brook; sweetly they slept
On the blue fields of heaven; and then there crept   10
A little noiseless noise among the leaves,
Born of the very sigh that silence heaves:
For not the faintest motion could be seen
Of all the shades that slanted o'er the green.
There was wide wand'ring for the greediest eye,   15
To peer about upon variety;
Far round the horizon's crystal air to skim,
And trace the dwindled edgings of its brim;

To picture out the quaint and curious bending
Of a fresh woodland alley, never ending; 20
Or by the bowery clefts, and leafy shelves,
Guess where the jaunty streams refresh themselves.
I gazed awhile, and felt as light and free
As though the fanning wings of Mercury
Had played upon my heels: I was light-hearted, 25
And many pleasures to my vision started;
So I straightway began to pluck a posey
Of luxuries bright, milky, soft, and rosy.

A bush of May flowers with the bees about them;
Ah, sure no tasteful nook would be without them; 30
And let a lush laburnum oversweep them,
And let long grass grow round the roots to keep them
Moist, cool, and green, and shade the violets,
That they may bind the moss in leafy nets.

A filbert hedge with wild briar overtwined, 35
And clumps of woodbine taking the soft wind
Upon their summer thrones; there too should be
The frequent chequer of a youngling tree,
That with a score of light green brethren shoots
From the quaint mossiness of aged roots; 40
Round which is heard a spring-head of clear waters
Babbling so wildly of its lovely daughters,
The spreading blue-bells: it may haply mourn
That such fair clusters should be rudely torn
From their fresh beds, and scattered thoughtlessly 45
By infant hands, left on the path to die.

Open afresh your round of starry folds,
Ye ardent marigolds!
Dry up the moisture from your golden lids,
For great Apollo bids 50
That in these days your praises should be sung
On many harps, which he has lately strung;
And when again your dewiness he kisses,
Tell him I have you in my world of blisses:
So haply when I rove in some far vale, 55
His mighty voice may come upon the gale.

Here are sweet peas, on tiptoe for a flight,
With wings of gentle flush o'er delicate white,
And taper fingers catching at all things,

To bind them all about with tiny rings.   60
    Linger awhile upon some bending planks
That lean against a streamlet's rushy banks,
And watch intently Nature's gentle doings;
They will be found softer than ring-dove's cooings.
How silent comes the water round that bend;   65
Not the minutest whisper does it send
To the o'erhanging sallows: blades of grass
Slowly across the chequered shadows pass;
Why, you might read two sonnets, ere they reach
To where the hurrying freshnesses aye preach   70
A natural sermon o'er their pebbly beds;
Where swarms of minnows show their little heads,
Staying their wavy bodies 'gainst the streams,
To taste the luxury of sunny beams
Tempered with coolness. How they ever wrestle   75
With their own sweet delight, and ever nestle
Their silver bellies on the pebbly sand.
If you but scantily hold out the hand,
That very instant not one will remain;
But turn your eye, and they are there again.   80
The ripples seem right glad to reach those cresses,
And cool themselves among the em'rald tresses;
The while they cool themselves, they freshness give,
And moisture, that the bowery green may live,
So keeping up an interchange of favours,   85
Like good men in the truth of their behaviours.
Sometimes goldfinches one by one will drop
From low-hung branches; little space they stop,
But sip, and twitter, and their feathers sleek,
Then off at once, as in a wanton freak,   90
Or, perhaps, to show their black and golden wings,
Pausing upon their yellow flutterings.
Were I in such a place, I sure should pray
That naught less sweet might call my thoughts away
Than the soft rustle of a maiden's gown   95
Fanning away the dandelion's down,
Than the light music of her nimble toes
Patting against the sorrel as she goes.
How she would start, and blush, thus to be caught
Playing in all her innocence of thought.   100

O let me lead her gently o'er the brook,
Watch her half-smiling lips and downward look;
O let me for one moment touch her wrist;
Let me one moment to her breathing list;
And as she leaves me may she often turn   105
Her fair eyes looking through her locks auburne.

1816.   1817.

FROM

ENDYMION

PROEM

A thing of beauty is a joy forever:
Its loveliness increases; it will never
Pass into nothingness; but still will keep
A bower quiet for us, and a sleep
Full of sweet dreams and health and quiet breathing.   5
Therefore, on every morrow, are we wreathing
A flowery band to bind us to the earth,
Spite of despondence, of the inhuman dearth
Of noble natures, of the gloomy days,
Of all the unhealthy and o'er-darkened ways   10
Made for our searching: yes, in spite of all,
Some shape of beauty moves away the pall
From our dark spirits. Such the sun, the moon,
Trees old and young, sprouting a shady boon
For simple sheep; and such are daffodils,   15
With the green world they live in; and clear rills
That for themselves a cooling covert make
'Gainst the hot season; the mid-forest brake,
Rich with a sprinkling of fair musk-rose blooms;
And such too is the grandeur of the dooms   20
We have imagined for the mighty dead;
All lovely tales that we have heard or read:
An endless fountain of immortal drink,
Pouring unto us from the heaven's brink.

    Nor do we merely feel these essences   25
For one short hour; no, even as the trees
That whisper round a temple become soon
Dear as the temple's self, so does the moon,
The passion poesy, glories infinite,

Haunt us till they become a cheering light　　30
Unto our souls, and bound to us so fast
That, whether there be shine, or gloom o'ercast,
They always must be with us, or we die.
　　　Therefore, 't is with full happiness that I
Will trace the story of Endymion.　　35
The very music of the name has gone
Into my being, and each pleasant scene
Is growing fresh before me as the green
Of our own valleys: so I will begin
Now while I cannot hear the city's din;　　40
Now while the early budders are just new,
And run in mazes of the youngest hue
About old forests; while the willow trails
Its delicate amber, and the dairy pails
Bring home increase of milk. And as the year　　45
Grows lush in juicy stalks, I'll smoothly steer
My little boat, for many quiet hours,
With streams that deepen freshly into bowers.
Many and many a verse I hope to write,
Before the daisies, vermeil-rimmed and white,　　50
Hide in deep herbage; and ere yet the bees
Hum about globes of clover and sweet peas,
I must be near the middle of my story.
O may no wintry season, bare and hoary,
See it half finished; but let autumn bold,　　55
With universal tinge of sober gold,
Be all about me when I make an end.
And now at once, adventuresome, I send
My herald thought into a wilderness:
There let its trumpet blow, and quickly dress　　60
My uncertain path with green, that I may speed
Easily onward, thorough flowers and weed.

1817　　　　　　　　　　　　　　　　　1818.

HYMN TO PAN

"O thou whose mighty palace-roof doth hang
From jaggèd trunks, and overshadoweth
Eternal whispers, glooms, the birth, life, death
Of unseen flowers in heavy peacefulness:
Who lov'st to see the hamadryads dress　　5

Their ruffled locks where meeting hazels darken;
And through whole solemn hours dost sit, and hearken
The dreary melody of bedded reeds,
In desolate places, where dank moisture breeds
The pipy hemlock to strange overgrowth,   10
Bethinking thee how melancholy loth
Thou wast to lose fair Syrinx,—do thou now,
By thy love's milky brow,
By all the trembling mazes that she ran,
Hear us, great Pan!   15

"O thou for whose soul-soothing quiet, turtles
Passion their voices cooingly 'mong myrtles,
What time thou wanderest at eventide
Through sunny meadows, that outskirt the side
Of thine enmossèd realms: O thou to whom   20
Broad-leavèd fig trees even now foredoom
Their ripened fruitage; yellow-girted bees
Their golden honeycombs; our village leas
Their fairest-blossomed beans and poppied corn;
The chuckling linnet its five young unborn,   25
To sing for thee; low-creeping strawberries
Their summer coolness; pent up butterflies
Their freckled wings; yea, the fresh budding year
All its completions,—be quickly near,
By every wind that nods the mountain pine,   30
O Forester Divine!

"Thou to whom every faun and satyr flies
For willing service; whether to surprise
The squatted hare while in half-sleeping fit;
Or upward ragged precipices flit   35
To save poor lambkins from the eagle's maw;
Or by mysterious enticement draw
Bewildered shepherds to their path again;
Or to tread breathless round the frothy main,
And gather up all fancifullest shells   40
For thee to tumble into naiads' cells,
And, being hidden, laugh at their out-peeping;
Or to delight thee with fantastic leaping,
The while they pelt each other on the crown

With silvery oak apples and fir cones brown,—   45
By all the echoes that about thee ring,
Hear us, O Satyr King!

"O Hearkener to the loud-clapping shears,
While ever and anon to his shorn peers
A ram goes bleating: Winder of the horn,   50
When snouted wild-boars routing tender corn
Anger our huntsmen: Breather round our farms,
To keep off mildews and all weather harms:
Strange Ministrant of undescribèd sounds,
That come a-swooning over hollow grounds,   . 55
And wither drearily on barren moors:
Dread Opener of the mysterious doors
Leading to universal knowledge,—see,
Great son of Dryope,
The many that are come to pay their vows   60
With leaves about their brows!

"Be still the unimaginable lodge
For solitary thinkings; such as dodge
Conception to the very bourne of heaven,
Then leave the naked brain: be still the leaven,   65
That spreading in this dull and clodded earth
Gives it a touch ethereal—a new birth:
Be still a symbol of immensity;
A firmament reflected in a sea;
An element filling the space between;   70
An unknown——but no more; we humbly screen
With uplift hands our foreheads, lowly bending,
And giving out a shout most heaven-rending,
Conjure thee to receive our humble paean,
Upon thy Mount Lycean!"   75

1817.   *1818.*

WHEN I HAVE FEARS THAT I MAY CEASE TO BE

When I have fears that I may cease to be
    Before my pen has gleaned my teeming brain,
Before high-pilèd books, in charact'ry,
    Hold like rich garners the full-ripened grain;

When I behold, upon the night's starred face,   5
    Huge cloudy symbols of a high romance,
And think that I may never live to trace
    Their shadows, with the magic hand of chance;
And when I feel, fair creature of an hour,
    That I shall never look upon thee more,   10
Never have relish in the faery power
    Of unreflecting love; then on the shore
Of the wide world I stand alone, and think,
Till love and fame to nothingness do sink.

1818.   *1848.*

ON SITTING DOWN TO READ "KING LEAR" ONCE AGAIN

O golden-tongued Romance, with serene lute!
    Fair plumèd Syren, Queen of far-away!
    Leave melodizing on this wintry day,
Shut up thine olden pages, and be mute:
Adieu! for once again the fierce dispute   5
    Betwixt damnation and impassioned clay
    Must I burn through; once more humbly assay
The bitter-sweet of this Shakespearian fruit.
Chief poet! and ye clouds of Albion,
    Begetters of our deep eternal theme!   10
When through the old oak forest I am gone,
    Let me not wander in a barren dream,
But when I am consumèd in the fire,
Give me new phœnix-wings to fly at my desire.

1818.   *1848.*

MOTHER OF HERMES, AND STILL YOUTHFUL MAIA

Mother of Hermes, and still youthful Maia,
    May I sing to thee
As thou wast hymnèd on the shores of Baiae?
    Or may I woo thee
In earlier Sicilian? or thy smiles   5
Seek as they once were sought, in Grecian isles,
By bards who died content on pleasant sward,
    Leaving great verse unto a little clan?

O, give me their old vigour; and unheard
   Save of the quiet primrose, and the span   10
      Of heaven, and few ears,
Rounded by thee, my song should die away
      Content as theirs,
Rich in the simple worship of a day.
1818.   *1848.*

FROM

HYPERION

Deep in the shady sadness of a vale
Far sunken from the healthy breath of morn,
Far from the fiery noon and eve's one star,
Sat grey-haired Saturn, quiet as a stone,
Still as the silence round about his lair;   5
Forest on forest hung about his head
Like cloud on cloud. No stir of air was there,
Not so much life as on a summer's day
Robs not one light seed from the feathered grass;
But where the dead leaf fell, there did it rest.   10
A stream went voiceless by, still deadened more
By reason of his fallen divinity
Spreading a shade; the naiad 'mid her reeds
Pressed her cold finger closer to her lips.

   Along the margin-sand large foot-marks went,   15
No further than to where his feet had strayed
And slept there since. Upon the sodden ground
His old right hand lay nerveless, listless, dead,
Unsceptred; and his realmless eyes were closed;
While his bowed head seemed list'ning to the Earth,   20
His ancient mother, for some comfort yet.
   It seemed no force could wake him from his place;
But there came one, who with a kindred hand
Touched his wide shoulders, after bending low
With reverence, though to one who knew it not.   25
She was a goddess of the infant world:
By her in stature the tall Amazon
Had stood a pigmy's height; she would have ta'en
Achilles by the hair and bent his neck,
Or with a finger stayed Ixion's wheel.   30

Her face was large as that of Memphian sphinx.
Pedestaled haply in a palace-court,
When sages looked to Egypt for their lore.
But, oh, how unlike marble was that face!
How beautiful, if sorrow had not made   35
Sorrow more beautiful than Beauty's self.
There was a listening fear in her regard,
As if calamity had but begun;
As if the vanward clouds of evil days
Had spent their malice, and the sullen rear   40
Was with its storèd thunder labouring up.
One hand she pressed upon that aching spot
Where beats the human heart, as if just there,
Though an immortal, she felt cruel pain;
The other upon Saturn's bended neck   45
She laid, and, to the level of his ear
Leaning with parted lips, some words she spake
In solemn tenour and deep organ tone,
Some mourning words, which in our feeble tongue
Would come in these like accents—O how frail   50
To that large utterance of the early gods!
    "Saturn, look up!—though wherefore, poor old king?
I have no comfort for thee, no not one:
I cannot say, 'O wherefore sleepest thou?'
For heaven is parted from thee, and the earth   55
Knows thee not, thus afflicted, for a god;
And ocean too, with all its solemn noise,
Has from thy sceptre passed; and all the air
Is emptied of thine hoary majesty.
Thy thunder, conscious of the new command,   60
Rumbles reluctant o'er our fallen house;
And thy sharp lightning in unpractised hands
Scorches and burns our once serene domain.
O aching time! O moments big as years!
All, as ye pass, swell out the monstrous truth,   65
And press it so upon our weary griefs
That unbelief has not a space to breathe.
Saturn, sleep on! O, thoughtless, why did I
Thus violate thy slumbrous solitude?
Why should I ope thy melancholy eyes?   70
Saturn, sleep on! while at thy feet I weep."

As when, upon a trancèd summer night,
Those green-robed senators of mighty woods,
Tall oaks, branch-charmèd by the earnest stars,
Dream, and so dream all night without a stir,   75
Save from one gradual solitary gust
Which comes upon the silence and dies off,
As if the ebbing air had but one wave;
So came these words and went, the while in tears
She touched her fair large forehead to the ground,   80
Just where her falling hair might be outspread
A soft and silken mat for Saturn's feet.

One moon, with alteration slow, had shed
Her silver seasons four upon the night,
And still these two were postured motionless   85
Like natural sculpture in cathedral cavern—
The frozen god still couchant on the earth,
And the sad goddess weeping at his feet;
Until at length old Saturn lifted up
His faded eyes, and saw his kingdom gone,   90
And all the gloom and sorrow of the place,
And that fair kneeling goddess; and then spake
As with a palsied tongue, and while his beard
Shook horrid with such aspen-malady:

"O tender spouse of gold Hyperion,   95
Thea, I feel thee ere I see thy face;
Look up, and let me see our doom in it;
Look up, and tell me if this feeble shape
Is Saturn's; tell me if thou hear'st the voice
Of Saturn; tell me if this wrinkling brow,   100
Naked and bare of its great diadem,
Peers like the front of Saturn. Who had power
To make me desolate? whence came the strength?
How was it nurtured to such bursting forth,
While Fate seemed strangled in my nervous grasp?   105
But it is so; and I am smothered up,
And buried from all godlike exercise
Of influence benign on planets pale,
Of admonitions to the winds and seas,
Of peaceful sway above man's harvesting,   110
And all those acts which Deity supreme
Doth ease its heart of love in.—I am gone

Away from my own bosom; I have left
My strong identity, my real self,
Somewhere between the throne and where I sit   115
Here on this spot of earth.   Search, Thea, search!
Open thine eyes eterne, and sphere them round
Upon all space: space starred, and lorn of light;
Space regioned with life-air, and barren void;
Spaces of fire, and all the yawn of hell.   120
Search, Thea, search! and tell me if thou seest
A certain shape or shadow making way
With wings or chariot fierce to repossess
A heaven he lost erewhile: it must—it must
Be of ripe progress—Saturn must be king.   125
Yes, there must be a golden victory;
There must be gods thrown down, and trumpets blown
Of triumph calm, and hymns of festival
Upon the gold clouds metropolitan,
Voices of soft proclaim, and silver stir   130
Of strings in hollow shells; and there shall be
Beautiful things made new, for the surprise
Of the sky-children: I will give command.—
Thea! Thea! Thea! where is Saturn?"

This passion lifted him upon his feet,   135
And made his hands to struggle in the air,
His druid locks to shake and ooze with sweat,
His eyes to fever out, his voice to cease.
He stood, and heard not Thea's sobbing deep.
A little time, and then again he snatched   140
Utterance thus: "But cannot I create?
Cannot I form?   Cannot I fashion forth
Another world, another universe,
To overbear and crumble this to naught?
Where is another chaos?   Where?"—That word   145
Found way unto Olympus, and made quake
The rebel three.—Thea was startled up,
And in her bearing was a sort of hope,
As thus she quick-voice spake, yet full of awe:

"This cheers our fallen house: come to our friends, 150
O Saturn! come away, and give them heart;
I know the covert, for thence came I hither."
Thus brief; then with beseeching eyes she went

With backward footing through the shade a space:
He followed, and she turned to lead the way   155
Through aged boughs, that yielded like the mist
Which eagles cleave upmounting from their nest.
1818–19   1820.

FANCY

Ever let the Fancy roam,
Pleasure never is at home;
At a touch sweet pleasure melteth,
Like to bubbles when rain pelteth.
Then let wingèd Fancy wander   5
Through the thought still spread beyond her;
Open wide the mind's cage-door,
She'll dart forth, and cloudward soar.
O sweet Fancy! let her loose:
Summer's joys are spoilt by use,   10
And the enjoying of the spring
Fades as does its blossoming;
Autumn's red-lipped fruitage too,
Blushing through the mist and dew,
Cloys with tasting. What do then?   15
Sit thee by the ingle, when
The sear faggot blazes bright,
Spirit of a winter's night;
When the soundless earth is muffled,
And the cakèd snow is shuffled   20
From the ploughboy's heavy shoon;
When the Night doth meet the Noon
In a dark conspiracy
To banish Even from her sky.
Sit thee there, and send abroad,   25
With a mind self-overawed,
Fancy, high-commissioned—send her!
She has vassals to attend her:
She will bring, in spite of frost,
Beauties that the earth hath lost;   30
She will bring thee, all together,
All delights of summer weather;
All the buds and bells of May,

From dewy sward or thorny spray;
All the heapèd autumn's wealth, 35
With a still, mysterious stealth.
She will mix these pleasures up
Like three fit wines in a cup,
And thou shalt quaff it:—thou shalt hear
Distant harvest-carols clear; 40
Rustle of the reapèd corn;
Sweet birds antheming the morn;
And in the same moment—hark!
'T is the early April lark,
Or the rooks, with busy caw, 45
Foraging for sticks and straw:
Thou shalt, at one glance, behold
The daisy and the marigold;
White-plumed lilies, and the first
Hedge-grown primrose that hath burst; 50
Shaded hyacinth, alway
Sapphire queen of the mid-May;
And every leaf and every flower
Pearlèd with the self-same shower:
Thou shalt see the field-mouse peep 55
Meagre from its cellèd sleep;
And the snake all winter-thin
Cast on sunny bank its skin:
Freckled nest-eggs thou shalt see
Hatching in the hawthorn-tree, 60
When the hen-bird's wing doth rest
Quiet on her mossy nest;
Then the hurry and alarm
When the bee-hive casts its swarm;
Acorns ripe down-pattering 65
While the autumn breezes sing.
    Oh, sweet Fancy! let her loose:
Every thing is spoilt by use.
Where's the cheek that doth not fade,
Too much gazed at? Where's the maid 70
Whose lip mature is ever new?
Where's the eye, however blue,
Doth not weary? Where's the face
One would meet in every place?

Where 's the voice, however soft,   75
One would hear so very oft?
At a touch sweet pleasure melteth
Like to bubbles when rain pelteth.
Let, then, wingèd Fancy find
Thee a mistress to thy mind: 80
Dulcet-eyed as Ceres' daughter
Ere the God of Torment taught her
How to frown and how to chide;
With a waist and with a side
White as Hebe's, when her zone   85
Slipt its golden clasp, and down
Fell her kirtle to her feet,
While she held the goblet sweet,
And Jove grew languid.—Break the mesh
Of the Fancy's silken leash;   90
Quickly break her prison-string
And such joys as these she 'll bring.
Let the wingèd Fancy roam,
Pleasure never is at home.

    1818.   *1820.*

ODE TO A NIGHTINGALE

My heart aches, and a drowsy numbness pains
  My sense, as though of hemlock I had drunk,
Or emptied some dull opiate to the drains
  One minute past, and Lethe-wards had sunk:
'T is not through envy of thy happy lot,   5
  But being too happy in thine happiness,—
    That thou, light-wingèd dryad of the trees,
      In some melodious plot
  Of beechen green, and shadows numberless,
    Singest of summer in full-throated ease.   10

O for a draught of vintage, that hath been
  Cooled a long age in the deep-delvèd earth,
Tasting of Flora and the country green,
  Dance, and Provençal song, and sunburnt mirth!
O for a beaker full of the warm South,   15
  Full of the true, the blushful Hippocrene,

With beaded bubbles winking at the brim,
    And purple-stainèd mouth;
That I might drink, and leave the world unseen,
    And with thee fade away into the forest dim:　20

Fade far away, dissolve, and quite forget
What thou among the leaves hast never known,
The weariness, the fever, and the fret
    Here, where men sit and hear each other groan;
Where Palsy shakes a few, sad, last gray hairs,　25
    Where Youth grows pale, and spectre-thin, and dies;
        Where but to think is to be full of sorrow
            And leaden-eyed despairs;
        Where Beauty cannot keep her lustrous eyes,
            Or new Love pine at them beyond to-morrow.　30

Away! away! for I will fly to thee,
    Not charioted by Bacchus and his pards,
But on the viewless wings of Poesy,
    Though the dull brain perplexes and retards:
Already with thee! tender is the night,　35
    And haply the Queen-Moon is on her throne,
        Clustered around by all her starry fays;
            But here there is no light,
Save what from heaven is with the breezes blown
    Through verdurous glooms and winding mossy ways.　40

I cannot see what flowers are at my feet,
    Nor what soft incense hangs upon the boughs,
But, in embalmèd darkness, guess each sweet
    Wherewith the seasonable month endows
The grass, the thicket, and the fruit-tree wild;　45
    White hawthorn, and the pastoral eglantine;
        Fast-fading violets covered up in leaves;
            And mid-May's eldest child,
The coming musk-rose, full of dewy wine,
    The murmurous haunt of flies on summer eves.　50

Darkling I listen; and, for many a time
    I have been half in love with easeful Death,
Called him soft names in many a musèd rhyme,
    To take into the air my quiet breath,
Now more than ever seems it rich to die,　55

To cease upon the midnight with no pain,
    While thou art pouring forth thy soul abroad
        In such an ecstasy!
Still wouldst thou sing, and I have ears in vain—
    To thy high requiem become a sod.   60

Thou wast not born for death, immortal bird!
    No hungry generations tread thee down:
The voice I hear this passing night was heard
    In ancient days by emperor and clown;
Perhaps the self-same song that found a path   65
    Through the sad heart of Ruth, when, sick for home,
        She stood in tears amid the alien corn;
            The same that oft-times hath
    Charmed magic casements, opening on the foam
        Of perilous seas, in faery lands forlorn.   70

Forlorn! the very word is like a bell
    To toll me back from thee to my sole self!
Adieu! the fancy cannot cheat so well
    As she is famed to do, deceiving elf.
Adieu! adieu! thy plaintive anthem fades   75
    Past the near meadows, over the still stream,
        Up the hillside; and now 't is buried deep
            In the next valley-glades:
    Was it a vision, or a waking dream?
        Fled is that music:—do I wake or sleep?   80
1819.   *1819.*

ODE ON A GRECIAN URN

Thou still unravished bride of quietness;
    Thou foster-child of silence and slow time;
Sylvan historian, who canst thus express
    A flowery tale more sweetly than our rhyme:
What leaf-fringed legend haunts about thy shape   5
    Of deities or mortals, or of both,
        In Tempe or the dales of Arcady?
    What men or gods are these? what maidens loth?
What mad pursuit? what struggle to escape?
        What pipes and timbrels? what wild ecstasy?   10

Heard melodies are sweet, but those unheard
    Are sweeter; therefore, ye soft pipes, play on,

Not to the sensual ear, but, more endeared,
    Pipe to the spirit ditties of no tone:
Fair youth, beneath the trees, thou canst not leave   15
    Thy song, nor ever can those trees be bare:
        Bold lover, never, never canst thou kiss,
Though winning near the goal—yet do not grieve;
    She cannot fade, though thou hast not thy bliss;
        Forever wilt thou love, and she be fair!   20

Ah, happy, happy boughs! that cannot shed
    Your leaves, nor ever bid the spring adieu;
And happy melodist, unwearièd,
    Forever piping songs forever new:
More happy love! more happy, happy love!   25
    Forever warm and still to be enjoyed,
        Forever panting, and forever young;
All breathing human passion far above,
    That leaves a heart high-sorrowful and cloyed,
        A burning forehead and a parching tongue.   30

Who are these coming to the sacrifice?
    To what green altar, O mysterious priest,
Lead'st thou that heifer lowing at the skies,
    And all her silken flanks with garlands drest?
What little town by river or sea-shore,   35
    Or mountain-built with peaceful citadel,
        Is emptied of this folk, this pious morn?
And, little town, thy streets forever more
    Will silent be; and not a soul to tell
        Why thou art desolate, can e'er return.   40

O Attic shape! fair attitude! with brede
    Of marble men and maidens overwrought,
With forest branches and the trodden weed;
    Thou, silent form! dost tease us out of thought
As doth eternity. Cold pastoral!   45
    When old age shall this generation waste,
        Thou shalt remain, in midst of other woe
Than ours, a friend to man, to whom thou say'st,
"Beauty is truth, truth beauty,"—that is all
        Ye know on earth, and all ye need to know.   50
    1819.   ·   1820.

TO AUTUMN

Season of mists and mellow fruitfulness,
    Close bosom-friend of the maturing Sun,
Conspiring with him how to load and bless
    With fruit the vines that round the thatch-eaves run;
To bend with apples the mossed cottage-trees,   5
    And fill all fruit with ripeness to the core;
        To swell the gourd, and plump the hazel shells
    With a sweet kernel; to set budding more,
And still more, later flowers for the bees,
Until they think warm days will never cease,   10
        For Summer has o'er-brimmed their clammy cells.

Who hath not seen thee oft amid thy store?
    Sometimes whoever seeks abroad may find
Thee sitting careless on a granary floor,
    Thy hair soft-lifted by the winnowing wind;   15
Or on a half-reaped furrow sound asleep,
    Drowsed with the fume of poppies, while thy hook
        Spares the next swath and all its twinèd flowers;
And sometimes like a gleaner thou dost keep
    Steady thy laden head across a brook;   20
    Or by a cider-press, with patient look,
        Thou watchest the last oozings hours by hours.

Where are the songs of Spring? Ay, where are they?
    Think not of them, thou hast thy music too:
While barrèd clouds bloom the soft-dying day,   25
    And touch the stubble-plains with rosy hue,
Then in a wailful choir the small gnats mourn
    Among the river sallows, borne aloft
        Or sinking as the light wind lives or dies;
And full-grown lambs loud bleat from hilly bourn;   30
    Hedge-crickets sing; and now with treble soft
    The red-breast whistles from a garden croft;
        And gathering swallows twitter in the skies.

1819.   1820.

ODE ON MELANCHOLY

No. no, go not to Lethe, neither twist
    Wolf's-bane, tight-rooted, for its poisonous wine;

Nor suffer thy pale forehead to be kissed
   By nightshade, ruby grape of Proserpine;
Make not your rosary of yew-berries,   5
   Nor let the beetle nor the death-moth be
      Your mournful Psyche, nor the downy owl
A partner in your sorrow's mysteries;
   For shade to shade will come too drowsily,
      And drown the wakeful anguish of the soul.   10

But when the melancholy fit shall fall
   Sudden from heaven like a weeping cloud,
That fosters the droop-headed flowers all,
   And hides the green hill in an April shroud;
Then glut thy sorrow on a morning rose,   15
   Or on the rainbow of the salt sand-wave,
      Or on the wealth of globèd peonies;
Or if thy mistress some rich anger shows,
   Emprison her soft hand, and let her rave,
      And feed deep, deep upon her peerless eyes.   20

She dwells with Beauty—Beauty that must die;
   And Joy, whose hand is ever at his lips
Bidding adieu; and aching Pleasure nigh,
   Turning to poison while the bee-mouth sips:
Ay, in the very temple of Delight   25
   Veiled Melancholy has her sovran shrine,
      Though seen of none save him whose strenuous tongue
Can burst Joy's grape against his palate fine;
   His soul shall taste the sadness of her might,
      And be among her cloudy trophies hung.   30
   1819?   1820.

THE EVE OF ST. AGNES

St. Agnes' Eve—ah, bitter chill it was!
The owl, for all his feathers, was a-cold;
The hare limped trembling through the frozen grass,
And silent was the flock in woolly fold;
Numb were the beadsman's fingers, while he told   5
His rosary, and while his frosted breath,
Like pious incense from a censer old,
   Seemed taking flight for heaven, without a death,
Past the sweet Virgin's picture, while his prayer he saith.

His prayer he saith, this patient, holy man;   10
Then takes his lamp, and riseth from his knees,
And back returneth, meagre, barefoot, wan,
Along the chapel aisle by slow degrees.
The sculptured dead, on each side, seem to freeze,
Emprisoned in black, purgatorial rails: 15
Knights, ladies, praying in dumb orat'ries,
He passeth by; and his weak spirit fails,
To think how they may ache in icy hoods and mails.

Northward he turneth through a little door,
And scarce three steps ere Music's golden tongue   20
Flattered to tears this aged man and poor;
But no—already had his death-bell rung;
The joys of all his life were said and sung;
His was harsh penance on St. Agnes' eve:
Another way he went, and soon among   25
Rough ashes sat he for his soul's reprieve,
And all night kept awake, for sinners' sake to grieve.

That ancient beadsman heard the prelude soft;
And so it chanced, for many a door was wide,
From hurry to and fro. Soon, up aloft,   30
The silver, snarling trumpets 'gan to chide;
The level chambers, ready with their pride,
Were glowing to receive a thousand guests;
The carvèd angels, ever eager-eyed,
Stared, where upon their heads the cornice rests,   35
With hair blown back, and wings put cross-wise on their
          breasts.

At length burst in the argent revelry,
With plume, tiara, and all rich array,
Numerous as shadows haunting faerily
The brain, new stuffed, in youth, with triumphs gay   40
Of old romance. These let us wish away,
And turn, sole-thoughted, to one lady there,
Whose heart had brooded, all that wintry day,
On love, and winged St. Agnes' saintly care,
As she had heard old dames full many times declare.   45

They told her how, upon St. Agnes' Eve,
Young virgins might have visions of delight,

And soft adorings from their loves receive
Upon the honeyed middle of the night,
If ceremonies due they did aright: 50
As, supperless to bed they must retire,
And couch supine their beauties, lily-white;
Nor look behind, nor sideways, but require
Of Heaven with upward eyes for all that they desire.

Full of this whim was thoughtful Madeline: 55
The music, yearning like a god in pain,
She scarcely heard; her maiden eyes divine,
Fixed on the floor, saw many a sweeping train
Pass by—she heeded not at all; in vain
Came many a tip-toe, amorous cavalier,   60
And back retired, not cooled by high disdain,
But she saw not—her heart was otherwhere:
She sighed for Agnes' dreams, the sweetest of the year.

She danced along with vague, regardless eyes,
Anxious her lips, her breathing quick and short: 65
The hallowed hour was near at hand; she sighs
Amid the timbrels, and the thronged resort
Of whisperers in anger or in sport;
'Mid looks of love, defiance, hate, and scorn,
Hoodwinked with faery fancy, all amort   70
Save to St. Agnes and her lambs unshorn,
And all the bliss to be before to-morrow morn.

So, purposing each moment to retire,
She lingered still. Meantime, across the moors,
Had come young Porphyro, with heart on fire   75
For Madeline. Beside the portal doors,
Buttressed from moonlight, stands he, and implores
All saints to give him sight of Madeline,
But for one moment in the tedious hours,
That he might gaze and worship all unseen;   80
Perchance speak, kneel, touch, kiss—in sooth such things
    have been.

He ventures in: let no buzzed whisper tell;
All eyes be muffled, or a hundred swords
Will storm his heart, Love's fev'rous citadel:

For him, those chambers held barbarian hordes,　　85
Hyena foemen, and hot-blooded lords,
Whose very dogs would execrations howl
Against his lineage; not one breast affords
Him any mercy, in that mansion foul,
Save one old beldame, weak in body and in soul.　　90

Ah, happy chance! the aged creature came,
Shuffling along with ivory-headed wand,
To where he stood, hid from the torch's flame,
Behind a broad hall-pillar, far beyond
The sound of merriment and chorus bland:　　95
He startled her; but soon she knew his face,
And grasped his fingers in her palsied hand,
Saying, "Mercy, Porphyro! hie thee from this place;
They are all here to-night, the whole blood-thirsty race!

"Get hence! get hence! there's dwarfish Hildebrand;　　100
He had a fever late, and in the fit
He cursèd thee and thine, both house and land.
Then there's that old Lord Maurice, not a whit
More tame for his gray hairs.—Alas me! flit!
Flit like a ghost away."—"Ah, gossip dear,　　105
We're safe enough; here in this arm-chair sit,
And tell me how"—"Good saints! not here, not here!
Follow me, child, or else these stones will be thy bier."

He followed through a lowly archèd way,
Brushing the cobwebs with his lofty plume;　　110
And as she muttered "Well-a—well-a-day!"
He found him in a little moonlight room,
Pale, latticed, chill, and silent as a tomb.
"Now tell me where is Madeline," said he,
"O tell me, Angela, by the holy loom　　115
Which none but secret sisterhood may see,
When they St. Agnes' wool are weaving piously."

"St. Agnes! ah, it is St. Agnes' Eve—
Yet men will murder upon holy days:
Thou must hold water in a witch's sieve,　　120
And be liege-lord of all the elves and fays,
To venture so; it fills me with amaze

To see thee, Porphyro!—St. Agnes's Eve!
God's help! my lady fair the conjuror plays
This very night: good angels her deceive!   125
But let me laugh awhile, I 've mickle time to grieve."

Feebly she laugheth in the languid moon,
While Porphyro upon her face doth look,
Like puzzled urchin on an aged crone
Who keepeth closed a wondrous riddle-book,   130
As spectacled she sits in chimney nook.
But soon his eyes grew brilliant, when she told
His lady's purpose; and he scarce could brook
Tears, at the thought of those enchantments cold,
And Madeline asleep in lap of legends old.   135

Sudden a thought came like a full-blown rose,
Flushing his brow, and in his painèd heart
Made purple riot; then doth he propose
A stratagem, that makes the beldame start:
"A cruel man and impious thou art!   140
Sweet lady, let her pray, and sleep, and dream
Alone with her good angels, far apart
From wicked men like thee. Go, go! I deem
Thou canst not surely be the same that thou didst seem."

"I will not harm her, by all saints I swear,"   145
Quoth Porphyro. "O may I ne'er find grace
When my weak voice shall whisper its last prayer,
If one of her soft ringlets I displace,
Or look with ruffian passion in her face!
Good Angela, believe me by these tears;   150
Or I will, even in a moment's space,
Awake, with horrid shout, my foemen's ears,
And beard them, though they be more fanged than wolves
    and bears."

"Ah, why wilt thou affright a feeble soul?
A poor, weak, palsy-stricken, churchyard thing,
Whose passing-bell may ere the midnight toll;   155
Whose prayers for thee, each morn and evening,
Were never missed." Thus plaining, doth she bring
A gentler speech from burning Porphyro;

So woeful, and of such deep sorrowing,   160
  That Angela gives promise she will do
Whatever he shall wish, betide her weal or woe.

Which was, to lead him, in close secrecy,
  Even to Madeline's chamber, and there hide
  Him in a closet, of such privacy   165
  That he might see her beauty unespied,
  And win perhaps that night a peerless bride,
  While legioned faeries paced the coverlet,
  And pale enchantment held her sleepy-eyed.
  Never on such a night have lovers met,   170
Since Merlin paid his demon all the monstrous debt.

"It shall be as thou wishest," said the dame:
  "All cates and dainties shall be storèd there
  Quickly on this feast-night; by the tambour frame
  Her own lute thou wilt see: no time to spare,   175
  For I am slow and feeble, and scarce dare
  On such a catering trust my dizzy head.
  Wait here, my child, with patience; kneel in prayer
  The while. Ah, thou must needs the lady wed,
Or may I never leave my grave among the dead."   180

So saying, she hobbled off with busy fear.
  The lover's endless minutes slowly passed.
  The dame returned, and whispered in his ear
  To follow her, with aged eyes aghast
  From fright of dim espial. Safe at last,   185
  Through many a dusky gallery, they gain
  The maiden's chamber, silken, hushed, and chaste,
  Where Porphyro took covert, pleased amain.
His poor guide hurried back, with agues in her brain.

Her faltering hand upon the balustrade,   190
  Old Angela was feeling for the stair,
  When Madeline, St. Agnes' charmèd maid,
  Rose, like a missioned spirit, unaware.
  With silver taper's light, and pious care,
  She turned, and down the aged gossip led   195
  To a safe level matting.—Now prepare,
  Young Porphyro, for gazing on that bed:
She comes, she comes again, like ring-dove frayed and fled.

Out went the taper as she hurried in;
Its little smoke, in pallid moonshine, died: 200
She closed the door, she panted, all akin
To spirits of the air and visions wide:
No uttered syllable, or woe betide!
But to her heart, her heart was voluble,
Paining with eloquence her balmy side,   205
As though a tongueless nightingale should swell
Her throat in vain, and die, heart-stifled, in her dell.

A casement high and triple-arched there was,
All garlanded with carven imageries
Of fruits and flowers and bunches of knot-grass,   210
And diamonded with panes of quaint device,
Innumerable of stains and splendid dyes
As are the tiger-moth's deep damasked wings;
And in the midst, 'mong thousand heraldries,
And twilight saints, and dim emblazonings,   215
A shielded scutcheon blushed with blood of queens and kings.

Full on this casement shone the wintry moon,
And threw warm gules on Madeline's fair breast,
As down she knelt for Heaven's grace and boon;
Rose-bloom fell on her hands, together prest,   220
And on her silver cross soft amethyst,
And on her hair a glory, like a saint:
She seemed a splendid angel, newly drest,
Save wings, for heaven.   Porphyro grew faint,
She knelt so pure a thing, so free from mortal taint.   225

Anon his heart revives: her vespers done,
Of all its wreathèd pearls her hair she frees;
Unclasps her warmèd jewels one by one;
Loosens her fragrant bodice; by degrees
Her rich attire creeps rustling to her knees;   230
Half-hidden, like a mermaid in sea-weed,
Pensive awhile she dreams awake, and sees,
In fancy, fair St. Agnes in her bed,
But dares not look behind or all the charm is fled.

Soon, trembling in her soft and chilly nest,   235
In sort of wakeful swoon, perplexed she lay,

Until the poppied warmth of sleep oppressed
Her soothèd limbs, and soul fatigued away;
Flown, like a thought, until the morrow-day;
Blissfully havened both from joy and pain;   240
Clasped like a missal where swart Paynims pray;
Blinded alike from sunshine and from rain,
As though a rose should shut, and be a bud again.

Stolen to this paradise, and so entranced,
Porphyro gazed upon her empty dress,   245
And listened to her breathing, if it chanced
To wake into a slumberous tenderness;
Which when he heard, that minute did he bless,
And breathed himself; then from the closet crept,
Noiseless as fear in a wide wilderness,   250
And over the hushed carpet, silent, stept,
And 'tween the curtains peeped, where, lo! how fast she
  slept.

Then by the bedside, where the faded moon
Made a dim, silver twilight, soft he set
A table, and, half-anguished, threw thereon   255
A cloth of woven crimson, gold, and jet—
O for some drowsy Morphean amulet!
The boisterous, midnight, festive clarion,
The kettle-drum, and far-heard clarionet
Affray his ears, though but in dying tone;   260
The hall door shuts again, and all the noise is gone.

And still she slept an azure-lidded sleep,
In blanchèd linen, smooth and lavendered,
While he from forth the closet brought a heap
Of candied apple, quince, and plum, and gourd;   265
With jellies soother than the creamy curd,
And lucent syrops, tinct with cinnamon;
Manna and dates, in argosy transferred
From Fez; and spicèd dainties, every one,
From silken Samarcand to cedared Lebanon.   270

These delicates he heaped with glowing hand
On golden dishes and in baskets bright
Of wreathèd silver; sumptuous they stand

In the retirèd quiet of the night,
Filling the chilly room with perfume light. 275
"And now, my love, my seraph fair, awake!
Thou art my heaven, and I thine eremite;
Open thine eyes, for meek St. Agnes' sake,
Or I shall drowse beside thee, so my soul doth ache."

Thus whispering, his warm, unnervèd arm 280
Sank in her pillow. Shaded was her dream
By the dusk curtains: 't was a midnight charm
Impossible to melt as icèd stream;
The lustrous salvers in the moonlight gleam;
Broad golden fringe upon the carpet lies. 285
It seemed he never, never could redeem
From such a stedfast spell his lady's eyes;
So mused awhile, entoiled in woofèd phantasies.

Awakening up, he took her hollow lute—
Tumultuous,—and in chords that tenderest be, 290
He played an ancient ditty, long since mute,
In Provence called "La belle dame sans mercy,"
Close to her ear touching the melody;
Wherewith disturbed, she uttered a soft moan;
He ceased—she panted quick—and suddenly 295
Her blue affrayèd eyes wide open shone;
Upon his knees he sank, pale as smooth-sculptured stone.

Her eyes were open, but she still beheld,
Now wide awake, the vision of her sleep:
There was a painful change that nigh expelled 300
The blisses of her dream so pure and deep;
At which fair Madeline began to weep,
And moan forth witless words with many a sigh,
While still her gaze on Porphyro would keep,
Who knelt, with joinèd hands and piteous eye, 305
Fearing to move or speak, she looked so dreamingly.

"Ah, Porphyro!" said she, "but even now
Thy voice was at sweet tremble in mine ear,
Made tuneable with every sweetest vow;
And those sad eyes were spritual and clear: 310
How changed thou art! how pallid, chill, and drear!

Give me that voice again, my Porphyro,
Those looks immortal, those complainings dear!
Oh leave me not in this eternal woe,
For if thou diest, my love, I know not where to go." 315

Beyond a mortal man impassioned far
At these voluptuous accents, he arose,
Ethereal, flushed, and like a throbbing star
Seen 'mid the sapphire heaven's deep repose;
Into her dream he melted, as the rose 320
Blendeth its odour with the violet—
Solution sweet: meantime the frost-wind blows
Like Love's alarum pattering the sharp sleet
Against the window-panes; St. Agnes' moon hath set.

'T is dark; quick pattereth the flaw-blown sleet. 325
"This is no dream, my bride, my Madeline!"
'T is dark; the icèd gusts still rave and beat.
"No dream, alas! alas! and woe is mine!
Porphyro will leave me here to fade and pine.—
Cruel! what traitor could thee hither bring? 330
I curse not, for my heart is lost in thine,
Though thou forsakest a deceivèd thing,
A dove forlorn and lost, with sick unprunèd wing."

"My Madeline! sweet dreamer! lovely bride!
Say, may I be for aye thy vassal blest? 335
Thy beauty's shield, heart-shaped and vermeil-dyed?
Ah, silver shrine, here will I take my rest
After so many hours of toil and quest,
A famished pilgrim—saved by miracle.
Though I have found, I will not rob, thy nest, 340
Saving of thy sweet self; if thou think'st well
To trust, fair Madeline, to no rude infidel.

"Hark! 't is an elfin-storm from faery land,
Of haggard seeming but a boon indeed:
Arise—arise! the morning is at hand; 345
The bloated wassailers will never heed.
Let us away, my love, with happy speed;
There are no ears to hear, or eyes to see,—
Drowned all in Rhenish and the sleepy mead.

Awake! arise! my love, and fearless be,   350
For o'er the southern moors I have a home for thee."

She hurried at his words, beset with fears,
For there were sleeping dragons all around,
At glaring watch, perhaps, with ready spears.—
Down the wide stairs a darkling way they found:— 355
In all the house was heard no human sound;
A chain-drooped lamp was flickering by each door;
The arras, rich with horseman, hawk, and hound,
Fluttered in the besieging wind's uproar;
And the long carpets rose along the gusty floor.   360

They glide, like phantoms, into the wide hall;
Like phantoms to the iron porch they glide,
Where lay the porter, in uneasy sprawl,
With a huge empty flaggon by his side.
The wakeful bloodhound rose, and shook his hide,   365
But his sagacious eye an inmate owns.
By one, and one, the bolts full easy slide;—
The chains lie silent on the footworn stones;—
The key turns, and the door upon its hinges groans.

And they are gone; aye, ages long ago   370
These lovers fled away into the storm.
That night the Baron dreamt of many a woe;
And all his warrior-guests, with shade and form
Of witch, and demon, and large coffin-worm,
Were long be-nightmared. Angela the old   375
Died palsy-twitched, with meagre face deform.
The beadsman, after thousand aves told,
For aye unsought-for slept among his ashes cold.
1819.   1820.

FROM

LAMIA

Upon a time, before the faery broods
Drove nymph and satyr from the prosperous woods,
Before King Oberon's bright diadem,
Sceptre, and mantle, clasped with dewy gem,
Frighted away the dryads and the fauns   5

From rushes green, and brakes, and cowslipped lawns,
The ever-smitten Hermes empty left
His golden throne, bent warm on amorous theft:
From high Olympus had he stolen light,
On this side of Jove's clouds, to escape the sight   10
Of his great summoner, and made retreat
Into a forest on the shores of Crete.
For somewhere in that sacred island dwelt
A nymph, to whom all hoofèd satyrs knelt;
At whose white feet the languid Tritons poured   15
Pearls, while on land they withered and adored.
Fast by the springs where she to bathe was wont,
And in those meads where sometime she might haunt,
Were strewn rich gifts, unknown to any Muse,
Though Fancy's casket were unlocked to choose.   20
Ah, what a world of love was at her feet!
So Hermes thought, and a celestial heat
Burnt from his wingèd heels to either ear,
That from a whiteness, as the lily clear,
Blushed into roses 'mid his golden hair,   25
Fallen in jealous curls about his shoulders bare.

   From vale to vale, from wood to wood, he flew,
Breathing upon the flowers his passion new,
And wound with many a river to its head,
To find where this sweet nymph prepared her secret bed: 30
In vain; the sweet nymph might nowhere be found,
And so he rested, on the lonely ground,
Pensive, and full of painful jealousies
Of the wood-gods and even the very trees.
There as he stood, he heard a mournful voice,   35
Such as, once heard, in gentle heart destroys
All pain but pity; thus the lone voice spake:
"When from this wreathèd tomb shall I awake!
When move in a sweet body fit for life,
And love, and pleasure, and the ruddy strife   40
Of hearts and lips! Ah, miserable me!"
The god, dove-footed, glided silently
Round bush and tree, soft-brushing, in his speed,
The taller grasses and full-flowering weed,
Until he found a palpitating snake,   45
Bright and cirque-couchant in a dusky brake.

She was a gordian shape of dazzling hue,
Vermilion-spotted, golden, green, and blue;
Striped like a zebra, freckled like a pard,
Eyed like a peacock, and all crimson barred;   50
And full of silver moons, that, as she breathed,
Dissolved, or brighter shone, or interwreathed
Their lustres with the gloomier tapestries;—
So rainbow-sided, touched with miseries,
She seemed, at once, some penanced lady elf,   55
Some demon's mistress, or the demon's self.
Upon her crest she wore a wannish fire
Sprinkled with stars, like Ariadne's tiar;
Her head was serpent, but ah, bitter-sweet!
She had a woman's mouth with all its pearls complete; 60
And for her eyes—what could such eyes do there
But weep, and weep, that they were born so fair,
As Proserpine still weeps for her Sicilian air?
Her throat was serpent, but the words she spake
Came, as through bubbling honey, for Love's sake,   65
And thus; while Hermes on his pinions lay,
Like a stooped falcon ere he takes his prey:—
  "Fair Hermes, crowned with feathers, fluttering light,
I had a splendid dream of thee last night:
I saw thee sitting, on a throne of gold,   70
Among the gods, upon Olympus old,
The only sad one; for thou didst not hear
The soft, lute-fingered Muses chaunting clear,
Nor even Apollo when he sang alone,
Deaf to his throbbing throat's long, long melodious moan. 75
I dreamt I saw thee, robed in purple flakes,
Break amorous through the clouds, as morning breaks,
And, swiftly as a bright Phoebean dart,
Strike for the Cretan isle; and here thou art!
Too gentle Hermes, hast thou found the maid?"   80
Whereat the star of Lethe not delayed
His rosy eloquence, and thus inquired:
"Thou smooth-lipped serpent, surely high inspired!
Thou beauteous wreath, with melancholy eyes,
Possess whatever bliss thou canst devise,   85
Telling me only where my nymph is fled,—
Where she doth breathe!" "Bright planet, thou hast said,"

Returned the snake, "but seal with oaths, fair god!"
"I swear," said Hermes, "by my serpent rod,
And by thine eyes, and by thy starry crown!" 90
Light flew his earnest words, among the blossoms blown.
Then thus again the brilliance feminine:
"Too frail of heart! for this lost nymph of thine,
Free as the air, invisibly, she strays
About these thornless wilds; her pleasant days 95
She tastes unseen; unseen her nimble feet
Leave traces in the grass and flowers sweet;
From weary tendrils, and bowed branches green,
She plucks the fruit unseen, she bathes unseen:
And by my power is her beauty veiled 100
To keep it unaffronted, unassailed
By the love-glances of unlovely eyes,
Of satyrs, fauns, and bleared Silenus' sighs.
Pale grew her immortality, for woe
Of all these lovers, and she grievèd so 105
I took compassion on her, bade her steep
Her hair in weird syrops, that would keep
Her loveliness invisible, yet free
To wander as she loves, in liberty.
Thou shalt behold her, Hermes, thou alone, 110
If thou wilt, as thou swearest, grant my boon!"
Then, once again, the charmèd god began
An oath, and through the serpent's ears it ran
Warm, tremulous, devout, psalterian.
Ravished, she lifted her Circean head, 115
Blushed a live damask, and swift-lisping said,
"I was a woman; let me have once more
A woman's shape, and charming as before.
I love a youth of Corinth—O the bliss!
Give me my woman's form, and place me where he is. 120
Stoop, Hermes, let me breathe upon thy brow,
And thou shalt see thy sweet nymph even now."
The god on half-shut feathers sank serene;
She breathed upon his eyes; and swift was seen
Of both the guarded nymph near-smiling on the green. 125
It was no dream; or say a dream it was,
Real are the dreams of gods, and smoothly pass
Their pleasures in a long immortal dream.
One warm, flushed moment, hovering, it might seem

Dashed by the wood-nymph's beauty, so he burned; 130
Then, lighting on the printless verdure, turned
To the swooned serpent, and with languid arm,
Delicate, put to proof the lithe Caducean charm.
So done, upon the nymph his eyes he bent
Full of adoring tears and blandishment, 135
And towards her stept; she, like a moon in wane,
Faded before him, cowered, nor could restrain
Her fearful sobs, self-folding like a flower
That faints into itself at evening hour.
But the god fostering her chillèd hand, 140
She felt the warmth, her eyelids opened bland,
And, like new flowers at morning song of bees,
Bloomed, and gave up her honey to the lees.
Into the green-recessèd woods they flew;
Nor grew they pale, as mortal lovers do. 145
    Left to herself, the serpent now began
To change: her elfin blood in madness ran,
Her mouth foamed, and the grass, therewith besprent,
Withered at dew so sweet and virulent;
Her eyes, in torture fixed and anguish drear, 150
Hot, glazed, and wide, with lid-lashes all sear,
Flashed phosphor and sharp sparks, without one cooling tear.
The colours all inflamed throughout her train,
She writhed about, convulsed with scarlet pain;
A deep volcanian yellow took the place 155
Of all her milder-moonèd body's grace,
And, as the lava ravishes the mead,
Spoilt all her silver mail and golden brede,
Made gloom of all her frecklings, streaks, and bars,
Eclipsed her crescents, and licked up her stars: 160
So that, in moments few, she was undrest
Of all her sapphires, greens, and amethyst,
And rubious-argent; of all these bereft,
Nothing but pain and ugliness were left.
Still shone her crown; that vanished, also she 165
Melted and disappeared as suddenly;
And in the air, her new voice luting soft,
Cried, "Lycius! gentle Lycius!"—Borne aloft
With the bright mists about the mountains hoar,
These words dissolved: Crete's forests heard no more. 170

1819.   1820.

LA BELLE DAME SANS MERCI

Ah, what can ail thee, wretched wight,
  Alone and palely loitering?
The sedge is withered from the lake,
  And no birds sing.

Ah, what can ail thee, wretched wight,   5
  So haggard and so woe-begone?
The squirrel's granary is full,
  And the harvest's done.

I see a lily on thy brow,
  With anguish moist and fever dew;   10
And on thy cheek a fading rose
  Fast withereth too.——

I met a lady in the meads,
  Full beautiful, a faery's child;
Her hair was long, her foot was light,   15
  And her eyes were wild.

I set her on my pacing steed,
  And nothing else saw all day long,
For sideways would she lean, and sing
  A faery's song.   20

I made a garland for her head,
  And bracelets too, and fragrant zone;
She looked at me as she did love,
  And made sweet moan.

She found me roots of relish sweet,   25
  And honey wild, and manna dew;
And sure in language strange she said,
  "I love thee true."

She took me to her elfin grot,
  And there she gazed and sighèd deep,   30
And there I shut her wild sad eyes—
  So kissed to sleep.

And there we slumbered on the moss;
  And there I dreamed, ah woe betide,
The latest dream I ever dreamed,   35
  On the cold hillside.

I saw pale kings and princes too,
    Pale warriors, death-pale were they all,
Who cried—"La belle dame sans merci
    Hath thee in thrall!"   40

I saw their starved lips in the gloom
    With horrid warning gapèd wide—
And I awoke, and found me here
    On the cold hillside.

And this is why I sojourn here,   45
    Alone and palely loitering,
Though the sedge is withered from the lake,
    And no birds sing.

1819.   *1820.*

BRIGHT STAR, WOULD I WERE STEADFAST
AS THOU ART

Bright star, would I were steadfast as thou art—
    Not in lone splendour hung aloft the night,
And watching, with eternal lids apart,
    Like Nature's patient, sleepless eremite,
The moving waters at their priest-like task   5
    Of pure ablution round earth's human shores,
Or gazing on the new soft-fallen mask
    Of snow upon the mountains and the moors:—
No; yet still steadfast, still unchangeable,
    Pillowed upon my fair love's ripening breast,   10
To feel forever its soft fall and swell,
    Awake forever in a sweet unrest;
Still, still to hear her tender-taken breath,
And so live ever—or else swoon to death.

1820.   *1846.*

WALTER SAVAGE LANDOR

AH, WHAT AVAILS THE SCEPTRED RACE

Ah, what avails the sceptred race,
    Ah, what the form divine!
What every virtue, every grace!
    Rose Aylmer, all were thine.

Rose Aylmer, whom these wakeful eyes   5
  May weep, but never see,
A night of memories and sighs
  I consecrate to thee.

                                        1806.

MILD IS THE PARTING YEAR, AND SWEET

Mild is the parting year, and sweet
  The odour of the falling spray;
Life passes on more rudely fleet,
  And balmless is its closing day.
I wait its close, I court its gloom,   5
  But mourn that never must there fall
Or on my breast or on my tomb
  The tear that would have soothed it all.

                                        1831.

A FIESOLAN IDYL

Here, where precipitate Spring with one light bound
Into hot Summer's lusty arms expires,
And where go forth at morn, at eve, at night,
Soft airs that want the lute to play with 'em,
And softer sighs that know not what they want,   5
Aside a wall, beneath an orange-tree,
Whose tallest flowers could tell the lowlier ones
Of sights in Fiesole right up above,
While I was gazing a few paces off
At what they seemed to show me with their nods,   10
Their frequent whispers and their pointing shoots,
A gentle maid came down the garden-steps
And gathered the pure treasure in her lap.
I heard the branches rustle, and stept forth
To drive the ox away, or mule, or goat,—   15
Such I believed it must be. How could I
Let beast o'erpower them? when hath wind or rain
Borne hard upon weak plant that wanted me,
And I (however they might bluster round)
Walkt off? 'T were most ungrateful; for sweet scents 20
Are the swift vehicles of still sweeter thoughts,
And nurse and pillow the dull memory

That would let drop without them her best stores.
They bring me tales of youth and tones of love,
And 't is and ever was my wish and way   25
To let all flowers live freely, and all die
(Whene'er their Genius bids their souls depart)
Among their kindred in their native place.
I never pluck the rose; the violet's head
Hath shaken with my breath upon its bank   30
And not reproacht me; the ever-sacred cup
Of the pure lily hath between my hands
Felt safe, unsoiled, nor lost one grain of gold.
I saw the light that made the glossy leaves
More glossy; the fair arm, the fairer cheek   35
Warmed by the eye intent on its pursuit;
I saw the foot that, although half-erect
From its gray slipper, could not lift her up
To what she wanted. I held down a branch
And gathered her some blossoms, since their hour   40
Was come, and bees had wounded them, and flies
Of harder wing were working their way thro'
And scattering them in fragments under foot.
So crisp were some, they rattled unevolved;
Others, ere broken off, fell into shells,   45
Unbending, brittle, lucid, white like snow,
And like snow not seen thro', by eye or sun;
Yet every one her gown received from me
Was fairer than the first. I thought not so,
But so she praised them to reward my care.   50
I said, "You find the largest." "This indeed,"
Cried she, "is large and sweet." She held one forth,
Whether for me to look at or to take
She knew not, nor did I; but taking it
Would best have solved (and this she felt) her doubt.   55
I dared not touch it; for it seemed a part
Of her own self—fresh, full, the most mature
Of blossoms, yet a blossom; with a touch
To fall, and yet unfallen. She drew back
The boon she tendered, and then, finding not   60
The ribbon at her waist to fix it in,
Dropt it, as loth to drop it, on the rest.

                                          1831.

THE DEATH OF ARTEMIDORA

"Artemidora! gods invisible,
 While thou art lying faint along the couch,
 Have tied the sandal to thy slender feet
 And stand beside thee, ready to convey
 Thy weary steps where other rivers flow.   5
 Refreshing shades will waft thy weariness
 Away, and voices like thy own come near
 And nearer, and solicit an embrace."
 Artemidora sighed, and would have prest
 The hand now pressing hers, but was too weak.   10
 Iris stood over her dark hair unseen
 While thus Elpenor spake. He lookt into
 Eyes that had given light and life erewhile
 To those above them, but now dim with tears
 And wakefulness. Again he spake of joy   15
 Eternal. At that word, that sad word *joy,*
 Faithful and fond her bosom heaved once more,
 Her head fell back: and now a loud deep sob
 Swelled through the darkened chamber; 't was not hers.

                                          1836.

THE HAMADRYAD

Rhaicos was born amid the hills wherefrom
Gnidos, the light of Caria, is discerned.
And small are the white-crested that play near,
And smaller onward are the purple waves.
Thence festal choirs were visible, all crowned   5
With rose and myrtle if they were inborn;
If from Pandion sprang they, on the coast
Where stern Athene raised her citadel,
Then olive was entwined with violets
Clustered in bosses, regular and large.   10
For various men wore various coronals,
But one was their devotion; 't was to her
Whose laws all follow, her whose smile withdraws
The sword from Ares, thunderbolt from Zeus,
And whom in his chill caves the mutable   15
Of mind, Poseidon, the sea-king, reveres,
And whom his brother, stubborn Dis, hath prayed

To turn in pity the averted cheek
Of her he bore away, with promises,
Nay, with loud oath before dread Styx itself,   20
To give her daily more and sweeter flowers
Than he made drop from her on Enna's dell.
　　Rhaicos was looking from his father's door
At the long trains that hastened to the town
From all the valleys, like bright rivulets   25
Gurgling with gladness, wave outrunning wave,
And thought it hard he might not also go
And offer up one prayer, and press one hand,
He knew not whose. The father called him in
And said, "Son Rhaicos! those are idle games;   30
Long enough I have lived to find them so."
And ere he ended, sighed; as old men do
Always, to think how idle such games are.
"I have not yet," thought Rhaicos in his heart,
And wanted proof. "Suppose thou go and help   35
Echeion at the hill, to bark yon oak
And lop its branches off, before we delve
About the trunk and ply the root with axe;
This we may do in winter."
　　　　　　　　　Rhaicos went;
For thence he could see farther, and see more   40
Of those who hurried to the city-gate.
Echeion he found there, with naked arm
Swart-haired, strong-sinewed, and his eyes intent
Upon the place where first the axe should fall:
He held it upright. "There are bees about,   45
Or wasps, or hornets," said the cautious eld,
"Look sharp, O son of Thallinos!" The youth
Inclined his ear, afar, and warily,
And caverned in his hand. He heard a buzz
At first, and then the sound grew soft and clear,   50
And then divided into what seemed tune,
And there were words upon it, plaintive words.
He turned, and said, "Echeion! do not strike
That tree; it must be hollow, for some god
Speaks from within. Come thyself near." Again   55
Both turned toward it; and behold! there sat
Upon the moss below, with her two palms

Pressing it, on each side, a maid in form.
Downcast were her long eyelashes, and pale
Her cheek, but never mountain-ash displayed   60
Berries of colour like her lips so pure,
Nor were the anemones about her hair
Soft, smooth, and wavering like the face beneath.
  "What dost thou here?" Echeion, half-afraid,
Half-angry, cried. She lifted up her eyes,   65
But nothing spake she. Rhaicos drew one step
Backward, for fear came likewise over him,
But not such fear: he panted, gaspt, drew in
His breath, and would have turned it into words,
But could not into one.

                        "O send away   70
That sad old man!" said she. The old man went
Without a warning from his master's son,
Glad to escape, for sorely he now feared;
And the axe shone behind him in their eyes.

    Hamad. And wouldst thou too shed the most innocent   75
Of blood? No vow demands it; no god wills
The oak to bleed.

    Rhaicos.   Who art thou? whence? why here?
And whither wouldst thou go? Among the robed
In white or saffron, or the hue that most
Resembles dawn or the clear sky, is none   80
Arrayed as thou art. What so beautiful
As that gray robe which clings about thee close,
Like moss to stones adhering, leaves to trees,
Yet lets thy bosom rise and fall in turn,
As, toucht by zephyrs, fall and rise the boughs   85
Of graceful platane by the river-side?

    Hamad. Lovest thou well thy father's house?
    Rhaicos.   Indeed
I love it, well I love it, yet would leave
For thine, where'er it be, my father's house,
With all the marks upon the door, that show   90
My growth at every birthday since the third,
And all the charms, o'erpowering evil eyes,
My mother nailed for me against my bed,
And the Cydonian bow (which thou shalt see)
Won in my race last spring from Eutychos.   95

Hamad. Bethink thee what it is to leave a home
Thou never yet hast left, one night, one day.
 Rhaicos. No, 't is not hard to leave it; 't is not hard
To leave, O maiden, that paternal home,
If there be one on earth whom we may love · 100
First, last, forever, one who says that she
Will love forever too. To say which word,
Only to say it, surely is enough—
It shows such kindness—if 't were possible
We at the moment think she would indeed.   105
 Hamad. Who taught thee all this folly at thy age?
 Rhaicos. I have seen lovers and have learnt to love.
 Hamad. But wilt thou spare the tree?
 Rhaicos.   My father wants
The bark; the tree may hold its place awhile.
 Hamad. Awhile! thy father numbers then my days? 110
 Rhaicos. Are there no others where the moss beneath
Is quite as tufty? Who would send thee forth,
Or ask thee why thou tarriest? Is thy flock
Anywhere near?
 Hamad.   I have no flock: I kill
Nothing that breathes, that stirs, that feels the air, 115
The sun, the dew. Why should the beautiful
(And thou art beautiful) disturb the source
Whence springs all beauty? Hast thou never heard
Of hamadryads?
 Rhaicos. Heard of them I have;
Tell me some tale about them. May I sit 120
Beside thy feet? Art thou not tired? The herbs
Are very soft; I will not come too nigh;
Do but sit there, nor tremble so, nor doubt.
Stay, stay an instant: let me first explore
If any acorn of last year be left   125
Within it; thy thin robe too ill protects
Thy dainty limbs against the harm one small
Acorn may do. Here's none. Another day
Trust me; till then let me sit opposite.
 Hamad. I seat me; be thou seated, and content. 130
 Rhaicos. O sight for gods! ye men below, adore
The Aphrodite! *Is* she there below?
Or sits she here before me? as she sate

Before the shepherd on those highths that shade
The Hellespont, and brought his kindred woe.   135
    Hamad. Reverence the higher Powers; nor deem amiss
Of her who pleads to thee, and would repay—
Ask not how much—but very much. Rise not—
No, Rhaicos, no! Without the nuptial vow
Love is unholy. Swear to me that none   140
Of mortal maids shall ever taste thy kiss,
Then take thou mine; then take it, not before.
    Rhaicos. Hearken, all gods above! O Aphrodite
O Herè! Let my vow be ratified!
But wilt thou come into my father's house?   145
    Hamad. Nay; and of mine I cannot give thee part.
    Rhaicos. Where is it?
    Hamad.   In this oak.
    Rhaicos.   Ay, now begins
The tale of hamadryad; tell it through.
    Hamad. Pray of thy father never to cut down
My tree; and promise him, as well thou mayst,   150
That every year he shall receive from me
More honey than will buy him nine fat sheep,
More wax than he will burn to all the gods.
Why fallest thou upon thy face? Some thorn
May scratch it, rash young man! Rise up; for shame!   155
    Rhaicos. For shame I cannot rise. O pity me!
I dare not sue for love—but do not hate!
Let me once more behold thee—not once more,
But many days; let me love on—unloved!
I aimed too high: on my own head the bolt   160
Falls back, and pierces to the very brain.
    Hamad. Go—rather go than make me say I love.
    Rhaicos. If happiness is immortality
(And whence enjoy it else the gods above?)
I am immortal too: my vow is heard—   165
Hark! on the left.—Nay, turn not from me now,
I claim my kiss.
    Hamad.   Do men take first, then claim?
Do thus the seasons run their course with them?
    Her lips were sealed; her head sank on his breast.
'T is said that laughs were heard within the wood;   170

But who should hear them? and whose laughs? and why?
 Savoury was the smell, and long past noon,
Thallinos, in thy house; for marjoram,
Basil and mint, and thyme and rosemary,
Were sprinkled on the kid's well-roasted length,   175
Awaiting Rhaicos. Home he came at last,
Not hungry, but pretending hunger keen,
With head and eyes just o'er the maple plate.
"Thou seest but badly, coming from the sun,
Boy Rhaicos!" said the father. "That oak's bark   180
Must have been tough, with little sap between;
It ought to run; but it and I are old."
Rhaicos, although each morsel of the bread
Increased by chewing, and the meat grew cold
And tasteless to his palate, took a draught   185
Of gold-bright wine, which, thirsty as he was,
He thought not of, until his father filled
The cup, averring water was amiss,
But wine had been at all times poured on kid—
It was religion.
    He, thus fortified,   190
Said, not quite boldly and not quite abasht,
"Father, that oak is Zeus's own; that oak
Year after year will bring thee wealth from wax
And honey. There is one who fears the gods
And the gods love;—that one" (he blushed, nor said   195
What one) "hast promist this, and may do more.
Thou hast not many moons to wait until
The bees have done their best; if then there come
Nor wax nor honey, let the tree be hewn."
 "Zeus hath bestowed on thee a prudent mind,"   200
Said the glad sire; "but look thou often there,
And gather all the honey thou canst find
In every crevice, over and above
What has been promist; would they reckon that?"
 Rhaicos went daily; but the nymph as oft,   205
Invisible. To play at love, she knew,
Stopping its breathings when it breathes most soft,
Is sweeter than to play on any pipe.
She played on his: she fed upon his sighs;
They pleased her when they gently waved her hair,   210

Cooling the pulses of her purple veins;
And when her absence brought them out, they pleased.
Even among the fondest of them all,
What mortal or immortal maid is more
Content with giving happiness than pain?   215
One day he was returning from the wood
Despondently. She pitied him, and said,
"Come back!" and twined her fingers in the hem
Above his shoulder. Then she led his steps
To a cool rill that ran o'er level sand   220
Through lentisk and through oleander; there
Bathed she his feet, lifting them on her lap
When bathed, and drying them in both her hands.
He dared complain; for those who most are loved
Most dare it; but not harsh was his complaint.   225
"O thou inconstant!" said he, "if stern law
Bind thee, or will, stronger than sternest law,
O, let me know henceforward when to hope
The fruit of love that grows for me but here."
He spake; and pluckt it from its pliant stem.   230
"Impatient Rhaicos! Why thus intercept
The answer I would give? There is a bee
Whom I have fed, a bee who knows my thoughts
And executes my wishes: I will send
That messenger. If ever thou art false,   235
Drawn by another, own it not, but drive
My bee away; then shall I know my fate,
And—for thou must be wretched—weep at thine.
But often as my heart persuades to lay
Its cares on thine and throb itself to rest,   240
Expect her with thee, whether it be morn
Or eve, at any time when woods are safe."
    Day after day the Hours beheld them blest,
And season after season: years had past,
Blest were they still. He who asserts that Love   245
Ever is sated of sweet things, the same
Sweet things he fretted for in earlier days,
Never, by Zeus! loved he a hamadryad.
    The nights had now grown longer, and perhaps
The hamadryads find them lone and dull   250
Among their woods; one did, alas! She called

Her faithful bee; 't was when all bees should sleep,
And all did sleep but hers. She was sent forth
To bring that light which never wintry blast
Blows out, nor rain nor snow extinguishes, 255
The light that shines from loving eyes upon
Eyes that love back, till they can see no more.
    Rhaicos was sitting at his father's hearth:
Between them stood the table, not o'erspread
With fruits which autumn now profusely bore, 260
Nor anise cakes, nor odorous wine, but there
The draft-board was expanded; at which game
Triumphant sat old Thallinos; the son
Was puzzled, vext, discomforted, distraught.
A buzz was at his ear; up went his hand, 265
And it was heard no longer. The poor bee
Returned (but not until the morn shone bright),
And found the hamadryad with her head
Upon her aching wrist, and showed one wing
Half broken off, the other's meshes marred, 270
And there were bruises which no eye could see
Saving a hamadryad's. At this sight
Down fell the languid brow, both hands fell down;
A shriek was carried to the ancient hall
Of Thallinos: he heard it not; his son 275
Heard it, and ran forthwith into the wood.
No bark was on the tree, no leaf was green,
The trunk was riven through. From that day forth
Nor word nor whisper soothed his ear, nor sound
Even of insect wing; but loud laments 280
The woodmen and the shepherds one long year
Heard day and night, for Rhaicos would not quit
The solitary place, but moaned and died.
    Hence milk and honey wonder not, O guest,
To find set duly on the hollow stone. 285

1846.

WITH AN ALBUM

I know not whether I am proud,
But this I know, I hate the crowd;
Therefore pray let me disengage
My verses from the motley page,

Where others far more sure to please　　　　5
Pour out their choral song with ease.
And yet perhaps, if some should tire
With too much froth or too much fire,
There is an ear that may incline
Even to words so dull as mine.　　　　　　10

1846.

TO AGE

Welcome, old friend! These many years
　　Have we lived door by door;
The Fates have laid aside their shears
　　Perhaps for some few more.

I was indocile at an age　　　　　　　　5
　　When better boys were taught;
But thou at length hast made me sage,
　　If I am sage in aught.

Little I know from other men,
　　Too little they from me;　　　　　　10
But thou hast pointed well the pen
　　That writes these lines to thee.

Thanks for expelling Fear and Hope—
　　One vile, the other vain;
One's scourge, the other's telescope,　　15
　　I shall not see again.

Rather what lies before my feet
　　My notice shall engage:
He who hath braved Youth's dizzy heat
　　Dreads not the frost of Age.　　　　20

1853.

I STROVE WITH NONE

I strove with none, for none was worth my strife.
Nature I loved, and, next to Nature, Art.
I warmed both hands before the fire of Life;
It sinks, and I am ready to depart.

1853.

ALFRED TENNYSON

CLARIBEL

A MELODY

Where Claribel low-lieth
  The breezes pause and die,
    Letting the rose-leaves fall;
But the solemn oak-tree sigheth,
    Thick-leaved, ambrosial,   5
  With an ancient melody
  Of an inward agony,
Where Claribel low-lieth.

At eve the beetle boometh
  Athwart the thicket lone;   10
At noon the wild bee hummeth
  About the mossed headstone;
At midnight the moon cometh,
  And looketh down alone.
Her song the lintwhite swelleth,   15
The clear-voiced mavis dwelleth,
  The callow throstle lispeth,
The slumbrous wave outwelleth,
  The babbling runnel crispeth,
The hollow grot replieth,   20
  Where Claribel low-lieth.

1830.

THE LADY OF SHALOTT

PART I

On either side the river lie
Long fields of barley and of rye,
That clothe the wold and meet the sky
And thro' the field the road runs by
    To many-towered Camelot;   5
And up and down the people go,
Gazing where the lilies blow
Round an island there below,
    The island of Shalott

Willows whiten, aspens quiver,   10
Little breezes dusk and shiver
Thro' the wave that runs forever
By the island in the river,
   Flowing down to Camelot.
Four gray walls, and four gray towers,   15
Overlook a space of flowers,
And the silent isle imbowers
   The Lady of Shalott.

By the margin, willow-veiled,
Slide the heavy barges trailed   20
By slow horses; and unhailed
The shallop flitteth silken-sailed,
   Skimming down to Camelot:
But who hath seen her wave her hand?
Or at the casement seen her stand?   25
Or is she known in all the land,
   The Lady of Shalott?

Only reapers, reaping early
In among the bearded barley,
Hear a song that echoes cheerly   30
From the river winding clearly,
   Down to towered Camelot:
And by the moon the reaper weary,
Piling sheaves in uplands airy,
Listening, whispers, " 'T is the fairy   35
   Lady of Shalott."

PART II

There she weaves by night and day
A magic web with colours gay.
She has heard a whisper say
A curse is on her if she stay   40
   To look down to Camelot.
She knows not what the curse may be,
And so she weaveth steadily,
And little other care hath she,
   The Lady of Shalott.   45

And moving thro' a mirror clear,
That hangs before her all the year,
Shadows of the world appear:
There she sees the highway near,
      Winding down to Camelot;   50
There the river eddy whirls,
And there the surly village-churls,
And the red cloaks of market girls,
      Pass onward from Shalott.

Sometimes a troop of damsels glad,   55
An abbot on an ambling pad,
Sometimes a curly shepherd-lad,
Or long-haired page in crimson clad,
      Goes by to towered Camelot;
And sometimes thro' the mirror blue   60
The knights come riding two and two:
She hath no loyal knight and true,
      The Lady of Shalott.

But in her web she still delights
To weave the mirror's magic sights,   65
For often thro' the silent nights
A funeral, with plumes and lights
      And music, went to Camelot;
Or when the moon was overhead,
Came two young lovers lately wed: 70
"I am half sick of shadows," said
      The Lady of Shalott.

PART III

A bow-shot from her bower-eaves,
He rode between the barley-sheaves;
The sun came dazzling thro' the leaves,   75
And flamed upon the brazen greaves
      Of bold Sir Lancelot.
A red-cross knight for ever kneeled
To a lady in his shield,
That sparkled on the yellow field,   80
      Beside remote Shalott.

The gemmy bridle glittered free,
Like to some branch of stars we see
Hung in the golden Galaxy;
The bridle bells rang merrily   85
       As he rode down to Camelot;
And, from his blazoned baldric slung,
A mighty silver bugle hung,
And as he rode his armour rung,
       Beside remote Shalott.   90

All in the blue unclouded weather
Thick jewelled shone the saddle-leather;
The helmet and the helmet-feather
Burned like one burning flame together,
       As he rode down to Camelot: 95
As often thro' the purple night,
Below the starry clusters bright,
Some bearded meteor, trailing light,
       Moves over still Shalott.

His broad clear brow in sunlight glowed;   100
On burnished hooves his war-horse trode;
From underneath his helmet flowed
His coal-black curls as on he rode,
       As he rode down to Camelot.
From the bank and from the river   105
He flashed into the crystal mirror.
"Tirra lirra," by the river
       Sang Sir Lancelot.

She left the web, she left the loom,
She made three paces thro' the room,   110
She saw the water-lily bloom,
She saw the helmet and the plume,
       She looked down to Camelot.
Out flew the web and floated wide;
The mirror cracked from side to side: 115
"The curse is come upon me," cried
       The Lady of Shalott.

PART IV

In the stormy east-wind straining,
The pale yellow woods were waning,
The broad stream in his banks complaining,   120
Heavily the low sky raining,
     Over towered Camelot.
Down she came and found a boat
Beneath a willow left afloat,
And round about the prow she wrote,   125
    The Lady of Shalott.

And down the river's dim expanse,
Like some bold seër in a trance,
Seeing all his own mischance,
With a glassy countenance   130
    Did she look to Camelot.
And at the closing of the day
She loosed the chain, and down she lay;
The broad stream bore her far away,
    The Lady of Shalott.   135

Lying, robed in snowy white
That loosely flew to left and right—
The leaves upon her falling light,—
Thro' the noises of the night
    She floated down to Camelot: 140
And as the boat-head wound along,
The willowy hills and fields among,
They heard her singing her last song,
    The Lady of Shalott:

Heard a carol, mournful, holy,   145
Chanted loudly, chanted lowly,
Till her blood was frozen slowly,
And her eyes were darkened wholly,
    Turned to towered Camelot;
For ere she reached upon the tide   150
The first house by the water-side,
Singing, in her song she died,
    The Lady of Shalott.

Under tower and balcony,
By garden-wall and gallery, 155
A gleaming shape she floated by,
Dead-pale between the houses high,
    Silent into Camelot.
Out upon the wharfs they came,
Knight and burgher, lord and dame, 160
And round the prow they read her name,
    The Lady of Shalott.

Who is this? and what is here?
And in the lighted palace near
Died the sound of royal cheer; 165
And they crossed themselves for fear,
    All the knights at Camelot.
But Lancelot mused a little space:
He said, "She has a lovely face;
God in his mercy lend her grace, 170
    The Lady of Shalott."

            1832.

THE PALACE OF ART

I built my soul a lordly pleasure-house,
    Wherein at ease for aye to dwell.
I said, "O soul, make merry and carouse,
    Dear soul, for all is well."

A huge crag-platform, smooth as burnished brass 5
    I chose. The rangèd ramparts bright
From level meadow-bases of deep grass
    Suddenly scaled the light.

Thereon I built it firm. Of ledge or shelf
    The rock rose clear, or winding stair. 10
My soul would live alone unto herself
    In her high palace there.

And "while the world runs round and round," I said,
    "Reign thou apart, a quiet king,
Still as, while Saturn whirls, his steadfast shade 15
    Sleeps on his luminous ring."

To which my soul made answer readily:
  "Trust me, in bliss I shall abide
In this great mansion that is built for me,
    So royal-rich and wide."   20

*   *   *   *   *   *   *   *   *   *
*   *   *   *   *   *   *   *   *   *

Four courts I made, east, west, and south, and north;
  In each a squarèd lawn, wherefrom
The golden gorge of dragons spouted forth
    A flood of fountain-foam.

And round the cool green courts there ran a row   25
  Of cloisters, branched like mighty woods,
Echoing all night to that sonorous flow
    Of spouted fountain-floods;

And round the roofs a gilded gallery,
  That lent broad verge to distant lands,   30
Far as the wild swan wings, to where the sky
    Dipt down to sea and sands.

From those four jets four currents in one swell
  Across the mountain streamed below
In misty folds, that, floating as they fell,   35
    Lit up a torrent-bow.

And high on every peak a statue seemed
  To hang on tiptoe, tossing up
A cloud of incense of all odour steamed
    From out a golden cup.   40

So that she thought, "And who shall gaze upon
  My palace with unblinded eyes,
While this great bow will waver in the sun,
    And that sweet incense rise?"

For that sweet incense rose and never failed;   45
  And, while day sank or mounted higher,
The light aerial gallery, golden-railed,
    Burnt like a fringe of fire.

Likewise the deep-set windows, stained and traced,
  Would seem slow-flaming crimson fires   50

From shadowed grots of arches interlaced,
    And tipt with frost-like spires.

*   *   *   *   *   *   *   *   *
*   *   *   *   *   *   *   *   *

Full of long-sounding corridors it was,
    That over-vaulted grateful gloom,
Thro' which the livelong day my soul did pass,   55
    Well-pleased, from room to room.

Full of great rooms and small the palace stood,
    All various, each a perfect whole
From living Nature, fit for every mood
    And change of my still soul.   60

For some were hung with arras green and blue,
    Showing a gaudy summer-morn,
Where with puffed cheek the belted hunter blew
    His wreathèd bugle-horn.

One seemed all dark and red—a tract of sand,   65
    And some one pacing there alone,
Who paced forever in a glimmering land,
    Lit with a low large moon.

One showed an iron coast and angry waves.
    You seemed to hear them climb and fall   70
And roar rock-thwarted under bellowing caves,
    Beneath the windy wall.

And one, a full-fed river winding slow
    By herds upon an endless plain,
The ragged rims of thunder brooding low,   75
    With shadow-streaks of rain.

And one, the reapers at their sultry toil:
    In front they bound the sheaves; behind
Were realms of upland, prodigal in oil,
    And hoary to the wind.   80

And one, a foreground black with stones and slags;
    Beyond, a line of heights; and higher,
All barred with long white cloud, the scornful crags;
    And highest, snow and fire.

And one, an English home—gray twilight poured   85
    On dewy pastures, dewy trees,
Softer than sleep; all things in order stored,
    A haunt of ancient Peace.

Nor these alone, but every landscape fair,
    As fit for every mood of mind,   90
Or gay, or grave, or sweet, or stern, was there,
    Not less than truth, designed.

*   *   *   *   *   *   *   *   *
*   *   *   *   *   *   *   *   *

Or the Maid-Mother by a crucifix,
    In tracts of pasture sunny-warm,
Beneath branch-work of costly sardonyx   95
    Sat smiling, babe in arm.

Or in a clear-walled city on the sea,
    Near gilded organ-pipes, her hair
Wound with white roses, slept St. Cecily;
    An angel looked at her.   100

Or, thronging all one porch of Paradise,
    A group of Houris bowed to see
The dying Islamite, with hands and eyes
    That said, "We wait for thee."

Or mythic Uther's deeply-wounded son   105
    In some fair space of sloping greens
Lay, dozing in the vale of Avalon,
    And watched by weeping queens.

Or, hollowing one hand against his ear,
    To list a foot-fall, ere he saw   110
The wood-nymph, stayed the Ausonian king to hear
    Of wisdom and of law.

Or over hills with peaky tops engrailed,
    And many a tract of palm and rice,
The throne of Indian Cama slowly sailed   115
    A summer fanned with spice.

Or sweet Europa's mantle blew unclasped,
　　From off her shoulder backward borne;
From one hand drooped a crocus; one hand grasped
　　　　The mild bull's golden horn.　　　　　　120

Or else flushed Ganymede, his rosy thigh
　　Half-buried in the eagle's down,
Sole as a flying star shot through the sky
　　　　Above the pillared town.

Nor these alone; but every legend fair　　　　125
　　Which the supreme Caucasian mind
Carved out of Nature for itself, was there,
　　　　Not less than life, designed.

*　　*　　*　　*　　*　　*　　*　　*　　*　　*
*　　*　　*　　*　　*　　*　　*　　*　　*

Then in the towers I placed great bells that swung,
　　Moved of themselves, with silver sound;　　130
And with choice paintings of wise men I hung
　　　　The royal dais round.

For there was Milton like a seraph strong,
　　Beside him Shakespeare bland and mild;
And there the world-worn Dante grasped his song,　　135
　　　　And somewhat grimly smiled.

And there the Ionian father of the rest;
　　A million wrinkles carved his skin;
A hundred winters snowed upon his breast,
　　　　From cheek and throat and chin.　　　　140

Above, the fair hall-ceiling, stately-set,
　　Many an arch high up did lift,
And angels rising and descending met
　　　　With interchange of gift.

Below was all mosaic choicely planned　　　　145
　　With cycles of the human tale
Of this wide world, the times of every land
　　　　So wrought they will not fail.

The people here, a beast of burden slow,
    Toiled onward, pricked with goads and stings;   150
Here played, a tiger, rolling to and fro
    The heads and crowns of kings;

Here rose, an athlete, strong to break or bind
    All force in bonds that might endure;
And here, once more, like some sick man declined,   155
    And trusted any cure.

But over these she trod; and those great bells
    Began to chime. She took her throne;
She sat betwixt the shining oriels,
    To sing her songs alone.   160

And through the topmost oriels' coloured flame
    Two godlike faces gazed below:
Plato the wise, and large-browed Verulam,
    The first of those who know.

And all those names that in their motion were   165
    Full-welling fountain-heads of change,
Betwixt the slender shafts were blazoned fair
    In diverse raiment strange;

Through which the lights, rose, amber, emerald, blue,
    Flushed in her temples and her eyes,   170
And from her lips, as morn from Memnon, drew
    Rivers of melodies.

No nightingale delighteth to prolong
    Her low preamble all alone,
More than my soul to hear her echoed song   175
    Throb through the ribbèd stone;

Singing and murmuring in her feastful mirth,
    Joying to feel herself alive,
Lord over Nature, lord of the visible earth,
    Lord of the senses five;   180

Communing with herself: "All these are mine;
    And let the world have peace or wars,
'T is one to me."   She—when young night divine
    Crowned dying day with stars,

Making sweet close of his delicious toils—   185
    Lit light in wreaths and anadems,
And pure quintessences of precious oils
    In hollowed moons of gems,

To mimic heaven; and clapt her hands and cried:
    "I marvel if my still delight   190
In this great house so royal-rich and wide
    Be flattered to the height.

"O all things fair to sate my various eyes!
    O shapes and hues that please me well!
O silent faces of the Great and Wise,   195
    My gods, with whom I dwell!

"O godlike isolation which art mine,
    I can but count thee perfect gain,
What time I watch the darknening droves of swine
    That range on yonder plain.   200

"In filthy sloughs they roll a prurient skin,
    They graze and wallow, breed and sleep;
And oft some brainless devil enters in,
    And drives them to the deep."

Then of the moral instinct would she prate   205
    And of the rising from the dead,
As hers by right of full-accomplished Fate;
    And at the last she said:

"I take possession of man's mind and deed.
    I care not what the sects may brawl.   210
I sit as God holding no form of creed,
    But contemplating all."

*   *   *   *   *   *   *   *   *
*   *   *   *   *   *   *   *   *

Full oft the riddle of the painful earth
 Flashed thro' her as she sat alone,
Yet not the less held she her solemn mirth,   215
 And intellectual throne.

And so she throve and prospered; so three years
 She prospered: on the fourth she fell,
Like Herod, when the shout was in his ears,
 Struck thro' with pangs of hell.   220

Lest she should fail and perish utterly,
 God, before whom ever lie bare
The abysmal deeps of Personality,
 Plagued her with sore despair.

When she would think, where'er she turned her sight 225
 The airy hand confusion wrought,
Wrote, "Mene, mene," and divided quite
 The kingdom of her thought.

Deep dread and loathing of her solitude
 Fell on her, from which mood was born   230
Scorn of herself; again, from out that mood,
 Laughter at her self-scorn.

"What! is not this my place of strength," she said,
 "My spacious mansion built for me,
Whereof the strong foundation-stones were laid 235
 Since my first memory?"

But in dark corners of her palace stood
 Uncertain shapes; and unawares
On white-eyed phantasms weeping tears of blood,
 And horrible nightmares,   240

And hollow shades enclosing hearts of flame,
 And, with dim fretted foreheads all,
On corpses three-months-old at noon she came
 That stood against the wall.

A spot of dull stagnation, without light   245
 Or power of movement, seemed my soul,
'Mid onward-sloping motions infinite
 Making for one sure goal:

A still salt pool, locked in with bars of sand,
 Left on the shore; that hears all night   250
The plunging seas draw backward from the land
 Their moon-led waters white:

A star that with the choral starry dance
 Joined not, but stood, and standing saw
The hollow orb of moving Circumstance   255
 Rolled round by one fixed law.

Back on herself her serpent pride had curled.
 "No voice," she shrieked in that lone hall,
"No voice breaks thro' the stillness of this world:
 One deep, deep silence all!"   260

She, mouldering with the dull earth's mouldering sod,
 Inwrapt tenfold in slothful shame,
Lay there exilèd from eternal God,
 Lost to her place and name.

And death and life she hated equally;   265
 And nothing saw, for her despair,
But dreadful time, dreadful eternity,
 No comfort anywhere;

Remaining utterly confused with fears,
 And ever worse with growing time,   270
And ever unrelieved by dismal tears,
 And all alone in crime.

Shut up as in a crumbling tomb girt round
 With blackness as a solid wall,
Far off she seemed to hear the dully sound   275
 Of human footsteps fall:

As in strange lands a traveller walking slow,
  In doubt and great perplexity,
A little before moon-rise hears the low
  Moan of an unknown sea;   280

And knows not if it be thunder, or a sound
  Of rocks thrown down, or one deep cry
Of great wild beasts; then thinketh, "I have found
  A new land, but I die."

She howled aloud: "I am on fire within!   285
  There comes no murmur of reply!
What is it that will take my sin,
  And save me lest I die?"

So when four years were wholly finishèd,
  She threw her royal robes away.   290
"Make me a cottage in the vale," she said,
  "Where I may mourn and pray.

"Yet pull not down my palace towers, that are
  So lightly, beautifully built:
Perchance I may return with others there   295
  When I have purged my guilt."

                                          1832

THE LOTUS-EATERS

"Courage!" he said, and pointed toward the land;
"This mounting wave will roll us shoreward soon."
In the afternoon they came unto a land
In which it seemèd always afternoon.
All round the coast the languid air did swoon,   5
Breathing like one that hath a weary dream.
Full-faced above the valley stood the moon;
And, like a downward smoke, the slender stream
Along the cliff to fall and pause and fall did seem.

A land of streams! some, like a downward smoke,   10
Slow-dropping veils of thinnest lawn, did go;
And some thro' wavering lights and shadows broke,
Rolling a slumbrous sheet of foam below.

They saw the gleaming river seaward flow
From the inner land; far off, three mountain-tops,   15
Three silent pinnacles of aged snow,
Stood sunset-flushed; and, dewed with showery drops,
Up-clomb the shadowy pine above the woven copse.

The charmèd sunset lingered low adown
In the red West; thro' mountain clefts the dale   20
Was seen far inland, and the yellow down
Bordered with palm, and many a winding vale
And meadow, set with slender galingale:
A land where all things always seemed the same!
And round about the keel, with faces pale,   25
Dark faces pale against that rosy flame,
The mild-eyed melancholy Lotus-eaters came.

Branches they bore of that enchanted stem,
Laden with flower and fruit, whereof they gave
To each; but whoso did receive of them   30
And taste, to him the gushing of the wave
Far, far away did seem to mourn and rave
On alien shores; and if his fellow spake,
His voice was thin, as voices from the grave;
And deep-asleep he seemed, yet all awake,   35
And music in his ears his beating heart did make.

They sat them down upon the yellow sand,
Between the sun and moon upon the shore;
And sweet it was to dream of Fatherland,
Of child, and wife, and slave; but evermore   40
Most weary seemed the sea, weary the oar,
Weary the wandering fields of barren foam.
Then some one said, "We will return no more";
And all at once they sang, "Our island home
Is far beyond the wave; we will no longer roam."   45

1832.

YOU ASK ME WHY, THO' ILL AT EASE

You ask me why, tho' ill at ease,
    Within this region I subsist,
    Whose spirits falter in the mist,
And languish for the purple seas,

It is the land that freemen till,   5
    That sober-suited Freedom chose;
    The land where, girt with friends or foes,
A man may speak the thing he will;

A land of settled government,
    A land of just and old renown,   10
    Where freedom slowly broadens down
From precedent to precedent;

Where faction seldom gathers head,
    But, by degrees to fullness wrought,
    The strength of some diffusive thought   15
Hath time and space to work and spread.

Should banded unions persecute
    Opinion, and induce a time
    When single thought is civil crime,
And individual freedom mute;   20

Tho' power should make from land to land
    The name of Britain trebly great,
    Tho' every channel of the State
Should fill and choke with golden sand,

Yet waft me from the harbour-mouth,   25
    Wild wind! I seek a warmer sky,
    And I will see before I die
The palms and temples of the South.

1833.   1842.

ULYSSES

It little profits that an idle king,
By this still hearth, among these barren crags,
Matched with an aged wife, I mete and dole
Unequal laws unto a savage race,
That hoard, and sleep, and feed, and know not me.   5
    I cannot rest from travel: I will drink
Life to the lees. All times I have enjoyed
Greatly, have suffered greatly, both with those
That loved me, and alone; on shore, and when
Thro' scudding drifts the rainy Hyades   10

Vext the dim sea. I am become a name;
For, always roaming with a hungry heart,
Much have I seen and known—cities of men
And manners, climates, councils, governments,
Myself not least, but honoured of them all;   15
And drunk delight of battle with my peers,
Far on the ringing plains of windy Troy.
I am a part of all that I have met;
Yet all experience is an arch wherethro'
Gleams that untravelled world whose margin fades   20
Forever and forever when I move.
How dull it is to pause, to make an end,
To rust unburnished, not to shine in use,
As tho' to breathe were life! Life piled on life
Were all too little, and of one to me   25
Little remains: but every hour is saved
From that eternal silence—something more,
A bringer of new things; and vile it were
For some three suns to store and hoard myself,
And this gray spirit yearning in desire   30
To follow knowledge like a sinking star,
Beyond the utmost bound of human thought.

    This is my son, mine own Telemachus,
To whom I leave the sceptre and the isle—
Well-loved of me discerning to fulfil   35
This labour, by slow prudence to make mild
A rugged people, and thro' soft degrees
Subdue them to the useful and the good.
Most blameless is he, centred in the sphere
Of common duties, decent not to fail   40
In offices of tenderness, and pay
Meet adoration to my household gods,
When I am gone. He works his work, I mine.

    There lies the port; the vessel puffs her sail;
There gloom the dark broad seas. My mariners,   45
Souls that have toiled, and wrought, and thought with
        me—
That ever with a frolic welcome took
The thunder and the sunshine, and opposed
Free hearts, free foreheads,—you and I are old;
Old age hath yet his honour and his toil: 50

Death closes all; but something ere the end,
Some work of noble note, may yet be done,
Not unbecoming men that strove with gods.
The lights begin to twinkle from the rocks;
The long day wanes; the slow moon climbs; the deep   55
Moans round with many voices. Come my friends,
'T is not too late to seek a newer world.
Push off, and, sitting well in order, smite
The sounding furrows; for my purpose holds
To sail beyond the sunset, and the baths   60
Of all the western stars, until I die.
It may be that the gulfs will wash us down;
It may be we shall touch the Happy Isles,
And see the great Achilles, whom we knew.
Tho' much is taken, much abides; and tho'   65
We are not now that strength which in old days
Moved earth and heaven, that which we are, we are—
One equal temper of heroic hearts,
Made weak by time and fate, but strong in will
To strive, to seek, to find, and not to yield.   70

About 1833.   1842.

MORTE D'ARTHUR

So all day long the noise of battle rolled
Among the mountains by the winter sea;
Until King Arthur's table, man by man,
Had fallen in Lyonesse about their lord,
King Arthur. Then, because his wound was deep,   5
The bold Sir Bedivere uplifted him,
Sir Bedivere, the last of all his knights,
And bore him to a chapel nigh the field,
A broken chancel with a broken cross,
That stood on a dark strait of barren land: 10
On one side lay the ocean, and on one
Lay a great water, and the moon was full.
    Then spake King Arthur to Sir Bedivere:
"The sequel of to-day unsolders all
The goodliest fellowship of famous knights   15
Whereof this world holds record. Such a sleep
They sleep—the men I loved. I think that we

Shall never more, at any future time,
Delight our souls with talk of knightly deeds,
Walking about the gardens and the halls   20
Of Camelot, as in the days that were.
I perish by this people which I made,—
Tho' Merlin sware that I should come again
To rule once more;—but let what will be, be,
I am so deeply smitten thro' the helm   25
That without help I cannot last till morn.
Thou therefore take my brand Excalibur,
Which was my pride: for thou rememberest how
In those old days, one summer noon, an arm
Rose up from out the bosom of the lake,   30
Clothed in white samite, mystic, wonderful,
Holding the sword; and how I rowed across
And took it, and have worn it, like a king;
And wheresoever I am sung or told
In after time, this also shall be known.   35
But now delay not: take Excalibur,
And fling him far into the middle mere;
Watch what thou seëst, and lightly bring me word."
     To him replied the bold Sir Bedivere:
"It is not meet, Sir King, to leave thee thus,   40
Aidless, alone, and smitten thro' the helm.
A little thing may harm a wounded man.
Yet I thy hest will all perform at full,
Watch what I see, and lightly bring thee word."
     So saying, from the ruined shrine he stept   45
And in the moon athwart the place of tombs,
Where lay the mighty bones of ancient men,
Old knights, and over them the sea-wind sang
Shrill, chill, with flakes of foam. He, stepping down
By zigzag paths, and juts of pointed rock,   50
Came on the shining levels of the lake.
     There drew he forth the brand Excalibur,
And o'er him, drawing it, the winter moon,
Brightening the skirts of a long cloud, ran forth
And sparkled keen with frost against the hilt;   55
For all the haft twinkled with diamond sparks,
Myriads of topaz-lights, and jacinth-work
Of subtlest jewellery. He gazed so long

That both his eyes were dazzled, as he stood,
This way and that dividing the swift mind,   60
In act to throw; but at the last it seemed
Better to leave Excalibur concealed
There in the many-knotted waterflags,
That whistled stiff and dry about the marge.
So strode he back slow to the wounded King.   65
    Then spake King Arthur to Sir Bedivere:
"Hast thou performed my mission which I gave?
What is it thou hast seen? or what hast heard?"
    And answer made the bold Sir Bedivere:
"I heard the ripple washing in the reeds,   70
And the wild water lapping on the crag."
    To whom replied King Arthur, faint and pale:
"Thou hast betrayed thy nature and thy name,
Not rendering true answer, as beseemed
Thy fealty, nor like a noble knight;   75
For surer sign had followed, either hand,
Or voice, or else a motion of the mere.
This is a shameful thing for men to lie.
Yet now, I charge thee, quickly go again,
As thou art lief and dear, and do the thing   80
I bade thee; watch, and lightly bring me word."
    Then went Sir Bedivere the second time
Across the ridge, and paced beside the mere,
Counting the dewy pebbles, fixed in thought;
But when he saw the wonder of the hilt,   85
How curiously and strangely chased, he smote
His palms together, and he cried aloud:
"And if indeed I cast the brand away,
Surely a precious thing, one worthy note,
Should thus be lost forever from the earth,   90
Which might have pleased the eyes of many men.
What good should follow this, if this were done?
What harm, undone? deep harm to disobey,
Seeing obedience is the bond of rule.
Were it well to obey, then, if a king demand   95
An act unprofitable, against himself?
The King is sick, and knows not what he does.
What record, or what relic of my lord
Should be to aftertime, but empty breath

And rumours of a doubt? But were this kept, 100
Stored in some treasure-house of mighty kings,
Some one might show it at a joust of arms,
Saying, 'King Arthur's sword, Excalibur,
Wrought by the lonely Maiden of the Lake;
Nine years she wrought it, sitting in the deeps 105
Upon the hidden bases of the hills.'
So might some old man speak in the aftertime
To all the people, winning reverence.
But now much honour and much fame were lost."

So spake he, clouded with his own conceit, 110
And hid Excalibur the second time,
And so strode back slow to the wounded King.

Then spoke King Arthur, breathing heavily:
"What is it thou hast seen? or what hast heard?"

And answer made the bold Sir Bedivere: 115
"I heard the water lapping on the crag,
And the long ripple washing in the reeds."

To whom replied King Arthur, much in wrath:
"Ah, miserable and unkind, untrue,
Unknightly, traitor-hearted! Woe is me! 120
Authority forgets a dying king,
Laid widowed of the power in his eye
That bowed the will. I see thee what thou art,
For thou, the latest-left of all my knights,
In whom should meet the offices of all, 125
Thou wouldst betray me for the precious hilt;
Either from lust of gold, or, like a girl,
Valuing the giddy pleasure of the eyes.
Yet, for a man may fail in duty twice,
And the third time may prosper, get thee hence; 130
But if thou spare to fling Excalibur,
I will arise and slay thee with my hands."

Then quickly rose Sir Bedivere, and ran,
And, leaping down the ridges lightly, plunged
Among the bulrush-beds, and clutched the sword, 135
And strongly wheeled and threw it. The great brand
Made lightnings in the splendour of the moon,
And flashing round and round, and whirled in an arch,
Shot like a streamer of the northern morn,
Seen where the moving isles of winter shock 140

By night, with noises of the northern sea.
So flashed and fell the brand Excalibur;
But ere he dipt the surface, rose an arm
Clothed in white samite, mystic, wonderful,
And caught him by the hilt, and brandished him   145
Three times, and drew him under in the mere.
And lightly went the other to the King.
    Then spoke King Arthur, drawing thicker breath:
"Now see I by thine eyes that this is done.
Speak out: what is it thou hast heard or seen?"   150
    And answer made the bold Sir Bedivere:
"Sir King, I closed mine eyelids, lest the gems
Should blind my purpose, for I never saw,
Nor shall see, here or elsewhere, till I die,
Not tho' I live three lives of mortal men,   155
So great a miracle as yonder hilt.
Then with both hands I flung him, wheeling him;
But when I looked again, behold an arm,
Clothed in white samite, mystic, wonderful,
That caught him by the hilt, and brandished him   160
Three times, and drew him under in the mere."
    And answer made King Arthur, breathing hard:
"My end draws nigh; 't is time that I were gone.
Make broad thy shoulders to receive my weight,
And bear me to the margin; yet I fear   165
My wound hath taken cold, and I shall die."
    So saying, from the pavement he half rose,
Slowly, with pain, reclining on his arm,
And looking wistfully with wide blue eyes
As in a picture. Him Sir Bedivere   170
Remorsefully regarded thro' his tears,
And would have spoken, but he found not words;
Then took with care, and, kneeling on one knee,
O'er both his shoulders drew the languid hands,
And, rising, bore him thro' the place of tombs.   175
    But, as he walked, King Arthur panted hard,
Like one that feels a nightmare on his bed
When all the house is mute. So sighed the King,
Muttering and murmuring at his ear, "Quick, quick!
I fear it is too late, and I shall die."   180
But the other swiftly strode from ridge to ridge,

Clothed with his breath, and looking, as he walked,
Larger than human on the frozen hills.
He heard the deep behind him, and a cry
Before. His own thought drove him, like a goad.   185
Dry clashed his harness in the icy caves
And barren chasms, and all to left and right
The bare black cliff clanged round him, as he based
His feet on juts of slippery crag that rang
Sharp-smitten with the dint of armèd heels—   190
And on a sudden, lo! the level lake,
And the long glories of the winter moon.

Then saw they how there hove a dusky barge,
Dark as a funeral scarf from stem to stern,
Beneath them; and, descending, they were ware   195
That all the decks were dense with stately forms
Black-stoled, black-hooded, like a dream; by these,
Three queens with crowns of gold; and from them rose
A cry that shivered to the tingling stars,
And, as it were one voice, an agony   200
Of lamentation, like a wind that shrills
All night in a waste land, where no one comes,
Or hath come, since the making of the world.

Then murmured Arthur, "Place me in the barge";
And to the barge they came. There those three queens 205
Put forth their hands, and took the king, and wept.
But she, that rose the tallest of them all
And fairest, laid his head upon her lap,
And loosed the shattered casque, and chafed his hands,
And called him by his name, complaining loud,   210
And dropping bitter tears against his brow
Striped with dark blood: for all his face was white
And colourless, and like the withered moon
Smote by the fresh beam of the springing east;
And all his greaves and cuisses dashed with drops   215
Of onset; and the light and lustrous curls—
That made his forehead like a rising sun
High from the dais-throne—were parched with dust,
Or, clotted into points and hanging loose,
Mixed with the knightly growth that fringed his lips.   220
So like a shattered column lay the King;
Not like that Arthur who, with lance in rest,

From spur to plume a star of tournament,
Shot thro' the lists at Camelot, and charged
Before the eyes of ladies and of kings.   225
    Then loudly cried the bold Sir Bedivere:
"Ah! my Lord Arthur, whither shall I go?
Where shall I hide my forehead and my eyes?
For now I see the true old times are dead,
When every morning brought a noble chance,   230
Every chance brought out a noble knight.
Such times have been not since the light that led
The holy Elders with the gift of myrrh.
But now the whole ROUND TABLE is dissolved,
Which was an image of the mighty world;   235
And I, the last, go forth companionless,
And the days darken round me, and the years,
Among new men, strange faces, other minds."
    And slowly answered Arthur from the barge:
"The old order changeth, yielding place to new,   240
And God fulfils Himself in many ways,
Lest one good custom should corrupt the world.
Comfort thyself: what comfort is in me?
I have lived my life, and that which I have done
May He within Himself make pure! But thou,   245
If thou shouldst never see my face again,
Pray for my soul. More things are wrought by prayer
Than this world dreams of. Wherefore, let thy voice
Rise like a fountain for me night and day.
For what are men better than sheep or goats   250
That nourish a blind life within the brain,
If, knowing God, they lift not hands of prayer
Both for themselves and those who call them friend?
For so the whole round earth is every way
Bound by gold chains about the feet of God.   255
But now farewell. I am going a long way
With these thou seëst—if indeed I go
(For all my mind is clouded with a doubt)—
To the island valley of Avilion,
Where falls not hail, or rain, or any snow,   260
Nor ever wind blows loudly; but it lies
Deep-meadowed, happy, fair with orchard-lawns
And bowery hollows crowned with summer sea;

Where I will heal me of my grievous wound."
   So said he; and the barge with oar and sail   265
Moved from the brink, like some full-breasted swan
That, fluting a wild carol ere her death,
Ruffles her pure cold plume, and takes the flood
With swarthy webs. Long stood Sir Bedivere,
Revolving many memories, till the hull   270
Looked one black dot against the verge of dawn,
And on the mere the wailing died away.

1834.   *1842.*

LOCKSLEY HALL

Comrades, leave me here a little, while as yet 't is early morn;
Leave me here, and when you want me, sound upon the bugle-horn.

'T is the place, and all around it, as of old, the curlews call,
Dreary gleams about the moorland flying over Locksley Hall;

Locksley Hall, that in the distance overlooks the sandy tracts,   5
And the hollow ocean-ridges roaring into cataracts.

Many a night from yonder ivied casement, ere I went to rest,
Did I look on great Orion sloping slowly to the west.

Many a night I saw the Pleiads, rising thro' the mellow shade,
Glitter like a swarm of fire-flies tangled in a silver braid.   10

Here about the beach I wandered, nourishing a youth sublime
With the fairy tales of science and the long result of Time;

When the centuries behind me like a fruitful land reposed;
When I clung to all the present for the promise that it closed;

When I dipt into the future far as human eye could see,   15
Saw the vision of the world and all the wonder that would be.——

In the spring a fuller crimson comes upon the robin's breast;
In the spring the wanton lapwing gets himself another crest;

In the spring a livelier iris changes on the burnished dove;
In the spring a young man's fancy lightly turns to thoughts of
    love.   20

Then her cheek was pale and thinner than should be for one so
    young,
And her eyes on all my motions with a mute observance hung.

And I said, "My cousin Amy, speak, and speak the truth to me;
Trust me, cousin, all the current of my being sets to thee."

On her pallid cheek and forehead came a colour and a light,   25
As I have seen the rosy red flushing in the northern night.

And she turned—her bosom shaken with a sudden storm of sighs,
All the spirit deeply dawning in the dark of hazel eyes,—

Saying, "I have hid my feelings, fearing they should do me
    wrong";
Saying, "Dost thou love me, cousin?" weeping, "I have loved thee
    long."   30

Love took up the glass of Time, and turned it in his glowing
    hands;
Every moment, lightly shaken, ran itself in golden sands.

Love took up the harp of Life, and smote on all the chords with
    might;
Smote the Chord of Self, that, trembling, passed in music out of
    sight.

Many a morning on the moorland did we hear the copses ring,   35
And her whisper thronged my pulses with the fullness of the
    spring.

Many an evening by the waters did we watch the stately ships,
And our spirits rushed together at the touching of the lips.

O my cousin, shallow-hearted! O my Amy, mine no more!
O the dreary, dreary moorland! O the barren, barren shore!   40

Falser than all fancy fathoms, falser than all songs have sung,
Puppet to a father's threat, and servile to a shrewish tongue!

Is it well to wish thee happy?—having known me, to decline
On a range of lower feelings and a narrower heart than mine!

Yet it shall be; thou shalt lower to his level, day by day,   45
What is fine within thee growing coarse to sympathise with clay.

As the husband is, the wife is; thou art mated with a clown,
And the grossness of his nature will have weight to drag thee
    down.

He will hold thee, when his passion shall have spent its novel
    force,
Something better than his dog, a little dearer than his horse.   50

What is this? his eyes are heavy: think not they are glazed with
    wine.
 Go to him—it is thy duty; kiss him; take his hand in thine.

It may be my lord is weary, that his brain is overwrought:
Soothe him with thy finer fancies, touch him with thy lighter
    thought.

He will answer to the purpose, easy things to understand—   55
Better thou wert dead before me, tho' I slew thee with my
    hand!

Better thou and I were lying, hidden from the heart's disgrace,
Rolled in one another's arms, and silent in a last embrace.

Cursèd be the social wants that sin against the strength of youth!
Cursèd be the social lies that warp us from the living truth!   60

Cursèd be the sickly forms that err from honest Nature's rule!
Cursèd be the gold that gilds the straitened forehead of the fool!

Well—'t is well that I should bluster!—Hadst thou less unworthy
    proved—
Would to God—for I had loved thee more than ever wife was
    loved.

Am I mad, that I should cherish that which bears but bitter fruit? 65
I will pluck it from thy bosom, tho' my heart be at the root.—

Never! tho' my mortal summers to such length of years should
    come
As the many-wintered crow that leads the clanging rookery home.

Where is comfort? in division of the records of the mind?
Can I part her from herself, and love her, as I knew her, kind?   70

I remember one that perished; sweetly did she speak and move:
Such a one do I remember, whom to look at was to love.

Can I think of her as dead, and love her for the love she bore?
No—she never loved me truly: love is love forevermore.

Comfort? comfort scorned of devils! this is truth the poet sings, 75
That a sorrow's crown of sorrow is remembering happier things.

Drug thy memories, lest thou learn it, lest thy heart be put to
    proof,
In the dead unhappy night, and when the rain is on the roof.

Like a dog, he hunts in dreams, and thou art staring at the wall,
Where the dying night-lamp flickers, and the shadows rise and
    fall. 80

Then a hand shall pass before thee, pointing to his drunken sleep,
To thy widowed marriage-pillows, to the tears that thou wilt
    weep.

Thou shalt hear the "Never, never," whispered by the phantom
    years,
And a song from out the distance in the ringing of thine ears;

And an eye shall vex thee, looking ancient kindness on thy pain. 85
Turn thee, turn thee on thy pillow; get thee to thy rest again.

Nay, but Nature brings thee solace; for a tender voice will cry.
'T is a purer life than thine; a lip to drain thy trouble dry.

Baby lips will laugh me down: my latest rival brings thee rest.
Baby fingers, waxen touches, press me from the mother's breast. 90

O, the child too clothes the father with a dearness not his due.
Half is thine and half is his: it will be worthy of the two.

O, I see thee, old and formal, fitted to thy petty part,
With a little hoard of maxims preaching down a daughter's heart:

"They were dangerous guides, the feelings—she herself was not
    exempt— 95
Truly, she herself had suffered."—Perish in thy self-contempt!

Overlive it—lower yet, be happy! wherefore should I care?
I myself must mix with action, lest I wither by despair.

What is that which I should turn to, lighting upon days like
    these?
Every door is barred with gold, and opens but to golden keys. 100

Every gate is thronged with suitors, all the markets overflow.
I have but an angry fancy: what is that which I should do?

I had been content to perish, falling on the foeman's ground,
When the ranks are rolled in vapour, and the winds are laid with
   sound.

But the jingling of the guinea helps the hurt that Honour feels, 105
And the nations do but murmur, snarling at each other's heels.——

Can I but relive in sadness? I will turn that earlier page.
Hide me from my deep emotion, O thou wondrous Mother-Age!

Make me feel the wild pulsation that I felt before the strife.
When I heard my days before me, and the tumult of my life; 110

Yearning for the large excitement that the coming years would
   yield,
Eager-hearted as a boy when first he leaves his father's field,

And at night along the dusky highway near and nearer drawn,
Sees in heaven the light of London flaring like a dreary dawn;

And his spirit leaps within him to be gone before him then, 115
Underneath the light he looks at, in among the throngs of men;

Men, my brothers, men the workers, ever reaping something new,
That which they have done but earnest of the things that they
   shall do!

For I dipt into the future, far as human eye could see,
Saw the vision of the world and all the wonder that would be; 120

Saw the heavens fill with commerce, argosies of magic sails,
Pilots of the purple twilight, dropping down with costly bales;

Heard the heavens fill with shouting, and there rained a ghastly
   dew
From the nations' airy navies grappling in the central blue;

Far along the world-wide whisper of the south-wind rushing
   warm,   125
With the standards of the peoples plunging thro' the thunder-
   storm;

Till the war-drum throbbed no longer, and the battle-flags were
    furled
In the Parliament of Man, the Federation of the World.

There the common sense of most shall hold a fretful realm in
    awe,
And the kindly earth shall slumber, lapt in universal law.   130

So I triumphed ere my passion, sweeping thro' me, left me dry,
Left me with the palsied heart, and left me with the jaundiced
    eye;

Eye to which all order festers, all things here are out of joint:
Science moves, but slowly, slowly, creeping on from point to
    point;

Slowly comes a hungry people, as a lion, creeping nigher,   135
Glares at one that nods and winks behind a slowly-dying fire.

Yet I doubt not thro' the ages one increasing purpose runs,
And the thoughts of men are widened with the process of the
    suns.

What is that to him that reaps not harvest of his youthful joys,
Tho' the deep heart of existence beat forever like a boy's?   140

Knowledge comes, but wisdom lingers, and I linger on the shore;
And the individual withers, and the world is more and more.

Knowledge comes, but wisdom lingers, and he bears a laden
    breast,
Full of sad experience, moving toward the stillness of his rest.

Hark, my merry comrades call me, sounding on the bugle-horn, 145
They to whom my foolish passion were a target for their scorn.

Shall it not be scorn to me to harp on such a mouldered string?
I am ashamed thro' all my nature to have loved so slight a thing.

Weakness to be wroth with weakness! woman's pleasure, woman's
    pain—
Nature made them blinder motions bounded in a shallower
    brain: 150

Woman is the lesser man; and all thy passions, matched with
  mine,
Are as moonlight unto sunlight, and as water unto wine.——

Here at least, where Nature sickens, nothing. Ah, for some
    retreat
Deep in yonder shining Orient, where my life began to beat;

Where in wild Mahratta-battle fell my father, evil-starred;— 155
I was left a trampled orphan, and a selfish uncle's ward.

Or to burst all links of habit—there to wander far away,
On from island unto island at the gateways of the day:

Larger constellations burning, mellow moons and happy skies,
Breadths of tropic shade and palms in cluster knots of Paradise. 160

Never comes the trader, never floats an European flag;
Slides the bird o'er lustrous woodland, swings the trailer from
    the crag;

Droops the heavy-blossomed bower, hangs the heavy-fruited tree—
Summer isles of Eden lying in dark-purple spheres of sea.

There methinks would be enjoyment more than in this march of
    mind,   165
In the steamship, in the railway, in the thoughts that shake
    mankind.

There the passions, cramped no longer, shall have scope and
    breathing space;
I will take some savage woman, she shall rear my dusky race.

Iron-jointed, supple-sinewed, they shall dive, and they shall run,
Catch the wild goat by the hair, and hurl their lances in the sun; 170

Whistle back the parrot's call, and leap the rainbows of the
    brooks,
Not with blinded eyesight poring over miserable books——

Fool, again the dream, the fancy! but I *know* my words are wild,
But I count the gray barbarian lower than the Christian child.

I, to herd with narrow foreheads, vacant of our glorious gains, 175
Like a beast with lower pleasures, like a beast with lower pains!

Mated with a squalid savage—what to me were sun or clime?
I the heir of all the ages, in the foremost files of time—

I that rather held it better men should perish one by one,
Than that earth should stand at gaze like Joshua's moon in
    Ajalon! 180

Not in vain the distance beacons. Forward, forward let us
    range!
Let the great world spin forever down the ringing grooves of
    change.

Thro' the shadow of the globe we sweep into the younger day:
Better fifty years of Europe than a cycle of Cathay.

Mother-Age (for mine I knew not), help me as when life begun: 185
Rift the hills, and roll the waters, flash the lightnings, weigh the
    sun.

O, I see the crescent promise of my spirit hath not set.
Ancient founts of inspiration well thro' all my fancy yet.

Howsoever these things be, a long farewell to Locksley Hall!
Now for me the woods may wither, now for me the roof-tree
    fall. 190

Comes a vapour from the margin, blackening over heath and holt,
Cramming all the blast before it, in its breast a thunderbolt.

Let it fall on Locksley Hall, with rain or hail, or fire or snow;
For the mighty wind arises, roaring seaward, and I go.

                      1842.

BREAK, BREAK, BREAK

    Break, break, break,
        On thy cold gray stones, O sea!
    And I would that my tongue could utter
        The thoughts that arise in me.

    O well for the fisherman's boy 5
        That he shouts with his sister at play!
    O well for the sailor lad
        That he sings in his boat on the bay!

And the stately ships go on
    To their haven under the hill;   10
But O for the touch of a vanished hand,
    And the sound of a voice that is still!

Break, break, break,
    At the foot of thy crags, O sea!
But the tender grace of a day that is dead   15
    Will never come back to me.

                      1842.

FROM

IN MEMORIAM A. H. H.

XXXIII

O thou that after toil and storm
    Mayst seem to have reached a purer air,
    Whose faith has centre everywhere,
Nor cares to fix itself to form,

Leave thou thy sister, when she prays,   5
    Her early heaven, her happy views;
    Nor thou with shadowed hint confuse
A life that leads melodious days.

Her faith thro' form is pure as thine,
    Her hands are quicker unto good: 10
    Oh, sacred be the flesh and blood
To which she links a truth divine!

See thou, that countest reason ripe
    In holding by the law within,
    Thou fail not in a world of sin,   15
And ev'n for want of such a type.

XXXIV

My own dim life should teach me this,
    That life shall live forevermore,
    Else earth is darkness at the core,
And dust and ashes all that is;

This round of green, this orb of flame,   5
    Fantastic beauty, such as lurks
    In some wild poet when he works
Without a conscience or an aim.

What then were God to such as I?
    'T were hardly worth my while to choose   10
    Of things all mortal, or to use
A little patience ere I die;

'T were best at once to sink to peace,
    Like birds the charming serpent draws,
    To drop head-foremost in the jaws   15
Of vacant darkness and to cease.

XLVII

That each, who seems a separate whole,
    Should move his rounds, and, fusing all
    The skirts of self again, should fall
Remerging in the general Soul,

Is faith as vague as all unsweet: 5
    Eternal form shall still divide
    The eternal soul from all beside,
And I shall know him when we meet;

And we shall sit at endless feast,
    Enjoying each the other's good.   10
    What vaster dream can hit the mood
Of Love on earth? He seeks at least

Upon the last and sharpest height,
    Before the spirits fade away,
    Some landing-place, to clasp and say,   15
"Farewell! We lose ourselves in light."

LIV

Oh yet we trust that somehow good
    Will be the final goal of ill,
    To pangs of nature, sins of will,
Defects of doubt, and taints of blood;

That nothing walks with aimless feet;   5
    That not one life shall be destroyed,
    Or cast as rubbish to the void,
When God hath made the pile complete;

That not a worm is cloven in vain;
   That not a moth with vain desire 10
   Is shrivelled in a fruitless fire,
Or but subserves another's gain.

Behold, we know not anything;
   I can but trust that good shall fall
   At last—far off—at last, to all, 15
And every winter change to spring.

So runs my dream: but what am I?
   An infant crying in the night;
   An infant crying for the light;
And with no language but a cry. 20

LV

The wish that of the living whole
   No life may fail beyond the grave,
   Derives it not from what we have
The likest God within the soul?

Are God and Nature, then, at strife, 5
   That Nature lends such evil dreams?
   So careful of the type she seems,
So careless of the single life,

That I, considering everywhere
   Her secret meaning in her deeds, 10
   And finding that of fifty seeds
She often brings but one to bear,

I falter where I firmly trod,
   And, falling with my weight of cares
   Upon the great world's altar-stairs 15
That slope thro' darkness up to God,

I stretch lame hands of faith, and grope,
   And gather dust and chaff, and call
   To what I feel is Lord of all,
And faintly trust the larger hope. 20

LVI

"So careful of the type?" but no.
  From scarpèd cliff and quarried stone
  She cries, "A thousand types are gone:
I care for nothing, all shall go.

"Thou makest thine appeal to me: 5
  I bring to life, I bring to death;
  The spirit does but mean the breath:
I know no more." And he, shall he,

Man, her last work, who seemed so fair,
  Such splendid purpose in his eyes,   10
  Who rolled the psalm to wintry skies,
Who built him fanes of fruitless prayer,

Who trusted God was love indeed
  And love Creation's final law—
  Tho' Nature, red in tooth and claw   15
With ravine, shrieked against his creed,—

Who loved, who suffered countless ills,
  Who battled for the True, the Just,—
  Be blown about the desert dust,
Or sealed within the iron hills?   20

No more? A monster, then, a dream,
  A discord. Dragons of the prime,
  That tare each other in their slime,
Were mellow music matched with him.

O life as futile, then, as frail!   25
  O for thy voice to soothe and bless!
  What hope of answer or redress?
Behind the veil, behind the veil.

XCVI

You say, but with no touch of scorn,
  Sweet-hearted, you, whose light-blue eyes
  Are tender over drowning flies,
You tell me, doubt is Devil-born.

I know not: one indeed I knew
    In many a subtle question versed,
    Who touched a jarring lyre at first,
But ever strove to make it true: 5

Perplext in faith, but pure in deeds,
    At last he beat his music out.   10
    There lives more faith in honest doubt,
Believe me, than in half the creeds.

He fought his doubts and gathered strength;
    He would not make his judgment blind;
    He faced the spectres of the mind   15
And laid them: thus he came at length

To find a stronger faith his own;
    And Power was with him in the night,
    Which makes the darkness and the light,
And dwells not in the light alone,   20

But in the darkness and the cloud,
    As over Sinai's peaks of old,
    While Israel made their gods of gold,
Altho' the trumpet blew so loud.

CXIV

Who loves not Knowledge? Who shall rail
    Against her beauty? May she mix
    With men and prosper! Who shall fix
Her pillars? Let her work prevail.

But on her forehead sits a fire: 5
    She sets her forward countenance
    And leaps into the future chance,
Submitting all things to desire.

Half-grown as yet, a child, and vain—
    She cannot fight the fear of death.   10
    What is she, cut from love and faith,
But some wild Pallas from the brain

Of demons? fiery-hot to burst
    All barriers in her onward race
    For power. Let her know her place;   15
She is the second, not the first.

A higher hand must make her mild,
 If all be not in vain, and guide
 Her footsteps, moving side by side
With Wisdom, like the younger child; 20

For she is earthly of the mind,
 But Wisdom heavenly of the soul.
 O, friend, who camest to thy goal
So early, leaving me behind,

I would the great world grew like thee, 25
 Who grewest not alone in power
 And knowledge, but by year and hour
In reverence and in charity.

CXVIII

Contemplate all this work of Time,
 The giant labouring in his youth;
 Nor dream of human love and truth
As dying Nature's earth and lime;

But trust that those we call the dead 5
 Are breathers of an ampler day
 For ever nobler ends. They say
The solid earth whereon we tread

In tracts of fluent heat began,
 And grew to seeming-random forms, 10
 The seeming prey of cyclic storms,
Till at the last arose the man;

Who throve and branched from clime to clime,
 The herald of a higher race,
 And of himself in higher place, 15
If so he type this work of Time

Within himself, from more to more;
 Or, crowned with attributes of woe
 Like glories, move his course, and show
That life is not as idle ore, 20

But iron dug from central gloom,
 And heated hot with burning fears,
 And dipt in baths of hissing tears,
And battered with the shocks of doom

To shape and use. Arise, and fly   25
   The reeling faun, the sensual feast;
   Move upward, working out the beast,
And let the ape and tiger die.

CXXIV

That which we dare invoke to bless;
   Our dearest faith; our ghastliest doubt;
   He, They, One, All; within, without;
The Power in darkness Whom we guess;

I found Him not in world or sun,   5
   Or eagle's wing, or insect's eye;
   Nor through the questions men may try,
The petty cobwebs we have spun.

If e'er, when faith had fall'n asleep,
   I heard a voice, "Believe no more,"   10
   And heard an ever-breaking shore
That tumbled in the Godless deep;

A warmth within the breast would melt
   The freezing reason's colder part,
   And like a man in wrath the heart   15
Stood up and answered, "I have felt."

No, like a child in doubt and fear:
   But that blind clamour made me wise;
   Then was I as a child that cries,
But, crying, knows his father near;   20

And what I am beheld again
   What is and no man understands;
   And out of darkness came the hands
That reach thro' Nature, moulding men.

1833–49.   1850.

TEARS, IDLE TEARS

Tears, idle tears, I know not what they mean.
Tears from the depth of some divine despair
Rise in the heart, and gather to the eyes,
In looking on the happy autumn-fields,
And thinking of the days that are no more.   5

Fresh as the first beam glittering on a sail
That brings our friends up from the underworld,
Sad as the last which reddens over one
That sinks with all we love below the verge;
So sad, so fresh, the days that are no more.   10

Ah, sad and strange as in dark summer dawns
The earliest pipe of half-awakened birds
To dying ears, when unto dying eyes
The casement slowly grows a glimmering square;
So sad, so strange, the days that are no more.   15

Dear as remembered kisses after death,
And sweet as those by hopeless fancy feigned
On lips that are for others; deep as love,
Deep as first love, and wild with all regret;
O death in life, the days that are no more.   20

                                            1847.

SWEET AND LOW

Sweet and low, sweet and low,
    Wind of the western sea,
Low, low, breathe and blow,
    Wind of the western sea!
Over the rolling waters go,   5
Come from the dying moon, and blow,
    Blow him again to me;
While my little one, while my pretty one, sleeps.

Sleep and rest, sleep and rest,
    Father will come to thee soon;   10
Rest, rest, on mother's breast,
    Father will come to thee soon;
Father will come to his babe in the nest,
Silver sails all out of the west
    Under the silver moon: 15
Sleep, my little one, sleep, my pretty one, sleep.

                                            1850.

THE SPLENDOUR FALLS ON CASTLE WALLS

The splendour falls on castle walls
    And snowy summits old in story;
The long light shakes across the lakes,
    And the wild cataract leaps in glory.
Blow, bugle, blow, set the wild echoes flying;   5
Blow, bugle; answer, echoes, dying, dying, dying.

O hark, O hear! how thin and clear,
    And thinner, clearer, farther going!
O sweet and far from cliff and scar,
    The horns of Elfland faintly blowing!   10
Blow, let us hear the purple glens replying;
Blow, bugle; answer, echoes, dying, dying, dying.

O love, they die in yon rich sky,
    They faint on hill or field or river:
Our echoes roll from soul to soul,   15
    And grow forever and forever.
Blow, bugle, blow, set the wild echoes flying;
And answer, echoes, answer, dying, dying, dying.

                1850.

THE BROOK

I come from haunts of coot and hern,
    I make a sudden sally,
And sparkle out among the fern,
    To bicker down a valley.

By thirty hills I hurry down,   5
    Or slip between the ridges,
By twenty thorps, a little town,
    And half a hundred bridges.

Till last by Philip's farm I flow
    To join the brimming river;   10
For men may come and men may go,
    But I go on forever.

I chatter over stony ways,
    In little sharps and trebles,
I bubble into eddying bays,   15
    I babble on the pebbles.

With many a curve my banks I fret
    By many a field and fallow,
And many a fairy foreland set
    With willow-weed and mallow.   20

I chatter, chatter, as I flow
    To join the brimming river;
For men may come and men may go,
    But I go on forever.

I wind about, and in and out,   25
    With here a blossom sailing,
And here and there a lusty trout,
    And here and there a grayling,

And here and there a foamy flake
    Upon me, as I travel   30
With many a silvery waterbreak
    Above the golden gravel,

And draw them all along, and flow
    To join the brimming river;
For men may come and men may go,   35
    But I go on forever.

I steal by lawns and grassy plots,
    I slide by hazel covers,
I move the sweet forget-me-nots
    That grow for happy lovers.   40

I slip, I slide, I gloom, I glance,
    Among my skimming swallows,
I make the netted sunbeam dance
    Against my sandy shallows.

I murmur under moon and stars   45
    In brambly wildernesses,
I linger by my shingly bars,
    I loiter round my cresses,

And out again I curve and flow
    To join the brimming river;
For men may come and men may go,   50
    But I go on forever.

                      1855.

NORTHERN FARMER
OLD STYLE

Wheer 'asta beän saw long and meä liggin' 'ere aloän?
Noorse? thourt nowt o' a noorse: whoy, Doctor 's·abeän an' agoän;
Says that I moänt 'a naw moor aäle: but I beänt a fool:
Git ma my aäle, fur I beänt a-gawin' to breäk my rule.

Doctors, they knaws nowt, fur a says what 's nawways true: 5
Naw soort o' koind o' use to saäy the things that a do.
I 've 'ed my point o' aäle ivry noight sin' I beän 'ere,
An' I 've 'ed my quart ivry market-noight for foorty year.

Parson 's a beän loikewoise, an' a sittin' 'ere o' my bed.
"The amoighty 's a taäkin o' you to 'issén, my friend," a said,   10
An' a towd ma my sins, an 's toithe were due, an' I gied it in hond;
I done moy duty boy 'um, as I 'a done boy the lond.

Larn'd a ma' beä. I reckons I 'annot sa mooch to larn.
But a cast oop, thot a did, 'bout Bessy Marris's barne.
Thaw a knaws I hallus voäted wi' Squoire an' choorch an' staäte,   15
An' i' the woost o' toimes I wur niver again the raäte.

An' I hallus coomed to 's chooch afoor moy Sally war deäd,
An' 'eärd 'um a bummin' awaäy loike a buzzard-clock ower my 'eäd,
An' I niver knaw'd whot a meäned but I thowt a 'ad summut to
          saäy,
An' I thowt a said whot a owt to 'a said an' I coomed awaäy.   20

Bessy Marris's barne! tha knaws she laäid it to meä.
Mowt a beän, mayhap, for she wur a bad un, sheä.
'Siver, I kep 'um, I kep 'um, my lass, tha mun understond;
I done moy duty boy 'um, as I 'a done boy the lond.

But Parson a cooms an' a goäs, an' a says it eäsy an' freeä,   25
"The amoighty 's a taäkin o' you to 'issén, my friend," says 'eä.
I weänt saäy men be loiars, thaw summun said it in 'aäste:
But 'e reäds wonn sarmin a weeäk, an' I 'a stubbed Thurnaby
          waäste.

D'ya moind the waäste, my lass? naw, naw, tha was not born
          then;
Theer wur a boggle in it, I often 'eärd 'um mysen;   30

Moäst loike a butter-bump, fur I 'eärd 'um about an' about,
But I stubbed 'um oop wi' the lot, an' raäved an' rembled 'um out.

Keäper's it wur; fo' they fun 'um theer a-laäid of 'is faäce
Down i' the woild 'enemies afoor I coomed to the plaäce.
Noäks or Thimbleby—toäner 'ed shot 'um as deäd as a naäil.   35
Noäks wur 'anged for it oop at 'soize—but git ma my aäle.

Dubbut looök at the waäste: theer warn't not feeäd for a cow;
Nowt at all but bracken an' fuzz, an' looök at it now—
Warnt worth nowt a haäcre, an' now theer 's lots o' feeäd,
Fourscoor yows upon it an' some on it down i' seeäd.   40

Nobbut a bit on it 's left, an' I meän to 'a stubbed it at fall,
Done it ta-year I meäned, an' runned plow thruff it an' all,
If godamoighty an' Parson 'ud nobbut let ma aloän,
Meä, wi' haäte hoonderd haäcre o' Squoire's, an' lond o' my oän.

Do godamoighty knaw what a 's doing a-taäkin' o' meä?   45
I beänt wonn as saws 'ere a beän an' yonder a peä;
An' Squoire 'ull be sa mad an' all—a' dear a' dear!
And I 'a managed for Squoire coom Michaelmas thutty year.

A mowt 'a taäen owd Joänes, as 'ant nor a 'aäpoth o' sense,
Or a mowt 'a taäen young Robins—a niver mended a fence: 50
But godamoighty a moost taäke meä an' taäke ma now
Wi' aäf the cows to cauve an' Thurnaby hoälms to plow!

Looök 'ow quoloty smoiles when they seeäs ma a passin' boy,
Says to thessén naw doubt "what a man a beä sewer-loy!"
Fur they knaws what I beän to Squoire sin fust a coomed to
     the 'All;
                                                              55
I done moy duty by Squoire an' I done moy duty boy hall.

Squoire 's i' Lunnon, an' summun I reckons 'ull 'a to wroite,
For whoä 's to howd the lond ater meä thot muddles ma quoit;
Sartin-sewer I beä, thot a weänt niver give it to Joänes,
Naw, nor a moänt to Robins—a niver rembles the stoäns.   60

But summun 'ull come ater meä mayhap wi' 'is kittle o' steäm
Huzzin' an' maäzin' the blessèd feälds wi' the Divil's oän teäm.
Sin' I mun doy I mun doy, thaw loife they says is sweet,
But sin' I mun doy I mun doy, for I couldn abeär to see it.

What atta stannin' theer fur, an' doesn bring ma the aäle?   65
Doctor 's a 'toättler, lass, an a 's hallus i' the owd taäle;
I weänt breäk rules fur Doctor, a knaws naw moor nor a floy;
Git ma my aäle I tell tha, an' if I mun doy I mun doy.

  1861.   *1864.*

MILTON

 O mighty-mouthed inventor of harmonies,
 O skilled to sing of Time or Eternity,
  God-gifted organ-voice of England,
   Milton, a name to resound for ages;
 Whose Titan angels, Gabriel, Abdiel,   5
 Starred from Jehovah's gorgeous armouries,
  Tower, as the deep-domed empyrëan
   Rings to the roar of an angel onset,—
 Me rather all that bowery loneliness,
 The brooks of Eden mazily murmuring,   10
  And bloom profuse and cedar arches
   Charm, as a wanderer out in ocean,
 Where some refulgent sunset of India
 Streams o'er a rich ambrosial ocean isle,
  And crimson-hued the stately palm-woods   15
   Whisper in odorous heights of even.

  1863.   *1863.*

WAGES

Glory of warrior, glory of orator, glory of song,
 Paid with a voice flying by to be lost on an endless sea;
Glory of Virtue, to fight, to struggle, to right the wrong—
 Nay, but she aimed not at glory, no lover of glory she:
Give her the glory of going on, and still to be.   5

The wages of sin is death: if the wages of Virtue be dust,
 Would she have heart to endure for the life of the
  worm and the fly?
She desires no isles of the blest, no quiet seats of the just,
 To rest in a golden grove, or to bask in a summer sky:
Give her the wages of going on, and not to die.   10

           1868.

RIZPAH

17—

Wailing, wailing, wailing, the wind over land and sea—
And Willy's voice in the wind, "O mother, come out to me."
Why should he call me to-night, when he knows that I cannot go?
For the downs are as bright as day, and the full moon stares at
    the snow.

We should be seen, my dear; they would spy us out of the town. 5
The loud black nights for us, and the storm rushing over the
    down,
When I cannot see my own hand, but am led by the creak of the
    chain,
And grovel and grope for my son till I find myself drenched with
    the rain.

Anything fallen again? nay—what was there left to fall?
I have taken them home, I have numbered the bones, I have hid-
    den them all. 10
What am I saying? and what are *you?* do you come as a spy?
Falls? what falls? who knows? As the tree falls so must it lie.

Who let her in? how long has she been? you—what have you
    heard?
Why did you sit so quiet? you never have spoken a word.
O—to pray with me—yes—a lady—none of their spies— 15
But the night has crept into my heart, and begun to darken my
    eyes.

Ah—you, that have lived so soft, what should *you* know of the
    night,
The blast and the burning shame and the bitter frost and the
    fright?
I have done it, while you were asleep—you were only made for
    the day.
I have gathered my baby together—and now you may go your
    way. 20

Nay—for it's kind of you, madam, to sit by an old dying wife.
But say nothing hard of my boy, I have only an hour of life.
I kissed my boy in the prison, before he went out to die.
"They dared me to do it," he said, and he never has told me a lie.

I whipt him for robbing an orchard once when he was but a
    child—   25
"The farmer dared me to do it," he said; he was always so wild—
And idle—and couldn't be idle—my Willy—he never could rest.
The King should have made him a soldier, he would have been
    one of his best.

But he lived with a lot of wild mates, and they never would let
    him be good;
They swore that he dare not rob the mail, and he swore that he
    would: 30
And he took no life, but he took one purse, and when all was done
He flung it among his fellows—"I 'll none of it," said my son.

I came into court to the judge and the lawyers. I told them my
    tale,
God's own truth—but they killed him, they killed him for robbing
    the mail.
They hanged him in chains for a show—we had always borne a
    good name—   35
To be hanged for a thief—and then put away—isn't that enough
    shame?
Dust to dust—low down—let us hide! but they set him so high
That all the ships of the world could stare at him, passing by.
God 'ill pardon the hell-black raven and horrible fowls of the air,
But not the black heart of the lawyer who killed him and hanged
    him there.   40

And the jailer forced me away. I had bid him my last goodbye;
They had fastened the door of his cell. "O mother!" I heard
    him cry.
I couldn't get back, tho' I tried; he had something further to say,
And now I never shall know it. The jailer forced me away.

Then, since I couldn't but hear that cry of my boy that was
    dead,   45
They seized me and shut me up; they fastened me down on my
    bed.
"Mother, O mother!" he called in the dark to me year after
    year—
They beat me for that, they beat me—you know that I couldn't
    but hear.

And then at the last they found I had grown so stupid and still
They let me abroad again—but the creatures had worked their
    will.   50

Flesh of my flesh was gone, but bone of my bone was left—
I stole them all from the lawyers—and you, will you call it a
    theft?—
My baby, the bones that had sucked me, the bones that had
    laughed and had cried—
Theirs? O no! they are mine—not theirs—they had moved in
    my side.

Do you think I was scared by the bones? I kissed 'em, I buried
    'em all—   55
I can't dig deep, I am old— in the night by the churchyard wall.
My Willy 'ill rise up whole when the trumpet of judgment 'ill
    sound,
But I charge you never to say that I laid him in holy ground:

They would scratch him up—they would hang him again on the
    cursèd tree.
Sin? O yes—we are sinners, I know—let all that be,   60
And read me a Bible verse of the Lord's good will toward men—
"Full of compassion and mercy, the Lord"—let me hear it again;
"Full of compassion and mercy—long-suffering." Yes, O yes!
For the lawyer is born but to murder—the Saviour lives but to
    bless.
He 'll never put on the black cap except for the worst of the
    worst,   65
And the first may be last—I have heard it in church—and the
    last may be first.
Suffering—O long-suffering—yes, as the Lord must know,
Year after year in the mist and the wind and the shower and the
    snow.

Heard, have you? what? they have told you he never repented
    his sin.
How do they know it? are *they* his mother? are *you* of his kin? 70
Heard! have you ever heard, when the storm on the downs began,
The wind that 'ill wail like a child and the sea that 'ill moan like
    a man?

Election, Election and Reprobation— it's all very well.
But I go to-night to my boy, and I shall not find him in hell;
For I cared so much for my boy that the Lord has looked into
    my care,   75
And He means me, I'm sure, to be happy with Willy, I know not
    where.

And if *he* be lost—but to save *my* soul, that is all your desire:
Do you think that I care for *my* soul if my boy be gone to the
    fire?
I have been with God in the dark—go, go, you may leave me
    alone—
You never have borne a child—you are just as hard as a stone.   80

Madam, I beg your pardon! I think that you mean to be kind,
But I cannot hear what you say for my Willy's voice in the wind—
The snow and the sky so bright—he used but to call in the dark,
And he calls to me now from the church and not from the gibbet—
    for hark!
Nay—you can hear it yourself—it is coming—shaking the walls— 85
Willy—the moon's in a cloud——Good-night. I am going. He
    calls.

                        1880.

TO VIRGIL

Roman Virgil, thou that singest
    Ilion's lofty temples robed in fire,
Ilion falling, Rome arising,
    wars, and filial faith, and Dido's pyre;

Landscape-lover, lord of language   5
    more than he that sang the Works and Days,
All the chosen coin of fancy
    flashing out from many a golden phrase;

Thou that singest wheat and woodland,
    tilth and vineyard, hive and horse and herd,   10
All the charm of all the Muses
    often flowering in a lonely word;

Poet of the happy Tityrus
   piping underneath his beechen bowers;
Poet of the poet-satyr   15
   whom the laughing shepherd bound with flowers;

Chanter of the Pollio, glorying
   in the blissful years again to be,
Summers of the snakeless meadow,
   unlaborious earth and oarless sea;   20

Thou that seëst Universal
   Nature moved by Universal Mind;
Thou majestic in thy sadness
   at the doubtful doom of human kind;

Light among the vanished ages;   25
   star that gildest yet this phantom shore;
Golden branch amid the shadows,
   kings and realms that pass to rise no more;

Now thy Forum roars no longer,
   fallen every purple Cæsar's dome—   30
Tho' thine ocean-roll of rhythm
   sound forever of Imperial Rome,—

Now the Rome of slaves hath perished,
   And the Rome of freemen holds her place,
I, from out the Northern Island   35
   sundered once from all the human race,

I salute thee, Mantovano,
   I that loved thee since my day began,
Wielder of the stateliest measure
   ever moulded by the lips of man.   40

1881.   1882.

VASTNESS

Many a hearth upon our dark globe sighs after many a vanished
   face;
Many a planet by many a sun may roll with the dust of a vanished
   race.

Raving politics, never at rest—as this poor earth's pale history
    runs,—

What is it all but a trouble of ants in the gleam of a million
    million of suns?

Lies upon this side, lies upon that side, truthless violence mourned
    by the Wise,   5

Thousands of voices drowning his own in a popular torrent of lies
    upon lies;

Stately purposes, valour in battle, glorious annals of army and
    fleet,

Death for the right cause, death for the wrong cause, trumpets
    of victory, groans of defeat;

Innocence seethed in her mother's milk, and Charity setting the
    martyr aflame;

Thraldom who walks with the banner of Freedom, and recks not
    to ruin a realm in her name;   10

Faith at her zenith, or all but lost in the gloom of doubts that
    darken the schools;

Craft with a bunch of all-heal in her hand, followed up by her
    vassal legion of fools;.

Trade flying over a thousand seas with her spice and her vintage,
    her silk and her corn;

Desolate offing, sailorless harbours, famishing populace, wharves
    forlorn;

Star of the morning, Hope in the sunrise; gloom of the evening,
    Life at a close;   15

Pleasure who flaunts on her wide down-way with her flying robe
    and her poisoned rose;

Pain, that has crawled from the corpse of Pleasure, a worm which
    writhes all day, and at night

Stirs up again in the heart of the sleeper, and stings him back
    to the curse of the light;

Wealth with his wines and his wedded harlots; honest Poverty,
    bare to the bone;

Opulent Avarice, lean as Poverty; Flattery gilding the rift in a
    throne;   20

Fame blowing out from her golden trumpet a jubilant challenge
    to Time and to Fate;
Slander, her shadow, sowing the nettle on all the laureled graves
    of the Great;

Love for the maiden, crowned with marriage, no regrets for
    aught that has been,
Household happiness, gracious children, debtless competence,
    golden mean;

National hatreds of whole generations, and pigmy spites of the
    village spire;   25
Vows that will last to the last death-ruckle, and vows that are snapt
    in a moment of fire;

He that has lived for the lust of the minute, and died in the doing
    it, flesh without mind;
He that has nailed all flesh to the Cross, till Self died out in the
    love of his kind;

Spring and Summer and Autumn and Winter, and all these old
    revolutions of earth;
All new-old revolutions of Empire—change of the tide—what is all
    of it worth?   30

What the philosophies, all the sciences, poesy, varying voices of
    prayer?
All that is noblest, all that is basest, all that is filthy with all that
    is fair?

What is it all, if we all of us end but in being our own corpse-
    coffins at last,
Swallowed in Vastness, lost in Silence, drowned in the deeps of a
    meaningless Past?

What but a murmur of gnats in the gloom, or a moment's anger of
    bees in their hive?—   35

*   *   *   *   *   *   *   *   *   *   *   *

Peace, let it be! for I loved him, and love him forever: the dead
    are not dead but alive.

                              1885.

CROSSING THE BAR

Sunset and evening star,
   And one clear call for me!
And may there be no moaning of the bar,
   When I put out to sea.

But such a tide as moving seems asleep,   5
   Too full for sound and foam,
When that which drew from out the boundless deep
   Turns again home.

Twilight and evening bell,
   And after that the dark!   10
And may there be no sadness of farewell,
   When I embark;

For tho' from out our bourne of Time and Place
   The flood may bear me far,
I hope to see my Pilot face to face,   15
   When I have crost the bar.

1889.   1889.

ELIZABETH BARRETT BROWNING

FROM

SONNETS FROM THE PORTUGUESE

I

I thought once how Theocritus had sung
Of the sweet years, the dear and wished-for years,
Who each one in a gracious hand appears
To bear a gift for mortals, old or young;
And as I mused it in his antique tongue,   5
I saw, in gradual vision through my tears,
The sweet, sad years, the melancholy years,
Those of my own life, who by turns had flung
A shadow across me. Straightway I was 'ware,
So weeping, how a mystic Shape did move   10
Behind me, and drew me backward by the hair;
And a voice said in mastery, while I strove,
"Guess now who holds thee?" "Death," I said. But there
The silver answer rang, "Not Death, but Love."

VI

Go from me. Yet I feel that I shall stand
Henceforward in thy shadow. Nevermore
Alone upon the threshold of my door
Of individual life, I shall command
The uses of my soul, nor lift my hand   5
Serenely in the sunshine as before,
Without the sense of that which I forbore—
Thy touch upon the palm. The widest land
Doom takes to part us, leaves thy heart in mine
With pulses that beat double. What I do   10
And what I dream include thee, as the wine
Must taste of its own grapes. And when I sue
God for myself, He hears that name of thine,
And sees within my eyes the tears of two.

XXVIII

My letters! all dead paper, mute and white!
And yet they seem alive and quivering
Against my tremulous hands, which loose the string
And let them drop down on my knee to-night.
This said he wished to have me in his sight   5
Once, as a friend. This fixed a day in spring
To come and touch my hand—a simple thing,
Yet I wept for it! This—the paper's light—
Said, *Dear, I love thee;* and I sank and quailed
As if God's future thundered on my past.   10
This said, *I am thine*—and so its ink has paled
With lying at my heart that beat too fast.
And this—O love, thy words have ill availed
If what this said I dared repeat at last!

XLIII

How do I love thee? Let me count the ways.
I love thee to the depth and breadth and height
My soul can reach, when feeling out of sight
For the ends of Being and ideal Grace.
I love thee to the level of everyday's   5
Most quiet need, by sun and candlelight.
I love thee freely, as men strive for Right;
I love thee purely, as they turn from Praise.

I love thee with the passion put to use
In my old griefs, and with my childhood's faith.   10
I love thee with a love I seemed to lose
With my lost saints. I love thee with the breath,
Smiles, tears, of all my life! and, if God choose,
I shall but love thee better after death.

1845–46.   (1847.)   1850.

A MUSICAL INSTRUMENT

What was he doing, the great god Pan,
    Down in the reeds by the river?
Spreading ruin and scattering ban,
Splashing and paddling with hoofs of a goat,
And breaking the golden lilies afloat   5
    With the dragon-fly on the river.

He tore out a reed, the great god Pan,
    From the deep cool bed of the river:
The limpid water turbidly ran,
And the broken lilies a-dying lay,   10
And the dragon-fly had fled away,
    Ere he brought it out of the river.

High on the shore sat the great god Pan,
    While turbidly flowed the river;
And hacked and hewed as a great god can,   15
With his hard bleak steel, at the patient reed,
Till there was not a sign of the leaf indeed
    To prove it fresh from the river.

He cut it short, did the great god Pan,
    (How tall it stood in the river!)   20
Then drew the pith, like the heart of a man,
Steadily from the outside ring,
And notched the poor dry empty thing
    In holes, as he sat by the river.

"This is the way," laughed the great god Pan   25
    (Laughed while he sat by the river),
"The only way, since gods began
To make sweet music, they could succeed."

Then, dropping his mouth to a hole in the reed,
    He blew in power by the river.   30

Sweet, sweet, sweet, O Pan!
    Piercing sweet by the river!
Blinding sweet, O great god Pan!
The sun on the hill forgot to die,
And the lilies revived, and the dragon-fly   35
    Came back to dream on the river.

Yet half a beast is the great god Pan,
    To laugh as he sits by the river,
Making a poet out of a man:
The true gods sigh for the cost and pain,   40
For the reed which grows nevermore again
    As a reed with the reeds in the river.

                          1860.

THE FORCED RECRUIT

In the ranks of the Austrian you found him,
    He died with his face to you all;
Yet bury him here where around him
    You honour your bravest that fall.

Venetian, fair-featured and slender,   5
    He lies shot to death in his youth,
With a smile on his lips over-tender
    For any mere soldier's dead mouth.

No stranger, and yet not a traitor,
    Though alien the cloth on his breast;   10
Underneath it how seldom a greater
    Young heart has a shot sent to rest!

By your enemy tortured and goaded
    To march with them, stand in their file,
His musket (see) never was loaded,   15
    He facing your guns with that smile!

As orphans yearn on to their mothers,
    He yearned to your patriot bands:—
"Let me die for our Italy, brothers,
    If not in your ranks, by your hands!   20

"Aim straightly, fire steadily! spare me
　　A ball in the body which may
Deliver my heart here, and tear me
　　This badge of the Austrian away!"

So thought he, so died he, this morning.　　　　　25
　　What then? many others have died.
Ay, but easy for men to die scorning
　　The death-stroke, who fought side by side—

One tricolor floating above them;
　　Struck down 'mid triumphant acclaims　　　30
Of an Italy rescued to love them
　　And blazon the brass with their names.

But he, without witness or honour,
　　Mixed, shamed in his country's regard,
With the tyrants who march in upon her,　　　35
　　Died faithful and passive: 't was hard.

'T was sublime. In a cruel restriction
　　Cut off from the guerdon of sons,
With most filial obedience, conviction,
　　His soul kissed the lips of her guns.　　　40

That moves you? Nay, grudge not to show it,
　　While digging a grave for him here:
The others who died, says your poet,
　　Have glory,—let *him* have a tear.

　　　　　　　　　　　　　　　1860.

ROBERT BROWNING

HEAP CASSIA, SANDAL-BUDS, AND STRIPES

Heap cassia, sandal-buds, and stripes
　　Of labdanum, and aloe-balls,
Smeared with dull nard an Indian wipes
　　From out her hair: such balsam falls
　　Down sea-side mountain pedestals,　　　　5
From tree-tops where tired winds are fain,
Spent with the vast and howling main,
To treasure half their island-gain.

And strew faint sweetness from some old
    Egyptian's fine worm-eaten shroud   10
Which breaks to dust when once unrolled;
    Or shredded perfume, like a cloud
    From closet long to quiet vowed,
With mothed and dropping arras hung,
Mouldering her lute and books among,   15
As when a queen, long dead, was young.

1835.

THE YEAR'S AT THE SPRING

    The year's at the spring,
    And day's at the morn;
    Morning's at seven;
    The hillside's dew-pearled;
    The lark's on the wing;   5
    The snail's on the thorn:
    God's in his heaven—
    All's right with the world!

1841.

CAVALIER TUNES

I. MARCHING ALONG

Kentish Sir Byng stood for his king,
Bidding the crop-headed Parliament swing;
And, pressing a troop unable to stoop
And see the rogues flourish and honest folk droop,
Marched them along, fifty-score strong,   5
Great-hearted gentlemen, singing this song.

God for King Charles! Pym and such carles
To the Devil that prompts 'em their treasonous parles!
Cavaliers, up! Lips from the cup,
Hands from the pasty, nor bite take nor sup   10
Till you're—
    CHORUS.—Marching along, fifty-score strong,
          Great-hearted gentlemen, singing this song.

Hampden to hell and his obsequies' knell!
Serve Hazelrig, Fiennes, and young Harry as well!

England, good cheer! Rupert is near!   15
Kentish and loyalists, keep we not here,
    CHORUS.—Marching along, fifty-score strong,
        Great-hearted gentlemen, singing this song?

Then, God for King Charles! Pym and his snarls
To the Devil that pricks on such pestilent carles!   20
Hold by the right, you double your might;
So onward to Nottingham, fresh for the fight,
    CHORUS—March we along, fifty-score strong,
        Great-hearted gentlemen, singing this song!

II. GIVE A ROUSE

King Charles, and who'll do him right now?
King Charles, and who's ripe for fight now?
Give a rouse: here's, in hell's despite now,
King Charles!

Who gave me the goods that went since?   5
Who raised me the house that sank once?
Who helped me to gold I spent since?
Who found me in wine you drank once?
    CHORUS—King Charles, and who'll do him right now?
        King Charles, and who's ripe for fight now?   10
        Give a rouse: here's, in hell's despite now,
        King Charles!

To whom used my boy George quaff else,
By the old fool's side that begot him?
For whom did he cheer and laugh else,   15
While Noll's damned troopers shot him?
    CHORUS—King Charles, and who'll do him right now?
        King Charles, and who's ripe for fight now?
        Give a rouse: here's, in hell's despite now,
        King Charles!   20

III. BOOT AND SADDLE

Boot, saddle, to horse, and away!
Rescue my castle before the hot day
Brightens to blue from its silvery grey.
    CHORUS.—Boot, saddle, to horse, and away!

Ride past the suburbs, asleep as you 'd say;   5
Many 's the friend there, will listen and pray,
"God's luck to gallants that strike up the lay—
    CHORUS.—Boot, saddle, to horse, and away!"

Forty miles off, like a roebuck at bay,
Flouts Castle Brancepeth the Roundheads' array;   10
Who laughs, "Good fellows ere this, by my fay,
    CHORUS.—Boot, saddle, to horse, and away!"

Who? My wife Gertrude, that, honest and gay,
Laughs when you talk of surrendering, "Nay!
I 've better counsellors; what counsel they?   15
    CHORUS.—Boot, saddle, to horse, and away!"

                           1842.

MY LAST DUCHESS

FERRARA

That 's my last Duchess painted on the wall,
Looking as if she were alive. I call
That piece a wonder, now: Frà Pandolf's hands
Worked busily a day, and there she stands.
Will 't please you sit and look at her? I said   5
"Frà Pandolf" by design, for never read
Strangers like you that pictured countenance,
The depth and passion of its earnest glance,
But to myself they turned (since none puts by
The curtain I have drawn for you, but I)   10
And seemed as they would ask me, if they durst,
How such a glance came there; so not the first
Are you to turn and ask thus. Sir, 't was not
Her husband's presence, only, called that spot
Of joy into the Duchess' cheek: perhaps   15
Frà Pandolf chanced to say, "Her mantle laps
Over my lady's wrist too much," or "Paint
Must never hope to reproduce the faint
Half-flush that dies along her throat;" such stuff
Was courtesy, she thought, and cause enough   20
For calling up that spot of joy. She had
A heart—how shall I say?—too soon made glad,
Too easily impressed; she liked whate'er

She looked on, and her looks went everywhere.
Sir, 't was all one! My favour at her breast,　　　25
The dropping of the daylight in the west,
The bough of cherries some officious fool
Broke in the orchard for her, the white mule
She rode with round the terrace—all and each
Would draw from her alike the approving speech,　　30
Or blush at least. She thanked men,—good! but thanked
Somehow—I know not how—as if she ranked
My gift of a nine-hundred-years-old name
With anybody's gift. Who 'd stoop to blame
This sort of trifling? Even had you skill　　　35
In speech (which I have not) to make your will
Quite clear to such an one, and say, "Just this
Or that in you disgusts me; here you miss,
Or there exceed, the mark,"—and if she let
Herself be lessoned so, nor plainly set　　　40
Her wits to yours, forsooth, and made excuse,
—E'en then would be some stooping; and I choose
Never to stoop. Oh, sir, she smiled, no doubt,
Whene'er I passed her; but who passed without
Much the same smile? This grew; I gave commands;　45
Then all smiles stopped together. There she stands
As if alive. Will 't please you rise? We 'll meet
The company below, then. I repeat,
The Count your master's known munificence
Is ample warrant that no just pretense　　　50
Of mine for dowry will be disallowed;
Though his fair daughter's self, as I avowed
At starting, is my object. Nay, we 'll go
Together down, sir. Notice Neptune, though,
Taming a sea-horse, thought a rarity,　　　55
Which Claus of Innsbruck cast in bronze for me!

　　　　　　　　　　　　　　　　1842.

THE LABORATORY

ANCIENT RÉGIME

Now that I, tying thy glass mask tightly,
May gaze through these faint smokes curling whitely,
As thou pliest thy trade in this devil's-smithy,—
Which is the poison to poison her, prithee?

He is with her, and they know that I know   5
Where they are, what they do: they believe my tears flow
While they laugh, laugh at me, at me fled to the drear
Empty church, to pray God in, for them!—I am here.

Grind away, moisten and mash up thy paste,
Pound at thy powder,—I am not in haste!   10
Better sit thus and observe thy strange things,
Than go where men wait me, and dance at the King's.

That in the mortar—you call it a gum?
Ah, the brave tree whence such gold oozings come!
And yonder soft vial, the exquisite blue,   15
Sure to taste sweetly,—is that poison too?

Had I but all of them, thee and thy treasures,
What a wild crowd of invisible pleasures!
To carry pure death in an ear-ring, a casket,
A signet, a fan-mount, a filigree basket!   20

Soon, at the King's, a mere lozenge to give,
And Pauline should have just thirty minutes to live!
But to light a pastile, and Elise, with her head
And her breast and her arms and her hands, should drop
          dead!

Quick—is it finished? The colour's too grim!   25
Why not soft like the phial's, enticing and dim?
Let it brighten her drink, let her turn it and stir,
And try it and taste, ere she fix and prefer!

What a drop! She's not little, no minion like me!
That's why she ensnared him: this never will free   30
The soul from those masculine eyes,—say "no!"
To that pulse's magnificent come-and-go.

For only last night, as they whispered, I brought
My own eyes to bear on her so, that I thought
Could I keep them one half-minute fixed, she would fall 35
Shrivelled; she fell not; yet this does it all!

Not that I bid you spare her the pain;
Let death be felt and the proof remain:
Brand, burn up, bite into its grace—
He is sure to remember her dying face!   40

Is it done? Take my mask off! Nay, be not morose;
It kills her, and this prevents seeing it close:
The delicate droplet, my whole fortune's fee!
If it hurts her, beside, can it ever hurt me?

Now, take all my jewels, gorge gold to your fill;   45
You may kiss me, old man, on my mouth if you will!
But brush this dust off me, lest horror it brings
Ere I know it—next moment I dance at the King's!

1844.

"HOW THEY BROUGHT THE GOOD NEWS FROM GHENT TO AIX"

16——

I sprang to the stirrup, and Joris, and he;
I galloped, Dirck galloped, we galloped all three;
"Good speed!" cried the watch, as the gate-bolts undrew;
"Speed!" echoed the wall to us galloping through;
Behind shut the postern, the lights sank to rest   5
And into the midnight we galloped abreast.

Not a word to each other; we kept the great pace
Neck by neck, stride by stride, never changing our place;
I turned in my saddle and made its girths tight,
Then shortened each stirrup, and set the pique right,   10
Rebuckled the cheek-strap, chained slacker the bit,
Nor galloped less steadily Roland a whit.

'T was moonset at starting; but while we drew near
Lokeren, the cocks crew and twilight dawned clear;
At Boom, a great yellow star came out to see;   15
At Düffeld, 't was morning as plain as could be;
And from Mecheln church-steeple we heard the half-chime,
So Joris broke silence with, "Yet there is time!"

At Aershot, up leaped of a sudden the sun,
And against him the cattle stood black every one,   20
To stare through the mist at us galloping past,
And I saw my stout galloper Roland at last,
With resolute shoulders, each butting away
The haze, as some bluff river-headland its spray;

And his low head and crest, just one sharp ear bent back   25
For my voice, and the other pricked out on his track;
And one eye's black intelligence—ever that glance
O'er its white edge at me, his own master, askance!
And the thick heavy spume-flakes which aye and anon
His fierce lips shook upwards in galloping on.   30

By Hasselt, Dirck groaned; and cried Joris, "Stay spur!
Your Roos galloped bravely, the fault's not in her,
We'll remember at Aix"—for one heard the quick wheeze
Of her chest, saw the stretched neck and staggering knees,
And sunk tail, and horrible heave of the flank,   35
As down on her haunches she shuddered and sank.

So we were left galloping, Joris and I,
Past Looz and past Tongres, no cloud in the sky;
The broad sun above laughed a pitiless laugh,
'Neath our feet broke the brittle bright stubble like chaff;   40
Till over by Dalhem a dome-spire sprang white,
And "Gallop," gasped Joris, "for Aix is in sight!"

"How they'll greet us!"—and all in a moment his roan
Rolled neck and croup over, lay dead as a stone;
And there was my Roland to bear the whole weight   45
Of the news which alone could save Aix from her fate,
With his nostrils like pits full of blood to the brim,
And with circles of red for his eye-sockets' rim.

Then I cast loose my buff-coat, each holster let fall,
Shook off both my jack-boots, let go belt and all,   50
Stood up in the stirrup, leaned, patted his ear,
Called my Roland his pet-name, my horse without peer,
Clapped my hands, laughed and sang, any noise, bad or good,
Till at length into Aix Roland galloped and stood.

And all I remember is, friends flocking round   55
As I sat with his head 'twixt my knees on the ground;
And no voice but was praising this Roland of mine,
As I poured down his throat our last measure of wine,
Which (the burgesses voted by common consent)
Was no more than his due who brought good news from
    Ghent.   60

1838.   *1845.*

THE LOST LEADER

Just for a handful of silver he left us,
    Just for a riband to stick in his coat—
Found the one gift of which fortune bereft us,
    Lost all the others she lets us devote.
They, with the gold to give, doled him out silver;   5
    So much was theirs who so little allowed:
How all our copper had gone for his service!
    Rags—were they purple, his heart had been proud!
We that had loved him so, followed him, honoured him,
    Lived in his mild and magnificent eye,   10
Learned his great language, caught his clear accents,
    Made him our pattern to live and to die!
Shakespeare was of us, Milton was for us,
    Burns, Shelley, were with us—they watch from their
        graves!
He alone breaks from the van and the freemen,   15
    He alone sinks to the rear and the slaves!

We shall march prospering—not through his presence;
    Songs may inspirit us—not from his lyre;
Deeds will be done—while he boasts his quiescence,
    Still bidding crouch whom the rest bade aspire.   20
Blot out his name, then, record one lost soul more,
    One task more declined, one more footpath untrod,
One more devils'-triumph and sorrow for angels,
    One wrong more to man, one more insult to God!
Life's night begins: let him never come back to us!   25
    There would be doubt, hesitation, and pain,
Forced praise on our part—the glimmer of twilight,
    Never glad confident morning again!
Best fight on well, for we taught him—strike gallantly,
    Menace our heart ere we master his own;   30
Then let him receive the new knowledge and wait us,
    Pardoned in heaven, the first by the throne!

                          1845.

HOME THOUGHTS, FROM ABROAD

Oh, to be in England now that April's there,
And whoever wakes in England sees, some morning,
    unaware,

That the lowest boughs and the brush-wood sheaf
Round the elm-tree bole are in tiny leaf,
While the chaffinch sings on the orchard bough   5
In England—now!

And after April, when May follows,
And the white-throat builds, and all the swallows!
Hark, where my blossomed pear-tree in the hedge
Leans to the field and scatters on the clover   10
Blossoms and dewdrops—at the bent spray's edge,—
That's the wise thrush; he sings each song twice over
Lest you should think he never could recapture
The first fine careless rapture!
And though the fields look rough with hoary dew,   15
All will be gay when noontide wakes anew
The buttercups, the little children's dower
—Far brighter than this gaudy melon-flower!

                                        1845.

HOME THOUGHTS, FROM THE SEA

Nobly, nobly Cape Saint Vincent to the northwest died away;
Sunset ran, one glorious blood-red, reeking into Cadiz Bay;
Bluish 'mid the burning water, full in face Trafalgar lay;
In the dimmest northeast distance dawned Gibraltar, grand and
    gray.
"Here and here did England help me: how can I help England?"
    say,   5
Whoso turns, as I, this evening, turn to God to praise and pray,
While Jove's planet rises yonder, silent over Africa.

    1838.   1845.

MEETING AT NIGHT

The grey sea and the long black land;
And the yellow half-moon large and low;
And the startled little waves that leap
In fiery ringlets from their sleep,
As I gain the cove with pushing prow,   5
And quench its speed i' the slushy sand.

Then a mile of warm sea-scented beach;
Three fields to cross till a farm appears;

A tap at the pane, the quick sharp scratch
And blue spurt of a lighted match,　　　　　　　　10
And a voice less loud, through its joys and fears,
Than the two hearts beating each to each!

　　　　　　　　　　　　　　　　　　1845.

PARTING AT MORNING

Round the cape of a sudden came the sea,
And the sun looked over the mountain's rim:
And straight was a path of gold for him,
And the need of a world of men for me.

　　　　　　　　　　　　　　　　　　1845.

THE BISHOP ORDERS HIS TOMB AT SAINT PRAXED'S CHURCH

ROME, 15——

Vanity, saith the Preacher, vanity!
Draw round my bed: is Anselm keeping back?
Nephews—sons mine—ah God, I know not! Well—
She men would have to be your mother once,
Old Gandolf envied me, so fair she was!　　　　　5
What's done is done, and she is dead beside,
Dead long ago, and I am Bishop since,
And as she died so must we die ourselves,
And thence ye may perceive the world's a dream.
Life, how and what is it? As here I lie　　　　　10
In this state-chamber, dying by degrees,
Hours and long hours in the dead night, I ask,
"Do I live, am I dead?" Peace, peace seems all.
Saint Praxed's ever was the church for peace;
And so, about this tomb of mine. I fought　　　　15
With tooth and nail to save my niche, ye know:
—Old Gandolf cozened me, despite my care;
Shrewd was that snatch from out the corner south
He graced his carrion with, God curse the same!
Yet still my niche is not so cramped but thence　　20
One sees the pulpit o' the epistle-side,
And somewhat of the choir, those silent seats,
And up into the aëry dome where live
The angels, and a sunbeam's sure to lurk.

And I shall fill my slab of basalt there,　　　　25
And 'neath my tabernacle take my rest,
With those nine columns round me, two and two,
The odd one at my feet where Anselm stands:
Peach-blossom marble all, the rare, the ripe
As fresh-poured red wine of a mighty pulse.　　30
—Old Gandolf with his paltry onion-stone,
Put me where I may look at him! True peach,
Rosy and flawless: how I earned the prize!
Draw close: that conflagration of my church
—What then? So much was saved if aught were missed! 35
My sons, ye would not be my death? Go dig
The white-grape vineyard where the oil-press stood,
Drop water gently till the surface sink,
And if ye find—ah God, I know not, I!—
Bedded in store of rotten fig-leaves soft,　　　　40
And corded up in a tight olive-frail,
Some lump, ah God, of *lapis lazuli,*
Big as a Jew's head cut off at the nape,
Blue as a vein o'er the Madonna's breast—
Sons, all have I bequeathed you, villas, all,　　45
That brave Frascati villa, with its bath,
So let the blue lump poise between my knees,
Like God the Father's globe on both His hands
Ye worship in the Jesu Church so gay,
For Gandolf shall not choose but see and burst!　50
Swift as a weaver's shuttle fleet our years:
Man goeth to the grave, and where is he?
Did I say basalt for my slab, sons? Black—
'T was ever antique-black I meant! How else
Shall ye contrast my frieze to come beneath?　55
The bas-relief in bronze ye promised me,
Those Pans and nymphs ye wot of, and perchance
Some tripod, thyrsus, with a vase or so,
The Saviour at his sermon on the mount,
Saint Praxed in a glory, and one Pan　　　　60
Ready to twitch the nymph's last garment off,
And Moses with the tables—but I know
Ye mark me not! What do they whisper thee,
Child of my bowels, Anselm? Ah, ye hope
To revel down my villas while I gasp　　　　65

Bricked o'er with beggar's mouldy travertine
Which Gandolf from his tomb-top chuckles at!
Nay, boys, ye love me—all of jasper, then!
'T is jasper ye stand pledged to, lest I grieve
My bath must needs be left behind, alas!   70
One block, pure green as a pistachio-nut;
There's plenty jasper somewhere in the world—
And have I not Saint Praxed's ear to pray
Horses for ye, and brown Greek manuscripts,
And mistresses with great smooth marbly limbs?   75
—That's if ye carve my epitaph aright,
Choice Latin, picked phrase, Tully's every word,
No gaudy ware like Gandolf's second line—
Tully, my masters? Ulpian serves his need!
And then how I shall lie through centuries,   80
And hear the blessed mutter of the mass,
And see God made and eaten all day long,
And feel the steady candle-flame, and taste
Good strong thick stupefying incense-smoke!
For as I lie here, hours of the dead night,   85
Dying in state and by such slow degrees,
I fold my arms as if they clasped a crook,
And stretch my feet forth straight as stone can point,
And let the bedclothes, for a mortcloth, drop
Into great laps and folds of sculptor's-work: 90
And as yon tapers dwindle, and strange thoughts
Grow, with a certain humming in my ears,
About the life before I lived this life,
And this life too, popes, cardinals, and priests,
Saint Praxed at his sermon on the mount,   95
Your tall pale mother with her talking-eyes,
And new-found agate urns as fresh as day,
And marble's language, Latin pure, discreet,
—Aha, ELUCESCEBAT quoth our friend?
No Tully, said I, Ulpian at the best!   100
Evil and brief hath been my pilgrimage.
All *lapis*, all, sons! Else I give the Pope
My villas! Will ye ever eat my heart?
Ever your eyes were as a lizard's quick,
They glitter like your mother's for my soul,   105
Or ye would heighten my impoverished frieze,

Piece out its starved design, and fill my vase
With grapes, and add a visor and a Term,
And to the tripod ye would tie a lynx
That in his struggle throws the thyrsus down,   110
To comfort me on my entablature
Whereon I am to lie till I must ask,
"Do I live, am I dead?" There, leave me, there!
For ye have stabbed me with ingratitude
To death—ye wish it—God, ye wish it! Stone—   115
Gritstone, a-crumble! Clammy squares which sweat
As if the corpse they keep were oozing through—
And no more *lapis* to delight the world!
Well, go! I bless ye. Fewer tapers there,
But in a row; and, going, turn your backs   120
—Ay, like departing altar-ministrants,—
And leave me in my church, the church for peace,
That I may watch at leisure if he leers—
Old Gandolf—at me, from his onion-stone,
As still he envied me, so fair she was!   125

1845.

SAUL

Said Abner, "At last thou art come! Ere I tell, ere thou speak,
Kiss my cheek, wish me well!" Then I wished it, and did kiss
   his cheek.
And he: "Since the King, O my friend, for thy countenance sent,
Neither drunken nor eaten have we; nor until from his tent
Thou return with the joyful assurance the King liveth yet,   5
Shall our lip with the honey be bright, with the water be wet.
For out of the black mid-tent's silence, a space of three days,
Not a sound hath escaped to thy servants, of prayer nor of praise,
To betoken that Saul and the spirit have ended their strife,
And that, faint in his triumph, the monarch sinks back upon life. 10

"Yet now my heart leaps, O belovèd! God's child with his dew
On thy gracious gold hair, and those lilies still living and blue
Just broken to twine round thy harp-strings, as if no wild heat
Were now raging to torture the desert!"

Then I, as was meet,
Knelt down to the God of my fathers, and rose on my feet,   15
And ran o'er the sand burnt to powder. The tent was unlooped;
I pulled up the spear that obstructed, and under I stooped;
Hands and knees on the slippery grass-patch, all withered and gone,
That extends to the second enclosure, I groped my way on,
Till I felt where the foldskirts fly open. Then once more I
          prayed,
                                                           20
And opened the foldskirts and entered, and was not afraid,
But spoke: "Here is David, thy servant!" And no voice replied.
At the first I saw naught but the blackness; but soon I descried
A something more black than the blackness—the vast, the upright
Main prop which sustains the pavilion; and slow into sight   25
Grew a figure against it, gigantic and blackest of all.
Then a sunbeam, that burst through the tent-roof, showed Saul.

He stood as erect as that tent-prop, both arms stretched out wide
On the great cross-support in the centre, that goes to each side;
He relaxed not a muscle, but hung there as, caught in his pangs 30
And waiting his change, the king serpent all heavily hangs,
Far away from his kind, in the pine, till deliverance come
With the spring-time,—so agonized Saul, drear and stark, blind
          and dumb.

Then I tuned my harp; took off the lilies we twine round its
          chords
Lest they snap 'neath the stress of the noontide—those sun-
          beams like swords!
                                                           35
And I first played the tune all our sheep know, as, one after one,
So docile they come to the pen-door till folding be done.
They are white, and untorn by the bushes, for lo, they have fed
Where the long grasses stifle the water within the stream's bed;
And now one after one seeks its lodging, as star follows star   40
Into eve and the blue far above us—so blue and so far!

Then the tune for which quails on the cornland will each leave
          his mate
To fly after the player; then, what makes the crickets elate
Till for boldness they fight one another; and then, what has weight
To set the quick jerboa a-musing outside his sand house—   45
There are none such as he for a wonder, half bird and half mouse!

God made all the creatures, and gave them our love and our fear,
To give sign we and they are his children, one family here.

Then I played the help-tune of our reapers, their wine-song,
    when hand
Grasps at hand, eye lights eye in good friendship, and great
    hearts expand   50
And grow one in the sense of this world's life. And then, the
    last song
When the dead man is praised on his journey—"Bear, bear him
    along
With his few faults shut up like dead flowerets! Are balm-seeds
    not here
To console us? The land has none left such as he on the bier.
Oh, would we might keep thee, my brother!" And then, the
    glad chaunt   55
Of the marriage—first go the young maidens; next, she whom
    we vaunt
As the beauty, the pride of our dwelling. And then, the great
    march
Wherein man runs to man to assist him and buttress an arch
Naught can break; who shall harm them, our friends? Then, the
    chorus intoned
As the Levites go up to the altar in glory enthroned.   60
But I stopped here; for here in the darkness Saul groaned.

And I paused, held my breath in such silence, and listened apart:
And the tent shook, for mighty Saul shuddered; and sparkles
    'gan dart
From the jewels that woke in his turban at once with a start,
All its lordly male-sapphires, and rubies courageous at heart.   65
So the head; but the body still moved not, still hung there erect.
And I bent once again to my playing, pursued it unchecked,
As I sang,—

    "Oh, our manhood's prime vigour! No spirit feels waste,
Not a muscle is stopped in its playing nor sinew unbraced.   70
Oh, the wild joys of living! the leaping from rock up to rock,
The strong rending of boughs from the fir-tree, the cool silver
    shock

Of the plunge in a pool's living water, the hunt of the bear,
And the sultriness showing the lion is couched in his lair.
And the meal, the rich dates yellowed over with gold dust divine, 75
And the locust-flesh steeped in the pitcher, the full draught of
    wine,
And the sleep in the dried river-channel where bulrushes tell
That the water was wont to go warbling so softly and well.
How good is man's life, the mere living! how fit to employ
All the heart and the soul and the senses forever in joy! 80
Hast thou loved the white locks of thy father, whose sword thou
    didst guard .
When he trusted thee forth with the armies, for glorious reward?
Didst thou see the thin hands of thy mother, held up as men sung
The low song of the nearly departed, and hear her faint tongue
Joining in while it could to the witness, 'Let one more attest, 85
I have lived, seen God's hand through a lifetime, and all was for
    best!'
Then they sung through their tears in strong triumph, not much,
    but the rest.
And thy brothers, the help and the contest, the working whence
    grew
Such result as, from seething grape-bundles, the spirit strained
    true:
And the friends of thy boyhood—that boyhood of wonder and
    hope, 90
Present promise and wealth of the future beyond the eye's scope,—
Till lo, thou art grown to a monarch; a people is thine;
And all gifts, which the world offers singly, on one head combine!
On one head, all the beauty and strength, love and rage (like
    the throe
That, a-work in the rock, helps its labour and lets the gold go), 95
High ambition and deeds which surpass it, fame crowning them,
    —all
Brought to blaze on the head of one creature—King Saul!"
And lo, with that leap of my spirit, heart, hand, harp, and voice,
Each lifting Saul's name out of sorrow, each bidding rejoice
Saul's fame in the light it was made for,—as when, dare I say, 100
The Lord's army, in rapture of service, strains through its array,
And upsoareth the cherubim-chariot,—"Saul!" cried I, and
    stopped,

And waited the thing that should follow. Then Saul, who hung
    propped
By the tent's cross-support in the centre, was struck by his name.
Have ye seen when Spring's arrowy summons goes right to the
    aim,   105
And some mountain, the last to withstand her,—that held (he
    alone,
While the vale laughed in freedom and flowers) on a broad
    bust of stone
A year's snow bound about for a breastplate,—leaves grasp of
    the sheet?
Fold on fold all at once it crowds thunderously down to his feet,
And there fronts you, stark, black, but alive yet, your mountain
    of old,   110
With his rents, the successive bequeathings of ages untold,
Yea, each harm got in fighting your battles, each furrow and scar
Of his head thrust 'twixt you and the tempest—all hail, there
    they are!
Now again to be softened with verdure, again hold the nest
Of the dove, tempt the goat and its young to the green on his
    crest   115
For their food in the ardours of summer. One long shudder
    thrilled
All the tent till the very air tingled, then sank and was stilled
At the King's self left standing before me, released and aware.
What was gone, what remained? All to traverse 'twixt hope and
    despair.
Death was past, life not come: so he waited. Awhile his right
    hand   120
Held the brow, helped the eyes, left too vacant, forthwith to
    remand
To their place what new objects should enter: 't was Saul as
    before.
I looked up, and dared gaze at those eyes, nor was hurt any more
Than by slow pallid sunsets in autumn, ye watch from the shore,
At their sad level gaze o'er the ocean—a sun's slow decline   125
Over hills which, resolved in stern silence, o'erlap and entwine
Base with base to knit strength more intensely; so arm folded
    arm
O'er the chest whose slow heavings subsided.

                         What spell or what charm
(For awhile there was trouble within me), what next should I
     urge
To sustain him where song had restored him? Song filled to
     the verge   130
His cup with the wine of this life, pressing all that it yields
Of mere fruitage, the strength and the beauty: beyond, on what
     fields
Glean a vintage more potent and perfect to brighten the eye
And bring blood to the lip, and commend them the cup they put
     by?
He saith, "It is good;" still he drinks not: he lets me praise life, 135
Gives assent, yet would die for his own part.

                         Then fancies grew rife
Which had come long ago on the pasture, when round me the
     sheep
Fed in silence—above, the one eagle wheeled slow as in sleep;
And I lay in my hollow and mused on the world that might lie
'Neath his ken, though I saw but the strip 'twixt the hill and
     the sky.   140
And I laughed—"Since my days are ordained to be passed with
     my flocks,
Let me people at least with my fancies the plains and rocks,
Dream the life I am never to mix with, and image the show
Of mankind as they live in those fashions I hardly shall know—
Schemes of life, its best rules and right uses, the courage that
     gains   145
And the prudence that keeps what men strive for!" And now
     these old trains
Of vague thought came again; I grew surer; so once more the
     string
Of my harp made response to my spirit, as thus:

                              "Yea, my King."
I began, "thou dost well in rejecting mere comforts that spring
From the mere mortal life held in common by man and by brute: 150
In our flesh grows the branch of this life, in our soul it bears fruit.
Thou hast marked the slow rise of the tree—how its stem trem-
     bled first
Till it passed the kid's lip, the stag's antler; then safely outburst

The fan-branches all round; and thou mindest when these too,
    in turn,
Broke a-bloom, and the palm-tree seemed perfect: yet more was
    to learn, 155
E'en the good that comes in with the palm-fruit. Our dates shall
    we slight,
When their juice brings a cure for all sorrow? or care for the
    plight
Of the palm's self whose slow growth produced them? Not so!
    stem and branch
Shall decay, nor be known in their place, while the palm-wine
    shall stanch
Every wound of man's spirit in winter. I pour thee such wine. 160
Leave the flesh to the fate it was fit for! the spirit be thine!
By the spirit, when age shall o'ercome thee, thou still shalt enjoy
More indeed, than at first when, inconscious, the life of a boy.
Crush that life, and behold its wine running! Each deed thou
    hast done
Dies, revives, goes to work in the world; until, e'en as the sun 165
Looking down on the earth, though clouds spoil him, though
    tempests efface,
Can find nothing his own deed produced not, must everywhere
    trace
The results of his past summer-prime, so each ray of thy will,
Every flash of thy passion and prowess, long over, shall thrill
Thy whole people, the countless, with ardour, till they too give
    forth 170
A like cheer to their sons, who in turn fill the South and the
    North
With the radiance thy deed was the germ of. Carouse in the
    past!
But the license of age has its limit; thou diest at last.
As the lion when age dims his eyeball, the rose at her height,
So with man—so his power and his beauty forever take flight. 175
No! Again a long draught of my soul-wine! Look forth o'er
    the years!
Thou hast done now with eyes for the actual; begin with the
    seer's!
Is Saul dead? In the depth of the vale make his tomb—bid arise
A grey mountain of marble heaped four-square, till, built to the
    skies,

Let it mark where the great First King slumbers: whose fame
　　would ye know?　　　　　　　　　　　　　　　　　　180
Up above see the rock's naked face, where the record shall go
In great characters cut by the scribe—Such was Saul, so he did,—
With the sages directing the work, by the populace chid,
For not half, they'll affirm, is comprised there!　Which fault to
　　amend,
In the grove with his kind grows the cedar, whereon they shall
　　spend　　　　　　　　　　　　　　　　　　　　　185
(See, in tablets 't is level before them) their praise, and record,
With the gold of the graver, Saul's story,—the statesman's great
　　word
Side by side with the poet's sweet comment. The river's a-wave
With smooth paper-reeds grazing each other when prophet-winds
　　rave;
So the pen gives unborn generations their due and their part　190
In thy being!　Then, first of the mighty, thank God that thou
　　art!"

And behold while I sang——but O Thou Who didst grant me,
　　that day,
And, before it, not seldom hast granted, Thy help to essay,
Carry on, and complete an adventure,—my shield and my sword
In that act where my soul was Thy servant, Thy word was my
　　word,—　　　　　　　　　　　　　　　　　　　　195
Still be with me, who then at the summit of human endeavour
And scaling the highest, man's thought could, gazed hopeless as
　　ever
On the new stretch of heaven above me,—till, mighty to save,
Just one lift of Thy hand cleared that distance—God's throne
　　from man's grave!
Let me tell out my tale to its ending—my voice to my heart,　200
Which can scarce dare believe in what marvels last night I took
　　part,
As this morning I gather the fragments, alone with my sheep,
And still fear lest the terrible glory evanish like sleep!
For I wake in the grey dewy covert, while Hebron upheaves
The dawn, struggling with night, on his shoulder, and Kidron
　　retrieves　　　　　　　　　　　　　　　　　　　205
Slow the damage of yesterday's sunshine.

　　　　　　　　　　　　　　　　I say, then, my song
While I sang thus, assuring the monarch, and, ever more strong,

Made a proffer of good to console him, he slowly resumed
His old motions and habitudes kingly. The right hand replumed
His black locks to their wonted composure, adjusted the swathes 210
Of his turban, and see—the huge sweat that his countenance
    bathes,
He wipes off with the robe; and he girds now his loins as of
    yore,
And feels slow for the armlets of price, with the clasp set before.
He is Saul ye remember in glory, ere error had bent
The broad brow from the daily communion; and still, though
    much spent 215
Be the life and the bearing that front you, the same God did
    choose
To receive what a man may waste, desecrate, never quite lose.
So sank he along by the tent-prop, till, stayed by the pile
Of his armour and war-cloak and garments, he leaned there
    awhile,
And sat out my singing,—one arm round the tent-prop, to raise 220
His bent head, and the other hung slack,—till I touched on the
    praise
I foresaw from all men in all time, to the man patient there;
And thus ended, the harp falling forward. Then first I was
    'ware
That he sat, as I say, with my head just above his vast knees
Which were thrust out on each side around me, like oak-roots
    which please 225
To encircle a lamb when it slumbers. I looked up to know
If the best I could do had brought solace: he spoke not, but slow
Lifted up the hand slack at his side, till he laid it with care
Soft and grave, but in mild settled will, on my brow; through my
    hair
The large fingers were pushed, and he bent back my head, with
    kind power— 230
All my face back, intent to peruse it, as men do a flower.
Thus held he me there with his great eyes that scrutinised mine—
And oh, all my heart how it loved him! but where was the sign?
I yearned—"Could I help thee, my father, inventing a bliss,
I would add, to that life of the past, both the future and this; 235
I would give thee new life altogether, as good, ages hence,
As this moment,—had love but the warrant love's heart to dis-
    pense!"

Then the truth came upon me. No harp more—no song more!
    outbroke—

"I have gone the whole round of creation: I saw and I spoke;
I, a work of God's hand for that purpose, received in my brain 240
And pronounced on the rest of His handwork—returned Him
    again
His creation's approval or censure; I spoke as I saw,
I report, as a man may of God's work, all 's love, yet all 's law.
Now I lay down the judgeship He lent me. Each faculty tasked
To perceive Him has gained an abyss where a dewdrop was
    asked. 245
Have I knowledge? confounded it shrivels at Wisdom laid bare.
Have I forethought? how purblind, how blank, to the Infinite
    Care!
Do I task any faculty highest, to image success?
I but open my eyes—and perfection, no more and no less,
In the kind I imagined, full-fronts me, and God is seen God 250
In the star, in the stone, in the flesh, in the soul and the clod.
And thus looking within and around me, I ever renew
(With that stoop of the soul which in bending upraises it too)
The submission of man's nothing-perfect to God's all-complete,
As by each new obeisance in spirit I climb to His feet. 255
Yet with all this abounding experience, this Deity known,
I shall dare to discover some province, some gift, of my own.
There 's a faculty pleasant to exercise, hard to hoodwink,
I am fain to keep still in abeyance (I laugh as I think),
Lest, insisting to claim and parade in it, wot ye, I worst 260
E'en the Giver in one gift. Behold, I could love if I durst!
But I sink the pretension as fearing a man may o'ertake
God's own speed in the one way of love; I abstain for love's
    sake.
—What, my soul? see thus far and no farther? when doors great
    and small,
Nine and ninety, flew ope at our touch, should the hundredth
    appal? 265
In the least things have faith, yet distrust in the greatest of all?
Do I find love so full in my nature, God's ultimate gift,
That I doubt His own love can compete with it? here the parts
    shift?
Here the creature surpass the Creator; the end, what began?

Would I fain in my impotent yearning do all for this man,   270
And dare doubt He alone shall not help him Who yet alone
    can?
Would it ever have entered my mind, the bare will, much less
    power,
To bestow on this Saul what I sang of, the marvellous dower
Of the life he was gifted and filled with? to make such a soul,
Such a body, and then such an earth for insphering the whole? 275
And doth it not enter my mind (as my warm tears attest),
These good things being given, to go on, and give one more, the
    best?
Ay, to save and redeem and restore him; maintain at the height
This perfection; succeed, with life's dayspring, death's minute
    of night;
Interpose at the difficult minute, snatch Saul the mistake,   280
Saul the failure, the ruin, he seems now, and bid him awake
From the dream, the probation, the prelude, to find himself set
Clear and safe in new light and new life,—a new harmony yet
To be run and continued, and ended—who knows?—or endure!
The man taught enough by life's dream, of the rest to make
    sure;   285
By the pain-throb, triumphantly winning intensified bliss,
And the next world's reward and repose by the struggles in this.

"I believe it! 'T is Thou, God, That givest, 't is I who receive:
In the First is the last, in Thy will is my power to believe.
All 's one gift: Thou canst grant it moreover, as prompt to my
    prayer,   290
As I breathe out this breath, as I open these arms to the air.
From Thy will stream the worlds, life and Nature, thy dread
    Sabaoth:
I will?—the mere atoms despise me! Why am I not loth
To look that, even that, in the face too? Why is it I dare
Think but lightly of such impuissance? What stops my despair? 295
This:—'t is not what man does which exalts him, but what man
    would do!
See the King—I would help him, but cannot; the wishes fall
    through.
Could I wrestle to raise him from sorrow, grow poor to enrich,
To fill up his life starve my own out, I would—knowing which,
I know that my service is perfect. Oh, speak through me now! 300

Would I suffer for him that I love? So wouldst Thou—so wilt
    Thou!
So shall crown Thee the topmost, ineffablest, uttermost crown;
And Thy love fill infinitude wholly, nor leave up nor down
One spot for the creature to stand in! It is by no breath,
Turn of eye, wave of hand, that salvation joins issue with
    death!   305
As Thy love is discovered almighty, almighty be proved
Thy power, that exists with and for it, of being beloved!
He Who did most shall bear most; the Strongest shall stand the
    most weak.
'T is the weakness in strength, that I cry for! my flesh, that I
    seek

In the Godhead! I seek and I find it. O Saul, it shall be   310
A Face like my face that receives thee; a Man like to me,
Thou shalt love and be loved by, forever; a Hand like this hand
Shall throw open the gates of new life to thee! See the Christ
    stand!"

I know not too well how I found my way home in the night.
There were witnesses, cohorts, about me, to left and to right; 315
Angels, powers, the unuttered, unseen, the alive, the aware:
I repressed, I got through them, as hardly, as strugglingly,
    there,
As a runner beset by the populace famished for news—
Life or death. The whole earth was awakened, hell loosed with
    her crews;
And the stars of night beat with emotion, and tingled and shot 320
Out in fire the strong pain of pent knowledge: but I fainted not,
For the Hand still impelled me at once and supported, sup-
    pressed
All the tumult, and quenched it with quiet, and holy behest,
Till the rapture was shut in itself, and the earth sank to rest.
Anon at the dawn, all that trouble had withered from earth— 325
Not so much but I saw it die out in the day's tender birth;
In the gathered intensity brought to the grey of the hills;
In the shuddering forests' held breath; in the sudden wind-thrills;
In the startled wild beasts that bore off, each with eye sidling
    still
Though averted with wonder and dread; in the birds stiff and
    chill,   330

That rose heavily as I approached them, made stupid with awe:
E'en the serpent that slid away silent—he felt the new law.
The same stared in the white humid faces upturned by the
    flowers,
The same worked in the heart of the cedar, and moved the vine-
    bowers;
And the little brooks witnessing murmured, persistent and low, 335
With their obstinate, all but hushed voices—"E'en so, it is so!"

1845, 1855.

LOVE AMONG THE RUINS

Where the quiet-coloured end of evening smiles
    Miles and miles
On the solitary pastures where our sheep,
    Half-asleep,
Tinkle homeward through the twilight, stray or stop   5
    As they crop,
Was the site once of a city great and gay
    (So they say),
Of our country's very capital, its prince
    Ages since   10
Held his court in, gathered councils, wielding far
    Peace or war.

Now the country does not even boast a tree,
    As you see,
To distinguish slopes of verdure, certain rills   15
    From the hills
Intersect and give a name to (else they run
    Into one),
Where the domed and daring palace shot its spires
    Up like fires   20
O'er the hundred-gated circuit of a wall
    Bounding all,
Made of marble, men might march on nor be pressed,
    Twelve abreast.

And such plenty and perfection, see, of grass   25
    Never was!
Such a carpet as, this summer-time, o'erspreads
    And embeds

Every vestige of the city, guessed alone,
    Stock or stone,—
Where a multitude of men breathed joy and woe   30
    Long ago;
Lust of glory pricked their hearts up, dread of shame
    Struck them tame;
And that glory and that shame alike the gold   35
    Bought and sold.

Now the single little turret that remains
    On the plains,
By the caper overrooted, by the gourd
    Overscored,   40
While the patching houseleek's head of blossom winks
    Through the chinks,
Marks the basement whence a tower in ancient time
    Sprang sublime,
And a burning ring, all round, the chariots traced   45
    As they raced,
And the monarch and his minions and his dames
    Viewed the games.

And I know, while thus the quiet-coloured eve
    Smiles to leave
To their folding all our many-tinkling fleece   50
    In such peace,
And the slopes and rills in undistinguished grey
    Melt away,
That a girl with eager eyes and yellow hair   55
    Waits me there
In the turret whence the charioteers caught soul
    For the goal,
When the king looked, where she looks now, breathless,
      dumb,
    Till I come.   60

But he looked upon the city, every side,
    Far and wide,
All the mountains topped with temples, all the glades'
    Colonnades,
All the causeys, bridges, aqueducts,—and then,   65
    All the men!

When I do come, she will speak not, she will stand,
    Either hand
On my shoulder, give her eyes the first embrace
    Of my face,   70
Ere we rush, ere we extinguish sight and speech
    Each on each.

In one year they sent a million fighters forth
    South and north,
And they built their gods a brazen pillar high   75
    As the sky,
Yet reserved a thousand chariots in full force—
    Gold, of course.
Oh heart! oh blood that freezes, blood that burns!
    Earth's returns   80
For whole centuries of folly, noise, and sin!
    Shut them in,
With their triumphs and their glories and the rest!
    Love is best.

                  1855.

FRA LIPPO LIPPI

I am poor brother Lippo, by your leave!
You need not clap your torches to my face.
Zooks! what's to blame? you think you see a monk!
What, 't is past midnight, and you go the rounds,
And here you catch me at an alley's end   5
Where sportive ladies leave their doors ajar?
The Carmine's my cloister: hunt it up,
Do,—harry out, if you must show your zeal,
Whatever rat, there, haps on his wrong hole,
And nip each softling of a wee white mouse,   10
Weke, weke, that's crept to keep him company!
Aha! you know your betters? Then you'll take
Your hand away that's fiddling on my throat,
And please to know me likewise. Who am I?
Why, one, sir, who is lodging with a friend   15
Three streets off—he's a certain—how d' ye call?
Master—a—Cosimo of the Medici,
I' the house that caps the corner. Boh! you were best!

Remember and tell me, the day you 're hanged,
How you affected such a gullet's-gripe!   20
But you, sir, it concerns you that your knaves
Pick up a manner, nor discredit you:
Zooks! are we pilchards, that they sweep the streets
And count fair prize what comes into their net?
He 's Judas to a tittle, that man is!   25
Just such a face! Why, sir, you make amends.
Lord, I 'm not angry! Bid your hang-dogs go
Drink out this quarter-florin to the health
Of the munificent House that harbours me
(And many more beside, lads! more beside!),   30
And all 's come square again. I 'd like his face—
His, elbowing on his comrade in the door
With the pike and lantern—for the slave that holds
John Baptist's head a-dangle by the hair
With one hand ("Look you, now," as who should say) 35
And his weapon in the other, yet unwiped!
It 's not your chance to have a bit of chalk,
A wood-coal, or the like? or you should see!
Yes, I 'm the painter, since you style me so.
What, brother Lippo's doings, up and down,   40
You know them, and they take you? like enough!
I saw the proper twinkle in your eye—
'Tell you, I liked your looks at very first.
Let 's sit and set things straight now, hip to haunch.
   Here 's spring come, and the nights one makes up
      bands   45
To roam the town and sing out carnival,
And I 've been three weeks shut within my mew,
A-painting for the great man, saints and saints
And saints again. I could not paint all night—
Ouf! I leaned out of window for fresh air.   50
There came a hurry of feet and little feet,
A sweep of lute-strings, laughs, and whifts of song—
Flower o' the broom,
Take away love, and our earth is a tomb!
Flower o' the quince,   55
I let Lisa go, and what good in life since?
Flower o' the thyme,—and so on. Round they went.
Scarce had they turned the corner when a titter

Like the skipping of rabbits by moonlight—three slim
    shapes,
And a face that looked up—zooks, sir, flesh and blood,   60
That's all I'm made of! Into shreds it went,
Curtain and counterpane and coverlet,
All the bed-furniture—a dozen knots,
There was a ladder! Down I let myself,
Hands and feet, scrambling somehow, and so dropped,   65
And after them. I came up with the fun
Hard by Saint Lawrence, hail fellow, well met,—
Flower o' the rose,
If I've been merry, what matter who knows?
And so, as I was stealing back again,   70
To get to bed and have a bit of sleep
Ere I rise up to-morrow and go work
On Jerome knocking at his poor old breast
With his great round stone to subdue the flesh,
You snap me of the sudden. Ah, I see!   75
Though your eye twinkles still, you shake your head—
Mine's shaved—a monk, you say—the sting's in that!
If Master Cosimo announced himself,
Mum's the word naturally; but a monk!
Come, what am I a beast for? tell us, now!   80
    I was a baby when my mother died,
And father died, and left me in the street.
I starved there, God knows how, a year or two,
On fig-skins, melon-parings, rinds and shucks,
Refuse and rubbish. One fine frosty day,   85
My stomach being empty as your hat,
The wind doubled me up and down I went.
Old aunt Lapaccia trussed me with one hand
(Its fellow was a stinger, as I knew),
And so along the wall, over the bridge,   90
By the straight cut to the convent. Six words there,
While I stood munching my first bread that month:
"So, boy, you're minded," quoth the good fat father,
Wiping his own mouth—'t was refection-time,—
"To quit this very miserable world?   95
Will you renounce"—"the mouthful of bread?" thought I;
"By no means!" Brief, they made a monk of me:
I did renounce the world, its pride and greed,

Palace, farm, villa, shop, and banking-house,
Trash, such as these poor devils of Medici　　　　　100
Have given their hearts to—all at eight years old.
Well, sir, I found in time, you may be sure,
'T was not for nothing—the good bellyful,
The warm serge and the rope that goes all round,
And day-long blessèd idleness beside!　　　　　105
"Let 's see what the urchin 's fit for"—that came next.
Not overmuch their way, I must confess,
Such a to-do! They tried me with their books:
Lord, they 'd have taught me Latin in pure waste!
Flower o' the clove,　　　　　110
All the Latin I construe is "amo," I love!
But, mind you, when a boy starves in the streets
Eight years together, as my fortune was,
Watching folk's faces to know who will fling
The bit of half-stripped grape-bunch he desires,　　　　　115
And who will curse or kick him for his pains,—
Which gentleman processional and fine,
Holding a candle to the sacrament,
Will wink and let him lift a plate and catch
The droppings of the wax to sell again,　　　　　120
Or holla for the Eight and have him whipped,—
How say I? nay, which dog bites, which lets drop
His bone from the heap of offal in the street,—
Why, soul and sense of him grow sharp alike;
He learns the look of things, and none the less　　　　　125
For admonition from the hunger-pinch.
I had a store of such remarks, be sure,
Which, after I found leisure, turned to use:
I drew men's faces on my copy-books,
Scrawled them within the antiphonary's marge,　　　　　130
Joined legs and arms to the long music-notes,
Found eyes and nose and chin for A's and B's,
And made a string of pictures of the world
Betwixt the ins and outs of verb and noun,
On the wall, the bench, the door. The monks looked
　　　black.　　　　　135
"Nay," quoth the Prior, "turn him out, d' ye say?
In no wise. Lose a crow and catch a lark.
What if at last we get our man of part·

We Carmelites, like those Camaldolese
And Preaching Friars, to do our church up fine   140
And put the front on it that ought to be!"
And hereupon he bade me daub away.
Thank you! my head being crammed, the walls a blank,
Never was such prompt disemburdening.
First, every sort of monk, the black and white,   145
I drew them, fat and lean: then, folk at church,
From good old gossips waiting to confess
Their cribs of barrel-droppings, candle-ends,
To the breathless fellow at the altar-foot,
Fresh from his murder, safe and sitting there   150
With the little children round him in a row
Of admiration, half for his beard, and half
For that white anger of his victim's son
Shaking a fist at him with one fierce arm,
Signing himself with the other because of Christ   155
(Whose sad face on the cross sees only this
After the passion of a thousand years),
Till some poor girl, her apron o'er her head
(Which the intense eyes looked through), came at eve
On tiptoe, said a word, dropped in a loaf,   160
Her pair of earrings, and a bunch of flowers,
(The brute took growling), prayed, and so was gone
I painted all, then cried, "'T is ask and have;
Choose, for more 's ready!" laid the ladder flat,
And showed my covered bit of cloister-wall.   165
The monks closed in a circle, and praised loud
Till checked, taught what to see and not to see,
Being simple bodies: "That 's the very man!
Look at the boy who stoops to pat the dog!
That woman 's like the Prior's niece who comes   170
To care about his asthma: it 's the life!"
But there my triumph's straw-fire flared and funked;
Their betters took their turn to see and say:
The Prior and the learnèd pulled a face,
And stopped all that in no time: "How? what 's here? 175
Quite from the mark of painting, bless us all!
Faces, arms, legs, and bodies like the true
As much as pea and pea! it 's devil's game!
Your business is not to catch men with show,

With homage to the perishable clay,   180
But lift them over it, ignore it all,
Make them forget there's such a thing as flesh,
Your business is to paint the souls of men—
Man's soul, and it's a fire, smoke—no, it's not—
It's vapour done up like a new-born babe   185
(In that shape when you die it leaves your mouth)—
It's—well, what matters talking, it's the soul!
Give us no more of body than shows soul!
Here's Giotto, with his saint a-praising God,
That sets us praising,—why not stop with him!   190
Why put all thoughts of praise out of our head
With wonder at lines, colours, and what not?
Paint the soul, never mind the legs and arms!
Rub all out, try at it a second time!
Oh, that white smallish female with the breasts,   195
She's just my niece—Herodias, I would say,—
Who went and danced, and got men's heads cut off!
Have it all out!" Now, is this sense, I ask?
A fine way to paint soul, by painting body
So ill the eye can't stop there, must go further,   200
And can't fare worse! Thus yellow does for white
When what you put for yellow's simply black,
And any sort of meaning looks intense
When all beside itself means and looks naught.
Why can't a painter lift each foot in turn,   205
Left foot and right foot, go a double step,
Make his flesh liker and his soul more like,
Both in their order? Take the prettiest face,
The Prior's niece—patron-saint,—is it so pretty
You can't discover if it means hope, fear,   210
Sorrow, or joy? won't beauty go with these?
Suppose I've made her eyes all right and blue,
Can't I take breath and try to add life's flash,
And then add soul and heighten them threefold?
Or say there's beauty with no soul at all   215
(I never saw it—put the case the same),
If you get simple beauty and naught else,
You get about the best thing God invents;
That's somewhat; and you'll find the soul you have missed,
Within yourself, when you return Him thanks.   220

"Rub all out!" Well, well, there's my life, in short,
And so the thing has gone on ever since.
I'm grown a man no doubt, I've broken bounds:
You should not take a fellow eight years old
And make him swear to never kiss the girls.   225
I'm my own master, paint now as I please—
Having a friend, you see, in the Corner-house!
Lord, it's fast holding by the rings in front—
Those great rings serve more purposes than just
To plant a flag in, or tie up a horse!   230
And yet the old schooling sticks, the old grave eyes
Are peeping o'er my shoulder as I work,
The heads shake still—"It's art's decline, my son!
You're not of the true painters, great and old;
Brother Angelico's the man, you'll find;   235
Brother Lorenzo stands his single peer:
Fag on at flesh, you'll never make the third!"
Flower o' the pine,
You keep your mistr—manners, and I'll stick to mine!
I'm not the third, then: bless us, they must know!   240
Don't you think they're the likeliest to know,
They with their Latin? So I swallow my rage,
Clench my teeth, suck my lips in tight, and paint
To please them—sometimes do, and sometimes don't;
For, doing most, there's pretty sure to come   245
A turn, some warm eve finds me at my saints—
A laugh, a cry, the business of the world—
(*Flower o' the peach,*
Death for us all, and his own life for each!)
And my whole soul revolves, the cup runs over,   250
The world and life's too big to pass for a dream,
And I do these wild things in sheer despite,
And play the fooleries you catch me at
In pure rage! The old mill-horse, out at grass
After hard years, throws up his stiff heels so,   255
Although the miller does not preach to him
The only good of grass is to make chaff.
What would men have? Do they like grass or no—
May they or mayn't they? all I want's the thing
Settled forever one way. As it is,   260
You tell too many lies and hurt yourself:

You don't like what you only like too much;
You do like what, if given you at your word,
You find abundantly detestable.
For me, I think I speak as I was taught: 265
I always see the garden, and God there
A-making man's wife; and my lesson learned,
The value and significance of flesh,
I can't unlearn ten minutes afterwards.

    You understand me: I'm a beast, I know.   270
But see, now—why, I see as certainly
As that the morning-star's about to shine,
What will hap some day. We've a youngster here
Comes to our convent, studies what I do,
Slouches and stares and lets no atom drop: 275
His name is Guidi—he'll not mind the monks—
They call him Hulking Tom, he lets them talk—
He picks my practice up—he'll paint apace,
I hope so—though I never live so long,
I know what's sure to follow. You be judge!   280
You speak no Latin more than I, belike;
However, you're my man, you've seen the world
—The beauty and the wonder and the power,
The shapes of things, their colours, lights, and shades,
Changes, surprises,—and God made it all!   285
—For what? Do you feel thankful, ay or no,
For this fair town's face, yonder river's line,
The mountain round it and the sky above,
Much more the figures of man, woman, child,
These are the frame to? What's it all about?   290
To be passed over, despised? or dwelt upon,
Wondered at? "Oh, this last of course!" you say.
But why not do as well as say,—paint these
Just as they are, careless what comes of it?
God's works—paint any one, and count it crime   295
To let a truth slip. Don't object, "His works
Are here already; Nature is complete:
Suppose you reproduce her (which you can't),
There's no advantage! you must beat her, then."
For, don't you mark? we're made so that we love   300
First when we see them painted, things we have passed
Perhaps a hundred times nor cared to see;

And so they are better, painted—better to us,
Which is the same thing. Art was given for that;
God uses us to help each other so,   305
Lending our minds out. Have you noticed, now,
Your cullion's hanging face? A bit of chalk,
And trust me but you should, though! How much more
If I drew higher things with the same truth!
That were to take the Prior's pulpit-place,   310
Interpret God to all of you! Oh, oh,
It makes me mad to see what men shall do
And we in our graves! This world's no blot for us,
Nor blank; it means intensely, and means good:
To find its meaning is my meat and drink.   315
"Ay, but you don't so instigate to prayer!"
Strikes in the Prior: "when your meaning's plain,
It does not say to folk, 'Remember matins!'
Or 'Mind you fast next Friday!'" Why, for this
What need of art at all? A skull and bones,   320
Two bits of stick nailed cross-wise, or, what's best,
A bell to chime the hour with, does as well.
I painted a Saint Lawrence six months since
At Prato, splashed the fresco in fine style.
"How looks my painting, now the scaffold's down?"   325
I ask a brother. "Hugely," he returns—
"Already not one phiz of your three slaves
Who turn the deacon off his toasted side,
But's scratched and prodded to our heart's content,
The pious people have so eased their own   330
With coming to say prayers there in a rage:
We get on fast to see the bricks beneath.
Expect another job this time next year,
For pity and religion grow i' the crowd—
Your painting serves its purpose!" Hang the fools!   335
—That is—you'll not mistake an idle word
Spoke in a huff by a poor monk, God wot,
Tasting the air this spicy night which turns
The unaccustomed head like Chianti wine!
Oh, the Church knows! don't misreport me, now!   340
It's natural a poor monk out of bounds
Should have his apt word to excuse himself.
And hearken how I plot to make amends.

I have bethought me: I shall paint a piece
—There's for you! Give me six months, then go, see　345
Something in Sant' Ambrogio's! Bless the nuns!
They want a cast o' my office. I shall paint
God in the midst, Madonna and her babe,
Ringed by a bowery, flowery angel-brood,
Lilies and vestments and white faces, sweet　　350
As puff on puff of grated orris-root
When ladies crowd to church at midsummer.
And then i' the front, of course a saint or two—
St. John, because he saves the Florentines;
St. Ambrose, who puts down in black and white　355
The convent's friends, and gives them a long day;
And Job, I must have him there past mistake,
The man of Uz (and Us without the z,
Painters who need his patience). Well, all these
Secured at their devotion, up shall come　　　360
Out of a corner when you least expect,
As one by a dark stair into a great light,
Music and talking, who but Lippo! I!—
Mazed, motionless, and moon-struck—I'm the man!
Back I shrink—what is this I see and hear?　　365
I, caught up with my monk's things by mistake,
My old serge gown and rope that goes all round,
I, in this presence, this pure company!
Where's a hole, where's a corner for escape?
Then steps a sweet angelic slip of a thing　　370
Forward, puts out a soft palm—"Not so fast!"
—Addresses the celestial presence: "Nay—
He made you and devised you, after all,
Though he's none of you! Could Saint John, there, draw—
His camel-hair make up a painting-brush?　　375
We come to brother Lippo for all that;
Iste perfecit opus!" So all smile—
I shuffle sideways with my blushing face,
Under the cover of a hundred wings
Thrown like a spread of kirtles when you're gay　380
And play hot cockles, all the doors being shut,
Till, wholly unexpected, in there pops
The hot-head husband! Thus I scuttle off
To some safe bench behind, not letting go

The palm of her, the little lily thing   385
That spoke the good word for me in the nick,
Like the Prior's niece—Saint Lucy, I would say.
And so all's saved for me, and for the church
A pretty picture gained. Go, six months hence!
Your hand, sir, and good-by: no lights, no lights!   390
The street's hushed, and I know my own way back,
Don't fear me! There's the gray beginning. Zooks!

                                        1855.

"CHILDE ROLAND TO THE DARK TOWER CAME"

My first thought was, he lied in every word,
    That hoary cripple, with malicious eye
    Askance to watch the working of his lie
On mine, and mouth scarce able to afford
Suppression of the glee, that pursed and scored   5
    Its edge, at one more victim gained thereby.

What else should he be set for, with his staff?
    What, save to waylay with his lies, insnare
    All travellers who might find him posted there,
And ask the road? I guessed what skull-like laugh   10
Would break, what crutch 'gin write my epitaph
    For pastime in the dusty thoroughfare,

If at his counsel I should turn aside
    Into that ominous tract which, all agree,
    Hides the Dark Tower. Yet acquiescingly   15
I did turn as he pointed; neither pride
Nor hope rekindling at the end descried,
    So much as gladness that some end might be.

For—what with my whole world-wide wandering,
    What with my search drawn out through years, my
        hope   20
    Dwindled into a ghost not fit to cope
With that obstreperous joy success would bring,—
I hardly tried now to rebuke the spring
    My heart made, finding failure in its scope.

As when a sick man very near to death   25
 Seems dead indeed, and feels begin and end
 The tears, and takes the farewell of each friend,
And hears one bid the other go, draw breath
Freelier outside ("since all is o'er," he saith,
 "And the blow fallen no grieving can amend") ;   30

While some discuss if near the other graves
 Be room enough for this, and when a day
 Suits best for carrying the corpse away,
With care about the banners, scarves, and staves;
And still the man hears all, and only craves   35
 He may not shame such tender love and stay :—

Thus I had so long suffered in this quest,
 Heard failure prophesied so oft, been writ
 So many times among "The Band"—to wit,
The knights who to the Dark Tower's search addressed   40
Their steps,—that just to fail as they, seemed best,
 And all the doubt was now—should I be fit?

So, quiet as despair, I turned from him,
 That hateful cripple, out of his highway
 Into the path he pointed. All the day   45
Had been a dreary one at best, and dim
Was settling to its close, yet shot one grim
 Red leer to see the plain catch its estray.

For mark! no sooner was I fairly found
 Pledged to the plain, after a pace or two,   50
 Than, pausing to throw backward a last view
O'er the safe road, 't was gone: grey plain all round;
Nothing but plain to the horizon's bound.
 I might go on; naught else remained to do.

So on I went. I think I never saw   55
 Such starved ignoble nature; nothing throve:
 For flowers—as well expect a cedar grove!
But cockle, spurge, according to their law
Might propagate their kind, with none to awe,
 You 'd think; a burr had been a treasure trove.   60

No! penury, inertness, and grimace,
   In some strange sort, were the land's portion. "See
   Or shut your eyes," said Nature peevishly;
"It nothing skills; I cannot help my case:
'T is the Last Judgment's fire must cure this place,   65
   Calcine its clods, and set my prisoners free."

If there pushed any ragged thistlestalk
   Above its mates, the head was chopped; the bents
   Were jealous else. What made those holes and rents
In the dock's harsh swarth leaves, bruised as to balk   70
All hope of greenness? 't is a brute must walk
   Pashing their life out, with a brute's intents.

As for the grass, it grew as scant as hair
   In leprosy; thin dry blades pricked the mud,
   Which underneath looked kneaded up with blood.   75
One stiff blind horse, his every bone a-stare,
Stood stupefied, however he came there,
   Thrust out past service from the Devil's stud!

Alive? he might be dead for aught I know,
   With that red, gaunt, and colloped neck a-strain,   80
   And shut eyes underneath the rusty mane.
Seldom went such grotesqueness with such woe:
I never saw a brute I hated so;
   He must be wicked to deserve such pain.

I shut my eyes and turned them on my heart.   85
   As a man calls for wine before he fights,
   I asked one draught of earlier, happier sights,
Ere fitly I could hope to play my part.
Think first, fight afterwards—the soldier's art:
   One taste of the old time sets all to rights.   90

Not it! I fancied Cuthbert's reddening face
   Beneath its garniture of curly gold,
   Dear fellow, till I almost felt him fold
An arm in mine to fix me to the place,
That way he used. Alas, one night's disgrace!   95
   Out went my heart's new fire and left it cold.

Giles, then, the soul of honour—there he stands
    Frank as ten years ago when knighted first.
    What honest man should dare (he said) he durst.
Good—but the scene shifts—faugh! what hangman
        hands   100
Pin to his breast a parchment? His own bands
    Read it. Poor traitor, spit upon and curst!

Better this present than a past like that;
    Back therefore to my darkening path again!
    No sound, no sight as far as eye could strain.   105
Will the night send a howlet or a bat?
I asked; when something on the dismal flat
    Came to arrest my thoughts and change their train.

A sudden little river crossed my path
    As unexpected as a serpent comes: 110
    No sluggish tide congenial to the glooms;
This, as it frothed by, might have been a bath
For the fiend's glowing hoof—to see the wrath
    Of its black eddy bespate with flakes and spumes.

So petty, yet so spiteful! All along,   115
    Low scrubby alders kneeled down over it;
    Drenched willows flung them headlong in a fit
Of mute despair, a suicidal throng:
The river which had done them all the wrong,
    Whate'er that was, rolled by, deterred no whit.   120

Which while I forded,—good saints, how I feared
    To set my foot upon a dead man's cheek,
    Each step, or feel the spear I thrust to seek
For hollows, tangled in his hair or beard!
—It may have been a water-rat I speared,   125
    But, ugh! it sounded like a baby's shriek.

Glad was I when I reached the other bank.
    Now for a better country. Vain presage!
    Who were the strugglers, what war did they wage,
Whose savage trample thus could pad the dank   130
Soil to a plash? Toads in a poisoned tank,
    Or wild cats in a red-hot iron cage—

The fight must so have seemed in that fell cirque.
　　What penned them there, with all the plain to choose?
　　No footprint leading to that horrid mews,　　135
None out of it. Mad brewage set to work
Their brains, no doubt, like galley-slaves the Turk
　　Pits for his pastime, Christians against Jews.

And more than that—a furlong on—why, there!
　　What bad use was that engine for, that wheel,　　140
　　Or brake, not wheel—that harrow fit to reel
Men's bodies out like silk? with all the air
Of Tophet's tool, on earth left unaware,
　　Or brought to sharpen its rusty teeth of steel.

Then came a bit of stubbed ground, once a wood,　　145
　　Next a marsh, it would seem, and now mere earth
　　Desperate and done with (so a fool finds mirth,
Makes a thing and then mars it, till his mood
Changes and off he goes!) : within a rood—
　　Bog, clay, and rubble, sand, and stark black dearth.　　150

Now blotches rankling, coloured gay and grim,
　　Now patches where some leanness of the soil's
　　Broke into moss or substances like boils;
Then came some palsied oak, a cleft in him
Like a distorted mouth that splits its rim　　155
　　Gaping at death, and dies while it recoils.

And just as far as ever from the end!
　　Naught in the distance but the evening, naught
　　To point my footstep further! At the thought,
A great black bird, Apollyon's bosom-friend,　　160
Sailed past, nor beat his wide wing, dragon-penned,
　　That brushed my cap—perchance the guide I sought.

For, looking up, aware I somehow grew,
　　'Spite of the dusk, the plain had given place
　　All round to mountains—with such name to grace　　165
Mere ugly heights and heaps now stolen in view.
How thus they had surprised me,—solve it, you!
　　How to get from them was no clearer case.

Yet half I seemed to recognise some trick
    Of mischief happened to me, God knows when—   170
    In a bad dream, perhaps. Here ended, then,
Progress this way. When, in the very nick
Of giving up one time more, came a click
    As when a trap shuts—you 're inside the den.

Burningly it came on me all at once,   175
    This was the place! those two hills on the right,
    Crouched like two bulls locked horn in horn in fight;
While to the left, a tall scalped mountain——dunce,
Dotard, a-dozing at the very nonce,
    After a life spent training for the sight!   180

What in the midst lay but the Tower itself?
    The round squat turret, blind as the fool's heart,
    Built of brown stone, without a counterpart
In the whole world. The tempest's mocking elf
Points to the shipman thus the unseen shelf   185
    He strikes on, only when the timbers start.

Not see? because of night perhaps?—why, day
    Came back again for that! before it left,
    The dying sunset kindled through a cleft:
The hills, like giants at a hunting, lay,   190
Chin upon hand, to see the game at bay,—
    "Now stab and end the creature—to the heft!"

Not hear? when noise was everywhere! it tolled
    Increasing like a bell. Names in my ears,
    Of all the lost adventurers my peers,—   195
How such a one was strong, and such was bold,
And such was fortunate, yet each of old
    Lost, lost! one moment knelled the woe of years.

There they stood, ranged along the hill-sides, met
    To view the last of me, a living frame   200
    For one more picture! in a sheet of flame
I saw them and I knew them all. And yet
Dauntless the slug-horn to my lips I set,
    And blew. *"Childe Roland to the Dark Tower came."*

                              1855.

THE LAST RIDE TOGETHER

I said, "Then, dearest, since 't is so,
Since now at length my fate I know,
Since nothing all my love avails,
Since all, my life seemed meant for, fails,
    Since this was written and needs must be,   5
My whole heart rises up to bless
Your name in pride and thankfulness!
Take back the hope you gave,—I claim
Only a memory of the same,
 —And this beside, if you will not blame,   10
    Your leave for one more last ride with me."

My mistress bent that brow of hers;
Those deep dark eyes, where pride demurs
When pity would be softening through,
Fixed me a breathing-while or two   15
    With life or death in the balance: right!
The blood replenished me again;
My last thought was at least not vain:
I and my mistress, side by side
Shall be together, breathe and ride;   20
So one day more am I deified.
    Who knows but the world may end to-night?

Hush! if you saw some western cloud
All billowy-bosomed, over-bowed
By many benedictions—sun's   25
And moon's and evening-star's at once,—
    And so you, looking and loving best,
Conscious grew your passion drew
Cloud, sunset, moonrise, star-shine too,
Down on you, near and yet more near,   30
Till flesh must fade for heaven was here!—
Thus leant she and lingered—joy and fear!
    Thus lay she a moment on my breast.

Then we began to ride. My soul
Smoothed itself out, a long-cramped scroll   35
Freshening and fluttering in the wind.

Past hopes already lay behind.
    What need to strive with a life awry?
Had I said that, had I done this,
So might I gain, so might I miss.   40
Might she have loved me? just as well
She might have hated, who can tell!
Where had I been now if the worst befell?
    And here we are riding, she and I.

Fail I alone, in words and deeds?   45
Why, all men strive, and who succeeds?
We rode; it seemed my spirit flew,
Saw other regions, cities new,
    As the world rushed by on either side.
I thought, All labour, yet no less   50
Bear up beneath their unsuccess.
Look at the end of work, contrast
The petty done, the undone vast,
This present of theirs with the hopeful past!
    I hoped she would love me: here we ride.   55

What hand and brain went ever paired?
What heart alike conceived and dared?
What act proved all its thought had been?
What will but felt the fleshly screen?
    We ride, and I see her bosom heave.   60
There's many a crown for who can reach.
Ten lines, a statesman's life in each!
The flag stuck on a heap of bones,
A soldier's doing! what atones?
They scratch his name on the Abbey stones.   65
    My riding is better, by their leave.

What does it all mean, poet? Well,
Your brains beat into rhythm, you tell
What we felt only; you expressed
You hold things beautiful the best,   70
    And place them in rhyme so, side by side.
'T is something, nay 't is much: but then,
Have you yourself what 's best for men?
Are you—poor, sick, old ere your time—

Nearer one whit your own sublime 75
Than we who never have turned a rhyme!
 Sing, Riding's a joy! For me, I ride.

And you, great sculptor—so you gave
A score of years to Art, her slave,
And that's your Venus, whence we turn 80
To yonder girl that fords the burn!
 You acquiesce, and shall I repine?
What, man of music, you grown grey
With notes and nothing else to say,
Is this your sole praise from a friend, 85
"Greatly his opera's strains intend,
But in music we know how fashions end!"
 I gave my youth; but we ride, in fine.

Who knows what's fit for us? Had fate
Proposed bliss here should sublimate 90
My being—had I signed the bond,—
Still one must lead some life beyond,
 Have a bliss to die with, dim-descried.
This foot once planted on the goal,
This glory-garland round my soul, 95
Could I descry such? Try and test!
I sink back shuddering from the quest.
Earth being so good, would heaven seem best?
 Now, heaven and she are beyond this ride.

And yet—she has not spoke so long! 100
What if heaven be that, fair and strong
At life's best, with our eyes upturned
Whither life's flower is first discerned,
 We, fixed so, ever should so abide?
What if we still ride on, we two, 105
With life forever old yet new,
Changed not in kind but in degree,
The instant made eternity,—
And heaven just prove that I and she
 Ride, ride together, forever ride? 110

     1855.

THE PATRIOT

AN OLD STORY

It was roses, roses, all the way,
   With myrtle mixed in my path like mad;
The house-roofs seemed to heave and sway;
   The church-spires flamed, such flags they had,
A year ago on this very day.   5

The air broke into a mist with bells;
   The old walls rocked with the crowd and cries.
Had I said, "Good folk, mere noise repels—
   But give me your sun from yonder skies!"
They had answered, "And afterward, what else?"   10

Alack, it was I who leaped at the sun
   To give it my loving friends to keep!
Naught man could do, have I left undone:
   And you see my harvest, what I reap
This very day, now a year is run.   15

There's nobody on the house-tops now—
   Just a palsied few at the windows set;
For the best of the sight is, all allow,
   At the Shambles' Gate—or, better yet,
By the very scaffold's foot, I trow.   20

I go in the rain, and, more than needs,
   A rope cuts both my wrists behind;
And I think, by the feel, my forehead bleeds,
   For they fling, whoever has a mind,
Stones at me for my year's misdeeds.   25

Thus I entered, and thus I go!
   In triumphs, people have dropped down dead:
"Paid by the world, what dost thou owe
   Me?" God might question; now, instead,
'T is God shall repay: I am safer so.   30

1855

A GRAMMARIAN'S FUNERAL

SHORTLY AFTER THE REVIVAL OF LEARNING IN EUROPE

Let us begin and carry up this corpse,
    Singing together.
Leave we the common crofts, the vulgar thorpes,
    Each in its tether
Sleeping safe on the bosom of the plain,   5
    Cared-for till cock-crow:
Look out if yonder be not day again
    Rimming the rock-row!
That's the appropriate country; there man's thought,
    Rarer, intenser,   10
Self-gathered for an outbreak, as it ought,
    Chafes in the censer.
Leave we the unlettered plain its herd and crop;
    Seek we sepulture
On a tall mountain, citied to the top,   15
    Crowded with culture!
All the peaks soar, but one the rest excels;
    Clouds overcome it;
No, yonder sparkle is the citadel's
    Circling its summit.   20
Thither our path lies; wind we up the heights;
    Wait ye the warning?
Our low life was the level's and the night's;
    He's for the morning.
Step to a tune, square chests, erect each head,   25
    'Ware the beholders!
This is our master, famous, calm and dead,
    Borne on our shoulders.
Sleep, crop and herd! sleep, darkling thorpe and croft,
    Safe from the weather!   30
He whom we convoy to his grave aloft,
    Singing together,
He was a man born with thy face and throat,
    Lyric Apollo!
Long he lived nameless: how should Spring take note   35
    Winter would follow?
Till lo, the little touch, and youth was gone!
    Cramped and diminished,

Moaned he, "New measures, other feet anon!
    My dance is finished"?   40
No, that's the world's way: (keep the mountain-side,
    Make for the city!)
He knew the signal, and stepped on with pride
    Over men's pity;
Left play for work, and grappled with the world   45
    Bent on escaping:
"What's in the scroll," quoth he, "thou keepest furled?
    Show me their shaping,
Theirs who most studied man, the bard and sage,—
    Give!" So he gowned him,   50
Straight got by heart that book to its last page:
    Learnèd, we found him.
Yea, but we found him bald too, eyes like lead,
    Accents uncertain:
"Time to taste life," another would have said;   55
    "Up with the curtain!"
This man said rather, "Actual life comes next?
    Patience a moment!
Grant I have mastered learning's crabbèd text,
    Still there's the comment.   60
Let me know all! Prate not of most or least,
    Painful or easy!
Even to the crumbs I'd fain eat up the feast,
    Ay, nor feel queasy."
Oh, such a life as he resolved to live,   65
    When he had learned it,
When he had gathered all books had to give!
    Sooner, he spurned it.
Image the whole, then execute the parts—
    Fancy the fabric   70
Quite, ere you build, ere steel strike fire from quartz,
    Ere mortar dab brick!
(Here's the town-gate reached: there's the market-place
    Gaping before us.)
Yea, this in him was the peculiar grace,   75
    (Hearten our chorus!)
That before living he'd learn how to live—
    No end to learning:

Earn the means first—God surely will contrive
    Use for our earning.   80
Others mistrust and say, "But time escapes:
    Live now or never!"
He said, "What's time? Leave Now for dogs and apes!
    Man has Forever."
Back to his book then: deeper drooped his head;   85
    Calculus racked him;
Leaden before, his eyes grew dross of lead;
    Tussis attacked him.
"Now, master, take a little rest!"—not he!
    (Caution redoubled!   90
Step two abreast, the way winds narrowly!)
    Not a whit troubled,
Back to his studies, fresher than at first,
    Fierce as a dragon
He (soul-hydroptic with a sacred thirst)   95
    Sucked at the flagon.
Oh, if we draw a circle premature,
    Heedless of far gain,
Greedy for quick returns of profit, sure
    Bad is our bargain!   100
Was it not great? did not he throw on God—
    (He loves the burthen)—
God's task to make the heavenly period
    Perfect the earthen?
Did not he magnify the mind, show clear   105
    Just what it all meant?
He would not discount life as fools do here,
    Paid by instalment.
He ventured neck or nothing—heaven's success
    Found, or earth's failure: 110
"Wilt thou trust death or not?" He answered, "Yes!
    Hence with life's pale lure!"
That low man seeks a little thing to do,
    Sees it and does it:
This high man, with a great thing to pursue,   115
    Dies ere he knows it.
That low man goes on adding one to one;
    His hundred's soon hit:

This high man, aiming at a million,
    Misses an unit.   120
That has the world here—should he need the next,
    Let the world mind him.
This throws himself on God, and, unperplexed,
    Seeking shall find him!
So, with the throttling hands of Death at strife,   125
    Ground he at grammar;
Still, through the rattle, parts of speech were rife:
    While he could stammer
He settled *Hoti's* business—let it be!
    Properly based *Oun*—   130
Gave us the doctrine of the enclitic *De*,
    Dead from the waist down.
Well, here's the platform, here's the proper place:
    Hail to your purlieus,
All ye highfliers of the feathered race,   135
    Swallows and curlews!
Here's the top-peak; the multitude below
    Live, for they can, there:
This man decided not to Live but Know—
    Bury this man there?   140
Here—here's his place, where meteors shoot, clouds form,
    Lightnings are loosened,
Stars come and go! Let joy break with the storm,
    Peace let the dew send!
Lofty designs must close in like effects: 145
    Loftily lying,
Leave him—still loftier than the world suspects,
    Living and dying.

                    1855.

PROSPICE

Fear death?—to feel the fog in my throat,
    The mist in my face,
When the snows begin, and the blasts denote
    I am nearing the place,
The power of the night, the press of the storm,   5
    The post of the foe,
Where he stands, the Arch Fear in a visible form,
    Yet the strong man must go;

For the journey is done and the summit attained,
    And the barriers fall,   10
Though a battle's to fight ere the guerdon be gained,
    The reward of it all.
I was ever a fighter, so—one fight more,
    The best and the last!
I would hate that Death bandaged my eyes, and forbore, 15
    And bade me creep past.
No! let me taste the whole of it, fare like my peers,
    The heroes of old,
Bear the brunt, in a minute pay glad life's arrears
    Of pain, darkness, and cold.   20
For sudden the worst turns the best to the brave,
    The black minute's at end,
And the elements' rage, the fiend-voices that rave,
    Shall dwindle, shall blend,
Shall change, shall become first a peace out of pain,   25
    Then a light, then thy breast,
O thou soul of my soul! I shall clasp thee again.
    And with God be the rest!

   1861.   1864.

AMONG THE ROCKS

Oh, good gigantic smile o' the brown old Earth,
    This autumn morning! How he sets his bones
To bask i' the sun, and thrusts out knees and feet
For the ripple to run over in its mirth,
    Listening the while where on the heap of stones   5
The white breast of the sea-lark twitters sweet.

That is the doctrine, simple, ancient, true;
    Such is life's trial, as old Earth smiles and knows.
If you loved only what were worth your love,
Love were clear gain, and wholly well for you: 10
    Make the low nature better by your throes!
Give earth yourself, go up for gain above!

                                 1864.

ABT VOGLER

AFTER HE HAS BEEN EXTEMPORISING UPON THE MUSICAL INSTRU-
MENT OF HIS INVENTION

Would that the structure brave, the manifold music I build,
    Bidding my organ obey, calling its keys to their work,
Claiming each slave of the sound, at a touch, as when Solomon
      willed
    Armies of angels that soar, legions of demons that lurk,
Man, brute, reptile, fly,—alien of end and of aim,   5
    Adverse, each from the other heaven-high, hell-deep removed,—
Should rush into sight at once as he named the ineffable Name,
    And pile him a palace straight, to pleasure the princess he loved!

Would it might tarry like his, the beautiful building of mine,
    This which my keys in a crowd pressed and importuned to
      raise!   10
Ah, one and all, how they helped, would dispart now and now
      combine,
    Zealous to hasten the work, heighten their master his praise!
And one would bury his brow with a blind plunge down to hell,
    Burrow awhile and build, broad on the roots of things,
Then up again swim into sight, having based me my palace well, 15
    Founded it, fearless of flame, flat on the nether springs.

And another would mount and march, like the excellent minion
      he was,
    Ay, another and yet another, one crowd but with many a crest,
Raising my rampired walls of gold as transparent as glass,
    Eager to do and die, yield each his place to the rest;   20
For higher still and higher (as a runner tips with fire,
    When a great illumination surprises a festal night—
Outlining round and round Rome's dome from space to spire)
    Up, the pinnacled glory reached, and the pride of my soul
      was in sight.

In sight? Not half! for it seemed, it was certain, to match man's
      birth,   25
    Nature in turn conceived, obeying an impulse as I;
And the emulous heaven yearned down, made effort to reach the
      earth,
    As the earth had done her best, in my passion, to scale the sky:

Novel splendours burst forth, grew familiar and dwelt with mine,
   Not a point nor peak but found and fixed its wandering star; 30
Meteor-moons, balls of blaze: and they did not pale nor pine,
     For earth had attained to heaven, there was no more near nor
      far.

Nay more; for there wanted not who walked in the glare and glow,
   Presences plain in the place; or, fresh from the Protoplast,
Furnished for ages to come, when a kindlier wind should blow, 35
   Lured now to begin and live, in a house to their liking at last;
Or else the wonderful dead who have passed through the body
     and gone,
     But were back once more to breathe in an old world worth
      their new:
What never had been, was now; what was, as it shall be anon;
     And what is—shall I say, matched both? for I was made per-
      fect too.
                                      40

All through my keys that gave their sounds to a wish of my soul,
   All through my soul that praised as its wish flowed visibly
     forth,
All through music and me! For think, had I painted the whole,
   Why, there it had stood, to see, nor the process so wonder-
     worth;
Had I written the same, made verse,—still, effect proceeds from
     cause, 45
   Ye know why the forms are fair, ye hear how the tale is told;
It is all triumphant art, but art in obedience to laws,
     Painter and poet are proud in the artist-list enrolled.

But here is the finger of God, a flash of the Will that can,
   Existent behind all laws, that made them and, lo, they are! 50
And I know not if, save in this, such gift be allowed to man,
     That out of three sounds he frame, not a fourth sound, but a
     star.
Consider it well: each tone of our scale in itself is naught;
   It is everywhere in the world—loud, soft, and all is said:
Give it to me to use! I mix it with two in my thought— 55
     And there! Ye have heard and seen: consider and bow the
     head!

Well, it is gone at last, the palace of music I reared;
   Gone! and the good tears start, the praises that come too slow;
For one is assured at first—one scarce can say that he feared,
   That he even gave it a thought—the gone thing was to go.   60
Never to be again! But many more of the kind
   As good, nay, better perchance: is this your comfort to me?
To me, who must be saved because I cling with my mind
   To the same, same self, same love, same God: ay, what was,
     shall be.

Therefore to whom turn I but to Thee, the ineffable Name?   65
   Builder and maker, Thou, of houses not made with hands!
What, have fear of change from Thee Who art ever the same?
   Doubt that Thy power can fill the heart that Thy power
     expands?
There shall never be one lost good! What was, shall live as
     before!
   The evil is null, is naught, is silence implying sound;   70
What was good shall be good, with, for evil, so much good more:
   On the earth, the broken arcs; in the heaven, a perfect round.

All we have willed or hoped or dreamed of good, shall exist;
   Not its semblance, but itself: no beauty, nor good, nor power
Whose voice has gone forth, but each survives for the melodist 75
   When eternity affirms the conception of an hour.
The high that proved too high, the heroic for earth too hard,
   The passion that left the ground to lose itself in the sky,
Are music sent up to God by the lover and the bard:
   Enough that He heard it once; we shall hear it by and by. 80

And what is our failure here but a triumph's evidence
   For the fullness of the days? Have we withered or agonised?
Why else was the pause prolonged but that singing might issue
     thence?
   Why rushed the discords in but that harmony should be prized?
Sorrow is hard to bear, and doubt is slow to clear;   85
   Each sufferer says his say, his scheme of the weal and woe:
But God has a few of us whom He whispers in the ear;
   The rest may reason, and welcome; 'tis we musicians know.

Well, it is earth with me; silence resumes her reign:
  I will be patient and proud, and soberly acquiesce.   90
Give me the keys. I feel for the common chord again,
  Sliding by semitones till I sink to the minor,—yes,
And I blunt it into a ninth, and I stand on alien ground,
  Surveying awhile the heights I rolled from into the deep;
Which, hark, I have dared and done, for my resting-place is found, 95
  The C Major of this life: so now I will try to sleep.

                                        1864.

RABBI BEN EZRA

  Grow old along with me!
  The best is yet to be,
  The last of life, for which the first was made:
  Our times are in His Hand
  Who saith, "A whole I planned;   5
  Youth shows but half: trust God, see all, nor be
          afraid!"

  Not that, amassing flowers,
  Youth sighed, "Which rose makes ours,
  Which lily leave and then as best recall?"
  Not that, admiring stars,   10
  It yearned, "Nor Jove, nor Mars;
  Mine be some figured flame which blends, transcends
          them all!"

  Not for such hopes and fears
  Annulling youth's brief years,
  Do I remonstrate: folly wide the mark!   15
  Rather I prize the doubt
  Low kinds exist without,
  Finished and finite clods, untroubled by a spark.

  Poor vaunt of life indeed,
  Were man but formed to feed   20
  On joy, to solely seek and find and feast:
  Such feasting ended, then
  As sure an end to men;
  Irks care the crop-full bird? frets doubt the maw-
          crammed beast?

Rejoice we are allied   25
To That which doth provide
And not partake, effect and not receive!
A spark disturbs our clod;
Nearer we hold of God
Who gives, than of His tribes that take, I must
    believe.   30

Then welcome each rebuff
That turns earth's smoothness rough,
Each sting that bids nor sit nor stand but go!
Be our joys three-parts pain!
Strive, and hold cheap the strain;   35
Learn, nor account the pang; dare, never grudge the
    throe!

For thence—a paradox
Which comforts while it mocks—
Shall life succeed in that it seems to fail:
What I aspired to be,   40
And was not, comforts me;
A brute I might have been, but would not sink i'
    the scale.

What is he but a brute
Whose flesh hath soul to suit,
Whose spirit works lest arms and legs want play?   45
To man propose this test—
Thy body at its best,
How far can that project thy soul on its lone way?

Yet gifts should prove their use:
I own the Past profuse   50
Of power each side, perfection every turn;
Eyes, ears took in their dole,
Brain treasured up the whole;
Should not the heart beat once, "How good to live
    and learn"?

Not once beat, "Praise be Thine!   55
I see the whole design;
I, who saw Power, see now Love perfect too:
Perfect I call Thy plan;

Thanks that I was a man!
Maker, remake, complete,—I trust what Thou shalt
    do!" 60

For pleasant is this flesh;
Our soul, in its rose-mesh
Pulled ever to the earth, still yearns for rest:
Would we some prize might hold
To match those manifold 65
Possessions of the brute,—gain most, as we did best!

Let us not always say,
"Spite of this flesh to-day
I strove, made head, gained ground upon the whole!"
As the bird wings and sings, 70
Let us cry, "All good things
Are ours, nor soul helps flesh more, now, than flesh
    helps soul!"

Therefore I summon age
To grant youth's heritage,
Life's struggle having so far reached its term: 75
Thence shall I pass, approved
A man, for aye removed
From the developed brute; a god though in the germ.

And I shall thereupon
Take rest, ere I be gone 80
Once more on my adventure brave and new;
Fearless and unperplexed,
When I wage battle next,
What weapons to select, what armour to indue.

Youth ended, I shall try 85
My gain or loss thereby;
Leave the fire ashes, what survives is gold.
And I shall weigh the same,
Give life its praise or blame:
Young, all lay in dispute; I shall know, being old. 90

For note, when evening shuts,
A certain moment cuts
The deed off, calls the glory from the grey:

A whisper from the west
Shoots, "Add this to the rest,   95
Take it and try its worth; here dies another day."

So, still within this life,
Though lifted o'er its strife,
Let me discern, compare, pronounce at last:
"This rage was right i' the main,   100
That acquiescence vain;
The Future I may face now I have proved the Past."

For more is not reserved
To man with soul just nerved
To act to-morrow what he learns to-day: 105
Here, work enough to watch
The Master work, and catch
Hints of the proper craft, tricks of the tool's true
       play.

As it was better youth
Should strive, through acts uncouth,   110
Toward making, than repose on aught found made;
So better age, exempt
From strife, should know, than tempt
Further. Thou waitedst age: wait death, nor be
       afraid!

Enough now if the Right   115
And Good and Infinite
Be named here, as thou callest thy hand thine own,
With knowledge absolute,
Subject to no dispute
From fools that crowded youth, nor let thee feel
       alone.   120

Be there, for once and all,
Severed great minds from small,
Announced to each his station in the Past!
Was I the world arraigned,
Were they my soul disdained,   125
Right? Let age speak the truth and give us peace
       at last!

Now, who shall arbitrate?
Ten men love what I hate,
Shun what I follow, slight what I receive;
Ten who in ears and eyes   130
Match me: we all surmise,
They this thing, and I that; whom shall my soul
    believe?

Not on the vulgar mass
Called "work" must sentence pass,
Things done, that took the eye and had the price; 135
O'er which, from level stand,
The low world laid its hand,
Found straightway to its mind, could value in a trice.

But all, the world's coarse thumb
And finger failed to plumb,   140
So passed in making up the main account;
All instincts immature,
All purposes unsure,
That weighed not as his work, yet swelled the man's
    amount;

Thoughts hardly to be packed   145
Into a narrow act,
Fancies that broke through language and escaped;
All I could never be,
All, men ignored in me,—
This I was worth to God, Whose wheel the pitcher
    shaped.   150

Ay, note that potter's wheel,
That metaphor! and feel
Why time spins fast, why passive lies our clay,—
Thou, to whom fools propound,
When the wine makes its round,   155
"Since life fleets, all is change, the Past gone, seize
    to-day!"

Fool! All that is, at all,
Lasts ever, past recall;
Earth changes, but thy soul and God stand sure:

What entered into thee,   160
That was, is, and shall be;
Time's wheel runs back or stops, Potter and clay
          endure.

He fixed thee 'mid this dance
Of plastic circumstance,
This Present thou, forsooth, wouldst fain arrest: 165
Machinery just meant
To give thy soul its bent,
Try thee and turn thee forth, sufficiently impressed.

What though the earlier grooves,
Which ran the laughing loves   170
Around thy base, no longer pause and press?
What though, about thy rim,
Skull-things in order grim
Grow out, in graver mood, obey the sterner stress?

Look not thou down but up!   175
To uses of a cup—
The festal board, lamp's flash, and trumpet's peal,
The new wine's foaming flow,
The Master's lips aglow!
Thou, heaven's consummate cup, what needst thou
          with earth's wheel?   180

But I need, now as then,
Thee, God, Who mouldest men:
And since, not even while the whirl was worst,
Did I—to the wheel of life
With shapes and colors rife,   185
Bound dizzily—mistake my end, to slake Thy thirst,

So take and use Thy work;
Amend what flaws may lurk,
What strain o' the stuff, what warpings past the aim!
My times be in Thy hand!   190
Perfect the cup as planned!
Let age approve of youth, and death complete the
          same!

                                             1864.

WANTING IS—WHAT?

Wanting is—what?
Summer redundant,
Blueness abundant,
—Where is the blot?
Beamy the world, yet a blank all the same,　　　　5
—Framework which waits for a picture to frame:
What of the leafage, what of the flower?
Roses embowering with naught they embower!
Come then, complete incompletion, O comer,
Pant through the blueness, perfect the summer!　　10
Breathe but one breath
Rose-beauty above,
And all that was death
Grows life, grows love,
Grows love!　　　　15

　　　　　　　　　　　　　　1883.

ADAM, LILITH, AND EVE

One day, it thundered and lightened.
Two women, fairly frightened,
Sank to their knees, transformed, transfixed,
At the feet of the man who sat betwixt;
And "Mercy!" cried each, "if I tell the truth　　5
Of a passage in my youth!"

Said This: "Do you mind the morning
I met your love with scorning?
As the worst of the venom left my lips,
I thought, 'If, despite this lie, he strips　　10
The mask from my soul with a kiss,—I crawl
His slave—soul, body, and all!'"

Said That: "We stood to be married;
The priest, or some one, tarried;
'If Paradise-door prove locked?' smiled you.　　15
I thought, as I nodded, smiling too,
'Did one, that's away, arrive,—nor late
Nor soon should unlock Hell's gate!'"

It ceased to lighten and thunder.
Up started both in wonder, 20
Looked round and saw that the sky was clear,
Then laughed, "Confess you believed us, dear!"
"I saw through the joke!" the man replied.
They re-seated themselves beside.

1883.

SUMMUM BONUM

All the breath and the bloom of the year in the bag of one bee;
   All the wonder and wealth of the mine in the heart of one gem;
In the core of one pearl all the shade and the shine of the sea;
   Breath and bloom, shade and shine, wonder, wealth, and—
      how far above them—
     Truth, that's brighter than gem, 5
     Trust, that's purer than pearl,—
Brightest truth, purest trust in the universe,—all were for me
   In the kiss of one girl.

1889.

EPILOGUE

At the midnight in the silence of the sleep-time,
   When you set your fancies free,
Will they pass to where—by death, fools think, imprisoned—
Low he lies who once so loved you, whom you loved so,
   —Pity me? 5

Oh to love so, be so loved, yet so mistaken!
   What had I on earth to do
With the slothful, with the mawkish, the unmanly?
Like the aimless, helpless, hopeless did I drivel
   —Being—who? 10

One who never turned his back but marched breast forward,
   Never doubted clouds would break,
Never dreamed, though right were worsted, wrong would
     triumph,
Held we fall to rise, are baffled to fight better,
   Sleep to wake 15

No, at noon-day in the bustle of man's work-time
  Greet the unseen with a cheer!
Bid him forward, breast and back as either should be,
"Strive and thrive!" cry, "Speed,—fight on, fare ever
  There as here!"   20

                                        1889

ARTHUR HUGH CLOUGH

SAY NOT THE STRUGGLE NAUGHT AVAILETH

Say not the struggle naught availeth,
  The labour and the wounds are vain,
The enemy faints not, nor faileth,
  And as things have been they remain.

If hopes were dupes, fears may be liars;   5
  It may be, in yon smoke concealed,
Your comrades chase e'en now the fliers,
  And, but for you, possess the field.

For while the tired waves, vainly breaking,
  Seem here no painful inch to gain,   10
Far back, through creeks and inlets making,
  Comes silent, flooding in, the main.

And not by eastern windows only,
  When daylight comes, comes in the light;
In front, the sun climbs slow, how slowly,   15
  But westward, look, the land is bright.
1849.   1862.

THE LATEST DECALOGUE

Thou shalt have one God only; who
Would be at the expense of two?
No graven images may be
Worshipped, except the currency:
Swear not at all; for, for thy curse   5
Thine enemy is none the worse:
At church on Sunday to attend
Will serve to keep the world thy friend:

Honour thy parents; that is, all
From whom advancement may befall: 10
Thou shalt not kill; but need'st not strive
Officiously to keep alive:
Do not adultery commit;
Advantage rarely comes of it:
Thou shalt not steal; an empty feat,   15
When it's so lucrative to cheat:
Bear not false witness; let the lie
Have time on its own wings to fly:
Thou shalt not covet; but tradition
Approves all forms of competition.   20

                                    1862.

HOPE EVERMORE AND BELIEVE

Hope evermore and believe, O man, for e'en as thy thought
    So are the things that thou see'st, e'en as thy hope and belief.
Cowardly art thou and timid? they rise to provoke thee against
    them;
    Hast thou courage? enough, see them exulting to yield.
Yea, the rough rock, the dull earth, the wild sea's furying waters 5
    (Violent say'st thou and hard, mighty thou think'st to destroy),
All with ineffable longing are waiting their Invader,
    All, with one varying voice, call to him, Come and subdue;
Still for their Conqueror call, and but for the joy of being
    conquered
    (Rapture they will not forego) dare to resist and rebel;   10
Still, when resisting and raging, in soft undervoice say unto him,
    Fear not, retire not, O man; hope evermore and believe.
Go from the east to the west, as the sun and the stars direct thee,
    Go with the girdle of man, go and encompass the earth:
Not for the gain of the gold, for the getting, the hoarding, the
    having;   15
    But for the joy of the deed, but for the duty to do.
Go with the spiritual life, the higher volition and action,
    With the great girdle of God, go and encompass the earth.
Go; say not in thy heart, And what then were it accomplished,
    Were the wild impulse allayed, what were the use or the good! 20
Go; when the instinct is stilled, and when the deed is accom-
    plished,
    What thou hast done and shalt do shall be declared to thee
    then.

Go with the sun and the stars, and yet evermore in thy spirit
　　Say to thyself, It is good, yet is there better than it;
This that I see is not all, and this that I do is but little;　　25
　　Nevertheless it is good, though there is better than it.

　　　　　　　　　　　　　　　　　　1862.

QUI LABORAT, ORAT

　　O only Source of all our light and life,
　　　　Whom as our truth, our strength, we see and feel,
　　But Whom the hours of mortal moral strife
　　　　Alone aright reveal!

　　Mine inmost soul, before Thee inly brought,　　　　5
　　　　Thy presence owns ineffable, divine;
　　Chastised each rebel, self-encentered thought,
　　　　My will adoreth Thine.

　　With eye down-dropt, if then this earthly mind
　　　　Speechless remain, or speechless e'en depart;　　10
　　Nor seek to see—for what of earthly kind
　　　　Can see Thee as Thou art?—

　　If well-assured 't is but profanely bold
　　　　In thought's abstractest forms to seem to see,
　　It dare not dare the dread communion hold　　　　15
　　　　In ways unworthy Thee,—

　　O not unowned, Thou shalt unnamed forgive;
　　　　In worldly walks the prayerless heart prepare;
　　And if in work its life it seem to live,
　　　　Shalt make that work be prayer.　　　　20

　　Nor times shall lack when, while the work it plies,
　　　　Unsummoned powers the blinding film shall part,
　　And, scarce by happy tears made dim, the eyes
　　　　In recognition start.

　　But, as Thou willest, give or e'en forbear　　　　25
　　　　The beatific supersensual sight,
　　So, with Thy blessing blest, that humbler prayer
　　　　Approach Thee morn and night.

　　　　　　　　　　　　　　　　　　1862.

ΎΜΝΟΣ ΆΥΜΝΟΣ

O Thou Whose image in the shrine
Of human spirits dwells divine;
Which from that precinct once conveyed,
To be to outer day displayed,

Doth vanish, part, and leave behind   5
Mere blank and void of empty mind,
Which wilful fancy seeks in vain
With casual shapes to fill again!

O Thou That in our bosom's shrine
Dost dwell, unknown because divine!   10
I thought to speak, I thought to say,
"The light is here," "behold the way,"
"The voice was thus," and "thus the word,"
And "thus I saw," and "that I heard;"
But from the lips that half essayed   15
The imperfect utterance fell unmade.

O Thou, in that mysterious shrine
Enthroned, as I must say, divine!
I will not frame one thought of what
Thou mayest either be or not.   20
I will not prate of "thus" and "so,"
And be profane with "yes" and "no."
Enough that in our soul and heart.
Thou, whatsoe'er Thou may'st be, art.

Unseen, secure in that high shrine,   25
Acknowledged present and divine,
I will not ask some upper air,
Some future day, to place Thee there;
Nor say, nor yet deny, such men
And women saw Thee thus and then,   30
Thy name was such, and there or here
To him or her Thou didst appear.

Do only Thou in that dim shrine,
Unknown or known, remain, divine;
There, or if not, at least in eyes   35
That scan the fact that round them lies,

The hand to sway, the judgment guide,
In sight and sense Thyself divide;
Be Thou but there,—in soul and heart,
I will not ask to feel Thou art.   40

                                    1862.

FROM
SONGS IN ABSENCE

Come back, come back! Behold with straining mast
And swelling sail, behold her steaming fast;
With one new sun to see her voyage o'er,
With morning light to touch her native shore.
    Come back, come back.   5

Come back, come back! while westward labouring by,
With sailless yards, a bare black hulk we fly.
See how the gale we fight with sweeps her back,
To our lost home, on our forsaken track.
    Come back, come back.   10

Come back, come back! Across the flying foam,
We hear faint far-off voices call us home:
"Come back," ye seem to say; "ye seek in vain;
We went, we sought, and homeward turned again."
    Come back, come back.   15

Come back, come back! And whither back or why?
To fan quenched hopes, forsaken schemes to try;
Walk the old fields; pace the familiar street;
Dream with the idlers, with the bards compete.
    Come back, come back.   20

Come back, come back! And whither and for what?
To finger idly some old Gordian knot,
Unskilled to sunder, and too weak to cleave,
And with much toil attain to half-believe.
    Come back, come back.   25

Come back, come back! Yea back, indeed, do go
Sighs panting thick, and tears that want to flow;
Fond fluttering hopes upraise their useless wings,
And wishes idly struggle in the strings.
    Come back, come back.   30

Come back, come back! More eager than the breeze,
The flying fancies sweep across the seas;
And lighter far than ocean's flying foam,
The heart's fond message hurries to its home.
      Come back, come back. .   35

Come back, come back!
Back flies the foam; the hoisted flag streams back;
The long smoke wavers on the homeward track;
Back fly with winds things which the winds obey:
The strong ship follows its appointed way.   40
1852.   1862.

"WITH WHOM IS NO VARIABLENESS, NEITHER SHADOW OF TURNING"

It fortifies my soul to know
That, though I perish, Truth is so;
That, howsoe'er I stray and range,
Whate'er I do, Thou dost not change.
I steadier step when I recall   5
That, if I slip, Thou dost not fall.

                    1862.

"PERCHÈ PENSA? PENSANDO S' INVECCHIA"

To spend uncounted years of pain,
Again, again, and yet again,
In working out in heart and brain
    The problem of our being here;
To gather facts from far and near,   5
Upon the mind to hold them clear,
And, knowing more may yet appear,
Unto one's latest breath to fear,
The premature result to draw—
Is this the object, end, and law,   10
    And purpose of our being here?

                    1869.

BLESSED ARE THEY THAT HAVE NOT SEEN

O happy they whose hearts receive
The implanted word with faith; believe
Because their fathers did before,

Because they learnt, and ask no more.
High triumphs of convictions wrought,   5
And won by individual thought,
The joy, delusive oft, but keen,
Of having with our own eyes seen,
What if they have not felt nor known?
An amplitude instead they own,   10
By no self-binding ordinance prest
To toil in labour they detest;
By no deceiving reasoning tied
Or this or that way to decide.

O happy they! above their head   15
The glory of the unseen is spread;
Their happy heart is free to range
Through largest tracts of pleasant change;
Their intellects encradled lie
In boundless possibility.   20
For impulses of varying kinds
The Ancient Home a lodging finds;
Each appetite our nature breeds,
It meets with viands for its needs.

Oh happy they! nor need they fear   25
The wordy strife that rages near;
All reason wastes by day, and more,
Will instinct in a night restore.
O happy, so their state but give
A clue by which a man can live;   30
O blest, unless 't is proved by fact
A dream impossible to act.

1869.

THE SHADOW

I dreamed a dream; I dreamt that I espied,
Upon a stone that was not rolled aside,
A Shadow sit upon a grave—a Shade,
As thin, as unsubstantial, as of old
Came, the Greek poet told,   5
To lick the life-blood in the trench Ulysses made—
As pale, as thin, and said:
"I am the Resurrection of the Dead.

The night is past, the morning is at hand,
And I must in my proper semblance stand,   10
Appear brief space and vanish;—listen! this is true:
I am that Jesus whom they slew."

    And shadows dim, I dreamed, the dead apostles came,
And bent their heads for sorrow and for shame—
Sorrow for their great loss, and shame   15
For what they did in that vain name.

    And in long ranges far behind there seemed
Pale, vapoury, angel forms—or was it cloud?—that kept
Strange watch; the women also stood beside and wept.

    And Peter spoke the word: 20
"O my own Lord,
What is it we must do?
Is it then all untrue?
Did we not see, and hear, and handle thee,
Yea, for whole hours   25
Upon the Mount in Galilee,
On the lake shore, and here at Bethany,
When thou ascendedst to thy God and ours?"

    And paler still became the distant cloud,
And at the word the women wept aloud.   30
And the Shade answered, "What ye say I know not;
    But it is true
    I am that Jesus whom they slew,
Whom ye have preached, but in what way I know not."

*   *   *   *   *   *   *   *   *   *   *

And the great World, it chanced, came by that way,   35
And stopped, and looked, and spoke to the police,
And said the thing, for order's sake and peace,
Most certainly must be suppressed, the nuisance cease.
His wife and daughter must have where to pray,
And whom to pray to, at the least one day   40
In seven, and something sensible to say.
Whether the fact so many years ago
Had, or not, happened, how was he to know?
Yet he had always heard that it was so.
As for himself, perhaps it was all one;   45
And yet he found it not unpleasant, too,
On Sunday morning in the roomy pew,
To see the thing with such decorum done.

As for himself, perhaps it was all one;
Yet on one's death-bed, all men always said, 50
It was a comfortable thing to think upon
The atonement and the resurrection of the dead.
So the great World, as having said his say,
Unto his country-house pursued his way.
And on the grave the Shadow sat all day. 55

* * * * * * * * *

And the poor Pope was sure it must be so,
Else wherefore did the people kiss his toe?
The subtle Jesuit cardinal shook his head,
And mildly looked and said
It mattered not a jot 60
Whether the thing, indeed, were so or not;
Religion must be kept up, and the Church preserved,
And for the people this best served.
And then he turned, and added most demurely,
"Whatever may befal, 65
We Catholics need no evidence at all,
The holy father is infallible, surely!"
    And English canons heard,
And quietly demurred.
Religion rests on evidence, of course, 70
And on inquiry we must put no force.
Difficulties still, upon whatever ground,
Are likely, almost certain, to be found.
The Theist scheme, the Pantheist, one and all,
Must with, or e'en before, the Christian fall. 75
And till the thing were plainer to our eyes,
To disturb faith was surely most unwise.
As for the Shade, who trusted such narration?—
Except, of course, in ancient revelation.
    And dignitaries of the Church came by. 80
It had been worth to some of them, they said,
Some hundred thousand pounds a year a head.
If it fetched so much in the market, truly,
'T was not a thing to be given up unduly.
It had been proved by Butler in one way, 85
By Paley better in a later day;
It had been proved in twenty ways at once,
By many a doctor plain to many a dunce;

There was no question but it must be so.
    And the Shade answered that he did not know;   90
He had no reading, and might be deceived,
But still he was the Christ, as he believed.
    And women, mild and pure,
Forth from still homes and village schools did pass,
And asked, if this indeed were thus, alas,   95
What should they teach their children and the poor?
    The Shade replied he could not know,
But it was truth, the fact was so.

*   *   *   *   *   *   *   *   *

Who had kept all commandments from his youth
Yet still found one thing lacking—even Truth: 100
And the Shade only answered, "Go, make haste,
Enjoy thy great possessions as thou may'st."

                        1869.

MATTHEW ARNOLD

TO A FRIEND

Who prop, thou ask'st, in these bad days, my mind?
He much, the old man, who, clearest-souled of men,
Saw The Wide Prospect, and the Asian Fen,
And Tmolus hill, and Smyrna bay, though blind.

Much he, whose friendship I not long since won,   5
That halting slave, who in Nicopolis
Taught Arrian, when Vespasian's brutal son
Cleared Rome of what most shamed him. But be his

My special thanks, whose even-balanced soul,
From first youth tested up to extreme old age,   10
Business could not make dull, nor passion wild;

Who saw life steadily, and saw it whole;
The mellow glory of the Attic stage,
Singer of sweet Colonus, and its child.

                      1849.

SHAKESPEARE

Others abide our question. Thou art free.
We ask and ask—thou smilest and art still,
Out-topping knowledge: for the loftiest hill,
Who to the stars uncrowns his majesty,

Planting his steadfast footsteps in the sea,   5
Making the heaven of heavens his dwelling-place,
Spares but the cloudy border of his base
To the foiled searching of mortality;

And thou, who didst the stars and sunbeams know,
Self-schooled, self-scanned, self-honoured, self-secure,   10
Didst tread on earth unguessed at.—Better so!

All pains the immortal spirit must endure,
All weakness which impairs, all griefs which bow,
Find their sole speech in that victorious brow.

                                        1849.

THE FORSAKEN MERMAN

Come, dear children, let us away;
Down and away below!
Now my brothers call from the bay,
Now the great winds shoreward blow,
Now the salt tides seaward flow,   5
Now the wild white horses play,
Champ and chafe and toss in the spray.
Children dear, let us away!
This way, this way!
    Call her once before you go—   10
Call once yet,
In a voice that she will know:
"Margaret! Margaret!"
Children's voices should be dear
(Call once more) to a mother's ear;   15
Children's voices, wild with pain—
Surely she will come again!
Call her once and come away;
This way, this way!
"Mother dear, we cannot stay!   20

The wild white horses foam and fret."
Margaret! Margaret!
Come, dear children, come away down;
Call no more!
One last look at the white-walled town,   25
And the little grey church on the windy shore;
Then come down!
She will not come though you call all day;
Come away, come away!
　　　Children dear, was it yesterday   30
We heard the sweet bells over the bay?
In the caverns where we lay,
Through the surf and through the swell,
The far-off sound of a silver bell?
Sand-strewn caverns, cool and deep,   35
Where the winds are all asleep,
Where the spent lights quiver and gleam,
Where the salt weed sways in the stream,
Where the sea-beasts, ranged all round,
Feed in the ooze of their pasture-ground,   40
Where the sea-snakes coil and twine,
Dry their mail and bask in the brine,
Where great whales come sailing by,
Sail and sail, with unshut eye,
Round the world for ever and aye?   45
When did music come this way?
Children dear, was it yesterday?
Children dear, was it yesterday
(Call yet once) that she went away?
Once she sate with you and me,   50
On a red gold throne in the heart of the sea,
And the youngest sate on her knee.
She combed its bright hair, and she tended it well,
When down swung the sound of a far-off bell.
She sighed, she looked up through the clear green sea;   55
She said: "I must go, for my kinsfolk pray
In the little grey church on the shore to-day.
'T will be Easter-time in the world—ah me!
And I lose my poor soul, merman! here with thee."
I said: "Go up, dear heart, through the waves;   60
Say thy prayer, and come back to the kind sea-caves!"

She smiled, she went up through the surf in the bay.
Children dear, was it yesterday?
    Children dear, were we long alone?
"The sea grows stormy, the little ones moan;   65
Long prayers," I said, "in the world they say;
Come!" I said; and we rose through the surf in the bay.
We went up the beach, by the sandy down
Where the sea-stocks bloom, to the white-walled town;
Through the narrow paved streets, where all was still,   70
To the little grey church on the windy hill.
From the church came a murmur of folk at their prayers,
But we stood without in the cold blowing airs.
We climbed on the graves, on the stones worn with rains,
And we gazed up the aisle through the small leaded panes. 75
She sate by the pillar; we saw her clear:
"Margaret, hist! come quick, we are here!
Dear heart!" I said, "we are long alone;
The sea grows stormy, the little ones moan."
But, ah, she gave me never a look,   80
For her eyes were sealed to the holy book!
Loud prays the priest; shut stands the door.
Come away, children, call no more!
Come away, come down, call no more!
    Down, down, down!   85
Down to the depths of the sea!
She sits at her wheel in the humming town,
Singing most joyfully.
Hark what she sings: "O joy, O joy,
For the humming street, and the child with its toy!   90
For the priest, and the bell, and the holy well;
For the wheel where I spun,
And the blessed light of the sun!"
And so she sings her fill,
Singing most joyfully,   95
Till the spindle drops from her hand,
And the whizzing wheel stands still.
She steals to the window, and looks at the sand,
And over the sand at the sea;
And her eyes are set in a stare;   100
And anon there breaks a sigh,
And anon there drops a tear.

From a sorrow-clouded eye,
And a heart sorrow-laden,—
A long, long sigh   105
For the cold strange eyes of a little mermaiden
And the gleam of her golden hair.
    Come away, away, children;
Come, children, come down!
The hoarse wind blows coldly;   110
Lights shine in the town.
She will start from her slumber
When gusts shake the door;
She will hear the winds howling,
Will hear the waves roar.   115
We shall see, while above us
The waves roar and whirl,
A ceiling of amber,
A pavement of pearl,
Singing, "Here came a mortal,   120
But faithless was she!
And alone dwell forever
The kings of the sea."
    But, children, at midnight,
When soft the winds blow,   125
When clear falls the moonlight,
When spring-tides are low;
When sweet airs come seaward
From heaths starred with broom,
And high rocks throw mildly   130
On the blanched sands a gloom;
Up the still, glistening beaches,
Up the creeks we will hie,
Over banks of bright seaweed
The ebb-tide leaves dry.   135
We will gaze, from the sand-hills,
At the white, sleeping town,
At the church on the hill-side,
And then come back down,
Singing, "There dwells a loved one,   140
But cruel is she!
She left lonely forever
The kings of the sea."

                                      1849.

SELF-DEPENDENCE

Weary of myself, and sick of asking
What I am and what I ought to be,
At this vessel's prow I stand, which bears me
Forwards, forwards, o'er the starlit sea.

And a look of passionate desire   5
O'er the sea and to the stars I send:
"Ye who from my childhood up have calmed me,
Calm me, ah, compose me to the end!

"Ah, once more," I cried, "ye stars, ye waters,
On my heart your mighty charm renew;   10
Still, still let me, as I gaze upon you,
Feel my soul becoming vast like you!"

From the intense, clear, star-sown vault of heaven,
Over the lit sea's unquiet way,
In the rustling night-air came the answer: 15
"Wouldst thou *be* as these are? *Live* as they.

"Unaffrighted by the silence round them,
Undistracted by the sights they see,
These demand not that the things without them
Yield them love, amusement, sympathy.   20

"And with joy the stars perform their shining,
And the sea its long moon-silvered roll;
For self-poised they live, nor pine with noting
All the fever of some differing soul.

"Bounded by themselves, and unregardful   25
In what state God's other works may be,
In their own tasks all their powers pouring,
These attain the mighty life you see."

O air-born voice! long since, severely clear,
A cry like thine in mine own heart I hear: 30
"Resolve to be thyself; and know that he
Who finds himself loses his misery!"

                                        1852.

THE FUTURE

A wanderer is man from his birth.
He was born in a ship
On the breast of the river of Time;
Brimming with wonder and joy
He spreads out his arms to the light,   5
Rivets his gaze on the banks of the stream.
    As what he sees is, so have his thoughts been.
Whether he wakes
Where the snowy mountainous pass,
Echoing the screams of the eagles,   10
Hems in its gorges the bed
Of the new-born, clear-flowing stream;
Whether he first sees light
Where the river in gleaming rings
Sluggishly winds through the plain;   15
Whether in sound of the swallowing sea,—
As is the world on the banks,
So is the mind of the man.
    Vainly does each, as he glides,
Fable and dream   20
Of the lands which the river of Time
Had left ere he woke on its breast,
Or shall reach when his eyes have been closed.
Only the tract where he sails
He wots of; only the thoughts   25
Raised by the objects he passes, are his.
    Who can see the green earth any more
As she was by the sources of Time?
Who imagines her fields as they lay
In the sunshine, unworn by the plough?   30
Who thinks as they thought,
The tribes who then roamed on her breast,
Her vigorous, primitive sons?
    What girl
Now reads in her bosom as clear   35
As Rebekah read, when she sate
At eve by the palm-shaded well?
Who guards in her breast
As deep, as pellucid a spring

Of feeling, as tranquil, as sure?   40
   What bard,
At the height of his vision, can deem
Of God, of the world, of the soul,
With a plainness as near,
As flashing, as Moses felt   45
When he lay in the night by his flock
On the starlit Arabian waste?
Can rise and obey
The beck of the Spirit, like him?
   This tract which the river Time   50
Now flows through with us, is the plain.
Gone is the calm of its earlier shore.
Bordered by cities and hoarse
With a thousand cries is its stream.
And we on its breast, our minds   55
Are confused as the cries which we hear,
Changing and shot as the sights which we see.
   And we say that repose has fled
Forever the course of the river of Time.
That cities will crowd to its edge   60
In a blacker, incessanter line;
That the din will be more on its banks,
Denser the trade on its stream,
Flatter the plain where it flows,
Fiercer the sun overhead.   65
That never will those on its breast
See an ennobling sight,
Drink of the feeling of quiet again.
   But what was before us we know not,
And we know not what shall succeed.   70
Haply, the river of Time—
As it grows, as the towns on its marge
Fling their wavering lights
On a wider, statelier stream—
May acquire, if not the calm   75
Of its early mountainous shore,
Yet a solemn peace of its own.
And the width of the waters, the hush
Of the grey expanse where he floats,
Freshening its current and spotted with foam   80

As it draws to the ocean, may strike
Peace to the soul of the man on its breast—
As the pale waste widens around him,
As the banks fade dimmer away,
As the stars come out, and the night-wind   85
Brings up the stream
Murmurs and scents of the Infinite Sea.

1852.

LINES

WRITTEN IN KENSINGTON GARDENS

In this lone, open glade I lie,
Screened by deep boughs on either hand;
And at its end, to stay the eye,
Those black-crowned, red-boled pine-trees stand.

Birds here make song, each bird has his,   5
Across the girdling city's hum.
How green under the boughs it is!
How thick the tremulous sheep-cries come!

Sometimes a child will cross the glade
To take his nurse his broken toy;   10
Sometimes a thrush flit overhead,
Deep in her unknown day's employ.

Here at my feet what wonders pass,
What endless, active life is here!
What blowing daisies, fragrant grass—   15
An air-stirred forest, fresh and clear.

Scarce fresher is the mountain-sod
Where the tired angler lies, stretched out,
And, eased of basket and of rod,
Counts his day's spoil, the spotted trout.   20

In the huge world, which roars hard by,
Be others happy if they can!
But in my helpless cradle I
Was breathed on by the rural Pan.

I, on men's impious uproar, hurled, 25
Think often, as I hear them rave,
That peace has left the upper world
And now keeps only in the grave.

Yet here is peace forever new:
When I who watch them am away, 30
Still all things in this glade go through
The changes of their quiet day.

Then to their happy rest they pass:
The flowers upclose, the birds are fed,
The night comes down upon the grass, 35
The child sleeps warmly in his bed.

Calm soul of all things! make it mine
To feel, amid the city's jar,
That there abides a peace of thine
Man did not make and cannot mar. 40

The will to neither strive nor cry,
The power to feel with others, give!
Calm, calm me more; nor let me die
Before I have begun to live!

1852.

THE SCHOLAR GIPSY

Go, for they call you, shepherd, from the hill;
  Go, shepherd, and untie the wattled cotes!
    No longer leave thy wistful flock unfed,
  Nor let thy bawling fellows rack their throats,
    Nor the cropped herbage shoot another head. 5
      But when the fields are still,
  And the tired men and dogs all gone to rest,
    And only the white sheep are sometimes seen
    Cross and recross the strips of moon-blanched green,
  Come, shepherd, and again begin the quest! 10

Here, where the reaper was at work of late—
  In this high field's dark corner, where he leaves
    His coat, his basket, and his earthen cruse,

And in the sun all morning binds the sheaves,
 Then here, at noon, comes back his stores to use,— 15
  Here will I sit and wait,
While to my ear from uplands far away
 The bleating of the folded flocks is borne,
 With distant cries of reapers in the corn—
All the live murmur of a summer's day.   20

Screened is this nook o'er the high, half-reaped field,
 And here till sun-down, shepherd, will I be.
  Through the thick corn the scarlet poppies peep,
And round green roots and yellowing stalks I see
 Pale pink convolvulus in tendrils creep; 25
  And air-swept lindens yield
Their scent, and rustle down their perfumed showers
 Of bloom on the bent grass where I am laid,
 And bower me from the August sun with shade;
And the eye travels down to Oxford's towers. 30

And near me on the grass lies Glanvil's book—
 Come, let me read the oft-read tale again!
  The story of the Oxford scholar poor,
Of pregnant parts and quick inventive brain,
 Who, tired of knocking at preferment's door, 35
  One summer-morn forsook
His friends, and went to learn the gipsy-lore,
 And roamed the world with that wild brotherhood,
 And came, as most men deemed, to little good,
But came to Oxford and his friends no more. 40

But once, years after, in the country lanes,
 Two scholars, whom at college erst he knew,
  Met him, and of his way of life enquired;
Whereat he answered that the gipsy-crew,
 His mates, had arts to rule as they desired 45
  The workings of men's brains,
And they can bind them to what thoughts they will.
 "And I," he said, "the secret of their art,
 When fully learned, will to the world impart;
But it needs heaven-sent moments for this skill." 50

This said, he left them, and returned no more.—
    But rumours hung about the country-side,
        That the lost scholar long was seen to stray,
    Seen by rare glimpses, pensive and tongue-tied,
        In hat of antique shape, and cloak of grey,   55
          The same the gipsies wore.
    Shepherds had met him on the Hurst in spring;
        At some lone alehouse in the Berkshire moors,
        On the warm ingle-bench, the smock-frocked boors
    Had found him seated at their entering,   60

But, 'mid their drink and clatter, he would fly.
    And I myself seem half to know thy looks,
        And put the shepherds, wanderer! on thy trace;
    And boys who in lone wheatfields scare the rooks
        I ask if thou hast passed their quiet place;   65
          Or in my boat I lie
    Moored to the cool bank in the summer-heats,
        'Mid wide grass meadows which the sunshine fills,
        And watch the warm, green-muffled Cumner hills,
    And wonder if thou haunt'st their shy retreats.   70

For most, I know, thou lov'st retired ground:
    Thee at the ferry Oxford riders blithe,
        Returning home on summer-nights, have met,
    Crossing the stripling Thames at Bab-lock-hithe,
        Trailing in the cool stream thy fingers wet,   75
          As the punt's rope chops round,
    And leaning backward in a pensive dream,
        And fostering in thy lap a heap of flowers
        Plucked in shy fields and distant Wychwood bowers,
    And thine eyes resting on the moonlit stream.   80

And then they land, and thou art seen no more!—
    Maidens, who from the distant hamlets come
        To dance around the Fyfield elm in May,
    Oft through the darkening fields have seen thee roam,
        Or cross a stile into the public way.   85
          Oft thou hast given them store

Of flowers—the frail-leafed, white anemone,
　　Dark bluebells drenched with dews of summer eves,
　　And purple orchises with spotted leaves,—
But none hath words she can report of thee.　　　　90

And above Godstow Bridge, when hay-time's here
　　In June, and many a scythe in sunshine flames,
　　　　Men who through those wide fields of breezy grass,
　　Where black-winged swallows haunt the glittering
　　　　　　Thames,
　　　　To bathe in the abandoned lasher pass,　　　95
　　　　　　Have often passed thee near,
　　Sitting upon the river bank o'ergrown;
　　　　Marked thine outlandish garb, thy figure spare,
　　　　Thy dark vague eyes, and soft abstracted air—
But when they came from bathing, thou wast gone!　100

At some lone homestead in the Cumner hills,
　　Where at her open door the housewife darns,
　　　　Thou hast been seen, or hanging on a gate
　　To watch the threshers in the mossy barns.
　　　　Children, who early range these slopes, and late,　105
　　　　　　For cresses from the rills,
　　Have known thee eying, all an April day,
　　　　The springing pastures and the feeding kine;
　　　　And marked thee, when the stars come out and
　　　　　　shine,
Through the long dewy grass move slow away.　　　110

In autumn, on the skirts of Bagley Wood—
　　Where most the gipsies by the turf-edged way
　　　　Pitch their smoked tents, and every bush you see
　　With scarlet patches tagged and shreds of grey,
　　　　Above the forest-ground called Thessaly,—　　115
　　　　　　The blackbird, picking food,
　　Sees thee, nor stops his meal, nor fears at all,
　　　　So often has he known thee past him stray,
　　　　Rapt, twirling in thy hand a withered spray,
And waiting for the spark from heaven to fall.　　　120

And once, in winter, on the causeway chill,
　　Where home through flooded fields foot-travellers go,
　　　Have I not passed thee on the wooden bridge,
　　Wrapt in thy cloak and battling with the snow,
　　　　Thy face tow'rd Hinksey and its wintry ridge?　125
　　　　　And thou hast climbed the hill,
　　And gained the white brow of the Cumner range;
　　　Turned once to watch, while thick the snowflakes
　　　　　fall,
　　　The line of festal light in Christ-Church hall—
Then sought thy straw in some sequestered grange.　130

But what—I dream! Two hundred years are flown
　　Since first thy story ran through Oxford halls,
　　　And the grave Glanvil did the tale inscribe
　　That thou wert wandered from the studious walls
　　　　To learn strange arts and join a gipsy-tribe;　135
　　　　　And thou from earth art gone
　　Long since, and in some quiet churchyard laid—
　　　Some country-nook, where o'er thy unknown grave
　　　Tall grasses and white flowering nettles wave,
Under a dark, red-fruited yew-tree's shade.　　　140

—No, no, thou hast not felt the lapse of hours!
　　For what wears out the life of mortal men?
　　　'T is that from change to change their being rolls;
　　'T is that repeated shocks, again, again,
　　　　Exhaust the energy of strongest souls,　　145
　　　　　And numb the elastic powers;
　　Till, having used our nerves with bliss and teen,
　　　And tired upon a thousand schemes our wit,
　　　To the just-pausing Genius we remit
Our worn-out life, and are—what we have been.　150

Thou hast not lived, why should'st thou perish, so?
　　Thou hadst *one* aim, *one* business, *one* desire;
　　　Else wert thou long since numbered with the dead!
　　Else hadst thou spent, like other men, thy fire!
　　　　The generations of thy peers are fled,　　155
　　　　　And we ourselves shall go;

But thou possessest an immortal lot,
 And we imagine thee exempt from age
 And living as thou liv'st on Glanvil's page,
Because thou hadst—what we, alas! have not.   160

For early didst thou leave the world, with powers
 Fresh, undiverted to the world without,
  Firm to their mark, not spent on other things;
 Free from the sick fatigue, the languid doubt
  Which much to have tried, in much been baffled,
   brings.   165
   O life unlike to ours!
Who fluctuate idly without term or scope,
 Of whom each strives, nor knows for what he
  strives,
 And each half lives a hundred different lives;
Who wait like thee, but not, like thee, in hope.   170

Thou waitest for the spark from heaven! and we,
 Light half-believers of our casual creeds,
  Who never deeply felt, nor clearly willed,
 Whose insight never has borne fruit in deeds,
  Whose vague resolves never have been fulfilled; 175
   For whom each year we see
Breeds new beginnings, disappointments new;
  Who hesitate and falter life away,
  And lose to-morrow the ground won to-day,—
Ah, do not we, wanderer! await it too?   180

Yes, we await it!—but it still delays,
 And then we suffer! and amongst us one,
  Who most has suffered, takes dejectedly
 His seat upon the intellectual throne;
  And all his store of sad experience he   185
   Lays bare of wretched days;
Tells us his misery's birth and growth and signs,
  And how the dying spark of hope was fed,
  And how the breast was soothed, and how the head,
And all his hourly varied anodynes.   190

This for our wisest! and we others pine,
 And wish the long unhappy dream would end,
  And waive all claim to bliss, and try to bear,
 With close-lipped patience for our only friend,
   Sad patience, too near neighbour to despair— 195
    But none has hope like thine!
Thou through the fields and through the woods dost
   stray,
  Roaming the country-side, a truant boy,
  Nursing thy project in unclouded joy,
 And every doubt long blown by time away.   200

O born in days when wits were fresh and clear,
 And life ran gaily as the sparkling Thames;
  Before this strange disease of modern life,
 With its sick hurry, its divided aims,
   Its heads o'ertaxed, its palsied hearts, was rife— 205
    Fly hence, our contact fear!
Still fly, plunge deeper in the bowering wood!
  Averse, as Dido did with gesture stern
  From her false friend's approach in Hades turn,
 Wave us away, and keep thy solitude!   210

Still nursing the unconquerable hope,
 Still clutching the inviolable shade,
  With a free, onward impulse brushing through,
 By night, the silvered branches of the glade—
   Far on the forest-skirts, where none pursue, 215
    On some mild pastoral slope
Emerge, and, resting on the moonlit pales,
  Freshen thy flowers as in former years
  With dew, or listen with enchanted ears,
 From the dark dingles, to the nightingales!   220

But fly our paths, our feverish contact fly!
 For strong the infection of our mental strife,
  Which, though it gives no bliss, yet spoils for rest;
 And we should win thee from thy own fair life,
   Like us distracted, and like us unblest.   225
    Soon, soon thy cheer would die,

Thy hopes grow timorous, and unfixed thy powers,
 And thy clear aims be cross and shifting made;
 And then thy glad perennial youth would fade,
Fade, and grow old at last, and die like ours. 230

Then fly our greetings, fly our speech and smiles!
 —As some grave Tyrian trader from the sea,
 Descried at sunrise an emerging prow
Lifting the cool-haired creepers stealthily,
 The fringes of a southward-facing brow 235
  Among the Ægæan isles;
And saw the merry Grecian coaster come,
 Freighted with amber grapes, and Chian wine,
 Green, bursting figs, and tunnies steeped in brine—
And knew the intruders on his ancient home, 240

The young, light-hearted masters of the waves—
 And snatched his rudder, and shook out more sail
 And day and night held on indignantly
O'er the blue Midland waters with the gale,
 Betwixt the Syrtes and soft Sicily, 245
  To where the Atlantic raves
Outside the western straits; and unbent sails
 There, where down cloudy cliffs, through sheets
  of foam,
 Shy traffickers, the dark Iberians come;
And on the beach undid his corded bales. 250

       1853.

YES! IN THE SEA OF LIFE ENISLED

Yes! in the sea of life enisled,
With echoing straits between us thrown,
Dotting the shoreless watery wild,
We mortal millions live *alone*.
The islands feel the enclasping flow, 5
And then their endless bounds they know.

But when the moon their hollows lights,
And they are swept by balms of spring,
And in their glens, on starry nights,

The nightingales divinely sing,   10
And lovely notes, from shore to shore,
Across the sounds and channels pour,—

Oh, then a longing like despair
Is to their farthest caverns sent;
For surely once, they feel, we were   15
Parts of a single continent!
Now round us spreads the watery plain—
Oh might our marges meet again!

Who ordered that their longing's fire
Should be, as soon as kindled, cooled?   20
Who renders vain their deep desire?
A god, a god their severance ruled!
And bade betwixt their shores to be
The unplumbed, salt, estranging sea.

            1853.

STANZAS FROM THE GRANDE CHARTREUSE

Through Alpine meadows soft-suffused
With rain, where thick the crocus blows,
Past the dark forges long disused,
The mule-track from Saint Laurent goes.
The bridge is crossed, and slow we ride,   5
Through forest, up the mountain-side.

The autumnal evening darkens round;
The wind is up, and drives the rain;
While, hark! far down, with strangled sound
Doth the Dead Guier's stream complain,   10
Where that wet smoke, among the woods,
Over his boiling cauldron broods.

Swift rush the spectral vapours white
Past limestone scars with ragged pines,
Showing—then blotting from our sight!   15
Halt—through the cloud-drift something shines!
High in the valley, wet and drear,
The huts of Courrerie appear.

Strike leftward! cries our guide; and higher
Mounts up the stony forest-way.   20
At last the encircling trees retire;
Look! through the showery twilight grey
What pointèd roofs are these advance?—
A palace of the kings of France?

Approach, for what we seek is here!   25
Alight, and sparely sup, and wait
For rest in this outbuilding near;
Then cross the sward and reach that gate;
Knock; pass the wicket! Thou art come
To the Carthusians' world-famed home.   30

The silent courts—where night and day
Into their stone-carved basins cold
The splashing icy fountains play,—
The humid corridors behold,
Where, ghostlike in the deepening night,   35
Cowled forms brush by in gleaming white!

The chapel, where no organ's peal
Invests the stern and naked prayer!—
With penitential cries they kneel
And wrestle; rising then, with bare   40
And white uplifted faces stand,
Passing the Host from hand to hand:

Each takes, and then his visage wan
Is buried in his cowl once more.
The cells!—the suffering Son of Man   45
Upon the wall—the knee-worn floor—
And where they sleep, that wooden bed,
Which shall their coffin be, when dead!

The library, where tract and tome
Not to feed priestly pride are there,   50
To hymn the conquering march of Rome,
Nor yet to amuse, as ours are;
They paint of souls the inner strife,
Their drops of blood, their death in life.

The garden, overgrown yet mild,— 55
See, fragrant herbs are flowering there!
Strong children of the Alpine wild
Whose culture is the brethren's care;
Of human tasks their only one,
And cheerful works beneath the sun. 60

Those halls, too, destined to contain
Each its own pilgrim-host of old,
From England, Germany, or Spain—
All are before me! I behold
The House, the Brotherhood austere!— 65
And what am I, that I am here?

For rigorous teachers seized my youth,
And purged its faith, and trimmed its fire;
Showed me the high, white star of Truth,
There bade me gaze, and there aspire. 70
Even now their whispers pierce the gloom:
What dost thou in this living tomb?

Forgive me, masters of the mind,
At whose behest I long ago
So much unlearnt, so much resigned. 75
I come not here to be your foe;
I seek these anchorites, not in ruth,
To curse and to deny your truth.

Not as their friend or child I speak;
But as, on some far northern strand, 80
Thinking of his own gods, a Greek
In pity and mournful awe might stand
Before some fallen Runic stone—
For both were faiths, and both are gone.

Wandering between two worlds, one dead, 85
The other powerless to be born,
With nowhere yet to rest my head,
Like these, on earth I wait forlorn.
Their faith, my tears, the world deride—
I come to shed them at their side. 90

Oh, hide me in your gloom profound,
Ye solemn seats of holy pain!
Take me, cowled forms, and fence me round,
Till I possess my soul again;
Till free my thoughts before me roll,   95
Not chafed by hourly false control!

For the world cries your faith is now
But a dead time's exploded dream;
My melancholy, sciolists say,
Is a passed mode, an outworn theme,—   100
As if the world had ever had
A faith, or sciolists been sad!

Ah, if it *be* passed, take away,
At least, the restlessness, the pain!
Be man henceforth no more a prey   105
To these out-dated stings again!
The nobleness of grief is gone—
Ah, leave us not the fret alone!

But if you cannot give us ease—
Last of the race of them who grieve,—   110
Here leave us to die out with these,
Last of the people who believe!
Silent, while years engrave the brow;
Silent—the best are silent now.

Achilles ponders in his tent,   115
The kings of modern thought are dumb;
Silent they are, though not content,
And wait to see the future come.
They have the grief men had of yore,
But they contend and cry no more.   120

Our fathers watered with their tears
This sea of Time whereon we sail;
Their voices were in all men's ears
Who passed within their puissant hail.
Still the same ocean round us raves,   125
But we stand mute and watch the waves.

For what availed it, all the noise
And outcry of the former men?
Say, have their sons achieved more joys?
Say, is life lighter now than then?   130
The sufferers died, they left their pain—
The pangs which tortured them remain.

What helps it now that Byron bore,
With haughty scorn which mocked the smart,
Through Europe to the Ætolian shore   135
The pageant of his bleeding heart?
That thousands counted every groan,
And Europe made his woe her own?

What boots it, Shelley, that the breeze
Carried thy lovely wail away,   140
Musical through Italian trees
Which fringe thy soft blue Spezzian bay?
Inheritors of thy distress,
Have restless hearts one throb the less?

Or are we easier to have read,   145
Oh Obermann, the sad, stern page,
Which tells us how thou hidd'st thy head
From the fierce tempest of thine age,
In the lone brakes of Fontainebleau,
Or chalets near the Alpine snow?   150

Ye slumber in your silent grave!—
The world, which for an idle day
Grace to your mood of sadness gave,
Long since hath flung her weeds away.
The eternal trifler breaks your spell;   155
But we—we learnt your lore too well!

Years hence, perhaps, may dawn an age,
More fortunate, alas, than we,
Which without hardness will be sage,
And gay without frivolity.   160
Sons of the world, oh, speed those years;
But while we wait, allow our tears!

Allow them! We admire with awe
The exulting thunder of your race;
You give the universe your law,   165
You triumph over time and space!
Your pride of life, your tireless powers,
We laud them, but they are not ours.

We are like children reared in shade
Beneath some old-world abbey wall,   170
Forgotten in a forest-glade,
And secret from the eyes of all.
Deep, deep the greenwood round them waves,
Their abbey, and its close of graves.

But, where the road runs near the stream,   175
Oft through the trees they catch a glance
Of passing troops in the sun's beam—
Pennon, and plume, and flashing lance!
Forth to the world those soldiers fare,
To life, to cities, and to war!   180

And through the wood, another way,
Faint bugle-notes from far are borne,
Where hunters gather, staghounds bay,
Round some fair forest-lodge at morn.
Gay dames are there, in sylvan green;   185
Laughter and cries, those notes between!

The banners flashing through the trees
Make their blood dance and chain their eyes;
That bugle-music on the breeze
Arrests them with a charmed surprise.   190
Banner by turns and bugle woo:
Ye shy recluses, follow too!

O children, what do ye reply?—
"Action and Pleasure, will ye roam
Through these secluded dells to cry   195
And call us?—but too late ye come!
Too late for us your call ye blow,
Whose bent was taken long ago.

"Long since we pace this shadowed nave;
    We watch those yellow tapers shine,   200
    Emblems of hope over the grave,
    In the high altar's depth divine.
    The organ carries to our ear
    Its accents of another sphere.

"Fenced early in this cloistral round   205
    Of reverie, of shade, of prayer,
    How should we grow in other ground?
    How can we flower in foreign air?
    —Pass, banners, pass; and bugles, cease;
    And leave our desert to its peace!"   210

                                        1855.

DOVER BEACH

The sea is calm to-night.
The tide is full, the moon lies fair
Upon the straits; on the French coast the light
Gleams and is gone; the cliffs of England stand,
Glimmering and vast, out in the tranquil bay.   5
Come to the window, sweet is the night-air!
Only, from the long line of spray
Where the sea meets the moon-blanched land,
Listen! you hear the grating roar
Of pebbles which the waves draw back, and fling,   10
At their return, up the high strand,
Begin, and cease, and then again begin,
With tremulous cadence slow, and bring
The eternal note of sadness in.
    Sophocles long ago   15
Heard it on the Ægean, and it brought
Into his mind the turbid ebb and flow
Of human misery; we
Find also in the sound a thought,
Hearing it by this distant northern sea.   20
    The sea of faith
Was once, too, at the full, and round earth's shore
Lay like the folds of a bright girdle furled.
But now I only hear

Its melancholy, long, withdrawing roar,   25
Retreating, to the breath
Of the night-wind, down the vast edges drear
And naked shingles of the world.
  Ah, love, let us be true
To one another! for the world which seems   30
To lie before us like a land of dreams,
So various, so beautiful, so new,
Hath really neither joy, nor love, nor light,
Nor certitude, nor peace, nor help for pain;
And we are here as on a darkling plain   35
Swept with confused alarms of struggle and flight,
Where ignorant armies clash by night.

         1867.

PALLADIUM

Set where the upper streams of Simois flow,
Was the Palladium, high 'mid rock and wood;
And Hector was in Ilium, far below,
And fought, and saw it not—but there it stood!

It stood, and sun and moonshine rained their light   5
On the pure columns of its glen-built hall.
Backward and forward rolled the waves of fight
Round Troy—but while this stood, Troy could not fall.

So, in its lovely moonlight, lives the soul.
Mountains surround it, and sweet virgin air;   10
Cold plashing, past it, crystal waters roll;
We visit it by moments, ah, too rare!

We shall renew the battle in the plain
To-morrow:—red with blood will Xanthus be;
Hector and Ajax will be there again;   15
Helen will come upon the wall to see.

Then we shall rust in shade, or shine in strife,
And fluctuate 'twixt blind hopes and blind despairs,
And fancy that we put forth all our life,
And never know how with the soul it fares.   20

Still doth the soul, from its lone fastness high,
Upon our life a ruling effluence send.
And when it fails, fight as we will, we die;
And while it lasts, we cannot wholly end.

1867.

WEST LONDON

Crouched on the pavement, close by Belgrave Square
A tramp I saw, ill, moody, and tongue-tied.
A babe was in her arms, and at her side
A girl; their clothes were rags, their feet were bare.

Some labouring men, whose work lay somewhere there,   5
Passed opposite; she touched her girl, who hied
Across, and begged, and came back satisfied.
The rich she had let pass with frozen stare.

Thought I: "Above her state this spirit towers;
She will not ask of aliens, but of friends,   10
Of sharers in a common human fate.

"She turns from that cold succour which attends
The unknown little from the unknowing great,
And points us to a better time than ours."

1867.

THE BETTER PART

Long fed on boundless hopes, O race of man,
How angrily thou spurn'st all simpler fare!
"Christ," some one says, "was human as we are;
No judge eyes us from heaven, our sin to scan;

"We live no more, when we have done our span."   5
"Well, then, for Christ," thou answerest, "who can care?
From sin, which Heaven records not, why forbear?
Live we like brutes our life, without a plan!"

So answerest thou; but why not rather say:
"Hath man no second life?—*Pitch this one high!*   10
Sits there no judge in heaven, our sin to see?—

"More strictly, then, the inward judge obey!
Was Christ a man like us? Ah, let us try
If we then, too, can be such men as he!"

                                        1869.

KAISER DEAD

What, Kaiser dead? The heavy news
Post-haste to Cobham calls the Muse,
From where in Farringford she brews
    The ode sublime,
Or with Pen-bryn's bold bard pursues   5
    A rival rhyme.

Kai's bracelet tail, Kai's busy feet,
Were known to all the village-street.
"What, poor Kai dead?" say all I meet;
    "A loss indeed!"   10
O for the croon pathetic, sweet,
    Of Robin's reed!

Six years ago I brought him down,
A baby dog, from London town;
Round his small throat of black and brown   15
    A ribbon blue,
And vouched by glorious renown
    A dachshound true.

His mother, most majestic dame,
Of blood unmixed, from Potsdam came;   20
And Kaiser's race we deemed the same—
    No lineage higher.
And so he bore the imperial name.
    But ah, his sire!

Soon, soon the days conviction bring: 25
The collie hair, the collie swing,
The tail's indomitable ring,
    The eye's unrest—
The case was clear; a mongrel thing
    Kai stood confest.   30

But all those virtues which commend
The humbler sort who serve and tend
Were thine in store, thou faithful friend.
    What sense, what cheer!
To us, declining tow'rds our end,   35
    A mate how dear!

For Max, thy brother-dog, began
To flag, and feel his narrowing span;
And cold, besides, his blue blood ran,
    Since, 'gainst the classes,   40
He heard, of late, the Grand Old Man
    Incite the masses.

Yes, Max and we grew slow and sad;
But Kai, a tireless shepherd-lad,
Teeming with plans, alert and glad   45
    In work or play,
Like sunshine went and came, and bade
    Live out the day!

Still, still I see the figure smart—
Trophy in mouth, agog to start,   50
Then, home returned, once more depart;
    Or prest together
Against thy mistress, loving heart,
    In winter weather.

I see the tail, like bracelet twirled,   55
In moments of disgrace uncurled,
Then at a pardoning word refurled,
    A conquering sign,
Crying, "Come on, and range the world,
    And never pine!"   60

Thine eye was bright, thy coat it shone;
Thou hadst thine errands, off and on;
In joy thy last morn flew: anon,
    A fit! All 's over;
And thou art gone where Geist hath gone,   65
    And Toss, and Rover.

Poor Max, with downcast, reverent head,
Regards his brother's form outspread;
Full well Max knows the friend is dead
    Whose cordial talk,   70
And jokes in doggish language said,
    Beguiled his walk.

And Glory, stretched at Burwood gate,
Thy passing by doth vainly wait;
And jealous Jock, thy only hate,   75
    The chiel from Skye,
Lets from his shaggy Highland pate
    Thy memory die.

Well, fetch his graven collar fine,
And rub the steel, and make it shine,   80
And leave it round thy neck to twine,
    Kai, in thy grave.
There of thy master keep that sign,
    And this plain stave.

1887.   1890.

DANTE GABRIEL ROSSETTI

THE BLESSED DAMOZEL

The blessed damozel leaned out
    From the gold bar of Heaven;
Her eyes were deeper than the depth
    Of waters stilled at even;
She had three lilies in her hand,   5
    And the stars in her hair were seven.

Her robe, ungirt from clasp to hem,
    No wrought flowers did adorn,
But a white rose of Mary's gift,
    For service meetly worn;   10
Her hair that lay along her back
    Was yellow like ripe corn.

Herseemed she scarce had been a day
    One of God's choristers;
The wonder was not yet quite gone   15
    From that still look of hers;
Albeit, to them she left, her day
    Had counted as ten years.

(To one, it is ten years of years.
    —Yet now, and in this place,   20
Surely she leaned o'er me—her hair
    Fell all about my face.—
Nothing: the autumn-fall of leaves.
    The whole year sets apace.)

It was the rampart of God's house
    That she was standing on;   25
By God built over the sheer depth
    The which is Space begun;
So high, that looking downward thence
    She scarce could see the sun.   30

It lies in Heaven, across the flood
    Of ether, as a bridge.
Beneath, the tides of day and night
    With flame and darkness ridge
The void, as low as where this earth   35
    Spins like a fretful midge.

Around her, lovers, newly met
    'Mid deathless love's acclaims,
Spoke evermore among themselves
    Their heart-remembered names;   40
And the souls mounting up to God
    Went by her like thin flames.

And still she bowed herself and stooped
    Out of the circling charm;
Until her bosom must have made   45
    The bar she leaned on warm,
And the lilies lay as if asleep
    Along her bended arm.

From the fixed place of Heaven she saw
    Time, like a pulse, shake fierce   50
Through all the worlds. Her gaze still strove
    Within the gulf to pierce
Its path; and now she spoke as when
    The stars sang in their spheres.

The sun was gone now; the curled moon   55
    Was like a little feather
Fluttering far down the gulf; and now
    She spoke through the still weather.
Her voice was like the voice the stars
    Had when they sang together.   60

(Ah sweet! Even now, in that bird's song,
    Strove not her accents there,
Fain to be hearkened? When those bells
    Possessed the mid-day air,
Strove not her steps to reach my side   65
    Down all the echoing stair?)

"I wish that he were come to me,
    For he will come," she said.
"Have I not prayed in Heaven?—on earth,
    Lord, Lord, has he not prayed?   70
Are not two prayers a perfect strength?
    And shall I feel afraid?

"When round his head the aureole clings,
    And he is clothed in white,
I'll take his hand and go with him   75
    To the deep wells of light;
As unto a stream we will step down,
    And bathe there in God's sight.

"We two will stand beside that shrine,
    Occult, withheld, untrod,   80
Whose lamps are stirred continually
    With prayer sent up to God;
And see our old prayers, granted, melt
    Each like a little cloud.

"We two will lie i' the shadow of   85
    That living mystic tree
Within whose secret growth the Dove
    Is sometimes felt to be,
While every leaf that His plumes touch
    Saith His Name audibly.   90

"And I myself will teach to him,
    I myself, lying so,
The songs I sing here; which his voice
    Shall pause in, hushed and slow,
And find some knowledge at each pause,   95
    Or some new thing to know."

(Alas! We two, we two, thou say'st!
    Yea, one wast thou with me
That once of old. But shall God lift
    To endless unity   100
The soul whose likeness with thy soul
    Was but its love for thee?)

"We two," she said, "will seek the groves
    Where the lady Mary is,
With her five handmaidens, whose names   105
    Are five sweet symphonies,
Cecily, Gertrude, Magdalen,
    Margaret, and Rosalys.

"Circlewise sit they, with bound locks
    And foreheads garlanded;   110
Into the fine cloth, white like flame,
    Weaving the golden thread,
To fashion the birth-robes for them
    Who are just born, being dead.

"He shall fear, haply, and be dumb: 115
    Then will I lay my cheek
To his, and tell about our love,
    Not once abashed or weak;
And the dear Mother will approve
    My pride, and let me speak.   120

"Herself shall bring us, hand in hand,
　　To Him round Whom all souls
Kneel, the clear-ranged unnumbered heads
　　Bowed with their aureoles;
And angels meeting us shall sing   125
　　To their citherns and citoles.

"There will I ask of Christ the Lord
　　Thus much for him and me:—
Only to live as once on earth
　　With Love,—only to be,   130
As then awhile, forever now
　　Together, I and he."

She gazed and listened, and then said,
　　Less sad of speech than mild,
"All this is when he comes." She ceased.   135
　　The light thrilled towards her, filled
With angels in strong level flight.
　　Her eyes prayed, and she smiled.

(I saw her smile.) But soon their path
　　Was vague in distant spheres: 140
And then she cast her arms along
　　The golden barriers,
And laid her face between her hands,
　　And wept. (I heard her tears.)

1847.   1850.

SISTER HELEN

"Why did you melt your waxen man,
　　　　　　　　Sister Helen?
To-day is the third since you began."
"The time was long, yet the time ran,
　　　　　　　　Little brother."   5
　　　　　(*O Mother, Mary Mother,*
Three days to-day, between Hell and Heaven!)

"But if you have done your work aright,
　　　　　　　　Sister Helen,
You'll let me play, for you said I might."   10

"Be very still in your play to-night,
        Little brother."
        (*O Mother, Mary Mother,*
Third night, to-night, between Hell and Heaven!)

"You said it must melt ere vesper-bell,   15
        Sister Helen;
If now it be molten, all is well."
"Even so—nay, peace! you cannot tell,
        Little brother."
        (*O Mother, Mary Mother,*   20
O what is this, between Hell and Heaven?)

"Oh the waxen knave was plump to-day,
        Sister Helen;
How like dead folk he has dropped away!"
"Nay now, of the dead what can you say,   25
        Little brother?"
        (*O Mother, Mary Mother,*
What of the dead, between Hell and Heaven?)

"See, see, the sunken pile of wood,
        Sister Helen,   30
Shines through the thin wax red as blood!"
"Nay now, when looked you yet on blood,
        Little brother."
        (*O Mother, Mary Mother,*
How pale she is, between Hell and Heaven!)   35

"Now close your eyes, for they 're sick and sore,
        Sister Helen,
And I 'll play without the gallery door."
"Aye, let me rest—I 'll lie on the floor,
        Little brother."   40
        (*O Mother, Mary Mother,*
What rest to-night, between Hell and Heaven?)

"Here high up in the balcony,
        Sister Helen,
The moon flies face to face with me."   45

"Aye, look and say whatever you see,
                         Little brother."
                  (*O Mother, Mary Mother,*
What sight to-night, between Hell and Heaven?)

"Outside it's merry in the wind's wake,   50
                         Sister Helen;
In the shaken trees the chill stars shake."
"Hush, heard you a horse-tread as you spake,
                         Little brother?"
                  (*O Mother, Mary Mother,*   55
What sound to-night, between Hell and Heaven?)

"I hear a horse-tread, and I see,
                         Sister Helen,
Three horsemen that ride terribly."
"Little brother, whence come the three,   60
                         Little brother?"
                  (*O Mother, Mary Mother,*
Whence should they come, between Hell and Heaven?)

"They come by the hill-verge from Boyne Bar,
                         Sister Helen,   65
And one draws nigh, but two are afar."
"Look, look, do you know them who they are,
                         Little brother?"
                  (*O Mother, Mary Mother,*
Who should they be, between Hell and Heaven?)   70

"Oh, it's Keith of Eastholm rides so fast,
                         Sister Helen,
For I know the white mane on the blast."
"The hour has come, has come at last,
                         Little brother!"   75
                  (*O Mother, Mary Mother,*
Her hour at last, between Hell and Heaven!)

"He has made a sign and called 'Halloo!'
                         Sister Helen,
And he says that he would speak with you."   80

"Oh tell him I fear the frozen dew,
                              Little brother."
                    (*O Mother, Mary Mother,*
Why laughs she thus, between Hell and Heaven?)

"The wind is loud, but I hear him cry,   85
                              Sister Helen,
That Keith of Ewern's like to die."
"And he and thou, and thou and I,
                              Little brother."
                    (*O Mother, Mary Mother,*   90
And they and we, between Hell and Heaven!)

"Three days ago, on his marriage-morn,
                              Sister Helen,
He sickened, and lies since then forlorn."
"For bridegroom's side is the bride a thorn,   95
                              Little brother?"
                    (*O Mother, Mary Mother,*
Cold bridal cheer, between Hell and Heaven!)

"Three days and nights he has lain abed,
                              Sister Helen,   100
And he prays in torment to be dead."
"The thing may chance, if he have prayed,
                              Little brother!"
                    (*O Mother, Mary Mother,*
If he have prayed, between Hell and Heaven!)   105

"But he has not ceased to cry to-day,
                              Sister Helen,
That you should take your curse away."
"*My* prayer was heard,—he need but pray,
                              Little brother!"   110
                    (*O Mother, Mary Mother,*
Shall God not hear, between Hell and Heaven?)

"But he says, till you take back your ban,
                              Sister Helen,
His soul would pass, yet never can."   115

"Nay then, shall I slay a living man,
                Little brother?"
                (*O Mother, Mary Mother,*
A living soul, between Hell and Heaven!)

"But he calls forever on your name,   120
                Sister Helen,
And says that he melts before a flame."
"My heart for his pleasure fared the same,
                Little brother."
                (*O Mother, Mary Mother,*   125
Fire at the heart, between Hell and Heaven!)

"Here's Keith of Westholm riding fast,
                Sister Helen,
For I know the white plume on the blast."
"The hour, the sweet hour I forecast,   130
                Little brother!"
                (*O Mother, Mary Mother,*
Is the hour sweet, between Hell and Heaven?)

"He stops to speak, and he stills his horse,
                Sister Helen;   135
But his words are drowned in the wind's course."
"Nay hear, nay hear, you must hear perforce,
                Little brother!"
                (*O Mother, Mary Mother,*
What word now heard, between Hell and Heaven?)   140

"Oh he says that Keith of Ewern's cry,
                Sister Helen,
Is ever to see you ere he die."
"In all that his soul sees, there am I,
                Little brother!"   145
                (*O Mother, Mary Mother,*
The soul's one sight, between Hell and Heaven!)

"He sends a ring and a broken coin,
                Sister Helen,
And bids you mind the banks of Boyne."   150

"What else he broke will he ever join,
     Little brother?"
    (*O Mother, Mary Mother,*
No, never joined, between Hell and Heaven!)

"He yields you these and craves full fain,   155
     Sister Helen,
You pardon him in his mortal pain."
"What else he took will he give again,
     Little brother?"
    (*O Mother, Mary Mother,*   160
Not twice to give, between Hell and Heaven!)

"He calls your name in an agony,
     Sister Helen,
That even dead Love must weep to see."
"Hate, born of Love, is blind as he,   165
     Little brother!"
    (*O Mother, Mary Mother,*
Love turned to hate, between Hell and Heaven!)

"Oh it's Keith of Keith now that rides fast,
     Sister Helen,   170
For I know the white hair on the blast."
"The short short hour will soon be past,
     Little brother!"
    (*O Mother, Mary Mother,*
Will soon be past, between Hell and Heaven!)   175

"He looks at me and he tries to speak,
     Sister Helen,
But oh his voice is sad and weak!"
"What here should the mighty Baron seek,
     Little brother?"   180
    (*O Mother, Mary Mother,*
Is this the end, between Hell and Heaven?)

"Oh his son still cries, if you forgive,
     Sister Helen,
The body dies but the soul shall live."   185

"Fire shall forgive me as I forgive,
                    Little brother!"
          (*O Mother, Mary Mother,*
As she forgives, between Hell and Heaven!)

"Oh he prays you, as his heart would rive,   190
                    Sister Helen,
To save his dear son's soul alive."
"Fire cannot slay it, it shall thrive,
                    Little brother."
          (*O Mother, Mary Mother,*   195
Alas, alas, between Hell and Heaven!)

"He cries to you, kneeling in the road,
                    Sister Helen,
To go with him for the love of God!"
"The way is long to his son's abode,   200
                    Little brother."
          (*O Mother, Mary Mother,*
The way is long, between Hell and Heaven!)

"A lady's here, by a dark steed brought,
                    Sister Helen,   205
So darkly clad, I saw her not."
"See her now or never see aught,
                    Little brother!"
          (*O Mother, Mary Mother,*
What more to see, between Hell and Heaven?)   210

"Her hood falls back, and the moon shines fair,
                    Sister Helen,
On the Lady of Ewern's golden hair."
"Blest hour of my power and her despair,
                    Little brother!"   215
          (*O Mother, Mary Mother,*
Hour blest and banned, between Hell and Heaven!)

"Pale, pale her cheeks, that in pride did glow,
                    Sister Helen,
'Neath the bridal-wreath three days ago."   220

"One morn for pride and three days for woe,
                    Little brother!"
                    (*O Mother, Mary Mother,*
Three days, three nights, between Hell and Heaven!)

"Her clasped hands stretch from her bending head,   225
                    Sister Helen;
With the loud wind's wail her sobs are wed."
"What wedding-strains hath her bridal-bed,
                    Little brother?"
                    (*O Mother, Mary Mother,*   230
What strains but death's, between Hell and Heaven!)

"She may not speak, she sinks in a swoon,
                    Sister Helen,—
She lifts her lips and gasps on the moon."
"Oh, might I but hear her soul's blithe tune,   235
                    Little brother!"
                    (*O Mother, Mary Mother,*
Her woe's dumb cry, between Hell and Heaven!)

"They 've caught her to Westholm's saddle-bow,
                    Sister Helen,   240
And her moonlit hair gleams white in its flow."
"Let it turn whiter than winter snow,
                    Little brother!"
                    (*O Mother, Mary Mother,*
Woe-withered gold, between Hell and Heaven!)   245

"O Sister Helen, you heard the bell,
                    Sister Helen;
More loud than the vesper-chime, it fell."
"No vesper-chime but a dying knell,
                    Little brother!"   250
                    (*O Mother, Mary Mother,*
His dying knell, between Hell and Heaven!)

"Alas! but I fear the heavy sound,
                    Sister Helen;
Is it in the sky or in the ground?"   255

"Say, have they turned their horses round,
>> Little brother?"
>>> (*O Mother, Mary Mother,*
What would she more, between Hell and Heaven?)

"They have raised the old man from his knee,   260
>> Sister Helen,
And they ride in silence hastily."
"More fast the naked soul doth flee,
>> Little brother!"
>>> (*O Mother, Mary Mother,*   265
The naked soul, between Hell and Heaven!)

"Flank to flank are the three steeds gone,
>> Sister Helen,
But the lady's dark steed goes alone."
"And lonely her bridegroom's soul hath flown,   270
>> Little brother."
>>> (*O Mother, Mary Mother,*
The lonely ghost, between Hell and Heaven!)

"Oh the wind is sad in the iron chill,
>> Sister Helen,   275
And weary sad they look by the hill."
"But he and I are sadder still,
>> Little brother!"
>>> (*O Mother, Mary Mother,*
Most sad of all, between Hell and Heaven!)   280

"See, see, the wax has dropped from its place,
>> Sister Helen,
And the flames are winning up apace!"
"Yet here they burn but for a space,
>> Little brother!"   285
>>> (*O Mother, Mary Mother,*
Here for a space, between Hell and Heaven!).

"Ah! what white thing at the door has crossed,
>> Sister Helen,
Ah! what is this that sighs in the frost?"   290

"A soul that's lost as mine is lost,
                               Little brother!"
                     (*O Mother, Mary Mother,*
     Lost, lost, all lost, between Hell and Heaven!)
1851.   1853.

FROM
THE HOUSE OF LIFE
LOVE ENTHRONED

I marked all kindred Powers the heart finds fair:—
     Truth, with awed lips; and Hope, with eyes upcast;
     And Fame, whose loud wings fan the ashen Past
To signal-fires, Oblivion's flight to scare;
And Youth, with still some single golden hair   5
     Unto his shoulder clinging, since the last
     Embrace wherein two sweet arms held him fast;
And Life, still wreathing flowers for Death to wear.

Love's throne was not with these; but far above
     All passionate wind of welcome and farewell   10
He sat in breathless bowers they dream not of,
     Though Truth foreknow Love's heart, and Hope foretell,
     And Fame be for Love's sake desirable,
And Youth be dear and Life be sweet to Love.

LOVESIGHT

When do I see thee most, beloved one?
     When in the light the spirits of mine eyes
     Before thy face, their altar, solemnize
The worship of that Love through thee made known?
Or when in the dusk hours (we two alone),   5
     Close-kissed and eloquent of still replies,
     Thy twilight-hidden glimmering visage lies,
And my soul only sees thy soul its own?

O love, my love! if I no more should see
Thyself, nor on the earth the shadow of thee,   10
     Nor image of thine eyes in any spring,—
How then should sound upon Life's darkening slope
The ground-whirl of the perished leaves of Hope,
     The wind of Death's imperishable wing?

HEART'S HOPE

By what word's power, the key of paths untrod,
　　Shall I the difficult deeps of Love explore,
　　Till parted waves of Song yield up the shore
Even as that sea which Israel crossed dryshod?
For lo! in some poor rhythmic period,　　　　　　　5
　　Lady, I fain would tell how evermore
　　Thy soul I know not from thy body, nor
Thee from myself, neither our love from God.

Yea, in God's name, and Love's, and thine, would I
　　Draw from one loving heart such evidence　　　10
As to all hearts all things shall signify;
　　Tender as dawn's first hill-fire, and intense
　　As instantaneous penetrating sense,
In Spring's birth-hour, of other Springs gone by.

SILENT NOON

Your hands lie open in the long fresh grass,—
　　The finger-points look through like rosy blooms;
　　Your eyes smile peace. The pasture gleams and glooms
'Neath billowing skies that scatter and amass.
All round our nest, far as the eye can pass,　　　5
　　Are golden kingcup-fields with silver edge,
　　Where the cow-parsley skirts the hawthorn-hedge.
'T is visible silence, still as the hour-glass.

Deep in the sun-searched growths the dragon-fly
Hangs like a blue thread loosened from the sky:—　10
　　So this winged hour is dropt to us from above.
Oh, clasp we to our hearts; for deathless dower,
This close-companioned, inarticulate hour
　　When twofold silence was the song of love.

THE DARK GLASS

Not I myself know all my love for thee:
　　How should I reach so far, who cannot weigh
　　To-morrow's dower by gage of yesterday?
Shall birth and death, and all dark names that be

As doors and windows bared to some loud sea,   5
    Lash deaf mine ears and blind my face with spray;
    And shall my sense pierce love—the last relay
And ultimate outpost of eternity?

Lo! what am I to Love, the lord of all?
    One murmuring shell he gathers from the sand;   10
    One little heart-flame sheltered in his hand.
Yet through thine eyes he grants me clearest call
And veriest touch of powers primordial
    That any hour-girt life may understand.

WILLOWWOOD

I.

I sat with Love upon a woodside well,
    Leaning across the water, I and he;
    Nor ever did he speak nor looked at me,
But touched his lute, wherein was audible
The certain secret thing he had to tell: 5
    Only our mirrored eyes met silently
    In the low wave; and that sound came to be
The passionate voice I knew; and my tears fell.

And at their fall, his eyes beneath grew hers;
And with his foot and with his wing-feathers   10
    He swept the spring that watered my heart's drouth.
Then the dark ripples spread to waving hair;
And as I stooped, her own lips, rising there,
    Bubbled with brimming kisses at my mouth.

II.

And now Love sang: but his was such a song,
    So meshed with half-remembrance hard to free,
    As souls disused in death's sterility
May sing when the new birthday tarries long.
And I was made aware of a dumb throng   5
    That stood aloof, one form by every tree;
    All mournful forms for each was I or she,
The shades of those our days that had no tongue.

They looked on us, and knew us and were known;
    While fast together, alive from the abyss,   10
    Clung the soul-wrung, implacable, close kiss;
And pity of self through all made broken moan
Which said, "For once, for once, for once alone!"
    And still Love sang, and what he sang was this:—

III.

"O ye, all ye that walk in Willowwood,
    That walk with hollow faces burning white,
What fathom-depth of soul-struck widowhood,
    What long, what longer hours, one lifelong night,
Ere ye again; who so in vain have wooed   5
    Your last hope lost, who so in vain invite
Your lips to that their unforgotten food,
    Ere ye, ere ye again shall see the light!

Alas! the bitter banks in Willowwood,
    With tear-spurge wan, with blood-wort burning red: 10
Alas! if ever such a pillow could
    Steep deep the soul in sleep till she were dead,
Better all life forget her than this thing,
    That Willowwood should hold her wandering!"

IV.

So sang he: and as meeting rose and rose
    Together cling through the wind's wellaway
    Nor change at once, yet near the end of day
The leaves drop loosened where the heart-stain glows,
So when the song died did the kiss unclose;   5
    And her face fell back drowned, and was as gray
    As its gray eyes; and if it ever may
Meet mine again I know not if Love knows.

Only I know that I leaned low, and drank
A long draught from the water where she sank—   10
    Her breath and all her tears and all her soul:
And as I leaned, I know I felt Love's face
Pressed on my neck with moan of pity and grace,
    Till both our heads were in his aureole.

THE CHOICE

I.

Eat thou and drink; to-morrow thou shalt die.
  Surely the earth, that's wise being very old,
  Needs not our help. Then loose me, love, and hold
Thy sultry hair up from my face; that I
May pour for thee this golden wine, brim-high,   5
  Till round the glass thy fingers glow like gold.
  We'll drown all hours: thy song, while hours are tolled,
Shall leap, as fountains veil the changing sky.

Now kiss, and think that there are really those,
  My own high-bosomed beauty, who increase   10
    Vain gold, vain lore, and yet might choose our way!
    Through many years they toil; then on a day
  They die not—for their life was death—but cease,
And round their narrow lips the mould falls close.

II.

Watch thou and fear; to-morrow thou shalt die.
  Or art thou sure thou shalt have time for death?
  Is not the day which God's word promiseth,
To come man knows not when? In yonder sky,
Now while we speak, the sun speeds forth: can I   5
  Or thou assure him of his goal? God's breath
  Even at this moment haply quickeneth
The air to a flame; till spirits, always nigh
Though screened and hid, shall walk the daylight here.
  And dost thou prate of all that man shall do?   10
    Canst thou, who hast but plagues, presume to be
    Glad in his gladness that comes after thee?
  Will *his* strength slay *thy* worm in hell? Go to:
Cover thy countenance, and watch, and fear.

III.

Think thou and act; to-morrow thou shalt die.
  Outstretched in the sun's warmth upon the shore,
    Thou say'st: "Man's measured path is all gone o'er;
Up all his years, steeply, with strain and sigh,

Man clomb until he touched the truth; and I,   5
  Even I, am he whom it was destined for."
How should this be? Art thou, then, so much more
Than they who sowed, that thou shouldst reap thereby?

Nay, come up hither. From this wave-washed mound
  Unto the furthest flood-brim look with me;   10
Then reach on with thy thought till it be drowned.
  Miles and miles distant though the last line be,
And though thy soul sail leagues and leagues beyond,
  Still, leagues beyond those leagues, there is more sea.

THE SUN'S SHAME

Beholding youth and hope in mockery caught
  From life; and mocking pulses that remain
  When the soul's death of bodily death is fain;
Honour unknown, and honour known unsought;
And penury's sedulous, self-torturing thought   5
  On gold, whose master therewith buys his bane;
  And longed-for woman longing all in vain
For lonely man with love's desire distraught;
And wealth, and strength, and power, and pleasantness
  Given unto bodies of whose souls men say,   10
  None poor and weak, slavish and foul, as they:—
Beholding these things, I behold no less
  The blushing morn and blushing eve confess
  The shame that loads the intolerable day.

THE ONE HOPE

When vain desire at last and vain regret
  Go hand in hand to death, and all is vain,
  What shall assuage the unforgotten pain
And teach the unforgetful to forget?
Shall Peace be still a sunk stream long unmet,   5
  Or may the soul at once in a green plain
  Stoop through the spray of some sweet life-fountain
And cull the dew-drenched flowering amulet?

Ah, when the wan soul in that golden air,
  Between the scriptured petals softly blown,   10
  Peers breathless for the gift of grace unknown,

Ah, let none other alien spell soe'er
But only the one Hope's one name be there,—
    Not less nor more, but even that word alone.

1847?–1881.   1869, 1870, 1881.

MARY'S GIRLHOOD

(*For a Picture*)

This is that blessed Mary, pre-elect
    God's Virgin. Gone is a great while, and she
    Dwelt young in Nazareth of Galilee.
Unto God's will she brought devout respect,
Profound simplicity of intellect,   5
    And supreme patience. From her mother's knee
    Faithful and hopeful; wise in charity;
Strong in grave peace; in pity circumspect.

So held she through her girlhood; as it were
    An angel-watered lily, that near God   10
        Grows and is quiet. Till, one dawn at home,
She woke in her white bed, and had no fear
    At all,—yet wept till sunshine, and felt awed:
        Because the fulness of the time was come.

1848–49.   1849.

FOR

A VENETIAN PASTORAL

BY GIORGIONE

Water, for anguish of the solstice:—nay,
    But dip the vessel slowly,—nay, but lean
    And hark how at its verge the wave sighs in
Reluctant. Hush! beyond all depth away
The heat lies silent at the brink of day: 5
    Now the hand trails upon the viol-string
    That sobs, and the brown faces cease to sing,
Sad with the whole of pleasure. Whither stray
Her eyes now, from whose mouth the slim pipes creep
    And leave it pouting, while the shadowed grass   10
        Is cool against her naked side? Let be:—

Say nothing now unto her lest she weep,
   Nor name this ever. Be it as it was—
   Life touching lips with Immortality.

                1850.

MARY MAGDALENE

AT THE DOOR OF SIMON THE PHARISEE

(*For a Drawing*)

"Why wilt thou cast the roses from thine hair?
   Nay, be thou all a rose—wreath, lips, and cheek.
   Nay, not this house—that banquet-house we seek;
See how they kiss and enter; come thou there.
This delicate day of love we two will share,   5
   Till at our ear love's whispering night shall speak.
   What, sweet one,—hold'st thou still the foolish freak?
Nay, when I kiss thy feet they'll leave the stair."

"Oh loose me! Seest thou not my Bridegroom's face
   That draws me to Him? For His feet my kiss,   10
   My hair, my tears He craves to-day:—and oh
What words can tell what other day and place
   Shall see me clasp those blood-stained feet of His?
   He needs me, calls me, loves me: let me go!"

1859?   1870.

FOR

THE WINE OF CIRCE

BY EDWARD BURNE JONES

Dusk-haired and gold-robed o'er the golden wine
   She stoops, wherein, distilled of death and shame,
   Sink the black drops; while, lit with fragrant flame,
Round her spread board the golden sunflowers shine.
Doth Helios here with Hecatè combine   5
   (O Circe, thou their votaress?) to proclaim
   For these thy guests all rapture in Love's name,
Till pitiless Night give Day the countersign?
Lords of their hour, they come. And by her knee
   Those cowering beasts, their equals heretofore,   10

Wait; who with them in new equality
   To-night shall echo back the sea's dull roar
   With a vain wail from passion's tide-strown shore
Where the dishevelled seaweed hates the sea.

1870.

THE WOODSPURGE

  The wind flapped loose, the wind was still,
  Shaken out dead from tree and hill:
  I had walked on at the wind's will;
  I sat now, for the wind was still.

  Between my knees my forehead was;   5
  My lips, drawn in, said not "Alas!"
  My hair was over in the grass;
  My naked ears heard the day pass.

  My eyes, wide open, had the run
  Of some ten weeds to fix upon;   10
  Among those few, out of the sun,
  The woodspurge flowered, three cups in one.

  From perfect grief there need not be
  Wisdom or even memory:
  One thing then learnt remains to me,   15
  The woodspurge has a cup of three.

1870.

JOHN KEATS

The weltering London ways, where children weep
  And girls whom none call maidens laugh,—strange road
  Miring his outward steps, who inly trode
The bright Castalian brink and Latmos' steep,—
Even such his life's cross-paths; till deathly deep   5
  He toiled through sands of Lethe; and long pain,
  Weary with labour spurned and love found vain,
In dead Rome's sheltering shadow wrapped his sleep.

O pang-dowered poet, whose reverberant lips
And heart-strung lyre awoke the moon's eclipse,   10
    Thou whom the daisies glory in growing o'er,
Their fragrance clings around thy name, not writ
But rumoured in water, while the fame of it
    Along Time's flood goes echoing evermore.

1881.

CHRISTINA ROSSETTI

SONG

When I am dead, my dearest,
    Sing no sad songs for me;
Plant thou no roses at my head,
    Nor shady cypress-tree:
Be the green grass above me   5
    With showers and dewdrops wet;
And if thou wilt, remember,
    And if thou wilt, forget.

I shall not see the shadows,
    I shall not feel the rain;   10
I shall not hear the nightingale
    Sing on, as if in pain:
And, dreaming through the twilight
    That doth not rise nor set,
Haply I may remember,   15
    And haply may forget.

1848.   1862.

THREE SEASONS

"A cup for hope!" she said,
In springtime ere the bloom was old;
The crimson wine was poor and cold
    By her mouth's richer red.

"A cup for love!" how low,   5
How soft the words; and all the while
Her blush was rippling with a smile
 Like summer after snow.

"A cup for memory!"
Cold cup that one must drain alone,   10
While autumn winds are up and moan
 Across the barren sea.

Hope, memory, love:
Hope for fair morn, and love for day,
And memory for the evening grey   15
 And solitary dove.

1853.   *1862.*

SLEEP AT SEA

Sound the deep waters:—
 Who shall sound that deep?
Too short the plummet,
 And the watchmen sleep.
Some dream of effort   5
 Up a toilsome steep;
Some dream of pasture grounds
 For harmless sheep.

White shapes flit to and fro
 From mast to mast;   10
They feel the distant tempest
 That nears them fast;
Great rocks are straight ahead,
 Great shoals not past;
They shout to one another   15
 Upon the blast.

O, soft the streams drop music
 Between the hills,
And musical the birds' nests
 Beside those rills;   20

The nests are types of home
  Love-hidden from ills,
The nests are types of spirits
  Love-music fills.

So dream the sleepers,   25
  Each man in his place;
The lightning shows the smile
  Upon each face;
The ship is driving, driving,
  It drives apace,   30
And sleepers smile, and spirits
  Bewail their case.

The lightning glares and reddens
  Across the skies;
It seems but sunset   35
  To those sleeping eyes.
When did the sun go down
  On such a wise?
From such a sunset
  When shall day arise?   40

"Wake!" call the spirits,
  But to heedless ears:
They have forgotten sorrows
  And hopes and fears;
They have forgotten perils   45
  And smiles and tears;
Their dream has held them long,
  Long years and years.

"Wake!" call the spirits again;
  But it would take   50
A louder summons
  To bid them awake.
Some dream of pleasure
  For another's sake;
Some dream, forgetful   55
  Of a lifelong ache.

One by one slowly,
  Ah, how sad and slow!
Wailing and praying,
  The spirits rise and go—   60
Clear stainless spirits,
  White, as white as snow;
Pale spirits, wailing
  For an overthrow.

One by one flitting,   65
  Like a mournful bird
Whose song is tired at last
  For no mate heard.
The loving voice is silent,
  The useless word;   70
One by one flitting,
  Sick with hope deferred.

Driving and driving,
  The ship drives amain,
While swift from mast to mast   75
  Shapes flit again,
Flit silent as the silence
  Where men lie slain;
Their shadow cast upon the sails
  Is like a stain.   80

No voice to call the sleepers,
  No hand to raise;
They sleep to death in dreaming
  Of length of days.
Vanity of vanities   85
  The Preacher says;
Vanity is the end
  Of all their ways.

1853.   *1862.*

UP-HILL

Does the road wind up-hill all the way?
  Yes, to the very end.
Will the day's journey take the whole long day?
  From morn to night, my friend.

But is there for the night a resting-place?　　　5
　　A roof for when the slow dark hours begin.
May not the darkness hide it from my face?
　　You cannot miss that inn.

Shall I meet other wayfarers at night?
　　Those who have gone before.　　　　　　10
Then must I knock, or call when just in sight?
　　They will not keep you standing at that door.

Shall I find comfort, travel-sore and weak?
　　Of labour you shall find the sum.
Will there be beds for me and all who seek?　　15
　　Yea, beds for all who come.

1858.　　　　　　　　　　　　　　*1861.*

WINTER RAIN

Every valley drinks,
　　Every dell and hollow;
Where the kind rain sinks and sinks,
　　Green of spring will follow.

Yet a lapse of weeks　　　　　　　　　5
　　Buds will burst their edges,
Strip their wool-coats, glue-coats, streaks,
　　In the woods and hedges;

Weave a bower of love
　　For birds to meet each other,　　　　10
Weave a canopy above
　　Nest and egg and mother.

But for fattening rain
　　We should have no flowers,
Never a bud or leaf again　　·　　　　　15
　　But for soaking showers;

Never a mated bird
　　In the rocking tree-tops,
Never indeed a flock or herd
　　To graze upon the lea-crops.　　　　20

Lambs so wholly white,
    Sheep the sun-bright leas on,
They could have no grass to bite
    But for rain in season.

We should find no moss   25
    In the shadiest places,
Find no waving meadow-grass
    Pied with broad-eyed daisies;

But miles of barren sand,
    With never a son or daughter,   30
Not a lily on the land,
    Or lily on the water.

1859.   *1862.*

YOUTH GONE, AND BEAUTY GONE

Youth gone, and beauty gone—if ever there
    Dwelt beauty in so poor a face as this,—
    Youth gone and beauty, what remains of bliss?
I will not bind fresh roses in my hair,
To shame a check at best but little fair,—   5
    Leave youth his roses who can bear a thorn;
I will not seek for blossoms anywhere,
    Except such common flowers as blow with corn.
Youth gone and beauty gone, what doth remain?
    The longing of a heart pent up forlorn,   10
        A silent heart whose silence loves and longs,
        The silence of a heart which sang its songs
    While youth and beauty made a summer morn,
Silence of love that cannot sing again.

                      1881.

THIS LIFE IS FULL OF NUMBNESS AND OF BALK

This Life is full of numbness and of balk,
    Of haltingness and baffled short-coming,
    Of promise unfulfilled, of everything
That is puffed vanity and empty talk:
Its very bud hangs cankered on the stalk,   5
    Its very song-bird trails a broken wing,
    Its very spring is not indeed like spring,

But sighs like autumn round an aimless walk.
This Life we live is dead for all its breath;
    Death's self it is, set off on pilgrimage,   10
    Travelling with tottering steps the first short stage:
      The second stage is one mere desert dust
        Where Death sits veiled amid creation's rust:—
Unveil thy face, O Death who art not Death.

                        1881.

WILLIAM MORRIS

AN APOLOGY

Of heaven or hell I have no power to sing,
I cannot ease the burden of your fears,
Or make quick-coming death a little thing,
Or bring again the pleasure of past years,
Nor for my words shall ye forget your tears,   5
Or hope again for aught that I can say,
The idle singer of an empty day.

But rather, when, aweary of your mirth,
From full hearts still unsatisfied ye sigh,
And, feeling kindly unto all the earth,   10
Grudge every minute as it passes by,
Made the more mindful that the sweet days die,
Remember me a little then, I pray,
The idle singer of an empty day.

The heavy trouble, the bewildering care   15
That weighs us down who live and earn our bread,
These idle verses have no power to bear;
So let me sing of names rememberèd,
Because they, living not, can ne'er be dead,
Or long time take their memory quite away   20
From us poor singers of an empty day.

Dreamer of dreams, born out of my due time,
Why should I strive to set the crooked straight?
Let it suffice me that my murmuring rhyme

Beats with light wing against the ivory gate, 25
Telling a tale not too importunate
To those who in the sleepy region stay,
Lulled by the singer of an empty day.

Folk say a wizard to a northern king
At Christmas-tide such wondrous things did show 30
That through one window men beheld the spring,
And through another saw the summer glow,
And through a third the fruited vines a-row,
While still, unheard, but in its wonted way,
Piped the drear wind of that December day. 35

So with this Earthly Paradise it is,
If ye will read aright, and pardon me,
Who strive to build a shadowy isle of bliss
Midmost the beating of the steely sea,
Where tossed about all hearts of men must be; 40
Whose ravening monsters mighty men shall slay,
Not the poor singer of an empty day.

1868.

THE DEATH OF PARIS

In the last month of Troy's beleaguerment,
When both sides, waiting for some god's great hand,
But seldom o'er the meads the war-shout sent,
Yet idle rage would sometimes drive a band
From town or tent about Troy-gate to stand 5
All armed, and there to bicker aimlessly;
And so at least the weary time wore by.

In such a fight, when wide the arrows flew,
And little glory fell to any there,
And naught there seemed for a stout man to do, 10
Rose Philoctetes from the ill-roofed lair
That hid his rage, and crept out into air,
And strung his bow, and slunk down to the fight,
'Twixt rusty helms, and shields that once were bright.

And even as he reached the foremost rank, 15
A glimmer as of polished steel and gold

Amid the war-worn Trojan folk, that shrank
To right and left, his fierce eyes could behold;
He heard a shout, as if one man were bold
About the streams of Simoeis that day—   20
One heart still ready to play out the play.

Therewith he heard a mighty bowstring twang,
And a shaft screamed 'twixt hostile band and band,
And close beside him fell, with clash and clang,
A well-tried warrior from the Cretan land,   25
And rolled in dust, clutching with desperate hand
At the gay feathers of the shaft that lay
Deep in his heart, well silenced from that day.

Then of the Greeks did man look upon man,
While Philoctetes from his quiver drew   30
A dreadful shaft, and through his fingers ran
The dull-red feathers; of strange steel and blue
The barbs were, such as archer never knew,
But black as death the thin-forged bitter point,
That with the worm's blood Fate did erst anoint.   35

He shook the shaft, and notched it, and therewith
Forth from the Trojans rang that shout again,
Whistled the arrow, and a Greek did writhe
Once more upon the earth in his last pain;
While the grey clouds, big with the threat of rain,   40
Parted a space, and on the Trojans shone,
And struck a glory from that shining one.

Then Philoctetes scowled, and cried, "O Fate,
I give thee this, thy strong man gave to me.
Do with it as thou wilt!—let small or great   45
E'en as thou wilt before its black point be!
Late grows the year, and stormy is the sea,
The oars lie rotten by the gunwales now
That nevermore a Grecian surf shall know."

He spake and drew the string with careless eyes,   50
And, as the shaft flew forth, he turned about
And tramped back slowly, noting in no wise

How from the Greeks uprose a joyous shout,
And from the Trojan host therewith brake out
Confusèd clamour, and folk cried the name   55
Of him wherethrough the weary struggle came,

Paris the son of Priam! Then once more
O'er head of leaguer and beleaguered town
Grey grew the sky; a cold sea-wind swept o'er
The ruined plain, and the small rain drove down;   60
While slowly underneath that chilling frown
Parted the hosts—sad Troy into its gates,
Greece to its tents, and waiting on the Fates.

Next day the seaward-looking gates none swung
Back on their hinges, whatso Greek might fare,   65
With seeming-careless mien, and bow unstrung,
Anigh them; whatso rough-voiced horn might dare,
With well-known notes, the war-worn warders there.
Troy slept amid its nightmares through the day,
And dull with waking dreams the leaguer lay.   70

Yet in the streets did man say unto man:
"Hector is dead, and Troilus is dead;
Aeneas turneth toward the waters wan;
In his fair house Antenor hides his head;
Fast from the tree of Troy the boughs are shred;   75
And now this Paris, now this joyous one,
Is the cry cried that biddeth him begone?"

But on the morrow's dawn, ere yet the sun
Had shone athwart the mists of last night's rain,
And shown the image of the Spotless One   80
Unto the tents and hovels of the plain
Whose girth of war she long had made all vain,
From out a postern looking towards the north
A little band of silent men went forth.

And in their midst a litter did they bear,   85
Whereon lay one with linen wrapped around,
Whose wan face turned unto the fresher air
As though a little pleasure he had found

Amidst of pain; some dreadful torturing wound
The man endured belike, and as a balm   90
Was the fresh morn, with all its rest and calm,

After the weary tossing of the night
And close dim-litten chamber, whose dusk seemed
Labouring with whispers fearful of the light,
Confused with images of dreams long dreamed,   95
Come back again, now that the lone torch gleamed
Dim before eyes that saw naught real as true
To vex the heart that naught of purpose knew.

Upon the late-passed night in e'en such wise
Had Paris lain. What time, like years of life,   100
Had passed before his weary heart and eyes!
What hopeless, nameless longings! what wild strife
'Gainst naught for naught, with wearying changes rife,
Had he gone through, till in the twilight grey
They bore him through the cold, deserted way.   105

Mocking and strange the streets looked now, most meet
For a dream's ending, for a vain life's end;
While sounded his strong litter-bearers' feet,
Like feet of men who through Death's country wend
Silent, for fear lest they should yet offend   110
The grim King, satisfied to let them go;
Hope bids them hurry, fear's chain makes them slow.

In feverish doze of time a-gone he thought,
When love was soft, life strong, and a sweet name,
The first sweet name that led him down love's ways,   115
Unbidden ever to his fresh lips came;
Half witting would he speak it, and for shame
Flush red, and think what folk would deem thereof
If they might know Oenone was his love.

And now,—Oenone no more love of his,   120
He worn with war and passion,—must he pray,
"O thou, I loved and love not, life and bliss
Lie in thine hands to give or take away;
O heal me, hate me not! think of the day

When as thou thinkest still, e'en so I thought 125
That all the world without thy love was naught."

Yea, he was borne forth such a prayer to make,
For she alone of all the world, they said,
The thirst of that dread poison now might slake;
For, midst the ancient wise ones nurturèd 130
On peaceful Ida, in the lore long dead,
Lost to the hurrying world, right wise she was,
Mighty to bring most wondrous things to pass.

Was the world worth the minute of that prayer,
If yet her love, despised and cast aside, 135
Should so shine forth that she should heal him there?
He knew not and he recked not; fear and pride
'Neath Helen's kiss and Helen's tears had died.
And life was love, and love too strong that he
Should catch at death to save him misery. 140

So, with soul drifting down the stream of love,
He let them bear him through the fresh fair morn,
From out Troy-gates; and no more now he strove
To battle with the wild dreams, newly born
From that past night of toil and pain forlorn; 145
No farewell did he mutter 'neath his breath
To failing Troy, no eyes he turned toward death.

Troy dwindled now behind them, and the way
That round about the feet of Ida wound
They left; and up a narrow vale, that lay, 150
Grassy and soft betwixt the pine-woods bound,
They went, and ever gained the higher ground,
For as a trench the little valley was
To catch the runnels that made green its grass.

Now ere that green vale narrowed to an end, 155
Blocked by a shaly slip thrust bleak and bare
From the dark pine-woods edge, as men who wend
Upon a well-known way they turned them there,
And through the pine-wood's dusk began to fare
By blind ways, till all noise of bird and wind 160
Amid that odorous night was left behind.

And in mean while deepened the languid doze
That lay on Paris into slumber deep;
O'er his unconscious heart, and eyes shut close,
The image of that very place 'gan creep,   165
And twelve years younger in his dreamful sleep,
Light-footed, through the awful wood he went,
With beating heart, on lovesome thoughts intent.

Dreaming, he went, till thinner and more thin
And bright with growing day, the pine-wood grew,   170
Then to an open rugged space did win;
Whence a close beech-wood was he passing through,
Whose every tall white stem full well he knew;
Then seemed to stay awhile for loving shame,
When to the brow of the steep bank he came.   175

Where still the beech-trunks o'er the mast-strewn ground
Stood close, and slim and tall, but hid not quite
A level grassy space they did surround
On every side save one, that to the light
Of the clear western sky, cold now but bright,   180
Was open, and the thought of the far sea,
Toward which a small brook tinkled merrily.

Himseemed he lingered there, then stepped adown
With troubled heart into the soft green place,
And up the eastmost of the beech-slopes brown   185
He turned about a lonesome, anxious face,
And stood to listen for a little space
If any came; but naught he seemed to hear
Save the brook's babble, and the beech-leaves' stir.

And then he dreamed great longing o'er him came—   190
Too great, too bitter, of those days to be,
Long past, when love was born amidst of shame;
He dreamed that, as he gazed full eagerly
Into the green dusk between tree and tree,
His trembling hand slid down the horn to take   195
Wherewith he erst was wont his herd to wake.

Trembling, he set it to his lips, and first
Breathed gently through it; then strained hard to blow,
For dumb, dumb was it grown, and no note burst
From its smooth throat. And ill thoughts poisoned now   200
The sweetness of his dream; he murmured low,
"Ah, dead and gone, and ne'er to come again;
Ah, passed away! ah, longed for long in vain!

"Lost love, sweet Helen, come again to me!"
Therewith he dreamed he fell upon the ground   205
And hid his face and wept out bitterly;
But woke with fall and torturing tears, and found
He lay upon his litter, and the sound
Of feet departing from him did he hear,
And rustling of the last year's leaves anear.   210

But in the self-same place he lay indeed,
Weeping and sobbing, and scarce knowing why;
His hand clutched hard the horn that erst did lead
The dew-lapped neat round Ida merrily;
He strove to raise himself, he strove to cry   215
That name of Helen once, but then withal
Upon him did the load of memory fall.

Quiet he lay a space, while o'er him drew
The dull, chill cloud of doubt and sordid fear,
As now he thought of what he came to do,   220
And what a dreadful minute drew anear;
He shut his eyes, and now no more could hear
His litter-bearers' feet; as lone he felt
As though amid the outer wastes he dwelt.

Amid that fear a minute naught and vain   225
His life and love seemed; with a dreadful sigh
He raised his arm, and soul's and body's pain
Tore at his heart with new-born agony,
As a thin quavering note, a ghost-like cry,
Rang from the long-unused lips of the horn,   230
Spoiling the sweetness of the happy morn.

He let the horn fall down upon his breast
And lie there, and his hand fell to his side;

And there indeed his body seemed to rest,
But restless was his soul, and wandered wide   235
Through a dim maze of lusts unsatisfied,
Thoughts half thought out, and words half said, and deeds
Half done, unfruitful, like o'er-shadowed weeds.

His eyes were shut now, and his dream's hot tears
Were dry upon his cheek; the sun grown high   240
Had slain the wind, when smote upon his ears
A sudden rustling in the beech-leaves dry;
Then came a pause; then footsteps drew anigh
O'er the deep grass; he shuddered, and in vain
He strove to turn, despite his burning pain.   245

Then through his half-shut eyes he seemed to see
A woman drawing near, and held his breath,
And clutched at the white linen eagerly,
And felt a greater fear than fear of death,
A greater pain than that love threateneth,   250
As soft, low breathing o'er his head he heard,
And thin fine linen raiment gently stirred.

Then spoke a sweet voice close, ah, close to him!
"Thou sleepest, Paris? would that I could sleep!
On the hillside do I lay limb to limb,   255
And lie day-long, watching the shadows creep
And change, till day is gone, and night is deep;
Yet sleep not ever, wearied with the thought
Of all a little lapse of time has brought.

"Sleep, though thou calledst me! Yet 'mid thy dream   260
Hearken, the while I tell about my life,
The life I led while 'mid the steely gleam
Thou wert made happy with the joyous strife,
Or in the soft arms of the Greek king's wife
Wouldst still moan out that day had come too soon,   265
Calling the dawn the glimmer of the moon.

"Wake not, wake not, before the tale is told!
Not long to tell, the tale of those ten years!
A gnawing pain that never groweth old,

A pain that shall not be washed out by tears; 270
A dreary road the weary foot-sole wears,
Knowing no rest, but going to and fro,
Treading it harder 'neath the weight of woe.

"No middle, no beginning, and no end;
No staying place, no thought of anything, 275
Bitter or sweet, with that one thought to blend;
No least joy left that I away might fling
And deem myself grown great; no hope to cling
About me; naught but dull, unresting pain,
That made all memory sick, all striving vain. 280

"Thou—hast thou thought thereof, perchance anights,
In early dawn, and shuddered, and then said,
'Alas, poor soul! yet hath she had delights,
For none are wholly hapless but the dead.'
Liar! O liar! my woe upon thine head, 285
My agony that naught can take away!
Awake, arise, O traitor, unto day!"

Her voice rose as she spoke, till loud and shrill
It rang about the place; but when at last
She ended, and the echoes from the hill, 290
Woful and wild, back o'er the place were cast,
From her lost love a little way she passed,
Trembling, and looking round as if afeared
At those ill sounds that through the morn she heard.

Then still she stood, her clenched hands slim and white 295
Relaxed, her drawn brow smoothed; with a great sigh
Her breast heaved, and she muttered: "Ere the light
Of yesterday had faded from the sky,
I knew that he would seek me certainly;
And, knowing it, yet feigned I knew it not, 300
Or with what hope, what hope, my heart was hot.

"That tumult in my breast I might not name—
Love should I call it? nay, my life was love
And pain these ten years;—should I call it shame?
What shame my weary waiting might reprove 305
After ten years?—or pride? what pride could move

After ten years this heart within my breast?
Alas! I lied—I lied, and called it rest.

"I called it rest, and wandered throught the night;
Upon my river's flowery bank I stood,   310
And thought its hurrying, changing black and white
Stood still beneath the moon, that hill and wood
Were moving round me, and I deemed it good
The world should change so, deemed it good that day
Forever into night had passed away.   315

"And still I wandered through the night, and still
Things changed, and changed not, round me; and the day—
This day wherein I am—had little will
With dreadful truth to drive the night away—
God knows if for its coming I did pray!   320
God knows if at the last in twilight-tide
My hope—my hope undone—I more might hide."

Then looked she toward the litter as she spake,
And slowly drew anigh it once again,
And from her worn, tried heart there did outbreak   325
Wild sobs and weeping, shameless of its pain;
Till, as the storm of passion 'gan to wane,
She looked and saw the shuddering misery
Wherein her love of the old days did lie.

Still she wept on, but gentler now withal,   330
And passed on till above the bier she stood,
Watching the well-wrought linen rise and fall
Beneath his faltering breath; and still her blood
Ran fiery hot with thoughts of ill and good,
Pity and scorn, and love and hate, as she,   335
Half dead herself, gazed on his misery.

At last she spake: "This tale I told e'en now,
Know'st thou 'mid dreams what woman suffered this?
Canst thou not dream of the old days, and how
Full oft thy lips would say 'twixt kiss and kiss,   340
That all of bliss was not enough of bliss
My loveliness and kindness to reward,
That for thy love the sweetest life was hard?

"Yea, Paris, have I not been kind to thee?
Did I not live thy wishes to fulfil? 345
Wert thou not happy when thou lovedst me?
What dream then did we have of change or ill?
Why must thou needs change? I am unchanged still;
I need no more than thee—what needest thou
But that we might be happy, yea e'en now?" 350

He opened hollow eyes and looked on her,
And stretched a trembling hand out; ah, who knows
With what strange, mingled look of hope and fear,
Of hate and love, their eyes met! Come so close
Once more, that everything they now might lose 355
Amid the flashing out of that old fire,
The short-lived uttermost of all desire.

He spake not,—shame and other love there lay
Too heavy on him; but she spake again:
"E'en now at the beginning of the day, 360
Weary with hope and fear and restless pain,
I said—'Alas,' I said, 'if all be vain
And he will have no pity, yet will I
Have pity—how shall kindness ere pass by?'"

He drew his hand aback and laid it now 365
Upon the swathings of his wound, but she
Set her slim hand upon her knitted brow
And gazed on him with bright eyes eagerly;
Nor cruel looked her lips that once would be
So kind, so longed for; neither spake awhile, 370
Till in her face there shone a sweet strange smile.

She touched him not, but yet so near she came
That on his very face he felt her breath;
She whispered, "Speak! thou wilt not speak for shame,
I will not grant for love, and grey-winged Death 375
Meanwhile above our folly hovereth.
Speak! was it not all false, is it not done?
Is not the dream dreamed out, the dull night gone?

"Hearkenest thou Paris? O look kind on me!
I hope no more indeed, but couldst thou turn 380

Kind eyes to me, then much for me and thee
Might love do yet. Doth not the old fire burn?
Doth not thine heart for words of old days yearn?
Canst thou not say—alas, what wilt thou say,
Since I have put by hope for many a day?   385

"Paris, I hope no more, yet while ago—
Take it not ill if I must needs say this—
A while ago I cried, 'Ah no, no, no!
It is no love at all, this love of his;
He loves her not, I it was had the bliss   390
Of being the well-beloved—dead is his love,
For surely none but I his heart may move.'"

She wept still; but his eyes grew wild and strange
With that last word, and harder his face grew,
Though her tear-blinded eyes saw not the change.   395
Long beat about his heart false words and true;
A veil of strange thought he might not pierce through,
Of hope he might not name, clung round about
His wavering heart, perplexed with death and doubt.

Then trembling did he speak: "I love thee still,   400
Surely I love thee." But a dreadful pain
Shot through his heart, and strange presage of ill,
As, like the ceasing of the summer rain,
Her tears stopped, and she drew aback again,
Silent a moment, till a bitter cry   405
Burst from her lips grown white with agony.

A look of pity came across his face
Despite his pain and horror, and her eyes
Saw it, and changed, and for a little space
Panting she stood, as one checked by surprise   410
Amidst of passion; then in tender wise,
Kneeling, she 'gan the bandages undo
That hid the place the bitter shaft tore through.

Then when the wound and his still face and white
Lay there before her, she 'gan tremble sore,   415
For images of hope and past delight,

Not to be named once, 'gan her heart flit o'er;
Blossomed the longing in her heart, and bore
A dreadful thought of uttermost despair,
That all if gained would be no longer fair.   420

In dull, low words she spake: "Yea, so it is,
That thou art near thy death, and this thy wound
I yet may heal, and give thee back what bliss
The ending of thy life may yet surround:
Mock not thyself with hope! the Trojan ground   425
Holds tombs, not houses now; all gods are gone
From out your temples but cold Death alone.

"Lo, if I heal thee, and thou goest again
Back unto Troy, and she, thy new love, sees
Thy lovesome body freed from all its pain,   430
And yet awhile amid the miseries
Of Troy ye twain lie loving, well at ease,
Yet 'midst of this, while she is asking thee
What kind soul made thee whole and well to be,

"And thou art holding back my name with lies,   435
And thinking, maybe, Paris, of this face,—
E'en then the Greekish flame shall sear your eyes,
The clatter of the Greeks fill all the place,
While she, my woe, the ruin of thy race,
Looking toward changed days, a new crown, shall stand, 440
Her fingers trembling in her husband's hand.

"Thou I called love once, wilt thou die e'en thus,
Ruined 'midst ruin, ruining, bereft
Of name and honour? O love, piteous
That but for this were all the hard things cleft   445
That lay 'twixt us and love, till naught was left
'Twixt thy lips and my lips! O hard that we
Were once so full of all felicity!

"O love, O Paris, know'st thou this of me,
That in these hills e'en such a name I have   450
As being akin to a divinity,
And lightly may I slay and lightly save;

Nor know I surely if the peaceful grave
Shall ever hide my body dead—behold,
Have ten long years of misery made me old?"   455

Sadly she laughed, and rising wearily
Stood by him in the fresh and sunny morn;
The image of his youth and faith gone by
She seemed to be, for one short minute born
To make his shamed, lost life seem more forlorn;   460
He shut his eyes and moaned, but once again
She knelt beside him, and the weary pain

Deepened upon her face. "Hearken!" she said,
'Death is anear thee; is then death so ill
With me anigh thee—since Troy is as dead,   465
Ere many tides the Xanthus' mouth shall fill,
And thou art reft of her that harmed me still,
What so may change—shall I heal thee for this,
That thou may'st die more mad for her last kiss?"

She gazed at him with straining eyes; and he—   470
Despite himself love touched his dying heart,
And from his eyes desire flashed suddenly,
And o'er his wan face the last blood did start
As with soft love his close-shut lips 'gan part.
She laughed out bitterly, and said, "Why, then,   475
Must I needs call thee falsest of all men,

"Seeing thou liest not to save thy life?
Yet listen once again—fair is this place,
That knew not the beginning of the strife
And recks not of its end—and this my face,   480
This body thou wouldst day-long once embrace
And deem thyself right happy, thine it is,
Thine only, Paris, shouldst thou deem it bliss."

He looked into her eyes, and deemed he saw
A strange and awful look a-gathering there,   485
And sick scorn at her quivering fine lip draw;
Yet trembling he stretched out his hand to her,
Although self-loathing and strange hate did tear

His heart that death made cold, e'en as he said,
"Whatso thou wilt shall be rememberèd;   490

"Whatso thou wilt, O love, shall be forgot,—
It may be I shall love thee as of old."
As thunder laughs she laughed—"Nay, touch me not!
Touch me not, fool!" she cried; "thou grow'st a-cold,
And I am Death, Death, Death!—the tale is told   495
Of all thy days! of all those joyous days
When, thinking naught of me, thou garneredst praise,

"Turn back again, and think no more of me!
I am thy death! woe for thy happy days!
For I must slay thee; ah, my misery!   500
Woe for the god-like wisdom thou wouldst praise!
Else I my love to life again might raise
A minute, ah, a minute! and be glad
While on my lips thy blessing lips I had!

"Would God that it were yesterday again!   505
Would God the red sun had died yester-eve,
And I were no more hapless now than then!
Would God that I could say, and not believe,
As yesterday, that years past hope did leave
My cold heart—that I lived a death in life—   510
Ah! then within my heart was yet a strife!

"But now, but now, is all come to an end—
Nay, speak not; think not of me! think of her
Who made me this; and back unto her wend,
Lest her lot, too, should be yet heavier!   515
I will depart for fear thou diest here,
Lest I should see thy woful ghost forlorn
Here wandering ever 'twixt the night and morn.

"—O heart grown wise, wilt thou not let me go?
Will ye be never satisfied, O eyes,   520
With gazing on my misery and my woe?
O foolish, quivering heart, now grown so wise,
What folly is it that from out thee cries
To be all close to him once more, once more,
Ere yet the dark stream cleaveth shore from shore?"   525

Her voice was a wail now; with quivering hand
At her white raiment did she clutch and tear
Unwitting, as she rose up and did stand
Bent over his wide eyes and pale face, where
No torturing hope was left, no pain, or fear;   530
For death's cold rest was gathering fast on him,
And toward his heart crept over foot and limb.

A little while she stood, and spake no word,
But hung above him, with white, heaving breast,
And moaning still as moans the grey-winged bird   535
In autumn-tide o'er his forgotten nest;
And then her hands about her throat she pressed,
As though to keep a cry back, then stooped down
And set her face to his, while spake her moan:

"O love, O cherished more than I can tell,   540
Through years of woe, O love, my life and bane,
My joy and grief, farewell, farewell, farewell!
Forgetfulness of grief I yet may gain;
In some wise may come ending to my pain;
It may be yet the gods will have me glad!   545
Yet, love, I would that thee and pain I had!

Alas! it may not be, it may not be,
The falling blossom of the late spring-tide
Shall hang a golden globe upon the tree
When through the vale the mists of autumn glide: 550
Yet would, O love, with thee I might abide!
Now, now that restful death is drawing nigh—
Farewell, farewell! how good it is to die!"

O strange, O strange, when on his lips once more
Her lips were laid! O strange that he must die   555
Now, when so clear a vision had come o'er
His failing heart, and keenest memory
Had shown him all his changing life passed by;
And what he was, and what he might have been,
Yea, and should be, perchance, so clear were seen!   560

Yea, then were all things laid within the scale—
Pleasure and lust, love and desire of fame,

Kindness, and hope, and folly—all the tale
Told in a moment, as across him came
That sudden flash, bright as the lightning-flame,   565
Showing the wanderer on the waste how he
Has gone astray 'mid dark and misery.

Ah, and her face upon his dying face,
That the sun warmed no more! that agony
Of dying love, wild with the tale of days   570
Long past, and strange with hope that might not be—
All was gone now, and what least part had he
In love at all, and why was life all gone?
Why must he meet the eyes of Death alone?

Alone, for she and ruth had left him there;   575
Alone, because the ending of the strife
He knew, well taught by death, drew surely near;
Alone, for all these years with pleasure rife
Should be a tale 'mid Helen's coming life,
And she and all the world should go its ways,   580
'Midst other troubles, other happy days.

And yet how was it with him? As if death
Strove yet with struggling life and love in vain,
With eyes grown deadly bright and rattling breath,
He raised himself, while wide his blood did stain   585
The linen fair, and seized the horn again,
And blew thereon a wild and shattering blast
Ere from his hand afar the thing he cast.

Then, as a man who in a failing fight
For a last onset gathers suddenly   590
All soul and strength, he faced the summer light,
And from his lips broke forth a mighty cry
Of "Helen, Helen, Helen!"—yet the sky
Changed not above his cast-back golden head,
And merry was the world though he was dead.   595

But now when every echo was as still
As were the lips of Paris, once more came
The litter-bearers down the beech-clad hill,

And stood about him crying out his name,
Lamenting for his beauty and his fame, 600
His love, his kindness, and his merry heart,
That still would thrust ill days and thoughts apart.

Homeward they bore him through the dark woods' gloom,
With heavy hearts presaging nothing good,
And when they entered Troy again, a tomb 605
For them and theirs it seemed.—Long has it stood,
But now indeed the labour and the blood,
The love, the patience, and good-heart are vain—
The Greeks may have what yet is left to gain.

I cannot tell what crop may clothe the hills, 610
The merry hills Troy whitened long ago;
Belike the sheaves, wherewith the reaper fills
His yellow wain, no whit the weaker grow
For that past harvest-tide of wrong and woe;
Belike the tale, wept over otherwhere, 615
Of those old days is clean forgotten there.

1869.

ALGERNON CHARLES SWINBURNE

A SONG IN TIME OF ORDER. 1852

Push hard across the sand,
    For the salt wind gathers breath;
Shoulder and wrist and hand,
    Push hard as the push of death.

The wind is as iron that rings, 5
    The foam-heads loosen and flee;
It swells and welters and swings,
    The pulse of the tide of the sea.

And up on the yellow cliff
    The long corn flickers and shakes; 10
Push, for the wind holds stiff,
    And the gunwale dips and rakes.

Good hap to the fresh fierce weather,
   The quiver and beat of the sea!
While three men hold together   15
   The kingdoms are less by three.

Out to the sea with her there,
   Out with her over the sand;
Let the kings keep the earth for their share!
   We have done with the sharers of land.   20

They have tied the world in a tether,
   They have bought over God with a fee;
While three men hold together,
   The kingdoms are less by three.

We have done with the kisses that sting,   25
   The thief's mouth red from the feast,
The blood on the hands of the king,
   And the lie at the lips of the priest.

Will they tie the winds in a tether,
   Put a bit in the jaws of the sea?
While three men hold together,   30
   The kingdoms are less by three.

Let our flag run out straight in the wind!
   The old red shall be floated again
When the ranks that are thin shall be thinned, 35
   When the names that were twenty are ten;

When the devil's riddle is mastered
   And the galley-bench creaks with a Pope,
We shall see Buonaparte the bastard
   Kick heels with his throat in a rope.   40

While the shepherd sets wolves on his sheep
   And the emperor halters his kine,
While Shame is a watchman asleep
   And Faith is a keeper of swine.

Let the wind shake our flag like a feather,   45
   Like the plumes of the foam of the sea!
While three men hold together,
   The kingdoms are less by three.

All the world has its burdens to bear,
    From Cayenne to the Austrian whips;   50
Forth, with the rain in our hair
    And the salt sweet foam in our lips;

In the teeth of the hard glad weather,
    In the blown wet face of the sea!
While three men hold together,   - 55
    The kingdoms are less by three.

        1862.

WHEN THE HOUNDS OF SPRING ARE ON WINTER'S TRACES

When the hounds of Spring are on Winter's traces,
    The Mother of Months in meadow or plain
Fills the shadows and windy places
    With lisp of leaves and ripple of rain;
And the brown bright nightingale amorous   5
Is half assuaged for Itylus,
For the Thracian ships and the foreign faces,
    The tongueless vigil and all the pain.

Come with bows bent and with emptying of quivers,
    Maiden most perfect, Lady of Light,   10
With a noise of winds and many rivers,
    With a clamour of waters, and with might;
Bind on thy sandals, O thou most fleet,
Over the splendour and speed of thy feet;
For the faint east quickens, the wan west shivers,   15
    Round the feet of the Day and the feet of the Night.

Where shall we find her, how shall we sing to her,
    Fold our hands round her knees, and cling?
O that man's heart were as fire and could spring to her,
    Fire, or the strength of the streams that spring!   20
For the stars and the winds are unto her
As raiment, as songs of the harp-player;
For the risen stars and the fallen cling to her,
    And the southwest-wind and the west-wind sing.

For winter's rains and ruins are over,   25
    And all the season of snows and sins;

The days dividing lover and lover,
   The light that loses, the night that wins;
And time remembered is grief forgotten,
And frosts are slain and flowers begotten,   30
And in green underwood and cover
   Blossom by blossom the spring begins.

The full streams feed on flower of rushes,
   Ripe grasses trammel a travelling foot,
The faint fresh flame of the young year flushes   35
   From leaf to flower and flower to fruit;
And fruit and leaf are as gold and fire,
And the oat is heard above the lyre,
And the hoofèd heel of a satyr crushes
   The chestnut-husk at the chestnut-root.   40

And Pan by noon and Bacchus by night,
   Fleeter of foot than the fleet-foot kid,
Follows with dancing and fills with delight
   The maenad and the Bassarid;
And soft as lips that laugh and hide,   45
The laughing leaves of the trees divide,
And screen from seeing and leave in sight
   The god pursuing, the maiden hid.

The ivy falls with the Bacchanal's hair
   Over her eyebrows hiding her eyes;   50
The wild vine slipping down leaves bare
   Her bright breast shortening into sighs;
The wild vine slips with the weight of its leaves,
But the berried ivy catches and cleaves
To the limbs that glitter, the feet that scare   55
   The wolf that follows, the faun that flies.

                            1865.

RONDEL

Kissing her hair I sat against her feet,
Wove and unwove it, wound and found it sweet;
Made fast therewith her hands, drew down her eyes,
Deep as deep flowers and dreamy like dim skies;
With her own tresses bound and found her fair,   5
   Kissing her hair.

Sleep were no sweeter than her face to me,
Sleep of cold sea-bloom under the cold sea;
What pain could get between my face and hers?
What new sweet thing would love not relish worse? 10
Unless, perhaps, white death had kissed me there,
     Kissing her hair?

                      1866.

A LEAVE-TAKING

Let us go hence, my songs; she will not hear.
Let us go hence together without fear;
Keep silence now, for singing-time is over,
And over all old things and all things dear.
She loves not you nor me as all we love her. 5
Yea, though we sang as angels in her ear,
     She would not hear.

Let us rise up and part; she will not know.
Let us go seaward as the great winds go,
Full of blown sand and foam; what help is here? 10
There is no help for all these things are so,
And all the world is bitter as a tear.
And how these things are, though ye strove to show,
     She would not know.

Let us go home and hence; she will not weep. 15
We gave love many dreams and days to keep,
Flowers without scent, and fruits that would not grow,
Saying, "If thou wilt, thrust in thy sickle, and reap."
All is reaped now; no grass is left to mow:
And we that sowed, though all we fell on sleep, 20
     She would not weep.

Let us go hence and rest; she will not love.
She shall not hear us if we sing hereof,
Nor see love's ways, how sore they are and steep.
Come hence, let be, lie still; it is enough. 25
Love is a barren sea, bitter and deep;
And though she saw all heaven in flower above,
     She would not love.

Let us give up, go down; she will not care.
Though all the stars made gold of all the air,   30
And the sea moving saw before it move
One moon-flower making all the foam-flowers fair,
Though all those waves went over us, and drove
Deep down the stifling lips and drowning hair,—
    She would not care.   35

Let us go hence, go hence; she will not see.
Sing all once more together; surely she,
She too, remembering days and words that were,
Will turn a little toward us, sighing; but we,
We are hence, we are gone, as though we had not been
    there.   40
Nay, and though all men seeing had pity on me,
    She would not see.

                    1866.

THE GARDEN OF PROSERPINE

Here, where the world is quiet,
  Here, where all trouble seems
Dead winds' and spent waves' riot
  In doubtful dreams of dreams,
I watch the green field growing,   5
For reaping folk and sowing,
For harvest-time and mowing,
  A sleepy world of streams.

I am tired of tears and laughter,
  And men that laugh and weep,   10
Of what may come hereafter
  For men that sow to reap;
I am weary of days and hours,
Blown buds of barren flowers,
Desires and dreams and powers,   15
  And everything but sleep.

Here life has death for neighbour,
  And far from eye or ear
Wan waves and wet winds labour,
  Weak ships and spirits steer;   20

They drive adrift, and whither
They wot not who make thither;
But no such winds blow hither,
    And no such things grow here.

No growth of moor or coppice,   25
    No heather-flower or vine,
But bloomless buds of poppies,
    Green grapes of Proserpine,
Pale beds of blowing rushes
Where no leaf blooms or blushes   30
Save this whereout she crushes
    For dead men deadly wine.

Pale, without name or number,
    In fruitless fields of corn,
They bow themselves and slumber   35
    All night till light is born;
And like a soul belated,
In hell and heaven unmated,
By cloud and mist abated
    Comes out of darkness morn.   40

Though one were strong as seven,
    He too with death shall dwell,
Nor wake with wings in heaven,
    Nor weep for pains in hell;
Though one were fair as roses,   45
His beauty clouds and closes;
And well though love reposes,
    In the end it is not well.

Pale, beyond porch and portal,
    Crowned with calm leaves, she stands   50
Who gathers all things mortal
    With cold immortal hands;
Her languid lips are sweeter
Than Love's, who fears to greet her,
To men that mix and meet her   55
    From many times and lands.

She waits for each and other,
    She waits for all men born;

Forgets the earth her mother,
   The life of fruits and corn; 60
And spring and seed and swallow
Take wing for her and follow
Where summer song rings hollow
   And flowers are put to scorn.

There go the loves that wither, 65
   The old loves with wearier wings;
And all dead years draw thither,
   And all disastrous things;
Dead dreams of days forsaken,
Blind buds that snows have shaken, 70
Wild leaves that winds have taken,
   Red strays of ruined springs.

We are not sure of sorrow,
   And joy was never sure;
To-day will die to-morrow; 75
   Time stoops to no man's lure;
And Love, grown faint and fretful,
With lips but half regretful,
Sighs, and with eyes forgetful
   Weeps that no loves endure. 80

From too much love of living,
   From hope and fear set free,
We thank with brief thanksgiving
   Whatever gods may be
That no life lives forever, 85
That dead men rise up never,
That even the weariest river
   Winds somewhere safe to sea.

Then star nor sun shall waken,
   Nor any change of light; 90
Nor sound of waters shaken,
   Nor any sound or sight;
Nor wintry leaves nor vernal,
Nor days nor things diurnal;
Only the sleep eternal 95
   In an eternal night.

1866.

HERTHA

I am that which began;
 Out of me the years roll;
Out of me God and man;
 I am equal and whole;
God changes, and man, and the form of them bodily; I am
  the soul. 5

Before ever land was,
 Before ever the sea,
Or soft hair of the grass,
 Or fair limbs of the tree,
Or the flesh-coloured fruit of my branches, I was, and thy
  soul was in me. 10

First life on my sources
 First drifted and swam;
Out of me are the forces
 That save it or damn;
Out of me man and woman, and wild-beast and bird; before
  God was, I am. 15

Beside or above me
 Naught is there to go;
Love or unlove me,
 Unknow me or know,
I am that which unloves me and loves; I am stricken, and I
  am the blow. 20

.I the mark that is missed
 And the arrows that miss,
I the mouth that is kissed
 And the breath in the kiss,
The search, and the sought, and the seeker, the soul and the
  body that is. 25

I am that thing which blesses
 My spirit elate;
That which caresses
 With hands uncreate
My limbs unbegotten that measure the length of the measure
  of fate. 30

But what thing dost thou now,
　　Looking Godward, to cry
"I am I, thou art thou,
　　I am low, thou art high"?
I am thou, whom thou seekest to find him; find thou but thy-
　　　　self, thou art I.　　　　　　　　　　　　　　35

I the grain and the furrow,
　　The plough-cloven clod,
And the ploughshare drawn thorough,
　　The germ and the sod,
The deed and the doer, the seed and the sower, the dust which
　　　　is God.　　　　　　　　　　　　　　　　　40

Hast thou known how I fashioned thee,
　　Child, underground?
Fire that impassioned thee,
　　Iron that bound,
Dim changes of water, what thing of all these hast thou
　　　　known of or found?　　　　　　　　　　　　45

Canst thou say in thine heart
　　Thou hast seen with thine eyes
With what cunning of art
　　Thou wast wrought in what wise,
By what force of what stuff thou wast shapen, and shown on
　　　　my breast to the skies?　　　　　　　　　　　50

Who hath given, who hath sold it thee,
　　Knowledge of me?
Hath the wilderness told it thee?
　　Hast thou learnt of the sea?
Hast thou communed in spirit with night? have the winds
　　　　taken counsel with thee?　　　　　　　　　　55

Have I set such a star
　　To show light on thy brow
That thou sawest from afar
　　What I show to thee now?
Have ye spoken as brethren together, the sun and the
　　　　mountains and thou?　　　　　　　　　　　　60

What is here, dost thou know it?
   What was, hast thou known?
Prophet nor poet
   Nor tripod nor throne
Nor spirit nor flesh can make answer, but only thy Mother
      alone.   65

Mother, not maker,
   Born, and not made;
Though her children forsake her,
   Allured or afraid,
Praying prayers to the God of their fashion, she stirs not for
      all that have prayed.   70

A creed is a rod,
   And a crown is of night;
But this thing is God—
   To be man with thy might,
To grow straight in the strength of thy spirit, and live out
      thy life as the light.   75

I am in thee to save thee,
   As my soul in thee saith;
Give thou, as I gave thee,
   Thy life-blood and breath,
Green leaves of thy labour, white flowers of thy thought,
      and red fruit of thy death.   80

Be the ways of thy giving
   As mine were to thee;
The free life of thy living,
   Be the gift of it free;
Not as servant to lord, nor as master to slave, shalt thou
      give thee to me.   85

O children of banishment,
   Souls overcast,
Were the lights ye see vanish meant
   Alway to last,
Ye would know not the sun overshining the shadows and stars
      overpast.   90

I, that saw where ye trod
 The dim paths of the night,
Set the shadow called God
 In your skies to give light;
But the morning of manhood is risen, and the shadowless
   soul is in sight.   95

The tree many-rooted
 That swells to the sky
With frondage red-fruited,
 The life-tree am I;
In the buds of your lives is the sap of my leaves: ye shall
   live and not die.   100

But the gods of your fashion
 That take and that give,
In their pity and passion
 That scourge and forgive,
They are worms that are bred in the bark that falls off; they
   shall die and not live.   105

My own blood is what stanches
 The wounds in my bark;
Stars caught in my branches
 Make day of the dark,
And are worshipped as suns till the sunrise shall tread out
   their fires as a spark.   110

Where dead ages hide under
 The live roots of the tree,
In my darkness the thunder
 Makes utterance of me;
In the clash of my boughs with each other ye hear the waves
   sound of the sea.   115

That noise is of Time
 As his feathers are spread
And his feet set to climb
 Through the boughs overhead,
And my foliage rings round him and rustles, and branches
   are bent with his tread.   120

The storm-winds of ages
　　Blow through me and cease,
The war-wind that rages,
　　The spring-wind of peace,
Ere the breath of them roughen my tresses, ere one of my
　　　　blossoms increase.   125

All sounds of all changes,
　　All shadows and lights
On the world's mountain-ranges
　　And stream-riven heights,
Whose tongue is the wind's tongue and language of storm-
　　　　clouds on earth-shaking nights;   130

All forms of all faces,
　　All works of all hands
In unsearchable places
　　Of time-stricken lands,
All death and all life, and all reigns and all ruins, drop
　　　　through me as sands.   135

Though sore be my burden
　　And more than ye know,
And my growth have no guerdon
　　But only to grow,
Yet I fail not of growing for lightnings above me or death-
　　　　worms below.   140

These too have their part in me,
　　As I too in these;
Such fire is at heart in me,
　　Such sap ·is this tree's,
Which hath in it all sounds and all secrets of infinite lands
　　　　and of seas.   145

In the spring-coloured hours
　　When my mind was as May's,
There brake forth of me flowers
　　By centuries of days,
Strong blossoms with perfume of manhood shot out from
　　　　my spirit as rays.   150

And the sound of them springing
    And smell of their shoots
Were as warmth and sweet singing
    And strength to my roots;
And the lives of my children made perfect with freedom of
            soul were my fruits.   155

    I bid you but be;
        I have need not of prayer;
    I have need of you free
        As your mouths of mine air,
That my heart may be greater within me, beholding the fruits
            of me fair.   160

    More fair than strange fruit is
        Of faiths ye espouse;
    In me only the root is
        That blooms in your boughs;
Behold now your God that ye made you, to feed him with
            faith of your vows.   165

    In the darkening and whitening
        Abysses adored,
    With dayspring and lightning
        For lamp and for sword,
God thunders in heaven, and his angels are red with the wrath
            of the Lord.   170

    O my sons, O too dutiful
        Toward gods not of me,
    Was not I enough beautiful?
        Was it hard to be free?
For behold, I am with you, am in you and of you; look forth
            now and see.   175

    Lo, winged with world's wonders,
        With miracles shod,
    With the fires of his thunders
        For raiment and rod,
God trembles in heaven, and his angels are white with the
            terror of God.   180

For his twilight is come on him,
    His anguish is here;
And his spirits gaze dumb on him,
    Grown grey from his fear;
And his hour taketh hold on him stricken, the last of his
            infinite year.   185

Thought made him and breaks him,
    Truth slays and forgives;
But to you, as time takes him,
    This new thing it gives,
Even love, the belovèd Republic, that feeds upon freedom and
            lives.   190

For truth only is living,
    Truth only is whole,
And the love of his giving
    Man's polestar and pole;
Man, pulse of my center, and fruit of my body, and seed of
            my soul.   195

One birth of my bosom;
    One beam of mine eye;
One topmost blossom
    That scales the sky;
Man, equal and one with me, man that is made of me, man
            that is I.   200

                    1871.

THE PILGRIMS

Who is your lady of love, O ye that pass
Singing? and is it for sorrow of that which was
    That ye sing sadly, or dream of what shall be?
        For gladly at once and sadly it seems ye sing.
—Our lady of love by you is unbeholden;   5
For hands she hath none, nor eyes, nor lips, nor golden
    Treasure of hair, nor face nor form; but we
        That love, we know her more fair than anything.

—Is she a queen, having great gifts to give?
—Yea, these: that whoso hath seen her shall not live   10

Except he serve her sorrowing, with strange pain,
    Travail and bloodshedding and bitterer tears;
And when she bids die he shall surely die.
And he shall leave all things under the sky
    And go forth naked under sun and rain   15
        And work and wait and watch out all his years.

—Hath she on earth no place of habitation?
—Age to age calling, nation answering nation,
    Cries out, Where is she? and there is none to say;
        For if she be not in the spirit of men,   20
For if in the inward soul she hath no place,
In vain they cry unto her, seeking her face,
    In vain their mouths make much of her; for they
        Cry with vain tongues, till the heart lives again.

—O ye that follow, and have ye no repentance?   25
For on your brows is written a mortal sentence,
    An hieroglyph of sorrow, a fiery sign,
        That in your lives ye shall not pause or rest,
Nor have the sure sweet common love, nor keep
Friends and safe days, nor joy of life nor sleep.   30
    —These have we not, who have one thing, the divine
    Face and clear eyes of faith and fruitful breast.

—And ye shall die before your thrones be won.
—Yea, and the changed world and the liberal sun
    Shall move and shine without us, and we lie   35
        Dead; but if she too move on earth and live,
But if the old world with all the old irons rent
Laugh and give thanks, shall we be not content?
    Nay, we shall rather live, we shall not die,
        Life being so little and death so good to give.   40

—And these men shall forget you.—Yea, but we
Shall be a part of the earth and the ancient sea,
    And heaven-high air august, and awful fire,
        And all things good; and no man's heart shall beat
But somewhat in it of our blood once shed   45
Shall quiver and quicken, as now in us the dead
    Blood of men slain and the old same life's desire
        Plants in their fiery footprints our fresh feet.

—But ye that might be clothed with all things pleasant,
Ye are foolish that put off the fair soft present,   50
   That clothe yourselves with the cold future air;
      When mother and father and tender sister and brother
And the old live love that was shall be as ye,
Dust, and no fruit of loving life shall be.
   —She shall be yet who is more than all these were,   55
      Than sister or wife or father unto us or mother.

—Is this worth life, is this, to win for wages?
Lo, the dead mouths of the awful grey-grown ages,
   The venerable, in the past that is their prison,
      In the outer darkness, in the unopening grave,   60
Laugh, knowing how many as ye now say have said,
How many, and all are fallen, are fallen and dead:
   Shall ye dead rise, and these dead have not risen?
      —Not we but she, who is tender and swift to save.

—Are ye not weary and faint not by the way,   65
Seeing night by night devoured of day by day,
   Seeing hour by hour consumed in sleepless fire?
      Sleepless: and ye too when shall ye too sleep?
—We are weary in heart and head, in hands and feet,
And surely more than all things sleep were sweet,   70
   Than all things save the inexorable desire
      Which whoso knoweth shall neither faint nor weep.

—Is this so sweet that one were fain to follow?
Is this so sure where all men's hopes are hollow,
   Even this your dream, that by much tribulation   75
      Ye shall make whole flawed hearts, and bowed necks
         straight?
—Nay, though our life were blind, our death were fruitless,
Not therefore were the whole world's high hope rootless;
   But man to man, nation would turn to nation,
      And the old life live, and the old great word be great. 80

—Pass on then and pass by us and let us be,
For what light think ye after life to see?
   And if the world fare better will ye know?
      And if man triumph who shall seek you and say?

—Enough of light is this for one life's span,   85
  That all men born are mortal, but not man;
    And we men bring death lives by night to sow,
      That man may reap and eat and live by day.

                    1871.

A FORSAKEN GARDEN

In a coign of the cliff between lowland and highland,
  At the sea-down's edge between windward and lee,
Walled round with rocks as an inland island,
  The ghost of a garden fronts the sea.
A girdle of brushwood and thorn encloses   5
  The steep square slope of the blossomless bed
Where the weeds that grew green from the graves of its roses
    Now lie dead.

The fields fall southward, abrupt and broken,
  To the low last edge of the long lone land.   10
If a step should sound or a word be spoken,
  Would a ghost not rise at the strange guest's hand?
So long have the grey bare walks lain guestless,
  Through branches and briers if a man make way,
He shall find no life but the sea-wind's, restless   15
    Night and day.

The dense hard passage is blind and stifled
  That crawls by a track none turn to climb
To the strait waste place that the years have rifled
  Of all but the thorns that are touched not of Time.   20
The thorns he spares when the rose is taken;
  The rocks are left when he wastes the plain.
The wind that wanders, the weeds wind-shaken,
    These remain.

Not a flower to be pressed of the foot that falls not;   25
  As the heart of a dead man the seed-plots are dry;
From the thicket of thorns whence the nightingale calls not,
  Could she call, there were never a rose to reply.
Over the meadows that blossom and wither
  Rings but the note of a sea-bird's song;   30
Only the sun and the rain come hither
    All year long.

The sun burns sere and the rain dishevels
　One gaunt bleak blossom of scentless breath.
Only the wind here hovers and revels　　　　　　　　　35
　In a round where life seems barren as death.
Here there was laughing of old, there was weeping,
　Haply, of lovers none ever will know,
Whose eyes went seaward a hundred sleeping
　　　Years ago.　　　　　　　　　　　　　　40

Heart handfast in heart as they stood, "Look thither,"
　Did he whisper? "Look forth from the flowers to the sea;
For the foam-flowers endure when the rose-blossoms wither,
　And men that love lightly may die—but we?"
And the same wind sang and the same waves whitened,　45
　And or ever the garden's last petals were shed,
In the lips that had whispered, the eyes that had lightened,
　　　Love was dead.

Or they loved their life through, and then went whither?
　And were one to the end—but what end who knows?　50
Love deep as the sea as a rose must wither,
　As the rose-red seaweed that mocks the rose.
Shall the dead take thought for the dead to love them?
　What love was ever as deep as a grave?
They are loveless now as the grass above them　　　55
　　　Or the wave.

All are at one now, roses and lovers,
　Not known of the cliffs and the fields and the sea.
Not a breath of the time that has been hovers
　In the air now soft with a summer to be.　　　　60
Not a breath shall there sweeten the seasons hereafter
　Of the flowers or the lovers that laugh now or weep,
When as they that are free now of weeping and laughter
　　　We shall sleep.

Here death may deal not again forever;　　　　　　65
　Here change may come not till all change end.
From the graves they have made they shall rise up never,
　Who have left naught living to ravage and rend.
Earth, stones, and thorns of the wild ground growing,
　While the sun and the rain live, these shall be;　　70
Till a last wind's breath, upon all these blowing,
　　　Roll the sea.

Till the slow sea rise and the sheer cliff crumble,
　　Till terrace and meadow the deep gulfs drink,
Till the strength of the waves of the high tides humble   75
　　The fields that lessen, the rocks that shrink,
. Here now in his triumph where all things falter,
　　Stretched out on the spoils that his own hand spread,
As a god self-slain on his own strange altar,
　　　　Death lies dead.   80

　　　　　　　　　　　　　　　1876.

THE SALT OF THE EARTH

　If childhood were not in the world,
　　　But only men and women grown;
　No baby-locks in tendrils curled,
　　　No baby-blossoms blown;

　Though men were stronger, women fairer,   5
　　　And nearer all delights in reach,
　And verse and music uttered rarer
　　　Tones of more godlike speech;

　Though the utmost life of life's best hours
　　　Found, as it cannot now find, words;   10
　Though desert sands were sweet as flowers
　　　And flowers could sing like birds,

　But children never heard them, never
　　　They felt a child's foot leap and run,—
　This were a drearier star than ever   15
　　　Yet looked upon the sun.

　　　　　　　　　　　　　　　1882.

HOPE AND FEAR

Beneath the shadow of dawn's aerial cope,
　　With eyes enkindled as the sun's own sphere,
　　Hope from the front of youth in godlike cheer
Looks Godward, past the shades where blind men grope
Round the dark door that prayers nor dreams can ope,   5
　　And makes for joy the very darkness dear
　　That gives her wide wings play; nor dreams that Fear

At noon may rise and pierce the heart of Hope.
Then, when the soul leaves off to dream and yearn,
May Truth first purge her eyesight to discern 10
What once being known leaves time no power to appal;
Till youth at last, ere yet youth be not, learn
The kind wise word that falls from years that fall—
"Hope thou not much, and fear thou not at all."

1882.

BEN JONSON

Broad-based, broad-fronted, bounteous, multiform,
With many a valley impleached with ivy and vine,
Wherein the springs of all the streams run wine,
And many a crag full-faced against the storm,
The mountain where thy Muse's feet made warm 5
Those lawns that revelled with her dance divine,
Shines yet with fire as it was wont to shine
From tossing torches round the dance a-swarm.

Nor less, high-stationed on the grey grave heights,
High-thoughted seers with heaven's heart-kindling lights 10
Hold converse; and the herd of meaner things
Knows, or by fiery scourge or fiery shaft,
When wrath on thy broad brows has risen, and laughed,
Darkening thy soul with shadow of thunderous wings.

1882.

THE SUNBOWS

Spray of song that springs in April, light of love that laughs
through May,
Live and die and live forever: naught of all things far less fair
Keeps a surer life than these that seem to pass like fire away.
In the souls they live which are but all the brighter that they were;
In the hearts that kindle, thinking what delight of old was there. 5
Wind that shapes and lifts and shifts them bids perpetual memory
play
Over dreams and in and out of deeds and thoughts which seem to
wear
Light that leaps and runs and revels through the springing flames
of spray.

Dawn is wild upon the waters where we drink of dawn to-day:
Wide, from wave to wave rekindling in rebound through radiant
    air,   10
Flash the fires unwoven and woven again of wind that works in
    play,
Working wonders more than heart may note or sight may wellnigh
    dare,
Wefts of rarer light than colours rain from heaven, though this
    be rare.
Arch on arch unbuilt in building, reared and ruined ray by ray,
Breaks and brightens, laughs and lessens, even till eyes may hardly
    bear   15
Light that leaps and runs and revels through the springing flames
    of spray.

Year on year sheds light and music, rolled and flashed from bay
    to bay
Round the summer capes of Time and winter headlands keen and
    bare,
Whence the soul keeps watch, and bids her vassal memory watch
    and pray,
If perchance the dawn may quicken, or perchance the midnight
    spare.   20
Silence quells not music, darkness takes not sunlight in her snare;
Shall not joys endure that perish? Yea, saith dawn, though night
    say nay:
Life on life goes out, but very life enkindles everywhere
Light that leaps and runs and revels through the springing flames
    of spray.

Friend, were life no more than this is, well would yet the living
    fare.   25
All aflower and all afire and all flung heavenward, who shall say
Such a flash of life were worthless? This is worth a world of
    care—
Light that leaps and runs and revels through the springing flames
    of spray.

                1884.

ROBERT BROWNING

He held no dream worth waking: so he said,
 He who stands now on death's triumphal steep,
 Awakened out of life wherein we sleep
And dream of what he knows and sees, being dead.
But never death for him was dark or dread: 5
 "Look forth" he bade the soul, and fear not. Weep,
 All ye that trust not in his truth, and keep
Vain memory's vision of a vanished head
As all that lives of all that once was he
Save that which lightens from his word; but we 10
 Who, seeing the sunset-coloured waters roll,
Yet know the sun subdued not of the sea,
 Nor weep nor doubt that still the spirit is whole,
 And life and death but shadows of the soul.

1889.   *1890.*

NOTES

NOTES

WILLIAM LISLE BOWLES

(1) "A poet by whose works, year after year, I was so enthusiastically delighted and inspired. . . . . My obligations to Mr. Bowles were indeed important and for radical good. At a very premature age, even before my fifteenth year, I had bewildered myself in metaphysics and in theological controversy. . . . . From this I was auspiciously withdrawn, ... chiefly . . . . by the genial influence of a style of poetry so tender and yet so manly, so natural and real and yet so dignified and harmonious, as the sonnets, etc., of Mr. Bowles." —Coleridge, *Biographia Literaria* (1817), chap. i.

SAMUEL ROGERS

(2) THE PLEASURES OF MEMORY. Part I. 1-20, 69-96. Cf. Akenside's "Pleasures of Imagination" (1744), with regard to subject and title; with regard to style, cf. Goldsmith's "Deserted Village" (1770).

WILLIAM WORDSWORTH

In the preface to the second edition of *Lyrical Ballads*, in 1800, Wordsworth wrote thus of poetry and of his purpose and method in the poems:

"The principal object, then, proposed in these poems was to choose incidents and situations from common life, and to relate or describe them throughout, as far as was possible, in a selection of language really used by men, and, at the same time, to throw over them a certain coloring of imagination, whereby ordinary things should be presented to the mind in an unusual aspect; and further, and above all, to make these incidents and situations interesting by tracing in them, truly though not ostentatiously, the primary laws of our nature: chiefly, as far as regards the manner in which we associate ideas in a state of excitement. Humble and rustic life was generally chosen, because in that condition the essential passions of the heart find a better soil in which they can attain their maturity, are less under restraint, and speak a plainer and more emphatic language. . . . . . The language, too, of these men has been adopted (purified indeed from what appear to be its real defects, from all lasting and rational causes of dislike or disgust), because such men hourly communicate with the best objects from which the best part of language is originally derived; and because, from their rank in society, and the sameness and narrow circle of their intercourse, being less under the influence of social vanity, they convey their feelings and notions in simple and unelaborated expressions. . . . . The reader will find that personifications of abstract ideas rarely occur in these volumes, and are utterly rejected as an ordinary device to elevate the style and raise it above prose. My purpose was to imitate, and, as far as possible, to adopt, the very language of men; and assuredly such personifications do not make any natural or regular part of that language. They are indeed a figure of speech occasionally prompted by passion, and I have made use of them as such; but have endeavored utterly to reject them as a mechanical device of style, or as a family language which writers in metre seem to lay claim to by prescription. . . . . There will also be found in these volumes little of what is usually called poetic diction; as much pains has been taken to avoid it as it is ordinarily taken to produce it; this has been done for the reason already alleged, to bring my language nearer to the language of men; and further, because the pleasure which I have proposed to myself to impart is of a kind very different from that which is supposed by many persons to be the proper object of poetry. Without being culpably particular, I do not know how to give my reader a more exact notion of the style in which it was my wish and intention to write than by informing him that I have at all times endeavored to look steadily at my subject; consequently there is, I hope, in these poems little falsehood of description, and my ideas are expressed in language fitted to their respective importance. . . . . If in a poem there should be found a series of lines, or even a single line, in which the language, though naturally arranged, and according to the strict laws of metre, does not differ from that of prose, there is a numerous class of critics who, when they stumble upon these prosaisms, as they call them, imagine that they have made a notable discovery, and exult over the poet as over a man ignorant of his own profession. Now, these men would establish a canon of criticism which the reader will conclude he must utterly reject if he wishes to be pleased with these volumes. And it would be a most easy task to prove to him that not only the language of a large portion of every good poem, even of the most elevated character, must necessarily, except with reference to the metre, in no respect differ from that of good prose, but likewise that some of the most interesting parts of the best poems will be found to be strictly the language of prose when prose is well written. . . . . We will go further. It may be safely affirmed that there neither is, nor can be, any *essential* difference between the language of prose and metrical composition. . . . .

"The knowledge both of the poet and the man of science is pleasure; but the knowledge of the one cleaves to us as a necessary part of our existence, our natural and unalienable inheritance; the other is a personal and individual acquisition, slow to come to us, and by no habitual and direct sympathy connecting us with our fellow-beings. The man of science seeks truth as a remote and unknown benefactor; he cherishes and loves it in his solitude. The poet, singing a song in which all human beings join with him, rejoices in the presence of truth as our visible friend and hourly companion. Poetry is the breath and finer spirit of all knowledge; it is the impassioned expression which is in the countenance of all science."

Notes signed "W." are by Wordsworth, being chiefly those that he dictated in 1834 to Miss Isabella Fenwick.

(3) An Evening Walk. Lines 323-44, 365-78. The text of the first edition is given, the better to illustrate Wordsworth's early manner in nature poetry. "There is not an image in it which I have not observed. . . . . The plan of it has not been confined to a particular walk or an individual place. . . . . The country is idealized rather than described in any one of its local aspects."—W.

(4) 28. *aerial:* in 1832, "spiritual." ¶ 35. In 1836, "The sportive outcry of the mocking owl."

(4) Simon Lee. "This old man had been huntsman to the squires of Alfoxden. . . . . The fact was as mentioned in the poem. . . . . The expression when the hounds were out, 'I dearly love their voice,' was word for word from his own lips."—W. In the first edition the style was even more bald and prosaic in places, as in the following lines:

> Of years he has upon his back,
> No doubt, a burden weighty;
> He says he is three score and ten,
> But others say he 's eighty.
> A long blue livery-coat has he,
> That 's fair behind, and fair before. . . . .
> His hunting feats have him bereft
> Of his right eye, as you may see.

(8) Expostulation and Reply. "The lines entitled 'Expostulation and Reply,' and those which follow, arose out of conversation with a friend who was somewhat unreasonably attached to modern books of moral philosophy."—W., in the preface to *Lyrical Ballads*, first edition. ¶ 30. *conversing*=communing; in this case, with the "mighty sum of things."

(10) Lines Composed a Few Miles above Tintern Abbey. "No poem of mine was composed under circumstances more pleasant for me to remember than this. I began

it upon leaving Tintern, after crossing the Wye, and concluded it just as I was entering Bristol in the evening, after a ramble of four or five days, with my sister. Not a line of it was altered, and not any part of it written down till I reached Bristol."—W. ¶ 29. *purer mind:* the comparison is not between two states of mind, but between mind, as pure spirit, and the body ("blood") and the emotions ("heart").

(11) 54. *hung upon*=weighed upon, oppressed. ¶ 67–72. Cf. "To the Daisy":

> In youth from rock to rock I went,
> From hill to hill in discontent
> Of pleasure high and turbulent,
> Most pleased when most uneasy.

(12) 85–111. Cf. "Ode: Intimations of Immortality," 175–203; "The Prelude," VIII. 340–56.

(13) 125. *inform*=give form to, mold, animate. ¶ 149. *past existence:* his own life in earlier years, when his love of nature was like hers now.

(14) THE SIMPLON PASS. Wordsworth crossed the Alps on foot in 1790. The lines are a part of "The Prelude" (VI. 621 ff.), but were first published separately.

(15) INFLUENCE OF NATURAL OBJECTS. The lines are a part of "The Prelude" (I. 401 ff.), but were first published separately.

(17) LUCY GRAY. "Founded on a circumstance told me by my sister. . . . . The way in which the incident was treated and the spiritualizing of the character might furnish hints for contrasting the imaginative influences which I have endeavored to throw over common life with Crabbe's matter-of-fact style of treating subjects of the same kind."—W.

(19) THE RECLUSE. Lines 754–835. The passage is taken from the unfinished part of a long poem, to be called "The Recluse," of which "The Prelude" and "The Excursion" were to have been parts; see the preface to "The Excursion." ¶ 24. *the bard:* Milton, in *Paradise Lost*, VII. 30, 31:

> Still govern thou my song,
> Urania, and fit audience find, though few.

(21) MICHAEL. "The character and circumstances of Luke were taken from a family to whom had belonged, many years before, the house we lived in at Townend. . . . . The name of the Evening Star was not in fact given to this house, but to another on the same side of the valley."—W. In a letter (1801) to his friend Thomas Poole, Wordsworth wrote thus of the poem: "I have attempted to give a picture of a man, of strong mind and lively sensibility, agitated by two of the most powerful affections of the human heart: the parental affection, and the love of property (*landed* property), including the feelings of inheritance, home, and personal and family independence. . . . . In writing it I had your character often before my eyes; and sometimes thought that I was delineating such a man as you yourself would have been under the same circumstances" (Knight's *Life of Wordsworth*, I. 215). In a letter (1801) to Charles James Fox, the statesman, Wordsworth said: "In the two poems, 'The Brothers' and 'Michael,' I have attempted to draw a picture of the domestic affections as I know they exist amongst a class of men who are now almost confined to the North of England. They are small, independent proprietors of land, here called Statesmen, men of respectable education, who daily labor in their own little properties. . . . . Their little tract of land serves as a kind of rallying point for their domestic feelings. . . . . The two poems which I have mentioned were written with a view to show that men who do not wear fine clothes can feel deeply. . . . . The poems are faithful copies from nature" (*ibid.*, II. 4). ¶ 2. *Ghyll:* "Ghyll, in the dialect of Cumberland and Westmoreland, is a short, and, for the most part, a steep narrow valley, with a stream running through it."—W., in a note to "The Idle Shepherd Boys."

(22) 24–26. Cf. "The Prelude," VIII. 345 ff. Wordsworth attributed his serene optimism and his insight into the nobility of human nature partly to the fact that the first

men in whom he became interested were of this superior shepherd class; see "The Prelude," VIII. 293 ff.

(23) 62–77. Wordsworth's view of the character of the shepherd's love of nature is made still clearer by lines about Michael preserved in Dorothy Wordsworth's journal and printed in Knight's *Life of Wordsworth* (I. 388):

> No doubt if you in terms direct had asked
> Whether he loved the mountains, true it is
> That with blunt repetition of your words
> He might have stared at you, and said that they
> Were frightful to behold, but had you then
> Discoursed with him . . . .
> Of his own business, and the goings on
> Of earth and sky, then truly had you seen
> That in his thoughts there were obscurities,
> Wonder and admiration, things that wrought
> Not less than a religion in his heart.

(27) 258. *Richard Bateman:* "The story alluded to is well known in the country."—W.

(32) 448. Cf. l. 416.

(35) LONDON, 1802. ¶ 4. *hall and bower:* the great room, and the private apartments (especially the women's), in a castle or mansion.

(37) THE SOLITARY REAPER. Dorothy Wordsworth wrote, under date of September 13, 1803, in her *Recollections of a Tour Made in Scotland*, that the poem was suggested by this sentence in Thomas Wilkinson's *Tour in Scotland:* "Passed a female who was reaping alone; she sung in Erse, as she bended over her sickle; the sweetest human voice I ever heard: her strains were tenderly melancholy, and felt delicious, long after they were heard no more." Wordsworth, in a note to the poem, in 1807, added that the last line of the poem was taken *verbatim* from the prose work.

(38) TO THE MEN OF KENT. England had declared war against France in May, 1803; and at the time of the writing of the sonnet, in October, Napoleon seemed to be planning to invade England. "The 'Men of Kent' is a technical expression applied to the inhabitants of that part of Kent who were never subdued in the Norman invasion, and who obtained glorious terms for themselves, on capitulation, receiving the confirmation of their own charters."—F. W. Robertson, *Lectures and Addresses* (1861). ¶ 2. *advance:* probably a reference to the fact that Kent projects out toward France, but, as Dowden suggests, the word may be used in the Shaksperean sense of "lift up," with a reference to the chalk cliffs along the coast; cf. "haughty." ¶ 13. Wordsworth's change of view about the French Revolution, and some of the steps of the process, appear in the following passages from "The Prelude" (XI. 105–12; X. 263–65, 283–88; XI. 205–14, 350–60):

> O pleasant exercise of hope and joy!
> For mighty were the auxiliars which then stood
> Upon our side, us who were strong in love.
> Bliss was it in that dawn to be alive,
> But to be young was very heaven! O times
> In which the meagre, stale, forbidding ways
> Of custom, law, and statute took at once
> The attraction of a country in romance!
> . . . .
> What, then, were my emotions, when in arms
> Britain put forth her freeborn strength in league,
> Oh, pity and shame! with those confederate Powers!
> . . . . I rejoiced,
> Yea, afterwards—truth most painful to record—
> Exulted, in the triumph of my soul,
> When Englishmen by thousands were o'erthrown,
> Left without glory on the field, or driven
> Brave hearts! to shameful flight.
> . . . . ¶ .

> But now, become oppressors in their turn,
> Frenchmen had changed a war of self-defence
> For one of conquest, losing sight of all
> Which they had struggled for: up mounted now,
> Openly in the eye of Earth and Heaven,
> The scale of Liberty. I read her doom,
> With anger vexed, with disappointment sore,
> But not dismayed, nor taking to the shame
> Of a false prophet.
> . . . .
>   Nature's self,
> By all varieties of human love
> Assisted, led me back through opening day
> To those sweet counsels between head and heart
> Whence grew that genuine knowledge, fraught with peace,
> Which, through the later sinkings of this cause,
> Hath still upheld me, and upholds me now
> In the catastrophe (for so they dream,
> And nothing less) when finally to close
> And seal up all the gains of France, a Pope
> Is summoned in to crown an Emperor.

Cf. Coleridge's "France: an Ode."

(38) SHE WAS A PHANTOM OF DELIGHT. "The germ of this poem was four lines, composed as a part of the verses on the Highland Girl. Though beginning in this way, it was written from my heart, as is sufficiently obvious."—W. Cf. another reference to his wife in "The Prelude," XIV. 268 ff.:

> She came, no more a phantom to adorn
> A moment, but an inmate of the heart,
> And yet a spirit, there for me enshrined
> To penetrate the lofty and the low.

(39) 22. *machine:* perhaps used for "body," as in *Hamlet*, II. ii. 124; "I rather think the whole woman with all her household routine is conceived as the organism of which the thoughtful soul is the animating principle."—Dowden.

(39) I WANDERED LONELY AS A CLOUD.

(40) 21, 22. Written by Mrs. Wordsworth.

(40) ODE TO DUTY. "This ode is on the model of Gray's 'Ode to Adversity.'"—W. ¶ 7. *vain temptations*=empty temptations, i. e., temptations to things which do not satisfy.

(41) 37. *unchartered*=unlimited, in contrast to rights and privileges under a charter, which are limited to those specified. ¶ 38. Cf. "Nuns Fret not at Their Convent's Narrow Room," l. 13. ¶ 45–48. Wordsworth here seems to unify moral law and physical law, or at least to assume a close analogy between the two, as alike manifestations of the divine order and beauty, the basis of the welfare of all things whether material or spiritual. This view was the easier for him because of his belief that God was "deeply interfused" in nature.

(41) ELEGIAC STANZAS. In memory of the poet's brother, Captain John Wordsworth, who went down with his ship in 1805.

(42) 18. *this:* the world of the picture.

(43) 54. *the kind*=its kind; here, the human race.

(44) PERSONAL TALK. The last two of a series of four sonnets.

(45) ODE: INTIMATIONS OF IMMORTALITY. "Two years at least passed between the writing of the four first stanzas [ll. 1–57] and the remaining part. . . . . Nothing was more difficult for me in childhood than to admit the notion of death as a state applicable to my own being. . . . . But it was not so much from feelings of animal vivacity that my difficulty came as from a sense of the indomitableness of the spirit within me. . . . . I was often unable to think of external things as having external existence, and I communed with all that I saw as something not apart from, but inherent in, my own immaterial nature. Many times while going to school have I grasped at a wall or tree to recall myself from this abyss

of idealism to the reality. At that time I was afraid of such processes. In later periods of life I have deplored, as we all have reason to do, a subjugation of an opposite character, and have rejoiced over the remembrances, as is expressed in the lines,

> Obstinate questionings
> Of sense and outward things,
> Fallings from us, vanishings, etc.

To that dream-like vividness and splendor which invest objects of sight in childhood, every one, I believe, if he would look back, could bear testimony, and I need not dwell upon it here; but having in the poem regarded it as presumptive evidence of a prior state of existence, I think it right to protest against a conclusion, which has given pain to some good and pious persons, that I meant to inculcate such a belief. It is far too shadowy a notion to be recommended to faith as more than an element in our instincts of immortality. But let us bear in mind that, though the idea is not advanced in revelation, there is nothing there to contradict it, and the fall of man presents an analogy in its favor. Accordingly, a pre-existent state has entered into the popular creeds of many nations, and, among all persons acquainted with classic literature, is known as an ingredient in Platonic philosophy."—W. Cf. Plato's *Phaedo*, from which the following passage is taken: "And if we acquired this knowledge before we were born and were born having it, then we also knew before we were born, and at the instant of birth, not only the equal or the greater or the less, but all other ideas; for we are not speaking only of equality absolute, but of beauty, good, justice, holiness, and all which we stamp with the name of essence. . . . . But if the knowledge which we acquired before birth was lost by us at birth, and if afterward by the use of the senses we recovered that which we previously knew, will not that which we call learning be a process of recovering our knowledge, and may not this be rightly termed recollection by us?"—Jowett's translation.

(46) 28. *fields of sleep:* "the yet reposeful, slumbering country-side; it is early morning, and the land is still, as it were, resting."—J. W. Hales, *Longer English Poems* (1872). ¶ 58–70. Cf. the following lines from Henry Vaughan's "Retreat" (1650):

> Happy those early days, when I
> Shined in my angel infancy!
> Before I understood this place
> Appointed for my second race,
> Or taught my soul to fancy aught
> But a white, celestial thought;
> When yet I had not walked above
> A mile or two from my first love,
> And looking back—at that short space—
> Could see a glimpse of His bright face;
> When on some gilded cloud or flower
> My gazing soul would dwell an hour,
> And in those weaker glories spy
> Some shadows of eternity.

(47) 72. *Nature's priest:* the emphasis is not upon a priest's sacrificial function in worship but upon his greater closeness to God and superior insight into divine truth; see the next two lines.

(48) 103, 104. The poet apparently had in mind Jaques's speech in *As You Like It* (II. vii. 139 ff.), on the seven ages of man. *humorous stage:* "humorous" is used in the Elizabethan sense (perhaps for that reason the phrase is quoted), and refers to the humors—or casts of mind, tempers, dominant moods—of men; the idea of the comic is absent; cf. the modern phrase, "I am not in the humor for it."

(49) 141, 142. *questionings of sense:* doubts as to the reality of material things revealed by the senses; see Wordsworth's statement above. ¶ 143. *Fallings from us, vanishings:* this does not refer to the passing away of "a glory from the earth," but to a sense of the unreality of the material world, which seems to fall away and vanish into mere thought. In addition

to the poet's words quoted above, the following statement, made by him in his old age to a friend, in interpretation of the phrase, is conclusive: "There was a time in my life when I had to push against something that resisted, to be sure that there was anything outside of me. I was sure of my own mind; everything else fell away, and vanished into thought" (Knight's edition of Wordsworth's poems, IV. 58).   ¶ 145. *worlds not realized:* this present world of matter, which in such moods does not seem real.   ¶ 154, 155. The lines admit of two interpretations: (1) our high spiritual instincts make our noisy years seem *only* moments in the Eternal Silence, and of little significance; (2) these instincts redeem our noisy years and make even them seem a part (though of course a very small part) of the Eternal Silence. The latter interpretation sorts rather better with the stanza as a whole, which exalts human life, not depreciates it.   But the former is the more natural, or at least the more obvious, interpretation, and is favored by the word "moments," which, if the second interpretation be correct, ought rather to be "portions."   The first interpretation is also made more probable by lines in Wordsworth's poem, "On the Power of Sound":

> O Silence! are man's noisy years
> No more than moments of thy life?

¶ 158. *Nor man nor boy:* a condensed expression for "manhood" and "boyhood," with the dulling of spiritual vision as years increase; cf. ll. 66–76.   ¶ 161. *in a season of calm weather:* cf. "Lines Composed a Few Miles above Tintern Abbey," ll. 41–49.

(50) 183–86. Cf. the same, ll. 86–102.   ¶ 187–93. Cf. the same, ll. 102–07, 153–55.   ¶ 196–99. The lines have been variously interpreted.   "A sunset reflection. The sun, 'like a strong man going forth to his race,' has now reached the goal and won the palm, and so with the life of a man when death comes."—Dowden.   "The meaning seems to be— The falling sun, with his bright train of colored clouds, yet brings the sobering thought of the race of men who, even in the poet's lifetime, had sunk to their setting, that their fellows might lord it in the zenith, crowned with victorious palm."—H. H. Turner, *Selections from Wordsworth* (1874.)   It is somewhat against both these explanations that they take the setting sun as a symbol of human death, whereas Wordsworth in his early poems seldom or never employs nature in this analogical way.   May not the meaning be simpler and more literal? The main thought in this stanza is that the poet still loves nature, partly because it is now associated in his mind with human life.   This is the thought with which the stanza ends; and in the lines about the sunset is another illustration of it.   As the poet looks at the setting sun, the clouds about it take coloring from his thoughts of human life—the coloring is sober, because human life is serious and on the whole sad.   The close of the day suggests the life of men during the day, in which they have run another day's race and won victories.   On this interpretation "man's mortality" means "man's mortal life"; cf. *Macbeth* (II. iii. 97, 98): "From this instant there's nothing serious in mortality."   ¶ 200–03. The lines are often taken as two disconnected couplets, whereas the first two lines are really introductory to the last two.   Professor Dowden well says: "These lines have been often quoted as an illustration of Wordsworth's sensibility to external nature; in reality, they testify to his enriching the sentiment of nature with feeling derived from the heart of man and from the experience of human life."   Cf. "Lines Composed a Few Miles above Tintern Abbey," ll. 89–94.

(50) INSIDE OF KING'S COLLEGE CHAPEL, CAMBRIDGE.   Wordsworth visited Cambridge in 1820, and this sonnet was probably written soon after.   ¶ 1. *royal saint:* Henry VI, who founded King's College in 1441, and probably laid the corner-stone of the chapel, which is generally considered one of the finest specimens of Gothic architecture.

(51) TO A SKYLARK.   Another stanza, coming second, Wordsworth transferred in 1845 to "A Morning Exercise."

(52) 11. This use of things in nature as symbols of things in human life is rare in Wordsworth's earlier poems, which teach rather the direct, dynamic influence of nature upon man.

In "The Prelude" (XIV. 315-19) he recognizes the symbolic use of nature as legitimate, but gives it a subordinate place:

> Nature's secondary grace
> Hath hitherto been barely touched upon,
> The charm more superficial that attends
> Her works, as they present to Fancy's choice
> Apt illustrations of the moral world.

This use of nature is more frequent in the later poems; see "A Flower Garden," "Once I could Hail," "This Lawn, a Carpet All Alive," "The Primrose of the Rock," etc.

CONTEMPORARY CRITICISM

Admirable as this poem ["The Female Vagrant"] is, the author seems to discover still superior powers in the "Lines Written near Tintern Abbey." On reading this production, it is impossible not to lament that he should ever have condescended to write such pieces as "The Last of the Flock," "The Convict," and most of the ballads. In the whole range of English poetry, we scarcely recollect anything superior to a part of the following passage. [Quotation of ll. 66-112.] The "experiment," we think, has failed, not because the language of conversation is little adapted to "the purposes of poetic pleasure," but because it has been tried upon uninteresting subjects. Yet every piece discovers genius; and, ill as the author has frequently employed his talents, they certainly rank him with the best of living poets.—*The Critical Review*, October, 1798, on *Lyrical Ballads*. (The article was written by Southey.)

Though we have been extremely entertained with the fancy, the facility, and (in general) the sentiments of these pieces, we cannot regard them as *poetry* of a class to be cultivated at the expense of a higher species of versification unknown in our language at the time when our elder writers, whom this author condescends to imitate, wrote their ballads. Would it not be degrading poetry, as well as the English language, to go back to the barbarous and uncouth numbers of Chaucer? Suppose, instead of modernizing the old bard, that the sweet and polished measures, on lofty subjects, of Dryden, Pope, and Gray, were to be transmuted into the dialect and versification of the fourteenth century, should we be gainers by the retrogradation? . . . . When we confess that our author has had the art of pleasing and interesting in no common way by his natural delineation of human passions, human characters, and human incidents, we must add that these effects were not produced by the *poetry:* we have been as much affected by pictures of misery and unmerited distress, in *prose*. The elevation of soul, when it is lifted into the higher regions of imagination, affords us a delight of a different kind from the sensation which is produced by the detail of common incidents. . . . . Distress from poverty and want is admirably described in the "true story of Goody Blake and Harry Gill"; but are we to imagine that Harry was bewitched by Goody Blake? The hardest heart must be softened into pity for the poor old woman; and yet, if all the poor are to help themselves, and supply their wants from the possessions of their neighbors, what imaginary wants and real anarchy would it not create? Goody Blake should have been relieved out of the *two millions* annually allowed by the state to the poor of this country, not by the plunder of an individual. "Lines on the First Mild Day of March" abound with beautiful sentiments from a polished mind. "Simon Lee, the Old Huntsman," is the portrait, admirably painted, of every huntsman who, by toil, age, and infirmities, is rendered unable to guide and govern his canine family. "Anecdote for Fathers": of this the dialogue is ingenious and natural; but the object of the child's choice and the inferences are not quite obvious. "We are Seven": innocent and pretty infantine prattle. . . . . "Lines Written near Tintern Abbey": the reflections of no common mind; poetical, beautiful, and philosophical, but somewhat tinctured with gloomy, narrow, and unsociable ideas of seclusion from the commerce of the world, as if men were born to live in woods and wilds, unconnected with each other. . . . . So much genius and originality are discovered in this publication that we wish to see another from the same hand, written on more elevated subjects and in a more cheerful disposition.—*The Monthly Review*, June, 1799, on *Lyrical Ballads*.

The *Lyrical Ballads* were unquestionably popular; and, we have no hesitation in saying, deservedly popular; for in spite of their occasional vulgarity, affectation, and silliness, they were undoubtedly characterized by a strong spirit of originality, of pathos, and natural feeling. . . . . It was precisely because the perverseness and bad taste of this new school was combined with a great deal of genius and of laudable feeling, that we were afraid of their spreading and gaining ground among us, and that we entered into the discussion with a degree of zeal and animosity which some might think unreasonable toward authors to whom so much merit had been conceded. . . . . Their peculiarities of diction alone are enough, perhaps, to render them ridiculous; but the author before us really seems anxious to court this literary martyrdom by a device still more infallible,—we mean, that of connecting his most lofty, tender, or impassioned conceptions with objects and incidents which the greater part of his readers will probably persist in thinking low, silly, or uninteresting. . . . . All the world laughs at elegiac stanzas to a sucking-pig—a hymn on washing-day—sonnets to one's grandmother—or pindarics on gooseberry-pye; and yet, we are afraid, it will not be quite easy to convince Mr. Wordsworth that the same ridicule must infallibly attach to most of the pathetic pieces in these volumes. . . . . The first is a kind of ode "To the Daisy,"—very flat, feeble, and affected; and in a diction as artificial. and as much encumbered with heavy expletives, as the theme of an unpracticed school-boy. . . . . Further on we find an "Ode to Duty," in which the lofty vein is very unsuccessfully attempted. . . . . The two last lines seem to be utterly without meaning; at least we have no sort of conception in what sense *Duty* can be said to keep the old skies *fresh* and the stars from wrong. . . . . Then we have elegiac stanzas "To the Spade of a Friend," beginning, "Spade! with which Wilkinson hath tilled his lands," but too dull to be quoted any further. After this there is a "Minstrel's Song, on the Restoration of Lord Clifford, the Shepherd," which is in a very different strain of poetry; and then the volume is wound up with an "O de," with no other title but the motto *Paulo majora canamus.* This is, beyond all doubt, the most illegible and unintelligible part of the publication. We can pretend to give no analysis or explanation of it; our readers must make what they can of the following extracts. [Quotation of "Ode: Intimations of Immortality," ll. 51–57, 129–67.] . . . . When we look at these ["On the Extinction of the Venetian Republic," and "I Grieved for Buonaparte"] and many still finer passages, in the writings of this author, it is impossible not to feel a mixture of indignation and compassion at that strange infatuation which has bound him up from the fair exercise of his talents, and withheld from the public the many excellent productions that would otherwise have taken the place of the trash now before us. Even in the worst of these productions there are, no doubt, occasional little traits of delicate feeling and original fancy; but these are quite lost and obscured in the mass of childishness and insipidity with which they are incorporated. . . . . We think there is every reason to hope that the lamentable consequences which have resulted from Mr. Wordsworth's open violation of the established laws of poetry will operate as a wholesome warning to those who might otherwise have been seduced by his example, and be the means of restoring to that ancient and venerable code its due honor and authority.—*The Edinburgh Review*, October, 1807, on *Poems*, by William Wordsworth, 1807. (The article was written by Francis Jeffrey.)

This will never do! It bears, no doubt, the stamp of the author's heart and fancy, but unfortunately not half so visibly as that of his peculiar system. His former poems were intended to recommend that system, and to bespeak favor for it by their individual merit; but this, we suspect, must be recommended by the system, and can only expect to succeed where it has been previously established. It is longer, weaker, and tamer than any of Mr. Wordsworth's other productions; with less boldness of originality, and less even of that extreme simplicity and lowliness of tone which wavered so prettily, in the *Lyrical Ballads*, between silliness and pathos. We have imitations of Cowper and even of Milton here; and grafted on the natural drawl of the Lakers, and all diluted into harmony by that profuse and irrepressible wordiness which deluges all the blank verse of this school of poetry, and lubricates and weakens the whole structure of their style. . . . . We now see clearly, however, how the case stands; and, making up our minds, though with the most sincere pain and reluctance, to consider him as finally lost to the good cause of poetry, shall endeavor to be thankful for the occasional gleams of tenderness and beauty which the natural force of his imagination and affections must still shed over all his productions, and to which we shall ever turn with delight, in spite of the affectation and mysticism and prolixity with which they are so abundantly contrasted.— *The Edinburgh Review*, November, 1814, on "The Excursion." (The article was written by Francis Jeffrey.)

The first characteristic, though only occasional, defect which I appear to myself to find in these poems is the inconstancy of the style. Under this name I refer to the sudden and unprepared transitions from lines or sentences of peculiar felicity (at all events striking and original) to a style not only unimpassioned but undistinguished. He sinks too often and too abruptly to that style which I should place in the second division of language, dividing it into the three species: first, that which is peculiar to poetry; second, that which is only proper in prose; and third, the neutral, or common to both. . . . . The second defect I could generalize with tolerable accuracy, if the reader will pardon an uncouth and new-coined word. There is, I should say, not seldom a *matter-of-factness* in certain poems. This may be divided into, first, a laborious minuteness and fidelity in the representation of objects and their positions, as they appeared to the poet himself: secondly, the insertion of accidental circumstances, in order to the full explanation of his living characters, their dispositions and actions—which circumstances might be necessary to establish the probability of a statement in real life, where nothing is taken for granted by the hearer, but appear superfluous in poetry, where the reader is willing to believe for his own sake. . . . . To these defects . . . . I may oppose . . . . the following (for the most part correspondent) excellences. First, an austere purity of language both grammatically and logically; in short, a perfect appropriateness of the words to the meaning. . . . . The second characteristic excellence of Mr. Wordsworth's works is a correspondent weight and sanity of the thoughts and sentiments, won, not from books, but from the poet's own meditative observation. They are fresh, and have the dew upon them. . . . . Third, ... the sinewy strength and originality of single lines and paragraphs: the frequent *curiosa felicitas* of his diction. . . . . Fourth, the perfect truth of nature in his images and descriptions as taken immediately from nature, and proving a long and genial intimacy with the very spirit which gives the physiognomic expression to all the works of nature. Like a green field reflected in a calm and perfectly transparent lake, the image is distinguished from the reality only by its greater softness and luster. . . . . Fifth, a meditative pathos, a union of deep and subtle thought with sensibility; a sympathy with man as man—the sympathy, indeed, of a contemplator rather than a fellow-sufferer or co-mate (*spectator, haud particeps*), but of a contemplator from whose view no difference of rank conceals the sameness of the nature; no injuries of wind or weather, of toil, or even of ignorance, wholly disguise the human face divine. . . . . Lastly, and pre-eminently, I challenge for this poet the gift of imagination in the highest and strictest sense of the word. In the play of fancy, Wordsworth, to my feelings, is not always graceful, and sometimes recondite. . . . . But in imaginative power he stands nearest of all modern writers to Shakespeare and Milton; and yet in a kind perfectly unborrowed and his own. To employ his own words, which are at once an instance and an illustration, he does indeed to all thoughts and to all objects

> add the gleam,
> The light that never was on sea or land,
> The consecration and the poet's dream.

—Coleridge, *Biographia Literaria* (1817), chap. xxii.

Criticism of the puerile and prosaic in Wordsworth's poetry took the form of satirical imitation in "The Baby's Debut" (in *Rejected Addresses*, 1812, by Horace and James Smith), of which the following is a part:

(Spoken in the character of Nancy Lake, a girl eight years of age, who is drawn upon the stage in a child's chaise by Samuel Hughes, her uncle's porter.)

My brother Jack was nine in May,
And I was eight on New-year's day;
    So in Kate Wilson's shop
Papa (he's my papa and Jack's)
Bought me, last week, a doll of wax,
    And brother Jack a top.

Jack's in the pouts, and this it is,—
He thinks mine came to more than his;
    So to my drawer he goes,
Takes out the doll, and, O my stars!
He pokes her head between the bars,
    And melts off half her nose!

Quite cross, a bit of string I beg,
And tie it to his peg-top's peg,
    And bang, with might and main,
Its head against the parlour door;
Off flies the head, and hits the floor,
    And breaks a window-pane.

.   .   .   .

Aunt Hannah heard the window break,
And cried, "O naughty Nancy Lake,
    Thus to distress your aunt:
No Drury Lane for you to-day!"
And while papa said, "Pooh, she may!"
    Mamma said, "No, she shan't!"

Well, after many a sad reproach,
They got into a hackney coach,
    And trotted down the street.
I saw them go: one horse was blind,
The tails of both hung down behind,
    Their shoes were on their feet.

The chaise in which poor brother Bill
Used to be drawn to Pentonville,
    Stood in the lumber-room:
I wiped the dust from off the top,
While Molly mopped it with a mop,
    And brushed it with a broom.

My uncle's porter, Samuel Hughes,
Came in at six to black the shoes
    (I always talk to Sam);
So what does he but takes and drags
Me in the chaise along the flags,
    And leaves me where I am.

My father's walls are made of brick,
But not so tall and not so thick
    As these; and, goodness me!
My father's beams are made of wood,
But never, never half so good
    As those that now I see.

SAMUEL TAYLOR COLERIDGE

Coleridge defined poetry as follows:

"Poetry is not the proper antithesis to prose, but to science. Poetry is opposed to science, and prose to metre. The proper and immediate object of science is the acquirement or communication of truth; the proper and immediate object of poetry is the communication of immediate pleasure. This definition is useful; but as it would include novels and other works of fiction, which yet we do not call poems, there must be some additional character by which poetry is not only divided from opposites but likewise distinguished from disparate, though similar, modes of composition. Now, how is this to be effected? In animated prose the beauties of nature, and the passions and accidents of human nature, are often expressed in that natural language which the contemplation of them would suggest to a pure and benevolent mind; yet still neither we nor the writers call such a work a poem, though no work could deserve that name which did not include all this, together with something else. What is this? It is that pleasurable emotion, that peculiar state and degree of excitement, which arises in the poet himself in the act of composition; and in order to understand this, we must combine a more than ordinary sympathy with the objects, emotions, or incidents contemplated by the poet, consequent on a more than common sensibility, with a more than ordinary activity of the mind in respect of the fancy and the imagination. Hence is produced a more vivid reflection of the truths of nature and of the human heart, united with a constant activity modifying and correcting these truths by that sort of pleasurable emotion which the exertion of all our faculties gives in a certain degree, but which can only be felt in perfection under the full play of those powers of mind which are spontaneous rather than voluntary, and in which the effort required bears no proportion to the activity enjoyed. This is the state which permits the production of a highly pleasurable whole of which each part shall also communicate for itself a distinct and conscious pleasure; and hence arises the definition, which I trust is now intelligible, that poetry, or rather a poem, is a species of composition, opposed to science as having intellectual pleasure for its object, and as attaining its end by the use of language natural to us in a state of excitement; but distinguished from other species of composition, not excluded by the former criterion, by permitting a pleasure from the whole consistent with a consciousness of pleasure from the component parts; and the perfection of which is to communicate from each part the greatest immediate pleasure compatible with the largest sum of pleasure on the whole. This, of course, will vary with the different modes of poetry; and that splendor of particular lines, which would be worthy of admiration in an impassioned elegy or a short indignant satire, would be a blemish and proof of vile taste in a tragedy or an epic poem.

"It is remarkable, by the way, that Milton in three incidental words has implied all which for the purposes of more distinct apprehension, which at first must be slow-paced in order to be distinct, I have endeavored to develop in a precise and strictly adequate definition. Speaking of poetry, he says, as in a parenthesis, 'which is simple, sensuous, passionate.' . . . . Had these three words only been properly understood by, and present in the minds of, general readers, not only almost a library of false poetry would have been either precluded or still-born, but, what is of more consequence, works truly excellent and capable of enlarging the understanding, warming and purifying the heart, and placing in the center of the whole being the germs of noble and manlike actions, would have been the common diet of the intellect instead. For the first condition, simplicity—while, on the one hand, it distinguishes poetry from the arduous processes of science laboring towards an end not yet arrived at, and supposes a smooth and finished road, on which the reader is to walk onward easily, with streams murmuring by his side, and trees and flowers and human dwellings to make his journey as delightful as the object of it is desirable, instead of having to toil with the pioneers and painfully make the road on which others are to travel,—precludes, on the other hand, every affectation and morbid peculiarity: the second condition, sensuousness, insures that framework of objectivity, that definiteness and articulation of imagery, and that modification of the images themselves, without which poetry becomes flattened into mere didactics of practice, or evaporated into a hazy, unthoughtful day-dreaming; and the third condition, passion, provides that neither thought nor imagery shall be simply objective, but that the *passio vera* of humanity shall warm and animate both."—*Lectures and Notes of 1818*, Section I.

(54) THE RIME OF THE ANCIENT MARINER. "During the first year that Mr. Words-

worth and I were neighbors, our conversations turned frequently on the two cardinal points of poetry, the power of exciting the sympathy of the reader by a faithful adherence to the truth of nature, and the power of giving the interest of novelty by the modifying colors of imagination. The sudden charm which accidents of light and shade, which moonlight or sunset, diffused over a known and familiar landscape, appeared to represent the practicability of combining both. These are the poetry of nature. The thought suggested itself (to which of us I do not recollect) that a series of poems might be composed of two sorts. In the one, the incidents and agents were to be, in part at least, supernatural; and the excellence aimed at was to consist in the interesting of the affections by the dramatic truth of such emotions as would naturally accompany such situations, supposing them real. . . . . For the second class, subjects were to be chosen from ordinary life. . . . . In this idea originated the plan of the *Lyrical Ballads;* in which it was agreed that my endeavors should be directed to persons and characters supernatural or at least romantic, yet so as to transfer from our inward nature a human interest and a semblance of truth sufficient to procure for these shadows of imagination that willing suspension of disbelief for the moment, which constitutes poetic faith. Mr. Wordsworth, on the other hand, was to propose to himself as his object to give the charm of novelty to things of every day, and to excite a feeling analogous to the super-natural, by awakening the mind's attention from the lethargy of custom and directing it to the loveliness and the wonders of the world before us. . . . . With this view I wrote 'The Ancient Mariner.' "—Coleridge, *Biographia Literaria* (1817), chap. xiv. "In the course of this walk was planned the poem of 'The Ancient Mariner,' founded on a dream, as Mr. Coleridge said, of his friend Mr. Cruikshank. Much the greatest part of the story was Mr. Coleridge's invention, but certain parts I suggested: for example, some crime was to be committed which should bring upon the Old Navigator, as Coleridge afterwards delighted to call him, the spectral persecution, as a consequence of that crime and his own wander-ings. I had been reading in Shelvocke's *Voyages,* a day or two before, that, while doubling Cape Horn, they frequently saw albatrosses in that latitude, the largest sort of sea-fowl, some extending their wings twelve or thirteen feet. 'Suppose,' said I, 'you represent him as having killed one of these birds on entering the South Sea, and that the tutelary spirits of these regions take upon them to avenge the crime.' The incident was thought fit for the purpose and adopted accordingly. I also suggested the navigation of the ship by the dead men, but do not recollect that I had anything more to do with the scheme of the poem. . . . . We began the composition together on that, to me, memorable evening. I furnished two or three lines at the beginning of the poem, in particular,

> And listened like a three years' child;
> The Mariner had his will."

—Dictated by Wordsworth to Miss Fenwick in 1843. "When . . . . Mr. Wordsworth was last in London, soon after the appearance of De Quincey's papers in *Tait's Magazine* [in 1834–35], he dined with me, ... and made the following statement, which, I am quite sure, I give to you correctly: 'The Ancient Mariner' was founded on a strange dream, which a friend of Coleridge had, who fancied he saw a skeleton ship, with figures in it. . . . . Besides the lines, ...

> And thou art long, and lank, and brown,
> As is the ribbed sea-sand,

I wrote the stanza, ...

> He holds him with his glittering eye—
> The Wedding Guest stood still,
> And listens like a three years' child:
> The Mariner hath his will,

and four or five lines more in different parts of the poem, which I could not now point out." —Alexander Dyce, in a letter to H. N. Coleridge, published in the 1852 edition of Coleridge's works. "Mrs. Barbauld once told me that she admired 'The Ancient Mariner' very much, but that there were two faults in it—it was improbable, and had no moral. As for the probability, I owned that that might admit some question; but as to the want of a moral, I told her that in my own judgment the poem had too much, and that the only or chief fault, if I might say so, was the obtrusion of the moral sentiment so openly on the reader as a principle or cause of action in a work of such pure imagination."—Coleridge, *Table Talk*, May 31, 1830.

The poem was printed in *Lyrical Ballads*, in 1798. The text was much changed in the second edition of the ballads, in 1800, and some changes were made in subsequent editions of the poem. The marginal notes were added in 1817. The complete text of the first edition may be found in J. D. Campbell's edition of Coleridge's poems. This first form of the poem had many archaisms, in imitation of the old ballads: "Ancyent Marinere," "ne" for "nor," "withouten," "ee" for "eye,' "yspread," etc.; most of these were changed in the second edition. A good many phrases and lines and some whole stanzas, in the first edition, were modified or dropped in subsequent editions; specimens of these changes are given below.

(54) 12. In 1798, "Or my staff shall make thee skip." *Eftsoons*=at once (literally, "soon after"; "aft," or "eft," is the positive, of which "after" is the comparative; cf. "aft" in nautical phraseology, meaning "behind," or "following").

(56) 51–70. Mr. Ivor James, in *The Source of "The Ancient Mariner"* (1890), argues that Coleridge got material for the poem from Captain Thomas James's *Strange and Dangerous Voyage* (1633). The book was in the Bristol city library, of which Coleridge was "a regular frequenter" the year before the poem was written. The following sentences are from *The Strange and Dangerous Voyage:* "We had Ice not farre off about vs, and some pieces as high as our Top-mast-head;" "The Ice . . . . crackt all ouer the Bay with a fearefull noyse;'' "These great pieces that came aground began to breake with a most terrible thundering noyse; '' "This morning . . . . we vnfastened our Ship and came to saile, steering betwixt great pieces of Ice that were a-ground in 40 fad., and twice as high as our top-mast head."—*Hakluyt Society's Publications*, No. 89 (1894). ¶ 67. In 1798, "The Marineres gave it biscuit-worms."

(58) 143–46. Not in the 1798 text, where Part III began abruptly, "I saw a something in the Sky."

(59) 164. *they for joy did grin.* "I took the thought of 'grinning for joy,' in that poem, from poor Burnett's remark to me, when we had climbed to the top of Plinlimmon, and were nearly dead with thirst. We could not speak from the constriction, till we found a little puddle under a stone. He said to me, 'You grinned like an idiot!' He had done the same." —Coleridge, *Table Talk*, May 31, 1830. "The mouth-spume changes to a tough collodion-like coating, which compresses and contracts the lips in a sardonic smile, changing to a canine grin."—"Thirst in the Desert," *The Atlantic Monthly*, April, 1898. ¶ 189. After this line the 1798 text had the following stanza:

> His bones were black with many a crack,
>   All black and bare, I ween;
> Jet-black and bare, save where with rust
> Of mouldy damps and charnel crust
>   They 're patched with purple and green.

(60) 193, 194. In 1798,

> And she is far liker Death than he;
>   Her flesh makes the still air cold.

¶ 198. After this line the 1798 text had the following stanza:

> A guste of wind sterte up behind
>   And whistled through his bones;
> Thro' the holes of his eyes and the hole of his mouth
>   Half-whistles and half-groans.

¶ 199, 200, 203–08. Not in the 1798 text.

(61) 242. *rotting:* in 1798, "eldritch."

(63) 297. *silly.* It is difficult to assign an exact meaning to the word here. Perhaps Coleridge had no precise sense in mind, using the word chiefly for its archaic flavor. Its earliest meaning was "blessed" (O.E. "sælig"); then it acquired the senses of "innocent," "harmless," "poor, pitiable," "helpless," "foolish," etc. Spenser uses it in the sense of "helpless": "my silly barke was tossed sore" ("Amoretti," lxiii); and that meaning, or "poor, pitiable," fits here as well as any.

(64) 347–49. It is possible that in addition to Wordsworth's suggestion that the ship should be navigated by the dead men, *The Letter of Saint Paulinus to Macarius* (1618) gave Coleridge a hint about animating the dead bodies with the spirits of angels. The letter tells of a wonderful voyage, in which one old man, sole survivor of the crew, was assisted in the navigation of a ship by Christ and the angels: "The mariner would rouse himself but scarce could he leap forward when he saw that angelic hands were busy about his task. No sooner did he touch a rope than the sail ran along the yard and stood swelling out, the mizzen was set, and the ship made way. . . . . Sometimes, indeed, it was vouchsafed him to behold an armed band—one may suppose of heavenly soldiers—who kept their watches on the deck and acted in all points as seamen. What crew, indeed, but a crew of angels was worthy to work that vessel which was steered by the Pilot of the world?"—*The Gentleman's Magazine,* October, 1853.

(65) 372. After this line came four stanzas in 1798, which were omitted in 1800; the last six lines were as follows:

> The Marineres all returned to work
> As silent as beforne.
>
> The Marineres all 'gan pull the ropes,
> But look at me they n' old:
> Thought I, I am as thin as air—
> They cannot me behold.

(66) 416, 417. Cf. Sir John Davies's "Orchestra" (1596), st. xlix, ll. 4, 5:

> For his [the sun's] great crystal eye is always cast
> Up to the Moon, and on her fixèd fast.

(68) 475. After this line came five stanzas in 1798, which were omitted in 1800. The first stanza was nearly the same as ll. 480–83. The third stanza was this:

> They lifted up their stiff right arms,
> They held them strait and tight;
> And each right-arm burnt like a torch,
> A torch that 's borne upright.
> Their stony eye-balls glittered on
> In the red and smoky light.

(70) 535. *ivy-tod*=ivy-bush.

(71) 582–85. In 1798 as follows:

> Since then at an uncertain hour,
> Now ofttimes and now fewer,
> That anguish comes and makes me tell
> My ghastly aventure.

(72) FRANCE: AN ODE. The ode was occasioned by France's invasion of Switzerland in 1798. For a similar change of view regarding France and the French Revolution, see the note on Wordsworth's "To the Men of Kent." The metrical scheme is the same in all the stanzas, although the indentation of the lines is not.

(73) 43. *Blasphemy's loud scream:* "On the 10th of November [1793], the Convention was invited by the Commune of Paris to celebrate the Feast of Reason in the church of Notre Dame; an actress, Mdlle. Maillard, was borne in triumph even to the altar. 'Legislators,' cried Chaumette, 'fanaticism has given way; it has given place to Reason, its blinking eyes

have not been able to support the brightness of its light; an immense people have assembled under these gothic arches, which for the first time have served as an echo to the truth."—Guizot's *History of France.*

(74) 66. *Helvetia's:* "Helvetia" was the Late Latin name for Switzerland (from "Helvetii," the Romans' name for the inhabitants of that region). ¶ 85–105. In an "Argument" prefixed to the ode in 1802, the fifth stanza is summarized thus: "An address to Liberty, in which the poet expresses his conviction that those feelings and that grand ideal of freedom which the mind attains by its contemplation of its individual nature and of the sublime surrounding objects (see stanza the first) do not belong to men as a society, nor can possibly be either gratified or realized under any form of human government, but belong to the individual man, so far as he is pure and inflamed with the love and adoration of God in nature."

(75) KUBLA KHAN. "In consequence of a slight indisposition, an anodyne had been prescribed, from the effects of which he [the author] fell asleep in his chair at the moment that he was reading the following sentence, or words of the same substance, in *Purchas's Pilgrimage:* 'Here the Khan Kubla commanded a palace to be built, and a stately garden thereunto. And thus ten miles of fertile ground were inclosed with a wall.' The author continued for about three hours in a profound sleep, at least of the external senses, during which time he has the most vivid confidence that he could not have composed less than from two to three hundred lines; if that indeed can be called composition in which all the images rose up before him as *things*, with a parallel production of the correspondent expressions, without any sensation or consciousness of effort. On awaking he appeared to himself to have a distinct recollection of the whole, and, taking his pen, ink, and paper, instantly and eagerly wrote down the lines that are here preserved. At this moment he was unfortunately called out by a person on business . . . . and detained by him above an hour, and on his return to his room found, to his no small surprise and mortification, that though he still retained some vague and dim recollection of the general purport of the vision, yet, with the exception of some eight or ten scattered lines and images, all the rest had passed away."—Preface to the poem, in 1816. The passage that Coleridge quotes loosely from memory is the following: "In Xaindu did Cublai Can build a stately Pallace, encompassing sixteene miles of plaine ground with a wall, wherein are fertile Meddowes, pleasant Springs, delightfull Streames, and all sorts of beasts of chase and game, and in the middest thereof a sumptuous house of pleasure."—*Purchas his Pilgrimage* (1614, 2d ed.), Book IV, chap. xiii. Professor Lane Cooper, in *Modern Philology*, January, 1906, throws light on the question why, in a poem the scene of which is Tartary, Coleridge brought in an Abyssinian maid, "singing of Mount Abora." Professor Cooper thinks that "Abora" is probably a variant of "Amara," a hill in Abyssinia and the seat of a terrestrial paradise like that described in the poem; hence the reference to it, for (as Coleridge implies in ll. 42–47) the maid's description of the one paradise would help him to describe the other. The article also contributes to a better understanding of the poem as a whole, of which Professor Cooper says, "This might preferably be termed a dream of the terrestrial, or even of the 'false,' paradise; since, aside from its unworthy, acquiescent admission of demoniac love within so-called 'holy' precincts, it reads like an arras of reminiscences from several accounts of natural or enchanted parks, and from various descriptions of that elusive and danger-fraught garden which mystic geographers have studied to locate from Florida to Cathay." Professor Cooper points out that Coleridge could have found a description of Mount Amara in the book he was reading when he fell asleep, for a whole chapter (Book VI, chap. v) is there given to it, from which the following sentences are taken: "It is situate in a great Plaine, largely extending it selfe euery way, without other hill in the same for the space of 30 leagues, the forme thereof round and circular. . . . . The way vp to it [the top] is cut out within the rocke, not with staires, but ascending by little and little, that one may ride vp with ease; it hath also hols cut to let in light. . . . . Halfe way vp is a faire and spacious Hall cut out of the same rock, with 3 windowes very large vpwards." Professor Cooper adds, "This sunlit and symmetrical hill, with its miracle of inner carven passages, may partially

explain Coleridge's 'sunny dome' and 'caves of ice' (why of *ice?*) which must have puzzled more than one reader in 'Kubla Khan.'" As to the caves of ice, may not the poet have thought of the rock as marble or alabaster, to heighten the beauty of the "pleasure dome" (cf. the description of the earthly paradise in *Paradise Lost*, IV. 543, 544); or may not the phrase have been used merely to suggest the delicious coolness of such caves in a hot climate?

(75) 1. *Xanadu:* a region in Tartary; in Purchas the form is "Zaindu," which Coleridge altered, apparently for the sake of euphony. *Khan:* the title of the sovereign princes in Tartar countries; also written "Cham."

(76) 32. *midway:* half-way between the fountain (l. 19) and the caverns into which the river plunged (l. 27).

(76) CHRISTABEL. The poem was intended for publication in the second edition of *Lyrical Ballads*, in 1800; but Coleridge could not or would not finish it, and it was handed about in manuscript (Scott heard it in 1801, and Byron in 1811) until 1816, when Murray published it on the recommendation of Byron. In the preface Coleridge said, "But as, in my very first conception of the tale, I had the whole present to my mind, with the wholeness no less than with the liveliness of a vision, I trust that I shall be able to embody in verse the three parts yet to come, in the course of the present year." In *Table Talk*, July 6, 1833, he said: "I could write as good verses now as ever I did, if I were perfectly free from vexations, and were I in the *ad libitum* hearing of fine music, which has a sensible effect in harmonizing my thoughts, and in animating and, as it were, lubricating my inventive faculty. The reason of my not finishing 'Christabel' is not that I don't know how to do it—for I have, as I always had, the whole plan entire from beginning to end in my mind; but I fear I could not carry on with equal success the execution of the idea, an extremely subtle and difficult one." Mr. Gillman, under whose care Coleridge was during the last years of his life, says, in his *Life of Coleridge* (1838), that the poet "explained the story of 'Christabel' to his friends," as follows: "The following relation was to have occupied a third and fourth canto, and to have closed the tale. Over the mountains, the Bard, as directed by Sir Leoline, hastes with his disciple; but in consequence of one of those inundations supposed to be common to this country, the spot only where the castle once stood is discovered—the edifice itself being washed away. He determines to return. Geraldine, being acquainted with all that is passing, like the weird sisters in *Macbeth*, vanishes. Reappearing, however, she awaits the return of the Bard, exciting in the meantime, by her wily arts, all the anger she could rouse in the Baron's breast, as well as that jealousy of which he is described to have been susceptible. The old Bard and the youth at length arrive, and therefore she can no longer personate the character of Geraldine, the daughter of Lord Roland de Vaux, but changes her appearance to that of the accepted though absent lover of Christabel. Now ensues a courtship most distressing to Christabel, who feels, she knows not why, great disgust for her once favored knight. This coldness is very painful to the Baron, who has no more conception than herself of the supernatural transformation. She at last yields to her father's entreaties, and consents to approach the altar with this hated suitor. The real lover, returning, enters at this moment, and produces the ring which she had once given him in sign of her betrothment. Thus defeated, the supernatural being Geraldine disappears. As predicted, the castle bell tolls, the mother's voice is heard, and, to the exceeding great joy of the parties, the rightful marriage takes place, after which follows a reconciliation and explanation between the father and daughter." On the other hand Justice Coleridge, nephew of the poet, reported as follows what Wordsworth said to him about the poem in 1836: "He said he had no idea how 'Christabel' was to have been finished, and he did not think my uncle had ever conceived, in his own mind, any definite plan for it; that the poem had been composed . . . . when there was the most unreserved intercourse between them as to all their literary projects and productions, and he had never heard from him any plan for finishing it. Not that he doubted my uncle's sincerity in his subsequent assertions to the contrary; because, he said, schemes of this sort passed rapidly and vividly through his mind, and so impressed him that he often fancied he had arranged things which

really, and upon trial, proved to be mere embryos."—*The Prose Works of William Words-worth*, edited by A. B. Grosart, III. 427. "The metre of the 'Christabel' is not, properly speaking, irregular, though it may seem so from its being founded on a new principle: namely, that of counting in each line the accents, not the syllables. Though the latter may vary from seven to twelve, yet in each line the accents will be found to be only four. Nevertheless this occasional variation in number of syllables is not introduced wantonly, or for the mere ends of convenience, but in correspondence with some transition in the nature of the imagery or passion."—Preface to the first edition.

(77) 7. *mastiff, which:* adopted in 1829; in 1816, "mastiff bitch."

(80) 129–34. The inability or reluctance of Geraldine to cross the threshold (which doubtless had been blessed by the Church) is the first hint that she is an evil spirit. ¶ 141, 142. The witch will not join in thanks to the Virgin Mary. ¶ 147–53. Animals were supposed to have a sense of the presence of supernatural beings. ¶ 156–59. Even the dying fire felt the supernatural presence.

(83) 252. In one of the extant manuscripts of the poem, says Mr. Campbell, after this line comes the line, "Are lean and old and foul of hue," suggesting a hag, or witch; cf. ll. 457, 458.

(85) 344. *Bratha Head:* the Brathay is a river flowing into Lake Windermere, in the Lake District. ¶ 350. *Pike*=Peak, a pointed hill. ¶ 351. *ghyll*=a ravine, with a stream running through it.

(93) 656–77. This so-called conclusion has little apparent relation to the poem, and probably was not originally meant to be a part of it. Mr. Campbell says that the lines are not in the three extant manuscripts of the poem. They were sent to Southey a year after Part II was composed, and probably were written later than it.

CONTEMPORARY CRITICISM

The author's first piece, the "Rime of the Ancyent Marinere," in imitation of the style as well as of the spirit of the elder poets, is the strangest story of a cock and a bull that we ever saw on paper; yet, though it seems a rhapsody of unintelligible wildness and incoherence (of which we do not perceive the drift, unless the joke lies in depriving the wedding-guest of his share of the feast), there are in it poetical touches of an exquisite kind.—*The Monthly Review*, June, 1799, on *Lyrical Ballads*.

This precious production ["Christabel"] is not finished, but we are to have more and more of it in future. It would be truly astonishing that such rude, unfashioned stuff should be tolerated, and still more that it should be praised by men of genius (witness Lord Byron and some others), were we not convinced that every principle of correct writing, as far as poetry is concerned, has been long *given up*, and that the observance rather than the breach of such rules is considered as an incontrovertible proof of rank stupidity. It is grand, in a word, it is sublime, to be lawless; and whoever writes the wildest nonsense in the quickest and newest manner is the popular poet of the day! Whether this sentence be considered as positive truth or as a splenetic effusion, by the different parties who *now* divide the literary world, we think that the time is fast approaching when all minds will be agreed on it, and when any versifier who widely differs from the established standard of our nobler authors will be directly remanded into that limbo of vanity from which he most certainly emerged. The fragment of "Kubla Khan" is declared to have been composed in a dream, and is published as the author wrote it. . . . . The poem itself is below criticism. . . . . We close the slight publication before us with unmingled regret. The author of *Remorse* may perhaps be able to explain our feeling better than ourselves; but that so much superior genius should be corrupted and debased by so much execrable taste must be a subject of sincere lamentation to every lover of the arts and to every friend of poetry.—*The Monthly Review*, January, 1817.

Then comes "The Lady Isabelle" and "The Cherub," in imitation of Mr. Coleridge; the former, in evident allusion to "The Lady Christabel," recently published, is quite as wandering and unintelligible as that long riddle, but it has none of those flowers of poetry which Mr. Coleridge has scattered over the dark pall that covers and conceals the meaning of "Christabel."—*The Quarterly Review*, July, 1816, on *The Poetic Mirror*, a collection of parodies.

Two other pieces in this miscellany [Byron's minor poems] recall to our mind the wild, unbridled, and fiery imagination of Coleridge. To this poet's high poetical genius we have always paid deference; though not uniformly perhaps, he has, too frequently for his own popularity, wandered into the wild and mystic, and left the reader at a loss accurately to determine his meaning.—*The Quarterly Review*, October, 1816, on "Childe Harold's Pilgrimage," etc.

Upon the whole, we look upon this publication as one of the most notable pieces of impertinence of which the press has lately been guilty, and one of the boldest experiments that has yet been made upon the patience or understanding of the public. It is impossible, however, to dismiss it without a remark or two. The other productions of the Lake School have generally exhibited talents thrown away upon subjects so mean that no power of genius could ennoble them, or perverted and rendered useless by a false theory of poetical composition. But even in the worst of them, if we except the "White Doe" of Mr. Wordsworth and some of the laureate odes, there were always some gleams of feeling or of fancy. But the thing now before us is utterly destitute of value. It exhibits from beginning to end not a ray of genius; and we defy any man to point out a passage of poetical merit in any of the three pieces which it contains, except, perhaps, the following lines, and even these are not very brilliant, nor is the leading thought original. [Quotation of "Christabel," ll. 408–13.] With this one exception there is literally not one couplet in the publication before us which would be reckoned poetry, or even sense, were it found in the corner of a newspaper or upon the window of an inn. Must we, then, be doomed to hear such a mixture of raving and driveling extolled as the work of a "wild and original" genius, simply because Mr. Coleridge has now and then written fine verses, and a brother poet chooses, in his milder mood, to laud him from courtesy or from interest?—*The Edinburgh Review*, September, 1816, on "Christabel," "Kubla Khan," etc. (The article was written by William Hazlitt.)

To speak of it ["The Ancient Mariner"] at all is extremely difficult; above all the poems with which we are acquainted in any language, it is a poem to be felt, cherished, mused upon, not to be talked about—not capable of being described, analyzed, or criticized. It is the wildest of all the creations of genius: it is not like a thing of the living, listening, moving world; the very music of its words is like the melancholy mysterious breath of something sung to the sleeping ear; its images have the beauty, the grandeur, the incoherence of some mighty vision. The loveliness and the terror glide before us in turns, with, at one moment, the awful shadowy dimness, at another, the yet more awful distinctness of a majestic dream. Dim and shadowy and incoherent, however, though it be, how blind, how wilfully or how foolishly blind, must they have been who refused to see any meaning or purpose in the Tale of the Mariner! . . . . We know not that there is any English poet who owes so much to this single element of power [the power of words] as Coleridge. It appears to us that there is not one of them, at least not one that has written since the age of Elizabeth, in whose use of *words* the most delicate sense of beauty concurs with so much exquisite subtlety of metaphysical perception. To illustrate this by individual examples is out of the question, but we think a little examination would satisfy any person who is accustomed to the study of language of the justice of what we have said. In the kind of poetry in which he has chiefly dealt, there can be no doubt the effect of his peculiar mastery over this instrument has been singularly happy—more so than, perhaps, it could have been in any other. The whole essence of his poetry is more akin to music than that of any other poetry we have ever met with.—*Blackwood's Magazine*, October, 1819.

ROBERT SOUTHEY

(97) THALABA THE DESTROYER. Book VII. xiii–xxiii. "In the continuation of the *Arabian Tales* the Domdaniel is mentioned—a seminary for evil magicians, under the roost of the sea. From this seed the present romance has grown. Let me not be supposed to prefer the rhythm in which it is written, abstractedly considered, to the regular blank verse, the noblest measure, in my judgment, of which our admirable language is capable. For the following poem I have preferred it, because it suits the varied subject: it is the Arabesque ornament of an Arabian tale. . . . . Verse is not enough favored by the English reader; perhaps this is owing to the obtrusiveness, the regular Jew's-harp twing-twang, of what has been foolishly called heroic measure. I do not wish the *improvisatoré* tune, but something that denotes the sense of harmony, something like the accent of feeling—like the tone which every poet necessarily gives to poetry."—Preface. Thalaba, who has been chosen by Allah to destroy the magicians, in his search for the Domdaniel caverns enters the Paradise of Sin, built by the sorcerer Aloadin in a valley encircled by mountains; there he finds his love Oneiza, recently brought thither by force, and plans to release her and himself by slaying Aloadin. At this point the selection begins.

(99) 55. *Zaccoum's fruit:* "It [the Zaccoum] is a tree which issueth from the bottom of hell; the fruit thereof resembleth the heads of devils; and the damned shall eat of the same."— *Koran,* chap. xxxvii. ¶65–67. *Homerites . . . . Himiar:* Arabian tribes whose women were skilful with the bow. ¶ 77. *Cassowar:* the cassowary, a bird nearly as large as the ostrich.

(101) MY DAYS AMONG THE DEAD ARE PASSED. Southey was a great lover of books and lived mostly in his library, which finally contained 14,000 volumes. De Quincey said that in conversation Southey's heart was "continually reverting to his wife, viz. his library. . . . . The library . . . . was in all senses a good one. The books were chiefly English, Spanish, and Portuguese; well selected, being the great cardinal classics of the three literatures; fine copies, and decorated externally with a reasonable elegance, so as to make them in harmony with the other embellishments of the room. This effect was aided by the horizontal arrangement upon brackets of many rare manuscripts, Spanish or Portuguese."— De Quincey, *Literary and Lake Reminiscences,* chap. v (1839). "On some authors, such as the old divines, he 'fed,' as he expressed it, slowly and carefully, dwelling on the page and taking in its contents deeply and deliberately, like an epicure with his wine, 'searching the subtle flavor.' . . . . For a considerable time after he had ceased to compose, he took pleasure in reading, and the habit continued after the power of comprehension was gone. . His dearly prized books, indeed, were a pleasure to him almost to the end, and he would walk slowly round his library, looking at them and taking them down mechanically."—*Life and Correspondence of Robert Southey* (1849), edited by his son, chaps. xxxii, xxxviii.

CONTEMPORARY CRITICISM

In the specimen of Jacobin poetry which we gave in our last number was developed a principle, perhaps one of the most universally recognized in the Jacobin creed, namely, "that the animadversion of human law upon human actions is for the most part nothing but gross oppression." . . . . Another principle, no less devoutly entertained, and no less sedulously disseminated, is the natural and eternal warfare of the poor and the rich. . . . . This principle is treated at large by many authors. It is versified in sonnets and elegies without end. We trace it particularly in a poem by the same author from whom we borrowed our former illustration of the Jacobin doctrine of crimes and punishments. In this poem the pathos of the matter is not a little relieved by the absurdity of the metre: . . . .

> Cold was the night wind; drifting fast the snows fell;
> Wide were the downs, and shelterless and naked;
> When a poor wand'rer struggled on her journey,
>   Weary and way-sore.

This is enough; unless the reader should wish to be informed how

> Fast o'er the bleak heath rattling drove a chariot;

or how, not long after,

> Loud blew the wind, unheard was her complaining—
> On went the horseman.

We proceed to give our imitation, which is of the Amœbœan or Collocutory kind.

SAPPHICS

THE FRIEND OF HUMANITY AND THE KNIFE-GRINDER

Friend of Humanity

Needy knife-grinder, whither are you going?
Rough is the road; your wheel is out of order;
Bleak blows the blast; your hat has got a hole in't,
    So have your breeches!

Weary knife-grinder, little think the proud ones,
Who in their coaches roll along the turnpike-
-road, what hard work 't is crying all day, "Knives and
    Scissors to grind O!"

Tell me, knife-grinder, how you came to grind knives?
Did some rich man tyrannically use you?
Was it the squire? or parson of the parish?
    Or the attorney?

Was it the squire, for killing of his game? or
Covetous parson, for his tithes distraining?
Or roguish lawyer, made you lose your little
    All in a lawsuit?

(Have you not read the Rights of Man, by Tom Paine?)
Drops of compassion tremble on my eyelids,
Ready to fall as soon as you have told your
    Pitiful story.

Knife-Grinder

Story! God bless you! I have none to tell, sir,
Only, last night, a-drinking at the Chequers,
This poor old hat and breeches, as you see, were
    Torn in a scuffle.

Constables came up for to take me into
Custody; they took me before the justice;
Justice Oldmixon put me in the parish-
    -Stocks for a vagrant.

I should be glad to drink your honour's health in
A pot of beer, if you will give me sixpence;
But for my part I never love to meddle
    With politics, sir.

Friend of Humanity

I give thee sixpence! I will see thee damned first—
Wretch! whom no sense of wrongs can rouse to vengeance—
Sordid, unfeeling, reprobate, degraded,
    Spiritless outcast!

(Kicks the knife-grinder, overturns his wheel, and exit in a transport of republican enthusiasm and universal philanthrophy.)

—*The Anti-Jacobin*, November 27, 1797. (This number was written by George Canning and J. H. Frere.)

Poetry has this much, at least, in common with religion, that its standards were fixed long ago by certain inspired writers, whose authority it is no longer lawful to call in question; and that many profess to be entirely devoted to it who have no *good works* to produce in support of their pretensions. . . . . The author who is now before us belongs to a *sect* of poets that has established itself in this country within these ten or twelve years, and is looked upon, we believe, as one of its chief champions and apostles. The peculiar doctrines of this sect it would not, perhaps, be very easy to explain; but that they are *dissenters* from the established systems in poetry and criticism, is admitted, and proved, indeed, by the whole tenor of their compositions. . . . . From this little sketch of the story [of "Thalaba"] our readers will easily perceive that it consists altogether of the most wild and extravagant fictions, and openly sets nature and probability at defiance. In its action it is not an imitation of anything, and excludes all rational criticism as to the choice and succession of its incidents. Tales of this sort may amuse children, and interest, for a moment, by the prodigies they exhibit and the multitude of events they bring together; but the interest expires with the novelty, and attention is frequently exhausted even before curiosity has been gratified. . . . . All the productions of this author, it appears to us, bear very distinctly the impression of an amiable mind, a cultivated fancy, and a perverted taste. · His genius seems naturally to delight in the representation of domestic virtues and pleasures and the brilliant delineation of external nature. In both these departments he is frequently very successful, but he seems to want vigor for the loftier flights of poetry. · He is often puerile, diffuse, and artificial, and seems to have but little acquaintance with those chaster and severer graces by whom the epic muse would be most suitably attended. His faults are always aggravated, and often created, by his partiality for the peculiar manner of that new school of poetry of which he is a faithful disciple, and to the glory of which he has sacrificed greater talents and acquisitions than can be boasted of by any of his associates.—*The Edinburgh Review*, October, 1802.

THOMAS CAMPBELL

(102) THE PLEASURES OF HOPE. Part I. 1–40. Cf. Akenside's "Pleasures of Imagination" (1744) and Roger's "Pleasures of Memory" (1792), with regard to subject and title, and the latter with regard also to verse and style.

(103) 31–40. The poet seems to combine the fable of Pandora, from whose box all the blessings but hope escaped, with the legend of the Iron Age, in which the gods and the virtues forsook the earth, and vices and evils took possession of it. ¶ 31. *Aonian:* Aonia was a district in Greece, where stood Mt. Helicon, the fabled abode of the Muses.

(103) YE MARINERS OF ENGLAND. First published in the London *Morning Chronicle*, with the title, "Alteration of the old ballad 'Ye Gentlemen of England, composed on the prospect of a Russian war." The tradition is that Campbell composed some, if not all, of the verses while living in Edinburgh, in 1799, after hearing the ballad sung at an evening reception; but the above title shows that he finished or revised them the latter part of the following year, during his residence in Germany. The patriotic pride and confidence of the poem was doubtless intensified by England's recent naval victories over the French, especially those of Cape St. Vincent (1797) and the Nile (1798). ¶ 15. *Blake:* Robert Blake, the famous admiral, who won brilliant victories over the Dutch and the Spanish, in Cromwell's time, died at sea, of disease, in 1657; he was buried in Westminster Abbey. *Nelson:* Lord Nelson, the greatest of English naval commanders, was killed on board his ship, in the battle of Trafalgar (1805), which shattered the naval power of France; he was buried in St. Paul's Cathedral. For neither Blake nor Nelson was the ocean a "grave," nor does the poet say so.

(104) 31. *meteor flag:* a double reference to the color of the British flag and to the old belief that meteors were portents of calamity.

(104) HOHENLINDEN. Hohenlinden is a village in Bavaria, about twenty miles from Munich; here the French inflicted a crushing defeat upon the Austrians, December 2, 1800. Campbell did not witness the battle (as was long erroneously believed); but he had been in Bavaria the summer before and saw some fighting, which no doubt heightened the vividness of his lines. ¶ 1. *Linden=*Hohenlinden.

(**105**) 23. *Frank:* the French. *Hun:* the Austrians; Campbell apparently confused the Hungarians, one of the peoples of Austria-Hungary, with the ancient Huns. ¶ 29. *Few, few shall part:* the battle was very bloody; some 15,000 men, about one-fourth of all the troops engaged, were killed or seriously wounded.

(**105**) BATTLE OF THE BALTIC. "It is an attempt to write an English ballad on the battle of Copenhagen, as much as possible in that plain, strong style peculiar to our old ballads which tell us the when, where, and how the event happened—without gaud or ornament but what the subject essentially and easily affords."—Campbell, in a letter to Dr. Currie, April 24, 1805. The battle of Copenhagen was fought on April 2, 1801. In the preceding December an armed neutrality league, directed against England, had been formed by Russia, Sweden, Prussia, and Denmark; England protested, and soon declared war. A fleet under Admirals Parker and Nelson was sent against the Danish fleet at Copenhagen; Parker remained in reserve with eight ships, while Nelson advanced to the attack with twelve ships of the line. The Danes had the advantage in position; three of the English ships went aground, and all were exposed to the fire of heavy land-batteries. The fight was so long and fierce that Parker signaled, "Discontinue the action." But Nelson, in reading the signal, applied his blind eye to the telescope and could make out nothing. He kept his own signal flying—"Move in closer!" At last the fire of the Danes began to slacken, and some of their ships were seen to be in flames; Nelson thereupon offered generous terms of surrender, which were accepted. The British loss in killed and severely wounded was more that 900; the Danish, from 1,600 to 1,800.

In its first form, in 1805, the poem contained 162 lines; but before publication Campbell reduced it to its present length by rejecting some stanzas and condensing and combining others. A few stanzas from the first draft will show the poet's method of revision:

> Of Nelson and the North
>   Sing the day,
> When, their haughty powers to vex,
> He engaged the Danish decks,
> And with twenty floating wrecks
>   Crowned the fray.
>
> All bright, in April's sun,
>   Shone the day;
> When a British fleet came down,
> Through the islands of the crown
> And by Copenhagen town
>   Took their stay.
>
> In arms the Danish shore
>   Proudly shone;
> By each gun the lighted brand
> In a bold determined hand;
> And the Prince of all the land
>   Led them on.
>
> For Denmark here had drawn
>   All her might;
> From her battle-ships so vast
> She had hewn away the mast,
> And at anchor to the last
>   Bade them fight.
>   .   .   .   .   .
> Three hours the raging fire
>   Did not slack;
> But the fourth, their signals drear
> Of distress and wreck appear,
> And the Dane a feeble cheer
>   Sent us back.
>   .   .   .   .   .

> The bells shall ring! the day
>   Shall not close,
> But a blaze of cities bright
>   Shall illuminate the night,
> And the wine-cup shine in light
>   As it flows.
>
> Yet, yet, amid the joy
>   And uproar,
> Let us think of them that sleep
> Full many a fathom deep
> All beside thy rocky steep,
>   Elsinore!

(106) 23. "*Hearts of oak*": the words are from the ballad, "Ye Gentlemen of England," long popular in England. ¶ 36. *gloom:* not night (cf. l. 51), but darkness caused by the smoke (cf. ll. 23–25).

(107) 63. *Elsinore:* a seaport near Copenhagen, at the entrance of the sound where the battle was fought; it contains the fortress of Kronborg, overlooking the sea, and is famous as the scene of *Hamlet.* ¶ 67. *Riou:* Captain Edward Riou, who commanded the frigates and smaller craft, fought most gallantly against the land-batteries; he was wounded severely in the head by a splinter, but was still directing his men, when a cannon ball cut him in two.

(107) LORD ULLIN'S DAUGHTER. Campbell's biographer, William Beattie, says that the poem was sketched among the scenes to which it refers, in the island of Mull, off the western coast of Scotland, where the poet spent five months as a private tutor in 1795; but it was not finished until the winter of 1804–05. ¶ 5. *Lochgyle:* a loch may be either a lake or a partially land-locked arm of the sea; here it is the latter, as the lovers were fleeing from the island to the Highlands, on the mainland. ¶ 7. *Ulva's isle:* a small island off the west shore of Mull.

CONTEMPORARY CRITICISM

"The Pleasures of Hope," a poem dear to every reader of poetry, bore, amidst many beauties, the mark of a juvenile composition, and received from the public the indulgence due to a promise of future excellence. Some license was also allowed for the didactic nature of the subject, which, prescribing no fixed plan, left the poet free to indulge his fancy in excursions as irregular as they are elegant and animated. . . . . But the hope of improvement was, in Mr. Campbell's case, hardly necessary to augment the expectation raised by the actual excellence of his first poem. The beauties of an highly polished versification, that animated and vigorous tone of moral feeling, that turn of expression, which united the sweetness of Goldsmith with the strength of Johnson, a structure of language alike remote from servile imitation of our more classical poets and from the babbling and jingling simplicity of ruder minstrels, new but not singular, elegant but not trite, justified the admirers of "The Pleasures of Hope" in elevating its author to a pre-eminent situation among living poets. . . . . Two beautiful war odes, entitled "The Mariners of England" and "The Battle of the Baltick," afford pleasing instances of that short and impetuous lyric sally in which Mr. Campbell excells all his contemporaries. Two ballads, "Glenara" and "Lord Ullin's Daughter," the former approaching the rude yet forcible simplicity of the ancient minstrels, the latter upon a more refined plan, conclude the volume. They were new to us, and are models in their several styles of composition.—*The Quarterly Review,* May, 1809.

There are probably few readers of English poetry who are not already familiar with the "Lochiel" and the "Hohenlinden"—the one by far the most spirited and poetical denunciation of woe since the days of Cassandra, the other the only representation of a modern battle which possesses either interest or sublimity. The song to "The Mariners of England" is also very generally known. It is a splendid instance of the most magnificent diction adapted to a familiar and even trivial metre. . . . . "The Battle of the Baltic," though we think it has been printed before, is much less known. Though written in a strange, and we think an unfortunate, metre, it has great force and grandeur both of conception and expression—that sort of force and grandeur which results from the simple and concise expression of great events and natural emotions, altogether unassisted by any splendor or amplification of expression. The characteristic merit in these, both of this piece and of "Hohenlinden," is that, by the forcible delineation of one or two great circumstances, they give a clear and most energetic representation of events as complicated as they are impressive, and thus impress the mind of the reader with all the terror and sublimity of the subject, while they rescue him from the fatigue and perplexity of its details.—*The Edinburgh Review*, April, 1809.

WALTER SCOTT

(**109**) THE LAY OF THE LAST MINSTREL. Canto I. i–xviii. "The poem now offered to the public is intended to illustrate the customs and manners which anciently prevailed on the borders of England and Scotland. . . . . The date of the tale itself is about the middle of the sixteenth century, when most of the personages actually flourished."—Preface to the first edition. In 1801 Scott received a visit from a Mr. Stoddart, a friend of the "Lake Poets," who recited to him some of their unpublished poems. "Amongst others was the striking fragment called 'Christabel,' by Mr. Colcridge, which, from the singularly irregular structure of the stanzas, and the liberty which it allowed the author to adapt the sound to the sense, seemed to be exactly suited to such an extravaganza as I meditated on the subject of Gilpin Horner [the germ of "The Lay of the Last Minstrel"]. . . . . It was in 'Christabel' that I first found it [this metre] used in serious poetry, and it is to Mr. Coleridge that I am bound to make the acknowledgment due from the pupil to his master."—Introduction (1831) to "The Lay of the Last Minstrel."

(**109**) 5. Cf. "Christabel," l. 54.

(**110**) 38. *barbed*=armored. ¶ 30. *Jedwood-axe:* a long-handled battle-axe, or partizan; so called from the town of Jedburgh, the coat-of-arms of which has such a weapon. ¶ 48. *Southern:* English. ¶ 61. *Dunedin*=Edinburgh. ("Dunedin," meaning the "hill of Edwin," is the name the Scots gave to Edinburgh, which was founded by Edwin, King of Northumbria, in the seventh century.)

(**111**) 63. *slogan's:* the slogan was the war-cry or gathering-word of a Highland clan (Gaelic "sluagh," army, and "gairm," a call).

(**112**) 112. *a clerk*=a learned man (Late Latin "clericus," a clergyman; also a learned man, because in the Middle Ages the clergy constituted the only educated class). ¶ 119. St Andrews, a town in Fifeshire, was the site of the cathedral of St. Andrew, where the "clerk of fame" was archbishop. ¶ 120. "The vulgar conceive that when a class of students have made a certain progress in their mystic studies, they are obliged to run through a subterranean hall, where the Devil literally catches the hindmost in the race, unless he crosses the hall so speedily that the arch-enemy can only apprehend his shadow. In the latter case, the person of the sage never after throws any shade; and those who have thus lost their shadow always prove the best magicians."—Scott. ¶ 126–43. Cf. "Christabel," ll. 1–52. ¶ 131. *scaur's:* a scaur is a precipitous bank. ¶ 137. *ban-dogs*=large, fierce dogs, usually kept chained ("band" and "dogs").

(**113**) 151. *fell*=a rocky hill. ¶ 156. *morris*=the morris dance (probably so called because of Moorish origin). ¶ 158. *emerald rings:* "Their [the fairies'] diversion was dancing hand-in-hand in a circle; and the traces of their tiny feet, which were held to be visible on the grass long afterwards, were called fairy rings. . . . . Ringlets of grass . . . . are very common in meadows, which are higher, sourer, and of a deeper green than the grass that grows round them, and by the common people are usually called 'fairy circles.'"—Brand's *Popular Antiquities.* ¶ 170. *Arthur's slow wain:* the seven brightest stars in the constellation *Ursa Major* (cf. "Northern Bear," l. 172); called a wain because of a fanciful resemblance to a cart with its tongue (the same as the Great Dipper); called Arthur's by a corruption of "Arcturus," the name of the brightest star in the group and often used for the whole.

(114) LOCHINVAR. From "Marmion" (Canto V. xii). "The ballad of 'Lochinvar' is in a very slight degree founded on a ballad called 'Katharine Janfarie,' which may be found in the *Minstrelsy of the Scottish Border*."—Scott.

(115) 20. *the Solway:* Solway Firth, an arm of the sea, separating Scotland from England; the tides in it are very swift (see *Redgauntlet*, chap. iv). ¶ 32. *galliard:* a spirited dance for two persons.

(115) CORONACH. From "The Lady of the Lake" (Canto III. xvi).

(116) 17. *correi:* "The hollow side of the hill, where game usually lies."—Scott. ¶ 18. *cumber*=distress, trouble (cf. "encumber").

(116) THE LADY OF THE LAKE. Canto VI. xv–xxi. The minstrel sings to the dying Roderick Dhu, in prison, an account of the battle between his Highland clan and the forces of James V, King of Scotland. "A skirmish actually took place at a pass thus called [Beal' an Duine] in the Trosachs, and closed with the remarkable incident mentioned in the text. It was greatly posterior in date to the reign of James V."—Scott. ¶ 9. *the erne*=the eagle.

(117) 26. *Saxon:* the Highlanders called the Lowlanders "Saxons" and themselves "Gaels." ¶ 36. *barbed*=armored.

(118) 84. *Tinchel:* "A circle of sportsmen who, by surrounding a great space and gradually narrowing, brought immense quantities of deer together, which usually made desperate efforts to break through the Tinchel."—Scott.

(119) 119. *Bracklinn's chasm:* the Falls of Bracklinn, in a wooded gorge, are not far from the scene of the battle. ¶ 120. *linn*=cataract.

(122) 218. *Bothwell's lord:* the exiled Douglas, in whose interest Roderick and his clan had taken up arms.

(122) PROUD MAISIE. From *The Heart of Mid-Lothian*, chap. xl. ¶ 7. *braw*= brave, stout, handsome.

(122) COUNTY GUY. From *Quentin Durward*, chap. iv. ¶ 5. *thrilled*=trilled.

(123) BONNY DUNDEE. From "The Doom of Devorgoil," II. ii. See *Old Mortality* for a portrait of Claverhouse at an earlier period than that of the ballad. John Graham of Claverhouse, Viscount of Dundee, a man of great personal fascination and a dashing soldier, was the chief agent of Charles II and James II in suppressing uprisings by the Scotch Covenanters. Even when James had fled to France, Claverhouse staunchly supported his cause, braving the Convention, or Scotch Parliament, as told in the poem, and marching out of Edinburgh at the head of fifty devoted followers. He failed in his attempt to persuade the Duke of Gordon to hold Edinburgh Castle for King James, but in the Highlands he raised an army which defeated the government forces at the battle of Killiecrankie, in 1689; he himself, however, was killed, saying almost with his last breath that "it was the less matter for him, seeing the day went well for his master." ¶ 10. *the bells are rung backward:* "To ring bells backward, to give an alarm by ringing the bells of a chime in the wrong order, beginning with the bass bell."—*Century Dictionary*. ¶ 11. *douce*=staid, prudent. ¶ 14. *the sanctified bends of the Bow:* Bow, or West Bow, a curving street in Edinburgh was inhabited chiefly by Covenanters. ¶ 15. *Ilk*=each. *carline*=middle-aged or old woman. *flyting*=scolding. *pow*=poll, head. ¶ 16. *couthie*=kindly, loving. *slee*=sly. ¶ 19. *Grassmarket:* at that time the place of executions. ¶ 24. *cowls of Kilmarnock:* Kilmarnock, a town west of Edinburgh, was formerly famous for the manufacture of "Kilmarnock cowls," or hooded garments. ¶ 25. *gullies*=large knives. ¶ 26. *close-heads:* the upper ends of narrow passages leading from the street.

(124) 31. *Mons Meg:* a great cannon, supposed to have been made in Mons, Belgium. *marrows*=mates. ¶ 35. *Montrose:* The Marquis of Montrose fought for the king in the Civil War, and was executed because of a royalist attack which he made on Scotland in 1650. ¶ 41. *Duniewassals:* Highland gentlemen of secondary rank. ¶ 44. *barkened*=tanned with bark.

CONTEMPORARY CRITICISM

There is nothing cold, creeping, or feeble in all Mr. Scott's poetry; no laborious little-ness, or puling classical affectation. He has his failures, indeed, like other people, but he always attempts vigorously, and never fails in his immediate object without accomplishing something far beyond the reach of an ordinary writer. Even when he wanders from the paths of pure taste, he leaves behind him the footsteps of a powerful genius, and molds the most humble of his materials into a form worthy of a nobler substance. Allied to this inherent vigor and animation, and in a great degree derived from it, is that air of facility and freedom which adds so peculiar a grace to most of Mr. Scott's compositions. . . . . These, we think, are the general characteristics of Mr. Scott's poetry. Among his minor peculiarities, we might notice his singular talent for description, and especially for the description of scenes abounding in *motion* or *action* of any kind. In this department, indeed, we conceive him to be almost without a rival, either among modern or ancient poets; and the character and process of his descriptions are as extraordinary as their effect is astonishing.—*The Edinburgh Review*, August, 1810, on "The Lady of the Lake." (The article was written by Francis Jeffrey.)

GEORGE GORDON BYRON

Notes signed "B." are by Byron.

(125) LACHIN Y GAIR. One of the poems in *Hours of Idleness.* "Lachin y Gair, or, as it is pronounced in the Erse, Loch na Garr, towers proudly pre-eminent in the Northern Highlands. . . . . Near Lachin y Gair I spent some of the early part of my life, the recol-lection of which has given birth to these stanzas."—B. ¶ 23. *my fathers:* "I allude here to my maternal ancestors, the Gordons, many of whom fought for the unfortunate Prince Charles, better known by the name of the Pretender."—B. ¶ 30. *Braemar:* a tract of the Highlands.

(126) ENGLISH BARDS AND SCOTCH REVIEWERS. Lines 143–64, 225–54, 438–59, 1037–70. Byron had begun to write a poem, "English Bards," in 1807; after the scathing criticism of *Hours of Idleness* in *The Edinburgh Review,* in 1808 (see p. 538), he enlarged the scope of the poem, as indicated by the later title, but his purpose was still, in part, to satirize the poetry of his day, of which he then and later had a low opinion. "With regard to poetry in general, I am convinced, the more I think of it, that he and *all* of us—Scott, Southey, Wordsworth, Moore, Campbell, I—are all in the wrong, one as much as another; that we are upon a wrong revolutionary poetical system, or systems, not worth a damn in itself, and from which none but Rogers and Crabbe are free. . . . . I am the more confirmed in this by having lately gone over some of our classics, particularly Pope, whom I tried in this way—I took Moore's poems and my own and some others, and went over them side by side with Pope's, and I was really astonished (I ought not to have been so) and mortified at the ineffable distance in point of sense, harmony, effect, and even *imagination,* passion, and *invention,* between the little Queen Anne's man and us of the Lower Empire."—Letter to Murray, September 15, 1817. But of the poem as a whole his mature judgment did not approve; in 1816, after re-reading it, he wrote on the margin: "The greater part of this satire I most sincerely wish had never been written—not only on account of the injustice of much of the critical and some of the personal part of it, but the tone and temper are such as I cannot approve."

(126) 26. *a fourth:* a fourth epic; "Joan of Arc," "Thalaba," and "Madoc" had already appeared. ¶ 29. *Berkley ballads:* an allusion to Southey's ballad, "The Old Woman of Berkley," in which an old woman is carried off by Beelzebub.

(127) 32. The first three words are quoted because, as Byron said in his note, they are "an evident plagiarism from the Anti-Jacobin to Mr. Southey on his dactylics"; the poem referred to contains the half-line, "God help thee, silly one." ¶ 37, 38. See "The Tables Turned." ¶ 40. See Wordsworth's preface to *Lyrical Ballads,* quoted on p. 506.

¶ 53. *Jeffrey:* Francis Jeffrey, editor of *The Edinburgh Review*, and long supposed to be the writer of the critique on *Hours of Idleness* (see p. 538). Byron changed his opinion of him later, when Jeffrey had praised generously his subsequent poems. In 1814 he wrote to Moore, "As for Jeffrey, it is a very handsome thing of him to speak well of an old antagonist, and what a mean mind dared not do"; and in "Don Juan" (X. xvi) he wrote thus in 1822:

> And all our little feuds, at least all *mine,*
>   Dear Jeffrey, once my most redoubted foe
> (As far as rhyme and criticism combine
>   To make such puppets of us things below),
> Are over: here's a health to "Auld Lang Syne!"
>   I do not know you, and may never know
> Your face—but you have acted on the whole
> Most nobly, and I own it from my soul.

¶ 54. *a judge:* the brutal and bloodthirsty Chief Justice Jeffreys, of the "Bloody Assizes" in 1685.

(128) 75–108. These lines were added in the second edition, in October, 1809. ¶ 77. *Hours of Idleness* was published anonymously, but the authorship was no secret. ¶ 81. *I tear the veil away:* the first edition of "English Bards and Scotch Reviewers," in March, was anonymous; the second bore Byron's name. ¶ 83. *Melbourne house:* Lord Melbourne was brother of George Lambe, a contributor to *The Edinburgh Review.* ¶ 84. *Holland's spouse:* "Certain it is, her ladyship is suspected of having displayed her matchless wit in *The Edinburgh Review.* However that may be, we know from good authority, that the manuscripts are submitted to her perusal—no doubt, for correction."—B. ¶ 85. *Jeffrey's harmless pistol:* "In 1806 Messrs. Jeffrey and Moore met at Chalk-Farm. The duel was prevented by the interference of the magistracy; and, on examination, the balls of the pistols were found to have evaporated."—B. ¶ 87. *buckram:* a coarse linen cloth used in binding books; the allusion to the bound volumes of the Review is obvious. ¶ 88. *"penetrable stuff":* Hamlet,* III. iv. 36. ¶ 105. *incondite*=unpolished, rude (Latin "inconditus," not put together).

(129) SHE WALKS IN BEAUTY. Included in *Hebrew Melodies;* but the stanzas were written about Lady Horton, whom the poet had recently seen at a ball, attired in mourning with numerous spangles on her dress.

(130) THE PRISONER OF CHILLON. Written in two days, at a small inn, where the poet was detained by bad weather during a tour of the Lake of Geneva with Shelley. François de Bonnivard (1496–1570?) was the head of a small priory outside Geneva. From political and religious motives he espoused the cause of the republic of Geneva against the Duke of Savoy, who had been granted seignorial rights over the city by the prince bishop. The duke imprisoned him in the castle of Chillon during the years 1530 to 1536, four of which he spent in the dungeon below the level of the Lake of Geneva. When Chillon was captured by the forces of his party, he was released, and was made a member of the council of Geneva, and given a pension; he married four times, having become a Protestant. It will be seen from these facts that Byron's prisoner is less the historical character than his own ideal conception of the heroic and pathetic victim of religious persecution. The meter of the poem perhaps shows somewhat the influence of "Christabel," which Byron had heard read and which he had recently advised Murray to publish.

(140) TO THOMAS MOORE. "This should have been written fifteen moons ago [just as Byron was leaving England forever]—the first stanza was."—Letter to Moore, July 10, 1817.

(141) CHILDE HAROLD'S PILGRIMAGE. "The following poem was written, for the most part, amidst the scenes which it attempts to describe. It was begun in Albania; and the parts relative to Spain and Portugal were composed from the author's observations in those countries. . . . . A fictitious character is introduced for the sake of giving some connection to the piece, which, however, makes no pretension to regularity. It has been sug-

gested to me . . . . that in this fictitious character, Childe Harold, I may incur the suspicion of having intended some real personage: this I beg leave, once for all, to disclaim."—Preface to the first edition of Cantos I and II. "Childe" is used as in the old romances and ballads, meaning a youth of a noble house, usually one not yet admitted to knighthood.

(141) *SPAIN.* Canto I. xxxv–xlii. When Byron visited Spain, in the summer of 1809, Spain and her ally, England, were at war with France, resisting the aggressions of Napoleon, who had seated his brother Joseph on the Spanish throne. The poet first appeals to the Spaniards to be worthy of their ancestors who fought against the Saracen invaders, and then describes the battle of Talavera, which occurred July 26–28; Byron visited the battlefield soon after. ¶ 2–4. Arabs and Moors invaded Spain in 711, aided by Count Julian, a Spanish nobleman; according to popular tradition, his motive was revenge for the violation of his daughter, Cava, by King Roderick, but it is far more probable that political discontent was the cause. The Saracens easily conquered all Spain except the mountainous northern portions, where Pelagio, whose standard was an oaken cross, repulsed them. *Gothic:* the ruling class in Spain were the descendants of the West Goths, who overran the country at the downfall of the Roman Empire. ¶ 7. *at last:* the Moors were finally driven from Spain in 1492, in the reign of Ferdinand and Isabella. ¶ 27. *Andalusia's shore:* Andalusia, the southern part of Spain, was the last stronghold of the Moors.

(142) 57. *flout*=mock at, with a reference here, apparently, to the contrast between "gaudy" and "pale blue." ¶ 59. *fond*=foolish, as often in early English (M. E. "fonned," p. p. of "fon," to act foolishly). ¶ 70. *hails:* here used in the sense of "welcomes."

(143) *GREECE.* Canto II. lxxiii, lxxxiv–xcl. ¶ 9. *Eurotas' banks:* a river in the country of the Spartans was selected for mention because the Spartans were in the desperate battle with the Persian hordes at Thermopylae. ¶ 10. *Lacedemon's:* Lacedemon was an ancient name for Laconia and its capital, Sparta. ¶ 11. *Epaminondas:* Thebes's greatest general. ¶ 29. *the cave:* "of Mount Pentelicus, from whence the marble was dug that constructed the public edifices of Athens. . . . . An immense cave, formed by the quarries, still remains."—B. ¶ 30. *Tritonia's*=Athena's; according to one tradition Athena was born near Lake Triton, in Libya. ¶ 31. *Colonna's cliff:* the promontory at the southern extremity of Attica, so named from the columns of a temple to Athena; the ancient Sunium.

(144) 40. *Hymettus:* a mountain near Athens, famous for its honey. ¶ 44. *Mendeli's:* Mendeli is the modern name for Pentelicus; see note on l. 29. ¶ 54. *Athena's tower*=the Parthenon, by a loose use of the word "tower." ¶ 55–72. Added in 1814. ¶ 56. *Its foreign lord:* Greece was then subject to Turkey.

(145) *BYRON AND CHILDE HAROLD.* Canto III. i–xvi. ¶ 1. Byron's daughter was only five weeks old when Lady Byron left him, and he never saw the child again.

(146) 43. *yet:* equivalent here to "but"; "yet rife" is in contrast to "lone." ¶ 64. *Something too much of this: Hamlet,* III. ii. 79. ¶ 65. *spell*=story, narrative. *silent seal* =seal of silence.

(147) 80. *pined*=pained. ¶ 99. *fond*=foolish.

(148) 123. *this clay*=the body.

(149) *WATERLOO.* Canto III. xvii–xxviii. The battle of Waterloo had been fought the year before Byron's visit. ¶ 9. *king-making victory:* the battle seated the kings of Europe more firmly on their thrones, which had been endangered first by the French Revolution and then by the ambition of Napoleon. ¶ 14. *"pride of place":* a term in falconry, meaning the highest point of flight. ¶ 36. Harmodius and Aristogeiton slew Hipparchus, one of the tyrants of Athens, in 514 B. C., at the Panathenaic festival, having concealed their swords in myrtle branches. ¶ 37. On the evening before the battle of Quatre-Bras (which occurred on June 16, 1815, two days before the battle of Waterloo), a ball was given in Brussels, and many of the British officers went to it. Wellington knew that Napoleon was near, and had made all preparations for the battle; but in order to keep the city ignorant of his plans he

let the ball go on. The Lady de Ros, a daughter of the Duchess of Richmond, who gave the ball, in her *Personal Recollections of the Great Duke of Wellington*, says: "When the duke arrived, rather late, at the ball, I was dancing, but at once went up to him to ask about the rumors. He said very gravely, 'Yes, they are true; we are off to-morrow.' This terrible news was circulated directly, and while some of the officers hurried away, others remained at the ball, and actually had not time to change their clothes, but fought in evening costume" (*Murray's Magazine*, January and February, 1889; in book form, as *A Sketch of the Life of Georgiana, Lady de Ros*, 1893).

(150) 61. The father of the Duke of Brunswick had been killed in the battle of Auerstädt, in 1806.

(151) 82. "*Cameron's Gathering*": the war-song which called together the Cameron clan. ¶83. *Lochiel:* Donald Cameron of Lochiel, the chief of the clan, who fought for the Young Pretender in 1745. *Albyn's:* "Albyn" is the Gaelic name for Scotland. ¶84. *Saxon*=English. ¶90. *Evan's:* Evan Cameron was grandfather of Donald, and had fought against Cromwell; his great-great-grandson commanded a regiment of Highlanders in the battle of Quatre-Bras, and was mortally wounded. ¶91. *Ardennes.* The forest was really that of Soignies: "The wood of Soignies is supposed to be a remnant of the forest of Ardennes, ... immortal in Shakespeare's *As You Like It*. . . . . I have ventured to adopt the name connected with nobler associations than those of mere slaughter."—B.

(151) *LAKE LEMAN IN CALM AND STORM.* Canto III. lxxxv–xcvii.

(152) 37–39. Cf. Wordsworth's "It Is a Beauteous Evening," etc., ll. 2, 3.

(153) 50–54. Cf. "Adonais," ll. 478–86. Byron was much in Shelley's company during the weeks when this canto was written, and evidently was influenced by the latter's idealistic pantheism, embodied later in "Adonais." *Cytherea's zone:* the girdle of Aphrodite, which made beautiful and awakened love for the person wearing it; see the *Iliad*, XIV. 214 ff. Aphrodite was called Cytherea from the island of Cythera, near which, according to one myth, she rose from the foam of the sea. ¶55–63. "It is to be recollected that the most beautiful and impressive doctrines of the divine Founder of Christianity were delivered, not in the Temple, but on the Mount. . . . . The Mussulmans . . . . are accustomed to repeat their prescribed orisons and prayers wherever they may be, at the stated hours—of course frequently in the open air, kneeling upon a light mat. . . . . On me the simple and entire sincerity of these men, and the spirit which appeared to be within and upon them, made a far greater impression than any general rite which was ever performed in places of worship."—B. ¶64. "The thunder-storm to which these lines refer occurred on the 13th of June, 1816, at midnight. I have seen, among the Acroceraunian mountains of Chimari, several more terrible, but none more beautiful."—B.

(154) 82–90. Cf. "Christabel," ll. 408–26; Byron had seen the poem in manuscript and it had recently been published by his advice; his stanza seems to be a direct reminiscence of Coleridge's lines. ¶102. *feeling:* see the preceding stanzas, in which the poet has attributed conscious life and emotion to the night and the storm. ¶104. *knoll:* apparently used in the sense of "signal-bell"; the dying away of the storm, which has absorbed his thought and temporarily taken him out of himself, recalls him to himself and the tempests within him.

(155) *VENICE.* Canto IV. i–iii. ¶1. *Bridge of Sighs.* "The communication between the ducal palace and the prisons of Venice is by a gloomy bridge, or covered gallery, high above the water, and divided by a stone wall into a passage and a cell. The state dungeons . . . . were sunk in the thick walls of the palace; and the prisoner, when taken out to die, was conducted across the gallery to the other side, and being then led back into the other compartment, or cell, upon the bridge, was there strangled."—Hobhouse. ¶8. *wingèd Lion's:* on a pillar near the ducal palace is the winged lion of St. Mark, the tutelary saint of Venice. ¶9. *her hundred isles:* Venice is built on some 117 islands. ¶10. *Cybele:* Cybele, the wife of Saturn, was sometimes regarded as the goddess of town life and as such wore a crown

fashioned like a turreted city wall. ¶ 13. At the height of her glory as a maritime power, in the fifteenth century, the republic of Venice had an enormous trade, a large fleet of war-galleys, and many possessions in the East, including most of the Greek islands. ¶ 19, 20. Before the capture of Venice by Napoleon, in 1797, the gondoliers were accustomed to sing, in alternation, stanzas from Tasso's *Jerusalem Delivered.* ¶ 27. *masque:* here about equivalent to "festivity" and "revel"; one kind of masque was an entertainment something like a modern mask-ball.

(155) *ROME AND FREEDOM.* Canto IV. lxxviii–lxxx, lxxxviii–xcviii.

(156) 10. *The Niobe of Nations:* the twelve children of Niobe, wife of the king of Thebes, were slain by the arrows of Apollo and Artemis because she had boasted of her superiority to their mother, Leto, in number of offspring. ¶ 19, 20. The Goths sacked Rome in 410 and later. Under Christian rule temples and other buildings were mutilated, to gratify religious fanaticism or to secure building material. ¶ 22, 23. The sense is that in the decay of the empire barbarian monarchs, who had captured Rome, rode up the Capitoline Hill, which in former days victorious Roman generals had climbed in their triumphal chariots, often with captive kings in their train. ¶ 28. *thunder-stricken nurse of Rome:* the bronze image, in the Capitoline Museum, of the wolf that suckled Romulus and Remus, the founders of Rome, is by some identified with the image mentioned by Cicero (*De divinatione,* ii. 20) as having been struck by lightning. ¶ 34. *ethereal:* coming from the ether, or upper air, whence Jove hurled his thunderbolts. ¶ 40. *things:* used loosely for the Roman Empire and its "men of iron"; modern nations have imitated the Romans by fighting and dying for conquest and glory. ¶ 44. *one vain man:* Napoleon.

(157) 53. *Alcides with the distaff:* while Hercules (called Alcides, because descended from Alceus) was the slave of Omphale, he wore woman's dress and spun wool with her handmaidens. ¶ 54. *At Cleopatra's feet:* when Julius Caesar was in Egypt he came under the spell of Cleopatra. ¶ 56. *his eagles:* the French regiments; from the Roman custom of having eagles on the military standards, the word came to be used for soldiers of any nation. *flee*=fly. The sense of this line and the next is that Napoleon wished to reduce his armies to mere tame instruments of his will, by which to win victories for his own power and glory.

(158) 97. *him:* Napoleon. ¶ 112. *deadly days:* the Reign of Terror during the French Revolution. ¶ 113. *vile ambition:* the military and political ambition of the new republic of France, which became the foe of the freedom of Europe, instead of its friend; cf. Coleridge's "France: an Ode." ¶ 115. *the base pageant:* apparently the empire and court of Napoleon. Some would take it to refer to the Congress of Vienna, the Holy Alliance, and the Second Treaty of Paris, all in 1815, and all designed to strengthen monarchy against the democratic tendencies of the age; but these could not rightly be called the "pretext" for the reactionary attempt to make political slavery perpetual ("the eternal thrall"), being rather a part of the attempt itself. ¶ 118–21. These lines show the keenness of Byron's political vision, no less than the strength and persistence of his passion for freedom. At a time when a monarchical reaction had set in strongly all over Europe, this English patrician saw and boldly proclaimed that the democratic tendency, although temporarily discredited, was really the strongest force of the times and would ultimately prevail. The simile from nature is as accurate as it is vigorous: the thunder-cloud, like freedom, is borne on the upper and main current of air; while the lower current, blowing in our faces and seeming to be the most important, is really only a temporary eddy, on a lower plane.

(159) *THE OCEAN.* Canto IV. clxxviii–clxxxiv. ¶ 1–9. Written later than the rest, in 1818. ¶ 27. *lay:* Byron made the same grammatical error, more common among educated people in his day than now, in "The Adieu," l. 94: "Where now my head must lay."

(160) 36. *The Armada's pride:* of the vast fleet which Spain sent against England, in 1588, more than half was destroyed by the sea in the terrible voyage northward, around the Orkney Islands, to avoid another battle with the English ships. *spoils of Trafalgar:* most of the French vessels captured by Nelson at Trafalgar were destroyed by a gale soon after.

¶ 30. *Thy waters washed them power:* in the first edition and in several later editions, the reading by mistake was, "Thy waters wasted them." "What does 'thy waters *wasted* them' mean . . . . ? *That is not me.* Consult the MS. *always.*"—Letter to Murray, September 24, 1818.

(160) DON JUAN. "You ask me for the plan of Donny Johnny: I have no plan— I had no plan; but I had or have materials. . . . . You are too earnest and eager about a work never intended to be serious. Do you suppose that I could have any intention but to giggle and make giggle?—a playful satire, with as little poetry as could be helped, was what I meant."—Letter to Murray, August 12, 1819. "Don Juan will be known, by and by, for what it is intended—a *satire* on *abuses* of the present states of society, and not an eulogy of vice."—Letter to Murray, October 25, 1822. Byron had already (1817) written a poem, "Beppo," in the same stanza and the same general manner. In a letter to Murray (March 25, 1818) he says of "Beppo": "Whistlecraft was my immediate model. . . . . But . . . . Berni is the father of that kind of writing, which, I think, suits our language, too, very well— we shall see by the experiment. If it does, I shall send you a volume in a year or two." Berni was an Italian poet of the sixteenth century. "Whistlecraft" was the pseudonym of J. H. Frere in "The Monks and the Giants" (1817); the first two stanzas of his poem will show how closely it anticipated "Beppo" and "Don Juan" in verse and style:

> I 've often wished that I could write a book
>   Such as all English people might peruse;
> I never should regret the pains it took,
>   That 's just the sort of fame that I should choose.
> To sail about the world like Captain Cook,
>   I 'd sling a cot up for my favourite Muse,
> And we 'd take verses out to Demarara,
> To New South Wales, and up to Niagara.
>
> Poets consume exciseable commodities,
>   They raise the nation's spirit when victorious,
> They drive an export trade in whims and oddities,
>   Making our commerce and revenue glorious;
> As an industrious and pains-taking body 't is
>   That poets should be reckoned meritorious:
> And therefore I submissively propose
> To erect one Board for Verse and one for Prose.

(160) *THE SHIPWRECK.* Canto II. xliv–liv, ciii–cx. "With regard to the charges about the shipwreck, I think that I told you and Mr. Hobhouse, years ago, that there was not a single circumstance of it not taken from fact; not, indeed, from any single ship- wreck, but all from actual facts of different wrecks."—Letter to Murray, August 23, 1821. The close parallel between the poet's narrative and Dalzell's *Shipwrecks and Disasters at Sea* (1812) was first pointed out in *The Monthly Magazine*, in 1821; a few passages (which, it should be said, are often taken from places widely apart) will show Byron's method of handling his material: "I perceived the ship settling by the head. . . . . Some appeared perfectly resigned, went to their hammocks, and desired their messmates to lash them in; others were securing themselves to gratings and small rafts; but the most predominant idea was that of putting on their best and cleanest clothes. The boats . . . . were got over the side. . . . . The yawl was stove alongside and sunk. . . . . One oar was erected for a mainmast, and the other broke to the breadth of the blankets for a yard. . . . . Spars, booms, hencoops, and everything buoyant was therefore cast loose, that the men might have some chance to save themselves. . . . . We had scarce quitted the ship, when she gave a heavy lurch to port, and then went down, head foremost. . . . . The crew had just time to leap overboard, which they did, uttering a most dreadful yell."

The ship in which Juan and his tutor, the licentiate Pedrillo, are sailing from Cadiz to Leghorn, is wrecked at sea by a prolonged gale. At this point the selection begins.

(163) 89. The long boat, after a terrible voyage, in which all but four of the thirty

occupants of the boat die, approaches one of the Cyclades, in the Aegean Sea. ¶ 110–12. "This morning I swam from Sestos to Abydos. The immediate distance is not above a mile, but the current renders it hazardous—so much so that I doubt whether Leander's conjugal affection must not have been a little chilled in his passage to Paradise. I attempted it a week ago and failed—owing to the north win... and the wonderful rapidity of the tide, —though I have been from my childhood a strong swimmer. But this morning being calmer, I succeeded, and crossed the 'broad Hellespont' in an hour and ten minutes."—Letter to Mr. Drury, May 3, 1810. Lieut. Ekenhead, of the British navy, accompanied the poet, and beat him by five minutes.

(165) *JUAN AND HAIDÉE.* Canto IV. clxxiv–clxxxv, cxcix–ccii. Haidée, the daughter of a Greek pirate, finds Juan, hides him in a cave, and nurses him back to life. At this point the selection begins. ¶ 7. According to one tradition, Io, the beautiful daughter of the king of Argos, was carried off by Phoenician traders. ¶ 8. Byron was careful to have his geography accurate: Ragusa is a port on the Adriatic Sea, and Scio is north of the Cyclades; a vessel bound from Ragusa to Scio would therefore pass among the islands, within easy reach of the pirate.

(168) *THE SCEPTIC AND HIS POEM.* Canto XIV. i–x.

(170) THE VISION OF JUDGMENT. Lines 744–848. Southey, in the preface to his "Vision of Judgment" (1821), vindicating George III, who had just died, went out of the way to attack the moral character of Byron. Byron, who thought Southey a Pharisee and a political turncoat as well as a poor poet, satirized him in this poem. The earlier stanzas describe a controversy at the gate of heaven, between the angelic and the infernal hosts, to decide whether George III should go to heaven or to hell; in the middle of the dispute a demon arrives with Southey under his wing, and the poet is given a chance to defend himself for writing "A Vision of Judgment." At this point the selection begins. ¶ 8. *"de se"*=upon himself (literally, "of himself ").

(171) 24. *"Wat Tyler"*: this poem, written in 1794 and expressing Southey's radical political opinions at that time, had been published surreptitiously in 1817, much to the author's annoyance. *"Rhymes on Blenheim"*: the familiar ballad, "The Battle of Blenheim" (1800), in which Southey insinuated that the great victory which the English won over the French in 1704 was a useless waste of life. *"Waterloo"*: "The Poet's Pilgrimage to Waterloo" (1816), in which Southey, now a conservative, rejoices over the downfall of the French and the collapse of the French Revolution. ¶ 29. *pantisocracy:* a scheme for a communistic colony (the word means "equal rule of all"), which Coleridge and Southey, in their youth, had dreamed of establishing in America; Byron's hint that the scheme had immoral features is a mere fling. ¶ 31. *anti-jacobin*=anti-radical, conservative. ("Jacobin" became a term or revolutionists during the French Revolution, when a society of revolutionists held their meetings in a Jacobin convent in Paris.) ¶ 41. *Wesley's:* Southey's life of the founder of Methodism had come out the year before.

(172) 63. *Like King Alphonso:* "Alfonso, speaking of the Ptolemean system, said that 'had he been consulted at the creation of the world, he would have spared the Maker some absurdities.' "—B.

(173) 104. *the hundredth psalm:* it begins, "Make a joyful noise unto the Lord."

(173) ON THIS DAY I COMPLETE MY THIRTY-SIXTH YEAR. Written at Missolonghi, Greece, January 22, 1824, three months before the poet's death. ¶ 5. *My days are in the yellow leaf:* cf. *Macbeth*, V. ii. 22, 23, "My way of life is fallen into the sear, the yellow leaf."

(174) 23, 24. The Spartan when killed or severely wounded in battle was borne off the field upon his shield. Byron implies that Greece was now animated by the same bold spirit of freedom which made the ancient Spartans fight to the death rather than yield; the Greeks were in the midst of their heroic and successful rebellion (1821–29) against Turkish rule. ¶ 26–28. Byron was justly proud of his ancestry. His mother was descended from James I.

His paternal ancestors can be traced back to the time of the Norman Conquest, and rendered distinguished service on many battlefields. Cf. the following stanzas from "On Leaving Newstead Abbey," one of the poems in *Hours of Idleness:*

> Of the mail-covered barons, who proudly to battle
>   Led their vassals from Europe to Palestine's plain,
> The escutcheon and shield, which with every blast rattle,
>   Are the only sad vestiges now that remain.
> .   .   .   .
>
> Paul and Hubert, too, sleep in the valley of Cressy;
>   For the safety of Edward and England they fell:
> My fathers! the tears of your country redress ye;
>   How you fought, how you died, still her annals can tell.
>
> On Marston, with Rupert, 'gainst traitors contending,
>   Four brothers enriched with their blood the bleak field,
> For the rights of a monarch their country defending,
>   Till death their attachment to royalty sealed.
>
> Shades of heroes, farewell! your descendant, departing
>   From the seat of his ancestors, bids you adieu!
> Abroad or at home, your remembrance imparting
>   New courage, he'll think upon glory and you.

CONTEMPORARY CRITICISM

The poesy of this young lord belongs to the class which neither gods nor men are said to permit. Indeed we do not recollect to have seen a quantity of verse with so few deviations in either direction from that exact standard. His effusions are spread over a dead flat, and can no more get above or below the level than if they were so much stagnant water. . . . . We must beg leave seriously to assure him that the mere rhyming of the final syllable, even when accompanied by the presence of a certain number of feet,—nay, although (which does not always happen) those feet should scan regularly, and have been all counted accurately upon the fingers,—is not the whole art of poetry. We would entreat him to believe that a certain portion of liveliness, somewhat of fancy, is necessary to constitute a poem; and that a poem in the present day, to be read, must contain at least one thought either in a little degree different from the ideas of former writers or differently expressed. . . . . But whatever judgment may be passed on the poems of this noble minor, it seems we must take them as we find them, and be content; for they are the last we shall ever have from him. He is at best, he says, but an intruder into the groves of Parnassus; he never lived in a garret, like thorough-bred poets; and "though he once roved a careless mountaineer in the Highlands of Scotland," he has not of late enjoyed this advantage. Moreover, he expects no profit from his publication; and whether it succeeds or not, "it is highly improbable, from his situation and pursuits hereafter," that he should again condescend to be an author. Therefore let us take what we get and be thankful. What right have we poor devils to be nice? We are well off to have got so much from a man of this lord's station, who does not live in a garret, but "has the sway" of Newstead Abbey. Again we say, let us be thankful; and, with honest Sancho, bid God bless the giver, nor look the gift-horse in the mouth.—*The Edinburgh Review*, January, 1808, on *Hours of Idleness.* (The article was attributed to Francis Jeffrey, but is now known to have been written by Henry Brougham, one of the founders of the *Review*, and Lord Chancellor of England in 1830–34.)

If the finest poetry be that which leaves the deepest impression on the minds of its readers —and this is not the worst test of its excellence—Lord Byron, we think, must be allowed to take precedence of all his distinguished contemporaries. He has not the variety of Scott, nor the delicacy of Campbell, nor the absolute truth of Crabbe, nor the polished sparkling of Moore; but in force of diction, and inextinguishable energy of sentiment, he clearly surpasses them all. "Words that breathe and thoughts that burn" are not merely the ornaments but the common staple of his poetry; and he is not inspired or impressive only in some happy passages, but through the whole body and tissue of his composition. It was an unavoidable condition, perhaps, of this higher excellence that his scene should be narrow and his persons few. To compass such ends as he had in view it was necessary to reject all ordinary agents and all trivial combinations. He could not possibly be amusing or ingenious or playful, or hope to maintain the requisite pitch of interest by the recitation of sprightly adventures or the opposition of common characters. To produce great effects, in short, he felt that it was necessary to deal only with the greater passions, with the exaltations of a daring fancy and the errors of a lofty intellect, with the pride, the terrors, and the agonies of strong emotion—the fire and air alone of our human elements. . . . . The great success of this singular production ["Childe Harold's Pilgrimage"], indeed, has always appeared to us an extraordinary proof of its merits; for, with all its genius, it does not belong to a sort of poetry that rises easily to popularity. It has no story or action, very little variety of character, and a great deal of reasoning and reflection of no very attractive tenor. It is substantially a contemplative and ethical work, diversified with fine description, and adorned or overshaded by the perpetual presence of one emphatic person, who is sometimes the author, and sometimes the object, of the reflections on which the interest is chiefly rested. It required, no doubt, great force of writing and a decided tone of originality to recommend a performance of this sort so powerfully as this has been recommended to public notice and admiration; and those high characteristics belong perhaps still more eminently to the part [Canto III] that is now before us than to any of the former. There is the same stern and lofty disdain of mankind and their ordinary pursuits and enjoyments, with the same bright gaze on Nature, and the same magic power of giving interest and effect to her delineations, but mixed up, we think, with deeper and more matured reflections and a more intense sensibility to all that is grand or lovely in the external world. . . . . Beautiful as this poetry is, it is a relief at last to close the volume. We cannot maintain our accustomed tone of levity, or even speak like calm literary judges, in the midst of these agonizing trances of a wounded and distempered spirit. Even our admiration is at last swallowed up in a most painful feeling of pity and of wonder. It is impossible to mistake these for fictitious sorrows, conjured up for the purpose of poetical effect. There is a dreadful tone of sincerity, and an energy that cannot be counterfeited, in the expression of wretchedness and alienation from human kind, which occurs in every page of this publication; and as the author has at last spoken out in his own person, and unbosomed his griefs a great deal too freely to his readers, the offense now would be to entertain a doubt of their reality. We certainly have no hope of preaching him into philanthropy and cheerfulness; but it is impossible not to mourn over such a catastrophe of such a mind.—*The Edinburgh Review*, December, 1816, on "Childe Harold's Pilgrimage," Canto III, "The Prisoner of Chillon," etc. (The article was written by Francis Jeffrey.)

That Lord Byron has never written anything more decisively and triumphantly expressive of the greatness of his genius, will be allowed by all who have read this poem. That (laying all its manifold and grievous offences for a moment out of our view) it is by far the most admirable specimen of the mixture of ease, strength, gayety, and seriousness extant in the whole body of English poetry, is a proposition to which we are almost as well persuaded, very few of them will refuse their assent. With sorrow and humiliation do we speak it, the poet has devoted his powers to the worst of purposes and passions; and it increases his guilt and our sorrow that he has devoted them entire. What the immediate effect of the poem may be on contemporary literature, we cannot pretend to guess, too happy could we hope that its lessons of boldness and vigor in language and versification and conception might be attended to, as they deserve to be, without any stain being suffered to fall on the purity of those who minister to the general shape and culture of the public mind, from the mischievous insults against all good principle and all good feeling which have been unworthily embodied in so many elements of fascination. The moral strain of the whole poem is pitched in the lowest key, and if the genius of the author lifts him now and then out of his pollution, it seems as if he regretted the elevation and made all haste to descend again. . . . . Love, honor, patriotism, religion, are mentioned only to be scoffed at and derided, as if their sole resting-place were, or ought to be, in the bosoms of fools. It appears, in short, as if this miserable man, having exhausted every species of sensual gratification, having drained the cup of sin even to its bitterest dregs, were resolved to show us that he is no longer a human being, even in his frailties, but a cool, unconcerned fiend, laughing with a detestable glee over the whole of the better and worse elements of which human life is composed—treating well nigh with equal derision the most pure of virtues and the most odious of vices, dead alike to the beauty of the one and the deformity of the other—a mere heartless despiser of that frail but noble humanity whose type was never exhibited in a shape of more deplorable degradation than in his own contemptuously distinct delineation of himself.—*Blackwood's Magazine*, August, 1819, on "Don Juan," Cantos I and II.

THOMAS MOORE

(**174**) THE HARP THAT ONCE THROUGH TARA'S HALLS. One of the *Irish Melodies*, which appeared at intervals during the years 1808–34. ¶ 1. *Tara's halls:* Tara, near Dublin, was a residence of the Irish kings.

(**175**) LESBIA HATH A BEAMING EYE. One of the *Irish Melodies*.

(**176**) OH, COME TO ME WHEN DAYLIGHT SETS. A Venetian air in *National Airs*, 1818–27.

(**177**) OFT, IN THE STILLY NIGHT. A Scotch air in *National Airs*.

(**177**) THE TWOPENNY POST-BAG. "The bag from which the following letters are selected was dropped by a twopenny postman about two months since, and picked up by an emissary of the Society for the Suppression of Vice, who, supposing it might materially assist the private researches of that institution, immediately took it to his employers. . . . . Unluckily, however, it turned out, upon examination, that the discoveries of profligacy which it enabled them to make lay chiefly in those upper regions of society which their well-bred regulations forbid them to molest or meddle with. In consequence . . . . the bag, with its violated contents, was sold for a trifle to a friend of mine. It happened that I had been just then seized with an ambition . . . . to publish something or other in the shape of a book; and it occurred to me that . . . . a few of these twopenny-post epistles, turned into easy verse, would be as light and popular a task as I could possibly select for a commencement."—Preface to the first edition.

(**178**) 9. *Townsend:* John T. Townshend, recently a lord of the treasury and lord of the bedchamber (cf. l. 13, where there seems also to be an allusion to Hermes, the patron of thieves and the conductor of the dead). ¶ 16. *R-g-nt:* Prince George, afterward George IV; he was made regent in 1811 because the king had become insane. ¶ 34. *Patriot monsters, from Spain:* the war against Napoleon had recently been raging in Spain, and the English were the Spaniards' allies. ¶ 38. *Lord George:* Byron, the first canto of whose "Childe Harold's Pilgrimage" treated mostly of Spain. ¶ 40. *Peninsular:* Spain was often referred to as "the Peninsula." ¶ 43. *Lord L-v-rp- -l's:* the Earl of Liverpool had until recently been secretary for war.

(**179**) 53. *monster:* "Alluding, I suppose, to the Latin advertisement of a *lusus naturae* in the newspapers lately."—Moore's note.

(**179**) LALLA ROOKH. Lines 1–119 in the last division, "The Light of the Haram." ¶ 1. *Vale of Cashmere:* Cashmere is north of India, in the region of the Himalayan Mountains; the inhabitants are mostly Mohammedan; the Vale of Cashmere, 5,000 feet above the sea, and encircled by high mountains, is of wonderful beauty. ¶ 12. *magian*=priest.

(**181**) 92–95. "It is the custom among the women to employ the *maazeen* to chaunt from the gallery of the nearest minaret, which on that occasion is illuminated; and the women assembled at the house respond at intervals with a *ziraleet*, or joyous chorus."—Russell, quoted by Moore. ¶ 97. *the silken swing.* "The swing is a favorite pastime in the East, as promoting a circulation of air extremely refreshing in those sultry climates."—

Richardson, quoted by Moore. "The swings are adorned with festoons. This pastime is accompanied with music of voices and of instruments, hired by the masters of the swings." —Thevenot, quoted by Moore. ¶ 108, 109. "An old commentator of the *Chou-King* says the ancients having remarked that a current of water made some of the stones near its banks send forth a sound, they detached some of them, and, being charmed with the delightful sound they emitted, constructed *king*, or musical instruments, of them."—Grosier, quoted by Moore.

PERCY BYSSHE SHELLEY

In "A Defence of Poetry" (1821) Shelley describes poetry and its function as follows: "Poetry is the record of the best and happiest moments of the happiest and best minds. We are aware of evanescent visitations of thought and feeling, sometimes associated with place or person, sometimes regarding our own mind alone, and always arising unforeseen and departing unbidden, but elevating and delightful beyond all expression. . . . . It is as it were the interpenetration of a diviner nature through our own; but its footsteps are like those of a wind over the sea, which the morning calm erases, and whose traces remain only, as on the wrinkled sand which paves it. These and corresponding conditions of being are experienced principally by those of the most delicate sensibility and the most enlarged imagination; and the state of mind produced by them is at war with every base desire. . . . . Poets are not only subject to these experiences as spirits of the most refined organization, but they can color all that they combine with the evanescent hues of this ethereal world. . . . . Poetry thus makes immortal all that is best and most beautiful in the world; it arrests the vanishing apparitions which haunt the interlunations of life, and, veiling them or in language or in form, sends them forth among mankind, bearing sweet news of kindred joy to those with whom their sisters abide—abide, because there is no portal of expression from the caverns of the spirit which they inhabit into the universe of things. Poetry redeems from decay the visitations of the divinity in man. Poetry turns all things to loveliness: it exalts the beauty of that which is most beautiful, and it adds beauty to that which it most deformed; it marries exultation and horror, grief and pleasure, eternity and change; it subdues to union under its light yoke all irreconcilable things. It transmutes all that it touches, and every form moving within the radiance of its presence is changed by wondrous sympathy to an incarnation of the spirit which it breathes; its secret alchemy turns to potable gold the poisonous waters which flow from death through life; it strips the veil of familiarity from the world, and lays bare the naked and sleeping beauty which is the spirit of its forms."

(182) QUEEN MAB. Sec. VII. 1–49. The passage is given as an example of Shelley's crude early thought and violent language about orthodox Christianity of his day. He himself in later years recognized the crudeness of the poem: "A poem, entitled 'Queen Mab,' was written by me, at the age of eighteen, I dare say in a sufficiently intemperate spirit. . . . . I doubt not but that it is perfectly worthless in point of literary composition; and that in all that concerns moral and political speculation, as well as in the subtler discriminations of metaphysical and religious doctrine, it is still more crude and immature."—Letter to *The Examiner*, June 22, 1821. The framework for the didacticism of the poem is simple. Queen Mab takes the spirit of Ianthe to her palace in the heavens:

> Yet likest evening's vault, that faery hall!
> As heaven, low resting on the wave, it spread
>   Its floors of flashing light,
>   Its vast and azure dome,
>   Its fertile golden islands
>   Floating on a silver sea;
> Whilst suns their mingling beamings darted
> Through clouds of circumambient darkness,
>   And pearly battlements around
>   Looked o'er the immense of heaven.

Here, as they survey past, present, and future, the fairy instructs the spirit of Ianthe in the true doctrine of man and God. ¶ 13. *There is no God.* "This negation must be understood solely to affect a creative Deity. The hypothesis of a pervading Spirit, coëternal with the universe, remains unshaken."—Shelley. ¶ 19. *term*=termination, limit.

(**183**) 23. *exterminable.* The word really means "capable of being exterminated," which would be nonsense here; Shelley may have used it, loosely, in the sense of "out of terms or bounds," "illimitable." W. M. Rossetti conjectured that the correct reading was "inexterminable" or "interminable." ¶ 30. *Seeva:* the third member of the Hindu Trinity; the same as "Shiva." *Foh:* the Chinese name for Buddha.

(**183**) ALASTOR. Lines 1–49. The passage is given partly as a specimen of Shelley's blank verse; cf. Wordsworth's "Lines Composed a Few Miles above Tintern Abbey," with regard to verse, style, and love of nature. Professor Alexander points out phrases taken from Wordsworth: "natural piety" (l. 3), and "obstinate questionings" (l. 26).

(**185**) HYMN TO INTELLECTUAL BEAUTY. "The 'Hymn to Intellectual Beauty' was conceived during his voyage around the lake [of Geneva] with Lord Byron."—Mrs. Shelley. Shelley's conception of the Eternal Beauty is based upon Plato; cf. the following passage from Plato's "Banquet," in Shelley's translation: "He who has been disciplined to this point in Love, by contemplating beautiful objects gradually, and in their order, now arriving at the end of all that concerns Love, on a sudden beholds a beauty wonderful in its nature. . . . . It is eternal, unproduced, indestructible; neither subject to increase nor decay: not, like other things, partly beautiful and partly deformed; not at one time beautiful and at another time not; not beautiful in relation to one thing and deformed in relation to another; not here beautiful and there deformed; not beautiful in the estimation of one person and deformed in that of another; nor can this supreme beauty be figured to the imagination, like a beautiful face or beautiful hands or any portion of the body, nor like any discourse nor any science. Nor does it subsist in any other that lives or is, either in earth, or in heaven, or in any other place; but it is eternally uniform and consistent, and monoeidic with itself. All other things are beautiful through a participation of it, with this one condition, that, although they are subject to production and decay, it never becomes more or less, or endures any change. . . . . Such a life as this, ... spent in the contemplation of the beautiful, is the life for men to live; which if you chance ever to experience you will esteem far beyond gold and rich garments, and even those lovely persons whom you and many others now gaze on with astonishment, and are prepared neither to eat nor drink so that you may behold and live forever with these objects of your love! What then shall we imagine to be the aspect of the supreme beauty itself, simple, pure, uncontaminated with the intermixture of human flesh and colors, and all other idle and unreal shapes attendant on mortality; the divine, the original, the supreme, the monoeidic beautiful itself? What must be the life of him who dwells with and gazes on that which it becomes us all to seek? Think you not that to him alone is accorded the prerogative of bringing forth, not images and shadows of virtue, for he is in contact not with a shadow but with reality, with virtue itself, in the production and nourishment of which he becomes dear to the gods, and, if such a privilege is conceded to any human being, himself immortal."

(**185**) 1–4. Cf. the extract from "A Defence of Poetry," on p. 541. ¶ 26. *these responses*=responses to these questions.

(**186**) 45, 46. Darkness is spoken of as nourishing the dying flame because it makes the flame seem brighter.

(**187**) ODE TO THE WEST WIND. "This poem was conceived and chiefly written in a wood that skirts the Arno, near Florence, and on a day when that tempestuous wind whose temperature is at once mild and animating was collecting the vapors which pour down the autumnal rains. They began, as I foresaw, at sunset with a violent tempest of hail and rain, attended by that magnificent thunder and lightning peculiar to the Cisalpine regions."—Shelley. ¶ 9. *Thine azure sister of the Spring:* the south wind, laden with blue haze in the springtime. ¶ 18. *angels*=messengers, carriers (Greek ἄγγελος, a messenger).

(**188**) 21. *maenad:* a priestess of Bacchus; the maenads celebrated the festivals of the god by frenzied songs and dances. ¶ 24. *closing night:* the night-sky closing down over the earth. ¶ 32–34. Baiae, a few miles from Naples, was a favorite seaside resort of the ancient Romans. Cf. the following lines from "Naples" in Roger's *Italy* (1822–28):

> Delicious Baiae. Here (what would they not ?)
> The masters of the earth, unsatisfied,
> Built in the sea; and now the boatman steers
> O'er many a crypt and vault yet glimmering,
> O'er many a broad and indestructible arch,
> The deep foundations of their palaces.

¶ 39–42. "The vegetation at the bottom of the sea, of rivers, and of lakes sympathizes with that of the land in the change of seasons, and is consequently influenced by the winds which announce it."—Shelley.

(**189**) 63. *dead thoughts:* Shelley's ideas about the reform of religion, society, and government had been ignored or rejected.

(**189**) THE INDIAN SERENADE. The poem exists in several different forms, and it is impossible to determine what was the final text adopted by Shelley. The verses were first published in *The Liberal*, in 1822; Mrs. Shelley published them among *Posthumous Poems*, in 1824. Three manuscripts of the poem are known: one given to Miss Sophia Stacey in 1819; another found on Shelley's person after his death, and described by Browning in a letter to Leigh Hunt, October 6, 1857; a third, in the Harvard library. The second manuscript is followed here.

(**190**) THE MASK OF ANARCHY. The mask described is of the earlier sort—merely a procession and pageant, with masks and disguising costumes. The manuscript sent to Hunt by Shelley has a sub-title, "Written on the Occasion of the Massacre at Manchester." The massacre occurred on August 16, 1819, and was occasioned by the holding of a mass-meeting in the interest of parliamentary reform. The meeting had been forbidden by the authorities, and three hundred hussars were ordered to disperse the crowd; six persons were killed, and some seventy-five injured. "He was residing near Leghorn . . . . when the news of the Manchester Massacre reached us; it aroused in him violent emotions of indignation and compassion. The great truth that the many, if accordant and resolute, could control the few, as was shown some years after, made him long to teach his injured country-men how to resist. Inspired by these feelings, he wrote 'The Mask of Anarchy,' which he sent to his friend, Leigh Hunt, to be inserted in the *Examiner*, of which Hunt was then editor. . . . . The poem was written for the people, and is therefore in a more popular tone than usual."—Mrs. Shelley. "You do not tell me whether you have received my lines on the Manchester affair. They are of the exoteric species. . . . . The great thing to do is to hold the balance between popular impatience and tyrannical obstinacy; to inculcate with fervor both the right of resistance and the duty of forbearance. You know my principles incite me to take all the good I can get in politics, forever aspiring to something more. I am one of those whom nothing will fully satisfy, but who are ready to be partially satisfied by all that is practicable. We shall see."—Letter to Hunt, November, 1819. Cf. Mrs. Shelley's note on "Queen Mab": "He did not in his youth look forward to gradual improvement; nay, in those days of intolerance, now almost forgotten, it seemed as easy to look forward to the sort of millennium of freedom and brotherhood, which he thought the proper state of mankind, as to the present reign of moderation and improvement."

(**190**) 6. *Castlereagh:* Viscount Castlereagh, who had been secretary for Ireland and secretary for war, was at this time foreign secretary; he was a leader of the aristocratic and reactionary party, freely expressing his contempt for the populace; in 1822 he committed suicide in a fit of insanity. ¶ 15. *Eldon:* Lord High Chancellor; he it was who had recently given a decision denying to Shelley the custody of his children by his first wife, because of his atheistical and immoral opinions in their relation to conduct and the rearing of British subjects; see ll. 18–21.

(191) 24. *Sidmouth:* Viscount Sidmouth, home secretary, who by his repressive measures was responsible for the massacre. ¶ 30–33. "And I looked, and behold a pale horse: and his name that sat on him was Death, and Hell followed with him."—Revelations 6: 8.

(193) 112. *grain*=color (at first, "red" from the small, grainlike bodies of insects used in making a red dye; then the meaning was extended to any kind of color).

(197) 244–49. A reference to the French Revolution and the union of the powers against France. ¶ 251. *like him following Christ:* Luke 18: 22.

(200) THE CLOUD. "There are others, such as the 'Ode to the Skylark' and 'The Cloud,' which in the opinion of many critics bear a purer poetical stamp than any other of his productions. They were written as his mind prompted, listening to the caroling of the bird, aloft in the azure sky of Italy, or marking the cloud as it sped across the heavens, while he floated in his boat on the Thames."—Mrs. Shelley.

(201) 33. *rack*=flying broken cloud.

(202) 81. *cenotaph*=an empty tomb; here, "the blue dome of air."

(203) TO A SKYLARK. "It was on a beautiful summer evening, while wandering among the lanes, whose myrtle hedges were the bowers of the butterflies, that we heard the caroling of the skylark, which inspired one of the most beautiful of his poems."—Mrs. Shelley. ¶ 15. *unbodied joy.* Professor Craik, without any authority, changed the first word to "embodied," on the ground that "unbodied" must have been a mistake. But both Shelley's edition and Mrs. Shelley's have "unbodied"; and in the Harvard manuscript (in which this poem is in Shelley's hand) the "un" is clear and unmistakable. Furthermore, "unbodied" goes better with the first stanza, in which the skylark is called a "spirit" because its song is so ethereal and heavenly; and it is also what would be expected from a Platonic idealist like Shelley, who believed that the body was a clog to the spirit and that to be freed from it was a blessing (cf. "Adonais," ll. 334–51). ¶ 22. *silver sphere:* the "star of heaven" (l. 18).

(204) 55. *these:* in the Harvard manuscript the word seems to be "those."

(205) 80. *knew:* for "knewest."

(206) EPIPSYCHIDION. Lines 388–591. "The meaning of this title has been much discussed. Without pretending to any classical authority, I may note that I cannot discern any significance beyond the simple one, 'a little poem about the soul.' "—Buxton Forman. "The title of this poem . . . . is translated by Shelley himself in the line [l. 238],

Whither 't was fled, this soul out of my soul,

and the word *Epipsychidion* is coined by him to express the idea of that line. It might mean something which is placed on a soul as if to complete or crown it. It was probably intended by Shelley to be also a diminutive of endearment from *epipsyche*. There is no such Greek word as ἐπι-ψυχή. But *epipsyche* would mean 'a soul upon a soul,' just as *epicycle*, in the Ptolemaic astronomy, meant 'a circle upon a circle.' Such 'a soul on a soul' might be paraphrased as a soul which is the complement of, and therefore responsive to, another soul like itself but in higher place and of a higher order. The lower would then seek to be united with the higher, because in such union it would be made perfect and the pre-established harmony between them be actually realized."—Stopford A. Brooke, in a note to "Epipsychidion," *Publications of the Shelley Society* (1887). One objection to this interpretation is that ψυχή, being feminine, would naturally take the feminine form of the adjective, and that to be correct the title would be "Epipsychidia." Another interpretation would derive the word from ἐπί, "upon," and ψυχίδιον, an actual Greek word, meaning "little soul," "darling," the same as the

Latin "animula"; "Epipsychidion" would then mean "upon my darling," or "a poem upon my darling." The lady to whom the poem is addressed was Emilia Viviani, the daughter of an Italian count, whose second wife had induced him to immure Emilia in a convent near Pisa. Shelley and Mrs. Shelley became deeply interested in her, and the poet idealized her into the embodiment of perfect beauty and love that he was forever seeking. He was afterward disillusioned, as his words below reveal. "It is to be published simply for the esoteric few; and I make its author a secret, to avoid the malignity of those who turn sweet food into poison, transforming all they touch into the corruption of their own natures."—Letter to Ollier, February 16, 1821. "The 'Epipsychidion' is a mystery; as to real flesh and blood, you know that I do not deal in those articles; you might as well go to a gin-shop for a leg of mutton as expect anything human or earthly from me."—Letter to Gisborne, October 22, 1821. "The 'Epipsychidion' I cannot look at; the person whom it celebrates was a cloud instead of a Juno, and poor Ixion starts from the centaur that was the offspring of his own embrace. . . . . It is an idealized history of my life and feelings. I think one is always in love with something or other; the error, and I confess it is not easy for spirits cased in flesh and blood to avoid it, consists in seeking in a mortal image the likeness of what is, perhaps, eternal."—Letter to Gisborne, June 18, 1822. In its conception of love the poem owes much to Plato's "Banquet," and something to Dante's "La Vita Nuova" and "Il Convito."

(206) 13. *continents:* used in the literal sense, "the things holding it in," as often in Shakspere.

(209) 120. *Parian:* Paros, an island in the Aegean Sea, was famous for its white marble.

(210) 170. *lights*=eyes.

(211) ADONAIS. "Adonais" is evidently a variant of "Adonis," the name of the beautiful youth, loved by Venus, who was killed by a wild boar; the analogy with Keats, whose early death Shelley ascribed to "savage criticism," is obvious. Why Shelley chose this particular form is not clear. Professor Hales thinks it may have been made, not quite correctly, on the analogy of such a word as "Thebais" ($\Theta\eta\beta\alpha\iota\varsigma$), "a song about Thebes," to designate at once the elegy and the subject of it. Dr. Furnivall suggested that it might be based on "Adonia" ($\mathrm{A}\delta\dot{\omega}\nu\iota\alpha$), the term for the women's yearly mourning for Adonis.

Shelley and Keats first met at Leigh Hunt's house, as early as 1817, but they never became intimate. "I knew personally but little of Keats; but on the news of his situation I wrote to him, suggesting the propriety of trying the Italian climate, and inviting him to join me. Unfortunately he did not allow me."—Canceled passage in Shelley's preface to "Adonais." "Keats's new volume has arrived to us, and the fragment called 'Hyperion' promises for him that he is destined to become one of the first writers of the age. His other things are imperfect enough. . . . . Where is Keats now? I am anxiously expecting him in Italy, when I shall take care to bestow every possible attention on him. . . . . I intend to be the physician both of his body and his soul,—to keep the one warm, and to teach the other Greek and Spanish. I am aware indeed, in part, that I am nourishing a rival who will far surpass me; and this is an additional motive, and will be an added pleasure."—Letter to Mrs. Hunt, November 11, 1820.

In the earlier stanzas Shelley imitated the Greek poets Bion and Moschus, of the third century B. C. The following passages from Shelley's unfinished metrical translation and from Mr. Lang's prose version afford interesting parallels with "Adonais":

> I mourn Adonis dead—loveliest Adonis—
> Dead, dead Adonis—and the Loves lament.
> Sleep no more, Venus, wrapped in purple woof.
> Wake, violet-stolèd queen, and weave the crown
> Of Death—'t is Misery calls—for he is dead.
>
> A deep, deep wound Adonis . . . .

A deeper Venus bears upon her heart.
See, his belovèd dogs are gathering round—
The oread nymphs are weeping. Aphrodite
With hair unbound is wandering through the woods,
Wildered, ungirt, unsandalled—the thorns pierce
Her hastening feet and drink her sacred blood.
Bitterly screaming out she is driven on
Through the long vales; and her Assyrian boy,
Her love, her husband, calls.

The oaks and mountains cry, Ai! ai! Adonis!
The springs their waters change to tears, and weep—
The flowers are withered up with grief . . . .
   Ai! ai!   Adonis is dead
Echo resounds   Adonis is dead.
Who will weep not thy dreadful woe, O Venus?
Soon as she saw and knew the mortal wound
Of her Adonis—saw the life-blood flow
From his fair thigh, now wasting, wailing loud
She clasped him, and cried   "Stay, Adonis!
Stay, dearest one,—
        and mix my lips with thine!
Wake yet a while, Adonis—oh, but once!
That I may kiss thee now for the last time—
But for as long as one short kiss may live!
          —Bion's "Lament for Adonis."

"This kiss will I treasure, even as thyself, Adonis, since, ah ill-fated, thou art fleeing me, thou art fleeing far, Adonis, and art faring to Acheron, to that hateful king and cruel, while wretched I yet live, being a goddess, and may not follow thee! . . . . For why, ah overbold, didst thou follow the chase, and, being so fair, why wert thou thus overhardy to fight with beasts? . . . . He reclines, the delicate Adonis, in his raiment of purple, and around him the Loves are weeping, and groaning aloud, clipping their locks for Adonis. And one upon his shafts, another on his bow is treading, and one hath loosed the sandal of Adonis, and another hath broken his own feathered quiver, and one in a golden vessel bears water, and another laves the wound, and another from behind him with his wings is fanning Adonis."—Bion's "Lament for Adonis."

Ye Dorian woods and waves, lament aloud;
Augment your tide, O streams, with fruitless tears;
For the belovèd Bion is no more.
Let every tender herb and plant and flower,
From each dejected bud and drooping bloom,
Shed dews of liquid sorrow, and with breath
Of melancholy sweetness on the wind
Diffuse its languid love; let roses blush,
Anemones grow paler for the loss
Their dells have known; and thou, O hyacinth,
Utter thy legend now—yet more, dumb flower,
Than "ah! alas!"—thine is no common grief—
Bion the sweetest singer is no more.
          —Moschus's "Lament for Bion."

"And Echo in the rocks laments that thou art silent, and no more she mimics thy voice. And in sorrow for thy fall the trees cast down their fruit, and all the flowers have faded. . . . . Poison came, Bion, to thy mouth, thou didst know poison. To such lips as thine did it come, and was not sweetened? What mortal was so cruel that could mix poison for thee, or who could give thee the venom that heard thy voice? surely he had no music in his soul."—Moschus's "Lament for Bion."

(211) 5. *obscure compeers:* the hours not marked by so memorable an event as the death of Keats. ¶ 12. *Urania.* Urania ("the heavenly one," from οὐρανός, the sky) was the muse of astronomy, and there seems to be no special fitness in calling her the mother of

Keats. But the name was also applied to Aphrodite, when she was thought of as the goddess of spiritual, heavenly love, in distinction from earthly love. Such love and beauty Shelley believed to be the central principle of the universe, and the inspiration of all high poetry; and this Urania might well be called the mother of Keats. ¶ 15. *one:* one Echo.

(212) 29. *He died:* the reference is to Milton. ¶ 31. *pride:* the object of "trampled" and "mocked," l. 33. ¶ 34. *lust and blood:* upon the restoration of the monarchy and of the established church in England, in 1660, loose living became the fashion; and leaders in the rebellion against Charles I were executed. ¶ 35. *clear sprite:* cf. "Lycidas," l. 70, "Fame is the spur that the clear spirit doth raise." ¶ 36. *the third:* if Shelley was thinking of poets in general, the other two would doubtless be Homer and Shakspere; but he may have been thinking of epic poets only, as in his "Defence of Poetry" (written in the same year with "Adonais"), in which he says, "Homer was the first and Dante the second epic poet; . . . . Milton was the third. ¶ 40. *tapers:* minor poets, happy in knowing their limitations and not attempting what they could not do well; their reward is that their works still live. ¶ 41. *suns:* either really great poets who have been undeservedly forgotten, or, more probably, poets who attempted greater things than they were capable of, and failed. *others more sublime:* great poets, like Lucan, Chatterton, and the others mentioned in ll. 396–405, who died before their powers matured. ¶ 44. *some yet live:* living poets, maligned or unappreciated, like Byron, Wordsworth, and Shelley himself. ¶ 47. *thy widowhood:* to say that the muse of high poetry is widowed implies that she is forsaken and forlorn, i. e., that poetry at that time was neglected and unappreciated, as was shown by the experience of Keats, Shelley, and others. ¶ 48, 49. An allusion to Keats's "Isabella, or the Pot of Basil," in which a maiden hides the head of her murdered lover in a pot of basil, and waters the plant with her tears. ¶ 55. *capital:* Rome, where Keats had gone for his health. ¶ 58. *Come away:* hasten to his death-chamber, while his body is still beautiful in death. Mr. Rossetti takes the words in the opposite sense—"Come away from the death chamber and leave him to his rest"; but the objection to this is that the following stanzas keep our thoughts in the presence of the dead and describe what takes place there.

(213) 67. *trace*=mark out. ¶ 68. *his extreme way:* Keats's last path. *her:* Corruption's. ¶ 69. *The eternal Hunger:* Corruption; some take the phrase to refer to Death, but in the preceding stanza Death is masculine, while the Hunger is feminine (see "her," l. 70). ¶ 80. *sweet pain:* apparently the pain of birth (cf. "whence they sprung," l. 79); in accordance with the personification of the dreams the pain is attributed to them, but the allusion, at bottom, is doubtless to the "sweet pain" of the poet in composition. ¶ 97, 98. The meaning seems to be that the Dream would lessen her grief by diverting her mind to a smaller loss, that of her bow and arrows. ¶ 99. *barbèd fire:* the barbèd arrows, which appear to be taken as symbols of the burning pain in her heart.

(214) 102–4. Keats's poetry won entrance even into the critical, scrutinizing intellect ("wit"), and it also moved the emotions. ¶ 107. *clips*=embraces. ¶ 133. Echo, spurned by Narcissus, pined away into a mere voice.

(215) 140, 141. Hyacinth, a beautiful youth, was beloved by Apollo; one day he was killed in a game of quoits, and the god made the flower, hyacinth, to spring up from his blood. Narcissus fell in love with his own reflection in the water, and pined to death; his body was turned into the flower, narcissus. ¶ 145. An allusion at once to the rich melody of Keats's verse and to his "Ode to a Nightingale." ¶ 151–53. Shelley believed, erroneously, that the criticism of Keats's poetry was directly responsible for his death: "The savage criticism on his 'Endymion,' which appeared in the *Quarterly Review* [see p. 561], produced the most violent effect on his susceptible mind; the agitation thus originated ended in the rupture of a blood-vessel in the lungs; a rapid consumption ensued, and the ensuing acknowledgements from more candid critics [see p. 563] of the true greatness of his powers, were ineffectual to heal the wound thus wantonly inflicted."—Shelley's preface. Cf. the less sympathetic reference by Byron ("Don Juan," XI. lix):

John Keats, who was killed off by one critique,
  Just as he really promised something great
If not intelligible, without Greek
  Contrived to talk about the gods of late,
Much as they might have been supposed to speak.
  Poor fellow! His was an untoward fate:
'T is strange the mind, that very fiery particle,
Should let itself be snuffed out by an article.

¶ 160. *brere*=briar. ¶ 177. *dies*=is annihilated. *that alone which knows:* the mind.

(216) 179. *sightless*=invisible; cf. *Macbeth*, I. vii. 23, "the sightless couriers of the air." *atom:* the mind. ¶ 180. *repose:* not necessarily annihilation; the poet is not yet answering his own question, but merely describing death as it appears to the senses. ¶ 186. *death, who lends what life must borrow.* "I think Shelley may intend to say that, in this our mortal state, death is the solid and permanent fact; it is rather a world of death than of life. The phenomena of life are but like a transitory loan from the great emporium, death."—W. M. Rossetti. ¶ 208–16. The lines describe the treatment that poetry and poets get in an unappreciative age, and their persistence in their mission; cf. "To a Skylark," ll. 36–40.

(217) 238. *unpastured*=unfed, and hence more ravenous. *dragon:* the critic. Shelley seems to have been aware that the lines attacking the critics are not of a piece with the rest of the poem: "It is a lament on the death of poor Keats, with some interposed stabs on the assassins of his peace and of his fame."—Letter to Ollier, June 8, 1821. "I have dipped my pen in consuming fire for his destroyers: otherwise the style is calm and solemn." —Letter to Gisborne, June 16, 1821. ¶ 240. *Wisdom the mirrored shield:* there is perhaps a twofold allusion to the shield of Athene, goddess of wisdom, and to the polished magic mirrors of the old romances, which dazzled the hostile beholder (see *Orlando Furioso*, Canto IV). ¶ 242. *filled its crescent sphere:* reached the maturity of its powers. ¶ 250. *The Pythian of the age:* Byron. "Pythian" was one of the titles of Apollo, because he slew the Python, a serpent who delivered oracles at Delphi. *one arrow:* "English Bards and Scotch Reviewers."

(218) 262. *mountain shepherds:* in accordance with the fiction of the older pastoral poetry, in which shepherds sing, to their pipes, songs of their own composition, the poet friends of Keats are spoken of as shepherds; "mountain" may be used merely as a general characterization of shepherds, but very likely it is meant to suggest the free spirit and elevated tone of the poets mentioned. ¶ 264. *Pilgrim of Eternity:* Byron; the name was suggested by his "Childe Harold's Pilgrimage." His grief was not so great as Shelley implies; see note on ll. 151–53. Keats's early poems Byron greatly disliked, partly for their attack on Pope. On receiving some books from Murray, he wrote him (October 12, 1820): "No more Keats, I entreat: flay him alive; if some of you don't, I must skin him myself. There is no bearing the driveling idiotism of the manikin." But in a letter to Shelley written April 26, 1821, or before "Adonais" was finished, Byron spoke in a different tone, and the reference to him in the poem may have been based upon this letter: "I am very sorry to hear what you say of Keats— is it *actually* true? I did not think that criticism had been so killing. Though I differ from you essentially in your estimate of his performances, I so much abhor all unnecessary pain that I would rather he had been seated on the highest peak of Parnassus than have perished in such a manner." ¶ 268. *Ierne:* an old name for Ireland. ¶ 269. *The sweetest lyrist:* Moore, who, however, had no personal relations with Keats. *her saddest wrong:* it is uncertain what Shelley had in mind, perhaps the suppression of the Irish insurrection of 1803; that was not Ireland's saddest wrong, but Shelley may have thought it was, and Moore had sung of the fate of Robert Emmett, a leader in the insurrection. ¶ 271. *of less note:* i. e., less notable than Byron and Moore, not less than "one frail form," which is Shelley himself. ¶ 276. *Actæon-like.* Actæon, a hunter, who saw Diana bathing, was turned into a stag and his own hounds hunted him to death. Shelley spiritualizes the myth, in a

characteristic way, and applies it to his own case: he had caught glimpses of the Absolute Beauty revealed in nature, and his life thereafter had been a restless pursuit of it; cf. "Alastor," "Hymn to Intellectual Beauty," and the letter of June 18, 1822, on p. 545. ¶ 280. *pardlike*=leopardlike. ¶ 281. *a love in desolation masked:* an antithesis between love and desolation is intended (cf. a similar one between power and weakness, in the next words); the poet really loves men and would help them, but being misunderstood and reviled he is compelled to live in sad seclusion, as if indifferent to his kind (cf. "neglected and apart," l. 296). ¶ 289. *pansies:* cf. *Hamlet,* IV. v. 176, 177, "there is pansies, that's for thoughts"; the word comes from the French *pensée. overblown:* cf. "my dead thoughts," in "Ode to the West Wind," l. 63. ¶ 290. *violets:* the violet is a symbol of modesty; cf. Shelley's "Remembrance" (1821), l. 19, "Violets for a maiden dead."

(219) 292. *ivy:* the ivy is a symbol of constancy in friendship. ¶ 300. The reference is to the cruel treatment that both had received; perhaps there is also an implication that Shelley, like Keats, would die early, partly because of that treatment. ¶ 301. *accents of an unknown land.* Mr. Rossetti thinks the meaning may be that he is writing in English, a tongue unknown to the Greek muse, Urania. Professor Alexander thinks that Shelley refers to the fact that his poetry is outside the range of most men's sympathy. May it not mean that he is writing upon the death of a modern poet ("new sorrow") in the manner of the old Greek elegy ("accents of an unknown land")? ¶ 306. *like Cain's or Christ's:* Shelley says, in effect, "The world brands and crowns with thorns two classes of men— enemies of the race, like Cain, or misunderstood benefactors of the race, like Christ; therefore, from the mere fact that my brow is branded and ensanguined you cannot tell to which class I belong." ¶ 307-15. The lines describe Leigh Hunt, Keats's early friend and patron. Severn, the artist, who cared for Keats in his last illness, thought that they referred to him; but Shelley explained, in the preface, that he did not know of Severn's devotion until the poem was ready for the press. ¶ 319. *nameless worm:* the criticism on Keats in the *Quarterly Review* was unsigned, as was the custom then. ¶ 322. *one breast alone:* Shelley seems not to have known that the review of "Endymion" in *Blackwood's Magazine* was still worse than the *Quarterly's;* see p. 562.

(220) 337. *thou:* the reviewer.

(221) 370-87. "He" and "his" throughout these lines refer to Keats. God ("that Power") is referred to throughout by neuter pronouns, to express Shelley's disbelief in the personality of the Supreme Principle. ¶ 381. *plastic*=molding, shaping. The Eternal Spirit of Beauty and Love is thought of as permeating the matter of the world, struggling with it from within, and molding it into forms of beauty; matter resists the process, and different portions of it yield to the Spirit in varying degrees, which accounts for the varying degrees of beauty in material things. Cf. Wordsworth's "Lines Composed a Few Miles above Tintern Abbey," ll. 95-102, and Spenser's "Hymne in Honour of Beautie," stanzas 5, 7:

> What time this world's great Work-maister did cast
> To make all things such as we now behold,
> It seemes that he before his eyes had plast
> A goodly Paterne, to whose perfect mould
> He fashiond them as comely as he could,
> That now so faire and seemely they appeare,
> As nought may be amended any wheare.

> Thereof as every earthly thing partakes
> Or more or lesse, by influence divine,
> So it more faire accordingly it makes,
> And the grosse matter of this earthly myne
> Which clotheth it thereafter doth refyne,
> Doing away the drosse which dims the light
> Of that faire beame which therein is empight.

The idea goes back to Plato: "The work of the Creator, whenever He looks to the unchangeable and fashions the form and nature of His work after an unchangeable pattern, must necessarily be made fair and perfect. . . . . Which of the patterns had the Artificer in view when He made the world—the pattern of the unchangeable, or of that which is created ? . . . . Every one will see that He must have looked to the eternal, for the world is the fairest of creations and He is the best of causes. . . . . Mind, the ruling power, persuaded necessity to bring the greater part of created things to perfection, and thus and after this manner in the beginning, when the influence of reason got the better of necessity, the universe was created. . . . . God made them [the four elements] the fairest and best, out of things which were not fair and good. . . . . And the ratios of their numbers, motions, and other properties, everywhere God, as far as necessity allowed or gave consent, has exactly perfected, and harmonized in due proportion."—"Timaeus," Jowett's translation. ¶ 384. *its:* the one Spirit's; so in the next two lines. ¶ 385. *as*=according as, to the degree that. ¶ 387. Shelley, who believed that the "one Spirit" is impersonal, naturally made the pure white light of heaven the highest physical expression of it. Cf. the lines by Wordsworth, referred to in the note on l. 381, in which the "mind of man" is made the climax. ¶ 394. *love and life:* life seems to mean here the lower side of life, against which love, the highest spiritual principle, contends. ¶ 395. *the dead live there:* in the young heart, by their uplifting influence. It is not clear whether the influence is exerted directly by them as a portion of nature (cf. ll. 373–76) or is the result of what they did, thought, and wrote while they had individual existence; ll. 407, 408 make it probable that the latter is meant. In either case the poet now affirms an immortality of influence in the world of men, as he previously did in the world of nature. Cf. "George Eliot's" lines:

> O may I join the choir invisible
> Of those immortal dead who live again
> In lives made better by their presence: live
> In pulses stirred to generosity,
> In deeds of daring rectitude, in scorn
> For miserable aims that end with self,
> In thoughts sublime that pierce the night like stars,
> And with their mild persistence urge man's search
> To vaster issues.

¶ 399. *Chatterton:* Thomas Chatterton committed suicide in his eighteenth year (1770); his poems, although variously appraised, at least showed wonderful promise. ¶ 401. *Sidney:* Sir Philip Sidney, poet, courtier, and soldier, was fatally wounded on the field of battle, in 1586, at the age of thirty-two; his chief poems are love sonnets. ¶ 403. *a spirit without spot:* the phrase, *sans peur et sans reproche*, has often been applied to Sidney. ¶ 404. *Lucan, by his death approved:* the Roman poet, author of the *Pharsalia*, an epic on the war between Caesar and Pompey, died in 65 A. D., at the age of twenty-six; he was implicated in a plot against the emperor Nero, and (it is alleged) turned informer against his own mother, hoping to save himself, but, being condemned to death, died bravely by opening his veins before the time.

(222) 410. That the ascription of personal, conscious life after death to these poets, and their welcome to Keats, are only a poetic fiction—a vivid way of saying that Keats deserves to rank with them—and not Shelley's real belief, appears not only from the previous references to the nature of Keats's immortality, but also from Shelley's essay, "On a Future State," written about 1815. ¶ 415–23. The sense seems to be this: "Foolish wretch, you will not mourn for Keats if you realize how superior his state is to yours; try to realize it by flying in imagination throughout the universe, which he pervades in reality; then, when you shrink back to your little pin-point of individual existence, you are more likely to be heavy-hearted for yourself than for him." ¶ 439 *a slope of green access:* "John Keats . . . . was buried in the romantic and lonely cemetery of the Protestants, ... under the pyramid which is the tomb of Cestius, and the massy walls and towers, now moldering and desolate, which formed the circuit of ancient Rome. The cemetery is an open space among the ruins, covered in winter with violets and daisies. It might make one in love with death to think that one should be buried in so sweet a place."—Shelley, in the preface.

(223) 460. Cf. "the one Spirit's" (l. 381), and "all new successions" (l. 383). ¶ 461. *shadows.* In conformity with his Platonic philosophy Shelley speaks of the most beautiful and brightest things on earth as only shadows compared with the Eternal Beauty of which they are imperfect manifestations (cf. l. 468); in addition to this contrast between "light" and "shadows," there is one between "forever" and "fly," i. e., earthly things have the unreality and transitoriness of shadows, but heavenly things are real and eternal. ¶ 464. The action of death is thought of as a blessing, because it releases us from individual human life, with its purblind and perverted vision (see l. 462), and admits us to "the white radiance of Eternity." ¶ 465. *that which thou dost seek:* not Keats, but Absolute Beauty (cf. "glory," l. 468, and "the fire for which all thirst," l. 485). ¶ 472-74. This note of despondency, of the loss of that youthful freshness and hope in which all things had been glorified, occurs often in Shelley's later poems, occasioned in part by the feverish haste of living which made him feel prematurely old and in part by the world's rejection of or indifference to his ideals; cf. "Stanzas Written in Dejection near Naples" (1818), "Ode to the West Wind" (1819), ll. 54-58, and "A Lament" (1821):

> Oh, world! oh, life! oh, time!
> On whose last steps I climb,
>   Trembling at that where I had stood before,
> When will return the glory of your prime?
>   No more—O, never more!
>
> Out of the day and night
> A joy has taken flight;
>   Fresh spring, and summer, and winter hoar
> Move my faint heart with grief, but with delight
>   No more—O, never more!

In expression and in the fact stated, the lines in "Adonais" are like Wordsworth's in "Ode: Intimations of Immortality," ll. 1-18, 176-79, but the reason for the fact is different. ¶ 480, 481. Cf. ll. 338, 339, and Wordsworth's "Ode: Intimations of Immortality," ll. 58-61.

(224) 484. Cf. ll. 384, 385. *as*=according as, to the degree that.

(224) THE WORLD'S GREAT AGE BEGINS ANEW. The final chorus in "Hellas," a lyrical drama upon the Greeks' war for independence from the Turks, which was then raging. Shelley believed, or hoped, that the revival among the Greeks of the free spirit of their ancestors was a prophecy of the coming Golden Age of freedom and love. ¶ 1. *The world's great age.* "From these unequal motions of the planets, mathematicians have called that the 'great year' in which the sun, moon, and five wandering stars, having finished their revolutions, are found in their original situation."—Cicero, *De natura deorum*, II. xx. Shelley thinks of human history as completing a similar great cycle and beginning afresh with a new and greater Golden Age. ¶ 4. *weeds*=garments. ¶ 5. *faiths and empires:* equivalent, in Shelley's dialect, to superstitions and tyrannies. ¶ 9. *Peneus:* the principal river of Thessaly, flowing through the beautiful vale of Tempe. ¶ 10. The general direction of the Peneus is northeastward. ¶ 12. *Cyclads:* the Cyclades, islands in the Aegean Sea. ¶ 13. *Argo:* the ship of Jason, in which, according to the fable, he brought back the golden fleece from Colchis. ¶ 15. *Orpheus:* Orpheus, son of Apollo and the muse Calliope, descended into Hades to recover his dead wife, Eurydice, and so charmed Pluto with the music of his lyre that he was allowed to lead Eurydice to the upper world on condition that he would not look back at her; failing to observe the condition and losing her, he wandered disconsolate through Thrace, and was dismembered by the Thracian Bacchantes, whose love he had spurned, and his body was cast into the river Hebrus. ¶ 18. *Calypso:* a nymph, on whose isle Ulysses was cast; she loved him, and offered to make him immortal, but he returned to his kingdom and his wife. ¶ 19-22. Thus far the poet has been recalling the glories of the early age of Greece—her natural beauty, the achievements of her mythical heroes, the power and pathos of her art, the wisdom and honor of her great men, and prophesying that the new Golden Age will equal or excel the old. But when he comes to the Trojan War, and the sorrows of the house of Laius (king of Thebes, whose son Oedipus unwittingly slew him and married his own mother), he expresses the hope that in the new age these events may have no parallels; death will still desolate the earth, but the case need not be made worse by war and violence.

(225) 23. *a subtler Sphinx:* a monster, the Sphinx, half woman and half lion, afflicted Thebes; she proposed a riddle to travelers who approached her rock by the highway, and if they could not solve it she killed them; Oedipus guessed her riddle, and she slew herself. By "subtler," Shelley means that the modern problems of life and thought are more difficult than those of the early ages. ¶ 31–36. "Saturn and Love were among the deities of a real or imaginary state of innocence and happiness. 'All those who fell,' or the gods of Greece, Asia, and Egypt; the 'One who rose,' or Jesus Christ, at whose appearance the idols of the pagan world were amerced of their worship; and the 'many unsubdued,' or the monstrous objects of the idolatry of China, India, the Antarctic islands, and the native tribes of America." —Shelley. ¶ 37. *O cease:* on the supposition that the history of the world will repeat itself, a new Iron Age of suffering and wrong will succeed the new Golden Age, and the poet does not wish to continue his prophecy to that period.

(226) To NIGHT. ¶ 1. *over:* in the Harvard manuscript, "o'er."

CONTEMPORARY CRITICISM

We have examined Mr. Shelley's system slightly, but, we hope, dispassionately; there will be those who will say that we have done so coldly. He has indeed, to the best of his ability, wounded us in the tenderest part. As far as in him lay, he has loosened the hold of our protecting laws, and sapped the principles of our venerable polity; he has invaded the purity and chilled the unsuspecting ardor of our fireside intimacies; he has slandered, ridiculed, and blasphemed our holy religion; yet these are all too sacred objects to be defended bitterly or unfairly. We have learned, too, though not in Mr. Shelley's school, to discriminate between a man and his opinions, and while we show no mercy to the sin, we can regard the sinner with allowance and pity. It is in this spirit that we conclude with a few lines which may serve for a warning to others, and for reproof, admonition, and even, if he so pleases, of encouragement to himself. We have already said what we think of his powers as a poet, and doubtless, with those powers, he might have risen to respectability in any honorable path which he had chosen to pursue, if to his talents he had added industry, subordination, and good principles. But of Mr. Shelley much may be said with truth which we not long since said of his friend and leader Mr. Hunt: he has not, indeed, all that is odious and contemptible in the character of that person; so far as we have seen he has never exhibited the bustling vulgarity, the ludicrous affectation, the factious flippancy, or the selfish heartlessness, which it is hard for our feelings to treat with the mere contempt they merit. Like him, however, Mr. Shelley is a very vain man; and, like most very vain men, he is but half-instructed in knowledge, and less than half-disciplined in his reasoning powers; his vanity, wanting the control of the faith which he derides, has been his ruin; it has made him too impatient of applause and distinction to earn them in the fair course of labor; like a speculator in trade, he would be rich without capital and without delay, and, as might have been anticipated, his speculations have ended only in disappointments.—*The Quarterly Review*, April, 1819, on "The Revolt of Islam."

There is not so much to find fault with in the mere silence of critics; but we do not hesitate to say, with all due respect for the general character of that journal, that Mr. Shelley has been infamously and stupidly treated in the *Quarterly Review*. His reviewer there, whoever he is, does not show himself a man of such lofty principles as to entitle him to ride the high horse in company with the author of the "Revolt of Islam." And when one compares the *vis inertiae* of his motionless prose with the "eagle-winged raptures" of Mr. Shelley's poetry, one does not think indeed of Satan reproving Sin, but one does think, we will say it in plain words and without a figure, of a dunce rating a man of genius. If that critic does not know that Mr. Shelley is a poet, almost in the very highest sense of that mysterious word, then we appeal to all those whom we have enabled to judge for themselves if he be not unfit to speak of poetry before the people of England. . . . . It is not in the power of all the critics alive to blind one true lover of poetry to the splendor of Mr. Shelley's genius; and the reader who, from mere curiosity, should turn to the "Revolt of Islam" to see what sort of trash it was that so moved the wrath and the spleen and the scorn of the reviewer, would soon feel that to understand the greatness of the poet, and the littleness of his traducer, nothing more was necessary than to recite to his delighted sense any six successive stanzas of that poem, so full of music, imagination, intellect, and passion.—*Blackwood's Magazine*, November, 1819.

We have already given some of our columns to this writer's merits, and we will not now repeat our convictions of his incurable absurdity. On the last occasion of our alluding to him, we were compelled to notice his horrid licentiousness and profaneness, his fearful offences to all the maxims that honorable minds are in the habit of respecting, and his plain defiance of Christianity. On the present occasion we are not met by so continued and regular a determination of insult, though there are atrocities to be found in the poem quite enough to make us caution our readers against its pages. "Adonais" is an elegy *after the manner of Moschus*, on a foolish young man, who, after writing some volumes of very weak, and, in the greater part, of very indecent, poetry, died some time since of a consumption, the breaking down of an infirm constitution having, in all probability, been accelerated by the discarding his neck-cloth, a practice of the Cockney poets, who look upon it as essential to genius, inasmuch as neither Michael Angelo, Raphael, or Tasso are supposed to have worn those anti-spiritual incumbrances. In short, as the vigor of Samson lay in his hair, the secret of talent in these persons lies in the neck; and what aspirations can be expected from a mind enveloped in muslin? Keats caught cold in training for a genius, and, after a lingering illness, died, to the great loss of the Independents of South America, whom he had intended to visit with an English epic poem, for the purpose of exciting them to liberty. But death, even the death of the radically presumptuous profligate, is a serious thing; and as we believe that Keats was made presumptuous chiefly by the treacherous puffing of his Cockney fellow-gossips, and profligate in his poems merely to make them saleable, we regret that he did not live long enough to acquire common-sense, and abjure the pestilent and perfidious gang who betrayed his weakness to the grave and are now panegyrising his memory into contempt. For what is the praise of Cockneys but disgrace, or what honorable inscription can be placed over the dead by the hands of notorious libellers, exiled adulterers, and avowed atheists? . . . .

We have some idea that this fragment of character ["Adonais," ll. 280–83] is intended for Mr. Shelley himself. It closes with a passage of memorable and ferocious blasphemy:

> He with a sudden hand
> Made bare his branded and ensanguined brow,
> Which was like Cain's or CHRIST's! ! !

What can be said to the wretched person capable of this daring profanation? The name of the first murderer—the accurst of God—brought into the same aspect image with that of the Saviour of the World! We are scarcely satisfied that even to quote such passages may not be criminal. The subject is too repulsive for us to proceed even in expressing our disgust for the general folly that makes the poem as miserable in point of authorship as in point of principle. We know that among a certain class this outrage and this inanity meet with some attempt at palliation, under the idea that frenzy holds the pen. That any man who insults the common order of society, and denies the being of God, is essentially mad we never doubted. But for the madness that retains enough of rationality to be wilfully mischievous we can have no more lenity than for the appetites of a wild beast. The poetry of the work is *contemptible*—a mere collection of bloated words heaped on each other without order, harmony, or meaning; the refuse of a school-boy's commonplace-book, full of the vulgarisms of pastoral poetry, yellow gems and blue stars, bright Phoebus and rosy-fingered Aurora; and of this stuff is Keats's wretched elegy compiled.—*The Literary Gazette*, December 8, 1821.

LEIGH HUNT

(227) The Story of Rimini. Canto III. 361–464. The story is that of Paola and Francesca, and the summer-house in the garden is the place where they first confessed their love to each other. The poem was published just as Keats was beginning to write, and its style, verse, and way of describing nature influenced his early poetry.

(229) 79. *Alcina or Morgana:* evil fays, the embodiments of sensual delights, who appear in Ariosto's *Orlando Furioso* and other romances on medieval subjects.

JOHN KEATS

(230) The following are some of Keats's utterances about poetry and human life, and his attitude toward both:

"We hate poetry that has a palpable design upon us, and, if we do not agree, seems to put its hand into its breeches' pocket. Poetry should be great and unobtrusive, a thing which enters into one's soul, and does not startle or amaze it with itself but with its object. How beautiful are the retired flowers! how would they lose their beauty were they to throng into the highway, crying out, 'Admire me, I am a violet! Dote upon me, I am a primrose!' " —Letter to Reynolds, February 3, 1818. "In poetry I have a few axioms, and you will see how far I am from their centre. 1st. I think poetry should surprise by a fine excess, and not by singularity; it should strike the reader as a wording of his own highest thoughts, and appear almost a remembrance. 2nd. Its touches of beauty should never be half-way, thereby making the reader breathless instead of content. The rise, the progress, the setting of imagery should, like the sun, come natural to him, shine over him, and set soberly, although in magnificence, leaving him in the luxury of twilight. . . . . Another axiom—that if poetry comes not as naturally as the leaves to a tree, it had better not come at all."—Letter to Taylor, February 27, 1818. "As to the poetical character itself (I mean that sort of which, if I am anything, I am a member; that sort distinguished from the Wordsworthian, or egotistical sublime, which is a thing *per se* and stands alone), it is not itself—it has no self—it is everything and nothing—it has no character—it enjoys light and shade; it lives in gusto, be it foul or fair, high or low, rich or poor, mean or elevated. It has as much delight in conceiving an Iago as an Imogen. What shocks the virtuous philosopher delights the chameleon poet. It does no harm from its relish of the dark side of things, any more than from its taste for the bright one, because they both end in speculation. A poet is the most unpoetical of anything in existence, because he has no identity—he is continually in for, and filling, some other body. . . . . In the second place, I will speak of my views, and of the life I purpose to myself. I am ambitious of doing the world some good: if I should be spared, that may be the work of maturer years—in the interval I will assay to reach to as high a summit in poetry as the nerve bestowed upon me will suffer. The faint conceptions I have of poems to come bring the blood frequently into my forehead. All I hope is that I may not lose all interest in human affairs—that the solitary indifference I feel for applause, even from the finest spirits, will not blunt any acuteness of vision I may have. I do not think it will. I feel assured I should write from the mere yearning and fondness I have for the beautiful, even if my night's labors should be burnt every morning and no eye ever shine upon them. But even now I am perhaps not speaking from myself, but from some character in whose soul I now live."—Letter to Woodhouse, October 27, 1818. "The imagination may be compared to Adam's dream,— he awoke and found it truth. I am more zealous in this affair, because I have never yet been able to perceive how anything can be known for truth by consecutive reasoning—and yet it must be. Can it be that even the greatest philosopher ever arrived at his goal without putting aside numerous objections? However it may be, O for a life of sensations rather than of thoughts."—Letter to Bailey, November 22, 1817. "I know nothing—I have read nothing—and I mean to follow Solomon's directions, 'Get learning—get understanding.' I find earlier days are gone by—I find that I can have no enjoyment in the world but continual drinking of knowledge. I find there is no worthy pursuit but the idea of doing some good to the world. Some do it with their society—some with their wit—some with their benevolence—some with a sort of power of conferring pleasure and good humor on all they meet—and in a thousand ways, all dutiful to the command of great Nature—there is but one way for me. The road lies through application, study, and thought. I will pursue it; and for that end purpose retiring for some years."—Letter to Taylor, April 24, 1818. "I have written to George for some books—shall learn Greek, and very likely Italian—and in other ways prepare myself to ask Hazlitt, in about a year's time, the best metaphysical road I can take. For although I take poetry to be chief, yet there is something else wanting to one who passes his life among books and thoughts on books—I long to feast upon old Homer as we have upon Shakspeare, and as I have lately upon Milton. If you understood Greek, and would read me passages now and then, explaining their meaning, 'twould be, from its mistiness, perhaps, a greater luxury than reading the thing one's self. I shall be happy when I can do the same for you."—Letter to Reynolds, April 27, 1818. "Were I to study physic or rather medicine again, I feel it would not make the least difference in my poetry; when the mind is in its infancy a bias is in reality a bias, but when we have acquired more strength a bias becomes no bias. Every department of knowledge we see excellent and calculated towards a great whole. . . . . An extensive knowledge is needful to thinking people—it takes away the heat and fever; and helps, by widening speculation, to ease the 'burden of the mystery,' a thing which I begin to understand a little. . . . . The difference of high sensations with and without knowledge appears to me this: in the latter case we are falling continually ten thousand fathoms deep and being blown up again, without wings, and with all the horror of a bare-shouldered creature—in the former case our shoulders are fledged, and we go through the same air and space without fear. . . . . I compare human life to a large mansion of many apartments, two of which I can only describe, the doors of the rest being as yet shut upon me. The first we step into we call the Infant, or Thoughtless, Chamber, in which we remain as long as we do not think. . . . . We no sooner get into the second chamber, which I shall call the Chamber of Maiden Thought, than we become intoxicated with the light and the atmosphere, we see nothing but pleasant wonders, and think of delaying there forever in delight. However, among the effects this breathing is father of is that tremendous one of sharpening one's vision into the heart and nature of man—of convincing one's nerves that the world is full of misery and heartbreak, pain, sickness, and oppression—whereby this chamber of Maiden Thought becomes gradually darkened, and at the same time, on all sides of it, many doors are set open—but all dark—all leading to dark passages. We see not the balance of good and evil; we are in a mist, *we* are now in that state, we feel the 'burden of the mystery.' To this point was Wordsworth come, as far as I can conceive, when he wrote 'Tintern Abbey,' and it seems to me that his genius is explorative of those dark passages. Now if we live, and go on thinking, we too shall explore them. He is a genius and superior to us in so far as he can, more than we, make discoveries and shed a light in them."—Letter to Reynolds, May 3, 1818.

(230) ON FIRST LOOKING INTO CHAPMAN'S HOMER. "We were put in possession of the Homer of Chapman, and to work we went, turning to some of the 'famousest' passages. . . . . One scene I could not fail to introduce to him—the shipwreck of Ulysses, in the fifth book of the 'Odysseis,' and I had the reward of one of his delighted stares, upon reading the following lines:

> Then forth he came, his both knees falt'ring, both
> His strong hands hanging down, and all with froth
> His cheeks and nostrils flowing, voice and breath
> Spent to all use, and down he sank to death.
> *The sea had soaked his heart through;* all his veins
> His toils had racked t' a labouring woman's pains.
> Dead-weary was he.

. . . . It was in the teeming wonderment of this his first introduction that, when I came down to breakfast the next morning, I found upon my table a letter with no other enclosure than his famous sonnet, 'On First Looking into Chapman's Homer.' We had parted . . . . at day-spring, yet he contrived that I should receive the poem from a distance of, may be, two miles, by ten o'clock."—"Recollections of John Keats," by Charles Cowden Clarke, in *The Gentleman's Magazine*, February, 1874. ¶ 3. *western islands:* Keats's reading was limited for the most part to the poets of England, the westernmost country of Europe, as Greece is the easternmost. ¶ 4. *in fealty:* the figure is taken from the feudal system; Apollo is the emperor of the "realms of gold," and the poets are his vassals. ¶ 6. *deep-browed:* an allusion to the overhanging brows and deep-set eyes of the familiar bust of Homer; in the manuscript the first reading was "low-browed." ¶ 8. *Chapman.* The translation of Homer by George Chapman, the Elizabethan dramatist and poet, came out during the years 1598–1616. Keats rightly characterized it in "loud and bold," as may be seen in the lines quoted above by Clarke and in the following (from the *Iliad*), which he says Keats and he also read together that night—they describe Neptune going in anger to the aid of the Greeks:

> The woods and all the great hills near trembled beneath the weight
> Of his immortal moving feet. Three steps he only took,
> Before he far-off Aegas reacht, but, with the fourth, it shook
> With his drad entry. In the depth of those seas he did hold
> His bright and glorious palace, built of never-rusting gold;
> And there arrived, he put in coach his brazen-footed steeds,
> All golden-maned, and pac't with wings; and all in golden weeds
> He clothed himself.

¶ 11. *Cortez:* it was Balboa, not Cortez, who discovered the Pacific Ocean, in 1513. The account given by Robertson in his *History of America*, which Clarke says Keats had read at school, is as follows: "At length the Indians assured them that from the top of the next mountain they should discover the ocean which was the object of their wishes. When, with infinite toil, they had climbed up the greater part of that steep ascent, Balboa commanded his men to halt, and advanced alone to the summit, that he might be the first who should enjoy a spectacle which he had so long desired. As soon as he beheld the South Sea stretching in endless prospect below him, he fell on his knees, and, lifting up his hands to heaven, returned thanks to God, Who had conducted him to a discovery so beneficial to his country and so honorable to himself. His followers, observing his transports of joy, rushed forward to join in his wonder, exultation, and gratitude."

(230) I Stood Tiptoe upon a Little Hill. Lines 1–106. "The poem . . . . was suggested to him by a delightful summer day, as he stood beside the gate that leads from the Battery on Hampstead Heath into a field by Caen Wood."—Leigh Hunt, in *Lord Byron and Some of his Contemporaries* (1828). Keats's style and verse in this poem, as in "Endymion," were evidently influenced by the poetry of Leigh Hunt (see p. 227) and of William Browne, whose *Britannia's Pastorals* (1613–16) furnished a motto for one section of the volume which included "I Stood Tiptoe upon a Little Hill." A passage from the pastorals (Book II, Song 1, ll. 782–96) will show how much nearer Keats was to Browne than to Dryden or Pope in his way of writing the pentameter couplet:

> First thick clouds rose from all the liquid plains;
> Then mists from marishes, and grounds whose veins
> Were conduit-pipes to many a crystal spring;
> From standing pools and fens were following
> Unhealthy fogs; each river, every rill
> Sent up their vapours to attend her will.
> These pitchy curtains drew 'twixt earth and heaven.
> And as Night's chariot through the air was driven,
> Clamour grew dumb, unheard was shepherd's song,
> And silence girt the woods; no warbling tongue
> Talked to the Echo; satyrs broke their dance,
> And all the upper world lay in a trance.
> Only the curled streams soft chidings kept;
> And little gales that from the green leaf swept
> Dry summer's dust, in fearful whisp'rings stirred,
> As loath to waken any singing bird.

(232) 67. *sallows*=willows.

(233) ENDYMION. *PROEM.* "Endymion," Book I, 1–62.

(234) 39, 40. "Endymion" was begun in Carisbrooke, Isle of Wight, whence the poet wrote to Reynolds, under date of April 18, 1817, "I shall forthwith begin my 'Endymion,' which I hope I shall have got some way with by the time you come, when we will read our verses in a delightful place I have set my heart upon, near the castle." ¶ 58, 59. "In 'Endymion' I leaped headlong into the sea, and thereby have become better acquainted with the soundings, the quicksands, and the rocks than if I had stayed upon the green shore, and piped a silly pipe, and took tea and comfortable advice. I was never afraid of failure; for I would sooner fail than not be among the greatest."—Letter to Hessey, October 9, 1818.

(234) *HYMN TO PAN.* "Endymion," Book I. 232–306.

(235) 12. *Syrinx:* Syrinx fled from the love of Pan to the water nymphs, who changed her into a clump of reeds by the river; when Pan embraced them and sighed over them, the reeds gave forth a sad melody, and the god made of them Pan's pipes, or the syrinx. ¶ 16. *turtles*=turtle-doves.

(236) 75. *Mount Lycean:* Mount Lyceum was in Arcadia, the favorite residence of Pan.

(236) WHEN I HAVE FEARS THAT I MAY CEASE TO BE. Cf. "Sleep and Poetry," ll. 96–98:

> O for ten years, that I may overwhelm
> Myself in poesy; so I may do the deed
> That my own soul has to itself decreed.

¶ 3. *in charact'ry*=in characters, in letters.

(237) 9. *fair creature:* not Fanny Brawne, whom Keats had not met at this time. ¶ 13, 14. Cf. Shakspere's *Sonnets*, cvii. 1, 2:

> Not mine own fears, nor the prophetic soul
> Of the wide world dreaming on things to come.

(237) ON SITTING DOWN TO READ "KING LEAR" ONCE AGAIN. ¶ 6. *damnation:* in the version written by Keats in a letter to George and Thomas Keats, January 23, 1818, the reading is "hell torment." ¶ 9. *clouds of Albion:* the story of Lear and his three daughters has come down to us from the cloudland of early British legend. ¶ 12–14. Keats was realizing more and more that he needed to nourish his poetical powers by studying the works of the great poets before him; cf. a statement, which precedes the sonnet, in the letter quoted above: "I think a little change has taken place in my intellect lately—I cannot bear to be uninterested or unemployed, I, who for so long a time have been addicted to passiveness. Nothing is finer for the purposes of great productions than a very gradual ripening of the intellectual powers. As an instance of this—observe—I sat down yesterday to read *King Lear* once again: the thing appeared to demand the prologue of a sonnet; I wrote it, and began to read."

(237) MOTHER OF HERMES, AND STILL YOUTHFUL MAIA. In a letter to Reynolds, May 3, 1818, Keats says that he wrote these lines on May Day. ¶ 1. Maia was the mother of Hermes. ¶ 3. *Baiae:* this seaside resort, near Naples, was in Magna Graecia, or that portion of southern Italy colonized by Greeks, who of course brought with them the worship of the Greek deities. ¶ 5. *Sicilian:* Sicily was also a Greek colony.

(238) HYPERION. Book I. 1–157. Saturn, the supreme god in the earlier classic mythology, was deposed by Jupiter, Neptune, and Pluto; the lines describe his stupor immediately after his overthrow. *Ixion's wheel:* Ixion, for boasting that Herè loved him, was bound to a revolving wheel in Tartarus.

(240) 95. *Hyperion:* god of the sun.

(242) FANCY.

(244) 81. *Ceres' daughter:* Proserpine, whom Pluto carried off to the lower world as his bride. 85. *Hebe's:* Hebe, the goddess of youth, was cup-bearer to the gods.

(**244**) ODE TO A NIGHTINGALE. ¶ 16. *Hippocrene:* a fountain on Mt. Helicon, sacred to the Muses, the waters of which were supposed to give poetic inspiration. (The fable was that the fountain gushed out where the hoof of Pegasus struck the ground; ἵππος, horse, κρήνη, fountain.)

(**245**) 26. The line was apparently suggested by the death of the poet's brother Tom, by consumption, a few months before. ¶ 32. *pards:* leopards drew the car of Bacchus. ¶ 33. *viewless*=invisible. ¶ 51. *for*=inasmuch as. ¶ 52. This was not merely a poetic fancy; cf. Keats's statement in a letter to Bailey, June 10, 1818: "Now I am never alone without rejoicing that there is such a thing as death—without placing my ultimate in the glory of dying for a great human purpose. Perhaps if my affairs were in a different state, I should not have written the above—you shall judge: I have two brothers; one is driven, by the 'burden of society,' to America; the other, with an exquisite love of life, is in a lingering state."

(**246**) 62. There seems to be a contrast implied between the bird and a poet like Keats himself in an age too hungry for material good to care much for poetry. ¶ 66. *Ruth:* cf. the second chapter of the Bible story of Ruth. ¶ 80. *do I wake or sleep?* The sense is, "In coming back to the ordinary world have I awaked into real life; or were those moments of beauty and joy with the nightingale real existence, in leaving which I have sunk into spiritual sleep?" Cf. a somewhat similar thought in "Adonais, ' ll. 343–48.

(**246**) ODE ON A GRECIAN URN. "There is some reason for thinking that the particular urn which inspired this beautiful poem is a somewhat weather-beaten work in marble still preserved in the garden of Holland House."—Buxton Forman. ¶ 3. *sylvan:* cf. "leaf-fringed," l. 5.

(**247**) 13. *sensual ear*=ear of sense; the idea of moral grossness is absent. ¶ 18–20. Cf. the "Ode on Melancholy," ll. 21–30. ¶ 31. Here begins a description of another group of figures, on the other side of the urn. ¶ 35. The "little town" is not represented on the urn, but is fancied by the poet. ¶ 41. *attitude:* the word refers to the poise of the whole urn. *brede*=braid, embroidery, ornament. ¶ 42. *marble:* see the note by Buxton Forman, quoted above. ¶ 44. *tease:* the basis of the sense of the word here is its earlier meaning of carding or combing a tangled mass, as of flax or wool; the quiet beauty of the old Greek vase smoothes the tangles out of our thoughts and gently leads us away from worries and frets into a calmer and higher mood, as the sense of eternity does. ¶ 49, 50. "I am certain of nothing but of the holiness of the heart's affections and the truth of imagination. What the imagination seizes as beauty must be truth—whether it existed before or not."—Keats, in a letter to Bailey November 22, 1817.

(**248**) TO AUTUMN. "How beautiful the season is now—how fine the air—a temperate sharpness about it. Really, without joking, chaste weather—Diana skies—I never liked stubble-field so much as now—aye, better than the chilly green of the spring. Somehow, a stubble-field looks warm—in the same way that some pictures look warm. This struck me so much in my Sunday's walk that I composed upon it."—Keats, in a letter to Reynolds, September 22, 1819. ¶ 28. *sallows*=willows. ¶ 30. *bourn*=boundary; sometimes used incorrectly for "region," and perhaps so here. ¶ 32. *garden-croft:* a croft is a small piece of inclosed ground.

(**248**) ODE ON MELANCHOLY. ¶ 2. *wolf's-bane:* a poisonous plant, of the aconite family.

(**249**) 6. *beetle:* the sacred beetle of Egypt was regarded as a symbol of the resurrection of the soul, and was placed in coffins. *death-moth:* a moth on whose back are markings that closely resemble the human skull. ¶ 7. *Psyche:* in Greek mythology the butterfly or the moth was often taken as a symbol of Psyche, the soul, because of its spirit-like emergence from the chrysalis of a worm; the death-moth would be the symbol of a soul made mournful by thoughts of death and its horrors.

(**249**) THE EVE OF ST. AGNES. St. Agnes was a Roman virgin who suffered martyrdom at the beginning of the fourth century. On account of her name (cf. Latin "agnus," lamb) and her youth and innocence, the lamb was associated with her in legend and picture. St. Agnes' Day is January 21; the eve is of course the night of January 20. "It was thought possible for a girl, on the eve of St. Agnes, to obtain, by divination, a knowledge of her future husband. . . . . Lying down on her back that night, with her hands under her head, the anxious maiden was led to expect that her future spouse would appear in a dream and salute her with a kiss."—Chambers, *Book of Days*. ¶ 8. *without a death*, i. e., without his having died.

(250) 14–16. The chapel is the chapel of a castle, and in it are the sarcophagi of the ancestors of the noble family; each sarcophagus is enclosed in an iron railing, and surmounted by a stone effigy of the person buried within, hands clasped on breast. *dumb orat'ries:* an oratory is a place of prayer (Latin "orare," to speak, to pray); these oratories are called dumb because the effigies can pray only by their posture. ¶ 18. *mails:* coats of mail. ¶ 21. *Flattered*. Keats, who was an ardent reader of Shakspere, may have used the word as Shakspere sometimes does, in the sense of "to soothe, to please." Leigh Hunt gave a more elaborate explanation: "In this word 'flattered' is the whole theory of the secret of tears, which are the tributes, more or less worthy, of self-pity to self-love. . . . . The poor old man was moved, by the sweet music, to think that so sweet a thing was intended for his comfort as well as for others. . . . . He began to consider how much he had suffered—how much he had suffered wrongly and mysteriously. . . . . Hence he found himself deserving of tears and self-pity, and he shed them, and felt soothed by his poor, old, loving self."—Hunt's *London Journal*, January 21, 1835. ¶ 37–41. Cf. "L'Allegro," ll. 119, 120, 127–30:

> Where throngs of knights and barons bold,
> In weeds of peace, high triumphs hold.
> . . . .
> And pomp, and feast, and revelry,
> With mask and antique pageantry;
> Such sights as youthful poets dream
> On summer eves by haunted stream.

(251) 58. *many a sweeping train:* "skirts sweeping along the floor."—Keats, in a letter to Taylor, June 11, 1820. ¶ 70. *Hoodwinked*=blinded (literally, having the eyes shut by a hood, as in the case of hunting-hawks). *amort*=dead.

(252) 90. *beldame*=an old woman. ("Not a direct adoption of the Fr. *belle dame*, 'fair lady,' but formed upon 'dam,' earlier 'dame,' in its Eng. sense of 'mother,' with 'bel'-employed to express relationship."—*A New English Dictionary*.) ¶ 105. *gossip*=god-mother (O. E. "god," God, and "sib," relation, alliance, the whole word meaning a God-relative, or sponsor at baptism). ¶ 116. *secret sisterhood:* nuns, who brought two lambs to St. Agnes' altar, and then spun and wove the wool.

(253) 133. *brook:* a misuse of the word, apparently for the rhyme; but Buxton Forman suggests that Keats may have meant to write "baulk."

(254) 168. *legioned:* as numerous as a legion. ¶ 170, 171. Merlin, the enchanter of King Arthur's court, while a furious storm was raging over the forest of Broceliande was magically imprisoned in a hawthorn-bush by his mistress, to whom he had revealed the spell, and was never seen again among men. (See Tennyson's "Merlin and Vivien.") Keats seems to have fused with this story the old notion that practicers of the black art sold themselves to the Devil, who claimed their souls at death. ¶ 172–75. Why Porphyro wanted the cates and the lute appears in a rejected stanza, which in the first draft came after stanza 6:

> 'T was said her future lord would there appear
> Offering as sacrifice—all in the dream—
> Delicious food even to her lips brought near:
> Viands and wine and fruit and sugared cream,
> To touch her palate with the fine extreme
> Of relish; then soft music heard; and then
> More pleasures followed in a dizzy stream
> Palpable almost; then to wake again
> Warm in the virgin morn, no weeping Magdalen.

(255) 218. *gules*=red color (a term in heraldry, derived probably from the red mouth —Latin "gula"—of the heraldic lion).

(256) 241. Hunt (*London Journal*, January 21, 1835) curiously misinterpreted the line: "Clasped like a missal in a land of Pagans: that is to say, where Christian prayer-books must not be seen, and are, therefore, doubly cherished for the danger." But "clasped" clearly means "fastened by its clasps, shut": Keats first wrote, "Shut like a missal"; and the thought in the next two lines makes this the natural interpretation. ¶ 266. *soother*= more soothing, pleasing. ¶ 268. *argosy*=a large merchant-vessel, richly laden. ¶ 269. *Fez:* the capital of Morocco. ¶ 270. *silken Samarcand:* a city in Turkestan, famous for its cottons and silks.

(257) 300. *a painful change:* cf. l. 311.

(259) 358. *arras:* tapestry hung on the walls, with inwoven figures (from Arras, a city in France, where the tapestry was made).

(259) LAMIA. Part I. 1–170. In Greek mythology Lamia was first a beautiful woman loved by Zeus, whom Herè turned into a man-eating monster; later she was thought of as an evil spirit, a vampire, who enticed men by her beauty and sucked their blood. (See Goethe's "Die Braut von Corinth.") In the Middle Ages witches were often called "Lamiae." Keats's poem is based upon a variation of the old legend, and combines the notions of a vampire and a snake-woman. In the first edition the following passage from Burton's *Anatomy of Melancholy* (1621) (Part III, Sec. 2, Mem. 1, subsec. 1) was printed as a note at the end of the poem: "Philostratus, in his fourth book *De vita Apollonii*, hath a memorable instance in this kind, which I may not omit, of one Menippus Lycius, a young man twenty-five years of age, that, going between Cenchreas and Corinth, met such a phantasm in the habit of a fair gentlewoman, which, taking him by the hand, carried him home to her house in the suburbs of Corinth, and told him she was a Phoenician by birth, and if he would tarry with her 'he would hear her sing and play, and drink such wine as never any drank, and no man should molest him, but she, being fair and lovely, would live and die with him that was fair and lovely to behold.' The young man, a philosopher, otherwise staid and discreet, able to moderate his passions, though not this of love, tarried with her awhile to his great content, and at last married her, to whose wedding, amongst other guests, came Apollonius, who, by some probable conjectures, found her out to be a serpent, a lamia, and that all her furniture was like Tantalus's gold described by Homer, no substance, but mere illusions. When she saw herself descried, she wept, and desired Apollonius to be silent, but he would not be moved, and thereupon she, plate, house, and all that was in it, vanished in an instant: 'many thousands took notice of this fact, for it was done in the midst of Greece.'"

(261) 47. *gordian shape*, i. e., twisted into an intricate knot, like the famous gordian knot. ¶ 49. *pard*=leopard. ¶ 63. *Sicilian air:* the vale of Enna, in which Proserpine was gathering flowers when Pluto seized her and carried her off to Hades, is in Sicily. ¶ 81. *star of Lethe:* Hermes was the sun-god during the hours when the sun was in the under-world.

(263) 133. *lythe Caducean charm:* Hermes' rod, entwined with serpents, was called Caduceus.

(264) LA BELLE DAME SANS MERCI. Cf. "The Eve of St. Agnes," l. 292. "Among the pieces printed at the end of Chaucer's works and attributed to him, is a translation, under this title ["La Belle Dame," etc.], of a poem of the celebrated Alain Chartier. . . . . It was the title which suggested to a friend the verses at the end of our present number."— Leigh Hunt, in *The Indicator*, May 10, 1820. Keats copied his poem into a journal-letter to George and Georgiana Keats, February–May, 1819; this earlier version has so many readings which to many lovers of Keats seem superior to the readings of the revised form that it is here printed entire:

> O what can ail thee, knight at arms,
>   Alone and palely loitering ?
> The sedge is withered from the lake,
>   And no birds sing !

O what can ail thee, knight at arms,
  So haggard and so woe-begone?
The squirrel's granary is full,
  And the harvest's done.

I see a lily on thy brow,
  With anguish moist and fever dew;
And on thy cheeks a fading rose
  Fast withereth too.—

I met a lady in the meads,
  Full beautiful, a faery's child;
Her hair was long, her foot was light,
  And her eyes were wild.

I made a garland for her head,
  And bracelets, too, and fragrant zone;
She looked at me as she did love,
  And made sweet moan.

I set her on my pacing steed,
  And nothing else saw, all day long;
For sidelong would she bend, and sing
  A faery's song.

She found me roots of relish sweet,
  And honey wild, and manna dew;
And sure in language strange she said,
  "I love thee true."

She took me to her elfin grot,
  And there she wept and sighed full sore;
And there I shut her wild, wild eyes
  With kisses four.

And there she lullèd me asleep,
  And there I dreamed, ah woe betide!
The latest dream I ever dreamt,
  On the cold hillside.

I saw pale kings, and princes too,
  Pale warriors, death-pale were they all,
Who cried, "La belle dame sans merci
  Thee hath in thrall!"

I saw their starved lips in the gloam
  With horrid warning gapèd wide—
And I awoke, and found me here,
  On the cold hill's side.

And this is why I sojourn here,
  Alone and palely loitering;
Though the sedge is withered from the lake,
  And no birds sing.

(265) BRIGHT STAR, WOULD I WERE STEDFAST AS THOU ART. Lord Houghton (R. M. Milnes) says that after Keats had set sail for Italy, in September, 1820, he "landed once more in England, on the Dorsetshire coast, after a weary fortnight spent in beating about the Channel; the bright beauty of the day and the scene revived the poet's drooping heart, and the inspiration remained on him for some time even after his return to the ship. It was then that he composed that sonnet of solemn tenderness, 'Bright Star, Would I Were Stedfast as Thou Art,' and wrote it out in a copy of Shakespeare's poems he had given to Severn a few days before. I know of nothing written afterwards."—*Life, Letters, and Literary Remains of John Keats* (1848).

CONTEMPORARY CRITICISM

Reviewers have been sometimes accused of not reading the works which they affected to criticize. On the present occasion we shall anticipate the author's complaint, and honestly confess that we have not read his work. Not that we have been wanting in our duty—far from it; indeed, we have made efforts almost as superhuman as the story itself appears to be, to get through it; but with the fullest stretch of our perseverance, we are forced to confess that we have not been able to struggle beyond the first of the four books of which this "Poetic Romance" consists. We should extremely lament this want of energy, or whatever it may be, on our part, were it not for one consolation—namely, that we are no better acquainted with the meaning of the book through which we have so painfully toiled than we are with that of the three which we have not looked into. It is not that Mr. Keats (if that be his real name, for we almost doubt that any man in his senses would put his real name to such a rhapsody), it is not, we say, that the author has not powers of language, rays of fancy, and gleams of genius—he has all these; but he is unhappily a disciple of the new school of what has been somewhere called Cockney poetry, which may be defined to consist of the most incongruous ideas in the most uncouth language. . . . .

Of the story we have been able to make out but little; it seems to be mythological, and probably relates to the loves of Diana and Endymion; but of this, as the scope of the work has altogether escaped us, we cannot speak with any degree of certainty, and must therefore content ourselves with giving some instances of its diction and versification—and here again we are perplexed and troubled. At first it appeared to us that Mr. Keats had been amusing himself and wearying his readers with an immeasurable game at *bouts-rimés;* but, if we recollect rightly, it is an indispensable condition at this play that the rhymes when filled up shall have a meaning; and our author, as we have already hinted, has no meaning. He seems to us to write a line at random, and then he follows, not the thought excited by this line, but that suggested by the *rhyme* with which it concludes. There is hardly a complete couplet enclosing a complete idea in the whole book. He wanders from one subject to another, from the association, not of the ideas, but of sounds, and the work is composed of hemistichs which, it is quite evident, have forced themselves upon the author by the mere force of the catchwords on which they turn.—*The Quarterly Review*, April (not published until September), 1818, on "Endymion." (The article was long attributed to William Gifford, editor of the Review, but is now known to have been written by J. W. Croker, the leading contributor.)

To witness the disease of any human understanding, however feeble, is distressing; but the spectacle of an able mind reduced to a state of insanity is of course ten times more afflicting. It is with such sorrow as this that we have contemplated the case of Mr. John Keats. This young man appears to have received from nature talents of an excellent, perhaps even of a superior, order—talents which, devoted to the purposes of any useful profession, must have rendered him a respectable if not an eminent citizen. His friends, we understand, destined him to the career of medicine, and he was bound apprentice some years ago to a worthy apothecary in town. But all has been undone by a sudden attack of the malady to which we have alluded. Whether Mr. John had been sent home with a diuretic or composing draught to some patient far gone in the poetical mania, we have not heard. This much is certain, that he has caught the infection and that thoroughly. For some time we were in hopes that he might get off with a violent fit or two; but of late the symptoms are terrible. The phrenzy of the "Poems" was bad enough in its way; but it did not alarm us half so seriously as the calm, settled, imperturbable, driveling idiocy of "Endymion." . . . .

And now good-morrow to the "Muses' son of Promise"; as for "the feats he yet may do," as we do not pretend to say, like himself, "Muse of my native land, am I inspired," we shall adhere to the safe old rule of *pauca verba*. We venture to make one small prophecy, that his bookseller will not a second time venture £50 upon anything he can write. It is a better and a wiser thing to be a starved apothecary than a starved poet; so back to the shop, Mr. John, back to "plasters, pills, and ointment boxes," etc. But, for Heaven's sake, young Sangrado, be a little more sparing of extenuatives and sporifics in your practice than you have been in your poetry.—*Blackwood's Magazine*, August, 1818, on "The Cockney School of Poetry."

Endymion is totally unlike all these, and all other poems. As we said before, it is not a *poem* at all. It is an ecstatic dream of poetry—a flush—a fever—a burning light—an involuntary outpouring of the spirit of poetry—that will not be controlled. . . . . It is the wanderings of the butterfly in the first hour of its birth, not as yet knowing one flower from another, but only that all *are* flowers. Its similitudes come crowding upon us from all delightful things. It is the May-day of poetry. . . . . It [the rhythm] combines more freedom, sweetness, and variety than are to be found in that of any other long poem written in the same measure, without any exception whatever. . . . . Is it credible that the foregoing extracts are taken, almost at random, from a work in which a writer in the most popular—we will say *deservedly* the most popular—critical journal of the day has been unable to discover anything worthy to redeem it from mere contempt? Those who have the most respect for the *Quarterly Review* will feel most pain at seeing its pages disgraced by such an article as that to which we allude.—*The London Magazine*, April, 1820.

We had never happened to see either of these volumes till very lately, and have been exceedingly struck with the genius they display and the spirit of poetry which breathes through all their extravagance. That imitation of our old writers, and especially of our older dramatists, to which we cannot help flattering ourselves that we have somewhat contributed, has brought on, as it were, a second spring in our poetry; and few of its blossoms are either more profuse of sweetness, or richer in promise, than this which is now before us. Mr. Keats, we understand, is still a very young man, and his whole works, indeed, bear evidence enough of the fact. They are full of extravagance and irregularity, rash attempts at originality, interminable wanderings, and excessive obscurity. They manifestly require, therefore, all the indulgence that can be claimed for a first attempt. But we think it no less plain that they deserve it, for they are flushed all over with the rich lights of fancy, and so colored and bestrewn with the flowers of poesy that, even while perplexed and bewildered in their labyrinths, it is impossible to resist the intoxication of their sweetness or to shut our hearts to the enchantments they so lavishly present. . . . . The following lines from an ode to a nightingale are equally distinguished for harmony and high poetic feeling. [Quotation of ll. 15-28, 63-70.] . . . . We know nothing at once so truly fresh, genuine, and English, and at the same time so full of poetical feeling and Greek elegance and simplicity, as this address to autumn. [Quotation of "To Autumn."] . . . . But the glory and charm of the poem ["The Eve of St. Agnes"] is in the description of the fair maiden's antique chamber, and of all that passes in that sweet and angel-guarded sanctuary; every part of which is touched with colors at once rich and delicate, and the whole chastened and harmonized, in the midst of its gorgeous distinctness, by a pervading grace and purity that indicate not less clearly the exaltation than the refinement of the author's fancy. . . . . Mr. Keats has unquestionably a very beautiful imagination, a perfect ear for harmony, and a great familiarity with the finest diction of English poetry; but he must learn not to misuse or misapply these advantages, and neither to waste the good gifts of nature and study on intractable themes nor to luxuriate too recklessly on such as are more suitable.—*The Edinburgh Review*, August, 1820. (The article was written by Francis Jeffrey.)

See also p. 553.

WALTER SAVAGE LANDOR

(265) AH, WHAT AVAILS THE SCEPTRED RACE. Rose Aylmer, daughter of Baron Aylmer, was Landor's friend and companion in his early years, in Wales; she went with her father to India, and died there in 1800. The poem was written after hearing of her death. Landor carried the memory of her to his grave, in his old age writing a poem about one of their days together, in which occur the following lines describing her treatment of a scratch he got in pulling roses for her:

> But then she saw a half-round bead,
> And cried, "Good gracious! how you bleed!"

Gently she wiped it off, and bound
With timorous touch that dreadful wound.
To lift it from its nurse's knee
I feared, and quite as much feared she,
For might it not increase the pain,
And make the wound burst out again?
She coaxed it to lie quiet there
With a low tune I bent to hear;
How close I bent I quite forget,
I only know I hear it yet.

(266) A FIESOLAN IDYL. Fiesole is a hamlet on a hill near Florence; Landor lived for some years in a villa on the hillside.

(268) THE DEATH OF ARTEMIDORA. In the first version, besides several minor differences, these lines occurred at the end:

With her that old boat incorruptible,
Unwearied, undiverted in its course,
Had plashed the water up the farther strand.

¶ 11. *Iris:* as the personification of the rainbow, uniting heaven and earth, she was the messenger of the gods.

(268) THE HAMADRYAD. A hamadryad was a nymph who was born and who died at the same time with the tree (usually an oak) of which she was the genius (ἅμα, together with; δρῦς, tree). The legend which Landor tells has been traced back to the fifth century B. C.; Landor follows closely the outline of the story as given by later Greek writers. Cf. Lowell's "Rhoecus." ¶ 2. *Gnidos:* the same as Cnidos, a city of Caria, Asia Minor, settled by Greeks, and a seat of the worship of Aphrodite. ¶ 7. *Pandion:* a legendary king of Athens. ¶ 9. The olive was sacred to Athene, who had produced it for the benefit of men. ¶ 12. *her:* Aphrodite.

(269) 19. *her:* Proserpine.

(270) 94. *Cydonian bow:* Cydonia was a city in the island of Crete, which was famous for its archers.

(272) 134, 135. The reference is to Paris, son of Priam king of Troy, whose award of the prize of beauty to Aphrodite awoke the jealousy of Herè and brought on the Trojan War. ¶ 166. *Hark! on the left:* thunder heard on the left was considered a favorable omen by the Greeks and Romans; cf. the *Aeneid*, II. 693.

(274) 221. *lentisk:* a sweet shrub. *oleander:* a poisonous evergreen shrub, with fragrant flowers.

ALFRED TENNYSON

(277) THE LADY OF SHALOTT. Palgrave says, in his edition of selected poems by Tennyson (1885), that the poem was suggested by an Italian *novella* upon the Donna di Scalotta, but the romance has not been identified. The poem departs considerably from the story as told by Malory (*Morte Darthur*, XVIII. ix-xx) and again by Tennyson in "Lancelot and Elaine." Canon Ainger, in his *Tennyson for the Young* (1891), says that Tennyson gave him this interpretation of the poem: "The newborn love for something, for some one, in the wide world from which she has been so long secluded, takes her out of the region of shadows into that of realities." Tennyson's son, in the *Memoir* (I. 116), says that the key to the poem is ll. 69-72. ¶ 3. *wold*=an open tract, a down (by change of meaning from O. E. "weald," forest). ¶ 5. *Camelot:* the capital city of King Arthur, the legendary king of Britain. ¶ 9. *Shalott:* a variant form, by way of the French, of "Astolat," the form in Malory and "Lancelot and Elaine."

(278) 19-27. In 1832 thus:

The little isle is all inrailed
With a rose-fence, and overtrailed
With roses; by the marge, unhailed,

> The shallop flitteth silken-sailed,
>> Skimming down to Camelot.
> A pearl-garland winds her head;
> She leaneth on a velvet bed,
> Full royally apparellèd,
>> The lady of Shalott.

(279) 80. *yellow field:* cf. "barley-sheaves," l. 74.

(281) 126. In 1832, after this line, came the following stanza:

> A cloud-white crown of pearl she dight,
> All raimented in snowy white
> That loosely flew (her zone in sight,
> Clasped with one blinding diamond bright),
>> Her wide eyes fixed on Camelot:
> Though the squally eastwind keenly
> Blew, with folded arms serenely
> By the water stood the queenly
>> Lady of Shalott.

(282) 163-71. In 1832 thus:

> They crossed themselves, their stars they blest,
> Knight, minstrel, abbot, squire, and guest.
> There lay a parchment on her breast,
> That puzzled more than all the rest
>> The well-fed wits at Camelot:
> "*The web was woven curiously,*
> *The charm is broken utterly,*
> *Draw near and fear not—this is I,*
>> *The Lady of Shalott.*"

(282) THE PALACE OF ART. The version of 1832 was greatly changed in 1842, many stanzas being omitted, altered, or transposed, while fourteen of the present stanzas were added (stanzas 18-20, 26, 28, 35-41, 53); in 1851 further revisions, mostly slight, were made, and stanzas 49-51 were added.

Tennyson prefixed the following explanatory lines:

> I send you here a sort of allegory
> (For you will understand it) of a soul,
> A sinful soul possessed of many gifts,
> A spacious garden full of flowering weeds,
> A glorious devil, large in heart and brain,
> That did love Beauty only (Beauty seen
> In all varieties of mould and mind);
> And Knowledge for its beauty; or if Good,
> Good only for its beauty; seeing not
> That Beauty, Good, and Knowledge are three sisters
> That doat upon each other, friends to man,
> Living together under the same roof,
> And never can be sundered without tears.
> And he that shuts Love out, in turn shall be
> Shut out from Love, and on her threshold lie
> Howling in outer darkness. Not for this
> Was common clay ta'en from the common earth,
> Moulded by God, and tempered with the tears
> Of angels to the perfect shape of man.

(283) 45-48. In 1832 thus:

> And round the terraces and round the walls,
>> While day sank lower or rose higher,
> To see those rails with all their knobs and balls,
>> Burn like a fringe of fire.

(284) 53-56. In 1832 thus:

> Full of long sounding corridors it was,
>> That over-vaulted grateful glooms,
> Roofed with thick plates of green and orange glass,
>> Ending in stately rooms.

¶ 65–68. In 1832 thus:

> Some were all dark and red, a glimmering land
>   Lit with a low round moon;
> Among brown rocks a man upon the sand
>   Went weeping all alone.

¶ 79. *prodigal in oil:* covered thick with olive trees, from whose fruit oil is made. ¶ 80. *hoary to the wind:* the under side of the olive leaf is ash-colored.

(285) 100. The legend is that an angel watched constantly over St. Cecilia, inventress of the organ. ¶ 105. *mythic Uther's:* Uther, according to the myth, was the father of King Arthur; cf. "Morte D'Arthur," ll. 256 ff. ¶ 111. *Ausonian king:* Numa Pompilius, one of the early legendary kings of Rome, who was reputed to receive counsel from the nymph Egeria; "Ausonia" was an old name for Campania, the district in which Rome is situated. ¶ 113. *engrailed*=indented. ¶ 115. *Indian Cama:* Camadeo, the Hindu god of love, who floated through the air, in spring and summer, on the back of a lory, or parrot.

(286) 117–20. Europa, while she was gathering flowers, was carried off by Zeus in the likeness of a bull, which swam with her on his back to Crete. In this stanza Tennyson followed Moschus, a Greek poet of the third century B. C.: "Meanwhile Europa, riding on the back of the divine bull, with one hand clasped the beast's great horn, and with the other caught up the purple fold of her garment, lest it might trail and be wet in the hoar sea's infinite spray. And her deep robe was swelled out by the winds, like the sail of a ship, and lightly still did waft the maiden onward."—*Idyls,* II. 121–26, Lang's translation. ¶ 121–24. Ganymede, a beautiful youth, was carried to Olympus by the eagle of Zeus, to serve as cupbearer to the gods. ¶ 133–40. In 1832 thus:

> There deep-haired Milton like an angel tall
>   Stood limnèd, Shakespeare bland and mild,
> Grim Dante pressed his lips, and from the wall
>   The bald blind Homer smiled.

¶ 137. *Ionian father:* Homer, who was supposed to be a native of Ionia, a region including the western part of Asia Minor, with adjacent islands, and settled by Ionian Greeks.

(287) 163. *Verulam:* Francis Bacon, who was made Baron Verulam. ¶ 164. *first*= foremost. ¶ 171. *Memnon:* a statue near Thebes, Egypt; according to legend, when the first rays of the sun struck the statue it gave forth a musical sound. ¶ 180. In 1832 there followed seven stanzas which were struck out in 1842; among them were these:

> With piles of flavorous fruits in basket-twine
>   Of gold, upheapèd, crushing down
> Musk-scented blooms—all taste—grape, gourd, or pine—
>   In bunch, or single-grown—
>
> Our growths, and such as brooding Indian heats
>   Make out of crimson blossoms deep,
> Ambrosial pulps and juices, sweets from sweets
>   Sun-changed, when sea-winds sleep.

(288) 186. In 1832, "She lit white streams of dazzling gas."

(289) 219. *Like Herod.* "And upon a set day Herod, arrayed in royal apparel, sat upon his throne, and made an oration unto them. And the people gave a shout, saying, 'It is the voice of a god, and not of a man.' And immediately the angel of the Lord smote him, because he gave not God the glory: and he was eaten of worms, and gave up the ghost." —Acts 12:21–23. ¶ 222, 223. The phrase seems to be taken almost without change from Arthur Hallam's *Remains:* "With Whom alone rest the abysmal secrets of personality." ¶ 227, 228. "This is the interpretation of the thing: MENE; God hath numbered thy kingdom, and finished it. TEKEL; Thou art weighed in the balances, and art found wanting. PERES; Thy kingdom is divided, and given to the Medes and Persians."—Daniel 5:26–28. ¶ 242. *fretted*=eaten into, here by worms (O. E. "fretan," to eat).

(291) THE LOTUS-EATERS. Cf. the *Odyssey,* IX. 83–97: "But on the tenth day we set foot on the land of the lotus-eaters, who eat a flowery food. So we stepped ashore and

drew water, and straightway my company took their midday meal by the swift ships. Now when we had tasted meat and drink I sent forth certain of my company to go and make search what manner of men they were who here live upon the earth by bread, and I chose out two of my fellows, and sent a third with them as herald. Then straightway they went and mixed with the men of the lotus-eaters, and so it was that the lotus-eaters devised not death for our fellows, but gave them of the lotus to taste. Now whosoever of them did eat the honey-sweet fruit of the lotus, had no more wish to bring tidings nor to come back, but there he chose to abide with the lotus-eating men, ever feeding on the lotus, and forgetful of his homeward way."—Butcher and Lang's translation. ¶ 1. *he:* Ulysses.

(292) 23. *galingale:* a flowering marsh-plant.

(292) You Ask Me Why, tho' Ill at Ease. ¶ 2. *this region:* foggy England. ¶ 4. *purple seas:* the blue seas of the South, reflecting unclouded skies.

(293) 6. *sober-suited:* quietly dressed, in contrast to the more ostentatious, flaring kind of freedom in some other lands, as France. ¶ 11, 12. Cf. Bacon's "Of Innovations": "It were good, therefore, that men in their innovations would follow the example of time itself, which indeed innovateth greatly, but quietly, and by degrees scarce to be perceived." Cf. also Gladstone's speech, "The Representation of the People," in 1866: "Changes that effect sudden and extensive transfer of power are attended by great temptations to human nature. . . . . The genius of our country and the history of our institutions dictate and recommend gradual progress."

(293) Ulysses. "'Ulysses' was written soon after Arthur Hallam's death, and gave my feeling about the need of going forward and braving the struggle of life, perhaps more simply than anything in 'In Memoriam.'"—*Memoir*, I. 196. Professor J. W. Hales (in his *Folia Litteraria*, 1893) finds in the poem the modern "passion for knowledge, for the exploration of its limitless fields, for the annexation of new kingdoms of science and thought." The poem, in which Tennyson said there was "an echo of Dante," seems to have been suggested by a passage in Dante's *La Divina Commedia* ("Inferno," XXVI. 91–142), in which Ulysses speaks: "When I departed from Circe, ... neither fondness for my son, nor filial devotion to my old father, nor the due love which should have made Penelope joyful, could conquer within me the ardor which I had to become experienced in the world and in human vices and worth. But I set sail on the deep open sea with only one ship and with that little company by which I had not been deserted. . . . . I and my companions were old and slow when we came to that narrow strait where Hercules set his landmarks as signs that man should go no farther. . . . . 'O brothers,' I said, 'who through a hundred thousand perils have reached the West, to this so small vigil of our senses that remains be not willing to deny the experience, following the sun, of the world without people. Consider your origin. You were not made to live like beasts, but to follow virtue and knowledge.' . . . . And having turned the stern toward the morning, we made wings of the oars for our wild flight. . . . . Already the night saw all the stars of the other pole, and our pole so low that it rose not above the floor of the sea. . . . . Out of the new land arose a whirlwind, and struck the forepart of the ship. Three times it whirled the ship about, with all the waters; the fourth time it raised the stern and made the stern go down, as pleased Another, until the sea was closed above us again." There is nothing of all this in the *Odyssey*. Tennyson, however, follows Homer and not Dante, in representing Ulysses as having returned to Ithaca, his rocky island kingdom, after ten years at the Trojan War and ten years more of wanderings. ¶ 10. *scudding drifts:* flying, broken clouds. *rainy Hyades:* a translation of Virgil's "pluvias Hyadas" (*Aeneid*, I. 744); the Hyades were seven stars in the constellation Taurus, which were supposed to bring rain. Mustard compares Horace, *Odes*, IV. xiv. 20–23:

> Indomitas prope qualis undas
> Exercet Auster, Pleiadum choro
> Scindente nubes, impiger hostium
> Vexare turmas.

"Almost as the South Wind drives the untamed waves, while the band of Pleiades rends the clouds, with untiring zeal to vex the squadrons of the foe."

(294) 17. *windy Troy:* translated from Homer's Ἴλιον ἠνεμόεσσαν (*Iliad*, XII. 115 ff.).

(295) 58, 59. Cf. the *Odyssey*, IV. 580: ἑξῆς δ' ἑζόμενοι πολιὴν ἅλα τύπτον ἐρετμοῖς, "and sitting in order they smote the gray sea with the oars." ¶ 60, 61. According to early Greek astronomy the stars sank into the ocean when they set; cf. the *Odyssey*, V. 275. ¶ 63. *Happy Isles:* the Greeks thought that the Islands of the Blessed were in the Atlantic Ocean, somewhere off the coast of Africa.

(295) Morte d'Arthur. The historical Arthur was a British king or general who, early in the sixth century, defeated the English invaders and thereby checked their conquest for half a century. Around this historical figure there began to gather legends which finally transformed him into a great king and surrounded him and his knights with the splendor of romance. Tennyson's poem is based upon a late compilation of these legends, Malory's *Morte Darthur* (1485), from which the following passages are taken: "And thus they fought all the long day, and never stinted till the noble knights were laid to the cold earth; and ever they fought still till it was near night, and by that time was there an hundred thousand laid dead upon the down. Then was Arthur wood wroth out of measure, when he saw his people so slain from him. Then the king looked about him, and then was he ware, of all his host and of all his good knights, were left no more alive but two knights; that one was Sir Lucan the butler, and his brother Sir Bedivere, and they were full sore wounded. Jesu mercy, said the king, where are all my worthy knights become? Alas that ever I should see this doleful day, for now, said Arthur, I am come to mine end. But would to God that I wist where were that traitor Sir Mordred, that hath caused all this mischief. Then was King Arthur ware where Sir Mordred leaned upon his sword among a great heap of dead men. . . . . Then the king gat his spear in both his hands, and ran toward Sir Mordred, crying: Traitor, now is thy death-day come. And when Sir Mordred heard Sir Arthur, he ran until him with his sword drawn in his hand. And there King Arthur smote Sir Mordred under the shield, with a foin of his spear, throughout the body, more than a fathom. And when Sir Mordred felt that he had his death wound he thrust himself with the might that he had up to the bur of King Arthur's spear. And right so he smote his father Arthur, with his sword holden in both his hands, on the side of the head, that the sword pierced the helmet and the brain-pan, and therewithal Sir Mordred fell stark dead to the earth; and the noble Arthur fell in a swoon to the earth, and there he swooned ofttimes. And Sir Lucan the butler and Sir Bedivere ofttimes heaved him up. And so weakly they led him betwixt them both, to a little chapel not far from the seaside. . . . . Then Sir Bedivere wept for the death of his brother. Leave this mourning and weeping, said the king, for all this will not avail me, for wit thou well an I might live myself, the death of Sir Lucan would grieve me evermore; but my time hieth fast, said the king. Therefore, said Arthur unto Sir Bedivere, take thou Excalibur, my good sword, and go with it to yonder water side, and when thou comest there I charge thee throw my sword in that water, and come again and tell me what thou there seest. My lord, said Bedivere, your commandment shall be done, and lightly bring you word again. So Sir Bedivere departed, and by the way he beheld that noble sword, that the pommel and the haft was all of precious stones; and then he said to himself: If I throw this rich sword in the water, thereof shall never come good, but harm and loss. And then Sir Bedivere hid Excalibur under a tree. And so, as soon as he might, he came again unto the king, and said he had been at the water, and had thrown the sword in the water. What saw thou there? said the king. Sir, he said, I saw nothing but waves and winds. That is untruly said of thee, said the king, therefore go thou lightly again, and do my commandment; as thou art to me lief and dear, spare not, but throw it in. Then Sir Bedivere returned again, and took the sword in his hand; and then him thought sin and shame to throw away that noble sword, and so eft he hid the sword, and returned again, and told to the king that he had been at the water, and done his commandment. What saw thou there? said the king.

Sir, he said, I saw nothing but the waters wappe and waves wanne. Ah, traitor untrue, said King Arthur, now hast thou betrayed me twice. Who would have weened that, thou that hast been to me so lief and dear? and thou art named a noble knight, and would betray me for the richness of the sword. But now go again lightly, for thy long tarrying putteth me in great jeopardy of my life, for I have taken cold. And but if thou do now as I bid thee, if ever I may see thee, I shall slay thee with mine own hands; for thou wouldst for my rich sword see me dead. Then Sir Bedivere departed, and went to the sword, and lightly took it up, and went to the water side; and there he bound the girdle about the hilts, and then he threw the sword as far into the water as he might; and there came an arm and a hand above the water and met it, and caught it, and so shook it thrice and brandished, and then vanished away the hand with the sword in the water. So Sir Bedivere came again to the king, and told him what he saw. Alas, said the king, help me hence, for I dread me I have tarried over long. Then Sir Bedivere took the king upon his back, and so went with him to that water side. And when they were at the water side, even fast by the bank hoved a little barge with many fair ladies in it, and among them all was a queen, and all they had black hoods, and all they wept and shrieked when they saw King Arthur. Now put me into the barge, said the king. And so he did softly; and there received him three queens with great mourning; and so they set them down, and in one of their laps King Arthur laid his head. And then that queen said: Ah, dear brother, why have ye tarried so long from me? alas, this wound on your head hath caught over-much cold. And so then they rowed from the land, and Sir Bedivere beheld all those ladies go from him. Then Sir Bedivere cried: Ah my lord Arthur, what shall become of me, now ye go from me and leave me here alone among mine enemies? Comfort thyself, said the king, and do as well as thou mayest, for in me is no trust for to trust in; for I will into the vale of Avilion to heal me of my grievous wound: and if thou hear never more of me, pray for my soul. But ever the queens and ladies wept and shrieked, that it was pity to hear. And as soon as Sir Bedivere had lost the sight of the barge, he wept and wailed, and so took the forest."—Book XXI, chaps. iv, v. ¶ 3. *table:* the Round Table, at which, according to legend, the king and his knights sat at meals. "Also Merlin made the Round Table in tokening of roundness of the world, for by the Round Table is the world signified by right, for all the world, Christian and heathen, repair unto the Round Table."—Malory's *Morte Darthur*, Book XIV, chap. ii; cf. l. 235. ¶ 4. *Lyonnesse:* a fabulous region near Cornwall, said now to be deep under water.

(296) 21. *Camelot:* Arthur's capital; see Tennyson's "Gareth and Lynette," ll. 184 ff., for a description of it. ¶ 22, 23. "Yet some men say in many parts of England that King Arthur is not dead, but had by the will of our Lord Jesu into another place; and men say that he shall come again."—Malory, *Morte Darthur*, Book XXI, chap. vii. Merlin, to whom Tennyson attributes the prophecy, was the magician and wizard of Arthur's court. ¶ 28-33. "So they rode till they came to a lake, the which was a fair water and broad, and in the midst of the lake Arthur was ware of an arm clothed in white samite, that held a fair sword in that hand. Lo! said Merlin, yonder is that sword that I spake of. With that they saw a damosel going upon the lake. What damosel is that? said Arthur. That is the Lady of the Lake, said Merlin. . . . . Sir Arthur, king, said the damosel, that sword is mine, and if ye will give me a gift when I ask it you, ye shall have it. By my faith, said Arthur, I will give you what gift ye will ask. Well! said the damosel, go ye into yonder barge, and row yourself to the sword, and take it and the scabbard with you, and I will ask my gift when I see the time. So Sir Arthur and Merlin alit and tied their horses to two trees, and so they went into the ship, and when they came to the sword that the hand held, Sir Arthur took it up by the handles, and took it with him, and the arm and the hand went under the water."— Malory, *Morte Darthur*, Book I, chap. xxv. ¶ 37. *middle mere:* classicism for "middle of the mere"; Mustard compares the *Aeneid*, X. 451, "medium procedit in aequor." ¶ 38. *lightly*=quickly, swiftly.

(297) 60. Translated from the *Aeneid*, IV. 285: "Atque animum nunc huc celerem,

nunc dividit illuc." ¶ 80. *lief*=beloved (O.E. "leof"; from the same root as "love"; cf. the adverbial use, still current, in "I had as lief go as not," etc.).

(298) 105, 106. Mustard compares the *Iliad*, XVIII. 400-03: "Nine years, in company with them, I wrought in bronze many skilful pieces of workmanship, ... in the hollow cave; and around me the ocean-stream with murmuring foam flowed endless." ¶ 110. *conceit*=conception, thought. ¶ 139. *a streamer of the northern morn:* the flames of the aurora borealis. ¶ 140. *moving isles of winter:* icebergs.

(299) 169, 170. Mustard compares Aeschylus, *Agamemnon*, l. 240: "She smote each of her sacrificers with a piteous glance from her eye, remarkable in her beauty as in a picture."

(300) 186. *dry:* the word seems here to be nearly equivalent to "grating," "harsh." Mustard compares a similar use of αὖος, "dry," "harsh," as in the *Iliad*, XII. 160: "And their helmets rang harsh"; and Van Dyke compares the use of "aridus" in Virgil's *Georgics*, I. 357: "A harsh noise begins to be heard upon the high mountains." ¶ 215. *greaves and cuisses:* armor for the calves and the thighs.

(301) 233. *holy Elders:* the Wise Men of the East, who brought offerings to the infant Christ. ¶ 240. Mustard compares Lucretius, *De rerum natura*, III. 964: "Cedit enim rerum novitate extrusa vetustas," "old things give way, being thrust out by new." ¶ 254, 255. Cf. the *Iliad*, VIII. 19 ff.; *Paradise Lost*, II. 1047 ff.; and Bacon's *Advancement of Learning*, i. 3: "Then, according to the allegory of the poets, he will easily believe that the highest link of nature's chain must needs be tied to the foot of Jupiter's chair." ¶ 259. *the island valley of Avilion:* the Land of the Blessed, in Celtic mythology, corresponding to the Happy Isles of the Greeks (see "Ulysses," l. 63). The next four lines seem to owe something to the description of Olympus, in the *Odyssey*, VI. 43, "it is not shaken by winds, nor drenched with rain, nor is there snow there"; and to the description of the island of Circe, in the *Odyssey*, X. 195, "the island, crowned round with the boundless deep."

(302) LOCKSLEY HALL. " 'Locksley Hall is an imaginary place (though the coast is Lincolnshire), and the hero is imaginary. The whole poem represents young life, its good side, its deficiencies, and its yearnings. Mr. Hallam said to me that the English people liked verse in trochaics, so I wrote the poem in this metre.' . . . . I remember my father saying that Sir William Jones' prose translation of the *Moâllakàt*, the seven Arabic poems (which are a selection from the work of pre-Mohammedan poets) hanging up in the temple of Mecca, gave him the idea of the poem."—*Memoir*, I. 195. In *Englische Studien*, XXVIII. 400, is a comparison of these Arabic poems with "Locksley Hall"; the similarity is not striking. ¶ 12. The reference is to the marvelous truths revealed by modern geology.

(304) 71. *one that perished:* the loving and true Amy; cf. ll. 70, 73.

(305) 75, 76. The poet is Dante, who says (*La Divina Commedia*, "Inferno," V. 121-23), "There is no greater grief than to remember a happy time in misery."

(306) 121-26. An anticipation of the perfecting of airships for use in commerce and war.

(308) 152. The original editions have nothing but a common dash at the end of the line; but the sense seems to require a full stop and a long dash, for the thought in the next line apparently goes back to the question asked in line 102. ¶ 155. *Mahratta-battle:* the Mahrattas are the most warlike of the races of India; they had been at war with the English in 1816-18.

(309) 180. *Joshua's moon:* see Joshua 10:13. ¶ 182. "When I went by the first train from Liverpool to Manchester (1830), I thought that the wheels ran in a groove. It was a black night and there was such a vast crowd round the train at the station that we could not see the wheels. Then I made this line."—Tennyson in the *Memoir*, I. 195.

(309) BREAK, BREAK, BREAK. The poem is in memory of Hallam. "It was made in a Lincolnshire lane at five o'clock in the morning."—Tennyson, quoted by A. Waugh, *Alfred Tennyson, a Study of His Life and Work* (1892).

(310) In Memoriam. The poem is in commemoration of Arthur Henry Hallam, son of the historian Hallam, who died in Vienna, September 15, 1833. He entered Cambridge University while Tennyson was in residence there, and between the two soon sprang up a friendship of peculiar intimacy. Hallam's sudden death stirred the poet's nature to its depths; for a while everything seemed blank to him, and the problems of life and death pressed upon him with crushing weight. Out of this spiritual experience arose "In Memoriam," the sections of which were written at intervals during the next sixteen years. The sections chosen for the present volume are only slightly elegiacal; they deal less with the poet's personal sorrow than with questions of modern religious thought, the discussion of which gives the poem its chief significance.

The stanza, which Tennyson supposed he had invented, had been used by several English poets before him, including Ben Jonson (1573–1637) in an elegy beginning thus:

> Though beauty be the mark of praise,
> And yours of whom I sing be such
> As not the world can praise too much,
> Yet is 't your virtue now I raise.

¶ *Section xxxiv.* 5. *round of green:* the earth. *orb of flame:* the sun.

(311) *Section xlvii.* Contrast Shelley's attitude in "Adonais," ll. 370–87. But in Section cxxx Tennyson comes nearer to Shelley's thought, although he doubtless still believes that his friend is in some sense individual and personal:

> Thy voice is on the rolling air;
> I hear thee where the waters run;
> Thou standest in the rising sun,
> And in the setting thou art fair.
>
> What art thou, then? I cannot guess;
> But tho' I seem in star and flower
> To feel thee some diffusive power,
> I do not therefore love thee less.
>
> My love involves the love before;
> My love is vaster passion now;
> Tho' mixt with God and Nature thou,
> I seem to love thee more and more.
>
> Far off thou art, but ever nigh;
> I have thee still, and I rejoice;
> I prosper, circled with thy voice;
> I shall not lose thee tho' I die.

(313) *Section lvi.* 2. *scarpèd* = cut down perpendicularly. The allusion is to fossils of extinct animals, often found in such cliffs. ¶ 26. *thy voice:* Hallam's. ¶ *Section xcvi.*

(314) 5. *one:* Hallam; cf. Section cix. ¶ 22–24. See Exodus, chap. 32. ¶ *Section cxiv.* 12. *Pallas:* according to Greek mythology, Pallas sprang, completely armed, from the head of Zeus. ¶ 16. Thomas Davidson, in his *Prolegomena to "In Memoriam"* (1889), remarks on this line, "Higher and truer than any clear conclusion which the understanding can draw from the physical facts of nature is the dim, half-formulated conclusion which the soul draws in response to its total experience, physical and spiritual."

(315) *Section cxviii.* 4. *earth and lime:* "Human love and truth are part of that living process, and have no resemblance to the 'earth and lime' of the fossil skeletons of extinct animals."—Davidson.

(316) 27. *the beast:* "Tennyson later accepted the evolutionary idea that man's body is evolved from the lower orders of life. . . . . But he wrote this passage several years before the publication of Darwin's *Origin of Species;* and it is by no means certain that the poet by 'beast' here meant anything more than the gross sensual passions."—Professor Squires.

(316) *Section cxxiv.* 3. *He:* the Supreme conceived as personal and one; theism. *They:* polytheism. *One:* the Supreme conceived as one but not necessarily personal; monism.

All: the Supreme conceived as the sum total of things; pantheism. *within, without:* in the soul, and in the world outside. ¶ 5–8. The first two lines refer to the argument for the existence of God derived from the order and apparent design in nature; the last two lines, to fine-spun metaphysical proofs. ¶ 21. *what I am:* the central essence of man, his spiritual being, with its direct intuition into spiritual truth. ¶ 22. *What is:* Absolute Being, the Supreme Existence.

(316) TEARS, IDLE TEARS. From "The Princess" (Part IV. 20–40). "The passion of the past, the abiding in the transient, was expressed in 'Tears,' which was written in the yellow autumn-tide at Tintern Abbey, full for me of its bygone memories. . . . . Not real woe, ... rather the yearning that young people occasionally experience for that which seems to have passed away from them forever."—Tennyson, in the *Memoir*, I. 253; II. 73.

(317) SWEET AND LOW. From "The Princess," between Parts II and III.

(318) THE SPLENDOUR FALLS ON CASTLE WALLS. From "The Princess," between Parts III and IV. The poem was inspired by the echoes on the lake at Killarney, during Tennyson's visit there in 1847 (*Memoir*, I. 253).

(318) THE BROOK. From the narrative poem with the same title. ¶ 7. *thorps*=hamlets. ¶ 9. *Philip's:* Philip is a character in the narrative poem.

(319) 19. *fairy foreland:* diminutive headland, or promontory; cf. "Aylmer's Field," ll. 91, 92:

> The little dells of cowslip, fairy palms,
> The petty mare's-tail forest, fairy pines.

(320) NORTHERN FARMER, OLD STYLE. "Roden Noel calls these two poems 'photographs,' but they are imaginative. The first is founded on the dying words of a farm-bailiff, as reported to me by a great-uncle of mine when verging upon 80—'God A'mighty little knows what He 's about, a-taking me. An' Squire will be so mad an' all.' I conjectured the man from that one saying."—*Memoir*, II. 9. ¶ 1. *'asta*=hast thou. ¶ 3. *moänt 'a*=may not have. ¶ 5. *a*=he. ¶ 10. *you:* "ou" as in "hour" (Tennyson's note). *'issèn*=himself. ¶ 11. *towd ma*=told me. ¶ 12. *boy 'um*=by him. ¶ 14. *barne*=bairn, child. ¶ 15. *Thaw*=though. ¶ 16. *raäte*=church rate, or tax. ¶ 18. *buzzard-clock*=cockchafer (Tennyson's note). ¶ 21. *tha*=thou. ¶ 23. *'Siver*=howsoever. ¶ 28. *stubbed*=dug up the stubs from. ¶ 30. *boggle*=bogle, haunting ghost.

(321) 31. *butter-bump*=bittern (Tennyson's note). ¶ 32. *raäved an' rembled*=tore up and threw away. ¶ 33. *Keäper's it wur*=gamekeeper's [ghost] it was. ¶ 34. *'enemies'*=anemones (Tennyson's note). ¶ 35. *toäner*=one or other. ¶ 36. *'soize*=the assizes, session of court. ¶ 40. *Fourscoor:* "ou" as in "hour" (Tennyson's note). *yows*=ewes. ¶ 42. *ta-year*=this year. ¶ 46. *wonn*=one. ¶ 49. *mowt*=might. *'ant*=haint. *'aäpoth*=half-penny-worth. ¶ 54. *sewer-loy*=surely. ¶ 60. *moänt*=mustn't.

(322) 65. *atta*=art thou. ¶ 66. *'loättler*=teetotaler. *hallus i' the owd taäle*=always in the old tale, i. e., always harping on the same string.

(322) MILTON. Tennyson printed this poem, with three others, under the general heading, "In Quantity," and these lines he designated, in a subtitle, as "Alcaics." "My alcaics are not intended for Horatian alcaics, nor are Horace's alcaics the Greek alcaics. . . . . The Greek alcaic, if we may judge from the two or three specimens left, had a much freer and lighter movement; and I have no doubt that an old Greek if he knew our language would admit my alcaics as legitimate, only 'Milton' must not be pronounced 'Mil*ton*.'"— *Memoir*, II. 11. The scheme of the Greek alcaic stanza is as follows:

$$\geqslant \mid - \smile \mid - \geqslant \mid - \smile \smile \mid - \smile \mid \asymp \wedge$$
$$\geqslant \mid - \smile \mid - \geqslant \mid - \smile \smile \mid - \smile \mid \asymp \wedge$$
$$\geqslant \mid - \smile \mid - \geqslant \mid - \smile \mid - \smile$$
$$- \smile \smile \mid - \smile \smile \mid - \smile \mid - \smile$$

(323) RIZPAH. The title is taken from the Old Testament story of Rizpah: "But the king took the two sons of Rizpah the daughter of Aiah, whom she bare unto Saul, ... and he delivered them into the hands of the Gibeonites, and they hanged them in the hill before the Lord. . . . . And Rizpah the daughter of Aiah took sackcloth, and spread it for her upon the rock, from the beginning of harvest until water dropped upon them out of heaven, and suffered neither the birds of the air to rest on them by day, nor the beasts of the field by night."—II Samuel 21: 8-10. Tennyson said (*Memoir*, II. 249-51) that the poem is founded on an incident, which he read in a cheap magazine, connected with the robbing of the mail by two men, Rooke and Howell, in the eighteenth century: "They were gibbeted on the spot where the robbery was committed, and there is an affecting story connected with the body of Rooke. When the elements had caused the clothes and flesh to decay, his aged mother, night after night, in all weathers, and the more tempestuous the weather the more frequent the visits, made a sacred pilgrimage to the lonely spot on the downs, and it was noticed that on her return she always brought something away with her in her apron. Upon being watched it was discovered that the bones of the hanging man were the objects of her search, and as the wind and rain scattered them on the ground she conveyed them to her home. There she kept them, and, when the gibbet was stripped of its horrid burden, in the dead silence of the night she interred them in the hallowed inclosure of Old Shoreham Church-yard."

(326) To VIRGIL. Subtitle, "Written at the Request of the Mantuans for the Nine-teenth Centenary of Virgil's Death." ¶ 1-4. This stanza refers to the *Aeneid.* ¶ 6. *he:* Hesiod, the Greek poet, of the eighth century B. C., whose *Works and Days* is somewhat like Virgil's *Georgics.* ¶ 9, 10. These lines refer to Virgil's *Georgics*, in which he gives directions about the care of fields, trees, domestic animals, and bees.

(327) 13, 14. These lines refer to the first of Virgil's *Eclogues.* ¶ 15, 16. These lines refer to the sixth eclogue, ll. 13-26. ¶ 17-20. These lines refer to the fourth eclogue, which is addressed to Pollio, one of Virgil's patrons, and prophesies the return of the Golden Age. ¶ 19. *Summers of the snakeless meadow:* cf. "Occidet et serpens" (*Eclogues*, IV. 24), "And the serpent shall die." ¶ 20. *unlaborious earth:* cf. "Non rastros patietur humus" (*Eclogues*, IV. 40), "The soil will not be hurt with mattocks." *oarless sea:* cf. "Cedet et ipse mari vector, nec nautica pinus mutabit merces: omnis feret omnia te lus" (*Eclogues*, IV. 38, 39), "The ocean-carrier himself will give up the sea, nor will the ship exchange merchandise, for every land will bear all things." ¶ 21, 22. Cf. the *Aeneid*, VI. 724-27:

> Principio caelum ac terras camposque liquentis
> Lucentemque globum Lunae Titaniaque astra
> Spiritus intus alit, totamque infusa per artus
> Mens agitat molem et magno se corpore miscet.

"In the first place, sky and earth and the liquid plains and the shining orb of Luna and the Titanian stars a spirit within nourishes, and, infused through the limbs, a mind agitates the whole mass and mingles with the great body." ¶ 27. An allusion to the golden branch ("aureus ramus") in the dark grove near the mouth of Hades, by which, as an offering to Proserpine, Aeneas gained admission to the lower world; see the *Aeneid*, VI. 136-43. ¶ 30. *purple Caesar:* the state robes of the Roman emperors were purple. ¶ 35, 36. Cf. Virgil's *Eclogues*, I. 67: "Et penitus toto divisos orbe Britannos," "And the Britains wholly cut off from the whole world." ¶ 37. *Mantovano:* Virgil, who was born near Mantua.

(330) CROSSING THE BAR. "Written in my father's eighty-first year, on a day in October when we came from Aldworth to Farringford. Before reaching Farringford he had the Moaning of the Bar in his mind, and after dinner he showed me this poem written out. I said, 'That is the crown of your life's work.' He answered, 'It came in a moment.' He explained the 'Pilot' as 'That Divine and Unseen Who is always guiding us.' A few days before my father's death he said to me: 'Mind you put "Crossing the Bar" at the end of all

editions of my poems.' "—*Memoir*, II. 366.   In going to Farringford, on the Isle of Wight, the poet crossed the Solent, the strait between the mainland and the island.

CONTEMPORARY CRITICISM

A prefatory sonnet opens to the reader the aspirations of the young author, in which, after the manner of sundry poets, ancient and modern, he expresses his own peculiar character by wishing himself to be something that he is not.   The amorous Catullus aspired to be a sparrow. . . . . Mr. Tennyson (though he, too, would, as far as his true love is concerned, not unwillingly "be an ear-ring," "a girdle," and "a necklace"') in the more serious and solemn exordium of his works ambitions a bolder metamorphosis—he wishes to be—*a river:*

> Mine be the strength of spirit fierce and free,
> Like some broad river rushing down alone—

rivers that travel in company are too common for his taste—

> With the self-same impulse wherewith he was thrown—

a beautiful and harmonious line—

> From his loud fount upon the echoing lea:
> Which, with increasing might, doth forward flee.

Every word of this line is valuable—the natural progress of human ambition is here strongly characterized—two lines ago he would have been satisfied with the *self-same* impulse—but now he must have *increasing* might; and indeed he would require all his might to accomplish his object of *fleeing forward*, that is, going backwards and forwards at the same time. . . . .

> doth forward flee
> By town, and tower, and hill, and cape, and isle,
> And in the middle of the green *salt* sea
> Keeps his blue waters fresh for many a mile.

A noble wish, beautifully expressed, that he may not be confounded with the deluge of ordinary poets, but, amidst their discolored and briny ocean, still preserve his own bright tints and sweet savor.   He may be at ease on this point—he never can be mistaken for any one else.   We have but too late become acquainted with him, yet we assure ourselves that if a thousand anonymous specimens were presented to us, we should unerringly distinguish his by the total absence of any particle of *salt*. . . . .

"The Lady of Shalott" is a poem in four parts, the story of which we decline to maim by such an analysis as we could give, but it opens thus:

> On either side the river lie
> Long fields of barley and of rye,
> That clothe the wold and *meet the sky*—
> And *through* the field the road runs *by*.

The Lady of Shalott was, it seems, a spinster who had, under some unnamed penalty, a certain web to weave. . . . . A knight, however, happens to ride past her window. . . . . The lady stepped to the window to look at the stranger, and forgot for an instant her web: —the curse fell on her, and she died; why, how, and wherefore, the following stanzas will clearly and pathetically explain. . . . . The "Lotus-eaters"—a kind of classical opium-eaters—are Ulysses and his crew.   They land on the "charmèd island," and "eat of the charmèd root," and then they sing:

> Long enough the winedark wave our weary bark did carry.
> This is lovelier and sweeter,
> Men of Ithaca, this is meeter,
> In the hollow rosy vale to tarry,
> Like a dreamy Lotus-eater—a delicious Lotus-eater!
> We will eat the Lotus, sweet
> As the yellow honeycomb;
> In the valley some, and some

> On the ancient heights divine,
> And no more roam,
> On the loud hoar foam,
> To the melancholy home,
> At the limits of the brine,
> The little isle of Ithaca, beneath the day's decline.

Our readers will, we think, agree that this is admirably characteristic and that the singers of this song must have made pretty free with the intoxicating fruit. How they got home you must read in Homer; Mr. Tennyson—himself, we presume, a dreamy lotus-eater, a delicious lotus-eater—leaves them in full song. . . . .

The other vision is "A Dream of Fair Women," in which the heroines of all ages—some, indeed, that belong to the times of "heathen goddesses most rare"—pass before his view. We have not time to notice them all, but the second, whom we take to be Iphigenia, touches the heart with a stroke of nature more powerful than even the veil that the Grecian painter threw over the head of her father.

> dimly I could descry
> The stern blackbearded kings with wolfish eyes,
> Watching to see me die.

> The tall masts quivered as they lay afloat,
> The temples, and the people, and the shore;
> One drew a sharp knife through my tender throat—
> Slowly,—and *nothing more!*

What touching simplicity—what pathetic resignation—he cut my throat—"*nothing more!*" One might indeed ask "what *more*" she would have?

But we must hasten on; and to tranquillize the reader's mind after this last affecting scene, we shall notice the only two pieces of a lighter strain which the volume affords. The first is elegant and playful; it is a description of the author's study, which he affectionately calls his "Darling Room."

> O darling room, my heart's delight;
> Dear room, the apple of my sight;
> With thy two couches, soft and white,
> There is no room so exquis*ite;*
> No little room so warm and bright,
> Wherein to read, wherein to write.

We entreat our readers to note how, even in this little trifle, the singular taste and genius of Mr. Tennyson break forth. In such a dear *little* room a narrow-minded scribbler would have been content with *one* sofa, and that one he would probably have covered with black mohair, or red cloth, or a good striped chintz; how infinitely more characteristic is white dimity!—'t is as it were a type of the purity of the poet's mind.—*The Quarterly Review*, April, 1833, on *Poems*, by Alfred Tennyson, 1833. (The article was written by J. G. Lockhart, Scott's biographer.)

In powers of narrative and scene-painting combined, this poem ["The Lady of Shalott"] must be ranked among the very first of its class. The delineation of outward objects, as in the greater number of Mr. Tennyson's poems, is, not picturesque, but (if we may use the term) statuesque, with brilliancy of color superadded. The forms are not, as in painting, of unequal degrees of definiteness; the tints do not melt gradually into each other, but each individual object stands out in bold relief, with a clear decided outline. . . . . Along with all this there is in the poem all that power of making a few touches do the whole work, which excites our admiration in Coleridge. Every line suggests so much more than it says that much may be left unsaid; the concentration, which is the soul of narrative, is obtained without the sacrifice of reality and life. Where the march of the story requires that the mind shall pause, details are specified; where rapidity is necessary, they are all brought before us in a flash. Except that the versification is less exquisite, the "Lady of Shalott" is entitled to a place by the side of "The Ancient Mariner" and "Christabel." . . . .

The length to which our quotations have extended, and the unsatisfactoriness of short extracts, prevent us from giving any specimen of one of the finest of Mr. Tennyson's poems, "The Lotus-Eaters." . . . . The poem is not of such sustained merit in the execution as some of the others; but the general impression resembles an effect of climate in a landscape: we see the objects through a drowsy, relaxing, but dreamy atmosphere, and the inhabitants seem to have inhaled the like. . . . .

The poems which we have quoted from Mr. Tennyson prove incontestably that he possesses, in an eminent degree, the natural endowment of a poet—the poetic temperament. And it appears clearly, not only from a comparison of the two volumes, but of different poems in the same volume, that, with him, the other element of poetic excellence—intellectual culture—is advancing both steadily and rapidly; that he is not destined, like so many others, to be remembered for what he might have done rather than for what he did; that he will not remain a poet of mere temperament, but is ripening into a true artist. . . . . We will not conclude without reminding Mr. Tennyson that if he wishes his poems to live he has still much to do in order to perfect himself in the merely mechanical parts of his craft. . . . . In some of the most beautiful of Mr. Tennyson's productions there are awkwardnesses and feeblenesses of expression, occasionally even absurdities, to be corrected, and which generally might be corrected without impairing a single beauty. His powers of versification are not yet of the highest order. In one great secret of his art, the adaptation of the music of his verse to the character of the subject, he is far from being a master: he often seems to take his metres almost at random. But this is little to set in the balance against so much excellence, and needed not have been mentioned except to indicate to Mr. Tennyson the points on which some of his warmest admirers see most room and most necessity for further effort on his part, if he would secure to himself the high place in our poetic literature for which so many of the qualifications are already his own.—*The London Review*, July, 1835. (The article was written by J. S. Mill.)

The first of these two volumes consists of republished poems, and may be regarded, we presume, as all that Mr. Tennyson wishes to preserve of his former editions. He has sifted in most cases his earlier harvests, and kept the better grain. There are some additions of verses and stanzas here and there, many minute changes, and also beneficial shortenings and condensations. The second volume, however, is on the whole far advanced in merit beyond the first. There is more clearness, solidity, and certainty of mind visible in it throughout; especially some of the blank-verse poems—a style almost unattempted in the earlier series—have a quiet completeness and depth, a sweetness arising from the happy balance of thought, feeling, and expression, that ranks them among the riches of our recent literature.—*The Quarterly Review*, September, 1842, on *Poems*, by Alfred Tennyson, 1842.

ELIZABETH BARRETT BROWNING

(**330**) SONNETS FROM THE PORTUGUESE. These sonnets were written during the courtship of Miss Barrett by Robert Browning, and were not shown to him until they had been married some months. In order to veil somewhat the personal element, she intended to call them "Sonnets Translated from the Bosnian." Mr. Browning suggested the present title, for its glancing reference to her "Catarina to Camoens," which was one of his favorite poems. They were privately printed in 1847, but not published until 1850.

(**330**) *Sonnet I.* 1-4. See Theocritus, *Idyls*, XV. 104, 105: "Tardiest of the Immortals are the beloved Hours, but dear and desired they come, for always, to all mortals, they bring some gift with them."—Lang's translation.

(**332**) A MUSICAL INSTRUMENT. For the Greek story about Pan's invention of the syrinx, see p. 557.

(**333**) THE FORCED RECRUIT. Based on an incident in the battle of Solferino, June 24, 1859, between the Austrians and the allied Italians and French, in the struggle for the liberation of Italy from Austria, a struggle in which Mrs. Browning was intensely interested.

ROBERT BROWNING

(334) HEAP CASSIA, SANDAL-BUDS, AND STRIPES. From "Paracelsus" (IV. 190–205). ¶ 1. *cassia:* a kind of cinnamon. ¶ 2. *labdanum:* a pungent gum resin. *aloe-balls:* aloe is a fragrant resin. ¶ 3. *nard*=spikenard.

(335) THE YEAR'S AT THE SPRING. From "Pippa Passes" (I. 221–28)

(335) CAVALIER TUNES. *I. Marching Along.* ¶ 1. *Kentish Sir Byng:* the Byngs were an old family in Kent, and stout loyalists. ¶ 7. *Pym:* John Pym was a leader in the Long Parliament, and aided in the impeachment of Strafford and Laud. ¶ 13. *Hampden:* John Hampden, who fought in the courts the attempt of Charles I to levy an obsolete tax, called ship-money; he died in 1643, apparently just before the time of this song. ¶ 14. *Hazelrig:* one of the five leaders of the long Parliament that Charles tried to arrest in 1642 just before the outbreak of civil war. *Fiennes:* John Fiennes, son of Viscount Saye and Sele, and prominent as a cavalry officer in the Civil War. *young Harry:* Sir Henry Vane the younger, who, after serving as governor of Massachusetts Bay Colony in 1636–37, returned to England and became prominent in the Long Parliament on the popular side.

(336) 15. *Rupert:* Prince Rupert, nephew of Charles I, the dashing leader of the king's cavalry. ¶ 22. *Nottingham:* at the outbreak of civil war the king raised the royal standard at Nottingham, and his supporters flocked to him there.

(336) *II. Give a Rouse.* ¶ 16. *Noll's:* Oliver Cromwell's.

(337) MY LAST DUCHESS.

(338) 45, 46. Professor Hiram Corson writes that Browning, in reply to his question, said, "Yes, I meant that the commands were that she be put to death," adding, after a pause, "or he might have had her shut up in a convent."

(338) THE LABORATORY. The scene of the poem is France.

(339) 37. The sense is, "My reason for wanting a larger dose is not that she may be killed quickly and without much pain."

(340) 44. The sense is, "Anything which hurts her is too sweet to me to hurt me."

(340) HOW THEY BROUGHT THE GOOD NEWS FROM GHENT TO AIX. "There is no sort of historical foundation about 'Good News from Ghent.' I wrote it under the bulwark of a vessel off the African coast, after I had been at sea long enough to appreciate even the fancy of a gallop on the back of a certain good horse 'York,' then in my stable at home. It was written in pencil on the fly-leaf of Bartoli's *Simboli*, I remember."—Browning. But the ride is described with considerable attention to verisimilitude. The distance from Ghent, in Flanders, to Aix-la-Chapelle, in west Prussia, is about ninety miles; most of the towns mentioned are in the direct route between the two places, and the distances are about what they should be—thus Düffeld, which they reach in the early morning, after starting at midnight, is some forty miles from Ghent, and Mecheln, from whose great cathedral tower they hear the chime, is a few miles south of their course, within earshot in the still of the morning. ¶ 10. *pique*=the peak or pommel of the saddle.

(342) THE LOST LEADER. In reply to a question whether Wordsworth was meant in this poem, Browning wrote, in 1875: "I *did* in my hasty youth presume to use the great and venerated personality of Wordsworth as a sort of painter's model; one from which this or the other particular feature may be selected and turned to account: had I intended more, above all, such a boldness as portraying the entire man, I should not have talked about 'handfuls of silver and bits of ribbon.' These never influenced the change of politics in the great poet; whose defection, nevertheless, accompanied as it was by a regular face-about of his special party, was to my juvenile apprehension, and even mature consideration, an event to deplore."—*The Prose Works of William Wordsworth,* edited by A. B. Grosart, I. xxxvii. ¶ 7. *had gone*=would have gone. ¶ 8. The sense is, "If the rags, which was all our poverty could furnish, had been royal robes, we would have arrayed him in them and he would have been proud of our devotion.' ¶ 29. *Best fight on well:* i. e., it is best for him to fight us gallantly, sticking to the side he has now chosen, instead of coming back to us.

(343) HOME THOUGHTS, FROM THE SEA.   The voyager is off the west coast of northern Africa, and southwest of Spain; stretched in a great arc before him, from west to east, lie Cape St. Vincent (where the English won a naval victory over the Spanish in 1797), Cadiz Bay, Cape Trafalgar (the scene of Nelson's great victory in 1805), and the straits of Gibraltar.

(344) PARTING AT MORNING.   ¶ 1. *came the sea:* as the lover's boat rounded the point? ¶ 3. *him:* the sun.   ¶ 4. *me:* the man.

(344) THE BISHOP ORDERS HIS TOMB AT ST. PRAXED'S CHURCH.   St. Praxed's Church, built in the ninth century, restored in the fifteenth, and containing some very old mosaics and rich stone-work, is one of the smaller churches of Rome and is situated in a quiet side-street.   For these reasons the weary old bishop, full of the Renaissance love of beautiful things, might naturally choose it for his last resting-place.   ¶ 1. The bishop is quoting Ecclesiastes 1: 2: "Vanity of vanities, saith the Preacher, vanity of vanities; all is vanity."   ¶ 3. *Nephews—sons mine:* he is accustomed, for propriety's sake, to call them his nephews although they are really his sons.   *I know not:* i. e., whether you are my sons or not; but cf. ll. 36, 64.   ¶ 4. *She, men:* supply "whom" after "she."   ¶ 5. *Gandolf:* a fellow ecclesiastic.

(345) 26. *tabernacle:* a stone canopy over the sarcophagus, supported by columns of peach-blossom marble; under it on the top of the sarcophagus, will be the recumbent statue of the bishop.   ¶ 31. *onion-stone:* a greenish marble, splitting into concentric coats like an onion (Italian "cipolino," a little onion); Gandolph's tomb is made of this inferior stone. ¶ 41. *olive-frail:* a basket of rushes, for olives.   ¶ 42. *lapis lazuli:* a rich blue stone.   ¶ 46. *Frascati villa:* Frascati, fifteen miles from Rome, on the north slope of the Alban hills, was a favorite summer resort for the wealthy inhabitants of Rome.   ¶ 47. *between my knees:* i. e., between the knees of his effigy on his tomb.   ¶ 48, 49. "The Gesu, the principal church of the Jesuits, one of the richest and most gorgeous in Rome. . . . . On the architrave above are two statues: God the Father, ... and Christ; . . . . between these, the globe of the earth, consisting of a single block of lapis lazuli (said to be the largest in existence)."— Baedeker's *Italy.*   ¶ 51, 52. Cf. Job 7: 6, 9: "My days are swifter than a weaver's shuttle, and are spent without hope; . . . . as the cloud is consumed and vanisheth away: so he that goeth down to the grave shall come up no more."   ¶ 55. *my frieze:* just below the top slab, and running around the sarcophagus, is to be a band of bronze with figures in bas-relief, which the bishop enumerates.   ¶ 58. *tripod:* associated with the oracle at Delphi, where the priestess sat on a tripod, over the rift in the earth whence came the fumes that were supposed to inspire her.   *thyrsus:* the thyrsus, a staff twined with ivy or the vine and topped with a pine-cone, was associated with the worship of Bacchus.

(346) 66. *travertine:* a white limestone.   ¶ 71. *pure green:* "Probably the variety known as bloodstone, deep green with blood-red spots; no stone takes a finer polish."—W. J. Rolfe, *Select Poems of Robert Browning* (1886).   ¶ 78. *Gandolf's second line:* cf. l. 99, where, apparently, we are given a specimen of the inferior Latin in the second line of Gandolf's epitaph.   ¶ 79. *Ulpian:* a Roman law-writer, living in the latter part of the second century A. D.; his Latin style is naturally less pure than that of Tully (Marcus Tullius Cicero). ¶ 87. *crook:* the statue of a bishop has a crosier, made somewhat like a shepherd's crook, the symbol of his function as a shepherd of souls.   ¶ 98. *marble's language:* i. e., language best adapted, by its conciseness and dignity, for inscriptions on marble.   ¶ 99. *elucescebat:* there is no such word in classical Latin.   ¶ 101. Cf. Genesis 47:9: "And Jacob said unto Pharaoh, The days of the years of my pilgrimage are an hundred and thirty years: few and evil have the days of the years of my life been."

(347) 108. *a Term:* a bust ending downward in a square block, like the statues of Terminus, the Roman god of boundaries, who was thus represented without feet, to suggest his fixity.

(347) SAUL. Lines 1–97 were published in 1845; the rest, in 1855. The poem is based upon I Samuel 16:14–23.   ¶ 1. *Abner;* the captain of Saul's host (I Samuel 14:50),

¶ 9. "But the Spirit of the Lord departed from Saul, and an evil spirit from the Lord troubled him."—I Samuel 16:14.

(348) 45. *jerboa:* a small jumping rodent, with a long tail.

(350) 101. *The Lord's army:* the host of angels.

(354) 204. *Hebron upheaves:* the city is on a hill.   ¶ 205. *Kidron:* a brook near Jerusalem; in hot countries small bodies of water may dwindle perceptibly, under the sun's rays, even in one day.

(355) 217. *what a man may waste:* God's anointing for a great work; see I Samuel 10: 1.

(357) 292. *Sabaoth*=armies, hosts; here, the hosts of angels.

(359) LOVE AMONG THE RUINS. The poem was written in Rome, and the scene of it seems to be the Roman Campagna, once the site of populous towns, in the prosperous days of the Roman Empire, now a desolate waste covered with ruins; but there was no city there as large as the city of the poem, except Rome.   ¶ 9. *capital:* supply "which."   ¶ 15. *verdure:* supply "which."   ¶ 17. *else:* i. e., if it were not for the rills.   ¶ 23. *marble:* supply "which."

(361) FRA LIPPO LIPPI. The poem is an interpretation of the personality and art of the Florentine painter, Fra Filippo Lippi (1406?–69), and is based upon Vasari's life of him. ¶ 2. *your torches:* his captors are the night-watch of Florence.   ¶ 7. *The Carmine:* a monastery of the Carmelite friars, in Florence.   ¶ 12. *you know your betters?* Apparently one of the watchmen had said that it was not for them to spy on the friars.   ¶ 17. *Cosimo of the Medici:* the Florentine banker, statesman, and patron of literature and art, who practically ruled the republic of Florence by putting his creatures into the chief offices; he lived from 1389 to 1464.   ¶ 18. *Boh! you were best!* On hearing that his patron is the great Cosimo, the watchman lets go of his throat.

(362) 21. *you, sir:* the head-watch.   ¶ 23. *pilchards:* cheap fish, somewhat like herring. ¶ 47. *shut within my mew:* it was often necessary to lock Fra Lippo Lippi in, to keep him at work.   ¶ 57. *Round they went:* the reference is to the song he heard, of the kind called "stornello," a folk-song, often extemporized, which went round the circle of singers, each inventing a few lines.

(363) 67. *Saint Lawrence:* the church of San Lorenzo.

(364) 117. *processional:* in a religious procession, where lighted candles are carried by some of the worshipers.   ¶ 121. *the Eight:* a magistracy of eight citizens, who administered the city government.   ¶ 127. *remarks*=observations, things noticed.   ¶ 130. *antiphonary's:* the antiphonary is the service-book, containing the musical responses and the antiphonal chants or songs, with the notes.

(365) 139. *Camaldolese:* the monks of the abbey of Camaldoli, a few miles from Florence; the church of the abbey, recently rebuilt, had many art treasures.   ¶ 140. *Preaching Friars:* the Dominican friars.   ¶ 145. *monk, the black and white:* Dominicans and Carmelites; so called from the color of their robes.

(366) 189. *Giotto:* a Florentine painter and architect (1266?–1336); his pictures have the defective technique and naïve simplicity of early Italian painting, but are full of religious feeling.   ¶ 196. *Herodias:* see Matthew, chap. 14.

(367) 235. *Brother Angelico:* Fra Angelico (1387–1455), although contemporary with Lippi, was of the earlier ascetic school.   ¶ 236. *Brother Lorenzo:* Lorenzo Monaco (1370?–1425), a painter of the conservative school and influenced by Fra Angelico; he was one of the Camaldolese monks.   ¶ 261–64. "You" here refers to the monks.

(368) 276. *Guidi:* Tommaso Guidi (1401–28 ?), usually called Masaccio (Tommasaccio, "Slovenly or Hulking Tom "), a Florentine painter and founder of the modern, naturalistic school, to which Fra Lippo Lippi belonged. "From his time and forward, religious painting in the old sense was at an end. Painters no longer attempted to transcend Nature, but to copy her, and to copy her in her loveliest aspects."—Ernest Radford, in *Browning Society's Illustrations.* Lippi was the pupil of Masaccio, not his master as Browning makes him, being

some years his junior. It would seem that Browning inverted their relation intentionally, to increase the artistic importance of the central figure of his poem; but a writer in the *Browning Society's Papers* (Part II, p. 160) says that Browning stated, in a letter to *The Pall Mall Gazette*, that "he followed the best authority he had access to, the last edition of Vasari."

(369) 324. *Prato:* a town near Florence; in the church there are frescoes by Lippi. ¶ 328. St. Lawrence, an archdeacon, suffered martyrdom in 258 A. D., by being roasted on a gridiron. ¶ 331. *rage:* i. e., at the sufferings of the martyr. ¶ 339. *Chianti:* a region a few miles south of Florence, famous for its excellent wines.

(370) 345. *There's for you:* he "tips" them again, to insure his release; cf. l. 27. ¶ 346. *Sant' Ambrogio's:* the convent of St. Ambrose, in Florence. ¶ 348. *God in the midst:* the picture, called "The Coronation of the Virgin," is now in the Academy of Fine Arts Florence. ¶ 354. *Saint John:* John the Baptist, the patron saint of Florence. ¶ 377. *Iste perfecit opus*="that one made the work." In the picture these words are on a scroll, which extends from the hand of one of the angels to Fra Lippo Lippi.

(371) CHILDE ROLAND TO THE DARK TOWER CAME. Browning printed a line under the title—"See Edgar's song in 'Lear.'" The song is the following (*King Lear*, III. iv):

> Child Rowland to the dark tower came,
>   His word was still,—Fie, foh, and fum,
> I smell the blood of a British man.

There is an old legend that Childe Roland went to elf-land to bring back his sister Ellen, who had been carried away by the fairies. (See *English and Scottish Popular Ballads*, edited by F. J. Child, I. 322.) "We are reduced to taking the poem as a simple work of fancy, built up of picturesque impressions which have, separately or collectively, produced themselves in the author's mind. I may venture to state that these picturesque materials included a tower which Mr. Browning once saw in the Carrara Mountains, a painting which caught his eye years later in Paris, and the figure of a horse in the tapestry in his own drawing-room—welded together in the remembrance of the line from *King Lear* which forms the heading of the poem."—Mrs. Orr's *Handbook to the Works of Robert Browning*. "I asked the poet what he had symbolized in the dark tower and Childe Roland's bugle-blast, thinking that he had intended to represent, by the tower, the stronghold of scepticism, of unbelief, of materialism, which would be razed to the ground when Science comprehends that the law which develops sound develops every natural law in the universe, and that at the first blast which she blows, with this knowledge, the dark tower must crumble. . . . . Mr. Browning replied that Childe Roland was 'only a *fantaisie*,' that he had written it 'because it pleased his fancy.'" —Clara Bloomfield-Moore, in *Lippincott's Magazine*, May, 1890. In a discussion at a meeting of the London Browning Society, after a paper by Mr. Kirkman (*Browning Society's Papers*, Part III, p. 21), Dr. Furnivall said "he had asked Browning if it was an allegory, and in answer had, on three separate occasions, received an emphatic 'no'; that it was simply a dramatic creation called forth by a line of Shakespeare's." "Upon the lengthwise wall of the room, above the Italian furniture, sombre and richly carved, was a long, wide band of tapestry, on which I thought I recognized the miserable horse of Childe Roland's pilgrimage. . . . . I asked Mr. Browning if the beast of the tapestry was the beast of the poem; and he said yes, and descanted somewhat on his lean monstrosity. . . . . I further asked him if he had said that he only wrote 'Childe Roland' for its realistic imagery, without any moral purpose,—a notion to which Mrs. Sutherland Orr has given currency; and he protested that he never had. When I asked him if constancy to an ideal—'He that endureth to the end shall be saved'—was not a sufficient understanding of the central purpose of the poem, he said, 'Yes, just about that.'"—The Rev. John W. Chadwick.

Childe: the word was used in old ballads for the son of a noble house, especially before he was admitted to knighthood,—a squire; but it was also used for a knight.

(373) 68. *the bents*=blades of coarse grass. ¶ 80. *colloped*="having ridges or bunches of flesh like collops."—*International Dictionary*. A collop is a slice or lump of meat

(375) 150. *rubble*=broken stones. ¶ 161. *dragon-penned*=like the wings of a dragon (Latin "penna," a feather, a wing).

(376) 182. *blind as the fool's heart:* cf. Psalms 14:1, "The fool hath said in his heart, There is no God." ¶ 203. *slug-horn:* a corruption of "slogan" (war-cry), incorrectly used here for a kind of horn.

(381) A GRAMMARIAN'S FUNERAL. ¶ 3. *crofts*=small farm inclosures. *thorpes* =villages. ¶ 18. *overcome*=pass over, overshadow.

(383) 86. *Calculus*=the stone. ¶ 88. *Tussis*=a cough. ¶ 95. *hydroptic*=thirsty, as in dropsy.

(384) 122. *mind*=attend to. ¶ 129. *Hoti's:* the Greek conjunction, ὅτι, "that," etc. ¶ 130. *Oun:* the Greek adverb οὖν, "then," "now then," etc. ¶ 131. *the enclitic De:* the Greek particle δε when it is attached to the preceding word. "To the Editor of *The Daily News*. Sir,—In a clever article this morning you speak of 'the doctrine of the enclitic *de*'— 'which, with all deference to Mr. Browning, in point of fact does not exist.' No, not to Mr. Browning: but pray defer to Herr Buttmann, whose fifth list of 'enclitics' ends 'with the inseparable *de*'—or to Curtius, whose fifth list ends also with '*de* (meaning "towards" and as a demonstrative appendage).' That this is not to be confounded with the accentuated '*de*, meaning *but*,' was the 'doctrine' which the Grammarian bequeathed to those capable of receiving it.—I am, sir, yours obediently, R. B."—Browning, in the London *Daily News*, November 21, 1874.

(384) PROSPICE. The poem was written a few months after Mrs. Browning's death; see the last three lines. The title means "Look Forward."

(385) AMONG THE ROCKS. Section vii of "James Lee's Wife."

(386) ABT VOGLER. Abt Vogler was born in Bavaria, in 1749; he was a Catholic priest, but devoted most of his time to music; he invented the orchestrion, a compact organ, composed operas and other works, and was famous as an extemporizer; he died in 1814. "He was indisputably the first organist of his age. . . . . His extempore playing never failed to create an impression, and in the elevated fugal style he easily distanced all rivals."—Grove's *Dictionary of Music and Musicians* (1879-89). *Abt:* the German form of "Abbé." ¶ 3. *as when Solomon willed.* Browning follows Mohammedan legends: "We also tried Solomon. ▪ . . . And we also put the devils in subjection under him; and among them such as were every way skilled in building, and in diving for pearls."—*The Koran*, chap. xxxviii, Sale's translation. "And Solomon was David's heir. . . . . And his armies were gathered together unto Solomon, consisting of genii and men and birds."—*Ibid.*, chap. xxvii. ¶ 9. *Would it might tarry:* this resumes the main sentence, begun in l. 1 and interrupted by the long comparison about Solomon. ¶ 17. *minion*=obsequious servant. ¶ 19. *rampired*=having ramparts, or bulwarks. ¶ 21. *a runner:* a running line of fire. ¶ 23. *Rome's dome:* the dome of St. Peter's. ¶ 25. *to match:* in order to match.

(387) 34. *Protoplast:* the type, or model, the original (Greek πρῶτος, first, and πλασστός, formed).

(388) 69. Cf. "Rabbi Ben Ezra," ll. 157-62. ¶ 73-80. Cf. Shelley's "Sensitive Plant," Part III. 130-37:

> That garden sweet, that lady fair,
> And all sweet shapes and odours there,
> In truth have never passed away:
> 'Tis we, 'tis ours, are changed; not they.
> For love and beauty and delight
> There is no death nor change: their might
> Exceeds our organs, which endure
> No light, being themselves obscure.

¶ 81-84. Cf. "The Last Ride Together," ll. 89-99, and "Rabbi Ben Ezra," ll. 37-42, 133-50.

(389) 91-96. "C Major is what may be called the natural scale, having no sharps or flats in its signature. A Minor, with A (a third below C) for its keynote, has the same signature, but sharps are introduced for the formation of correct intervals. Pauer says that minor

keys are chosen for expressing 'intense seriousness, soft melancholy, longing, sadness, and passionate grief.' . . . . Perhaps Browning chose C Major for the key, as the one most. allied to matters of everyday life, including rest and sleep. The common chord, as it is called, the keynote with its third and fifth, contains the rudiments of all music."—Helen J. Ormerod, "Some Notes on Browning's Poems Relating to Music," *Browning Society's Papers*, Part IX.

(389) RABBI BEN EZRA. "One of the most eminent of the Jewish *literati* of the Middle Ages. He was born at Toledo about 1090; left Spain for Rome about 1140; resided afterwards . . . . in England (1159); and died probably in 1168. He was distinguished as a philosopher, astronomer, physician, and poet, but especially as a grammarian and commentator. The works by which he is best known form a series of commentaries on the books of the Old Testament. . . . . Abenezra's commentaries are acknowledged to be of very great value; he was the first who raised biblical exegesis to the rank of a science, interpreting the text according to its literal sense, and illustrating it from cognate languages. His style is elegant, but so concise as to be sometimes obscure; and he occasionally indulges in epigram." —*Encyclopaedia Britannica*. The rabbi, as a religious teacher who attained to a good old age, might well have been taken as the mouth-piece of the poet in this poem, without special regard to the particular doctrines which the Hebrew sage really taught. But Browning seems also to have based the poem in part upon the actual philosophy of Rabbi Ben Ezra, so far as this agreed with his own way of thinking. ¶ 4. *Our times are in His hand:* cf. "In Thy hand lies my history," a line from a poem by Rabbi Ben Ezra (according to Dr. Michael Sachs in his *Die religiöse Poesie der Juden in Spanien*). ¶ 7-12. The thought in these lines is summed up in "such hopes and fears" (l. 13), and the whole depends, grammatically, upon "remonstrate" (l. 15): "I do not remonstrate that youth, amassing flowers, sighed," etc. *figured*=imagined. ¶ 16. *doubt:* cf. ll. 8, 9; but here the word seems to be used also for all the restlessness and discontent of spirit which attend the striving to attain a high ideal, the "troubling" and "disturbing" of the "clod" by a divine "spark." ¶ 17. *low kinds:* the lower animals (cf. ll. 24, 30, 42); the reference is not to lower kinds of men, for man as man is being contrasted with the creatures below him. ¶ 24. *care:* the subject of "irks." *doubt:* the subject of "frets."

(390) 33. Contrast l. 22. ¶ 40-42. Cf. "Saul," l. 296. ¶ 44. *to suit:* i. e., merely to suit, or fit, the flesh. ¶ 45. *lest arms and legs want play:* i. e., merely to move the body. ¶ 48. *thy soul on its lone way.* "The soul of man is called lonely because it is separated, during its union with the body, from the Universal Soul, into which it is again received when it departs from its earthly companion."—Rabbi Ben Ezra, in his commentary on the Psalms. ¶ 49. *gifts:* the bodily powers; cf. ll. 52, 53. ¶ 50. *the past:* the past years of his own life, in which, by the use of his senses and brain, he had been getting impressions of the power and perfection in the works of God. ¶ 54. *once:* in youth, the time of activity and acquisition of knowledge of the external world. ¶ 55. *once:* in old age. ¶ 57. Cf. "Saul," ll. 239-304.

(391) 60. *I trust what Thou shalt do:* i. e., in old age, supplementing the more fleshly life of youth and manhood ("Thanks that I was a man," l. 59) with the spirituality of age. ¶ 61. The thought is continuous with that in the preceding line: "Maker, complete my nature by rounding it out on the spiritual side; there is need of it, for the attraction of fleshly pleasures is relatively too great." ¶ 63. *rest:* rest from spiritual struggle. ¶ 64. *some prize:* of a spiritual nature. ¶ 66. *brute:* our own fleshly natures. *gain most, as we did best:* i. e., would we might gain the greatest and most pleasant returns when we live in the best and highest way. ¶ 67. *always:* i. e., as we did in youth and manhood. ¶ 71. *Let us cry:* i. e., in old age, when God shall have made us more spiritual, and the "rose-mesh" of the flesh holds us less firmly. ¶ 74. *To grant youth's heritage:* i. e., to grant him, in old age, all that he has earned by the experience of life so far. ¶ 76. *Thence:* from the "term," or temporary end, of life's struggle, which he has reached at the beginning of old age. ¶ 79. *thereupon:* in old age. ¶ 80. *ere I be gone:* at death. ¶ 84. *indue*=put on.

(392) 124, 125. Understand "whom" after "I" and "they."

(393) 151. *potter's wheel:* "But now, O Lord, thou art our father; we are the clay, and thou our potter; and we are all the work of thy hand."—Isaiah 64:8.

(394) 164. *plastic*=molding. ¶ 168. *impressed*=molded.

(395) ADAM, LILITH, AND EVE. According to a rabbinical legend, Adam had a wife, Lilith, before Eve. The poem has no connection with the legend except in the use of the names.

CONTEMPORARY CRITICISM

It is really high time that this sort of thing should, if possible, be stopped. Here is another book of madness and mysticism, another melancholy specimen of power wantonly wasted and talent deliberately perverted, another act of self-prostration before that demon of bad taste who now seems to hold in absolute possession the fashionable masters of our ideal literature. It is a strong case for the correctional justice of criticism, which has too long abdicated its proper functions. . . . . Here is Robert Browning, for instance—no one can doubt that he is capable of better things—no one, while deploring the obscurities that deface the "Paracelsus" and the *Dramatic Lyrics,* can deny the less questionable qualities which characterized those remarkable poems; but can any of his devotees be found to uphold his present elaborate experiment on the patience of the public? Take any of his worshipers you please—let him be "well up" in the transcendental poets of the day—take him fresh from Alexander Smith, or Alfred Tennyson's "Maud," or the "Mystic" of Bailey—and we will engage to find him at least ten passages in the first ten pages of *Men and Women,* some of which, even after profound study, he will not be able to construe at all, and not one of which will he be able to read off at sight. . . . .

And it is on this beauty of form, this exquisite perfection of style, that the Baileys and the Brownings would have us believe that they set small account, that they purposely and scornfully trample. We do not believe it. We believe that it is only because they are half-gifted that they are but half-intelligible. Their mysticism is weakness—weakness writhing itself into contortions that it may ape the muscles of strength. Artistic genius, in its higher degrees, necessarily involves the power of beautiful self-expression. It is but a weak and watery sun that allows the fogs to hang heavy between the objects on which it shines and the eyes it would enlighten; the true day-star chases the mists at once, and shows us the world at a glance.

Our main object has been to protest against what we feel to be the false teachings of a perverted school of art; and we have used this book of Mr. Browning's chiefly as a means of showing the extravagant lengths of absurdity to which the tenets of that school can lead a man of admitted powers. We should regret, however, in the pursuit of this object, to inflict injustice on Mr. Browning. This last book of his, like most of its predecessors, contains some undeniable beauties—subtle thoughts, graceful fancies, and occasionally a strain of music, which only makes the chaos of surrounding discords jar more harshly on the ear. The dramatic scenes, "In a Balcony," are finely conceived and vigorously written; "Bishop Blougram's Apology" and "Cleon" are well worth reading and thinking over; and there is a certain grace and beauty in several of the minor poems. That which, on the whole, has pleased us most—really, perhaps, because we could read it off-hand—is "The Statue and the Bust." . . . . Why should a man who, with so little apparent labor, can write naturally and well, take so much apparent labor to write affectedly and ill? . . . . Frequently the conclusion is almost irresistible that Mr. Browning's mysticism must be of *malice prepense;* on the whole, however, we are inclined to clear his honesty at the expense of his powers, and to conclude that he is obscure, not so much because he has the vanity to be thought original, as because he lacks sufficient genius to make himself clear.—*The Saturday Review,* November 24, 1855, on *Men and Women.*

ARTHUR HUGH CLOUGH

(399) QUI LABORAT, ORAT. The title means, "Who Labors, Prays"; see l. 20. ¶ 26. *The beatific supersensual sight:* the "beatific vision" of mediaeval theology, or "blissful sight" of God by the eye of the soul, vouchsafed to angels and saints.

(400) Ύμνος Άυμνος. The title means, "A Hymn That Is Not a Hymn," or "A Hymn Unsung."

(401) SONGS IN ABSENCE. Written during the poet's voyage to America or during his stay there.

(402) "WITH WHOM IS NO VARIABLENESS, NEITHER SHADOW OF TURNING." The title is taken from James 1:17.

(402) "PERCHE PENSA? PENSANDO S'INVECCHIA." The title means, "Why Does He Think? Through Thinking, One Grows Old."

(403) THE SHADOW. The poem was not completed; the manuscript consists of several fragments, which are here separated from each other by stars. ¶ 5, 6. "I drew my sharp sword from my thigh, and dug a pit, as it were a cubit in length and breadth, and about it poured a drink-offering to all the dead. . . . . But when I had besought the tribes of the dead with vows and prayers, I took the sheep and cut their throats over the trench, and the dark blood flowed forth, and lo, the spirits of the dead that be departed gathered them from out of Erebus."—*Odyssey*, XI. 24–37, Butcher and Lang's translation.

(405) 71. *on inquiry we must put no force:* i. e., we must not check free inquiry. ¶ 85. *Butler:* Bishop Joseph Butler, of the English Church, author of *The Analogy of Religion, Natural and Revealed, to the Constitution and Course of Nature* (1736). ¶ 86. *Paley:* William Paley, an Anglican clergyman, author of *Evidences of Christianity* (1794).

(406) 99–102. Cf. Matthew 19:20–22.

MATTHEW ARNOLD

Arnold's theory of poetry is contained in the following sentences from his essay on Wordsworth (1879):

"Long ago, in speaking of Homer, I said that the noble and profound application of ideas to life is the most essential part of poetic greatness. I said that a great poet receives his distinctive character of superiority from his application, under the conditions immutably fixed by the laws of poetic beauty and poetic truth, from his application, I say, to his subject, whatever it may be, of the ideas

On man, on Nature, and on human life,

which he has acquired for himself. . . . . Voltaire, with his signal acuteness, most truly remarked that 'no nation has treated in poetry moral ideas with more energy and depth than the English nation.' And he adds, 'There, it seems to me, is the great merit of the English poets.' Voltaire does not mean, by 'treating in poetry moral ideas,' the composing moral and didactic poems;—that brings us but a very little way in poetry. He means just the same thing as was meant when I spoke above 'of the noble and profound application of ideas to life'; and he means the application of these ideas under the conditions fixed for us by the laws of poetic beauty and poetic truth. If it is said that to call these ideas *moral* ideas is to introduce a strong and injurious limitation, I answer that it is to do nothing of the kind, because moral ideas are really so main a part of human life. The question, *how to live,* is itself a moral idea; and it is the question which most interests every man, and with which, in some way or other, he is perpetually occupied. A large sense is of course to be given to the term *moral.* Whatever bears upon the question, 'how to live,' comes under it.

Nor love thy life, nor hate; but, what thou liv'st,
Live well; how long or short, permit to Heaven.

In those fine lines Milton utters, as every one at once perceives, a moral idea. Yes, but so too, when Keats consoles the forward-bending lover on the Grecian Urn, the lover arrested and presented in immortal relief by the sculptor's hand before he can kiss, with the line,

> Forever wilt thou love, and she be fair,

he utters a moral idea. When Shakespeare says that

> We are such stuff
> As dreams are made of, and our little life
> Is rounded with a sleep,

he utters a moral idea. . . . . Morals are often treated in a narrow and false fashion; they are bound up with systems of thought and belief which have had their day; they are fallen into the hands of pedants and professional dealers; they grow tiresome to some of us. We find attraction, at times, even in a poetry of revolt against them; in a poetry which might take for its motto Omar Kheyam's words, 'Let us make up in the tavern for the time which we have wasted in the mosque.' Or we find attractions in a poetry indifferent to them; in a poetry where the contents may be what they will, but where the form is studied and exquisite. We delude ourselves in either case; and the best cure for our delusion is to let our minds rest upon that great and inexhaustible word *life*, until we learn to enter into its meaning. A poetry of revolt against moral ideas is a poetry of revolt against *life;* a poetry of indifference towards moral ideas is a poetry of indifference towards *life*."

(406) TO A FRIEND. ¶ 2. *the old man:* Homer. ¶ 3. *The Wide Prospect, and the Asian Fen.* "The name 'Europe' (Εὐρώπη, the wide prospect) probably describes the appearance of the European coast to the Greeks on the coast of Asia Minor opposite. The name 'Asia,' again, comes, it has been thought, from the muddy fens of the rivers of Asia Minor, such as the Cayster or Maeander, which struck the imagination of the Greeks living near them."—Arnold's note. (Ἀσία is the feminine form of the Greek adjective meaning "marshy.") ¶ 4. *Tmolus hill:* a mountain range beginning near Smyrna, on the western coast of Asia Minor; Smyrna is one of the cities claiming to be the birthplace of Homer. ¶ 5. *he:* Epictetus, the lame Stoic philosopher, who had been a slave; when Domitian, the son of Vespasian, banished the philosophers from Rome, in 89 A. D., Epictetus went to Nicopolis, in Epirus; his pupil, Arrian, compiled a manual of his doctrines. ¶ 14. *Colonus, and its child:* Sophocles, who in his tragedy *Oedipus at Colonus* described the city and its grove of nightingales, was born at Colonus in 495 B. C.

(407) THE FORSAKEN MERMAN. The poem is based on one form of an old legend found in the ballads of many nations: see the German ballad, "Die Schöne Agnese"; and consult *English and Scottish Popular Ballads*, edited by F. J. Child, I. 360, for an account of the various forms of the legend.

(412) THE FUTURE. ¶ 36. *Rebekah:* see Genesis, chap. 24.

(413) 45. *Moses:* see Exodus, chap. 3. ¶ 57. *shot* = varying (used chiefly of fabrics, as silks, so woven as to present changeable tints).

(414) LINES WRITTEN IN KENSINGTON GARDENS. The gardens are in London.

(415) THE SCHOLAR GIPSY. "There was very lately a lad in the University of Oxford, who was by his poverty forced to leave his studies there, and at last to join himself to a company of vagabond gipsies. Among these extravagant people, by the insinuating subtility of his carriage, he quickly got so much of their love and esteem as that they discovered to him their mystery. After he had been a pretty while exercised in the trade, there chanced to ride by a couple of scholars, who had formerly been of his acquaintance. They quickly spied out their old friend among the gipsies; and he gave them an account of the necessity which drove him to that kind of life, and told them that the people he went with were not such impostors as they were taken for, but that they had a traditional kind of learning among them, and could do wonders by the power of imagination, their fancy binding that of others; that himself had learned much of their art, and when he had compassed the whole secret,

he intended, he said, to leave their company, and give the world an account of what he had learned."—J. Glanvil's *Vanity of Dogmatizing* (1661). quoted by Arnold as a note.

(417) 79. *Wychwood bowers:* Wychwood Forest is about ten miles from Oxford.

(418) 95. *lasher*=a dam in a river.

(419) 129. *Christ-Church hall:* the hall, or dining-room, of Christ Church College, one of the largest colleges in Oxford University.

(421) 209. *her false friend's approach:* Aeneas, during his visit to the lower world, saw and spoke to the shade of Dido, who had killed herself when he forsook her; "she, turned away, held her eyes fixed upon the ground" (*Aeneid*, VI. 469).

(422) 239. *tunnies:* the tunny has been a favorite food-fish in the Mediterranean from the earliest times. ¶ 244. *Midland*=Mediterranean. ¶ 245. *Syrtes:* shoals off the northern coast of Africa. ¶ 249. *Iberians:* the ancient inhabitants of Spain and Portugal; the peninsula was formerly called Iberia.

(422) Yes, in the Sea of Life Enisled. From "Switzerland" (fifth section).

(423) Stanzas from the Grande Chartreuse. La Grande Chartreuse is the chief monastery of the Carthusian monks, founded in the eleventh century; it is situated in the Alps, in southeastern France. ¶ 4. *Saint Laurent:* a village. ¶ 10. *Dead Guier's:* the river, *Guiers Morte*, a tributary of the Rhone.

(425) 62. *pilgrim-host:* Carthusian monks on pilgrimage.

(426) 99. *sciolists*=pretenders to scientific knowledge, smatterers.

(427) 135. *Aetolian*=Grecian (Aetolia was a district of Greece). ¶ 142. *Spezzian bay:* Shelley spent the last months of his life on the shores of the Gulf of Spezzia, on the north-western coast of Italy. ¶ 146. *Obermann.* "The author of *Obermann*, Etienne Pivert de Senancour, has little celebrity in France, his own country, and out of France he is almost unknown. But the profound inwardness, the austere sincerity, of his principal work, *Obermann*, the delicate feeling for nature which it exhibits, and the melancholy eloquence of many passages of it, have attracted and charmed some of the most remarkable spirits of this century, such as George Sand and Sainte-Beuve. . . . . Senancour was born in 1770."—Arnold's note to his poem, "Stanzas in Memory of the Author of Obermann."

(430) Palladium. At the time of the building of Troy, a stone image of Athene fell from heaven near the site of the new city, and Athene was accordingly taken as the special divinity of Troy. The heaven-sent image, called the Palladium (from "Pallas," another name for Athene), was given a shrine in the upper city; and the belief became current that while it remained in the shrine the city could not be captured and destroyed. ¶ 1. *Simois:* one of the rivers of the Trojan plain. ¶ 14. *Xanthus:* a river flowing through the plain before Troy, which was the battlefield of the Greeks and Trojans.

(432) Kaiser Dead. ¶ 2. *Cobham:* Arnold's home at this time. ¶ 3. *Farringford:* Tennyson's home on the Isle of Wight. ¶ 5. *Pen-bryn's bold bard:* William Morris. ¶ 12. In a note Arnold quotes the following lines from "Poor Mailie's Elegy," in which Burns, referring to himself as "Robin," laments the death of his pet ewe:

> Come, join the melancholius croon
> O' Robin's reed.

¶ 20. *Potsdam:* a residence of the German emperors; cf. l. 23. ¶ 41. *the Grand Old Man:* Gladstone; in his later years he advocated home rule for Ireland and further extension of the suffrage, but never incited the masses against the classes.

DANTE GABRIEL ROSSETTI

(434) The Blessed Damozel. "I saw that Poe [in "The Raven"] had done the utmost it was possible to do with the grief of the lover on earth, and so I determined to reverse the conditions, and give utterance to the yearning of the loved one in heaven."—Rossetti, as reported by Hall Caine in his *Recollections of Dante Gabriel Rossetti* (1882). "Such inspi-

ration as is traceable to any source whatever belongs assumably to the pictures of those early Italian painters whom Rossetti had lovingly studied, and to domestic influences to which he yielded."—Joseph Knight, *The Life of Dante Gabriel Rossetti* (1887). The poem was first published in *The Germ*, the short-lived periodical of the pre-Raphaelite movement; it was considerably revised in later editions; the first text is given in William Sharp's *Dante Gabriel Rossetti* (1882). ¶ 1. *blessed:* i. e., one of the blessed in heaven. *damozel:* an old form of "damsel" (cf. French "mademoiselle").

(435) 13. *herseemed*=it seemed to her (by analogy with "me seems," not uncommon in early English: "Me seemeth good."—*Richard III*, II. ii. 120).

(438) SISTER HELEN. The poem was first published in the English edition of *The Düsseldorf Artists' Annual;* the text was somewhat revised in the edition of 1870, and again in the edition of 1881, the stanzas about the Lady of Ewern (ll. 204–45, 267–73) being added at the latter date. ¶ 1. *waxen man:* " 'The Devil teacheth how to make pictures [images] of wax or clay, that, by roasting thereof, the persons that they bear the name of may be continually melted, or dried away by continual sickness,' is the dictum of King James."—Brand's *Popular Antiquities*.

(447) THE HOUSE OF LIFE. Sonnets 1, 4, 5, 19, 34, 49–52, 71–73, 92, 101. Rossetti prefixed to the series the following sonnet on the sonnet:

> A sonnet is a moment's monument,—
> Memorial from the soul's eternity
> To one dead deathless hour. Look that it be,
> Whether for lustral rite or dire portent,
> Of its own arduous fullness reverent:
> Carve it in ivory or in ebony,
> As Day or Night may rule; and let Time see
> Its flowering crest impearled and orient.
>
> A sonnet is a coin: its face reveals
> The soul; its converse, to what Power 't is due—
> Whether for tribute to the august appeals
> Of Life, or dower in Love's high retinue,
> It serve; or, 'mid the dark wharf's cavernous breath,
> In Charon's palm it pay the toll to Death.

(453) MARY'S GIRLHOOD. The sonnet was first published in an art catalogue, and illustrated the poet's picture, "The Girlhood of the Virgin Mary."

(453) FOR "A VENETIAN PASTORAL." The sonnet was published in *The Germ*. ¶ 14. Cf. Keats's "Ode on a Grecian Urn," ll. 11–20.

(454) MARY MAGDALENE. The sonnet was written for one of Rossetti's drawings. "In the drawing Mary has left a procession of revelers, and is ascending by a sudden impulse the steps of the house where she sees Christ. Her lover has followed her, and is trying to turn her back."—Rossetti's note. ¶ 10, 11. See John 12:3; Matthew 26:6, 7; Luke 8:2. ¶ 12, 13. See Matthew 28: 1–9.

(454) FOR "THE WINE OF CIRCE." The picture is the well-known one by Edward Burne Jones. Cf. Homer's account of Circe: "In the forest glades they found the halls of Circe builded, of polished stone, in a place with wide prospect. And all around the palace mountain-bred wolves and lions were roaming, whom she herself had bewitched with evil drugs that she gave them. Yet the beasts did not set on my men, but lo, they ramped about them and fawned on them, wagging their long tails. . . . . So she led them in and set them upon chairs and high seats, and made them a mess of cheese and barley-meal and yellow honey with Pramnian wine, and mixed harmful drugs with the food to make them utterly forget their own country. Now when she had given them the cup and they had drunk it off, presently she smote them with a wand, and in the styes of the swine she penned them. So they had the head and voice, the bristles and the shape of swine, but their mind abode even as of old. Thus were they penned there weeping."—*Odyssey*, X. 210–41, Butcher and Lang's translation.

(455) John Keats. ¶ 4. *Castalian:* Castalia was a fountain on Mount Parnassus, in Greece, sacred to the Muses. *Latmos' steep:* Latmos, a mountain in Asia Minor, was the scene of the fabled loves of Endymion and Diana; see Keats's "Endymion."

(456) 10. *awoke the moon's eclipse:* an allusion to Keats's revival of the myth of Diana and Endymion. ¶ 11. "A little before he died he said that he 'felt the daisies growing over him.'"—Leigh Hunt, *Autobiography*, chap. xvi. ¶ 12, 13. *not writ But rumoured in water:* cf. the epitaph which Keats desired should be placed on his grave-stone, "Here lies one whose name was writ in water."

CHRISTINA ROSSETTI

(461) Youth Gone, and Beauty Gone. No. 14 in "Monna Innominata."
(461) This Life is Full of Numbness and of Balk. No. 26 in "Later Life."

WILLIAM MORRIS

(462) An Apology. Prefixed to *The Earthly Paradise.*

(463) 25. *ivory gate:* there were two gates to the realm of Morpheus, one of horn and one of ivory; untrue dreams issued through the latter.

(463) The Death of Paris. In *The Earthly Paradise*, "September." Cf. Tennyson's "Death of Oenone." The legend was a gradual growth. Sophocles (495–406 B. C.) in his *Philoctetes* refers to the death of Paris by a poisoned arrow of Philoctetes. Lycophron, of the third century B. C., in his *Alexandra* makes Cassandra predict the consequences of Paris's elopement with Helen, including the death of Paris by the poisoned arrow; he represents Oenone as prevented by her father from curing Paris, and says that when Paris was dead she threw herself down from a tower and perished on his body. Apollodorus, who lived about 140 B. C., tells the story thus: "Now Hector married Andromache, the daughter of Eëtion, and Alexander [Paris] married Oenone, the daughter of the river Kebren. She, having learned the art of prophecy from Rhea, warned Alexander not to sail away after Helen; but, failing to persuade him, she told him if he should be wounded to come to her, for she alone could heal him. He carried off Helen from Sparta; and when war was made upon Troy, and he was shot by Philoctetes with the bow of Heracles, he went up into Mount Ida to Oenone. But she, remembering her wrongs, refused to heal him. So Alexander died, while being carried back to Troy; and Oenone, changing her mind, brought the medicines to heal him, and when she found him dead she hanged herself."—*Bibliotheca*, III. xii. 6. ¶ 11. *Philoctetes:* one of the Greeks at the siege of Troy, to which he brought some poisoned arrows that his friend Hercules had given him; he was famous as an archer, and had the bow of Hercules.

(464) 35. *worm's:* the reference is to the hundred-headed Hydra, which Hercules slew. ¶ 42. *thats hining one:* Paris; cf. l. 16.

(465) 58. *leaguer:* the besieging army. ¶ 80. *the Spotless One:* Athene, whose temple and statue were upon the citadel of Troy (*Iliad*, VI. 88, 297, 303); although aiding the Greeks throughout the war, she was still regarded by the Trojans as "protector of the city" (*Iliad*, VI. 305), and it was believed that Troy could not fall while her statue, the Palladium remained in its place. Cf. note on "Palladium," p. 536.

(468) 176. *mast-strewn:* strewn with beech-nuts.

(469) 214. *dew-lapped*=having dew-laps, the pendulous skin under the throat of an ox (so called because it laps the dew). *neat*=cattle (O.E. "neat," cattle). Although Paris was the son of Priam, king of Troy, he was exposed on Mount Ida to die, because his mother had a dream, before his birth, that she had borne a firebrand which destroyed the city; he was saved and reared by a shepherd.

ALGERNON CHARLES SWINBURNE

Swinburne expressed his poetic creed, in his essay "Wordsworth and Byron" (1884), as follows:

"Mr. Arnold has at once a passion and a genius for definitions. It is doubtless good to have such a genius, but it is surely dangerous to have such a passion. All sane men must be willing to concede the truth of an assertion which he seems to fling down as a challenge from the ethical critic to the aesthetic—that a school of poetry divorced from any moral idea is a school of poetry divorced from life. Even John Keats himself, except in his most hectic moments of sensuous or spiritual debility, would hardly, I should imagine, have undertaken to deny this. What may reasonably be maintained is a thesis very different from such a denial; namely, that a school of poetry subordinated to any school of doctrine, subjugated and shaped and utilized by any moral idea to the exclusion of native impulse and spiritual instinct, will produce work fit to live when the noblest specimens of humanity are produced by artificial incubation. . . . . Before entering on the question, what criticism of life in any intelligible sense of the phrase may be derivable or deducible from the writings of Wordsworth or Byron, I would venture to put forward, by no means a counter theory or a rival definition to Mr. Arnold's theory or definition of poetry, but a simple postulate, or at least a simple assumption, on which I would rest my argument. If it be not admitted, there is an end of the matter: it would be absolute waste of time, for one who assumes it as indisputable, to enter into controversy with one who holds it as disputable, that the two primary and essential qualities of poetry are imagination and harmony; that where these qualities are wanting there can be no poetry, properly so called; and that where these qualities are perceptible in the highest degree, there, even though they should be unaccompanied and unsupported by any other great quality whatever—even though the ethical or critical faculty should be conspicuous by its absence—there, and only there, is the best and highest poetry."

(480) A SONG IN TIME OF ORDER, 1852. The second republic in France was overthrown in 1851 by Louis Napoleon (nephew of Napoleon the Great), who became emperor in 1852.

(481) 34. *The old red:* the flag of the revolution which had resulted in the establishment of a French republic in 1848. ¶ 38. *galley-bench:* criminals were formerly condemned to the galleys, where the terrible labor at the oars soon broke down all but the strongest. ¶ 39. *Buonaparte the bastard:* Napoleon III's title to the throne of France was disputed.

(482) 50. *Cayenne:* the capital of French Guiana, where political prisoners were sent. *the Austrian whips:* Austria was a leader in the reaction against popular government, and had recently repressed revolutionary uprisings within her own limits and in Italy, portions of which were subject to her.

(482) WHEN THE HOUNDS OF SPRING ARE ON WINTER'S TRACES. A chorus in *Atalanta in Calydon*, ll. 65–120. ¶ 2. *The Mother of Months:* Artemis, goddess of the moon. ¶ 5–8. King Tereus, of Thrace, pretending that his wife Procne was dead, married her sister, Philomela; when she discovered the truth, he cut out her tongue, but she wove the story into a robe and sent it to Procne; the sisters then took revenge upon Tereus by serving up to him at table Itys ("Itylus" is the diminutive form), son of Tereus and Procne; the gods finally changed all four into birds, Philomela becoming a nightingale, and Procne a swallow. Cf. Swinburne's "Itylus," ll. 55–60:

> O sister, sister, thy first-begotten!
> The hands that cling and the feet that follow,
> The voice of the child's blood crying yet,
> *Who hath remembered me? Who hath forgotten?*
> Thou hast forgotten, O summer swallow,
> But the world shall end when I forget.

(483) 44. *The maenad and the Bassarid:* Bacchantes, or worshipers of Bacchus ("Bassarid" is a patronymic from "Bassareus," a surname of Dionysus, or Bacchus).

(488) Hertha.   Hertha was a goddess of the ancient Germans, whom Tacitus says (*Germania*, xl) was "Mother Earth."   But Swinburne takes the name for a vaguer and vaster divinity, like that of oriental thought, the All, Absolute Being, the source, home, and element of all things.   Cf. Emerson's "Brahma":

> If the red slayer think he slays,
>   Or if the slain think he is slain,
> They know not well the subtle ways
>   I keep, and pass, and turn again.
>
> Far or forgot to me is near;
>   Shadow and sunlight are the same;
> The vanished gods to me appear;
>   And one to me are shame and fame.
>
> They reckon ill who leave me out;
>   When me they fly, I am the wings;
> I am the doubter and the doubt,
>   And I the hymn the Brahmin sings.
>
> The strong gods pine for my abode,
>   And pine in vain the sacred Seven;
> But thou, meek lover of the good!
>   Find me, and turn thy back on heaven.

BIBLIOGRAPHY

BIBLIOGRAPHY

GENERAL WORKS

HISTORY AND SOCIAL CONDITIONS. A History of England (1815–58), by Spencer Walpole, 6 vols. (Longmans, 1890). A History of Modern England (1846–95), by Herbert Paul, 5 vols. (Macmillan, 1904–6). The Story of the People of England in the Nineteenth Century, by Justin McCarthy (Putnam, 1899). A History of Our Own Times (1837–1901), by Justin McCarthy, 5 vols. (Harper). Social England, ed. by H. D. Traill, Vols. 5, 6 (Putnam, 1896–97).

LITERATURE. Histoire de la littérature anglaise, by H. A. Taine, Vol. 4 (Paris, 1863); translation by H. van Laun, 1871 (Holt, 1896). A History of Nineteenth Century Literature, by George Saintsbury (Macmillan, 1896). The Literary History of England in the End of the Eighteenth and Beginning of the Nineteenth Century, by Margaret Oliphant (Macmillan, 1883, new ed.). Chambers' Cyclopaedia of English Literature, 3 vols. (Lippincott, 1902–4, new ed.). The Encyclopaedia Britannica. Dictionary of National Biography. The Makers of English Poetry, by W. J. Dawson (Revell, 1906; rewritten form of Makers of Modern English, 1890). Landscape in Poetry, by F. T. Palgrave (Macmillan, 1897). A History of English Romanticism in the Nineteenth Century, by H. A. Beers (Holt, 1901). On Poetic Interpretation of Nature, by J. C. Shairp (Edinburgh, 1877). Aspects of Poetry, by J. C. Shairp (Clarendon Press, 1881): Poetic Style in Modern English Poetry. The Literature of the Georgian Era, by William Minto (Blackwood, 1894). Main Currents in Nineteenth Century Literature, by George Brandes, 6 vols. (Macmillan, 1901–5): Vol. 4, Naturalism in England (to the death of Byron). The Age of Wordsworth, by C. H. Herford (Bell, 1894). The French Revolution and Literature, by Edward Dowden (Scribner, 1897). The French Revolution and the English Poets, by A. E Hancock (Holt, 1899). The Liberal Movement in English Literature, by W. J. Courthope (Murray, 1895). Studies in Literature, by Edward Dowden (Paul, 1878). Studies and Appreciations, by L. E. Gates (Macmillan, 1900): The Romantic Movement; The Return to Conventional Life. The Age of Tennyson, by Hugh Walker (Bell, 1897). Transcripts and Studies, by Edward Dowden (Paul, 1888): Victorian Literature. The Victorian Age of English Literature, by Margaret Oliphant (Percival, 1892). Studies in Early Victorian Literature, by Frederic Harrison (Arnold, 1906): Characteristics of Victorian Literature. Our Living Poets, by H. B. Forman (Tinsley, 1871). Victorian Poets, by E. C. Stedman (Boston, 1875; Houghton, 1887, rev. ed.). Early Reviews of Great Writers (1786–1832), ed. by E. Stevenson (Scott, 1906). Edinburgh, Quarterly, and Blackwood Reviews, ed. by W. H. Griffin (Heath, in preparation; Belles Lettres series). Early Reviews of English Poets (1757–1855), ed. by J. L. Haney (Philadelphia, Egerton Press, 1904).

WILLIAM LISLE BOWLES

EDITIONS. The Poetical Works (Cassell, 1879). The Poetical Works, ed. by W. Tirebuck (Scott, 1887; Canterbury Poets ed., with Lamb and H. Coleridge).

CRITICISMS. Quarterly Review, November, 1809. Biographia Literaria, by S. T. Coleridge, chap. i (London, 1817).

SAMUEL ROGERS

EDITIONS. The Poetical Works, ed. by E. Bell (Bell, 1875; Aldine ed.). Poems, and Italy (Routledge, 1890; two volumes, Handy Volume ed.).

CRITICISMS. Quarterly Review, March, 1813. Edinburgh Review, October, 1813; March, 1819.

WILLIAM WORDSWORTH

EDITIONS. The Poetical Works, 8 vols., ed. by William Knight (Paterson, 1882–86; Macmillan). The Poetical Works, 7 vols., ed. by Edward Dowden (Bell, 1892–93; Aldine ed.). The Complete Poetical Works, ed. by John Morley (Macmillan, 1888; Globe ed.). The Complete Poems, ed. by Thomas Hutchinson (Oxford University Press, 1896). The Complete Poetical Works, ed. by A. J. George (Houghton, 1904; Cambridge ed.). Poems (selected), ed. by Edward Dowden (Ginn, 1897; Athenaeum Press ed.). Lyrical Ballads, 1798, a reprint ed. by Thomas Hutchinson (Duckworth, 1898). Poems, 1807, a reprint, ed. by Thomas Hutchinson (Nutt, 1897). The Prose Works, 3 vols., ed. by A. B. Grosart (Moxon, 1876). The Prose Works, 2 vols., ed. by William Knight (Macmillan, 1896). Wordsworth's Guide to the Lakes, 1835, a reprint, ed. by Ernest de Sélincourt (Oxford University Press, 1906). Wordsworth's Prefaces (with Coleridge's chapters on Wordsworth in Biographia Literaria), ed. by A. J. George (Heath, 1906; Belles Lettres series). Wordsworth's Literary Criticism, ed. by Nowell Smith (Frowde, 1906).

BIOGRAPHY. The Life of William Wordsworth, 3 vols., by William Knight (Paterson, 1889; Macmillan). Wordsworth, by F. W. H. Myers (Macmillan, 1881; English Men of Letters series). The Prelude, by William Wordsworth. Journals of Dorothy Wordsworth, 2 vols., ed. by William Knight (Macmillan, 1897). Diary, Reminiscences, and Correspondence of H. C. Robinson, ed. by Thomas Sadler (Macmillan, 1869; with additions, 1872). My First Acquaintance with Poets, by William Hazlitt, in Literary Remains (Vol. 12, in his collected works, Dent, 1902–4). The Life and Correspondence of Robert Southey, ed. by his son (London, 1849–50). Literary and Lake Reminiscences (1839), chaps. iii–v, by Thomas DeQuincey (Vol. 2, in the new edition of DeQuincey, by David Masson; Black, 1889–90). Wordsworthiana, ed. by William Knight (Macmillan, 1889): Reminiscences of Wordsworth amongst the Peasantry of Westmoreland. Yesterdays with Authors, by J. T. Fields (Houghton, 1872). La Jeunesse de William Wordsworth, by Emile Legouis (Paris, 1896); translated by J. W. Matthews, The Early Life of William Wordsworth (Dent, 1897). Studies of a Biographer, by Leslie Stephen (Putnam, 1899); Wordsworth's Youth. Homes and Haunts of the British Poets, by William Howitt (Routledge, 1894). Literary Associations of the English Lakes, by H. D. Rawnsley (MacLehose, 1894; Macmillan).

CRITICISMS. Matthew Arnold: Essays in Criticism, second series (Macmillan, 1888; the essay on Wordsworth, 1879). Walter Bagehot: Literary Studies (Longmans, 1878–79). George Brimley: Essays (Macmillan, 1858; reissue, 1882). S. A. Brooke: Theology in the English Poets (London, 1874). John Burroughs: Fresh Fields (Houghton, 1885). Edward Caird: Essays on Literature and Philosophy (MacLehose, 1892). R. W. Church: Dante and Other Essays (Macmillan, 1888). Thomas De Quincey: On Wordsworth's Poetry, 1845 (in Vol. 11 of Masson's new edition of De Quincey). Aubrey De Vere; Essays, chiefly on Poetry (Macmillan, 1887). Edinburgh Review: October, 1807, Poems; November, 1814, The Excursion; October, 1815, The White Doe of Rylstone; November, 1822, Memorials of a Tour on the Continent. R. H. Hutton: Essays, Theological and Literary (Strahan, 1871). H. N. Hudson: Studies in Wordsworth (Little, 1884). William Knight: Studies in Philosophy and Literature (Nature as Interpreted by Wordsworth) (Edinburgh, 1868). J. R. Lowell: Among My Books, second series, 1876 (Literary Essays, Vol. 4, in his collected works; Houghton); Wordsworth, 1884 (Literary and Political Addresses, in his collected works). L. Magnus: A Primer of Wordsworth (Methuen, 1897). David Masson: Wordsworth, Shelley, Keats (Macmillan, 1874). John Morley: Studies in Literature (Macmillan, 1891). Walter Pater: Appreciations (Macmillan, 1889; the essay on Wordsworth, 1874). Quarterly Review: October, 1814, The Excursion (by Charles Lamb); October, 1815, Poems, and The White Doe of Rylstone. Walter Raleigh: Wordsworth (Arnold, 1903). Edmond Scherer: Essays on English Literature (translated by George Saintsbury from Etudes critiques) (Scribner, 1891). J. C. Shairp: Studies in Poetry and Philosophy (Edinburgh, 1868; Houghton). Leslie Stephen: Hours in a Library, Vol. 2 (Wordsworth's Ethics) (Smith, 1874–79; Putnam, 1892, new ed., with additions). A. C. Swinburne: Miscellanies (Chatto, 1886). W. H. White: An Examination of the Charge of Apostasy against Wordsworth (Longmans, 1898). G. E. Woodberry: Studies in Letters and Life (Houghton, 1890); The Torch (McClure, 1905). Wordsworthiana, a selection from papers read to the Wordsworth Society (papers by Ainger, Arnold, De Vere, Dowden, Noel, and others) (Macmillan, 1889). See also above, under "General Works, Literature," Saintsbury, Oliphant, Chambers, Encyclopaedia Britannica, Dawson, Palgrave, Beers, Minto, Brandes, Herford, Dowden, Hancock, Courthope, Gates.

SAMUEL TAYLOR COLERIDGE

EDITIONS. Complete Works, 7 vols., ed. by W. G. T. Shedd (1858; reissue, Harper, 1884). The Poetical Works, ed. by J. D. Campbell (Macmillan, 1893; Globe ed.). The Poetry, ed. by Richard Garnett (Scribner, 1898; Muses' Library ed.). The Poetical Works, 2 vols., ed. by T. Ashe (Bell, 1885; Aldine ed.). Prose Works, ed. by T. Ashe, 6 vols. (Bell, 1885; Bohn ed.). Table Talk, ed. by Henry Morley (Routledge, 1883; Morley's Universal Library ed.). Anima Poetae, from Coleridge's unpublished notebooks, ed. by E. H. Coleridge (Houghton, 1895).

BIOGRAPHY. S. T. Coleridge und die englische Romantik, by Alois Brandl (Berlin, 1886); translation by Lady Eastlake, S. T. Coleridge and the English Romantic School (Murray, 1887). Coleridge, by H. D. Traill (Macmillan, 1884; English Men of Letters series). Life of S. T. Coleridge, by Hall Caine (Scott, 1887; Great Writers series). S. T. Coleridge, a Narrative of the Events of His Life, by J. D. Campbell (Macmillan, 1894). (See also Campbell's introduction to his edition of Coleridge.) Early Recollections, chiefly relating to the late S. T. Coleridge, by Joseph Cottle (London, 1837). The Life of S. T. Coleridge, by James Gillman (London, 1838; only one volume published). Letters of S. T. Coleridge, ed. by E. H. Coleridge (Heinemann, 1895; Houghton). Biographia Literaria, by S. T. Coleridge, 1817 (Bell, 1885; Bohn ed.). Coleridge and Opium-Eating (1845), by Thomas De Quincey (Vol. 5, in Masson's new edition of De Quincey's works). The Autobiography of Leigh Hunt, chap. xvi (London, 1850). The Life of John Sterling (1851), by Thomas Carlyle, chap. viii. See also above under "Wordsworth, Biography," Dorothy Wordsworth, Robinson, Southey, De Quincey (Literary and Lake Reminiscences, chap. ii), Hazlitt.

CRITICISMS. Peter Bayne: Essays in Biography and Criticism, second series (Boston, 1858). Blackwood's Magazine: October, 1817, Biographia Literaria; October, 1819, The Lake School of Poets; October, 1834, Coleridge's Poetical Works. Edward Dowden: New Studies in Literature (Coleridge as a Poet) (Houghton, 1895). Edinburgh Review: September, 1816, Christabel; August, 1817, Biographia Literaria. John Forster: Great Teachers (Redway, 1898). Richard Garnett: Essays of an ex-Librarian (Heinemann, 1901). J. R. Lowell: Democracy and Other Addresses (Houghton, 1887; in Latest Literary and Political Addresses, in the collected edition of his works). Walter Pater: Appreciations (Macmillan, 1889; the essay on Coleridge, 1865 and 1880). Quarterly Review: April, 1814, Remorse (also a general discussion of Coleridge's poetry). J. M. Robertson: New Essays towards a Critical Method (Lane, 1897). J. C. Shairp: Studies in Poetry and Philosophy (Edinburgh, 1868; Houghton). Leslie Stephen: Hours in a Library, Vol. 3 (Smith, 1874–79: Putnam, 1892, new ed., with additions). A. C. Swinburne: Essays and Studies (Chatto, 1875). William Watson: Excursions in Criticism (Coleridge's Supernaturalism) (Macmillan, 1893). G. E. Woodberry: Studies in Letters and Life (Houghton, 1890); Makers of Literature (Macmillan, 1900). See also above, under "General Works, Literature," Saintsbury, Oliphant, Chambers, Encyclopaedia Britannica, Dictionary of National Biography, Dawson, Palgrave, Beers, Brandes, Minto, Herford, Dowden, Hancock, Courthope, Gates, Stevenson, Griffin, Haney.

BIBLIOGRAPHY. By J. P. Anderson, in Caine's Life of Coleridge. J. L. Haney: A Bibliography of S. T. Coleridge (privately printed, 1903).

ROBERT SOUTHEY

EDITIONS. The Poetical Works, collected by himself, 10 vols. (Longmans, 1837–38). Poems, chosen and arranged by Edward Dowden (Macmillan, 1895; Golden Treasury ed.). Selections from the Poems, ed. by S. R. Thompson (Scott, 1888; Canterbury Poets ed.). Ballads and Other Poems, ed. by C. J. Battersby (Blackie, 1899).

BIOGRAPHY. The Life and Correspondence of Robert Southey, ed. by his son (London, 1849–50). Southey, by Edward Dowden (Macmillan, 1876; English Men of Letters series). Literary and Lake Reminiscences, by Thomas De Quincey, chaps. iv, v (Vol. 2, in Masson's new edition of De Quincey). See also above, under "Wordsworth, Biography," De Quincey, Robinson.

CRITICISMS. Blackwood's Magazine, March and April, 1851. Edinburgh Review: October, 1802, Thalaba; October, 1805, Madoc; February, 1811, The Curse of Kehama; June, 1815, Roderick; March, 1817, Wat Tyler; July, 1821, A Vision of Judgment. Quarterly Review: February, 1811, The Curse of Kehama; April, 1815, Roderick. George Saintsbury: Essays in English Literature, second series (Dent, 1895). Leslie Stephen: Studies of a Biographer, Vol. 4 (Southey's Letters) (Putnam, 1902). See also above, under "General Works, Literature," Saintsbury, Oliphant, Dictionary of National Biography, Minto, Dawson.

THOMAS CAMPBELL

EDITIONS. The Poetical Works, ed. by W. A. Hill, with a sketch of Campbell's life by W. Allingham (Bell, 1875; Aldine ed.). The Poetical Works, ed. by W. M. Rossetti (London and Edinburgh, 1871; the same in Moxon's Popular Poets series, 1880). Poems (Scott, 1885; Canterbury Poets ed.). Poems, selected by L. Campbell (Macmillan, 1904: Golden Treasury ed.).

BIOGRAPHY. The Life and Letters of Thomas Campbell, by William Beattie (Moxon, 1849).

CRITICISMS. Blackwood's Magazine: January, 1825, Theodoric. Edinburgh Review: April, 1809, Gertrude of Wyoming; January, 1825, Theodoric. Quarterly Review: May, 1809, Gertrude of Wyoming. George Saintsbury: Essays in English Literature, second series (Dent, 1905). See also above, under "General Works, Literature," Saintsbury, Oliphant, Chambers, Encyclopaedia Britannica, Dawson, Minto.

WALTER SCOTT

EDITIONS. The Complete Poetical Works, with introductions and notes by Andrew Lang, 6 vols. (Estes, 1902). The Poetical Works, with the author's introductions, notes, and appendices, together with the annotations of J. G. Lockhart and others, 4 vols. (Oliphant, 1898; Lippincott, 1900). The Poems, ed. by J. Dennis, 5 vols. (Bell, 1892; Aldine ed.). The Poetical Works, ed. by William Minto, 2 vols. (Black, 1887–88). The Complete Poetical Works, ed. by H. E. Scudder (Houghton, 1900; Cambridge ed.). The Poems, ed. by J. L. Robertson (Oxford University Press, 1906). Poetical Works (not complete), ed. by F. T. Palgrave (Macmillan, 1866; Globe ed.).

BIOGRAPHY. Memoirs of the Life of Sir Walter Scott, by J. G. Lockhart, 1837 (Houghton, 1901; new ed.). Sir Walter Scott, by R. H. Hutton (Macmillan, 1878; English Men of Letters series). Life of Sir Walter Scott, by C. D. Yonge (Scott, 1888; Great Writers series). The Journal of Sir Walter Scott (1825–32), ed. by David Douglas, 2 vols. (Harper, 1900). Familiar Letters of Sir Walter Scott, ed. by David Douglas, 2 vols. (Douglas, 1894; Houghton). Abbotsford and Newstead Abbey, by Washington Irving (London, 1850). Studies of a Biographer, by Leslie Stephen, Vol. 2 (The Story of Scott's Ruin) (Putnam, 1899). The Homes and Haunts of Sir Walter Scott, by G. S. Napier (MacLehose, 1897; Macmillan). The Scott Country, by S. R. Crockett (Macmillan, 1902).

CRITICISMS. Blackwood's Magazine, April, 1817. Thomas Carlyle: Critical and Miscellaneous Essays, Vol. 3 (the essay on Scott, in London and Westminster Review, 1838). Edinburgh Review: April, 1805, The Lay of the Last Minstrel; April, 1808, Marmion; August, 1810, The Lady of the Lake; August, 1811, The Vision of Don Roderick; February, 1815, The Lord of the Isles. John Hay: Addresses (Sir Walter Scott, address at the unveiling of the bust of Scott in Westminster Abbey, 1897) (Century Co., 1906). Victor Hugo: Littérature et Philosophie (Paris, 1834). Andrew Lang: Essays in Little (Scribner, 1891). F. T. Palgrave: Biographical and Critical Memoir, prefixed to his edition of Scott. Quarterly Review: May, 1810, The Lady of the Lake; October, 1811, The Vision of Don Roderick; December, 1812, Rokeby; July, 1815, The Lord of the Isles. John Ruskin: Modern Painters, Part IV, chap. xvi (Scott's descriptions of nature) (London, 1856). J. C. Shairp: Aspects of Poetry (The Homeric Spirit in Walter Scott) (Clarendon Press, 1881). Leslie Stephen: Hours in a Library, Vol. 1 (Smith, 1874–79). A. C. Swinburne: Studies in Prose and Poetry (The Journal of Sir Walter Scott) (Chatto, 1897). Arthur Symons: Was Sir Walter Scott a Poet? (Atlantic Monthly, November, 1904). See also above, under "General Works, Literature," Saintsbury, Oliphant, Chambers, Dictionary of National Biography, Dawson, Palgrave, Beers, Brandes, Minto, Herford, Gates.

BIBLIOGRAPHY. By J. P. Anderson, in Yonge's Life of Scott.

GEORGE GORDON BYRON

EDITIONS. The Works: Poetry, ed. by E. H. Coleridge, 7 vols.; Letter and Journals, ed. by R. E. Prothero, 6 vols. (Murray, 1898–1904). The Poetical Works, ed. with a memoir by E. H. Coleridge (Murray, 1906; Scribner). The Complete Poetical Works, ed. by P. E. More (Houghton, 1906; Cambridge ed.). The Poems (Oxford University Press, 1896). Childe Harold, ed. by H. F. Tozer (Clarendon Press, 1885). Childe Harold, ed. by W. J. Rolfe (Houghton, 1885).

BIOGRAPHY. The Life of Lord Byron, with His Letters and Journals, and Illustrative Notes, by Thomas Moore (Murray, 1830). Lord Byron, a Biography, with a Critical Essay on His Place in Literature, by Karl Elze (Murray, 1872; translation of the German edition of 1870). Byron, by John Nichol (Macmillan, 1880; English Men of Letters series). Life of Lord Byron, by Roden Noel (Scott, 1890; Great Writer series). Letters of Lord Byron (1804–13), ed. by W. E. Henley (Macmillan, 1897). Journal of the Conversations of Lord Byron, by Thomas Medwin (London, 1824). Recollections of the Life of Lord Byron from 1808 to 1814, by R. C. Dallas (London, 1824). A Narrative of Lord Byron's Last Journey to Greece, by Pietro Gamba (London, 1825). Lord Byron and Some of His Contemporaries, by Leigh Hunt (London, 1828). The Autobiography of Leigh Hunt, chaps. xv–xix (London, 1850). Recollections of the Last Days of Shelley and Byron, by E. J. Trelawny (London, 1858; reissue, Frowde, 1906). Lord Byron jugé par les temoins de sa vie, by Countess Guiccioli (Paris, 1868); translation by H. E. H. Jerningham, My Recollections of Lord Byron and Those of Eye-Witnesses of His Life (London, 1869). Byron and the Greek Patriots (Harper's Magazine, February, 1894). See also above, under "Wordsworth, Biography," Robinson.

CRITICISMS. Matthew Arnold: Essays in Criticism, second series (Macmillan, 1888). Blackwood's Magazine: June, 1817, Manfred; November, 1817, The Lament of Tasso; May, 1818, Childe Harold, Canto IV; July, 1819, Mazeppa; August, 1819, Don Juan; April, 1821, The Doge of Venice; December, 1822, Werner; January, 1823, Heaven and Earth; July, 1823, Don Juan; February, 1825, Byron's Character and Writings. George Brandes: Shelley und Lord Byron (Leipzig, 1894). G. K. Chesterton: Varied Types (The Optimism of Byron) (Dodd, 1903). J. C. Collins: Studies in Poetry and Criticism (The Collected Works of Lord Byron) (Bell, 1905; this essay appeared in the Quarterly Review, April, 1905). Edinburgh Review: January, 1808, Hours of Idleness; February, 1812, Childe Harold, Cantos I and II; July, 1813, The Giaour; April, 1814, The

Corsair, The Bride of Abydos; December, 1816, Childe Harold, Canto III, The Prisoner
of Chillon, etc.; August, 1817, Manfred; February, 1818, Beppo; June, 1818, Childe Harold,
Canto IV; July, 1821, Marino Faliero, The Prophecy of Dante; February, 1822, Sardanapalus,
The Two Foscari, Cain. Goethe: Eckermann's Conversations with Goethe, translated from
the German by S. M. Fuller (Boston, 1839). W. E. Henley: Views and Reviews (Scribner,
1890). T. B. Macaulay: Critical, Historical, and Miscellaneous Essays (Moore's Life of
Lord Byron; in Edinburgh Review, June, 1831). P. E. More: The Wholesome Revival of
Byron (Atlantic Monthly, December, 1898); Shelburne Essays, third series (A Note on
Byron's Don Juan) (Putnam, 1906). John Morley: Critical Miscellanies, first series (Mac-
millan, 1871). J. F. A. Pyre: Byron in Our Day (Atlantic Monthly, April, 1907). Quar-
terly Review: March, 1812, Childe Harold, Cantos I and II; January, 1814, The Giaour,
The Bride of Abydos; July, 1814, The Corsair, Lara; October, 1816, Childe Harold, Canto
III, The Prisoner of Chillon, etc.; April, 1818, Childe Harold, Canto IV; July, 1822, Marino
Faliero, Sardanapalus, The Two Foscari, Cain. C.-A. Sainte-Beuve: Chateaubriand et
son groupe littéraire sous l'Empire, Vol. 1, chap. xv (Paris, 1848–49). Otto Schmidt: Rous-
seau und Byron (Oppeln, 1890). A. C. Swinburne: Essays and Studies (Chatto, 1875);
Miscellanies (Chatto, 1886). G. E. Woodberry: Studies in Letters and Life (Houghton,
1890). See also above, under "General Works, Literature," Taine, Saintsbury, Oliphant,
Chambers, Encyclopaedia Britannica, Dictionary of National Biography, Dawson, Palgrave,
Beers, Brandes, Minto, Herford, Dowden, Hancock, Courthope, Gates, Stevenson, Griffin,
Haney.

BIBLIOGRAPHY. By J. P. Anderson, in Noel's Life of Byron. By E. H. Coleridge, in
his edition of Byron's poems, Vol. 7.

THOMAS MOORE

EDITIONS. Complete Poetical Works, collected by himself, with explanatory notes
and biographical introduction, 2 vols. (Crowell, 1895). The Poetical Works, ed. by W. M.
Rossetti (Moxon, 1880; Popular Poets ed.). The Poetical Works (Bliss, 1897; Apollo
Poets ed.). Poems, selected by C. L. Falkiner (Macmillan, 1903; Golden Treasury ed.).

BIOGRAPHY. Thomas Moore, His Life and Works, by A. J. Symington (Black, 1880).

CRITICISMS. Blackwood's Magazine: June, 1817, Lalla Rookh; May, 1818, The
Fudge Family in Paris; October, 1818; January, 1822, Irish Melodies; January, 1823,
The Loves of the Angels; May, 1852. Edinburgh Review: July, 1803, translation of Ana-
creon; July, 1806; November, 1817, Lalla Rookh. Quarterly Review: June, 1812, and
October, 1822, Irish Melodies. George Saintsbury: Essays in English Literature, first
series (Percival, 1890). See also above, under "General Works, Literature," Chambers,
Encyclopaedia Britannica, Dictionary of National Biography, Beers, Minto.

PERCY BYSSHE SHELLEY

EDITIONS. The Poetical Works, 4 vols., The Prose Works, 4 vols., ed. by H. B. Forman
(Reeves, 1876–80). The Poetical Works, ed. by R. H. Shepherd, 3 vols. (Chatto, 1888).
The Complete Poetical Works, ed. by G. E. Woodberry, 4 vols. (Houghton, 1892). The
Poetical Works, ed. by H. B. Forman, 5 vols. (Macmillan, 1892; Aldine ed.).

The Poetical Works, ed. by Edward Dowden (Macmillan, 1890; Globe ed.). The
Complete Poetical Works, ed. by G. E. Woodberry (Houghton, 1901; Cambridge ed.). Select
Poems, ed. by W. J. Alexander (Ginn, 1898; Athenaeum Press ed.). Essays and Letters,
ed. by Ernest Rhys (Scott, 1886; Camelot Classics ed.). A Defense of Poetry, ed. by A. S.
Cook (Ginn, 1890). An Apology for Poetry, ed. by L. Winstanley (Heath, in preparation;
Belles Lettres series, with Browning's Essay on Shelley). Original Poetry by Victor and
Cazire [P. B. Shelley and Elizabeth Shelley] (1810), a reprint, ed. by Richard Garnett (Lane,
1897). Notes on the MS. volume of Shelley's Poems in the Library of Harvard College,

by G. E. Woodberry [with a facsimile of the MS. of To a Skylark] (issued by the Library of Harvard University, 1889).

BIOGRAPHY. The Life of P. B. Shelley, by Edward Dowden, 2 vols. (Paul, 1886; Lippincott). Shelley, by J. A. Symonds (Macmillan, 1878; English Men of Letters series). Life of P. B. Shelley, by William Sharp (Scott, 1887; Great Writers series). P. B. Shelley, Poet and Pioneer, a Biographical Study, by H. S. Salt (Reeves, 1896). Memoirs of P. B. Shelley, by T. L. Peacock (London, 1875; reprinted from Fraser's Magazine, 1858-60). The Life of P. B. Shelley, by T. J. Hogg (Moxon, 1858; reissue, Dutton, 1896). Shelley Memorials, ed. by Lady Shelley (King, 1859). William Godwin, His Friends and Contemporaries, by C. K. Paul (London, 1876). See also above, under "Byron, Biography," Trelawny, Hunt.

CRITICISMS. Matthew Arnold: Essays in Critici,m, second series (Macmillan, 1888). Walter Bagehot: Literary Studies (Longmans, 1878-79). Blackwood's Magazine: January, 1819, The Revolt of Islam; June, 1819, Rosalind and Helen; November, 1819, Alastor; September, 1820, Prometheus Unbound; December, 1821, Adonais. Robert Browning: An Essay on Shelley, 1852 (Shelley Society's Papers, London, 1888; in the Cambridge edition of Browning). Aubrey De Vere: Essays, chiefly on Poetry (Macmillan, 1887). Edinburgh Review: July, 1824, posthumous poems. Joseph Forster: Great Teachers (Redway, 1898). Edmund Gosse: Questions at Issue (Appleton, 1893). R. H. Hutton: Essays Theological and Literary (Strahan, 1871). Andrew Lang: Letters to Dead Authors (Scribner, 1893). David Masson: Wordsworth, Shelley, Keats (Macmillan, 1874). Quarterly Review: April, 1819, The Revolt of Islam; October, 1821, Prometheus Unbound. J. M. Robertson: New Essays towards a Critical Method (Lane, 1897). H. S. Salt: A Shelley Primer (Shelley Society's Papers, London, 1887). J. C. Shairp: Aspects of Poetry (Shelley as a Lyric Poet) (Clarendon Press, 1881). Shelley Society's Papers (London, 1886-). Leslie Stephen: Hours in a Library, Vol. 3 (Godwin and Shelley) (Smith, 1874-79). A. C. Swinburne: Essays and Studies (Notes on the Text of Shelley) (Chatto, 1875). John Todhunter: A Study of Shelley (Paul, 1880). W. P. Trent: Authority of Criticism (Scribner, 1899). G. E. Woodberry: Studies in Letters and Life (Houghton 1890); Makers of Literature (Macmillan, 1900); The Torch (McClure, 1905). See also above, under "General Works, Literature," Saintsbury, Oliphant, Chambers, Encyclopaedia Britannica, Dictionary of National Biography, Dawson, Palgrave, Beers, Brandes, Minto, Herford, Dowden, Hancock, Courthope, Gates, Stevenson, Griffin, Haney.

CONCORDANCE. F. S. Ellis: A Lexical Concordance to the Poetical Works of P. B. Shelley (Quaritch, 1892).

BIBLIOGRAPHY. H. B. Forman: The Shelley Library, an Essay in Bibliography (Reeves, 1886). By J. P. Anderson, in Sharp's Life of Shelley.

LEIGH HUNT

EDITIONS. The Poetical Works (Moxon, 1883; Popular Poets ed.). Poems (selected), ed. by J. H. Panting (Scott, 1889; Canterbury Poets ed., with Hood's poems). Essays (selected), ed. by Arthur Symons (Scott, 1887; Camelot Classics ed.). Essays (selected), ed. by Arthur Seymour (Dutton, 1904).

BIOGRAPHY. Life of Leigh Hunt, by Cosmo Monkhouse (Scott, 1893; Great Writers series). The Autobiography of Leigh Hunt (London, 1850).

CRITICISMS. Blackwood's Magazine: October, November, 1817, and July, 1818, On the Cockney School of Poetry; October, 1819, Foliage, Poems Original and Translated. Edinburgh Review: June, 1816, The Story of Rimini. Quarterly Review: January, 1816 The Story of Rimini; May, 1818, Foliage. George Saintsbury: Essays in English Literature, first series (Percival, 1890). See also above, under "General Works, Literature," Saintsbury, Chambers, Encyclopaedia Britannica, Dictionary of National Biography.

BIBLIOGRAPHY. By J. P. Anderson, in Monkhouse's Life of Hunt.

JOHN KEATS

EDITIONS. The Poetical Works and Other Writings, ed. by H. B. Forman, 4 vols. (Reeves, 1883). The Complete Works, ed. by H. B. Forman, 5 vols. (Crowell, 1901). The Poems, with an introduction by R. S. Bridges (Bullen, 1896; Scribner; Muses' Library ed.). The Complete Poetical Works and Letters, ed. by H. E. Scudder (Houghton, 1899; Cambridge ed.). Poetical Works (Macmillan, 1902; Globe ed.). Poetical Works, ed. by F. T. Palgrave (Macmillan, 1884; Golden Treasury ed.). Letters, ed. by Sidney Colvin (Macmillan, 1891).

BIOGRAPHY. Keats, by Sidney Colvin (Macmillan, 1887; English Men of Letters series). Life of John Keats, by W. M. Rossetti (Scott, 1887; Great Writers series). Life, Letters, and Literary Remains of John Keats, ed. by R. M. Milnes (Lord Houghton) (London, 1848; rev. ed., 1867). Recollections of Writers, by Charles and Mary Cowden Clarke (London, 1878). Recollections of John Keats, by C. C. Clarke (The Gentleman's Magazine, February, 1874). Keats in Hampstead, by Kenyon West (Century Magazine, October, 1895). See also above, under "Byron, Biography," Hunt.

CRITICISMS. Matthew Arnold: Essays in Criticism, second series (Macmillan, 1888). Blackwood's Magazine: August, 1818, On the Cockney School of Poetry (Endymion). R. S. Bridges: Keats, a Critical Essay (privately printed, 1895). Aubrey De Vere: Essays, chiefly on Poetry (Macmillan, 1887). Edmund Gosse: Critical Kit-Kats (Keats in 1894) (Dodd, 1896). Edinburgh Review: August, 1820, Endymion, Lamia, etc. Andrew Lang: Letters on Literature (Longmans, 1889). J. R. Lowell: Among My Books, second series (Keats, 1854) (Literary Essays, Vol. I, in Lowell's collected works). H. W. Mabie: Essays in Literary Interpretation (Dodd, 1892). David Masson: Wordsworth, Shelley, Keats (Macmillan, 1874). P. E. More: Shelburne Essays, fourth series (Putnam, 1906). Quarterly Review: April, 1818, Endymion. J. M. Robertson: New Essays towards a Critical Method (The Art of Keats) (Lane, 1897). E. C. Stedman: Keats (Century Magazine, February, 1884). William Watson: Excursions in Criticism (Keats's letters) (Macmillan, 1893). Henry Van Dyke: The Influence of Keats (Century Magazine, October, 1895). G. E. Woodberry: Studies in Letters and Life (On the Promise of Keats) (Houghton, 1890). See also above, under "General Works, Literature," Saintsbury, Oliphant, Chambers, Encyclopaedia Britannica, Dictionary of National Biography, Dawson, Palgrave, Beers, Brandes, Minto, Herford, Courthope, Gates, Stevenson, Griffin, Haney.

BIBLIOGRAPHY. By J. P. Anderson, in Rossetti's Life of Keats.

WALTER SAVAGE LANDOR

EDITIONS. Works, ed. by John Forster, 8 vols. (Chapman, 1874–76). Works, ed. by C. G. Crump, 10 vols. (Dent, 1891–93; Poems, Dialogues in Verse, and Epigrams, 2 vols). Letters and Other Unpublished Writings, ed. by Stephen Wheeler (Bentley, 1897). Letters, Private and Public, ed. by Stephen Wheeler (Duckworth, 1899). Selections (verse and prose), ed. by Sidney Colvin (Macmillan, 1882; Golden Treasury ed.). Selections (mostly prose), ed. by W. B. S. Clymer (Ginn, 1898; Athenaeum Press ed.). Selections from the Imaginary Conversations (prose only), ed. by A. G. Newcomer (Holt, 1899). Imaginary Conversations (selections), ed. by Havelock Ellis, 3 vols. (Scott, 1889; Camelot Classics ed.). Poems (selected), ed. by Ernest Radford (Scott, 1887; Canterbury Poets ed.).

BIOGRAPHY. W. S. Landor, by John Forster, 2 vols. (Chapman, 1869; abridged, as Vol. I of the works, 1874). Landor, by Sidney Colvin (Macmillan, 1878; English Men of Letters series). Last Days of Landor, by Kate Field (Atlantic Monthly, April, May, June, 1866). See also above, under "Wordsworth, Biography," Robinson (Vol. 2, chap. xii, and index).

CRITICISMS. Blackwood's Magazine: April, 1824, March and April, 1837, Imaginary Conversations; January, 1854, Last Fruit off an Old Tree. H. W. Boynton: The Poetry of Landor (Atlantic Monthly, July, 1902). Contemporary Review, August, 1871. Thomas De Quincey: three articles on Landor, 1847 (in Vol. 11 of Masson's new edition of De Quincey). Aubrey De Vere: Essays, chiefly on Poetry (Macmillan, 1887). Edward Dowden: Studies in Literature (Paul, 1878). Edinburgh Review: March, 1824, Imaginary Conversations; April, 1850, Hellenics, etc. W. E. Henley: Views and Reviews (Scribner, 1890). J. R. Lowell: Latest Literary Essays and Addresses. North American Review, January, 1877. George Saintsbury: Essays in English Literature, second series (Scribner, 1895). H. E. Scudder: Men and Letters (Landor as a Classic) (Houghton, 1887). Leslie Stephen: Hours in a Library, Vol. 2 (Smith, 1874–79; new and enlarged ed., 1892). A. C. Swinburne: Miscellanies (Chatto, 1886; the article on Landor, in the Encyclopaedia Britannica). Arthur Symons: The Poetry of Landor (compares English and Latin versions of some poems) (Atlantic Monthly, June, 1906). G. E. Woodberry: Studies in Literature and Life (Houghton, 1890). See also above, under "General Works, Literature," Saintsbury, Chambers, Dictionary of National Biography, Walker, Oliphant, Stedman.

BIBLIOGRAPHY. By Stephen Wheeler, in Letters and Other Unpublished Writings of W. S. Landor.

ALFRED TENNYSON

EDITIONS. Complete Works, 6 vols. (Macmillan, 1903; new library ed.). The Life and Works, 10 vols. (Macmillan, 1899, new ed.; the life is the memoir by Tennyson's son, 4 vols.). The Poetical Works, 7 vols. (Houghton, 1904; new Riverside ed.). The Poetical and Dramatic Works, 3 vols. (Houghton, 1906). The Works (Macmillan, 1893; Globe ed.). The Poetic and Dramatic Works, ed. by W. J. Rolfe (Houghton, 1898; Cambridge ed.; does not contain the latest poems, but has selections from Poems by Two Brothers, Timbuctoo, and the suppressed poems of 1830 and 1832). Poems by Two Brothers (Macmillan, 1893; reprint of the edition of 1827); the same (Crowell, 1902). The Early Poems, ed. by J. C. Collins (Putnam, 1899; reprint of Poems, 1842, with the various readings and suppressed poems). Suppressed Poems, ed. by J. C. Thomson (Harper, 1903). Poems, ed. by Henry Van Dyke (Ginn, 1903; Athenaeum Press ed.). Selections, ed. by F. J. Rowe and W. T. Webb (Macmillan, 1893). In Memoriam, ed. by W. J. Rolfe (Houghton, 1895); ed. by C. Mansford (Swan, 1903); ed. by V. P. Squires (Silver, 1906).

BIOGRAPHY. Alfred, Lord Tennyson, a Memoir, by his Son, 2 vols. (Macmillan, 1897; one-vol. ed., 1905). Tennyson, by A. C. Lyall (Macmillan, 1902; English Men of Letters series). Alfred Tennyson, by Andrew Lang (Dodd, 1901; Modern English Writers series). Tennyson, by G. K. Chesterton and Richard Garnett (Pott, 1904; Bookman Biographies series). Yesterdays with Authors, by J. T. Fields (Houghton, 1872). Records of Tennyson, Ruskin, Browning, by Anne T. Ritchie (Harper, 1892). A Day with Tennyson, by Edwin Arnold (Forum, December, 1891, Vol. 12, p. 536). Tennyson, a Personal Reminiscence, by James Knowles (Nineteenth Century, January, 1893). The Voice of Tennyson, by Henry Van Dyke (Century Magazine, February, 1893). Recollections of Lord Tennyson, by J. A. Symonds (Century Magazine, May, 1893). Memories of the Tennysons, by H. D. Rawnsley (MacLehose, 1900; Macmillan). Personal Recollections of Tennyson, by W. G. McCabe (Century Magazine, March, 1902). A Child's Recollections of Tennyson, by E. N. Ellison (Dutton, 1906). The Laureate's Country, by A. J. Church (Seeley, 1891). The Homes and Haunts of Alfred, Lord Tennyson, by G. S. Napier (MacLehose, 1892).

CRITICISMS. Walter Bagehot: Literary Studies (Wordsworth, Tennyson, Browning, or Pure, Ornate, and Grotesque Art in English Poetry) (Longmans, 1878–79; this essay, in the National Review, November, 1864). Peter Bayne: Essays in Biography and Criticism, first series (Tennyson and His Teachers) (Boston, 1857). Blackwood's Magazine: May, 1832, Poems, Chiefly Lyrical; April, 1849, Poems, The Princess; September, 1855, Maud; November, 1859, Idylls of the King; November, 1864, Enoch Arden, etc. George Brimley:

Essays (Macmillan, 1858; reissue, 1882; the essay on Tennyson, in Cambridge Essays, 1855).
S. A. Brooke: Tennyson, His Art and Relation to Modern Life (Putnam, 1894). G. K.
Chesterton: Varied Types (Dodd, 1903). J. C. Collins: Illustrations of Tennyson (Chatto,
1891). W. M. Dixon: A Primer of Tennyson (Dodd, 1896). Edward Dowden: Studies
in Literature (Mr. Tennyson and Mr. Browning) (Paul, 1878). Edinburgh Review: April,
1843, Poems; October, 1849, The Princess; October, 1855, Maud, In Memoriam; April,
1870, Idylls of the King. C. C. Everett: Essays Theological and Literary (Houghton, 1891).
Joseph Forster: Great Teachers (Redway, 1898). L. E. Gates: Studies and Appreciations
(Tennyson's Relation to Common Life; Nature in Tennyson's Poetry) (Macmillan, 1890).
W. C. Gordon: The Social Ideals of Alfred Tennyson (University of Chicago Press, 1906).
Edmund Gosse: Questions at Issue (Tennyson—and After) (Appleton, 1893). A. H. Hallam:
Literary Remains (On Some of the Characteristics of Modern Poetry, and on the Lyrical
Poems of Alfred Tennyson) (London, 1853; this essay, in the Englishman's Magazine, August,
1831). Frederic Harrison: Tennyson, Ruskin, Mill, and Other Literary Estimates (Mac-
millan, 1899). W. E. Henley: Views and Reviews (Scribner, 1890). R. H. Hutton: Literary
Essays (Macmillan, 1888). Morton Luce: A Handbook to the Works of Alfred, Lord Tennyson (Bell, 1895). J. S. Mill: Early Essays (Tennyson's Poems) (Bell, 1897; this essay, in
the London Review, July, 1835). Emile Montégut: Ecrivains modernes de l'Angleterre,
second series (Paris, 1889). W. P. Mustard: Classical Echoes in Tennyson (Macmillan, 1904).
F. W. H. Myers: Science and a Future Life (Tennyson as a Prophet) (Macmillan, 1893;
this essay, in the Nineteenth Century, March, 1889). Herbert Paul: Men and Letters (The
Classical Poems of Tennyson) (Lane, 1901; this essay, in the Nineteenth Century, March,
1893). Quarterly Review: April, 1833; January, 1859. Revue des Deux Mondes: Vol.
35, p. 345 (1851). J. M. Robertson: Essays towards a Critical Method (The Art of Tenny-
son) (Unwin, 1899). Josiah Royce: Studies of Good and Evil (Tennyson and Pessimism)
(Appleton, 1898). George Saintsbury: Corrected Impressions (Heinemann, 1895). H. S.
Salt: Tennyson as a Thinker (Reeves, 1893). Leslie Stephen: Studies of a Biographer
Vol. 3 (The Life of Tennyson) (Putnam, 1899). A. C. Swinburne: Miscellanies (Tennyson
and Musset) (Chatto, 1886; Scribner); Studies in Prose and Poetry (Tennyson or Darwin?)
(Chatto, 1894; Scribner). H. D. Traill: Aspects of Tennyson (Nineteenth Century, Decem-
ber, 1892). Henry Van Dyke: The Poetry of Tennyson (Scribner, 1889). T. H. Warren:
Essays of Poets and Poetry (In Memoriam after Fifty Years; Virgil and Tennyson; Tenny-
son and Dante) (Murray, forthcoming). Theodore Watts: Tennyson as a Nature Poet;
Tennyson as the Poet of Evolution (Nineteenth Century, May and October, 1893). West-
minster Review: January, 1831, Poems, Chiefly Lyrical; August, 1891, Tennyson's Lincolnshire Farmers. See also above, under "General Works, Literature," Taine, Saintsbury,
Chambers, Dictionary of National Biography, Dawson, Palgrave, Walker, Oliphant, Forman,
Stedman, Stevenson, Griffin, Haney.

On In Memoriam. In Memoriam, annotated by the Author (Macmillan, 1906). Brother
Azarias (P. F. Mullany): The Spiritual Sense of In Memoriam (Houghton, 1892). Elizabeth
Chapman: A Companion to In Memoriam (Macmillan, 1888). Thomas Davidson: Prolego-
mena to In Memoriam (Houghton, 1889). Alfred Gatty: A Key to Tennyson's In Memoriam
(Bell, 1881). J. F. Genung: Tennyson's In Memoriam, Its Purpose and Its Structure (Hough-
ton, 1884).

On The Idylls of the King. Richard Jones: The Growth of the Idylls of the King
(Lippincott, 1895). Harold Littledale: Essays on Lord Tennyson's Idylls of the King
(Macmillan, 1893). M. W. MacCallum: Tennyson's Idylls of the King and Arthurian
Story from the Sixteenth Century (Macmillan, 1894). Howard Maynadier: The Arthur
of the English Poets (Houghton, 1907).

CONCORDANCES. D. B. Brightwell: A Concordance to the Entire Works of Alfred
Tennyson (Moxon, 1869). Concordance to the Works of Alfred Tennyson (Strahan, 1870).

BIBLIOGRAPHY. R. H. Shepherd: Bibliography of Tennyson (London, 1896). L. S.

Livingston: Bibliography of the First Editions in Book Form of the Works of Alfred Tennyson (Dodd, 1902). In the Providence Public Library's Monthly Bulletin, October, 1897. In Dixon's Primer of Tennyson, and Luce's Handbook to the Works of Tennyson.

ELIZABETH BARRETT BROWNING

EDITIONS. The Poetical Works, 6 vols. (Smith, 1889-90; Scribner). The Poetical Works, ed. by Charlotte Porter and H. A. Clarke, 6 vols. (Crowell, 1900). The Poetical Works, ed. by F. G. Kenyon (Macmillan, 1897; Globe ed.). The Complete Poetical Works, ed. by H. W. Preston (Houghton, 1900; Cambridge ed.).

BIOGRAPHY. E. B. Browning, by J. H. Ingram (Roberts, 1888; Famous Women series). The Letters of E. B. Browning, ed. by F. G. Kenyon, 2 vols. (Smith, 1897). The Letters of Robert Browning and Elizabeth Barrett Barrett (1845-46), ed. by R. B. Browning (Smith, 1899). Records of Tennyson, Ruskin, Browning, by A. T. Ritchie (Harper, 1892). W. W. Story and His Friends, ed. by Henry James (Houghton, 1903).

CRITICISMS. Peter Bayne: Essays in Biography and Criticism, first series (Boston, 1857); Two Great Englishwomen (Clarke, 1881). Blackwood's Magazine: November, 1844, Poems; January, 1857, Aurora Leigh; April, 1860, Poems before Congress; April, 1862. G. K. Chesterton: Varied Types (Dodd, 1903). L. E. Gates: Studies and Appreciations (The Return to Conventional Life) (Macmillan, 1900). E. W. Gosse: Critical Kit-Kats (The Sonnets from the Portuguese) (Dodd, 1896). Emile Montégut: Ecrivains modernes de l'Angleterre, second series (Paris, 1889). Lilian Whiting: A Study of E. B. Browning (Little, 1899). See also above, under "General Works, Literature," Saintsbury, Chambers, Encyclopaedia Britannica, Dictionary of National Biography, Walker, Oliphant, Stedman.

ROBERT BROWNING

EDITIONS. The Poetical Works, 9 vols. (Macmillan, 1894; new and complete ed.). The Complete Poetical and Dramatic Works, ed. by G. W. Cooke, 6 vols. (Houghton, 1899; new Riverside ed.). The Poetical Works, ed. by Augustine Birrell, 2 vols. (Macmillan, 1896; Globe ed.). The Poetical and Dramatic Works, 3 vols. (Houghton, 1906). The Complete Poetical and Dramatic Works, ed. by H. E. Scudder (Houghton, 1895; Cambridge ed.). Poems, from the Author's revised text of 1889, his own selections, with additions from his latest works, ed. with notes by Charlotte Porter and H. A. Clarke, 2 vols. (Crowell, 1896). The Ring and the Book, annotated, with introduction, by Charlotte Porter and H. A. Clarke (Crowell, 1897).

BIOGRAPHY. The Life and Letters of Robert Browning, by Mrs. Sutherland Orr (Houghton, 1891). Life of Robert Browning, by William Sharp (Scott, 1890; Great Writers series). Robert Browning, by G. K. Chesterton (Macmillan, 1903; English Men of Letters series). Browning, by Edward Dowden (Dutton, 1904; Temple Biographies series). Robert Browning, by James Douglas (Pott, 1904; Bookman Biographies series). The Letters of Robert Browning and Elizabeth Barrett Barrett (1845-46), ed. by R. B. Browning (Smith, 1899). Robert Browning, Personalia, by Edmund Gosse (Houghton 1890). Records of Tennyson, Ruskin, Browning, by A. T. Ritchie (Harper, 1892). W. W. Story and His Friends, ed. by Henry James (Houghton, 1903). Browning in Asolo; Browning in Venice; by K. C. Bronson (Century Magazine, April, 1900; February, 1902).

INTRODUCTIONS, HANDBOOKS, and CRITICISMS. W. J. Alexander: An Introduction to the Poetry of Robert Browning (Ginn, 1889). Edward Berdoe: The Browning Cyclopaedia (Macmillan, 1892); Browning's Message to His Time—His Religion, Philosophy, and Science (Macmillan, 1890). Augustine Birrell: Obiter Dicta, first series (On the Alleged Obscurity of Mr. Browning's Poetry) (Stock, 1884; Scribner); Essays and Addresses (Scribner, 1901). Blackwood's Magazine: May, 1871, Prolixity (The Ring and the Book). S. A. Brooke: The Poetry of Robert Browning (Crowell, 1902). Boston Browning Society Papers, 1886-97

(J. W. Chadwick, Luria; C. C. Everett, Sordello; Henry Jones, Browning as a Dramatic Poet; Josiah Royce, Browning's Theism, and the Problem of Paracelsus; V. D. Scudder, The Greek Spirit in Shelley and Browning, etc.) (Macmillan, 1897). Browning Society Papers (Trubner, 1881—). Browning Studies, select papers by members of the Browning Society, ed. by Edward Berdoe (Allen, 1895). J. J. Chapman: Emerson and Other Essays (Scribner, 1898). R. W. Church: Dante and Other Essays (Sordello) (Macmillan, 1888). Contemporary Review, January, 1867, Vol. 4, pp. 1, 133. G. W. Cooke: A Guide-Book to the Poetic and Dramatic Works of Robert Browning (Houghton, 1891). Hiram Corson: An Introduction to the Study of Robert Browning's Poetry (Heath, 1886). Edward Dowden: Studies in Literature (Mr. Tennyson and Mr. Browning) (Paul, 1878); Transcripts and Studies (Mr. Browning's Sordello) (Paul, 1887). Edinburgh Review: October, 1864, Poems, Dramatis Personae. C. C. Everett: Essays Theological and Literary (Houghton, 1901). Joseph Forster: Great Teachers (Allen, 1890; Redway, 1898, enlarged ed.). Fraser's Magazine: February, 1863. C. H. Herford: Robert Browning (Blackwood, 1905; Modern English Writers series). R. H. Hutton: Essays Theological and Literary (Strahan, 1871). Henry Jones: Browning as a Philosophical and Religious Teacher (Macmillan, 1891). J. R. Lowell: Browning's Plays and Poems (North American Review, 1848). H. W. Mabie: Essays in Literary Interpretation (Dodd, 1892). M. A. Molineux: A Phrase Book from the Poetic and Dramatic Works of Robert Browning, with an index of significant words not elsewhere noted (Houghton, 1896). P. E. More: Shelburne Essays, third series (Why Is Browning Popular?) (Putnam, 1906). John Morley: Studies in Literature (On the Ring and the Book) (Macmillan, 1891). Quarterly Review: July, 1865, Poems, Dramatis Personae. Revue des Deux Mondes: Vol. 35, p. 661 (1851); Vol. 85, p. 704 (1870). George Saintsbury: Corrected Impressions (Heinemann, 1895). George Santayana: Interpretations of Poetry and Religion (The Poetry of Barbarism—Walt Whitman, Robert Browning) (Scribner, 1900). Leslie Stephen: Studies of a Biographer, Vol. 3 (The Browning Letters) (Putnam, 1902). A. C. Swinburne: George Chapman, a Critical Essay (Chatto, 1875; Scribner). G. E. Woodberry: Studies in Letters and Life (Houghton, 1890). See also above, under "General Works, Literature," Saintsbury, Chambers, Dictionary of National Biography (Supplement), Dawson, Palgrave, Oliphant, Forman, Haney; and under "Tennyson, Criticisms," Bagehot.

BIBLIOGRAPHY. F. J. Furnivall: A Bibliography of Robert Browning from 1833 to 1881 (Browning Society Papers, 1881–84). By J. P. Anderson, in Sharp's Life of Browning. W. M. Nicoll and T. Wise: Literary Anecdotes of the Nineteenth Century (Materials for a Bibliography of Robert Browning) (1895).

ARTHUR HUGH CLOUGH

EDITIONS. Poems and Prose Remains, with a memoir, ed. by his wife, 2 vols. (Macmillan, 1869). Poems (Macmillan, 1888). Prose Remains, with a selection from his letters, and a memoir, ed. by his wife (Macmillan, 1888). Selections from the Poems, ed. by B. M. S. C. (Macmillan, 1894; Golden Treasury ed.).

BIOGRAPHY. Memoir by Mrs. Clough (see above). Memoir by C. E. Norton, prefixed to an edition of the Poems (Ticknor, 1862; first in the Atlantic Monthly, April, 1862). Portraits of Friends, by J. C. Shairp (Houghton, 1889).

CRITICISMS. Walter Bagehot: Literary Studies (Longmans, 1878–79). Edward Dowden: Studies in Literature (The Transcendental Movement and Literature) (Paul, 1878). R. H. Hutton: Essays Theological and Literary (Strahan, 1871). North American Review: October, 1867, A. H. Clough. F. T. Palgrave: A. H. Clough (Fraser's Magazine, April, 1862). T. S. Perry: Arthur Hugh Clough (Atlantic Monthly, October, 1875). J. M. Robertson: New Essays towards a Critical Method (Lane, 1897). J. A. Symonds: A. H. Clough (Fortnightly Review, December, 1868). S. Waddington: A. H. Clough, a Monograph (Bell, 1883). See also above, under "General Works, Literature," Saintsbury, Chambers, Dictionary of National Biography, Oliphant, Stedman.

MATTHEW ARNOLD

EDITIONS. Poetical Works (Macmillan, 1890; Globe ed.). Poetical Works, 3 vols. (Macmillan, 1895). Selected Poems (Macmillan; Golden Treasury ed.). Prose Works (Macmillan).

BIOGRAPHY. Letters of Matthew Arnold (1848–88), ed. by G. W. E. Russell, 2 vols. (Macmillan, 1895). Life of Matthew Arnold, by George Saintsbury (Dodd, 1899; Modern English Writers series). Matthew Arnold, by H. W. Paul (Macmillan, 1902; English Men of Letters series). Matthew Arnold, by G. W. E. Russell (Scribner, 1904; Literary Lives series). Recollections of Eminent Men, by E. P. Whipple (Ticknor, 1887).

CRITICISMS. Augustine Birrell: Res Judicatae (Stock, 1892; Scribner). Blackwood's Magazine: September, 1849, The Strayed Reveller; March, 1854, Poems (Sohrab and Rustum, etc.). A. H. Clough: Prose Remains (Review of Some Poems by Alexander Smith and Matthew Arnold) (Macmillan, 1869; this essay, as Recent English Poetry, in the North American Review, July, 1853). Edward Dowden: Transcripts and Studies (Paul, 1887). Edinburgh Review: October, 1856. Richard Garnett: Essays of an Ex-Librarian (Heinemann, 1901). L. E. Gates: Three Studies in Literature (Arnold's prose works) (Macmillan, 1899). Frederic Harrison: Tennyson, Ruskin, Mill, and Other Literary Estimates (Macmillan, 1899). W. E. Henley: Views and Reviews (Scribner, 1890). R. H. Hutton: Literary Essays (Macmillan, 1888). H. W. Paul: Men and Letters (Matthew Arnold's Letters) (Lane, 1901). W. C. Roscoe: Poems and Essays (The Classical School of English Poetry—Matthew Arnold) (Chapman, 1860). George Saintsbury: Corrected Impressions (Heinemann, 1895). Leslie Stephen: Studies of a Biographer, Vol. 2 (Putnam, 1899). A. C. Swinburne: Essays and Studies (Matthew Arnold's New Poems, 1867) (Chatto, 1875). T. Herbert Warren: Essays of Poets and Poetry (Murray, forthcoming). G. E. Woodberry: Makers of Literature (Macmillan, 1900). See also above, under "General Works, Literature," Saintsbury, Chambers, Dictionary of National Biography, Dawson, Palgrave, Gates, Walker, Oliphant, Forman, Stedman.

BIBLIOGRAPHY. T. B. Smart: The Bibliography of Matthew Arnold (Davy, 1892).

DANTE GABRIEL ROSSETTI

EDITIONS. The Collected Works, ed. by W. M. Rossetti, 2 vols. (Ellis, 1886; Roberts). Poems, ed. by W. M. Rossetti, 7 vols. (Ellis, 1898–1901; Siddal ed.). See also, for the first edition of The Blessed Damozel, a facsimile reprint of The Germ (1850), the literary organ of the Pre-Raphaelite brotherhood (Stock, 1901).

BIOGRAPHY. Pre-Raphaelite Diaries and Letters (1835–56), ed. by W. M. Rossetti (London, 1900). Ruskin, Rossetti, Pre-Raphaelitism (Papers, 1854–62), ed. by W. M. Rossetti (Allen, 1899; Dodd). Rossetti Papers (1862–70), ed. by W. M. Rossetti (Scribner, 1903). D. G. Rossetti, His Family Letters, with a memoir, ed. by W. M. Rossetti (Ellis, 1895; Roberts). Letters of D. G. Rossetti to William Allingham (1854–70), ed. by G. B. Hill (Unwin, 1897; Stokes). Recollections of D. G. Rossetti, by Hall Caine (Stock, 1882). D. G. Rossetti, a Record and a Study, by William Sharp (Macmillan, 1882). Life of D. G. Rossetti, by Joseph Knight (Scott, 1887; Great Writers series). Dante Rossetti and the Pre-Raphaelite Movement, by Esther Wood (Low, 1894; Scribner). D. G. Rossetti, an Illustrated Memorial of His Art and Life, by H. C. Marillier (Bell, 1899). The Rossettis, Dante Gabriel and Christina, by E. L. Cary (Putnam, 1900). Rossetti, by A. C. Benson (Macmillan, 1904; English Men of Letters series). Recollections of D. G. Rossetti and His Circle, by H. T. Dunn (Pott, 1904). The English Pre-Raphaelite Painters, by P. H. Bate (Bell, 1899; Macmillan). The Pre-Raphaelite Brotherhood, by W. Holman Hunt (Contemporary Review, April, May, June, 1886).

CRITICISMS. Blackwood's Magazine, August, 1870. R. W. Buchanan: The Fleshly School of Poetry, and Other Phenomena of the Day (London, 1872; first in the Contemporary

Review, October, 1871). Edinburgh Review: April, 1900, Morris and Rossetti. H. W. Mabie: Essays in Literary Interpretation (Dodd, 1892). F. W. H. Myers: Essays, Modern (Rossetti and the Religion of Beauty) (Macmillan, 1883). Walter Pater: Appreciations (Macmillan, 1889; the essay on Rossetti, 1883). A. C. Swinburne: Essays and Studies (Chatto, 1875). Theodore Watts: The Truth about Rossetti (Nineteenth Century, March, 1883). See also above, under "General Works, Literature," Saintsbury, Chambers, Encyclopaedia Britannica, Dictionary of National Biography, Dawson, Beers, Oliphant, Forman, Stedman.

BIBLIOGRAPHY. By J. P. Anderson, in Knight's Life of Rossetti.

CHRISTINA ROSSETTI

EDITIONS. The Poetical Works, with a memoir and notes by W. M. Rossetti (Macmillan, 1904).

BIOGRAPHY. Christina Rossetti, a Biographical and Critical Study, by Mackenzie Bell (Roberts, 1898). Memoir by W. M. Rossetti (see above). , See also above, under "D. G. Rossetti, Biography."

CRITICISMS. A. C. Benson: Christina Rossetti (Littell's Living Age, Mar. 9, 1895). Edmund Gosse: Critical Kit-Kats (Dodd, 1896). P. E. More: Shelburne Essays, third series (Putnam, 1906). Westminster Review: Vol. 143, p. 444 (1895), The Poetry of Christina Rossetti. See also above, under "General Works, Literature," Saintsbury, Chambers, Dictionary of National Biography, Oliphant, Stedman.

WILLIAM MORRIS

EDITIONS. The Poetical Works, 11 vols. (Longmans, 1896–98). The Earthly Paradise (Longmans, one-vol. ed.). The Earthly Paradise (Reeves, 1890; one-vol. ed.).

BIOGRAPHY. The Life of William Morris, by J. W. Mackail, 2 vols. (Longmans, 1899). William Morris, His Art, His Writings, and His Public Life, by Aymer Vallance (Macmillan, 1897). William Morris, Poet, Craftsman, Socialist, by E. L. Cary (Putnam, 1902). See also above, under "D. G. Rossetti, Biography."

CRITICISMS. Mackenzie Bell: William Morris, a Eulogy (Fortnightly Review, November, 1896). Blackwood's Magazine: July, 1869, The Life and Death of Jason, The Earthly Paradise, Parts I and II; May, 1870. G. K. Chesterton: Varied Types (William Morris and His School) (Dodd, 1903). Walter Crane: William Morris (Scribner's Magazine, July, 1897; on his art work). Edinburgh Review: January, 1871, The Earthly Paradise; January, 1897, William Morris, Poet and Craftsman; April, 1900, Morris and Rossetti. Andrew Lang: The Poetry of William Morris (Contemporary Review, August, 1882). F. W. H. Myers: Modern Poets and the Meaning of Life (Nineteenth Century, January, 1893). George Saintsbury: Corrected Impressions (Heinemann, 1895). William Sharp: William Morris, the Man and His Work (Atlantic Monthly, December, 1896). A. C. Swinburne: Essays and Studies (Morris's Life and Death of Jason) (Chatto, 1875; Scribner). Arthur Symons: Studies in Two Literatures (Smithers, 1897). Theodore Watts (Watts-Dunton): William Morris (Athenaeum, October 10, 1896). Julius von Riegel: Die Quellen von William Morris Dichtung, The Earthly Paradise (Varnhagen's Erlanger Beiträge zur englischen Philologie, No. 9 [1890]. See also above, under "General Works, Literature," Saintsbury, Chambers, Dictionary of National Biography, Dawson, Walker, Oliphant, Stedman.

BIBLIOGRAPHY. Temple Scott: A Bibliography of the Works of William Morris (Bell, 1897). H. B. Forman: The Books of William Morris Described, with some account of his doings in literature and in the allied crafts (Hollings, 1897). In The Dial, Vol. 21, p. 209.

ALGERNON CHARLES SWINBURNE

EDITIONS. The Poems, 6 vols. (Harper, 1904). (The dramas and essays are to appear in six volumes, in the same series. Chatto and Windus publish all the works.) Selections from the Poetical Works (Chatto, 1887). Selections from the Poetical Works, ed. by R. H. Stoddard (Crowell, 1884). Selected Poems, ed. by W. M. Payne (Heath, 1906; Belles Lettres series).

BIOGRAPHY. A. C. Swinburne, a Study, by Theodore Wratislaw (Wessels, 1900; English Writers of To-Day series). The New International Encyclopaedia, The Encyclopedia Americana, Men and Women of the Time, etc.

CRITICISMS. Peter Bayne: Mr. Arnold and Mr. Swinburne (Contemporary Review, 1867, Vol. 6, p. 337). Robert Buchanan: The Fleshly School of Poetry, and Other Phenomena of the Day (London, 1872; first in the Contemporary Review, October, 1871). Edinburgh Review: July, 1865, Atalanta in Calydon. Fraser's Magazine: November, 1866, Mr. Swinburne and His Critics. Edmund Gosse: Mr. Swinburne (Century Magazine, May, 1902). J. R. Lowell: My Study Windows (Swinburne's Tragedies) (Literary Essays, Vol. 2, in Lowell's collected works; the essay on Swinburne appeared in 1866). R. M. Milnes (Lord Houghton): Mr. Swinburne's Bothwell (Fortnightly Review, July, 1874). P. E. More: Shelburne Essays, third series (Putnam, 1906). F. W. H. Myers: Modern Poets and the Meaning of Life (Nineteenth Century, January, 1893). W. M. Rossetti: Swinburne's Poems and Ballads, a Criticism (London, 1866). George Saintsbury: Corrected Impressions (Heinemann, 1895). A. C. Swinburne: Notes on Poems and Reviews (London, 1866); Under the Microscope (White, 1872). G. E. Woodberry: The Torch (McClure, 1905). See also above, under "General Works, Literature," Chambers, Dawson, Walker, Forman, Stedman.

BIBLIOGRAPHY. R. H. Shepherd: The Bibliography of Swinburne (Redway, 1887). T. J. Wise: A Bibliographical List of the Scarcer Works and Uncollected Writings of Swinburne (London, privately printed, 1897).

INDICES

INDEX TO FIRST LINES